UNEMPLOYMENT INSURANCE

LA FOLLETTE PUBLIC POLICY SERIES

The Robert M. La Follette
Institute of Public Affairs

Robert H. Haveman, Director

UNEMPLOYMENT INSURANCE

THE SECOND HALF-CENTURY

EDITED BY

W. LEE HANSEN

JAMES F. BYERS

With the assistance of Jan Levine Thal

THE UNIVERSITY OF WISCONSIN PRESS

The University of Wisconsin Press
114 North Murray Street
Madison, Wisconsin 53715

3 Henrietta Street
London WC2E 8LU, England

5 4 3 2 1

Printed in the United States of America

Library of Congress Cataloging-in-Publication Data

Unemployment insurance.
   (La Follette public policy series)
   Includes bibliographical references.
   1. Insurance, Unemployment—United States—History.
I. Hansen, W. Lee. II. Byers, James F., 1945–   .
III. Thal, Jan Levine. IV. Series.
HD7096.U5U6378   1989   368.4′4′00973   89-40257
ISBN 0-299-12350-2
ISBN 0-299-12354-5 (pbk.)

In memory of Wilbur Cohen

Contents

PART TWO   NEW DIRECTIONS

PART THREE   THE WISCONSIN CASE

Figures

Tables

Preface

It is fitting that this volume be dedicated to the memory of Wilbur Cohen because it was he who suggested this conference, pressed for its scheduling, and then contributed so much to its success. His untimely death in May 1987 prevented him from writing the foreword to this conference volume.

Wilbur Cohen was a lifelong analyst and champion of the unemployment insurance system. His interest was whetted during his undergraduate days at the University of Wisconsin–Madison, where he studied economics under such illustrious faculty members as John R. Commons, Edwin Witte, and Harold Groves. These scholars had taken the lead in designing and then securing passage of Wisconsin's UI program in 1931: the legendary Commons had been promoting the idea of unemployment insurance for more than a decade; Witte worked actively to promote UI and was responsible for giving shape to the Federal UI program a few years later; and the young instructor Groves sought and won election to the state legislature for the specific purpose of spearheading efforts to enact the legislation. Equally important were two of Commons's students, Paul Raushenbush and Elizabeth Brandeis ("EB") Raushenbush, who assisted in drafting the legislation and securing its passage; EB was by then a member of the economics faculty and her husband Paul, an instructor, became the administrator of Wisconsin's UI program after its enactment, a position he held for thirty-five years. Cohen witnessed passage of the UI bill in the state Capitol in the company of several other students and his economics instructor, Paul Raushenbush.

Cohen's interest and connections paid off immediately after he received his B.A. degree in 1934. That same year President Roosevelt invited Witte to Washington to serve as executive director of the cabinet Committee on Economic Security, and Witte asked Cohen to join him as his research assistant. The following year Cohen became the first employee of the new Social Security Board.

Cohen thrived on these experiences, and they left their mark, leading him to become a firm and effective advocate of UI throughout the rest of his life. He rose to become the top federal administrator of the Social Security program, and later undersecretary and then secretary of the Department of Health, Education, and Welfare in the 1960s. After leaving government, he became a professor of social work at the University of Michigan and subsequently professor of public affairs at the Lyndon B. Johnson School of Public Policy, University of Texas in Austin. From 1978 to 1980 he served as chair of the National Commission on Unemployment Compensation.

Cohen took a very active part in the UI conference discussions, and he offered a long research agenda at the close of the conference. He looked forward to the publication of this volume and had promised his comments.

Our hopes of including Cohen's full range of insights have been thwarted by his untimely death. Lest his strong and wide-ranging opinions be lost, I have put together something that I hope approximates what he himself might have written. For this I draw on an incomplete audiotape of his concluding comments at the conference and on a 1984 public lecture on UI that was sponsored by the La Follette Institute.

In concluding the La Follette Institute's first public lecture, Cohen offered for consideration an agenda not unlike that which he advocated at the conference. Here is what he said:

> After fifty years, however, there is a reasonable basis for arguing that some important changes and reforms are necessary and desirable in the federal-state unemployment compensation program. I would list five controversial changes as follows:
>
> 1. Some specific federal benefit standards to assure a reasonable degree of long-run adequacy of benefits.
> 2. A federal-state reinsurance plan to assist in a more equitable system of financing state costs when high levels of unemployment occur.
> 3. A more adequate revenue base, including an increase in the federal maximum earnings base.
> 4. Some modification of the federal revenue funding and budgeting arrangements to assure a more effective administration of both unemployment insurance and the employment service.
> 5. A supplementary system of federal and state financial aid primarily for those unemployed persons who are not beneficiaries of unemployment insurance.

The conference papers and discussion prompted Cohen to offer some additional reflections and to call for new thinking on the UI program. In the most fundamental sense he called for a reexamination of the basic federal-state relationship underpinning the UI program and for exploring the implications of changing this relationship.

Responding to Robert Topel's paper and the ensuing discussion, Cohen suggested rethinking the concept of experience rating. He indicated that although there may have been merit in the original idea of penalizing employers who did not regularize their employment and thus reduce their unemployment, the differential incidence of unemployment among firms and across industries results less from employer negligence than from national economic conditions which are beyond the control of individual employers. To assure that the costs of the UI program are met, he proposed that perhaps some combination of experience rating and flat rates might be established. He wondered why there had not been more evaluation of the impact of experience rating during the fifty-year history of the UI program. He also asked why states could not be given more latitude in setting their own tax rates, including the option of using different combinations of experience and flat rates.

Cohen furthermore expressed concern about interstate UI tax competition in the current economic environment. Because of the unevenness of the economic forces affecting unemployment levels among the states, UI tax rates are almost certain to differ from one state to another. This circumstance is likely to foster competition among states as they compete for new industry and try at the same time to retain firms that are now located in their jurisdictions. Such competition is likely to restrict the size of their UI benefit levels, thereby undercutting the basic purposes of the program: minimizing unemployment and providing some measure of compensation to those who are unemployed.

Cohen suggested that the funding of UI administrative costs be shared by the states and the federal government so as to reduce the degree of federal control over the UI system. This would enable individual states to become more effective in their administration of the UI program. The effect of such a change deserves further investigation.

These observations prompted him to conclude that although always an ardent federalist, he could well see making UI an all-state system, one completely divorced from federal controls and responsibility.

Wilbur Cohen's suggestions represent a combination of practical advice and distilled wisdom from perhaps the most knowledgeable expert on unemployment insurance in this country. They are also symbolic of his lifetime dedication and concern for the program he helped to shape. That commitment constantly energized him to seek improvements in the benefit delivery system, which is the purpose of the program; in funding stability, which guarantees the permanence of this cornerstone of our employment security safety net; and in the always difficult federal-state partnership that uniquely characterizes this country's UI system.

W. Lee Hansen

Acknowledgments

We are indebted for their generous support to the Robert M. La Follette Institute of Public Affairs and to the Industrial Relations Research Institute. The past and current directors of the La Follette Institute, Dennis M. Dresang and Robert H. Haveman, respectively, have been extremely helpful in both their intellectual and their financial support. We also appreciate the generosity of the Johnson Foundation of Racine, Wisconsin, for offering the use of its Frank Lloyd Wright–designed Wingspread for the conference, which was held in February 1986.

Additional thanks go to Jan Levine Thal, who helped with the many details of organizing the conference, seeing to its smooth operation, and editing the conference papers. Sandra Engelsby of the Industrial Relations Research Institute provided significant help before, during, and since the conference; and Rhonda Danielson of the La Follette Institute did much to lighten the administrative burdens associated with the project.

We should also note here that the views expressed in these papers are solely those of the authors and do not necessarily reflect those of the institution sponsoring the conference or the institutions with which the contributors are affiliated.

UNEMPLOYMENT INSURANCE

Introduction

W. LEE HANSEN AND JAMES F. BYERS

This volume of research papers looks both backward and forward, establishing the links between the past and the future on the fiftieth anniversary of Wisconsin's unemployment insurance program, the first in the nation, which was enacted in 1931.

A backward look establishes the context in which UI programs evolved over the past half century under joint federal-state sponsorship. A forward look points the direction the UI program might take during its second fifty years. And an examination of current issues in UI policy and practice sharpens our understanding of the success of past efforts to mold the UI program so that it can deal with the very different economic and social environment of the 1980s and beyond.

The motivations for undertaking this task are several. One was that Wilbur Cohen kept pressing for some formal recognition of Wisconsin's pathbreaking UI legislation, which represented another in a long series of state capital–University of Wisconsin collaborations known as the "Wisconsin Idea." Essentially, this term describes the effective partnership in Wisconsin between scholars and practitioners in trying to generate practical solutions to the state's varied social problems. This partnership began in the early part of this century with strong guidance and help from Governor Robert La Follette and Charles Van Hise, president of the University of Wisconsin.

Another motivation for this project arose out of the serious difficulties the state of Wisconsin experienced in the early 1980s with its UI program, long considered to be a model program. Over the years the levels of benefits offered by and taxes needed to support the program had evolved separately. Responding more often to political expediency than sound policy, those in charge of the program lowered taxes while steadily increasing benefit levels, thereby endangering the fiscal integrity of UI. In part because of the onset of substantially higher and more prolonged unemployment in the late 1970s and early 1980s, and in part because the federal government mandated that states pay extended benefits, the Wisconsin program experienced serious financial difficulties as of early 1983, prompting calls for substantial restructuring.

Most other states experienced similar problems, resulting from a combination of higher unemployment rates and a failure to ensure that the fiscal basis of UI programs remained sound, and they found it increasingly necessary to borrow from the federal government to continue paying benefits. With the sharp rise in unemployment rates in 1982 the full extent of the crisis became apparent. As a result of increased federal pressures, the states began to overhaul their programs by paring back benefits and raising UI taxes. How this restructuring should be accomplished proved to be more complicated than people had realized, and it prompted increased attention by academic experts, program managers, and politicians who were forced to devise new ways to deal with this unwelcome problem.

The reasons for the concern about the vitality of UI programs are apparent. Over the years UI has evolved into a program that exerts a profound effect on the security of working people and their families, on employers, and on society as a whole.

— For over half a century UI payments have sustained workers during the interruption of income due to layoffs and also protected them from having to take the first job available to them after becoming unemployed.

— UI has allowed businesses greater freedom to respond to changing demands in the marketplace and particularly to reduce their work forces without fear of permanently losing skilled and valuable employees.

— UI has through its self-financing scheme operated as an important countercyclical force that minimizes the effects of disruptive cycles in the pace of economic activity.

— UI has accomplished all this without ever missing a benefit payment, defaulting on a loan, or requiring a bailout from general revenues.

Despite these successes, the size and scope of the UI program requires that it be reexamined periodically to ensure that it continues to perform as intended. Such a reexamination may even offer some lessons for other social welfare programs.

To facilitate this reexamination, the Wingspread conference brought together academic experts on UI, state and federal officials working in UI programs, and state political leaders concerned about the present and future effectiveness of the UI system. Despite significant differences in points of view, these disparate groups were able to come together and discuss in productive ways how UI can better meet the needs of workers, employers, and the public in today's economy and over the next half century as well.

Current Issues

The first group of papers concentrates on a variety of issues that have arisen only recently. One is the substantially higher unemployment rates of the late 1970s and early 1980s. Another is the breakdown in the effectiveness of UI programs because total benefit payments exceeded the employer taxes levied to finance the UI program.

The nature of the UI crisis, its development, and the legislative remedies of the early 1980s are reviewed by Wayne Vroman. He concludes that UI was less successful in the 1980s than it had been during earlier recessions in reducing earnings losses to unemployed workers and in serving as an automatic stabilizer for the economy. He also finds higher poverty rates for the unemployed in 1983 than in 1976, reflecting the longer duration of unemployment in the 1980s and also the cutbacks in both UI benefit levels and duration of benefit payments. Vroman concludes that the most pressing problem for the UI system is adapting it to better serve the long-term unemployed, whose benefits typically run out after twenty-six weeks or less.

Sheldon Danziger and Peter Gottschalk develop more fully than Vroman the linkages between UI and economic welfare, focusing on how much UI benefits and other transfer payments affected the extent of poverty in 1976 and again in 1984. They find that most unemployed heads of households with low weekly earnings received no UI benefits in either year. Moreover, the proportion of this group receiving UI decreased substantially over the period. Because unemployed low earners, irrespective of whether they obtained UI benefits, generally received relatively small amounts of in-kind and cash benefits from transfer programs, they were more likely to be poor. By contrast, the unemployed who were not low earners fared better; they were more likely to receive UI benefits and not very likely to be poor. Thus, although UI helps eliminate poverty among UI recipients, the number of such persons is rather small. As a result, UI is not a very potent weapon in the fight against poverty.

Gary Burtless offers a comprehensive review of the impact of UI on labor supply. Interest in labor supply effects arose as a result of proposals in the 1960s for a negative income tax. Since then economists have given significant attention to these effects, particularly those resulting from UI. Indeed, research by Feldstein and others indicates that UI has important adverse effects on labor supply. Considerable theoretical work has been done which illustrates a variety of possible effects, many of which are offsetting. Which of these effects is strongest remains unknown, and hence Burtless's call for continued empirical investigations. Most of the available empirical research focuses first on the adverse incentives to insured unemployed workers for seeking employment and second on the layoff behavior of employers. This research indicates that in the more generous programs employers are more likely to lay off workers, and better insured workers spend longer periods being unemployed. Burtless concludes that although this research demonstrates both the beneficial and adverse effects of UI on labor supply, the impact on aggregate work effort in the economy as a whole remains unknown.

The question of how to modify the financing of UI cropped up dramati-

cally in the early 1980s after substantially higher unemployment rates
drained state UI reserve funds and forced them to borrow from the federal
government. A central feature of UI finance is the concept of experience
rating (a Wisconsin invention), which means that tax rates on employers
are based at least in part on how much of the unemployment they generate
requires the payment of UI benefits. Robert Topel shows that the structure of the payroll tax system encourages higher unemployment rates,
largely because firms with unstable employment are not liable for the full
cost of the UI benefits they generate for their workers through layoffs.
This is the result of imperfect experience rating. Topel goes on to propose
a number of financing reforms that would reduce the incentives that lead
to higher layoffs. He also suggests extending the concept of experience
rating to workers so that they share in the costs of unemployment. What
this would mean for the decision-making process is not clear: would a
firm's workers have to agree to the firm's decision to lay off workers?
Clearly, many details would have to be worked out before it would be
possible to assess the feasibility of such a plan. Topel's provocative suggestions generated considerable discussion at the conference.

A perennial difficulty with social programs is deciding who is eligible
and then finding an efficient method for ensuring compliance with the
eligibility requirements. Equally important is recognition that incentives
exist for noncompliance. Based on data for Arizona, Paul Burgess and
Jerry Kingston find evidence of a significant problem of noncompliance
with UI eligibility requirements. They go on to discuss possible programmatic responses, such as eliminating the work search requirement and
improving program administration through the use of statistical profiles
which help to identify situations in which abuses occur. Because of political
concerns, they are not optimistic that the work search requirement will
ever be eliminated. They do believe that their statistical profiles can be
effective in dealing with the work requirement issue and would involve
little or no additional cost.

Discussions of public policy can usually be informed by comparative
data summarizing the experience of other countries. Beatrice Reubens has
pulled together the information that is available on UI programs for
Western European countries, focusing on their responses to increased
unemployment rates since 1973. Though UI systems differ substantially
from country to country, it is surprising how similar the issues confront-
ing various countries are. One recent development of interest is the coverage afforded in European countries to part-time employees, an issue we
have not yet dealt with here in the United States. Other proposals for
altering the UI system in Western Europe would allow unemployed workers
to receive benefits while seeking to improve their labor skills or helping
them establish their own businesses through grants. Still another proposal

would allow UI reserve funds to be used to facilitate training, early retirement, temporary employment, and employment subsidies to employers. Many of these proposals are under active consideration and have been emerging here in the United States as well.

To understand UI programs requires knowing a good deal about the complex federal-state relationships that govern the determination of policy and the operation of the UI system. Murray Rubin, a longtime federal administrator in the UI program, describes the evolution of these relationships, their effectiveness, and what might be done to alter them in light of the economic conditions of the 1980s. Much of the conflict over UI policy and the UI crisis in the late 1970s and early 1980s can be traced to the peculiar division of responsibility that has evolved between the states and the federal government. The key question is whether and how these relationships can be improved; if they cannot, is there a need to shift the focus of responsibility more heavily toward the states?

All public programs are soon surrounded by a network of regulations, rules, and the like, that are designed to ensure the smooth and efficient functioning of the program. UI is no exception. Edwin Kehl, an administrator of the UI program in Wisconsin, offers his suggestions for simplifying the administration of UI. Perhaps his most important suggestion is that responsibility for operating the UI program reside with the same agency that funds it; this calls for downplaying the federal role and emphasizing that of the state. He also proposes simplifications, among them establishing additional incentives to maintain the solvency of trust funds rather than using the punitive approach that has been employed. He also advocates giving the states more flexibility in operating their own programs by eliminating various federal mandates and other pressures. Finally, he favors adequate compensation to state governments for the administrative costs they incur in operating UI programs. Kehl does not, however, favor devolvement — the shifting of responsibility for the UI program back to the states — an idea that was receiving considerable attention at the time he prepared his paper.

New Directions

New ideas for changing UI systems have cropped up for years, but there is nothing like a crisis to bring them out into the open. Two much-discussed issues are investigated in this section. One is the proposal to use UI and its trust funds to help underwrite the costs of training for the unemployed. The other is to make UI benefits available for people who work less than full-time. A third issue which has received much less attention is the usefulness of trying to learn more through controlled experiments about how the UI system operates.

W. Lee Hansen and James Byers lead off this section by examining the effects of the many proposals to incorporate retraining into UI programs. After examining the long history and development of the UI system and its single-minded focus on providing benefits to unemployed workers, they review a number of recent proposals that would link retraining and similar proposals to the UI system. They end up arguing against these proposals, showing that such uses of UI funds would be at odds with the central purpose of the system, would add considerably to its cost, and would probably not be all that effective. The retraining function does not fit easily into the current UI system, whose principal purpose is to use an experience-rated tax system to provide benefits to unemployed workers. The Hansen-Byers view is not universally popular but, even so, merging the retraining function into the UI system poses formidable administrative and policy problems.

Martin Morand's exploration of recent developments in short-time compensation has a different tone. Morand has studied these programs in detail, and is at times as much an advocate as an analyst of plans to permit the award of UI benefits to persons who work less than full-time. The paper brings to our attention the rich body of recent information that is available as a result of the case study approach. Reading these accounts makes one appreciate the enormous complexities of programs that attempt to incorporate new goals. Even though short-time UI compensation has gained a foothold in Europe, the demand for it here is not sufficient to predict its adoption any time soon. This is probably good because additional experimentation is needed to help assess the desirability and feasibility of this approach in the U.S. context.

In this age of social experiments, when not only proposed programs but also new programs are often tested to evaluate their effectiveness, older existing programs have been neglected. Yet the potential for learning more about how established programs work is probably just as great, if not greater, than for entirely new programs. Thus, the controlled experiments carried out by Robert Spiegelman and Stephen Woodbury under the auspices of the W. E. Upjohn Institute were most revealing. In two carefully controlled experiments in Illinois, special bonuses were offered, in the first case to employees who became reemployed within eleven weeks of being laid off, and in the other case to employers who hired UI recipients. The preliminary results indicate the high ratio of benefits to costs; substantial savings in benefits payments accrue as a result of the bonus payments to employees and employers. The authors then go on to summarize other experiments with UI programs, concluding that such experiments have much to offer in improving the effectiveness and efficiency of the UI system.

The Wisconsin Case

An important purpose of the conference was to bring together scholars and practitioners while at the same time focusing on the experience of individual states. Because of Wisconsin's historic role in the development of UI and its aggressive actions in 1983 and 1984 to get its UI program back on track, it was only natural that two of the papers discuss the Wisconsin case.

Raymond Munts, a former staff director of the National Commission on Unemployment Compensation, reviews the early developments of the Wisconsin program, compares recent benefits levels, and then speculates about the future directions of the program.

The early history of Wisconsin's UI program is of substantial interest, but the more intriguing story is how it coped with the difficult financial problems that were finally recognized in 1983. Clifford Miller, who lays out this fascinating story, served as the chief architect of the plans to reestablish Wisconsin's UI program on a solid footing. The extensive detail he provides is important in understanding the complexity of the program, its complicated financing, the financial difficulties that arose, and the political environment in which reforms were hammered out. As his paper shows, it was not enough to deal with the financing problems. It was also essential to recreate a policy group that would oversee the program and ensure its future integrity. Although Miller is obviously pleased with the success of the recent legislative and administrative changes in putting the Wisconsin UI program back on a sound financial footing, much remains to be done. He cautions that in an era of tight resources it is imperative to monitor the UI program closely because the margin for error—say, if the trust fund were to go into debt—is so small.

The Research Agenda

The need for research in unemployment compensation to illuminate a number of unresolved key issues emerged as a major conclusion of the UI conference at Wingspread. The papers presented there, the ensuing interplay of discussion, and later comments from participants identified some of these ssues and highlighted others.

Distilling these into a succinct summary without preparing an abbreviated set of research proposals proved to be difficult, however. We are not certain that we have done justice to the various ideas that came forth, nor that our grouping of them is in any sense optimal. But we are certain that a forward view is needed, one that can serve to guide policymaking in Wisconsin and in the nation as a whole. A continuing concern, however, is that the unemployment insurance program has increasingly come to be viewed as a vehicle for accomplishing related social goals. Whether it can carry this burden while pursuing its original goals continues to be a central question to any UI research agenda.

We begin by listing a wide array of research questions and then highlight those that are of particular significance for Wisconsin.

1. Federal-State Relations

Political and legal considerations led to the adoption of our bipartite UI system. What lessons have we learned from our first half century of UI federalism?

— One justification for fifty state programs rather than a single federal program is the advantages coming from multiple approaches to the problem — the idea of creating fifty "little laboratories" in which to test alternative approaches. What experiments have been tried? Which have failed, and which succeeded? What forces have spurred or retarded experimentation? Have the successes spread to other states? What explains the patterns of imitation?

— A guiding principle of the UI system has been federal standards to ensure uniformity. Are such standards necessary? What criteria can be used to assess the need for uniformity? More important, are more or fewer standards necessary? What kinds of standards?

— Recently there have been proposals for the devolvement of federal authority to the states. One such proposal calls for devolvement of administrative funding and spending to states. Has federal control over administrative funding limited state initiative and innovation, and if so, how? Would devolvement remedy this problem? What other changes might accompany devolvement?

— The investment of UI reserve funds has also been controlled by the federal government. Should jurisdiction of trust funds also be devolved to the states? What alternate investments of these reserve funds should be considered?

— Might there be any reason for further development of the UI system so that states might also be able to set UI tax rates to reflect the varying conditions of the different states?

2. Lessons from Foreign Experiences with UI

This country's UI system has never imitated the European systems of UI which were already long in place, and yet it has learned from them.

— What is the record of attempts to transplant elements of European UI programs to the United States — for example, dependents' benefits, retraining, and worksharing?

—Most European systems are funded on a tripartite basis; employer taxes, worker taxes, and general revenues all contribute to UI reserve funds. What has been the impact of this joint financing system on the viability of UI programs? How has this affected employee and employer behavior? What might be the impact of incorporating this concept into the U.S. UI system?

3. Impact of UI on Worker Behavior

UI is predicated on the notion that unemployed workers engage in an active search for new jobs.

—How extensive is this search activity? Are there any ways to enhance the success of job search efforts by UI recipients? What is the role of the Job Service and of private employment agencies in helping the unemployed find employment? When plant shutdowns make job search in the immediate area futile, what alternative policies might facilitate the reemployment of UI recipients?

—To what extent does receipt of UI benefits affect patterns of income and consumption in light of the changed composition of households since UI was established? How do these effects differ in multi- as compared to single-earner households?

—What is the relationship between unemployment and poverty status for UI recipients, both while they receive benefits and subsequently? Should UI be integrated with other types of transfer payments?

4. Impact of UI on Employers

A central argument for UI is that by shifting some of the costs of unemployment to employers the overall level of unemployment would be reduced.

—Do the costs of UI cause employers to try to minimize layoffs? How much of a deterrence are these costs? How do these costs vary across industries and for different occupational groups?

—What is the relationship between the taxes paid by individual employers and their tendency to lay off workers subsequently?

5. Benefit Payments

Payment of benefits to unemployed workers is the central purpose of UI. Yet only in this country are benefit levels tied to previous wages and limited in duration (e.g., twenty-six weeks).

—The original intent of the UI system was to replace roughly 50 percent of wages received before layoff, enough to provide for "non-deferrable"

expenses but not so much as to introduce a "moral hazard" that would
encourage people to want to remain unemployed for long. What do we
know about the appropriateness of current benefit levels? As much as a
quarter of total compensation now comes as fringe benefits which are
ignored in the calculation of UI. Has the 50 percent target thus been eroded?
— Some industries have negotiated union contracts with supplemental unemployment benefits (SUBs) that provide laid-off workers with 90 percent
or more of their regular wages. What is the impact of such agreements
on workers, employers, and the UI system? Has this put pressure on the
system to pay higher benefits for all unemployed workers?

6. Tax Policy

The reserve fund and the taxes that generate the fund are crucial to the
fabric of a social insurance program such as UI. Indeed, the major and
most obvious problem with the UI system over the past decade has been
the drain on reserve funds as a result of prolonged unemployment and
an imbalance in the structure of taxes and benefits.

— The tax wage base has been capped at $7,000, in contrast with Social
Security, whose tax base now exceeds $40,000, even though both pro-
grams were originally created by the same legislation. What would be the
effect of raising the tax base on the reserve funds? Would such an increase
add pressure to raise benefit levels? What would be the implications for
experience rating?
— With UI benefits now subject to a 50 percent tax rate because of 1986 tax
reform legislation, how has this affected net benefit levels across the income
distribution? Should the additional tax revenues go into general revenue,
or should they go directly into the trust funds, as is the case with taxes
on Social Security benefits? Would federal taxation pave the way for states
to tax these benefits?
— Periodically someone proposes that workers also be taxed for UI. What
are the implications of such a tax? How might it affect the balance of power
in decision making on UI policy? What expectations might it raise on the
part of workers? Would such a change affect the attractiveness of uncapping
the taxable wage base? Are there any technical difficulties in collecting such
a tax? What has been the experience of the several states that do tax
employees?
— Full and complete experience rating is rarely utilized. What are the effects
on employers of moving toward more complete experience rating? How
would this affect the extent of cross-subsidies among employers in different
industries?

7. Trust Funds

Trust funds provide the fiscal and philosophical underpinnings for the
UI program. At the same time these funds were drawn down perilously

during the late 1970s and early 1980s. This accounts for the widespread concern in recent years about the crisis in UI.

— What is the optimal size of a state's UI reserve fund? How can the size of the fund be made responsive to the likely demands on it? How is it possible for state legislators to be made more keenly aware of the impact on the reserve fund of the tax rates and benefit levels they legislate? Why do so many states have such small reserve funds after several years of improved economic conditions?

— For many years the federal government made loans to states when their reserve funds were low. How did these federal loan policies shape state attitudes toward their reserve funds? More recently, how has federal imposition of interest charges and penalties altered these attitudes? To what extent have these changes altered federal-state relations?

— Numerous bills are before Congress that would allow UI trust fund monies to be used to pay for retraining, relocation, and self-employment ventures. In what sense do these proposals complement or conflict with the goals of UI and with the larger social goal of reducing unemployment? Should there be rules governing the solvency of these funds — that is, restricting the use of these funds for related purposes unless they meet appropriate solvency standards?

8. Retraining

Retraining has never been an official goal of UI. Yet since 1960 use of UI benefits has been broadened to include use of UI funds to support training for displaced workers.

— Is retraining and its suspension of work search requirements consistent with the purposes of UI? If retraining is a necessary response to unemployment, should it be incorporated into UI or made a separate program? If part of the UI program, how should the costs of retraining be paid? Is the establishment of a separate trust fund for retraining a solution?

— How do states define approved training which the unemployed can obtain without sacrificing their UI benefit payments? How many UI recipients avail themselves of training programs? What fraction of UI payments go to support persons receiving training?

— Should enrollment in a retraining program be required for persons receiving extended UI benefits?

— If increased labor mobility is required to deal with structural unemployment, might relocation funds be more useful than retraining to some workers? If so, should these funds come from UI resources?

9. New Approaches

Several new approaches to UI have been proposed recently.

— One approach is short-time compensation, which would involve the sharing of unemployment by workers through reduction in hours and prorated UI benefits. What are the likely effects of such a program? Would liberalization of the partial benefits formula accomplish the same purpose? How does Wisconsin's approach compare with that of California and other states having these programs?

— Another proposal is privatization, which argues that the UI program should be in the private sector. What arguments can be made for and against a system of private UI? What forces prevented adoption of a private-sector solution when UI was first considered fifty years ago?

— Still another proposal is to replace UI with a program that would provide loans to unemployed workers. By allowing workers to decide how to allocate their benefit money — for living expenses, retraining, relocation, or entrepreneurial capital — would this make the UI system more flexible?

— If loans are not to replace UI benefits, would it be appropriate for unemployed workers to borrow from the UI system after the expiration of their regular benefits?

10. Issues of Special Concern to Wisconsin

UI originated in Wisconsin, which has since frequently anticipated problems that later emerged throughout the UI system. Wisconsin's unique situation suggests special attention to these topics.

— Wisconsin does not require laid-off workers to wait a week before eligibility for UI benefits begins. Legislators agree that this policy emerged as a result of political rather than economic considerations. What would be the effect of introducing a one-week eligibility period before payments can begin? Or is there some other way to prevent abuse of the current situation, which favors workers and employers in industries where unemployment spells are frequent and often short as well?

— Wisconsin utilizes experience rating, but extensive cross-industry subsidies still result. What are the likely effects on employer costs and behavior of increasing the extent of experience rating in setting UI taxes? What would be the effect in different industries? How might such a change be phased in to smooth the transition?

— Wisconsin also utilizes a rate limiter, but its use prevents revenues from increasing as fast as the need for UI increases. Should the rate limiter be raised from 1 to 2 percent?

— Wisconsin has a low taxable wage base relative to Social Security. What would be the effect of raising the taxable wage base to, say, $20,000? How would such an increase affect the financial soundness of the state's UI system? How would it affect business competitiveness, particularly if it were combined with a greater degree of experience rating?

— Some workers spend a lifetime in the labor market without ever making a UI benefit claim, while others collect several weeks of benefits every year because of seasonal unemployment. What is the lifetime distribution of benefits to different workers or groups of workers? How would elimination of seasonal unemployment affect this distribution? Should seasonal unemployment be excluded from coverage and benefit eligibility? If so, how might this be accomplished?

— Wisconsin made substantial revisions in its UI program in 1983. Did these changes go far enough to keep the program solvent over the long run, particularly in view of future developments that could substantially affect the demands made on UI funds?

PART ONE

CURRENT ISSUES

1

The Aggregate Performance of Unemployment Insurance, 1980–1985

WAYNE VROMAN

Introduction

Unemployment insurance pays benefits that provide partial wage loss replacement to the unemployed. It has been an important U.S. income security program for nearly fifty years. The present paper examines major legislative developments and the economic performance of the program since 1979. Program benefits, especially for long-term unemployment, have been less available in the 1980s than in earlier periods. The causes for cutbacks in benefit availability are twofold: policy actions initiated by the Reagan administration and state legislative actions undertaken to reduce trust fund inadequacies. This paper estimates by year and category the dollar amount of the benefit cutbacks experienced in the years 1980 to 1984. It also examines the income of the unemployed and compares their poverty rates in 1983 with poverty rates in 1976. The purpose of the poverty analysis is to document the distributional consequences of the recent reductions in benefit availability.

Unemployment insurance developments in the 1980s have been dominated by cyclical changes in the macroeconomy. The years 1980 through 1983 witnessed two recessions, and unemployment rates in both 1982 and 1983 exceeded 9.5 percent of the civilian labor force. There were several legislative developments in these years (both at the federal level and in the states) that were driven by unemployment insurance funding problems experienced by many states. In 1984 and 1985 unemployment has declined, trust fund rebuilding has occurred, and there have been fewer important legislative developments. This paper focuses less on 1984–85 than the earlier years when unemployment insurance funding problems were immediate and acute.

1. An Overview of Unemployment Insurance

State unemployment insurance, created by the Social Security Act of 1935, was intended to be a self-financing social insurance program which levied payroll taxes on covered employers and paid benefits to eligible unemployed workers. Workers laid off by their employers are potentially eligible to collect benefits for only a limited time, usually twenty-six weeks, until they are recalled, find another job, exhaust their benefits, or leave the labor force. Although states have sole authority to determine eligibility criteria and payment levels, most jurisdictions pay benefits that are 50 to 60 percent of previous wages subject to a weekly benefit maximum. States also have the responsibility of determining the tax rates levied on covered employers to finance program benefits.

A long-standing policy issue dating from the inception of state UI is the appropriate duration of program benefits. The original state laws enacted in the 1930s typically allowed a maximum of from twelve to sixteen weeks of benefits per year. As experience accumulated in the 1940s and 1950s initial concerns about excessive claim loads diminished, and the program proved to be less expensive than anticipated. Maximum benefit durations were gradually extended and a norm of twenty-six weeks became widespread. By 1960 no state had a maximum duration of less than twenty weeks and only nine had maximum durations shorter than twenty-six weeks.[1]

Experience with widespread benefit exhaustion in the late 1950s and early 1960s led to temporary extensions of maximum duration up to thirty-nine weeks, with the last thirteen weeks provided under emergency federal programs. The practice of extending benefits an additional thirteen weeks during recessions was made an automatic feature of state UI in 1970 with the creation of the federal-state extended benefit (EB) program (P.L. 91-373). Financed jointly by federal and state payroll taxes on covered employers, the EB program was "triggered on" when state unemployment rates or the national rate (based on UI claims data) exceeded predetermined thresholds. The final part of pre-1980 duration legislation was a third tier of potential benefits beyond EB which were also available to the long-term unemployed in 1972–73 and 1975–77. Maximum durations could be as long as fifty-two weeks in the 1972–73 and sixty-five weeks in the 1975–77 downturns. Thus from 1937 to 1977 there was a strong trend toward longer maximum potential durations of benefits in state UI, particularly during recessions, due both to increased duration in regular state UI and to programs targeted on the long-term unemployed.

As unemployment insurance has evolved, concerns have grown regarding possible labor market distortions caused by program provisions. Long potential benefit durations and high replacement rates (benefits relative to previous wages) could induce some workers to prolong their spells of measured unemployment. Estimates of the size of the labor market distortions vary, but in a recent high employment year like 1979 some 0.5 to 1.0 percentage points of the total 5.8 percent unemployment rate could be attributed to state UI.[2] Federal policy initiatives of the 1980s to restrict UI benefits are partly a response to these concerns about labor market distortions.

During the 1970s a financing problem in state UI became apparent which has emerged as an even more serious problem in the 1980s. Between 1972 and 1979, twenty-five of the fifty-three "states" (including the District of Columbia, Puerto Rico, and the Virgin Islands) needed U.S. Treasury loans totaling $5.6 billion to make benefit payments. Between January 1, 1980, and December 31, 1984, almost $18 billion of additional loans was disbursed among thirty-three jurisdictions. The total indebtedness of the state UI system was about $13.3 billion at the end of December 1983. At the end of 1985 roughly $6 billion in debts was still outstanding.

The state UI funding problem has several causes. Four economic contractions since 1970, including two very severe recessions, have resulted in a heavy demand for benefits, particularly during 1975–77 and 1981–83. The high inflation of the past decade has contributed to the funding problem because weekly benefit maximums have risen with average wages while the program's tax base has lagged behind. About half of total wages in covered employment are now taxable. Tax rates could be raised to offset the slow growth of the federal tax base ($7,000 per employee in 1985), or states could raise their own tax bases, but such actions have not always occurred at the state level, partly because of concern that employers will relocate in response to higher taxes. Finally, the EB program has cost more than anticipated. For all of these reasons benefit outlays have shown a pronounced tendency to exceed taxes in the years since 1969. A major motivating force behind recent UI legislation at both the state and federal level has been the deficits and debts due to inadequate program financing.

2. Recent Legislative Developments

State UI has been an active area of both federal and state legislation, particularly in the years 1981 to 1983.[3] The Reagan administration's initial UI legislative proposals of 1981 were designed to restrict the availability of jobless benefits, encouraging workers to actively seek reemployment and limiting future state UI trust fund deficits. Before discussing these proposals, however, it will be useful to review earlier legislation dating from the mid-1970s, a period when several UI programs first experienced serious funding problems.[4]

The first federal loans to states in the 1970s to cover claims for UI benefits were granted between 1972 and 1974 to three states, Connecticut, Vermont, and Washington. Then in 1975 and 1976, years of very high unemployment, emergency loans were extended to twenty-three states. These loans, provided on an interest-free basis, were to be repaid in subsequent years after economic prosperity had returned. Altogether twenty-five programs received loans totaling $5.6 billion during the 1970s. Some repaid their advances promptly, whereas others made no effort to repay the federal loans.

Through penalty tax rates added to the Federal Unemployment Tax (FUT), which supports the costs of UI program administration and half of the EB program, a mechanism existed to ensure gradual loan repayment by the states; however, these penalties were not allowed to take effect as scheduled. Laws enacted in 1975 (P.L. 94-45) and 1977 (P.L. 95-19) deferred to 1978 and then to 1980 the effective date of the penalty tax provisions applicable to most states with loans more than two years old.[5] A further deferral of FUT penalty taxes was not seriously proposed in 1979, and they took effect in 1980 in nine states. Thus, at the end of 1979 three of the largest debtor states (New Jersey, Illinois, and Pennsylvania) had practically all of their original loans still outstanding even though they had been received mainly during the 1975–77 period.[6] Thirteen debtor jurisdictions owed a combined total of $3.8 billion at the end of 1979, while twelve had completely repaid their earlier loans. Failure of many states to make prompt debt repayments was a consideration in later deficit legislation.

Another legislative development of the 1970s was the taxation of UI benefits under the federal personal income tax. The Revenue Act of 1978 (P.L. 95-600) made UI benefits taxable as ordinary income starting in 1979 for single persons with income above $20,000 and couples filing joint returns with income above $25,000. This tax provision, which included a phase-in interval to prevent notch problems, was intended to prevent occurrences of high replacement rates (benefits as a proportion of after-tax wages) and was not viewed as an important increment to tax revenues. The tax proceeds were treated as other federal income tax revenues and not earmarked for state UI programs in any way. The legislation was important in two ways: it restricted benefits to some high-income families, and it established a precedent for taxing government transfer payments which previously had always been received as nontaxable income.

Shortly after Ronald Reagan took office in January 1981, the new administration proposed a series of changes in the UI program as part of its overall package of domestic social legislation. Several proposals regarding UI benefits and program financing were included in the Omnibus

Budget Reconciliation Act of 1981 (P.L. 97-35).[7] Four important changes in UI were the following: (1) the law sharply restricted worker access to benefits under the EB program by changing the EB triggering mechanism; (2) it raised the cost of future state UI indebtedness by requiring interest payments on loans made after April 1, 1982; (3) it substantially reduced worker access to benefits under the Trade Adjustment Assistance (TAA) program; and (4) it curtailed the availability of UI benefits to persons who voluntarily leave military service, that is, unemployment compensation for ex-servicemen (known as UCX).[8] All four changes have implications for benefit availability, either directly or because the increased cost of loans would make states more likely to limit UI benefits in order to avoid future deficits. Estimates prepared by the Congressional Budget Office indicate that the four changes caused a total federal budget savings of $4.6 billion in fiscal year 1983, of which $3.7 billion was due to changes in the EB triggers.[9] Because of the importance of these changes, they are discussed in more detail.

Extended benefits are intended to alleviate the hardships of recession-induced long-term unemployment. As originally created in 1970, the EB program provided a mechanism for automatically extending maximum benefit duration by half, that is, allowing thirteen additional weeks of benefits during economic downturns for those entitled to twenty-six weeks' coverage under regular state UI. Benefit eligibility under EB was triggered on when the insured unemployment rate (IUR, figured as the proportion of UI claimants to covered employment) exceeded a predetermined threshold rate. An automatic trigger activated the program whenever the IUR for a given thirteen-week period exceeded 4 percent and was also at least 20 percent higher than the average rate for the same period in the preceding two years. An optional EB trigger was available for states to use whenever the state IUR exceeded 5 percent (regardless of the average in the previous two years). There was also a trigger based on national data that would activate the EB program in all states whenever the national IUR reached 4.5 percent.

The effect of the Reagan administration's EB initiatives was threefold. First, the national trigger was eliminated. Henceforth the program was activated in states only when state threshold rates were exceeded. Second, those receiving EB were excluded from state IUR computations. Finally, the level of automatic and optional state IUR triggers was raised, respectively, to 5 and 6 percent of covered employment (one percentage point above their previous level). The latter two provisions have made it more difficult for states to activate the EB program, especially since September 25, 1982, when the higher trigger thresholds became effective. Combined with the elimination of the national trigger (effective August 14, 1981), these changes greatly reduced EB availability in the 1981–83 period. We will further examine the reduction in EB payments in the next section.

The 1981 legislation could be characterized as restricting jobless benefit eligibility to target UI more effectively on the long-term unemployed. Eliminating the national EB trigger targeted the program on those states with high unemployment. The modifications of TAA effectively reoriented the program from providing short-term cash benefits (coincident with UI benefits) to providing cash benefits only after UI was exhausted and encouraging positive adjustments such as retraining, job search assistance, and relocation allowances. Total support payments under TAA were sharply reduced. The UCX change reduced benefits to a group whose joblessness is partly the result of their own voluntary decision, that is, not to reenlist in the military.[10]

Regardless of the motive for the changes, they have had the effect of reducing benefit eligibility to unemployed workers in a period of economic recession. As the recession deepened in late 1981 and into 1982, congressional sentiment evolved to the point that subsequent federal legislation was designed to increase benefit availability for the long-term unemployed. Although the Reagan administration initially opposed the congressional initiatives in this area, the president ultimately acceded to new extensions of jobless benefits.

The Tax Equity and Fiscal Responsibility Act of 1982 (P.L. 97-248, commonly known as TEFRA) contained several provisions relating to UI benefits and financing. (1) It created the Federal Supplemental Compensation (FSC) program, which made from six to ten additional weeks of benefits available to exhaustees (whose qualification for regular state UI benefits included at least twenty weeks of base period employment). The extra weeks of benefits (later increased to eight to sixteen weeks) were available in the period from mid-September 1982 to the end of March 1983, with the potential number of weeks linked to the state's IUR. Benefits were payable in all states regardless of the availability of EB. (2) The tax base and tax rate for FUT were raised from $6,000 to $7,000 and 0.7 to 0.8 percent effective January 1, 1983. (3) Some of the loan and interest repayment provisions were eased for selected debtor states.[11] (4) The income limits for taxing UI benefits as ordinary income in 1983 were reduced to $12,000 for single persons and $18,000 for couples filing joint returns.

These TEFRA provisions are interesting because they addressed several different state UI problem areas. The FSC program provided benefits to the long-term unemployed while the income tax provisions reduced net benefits to many others in families with moderate annual incomes. Increased FUT taxes, designed to speed the repayment of old debts associated with extended benefit programs of earlier recessions, also raised taxes on employers in many states since the state taxable maximum must be at least equal to the FUT taxable maximum. The loan and debt repayment provisions recognized that increased tax burdens on states during recessions would not be beneficial if a state was already experiencing a major fiscal crisis. Several of these same concerns were also addressed in subsequent legislation.

The Social Security Amendments of March 1983 (P.L. 98-21) included two important groups of UI provisions. The FSC program was extended for six months, to the end of September 1983, and eligible persons were permitted to receive from eight to fourteen weeks of FSC (depending on the level of the state's IUR) if they had not already started to collect FSC, and from six to ten additional weeks if they had previously exhausted FSC eligibility. Thus, a March 1983 FSC exhaustee could potentially collect sixty-five weeks of benefits: twenty-six of regular state UI, thirteen of EB, and twenty-six of FSC, equaling the longest potential duration available in the 1975–77 period. Furthermore, interest and debt repayment terms were made potentially easier for debtor state UI programs. If a debtor state maintained its tax effort and increased its net solvency in 1983 (or the first year of indebtedness) through tax increases and/or benefit reductions by 25 percent (and then by more in subsequent years) it would be allowed during fiscal years 1983, 1984, and 1985 to defer until later years at no cost 80 percent of the interest payments on federal loans made after April 1, 1982.[12] Also, if the state satisfied certain solvency requirements, the annual increment in its FUT penalty tax rate would be reduced. Both provisions had the effect of allowing states to defer financial obligations associated with their debts. Because these provisions made it attractive for states to improve program solvency, legislation was enacted in nearly all the large debtor states.[13] The U.S. Labor Department was to determine if states had satisfied the net solvency requirements. One effect of state legislation, of course, was to further restrict eligibility for regular state UI in all years after 1983.

The UI changes made in the 1983 Social Security Amendments were clearly designed to provide income to the long-term unemployed and to lighten financial burdens on debtor states. The carrot and stick approach to the latter problem also meant that the financial balance in several state programs would be improved in later years. Like the TEFRA changes, these initiatives came more from the Congress than from the Reagan administration. In fact, the 1983 administration proposals prior to the Social Security Amendments had called for further restricting FSC eligibility (by mandating a thirty rather than twenty weeks-of-work qualifying requirement and automatically disqualifying all job leavers) and fostering increased job seeking and other financial incentives to reemployment, such as job vouchers. When the Congress passed its own proposals, however, the president acceded to its initiative even though administration provisions were not included in the legislation.

The most recent important federal legislation affecting state UI, again a congressional initiative, was that provided in the Federal Supplemental Compensation Amendments of 1983 (P.L. 98-135), which extend the FSC program from late October 1983 through the end of March 1985. During this period persons exhausting regular state UI or EB were eligible for eight to fourteen weeks of FSC, with the exact number depending on each state's IUR.[14] Other provisions permitted the payment of some benefits for those exhausting FSC eligibility during the March–October 1983 period as well as persons with part of their earlier FSC entitlement remaining at the start of the final phase of the FSC program. These latter two provisions, respectively covering so-called reach-back and transitional benefits, provide even fewer additional weeks than the eight to fourteen weeks available to new FSC recipients.

The 1983 FSC legislation carried the program through the 1984 election year and into 1985. It was projected to cost $3.4 and $1.3 billion in fiscal years 1984 and 1985. Two aspects of the legislation are noteworthy. First, it did nothing to change the existing trigger formulas in the EB program. As a result EB continued to be of very minor importance during 1984 and 1985. Second, the legislation covered a seventy-eight-week period but provided only a maximum of fourteen weeks of FSC benefits. Combined with twenty-six weeks of regular state UI, maximum potential benefit duration from the two programs was forty weeks. Thus certain long-term unemployed workers could experience lengthy spells of uncompensated unemployment.

The Reagan administration's policy objectives in unemployment insurance have been consistent over the 1981–85 period. The major objective was to reorient the program from an almost exclusive emphasis on income maintenance (providing cash benefits to the unemployed) toward a greater emphasis on positive adjustments by unemployed workers. The latter encompasses retraining and relocation allowances as well as financial incentives such as job vouchers for employers to hire the unemployed. To accomplish this reorientation the administration has restricted benefit availability in several ways, the most notable being the changes in the EB triggers. The size of the benefit restrictions has far outweighed the increased resources devoted to positive adjustments by jobless workers. Thus, the size of state UI programs has in effect been cut substantially, and this has been done in a period of unusually high unemployment. The administration has also wanted to reduce the federal role in UI financing by encouraging the states to achieve a better balance between program revenues and benefits.

The deep recession that began in late 1981 was the motivating force behind the three major pieces of federal UI legislation enacted in 1982 and 1983. Congress has acted to increase benefit availability to the long-term unemployed and to lessen financial burdens on debtor states. In each instance FSC has been used to provide long-term benefits, while the earlier changes in the EB triggers have not been altered. The Reagan administration acquiesced to these initiatives even though they were at variance with the basic thrust of its own UI legislative agenda.

As noted earlier, the macroeconomy in 1984 and 1985 has been characterized by large increases in real GNP and declining unemployment. At the federal level there was no major UI legislation. State trust fund balances have been growing, and there has been no immediate need for most states to enact additional UI financing legislation.

3. Aggregate Unemployment Insurance Benefit Payments

The primary objective of unemployment insurance is to reduce the economic hardships caused by joblessness. Aggregate benefit payments increase sharply in recessions, and this was observed during 1980–83 as in earlier downturns. What has been unusual about the 1980s is that benefit availability was deliberately reduced by policy actions while the economy was in recession. Thus, although aggregate benefits increased during 1980–83, the key analytic question is, How much did Reagan administration policy initiatives restrain the growth in benefit payments during this period?

Descriptive data on UI benefit payments for the years 1969 to 1984 are presented in Table 1.1. One obvious feature of the table is the large number of public programs that pay jobless benefits to unemployed workers. In addition to regular state UI, eight other programs are identified that currently compensate the unemployed or did in the 1970s. The three recessionary periods covered by the table (1970–71, 1974–76, and 1980–83) all show sharp increases in benefit payments. Although regular state UI is by far the largest program and accounts for much of the cyclical increase in benefit payments, countercyclical payment patterns are observed for several of the other programs as well.

Specific institutional circumstances cause the unusual time series patterns of benefit payments for supplemental unemployment assistance, trade adjustment assistance, and public service joblessness. Supplemental unemployment assistance (SUA) was a temporary program enacted in the 1974–76 recession to provide benefits to persons previously employed in noncovered sectors and to some who did not qualify under the regular state UI programs. The program lapsed in 1978, and there was no attempt to enact a similar program in the 1980–83 period.[15] The unusual bulge in TAA payments in 1980 and, to a lesser extent, 1981 mainly reflects

Table 1.1. Unemployment Insurance Benefit Payments by Year, 1969–84 (in millions)

| | State Unemployment Insurance | | | | Other Unemployment Programs | | | | | | |
| | Total | Regular State UI[a] | Federal State Extended Benefits[a] | Temporary Programs[a] | Railroad | Federal Employees | Ex-Service Men | Supplemental Unemployment Assistance | Trade Adjustment Assistance | Public Service Jobless[a] | Total All Programs |
Year	(1)	(2)	(3)	(4)	(5)	(6)	(7)	(8)	(9)	(10)	(11)
1969	2100	2100	0	0	94	47	86	0	0	0	2327
1970	3811	3811	0	0	95	79	201	0	0	0	4186
1971	5582	4916	665	0	120	109	349	0	0	0	6160
1972	5454	4467	466	521	87	128	364	0	18	0	6051
1973	4188	4034	143	11	58	124	200	0	17	0	4587
1974	6570	6031	539	0	52	152	247	0	17	0	7038
1975	16,548	11,884	2527	2137	137	270	521	664	37	0	18,177
1976	14,280	9211	2308	2762	219	310	602	975	165	0	16,551
1977	11,533	8577	1733	1224	174	274	468	680	159	3	13,291
1978	8612	7915	628	15	191	175	276	163	292	583	10,292
1979	9100	8878	221	0	143	163	286	0	277	370	10,339
1980	15,331	13,737	1595	0	238	177	351	0	2241	325	18,663
1981	15,087	13,757	1330	0	266	221	311	0	863	284	17,032
1982	24,473	20,944	2413	1116	394	261	79	0	51	60	25,318
1983	25,488	18,314	1704	5470	378	241	184	0	34	42	26,387
1984	15,533	13,453	42	2038	182	196	132	0	67	11	16,121

Source: Based on data from Table 3.11 of the National Income Accounts. See U.S. Department of Commerce, *The National Income and Product Accounts of the United States, 1929–1976, Statistical Tables* (Washington, D.C.: U.S. Department of Commerce, 1981), and subsequent July issues of the *Survey of Current Business*. The detail for 1984 is based on unpublished data.

[a]Based on unpublished detail from Table 3.11 of the National Income Accounts. Column (2) includes reimbursable benefits. Column (4) encompasses Temporary Compensation of 1972–73, Federal Supplemental Benefits of 1975–78, and Federal Supplemental Compensation of 1982–84.

increased payments to unemployed autoworkers who were particularly affected by the auto industry slump that began in the fall of 1979. After their eligibility had been exhausted, payment levels for the program would probably have returned to 1978–79 levels, roughly $300 million a year, if the Reagan administration's TAA initiatives had not been enacted. The high level of Public Service Jobless benefit payments in 1978 reflects the combined effects of first-time eligibility for UI benefits and unusual numbers of layoffs due to the 1977 Comprehensive Employment and Training Act (CETA) legislation, which stipulated that federally financed public service jobs could last no more than eighteen months.

For three of the smaller programs identified in Table 1.1 there is a clear evidence of benefit reductions in 1982 and 1983 due to the Reagan administration's policies. Unemployment compensation for ex-servicemen (column 7) paid only $79 million in 1982 and $184 million in 1983.[16] From the pattern of payments made during the 1973–76 period, the 1982–83 amounts appear to be $350–$500 million less per year than would have been paid if program eligibility had not been sharply restricted.[17] As noted, TAA payments would have been lower in 1982–83 even if the program had not been modified. The reductions in annual benefits due to policy changes fall into the $250–$350 million range. The elimination of public service employment between January and October of 1981 meant that the associated jobless benefits were also terminated. From the table it appears that annual benefit reductions in 1982 and 1983 were roughly $250–$300 million when compared with payments in 1980. Although the exact magnitude of the benefit reductions is not known precisely, it is clear that total reductions under the special programs were roughly $1 billion in both 1982 and 1983. In these two years the six programs included in columns 5–10 paid combined benefits of $845 and $879 million, whereas the corresponding totals in 1975 and 1976 were respectively $1.629 and $2.271 billion.[18] Much of the difference is due to Reagan administration policy initiatives.

Table 1.1 shows that the bulk of jobless benefits are paid out under the three tiers of state unemployment insurance programs: regular state UI, federal-state extended benefits, and federal temporary compensation (TC) programs. Combined outlays under these programs rose from $9.1 billion in 1979 to $24.5 billion in 1982 and $25.5 billion in 1983. For the latter two programs that provide benefits to the long-term unemployed, 1975 and 1976 aggregate payments (measured in current dollars) nearly equaled those of 1982 and 1983, $9.734 versus $10.703 billion. In real terms 1982–83 benefits to the long-term unemployed were 33 percent less than in 1975–76.[19] Lower real benefits were paid despite the fact that long-term joblessness was much more prevalent in 1982–83 compared with the earlier period.[20]

Because of the size and importance of the three state UI programs a multiple regression analysis of their performance in the 1980–83 period was undertaken. The table illustrates that UI outlays are highly cyclical. It seemed prudent to include several business cycles in the regressions in order to obtain accurate parameter estimates for the cyclical component of benefit payments. By including quarterly data back to 1957 a data base was assembled that covered four recessions prior to the downturns of 1980–83. Starting with the 1957–58 recession, a federal temporary compensation program has been enacted in each recession to provide long-term jobless benefits to workers exhausting their regular state UI benefits. Thus the data base has the maximum number of observations of these TC programs.

Benefit payments in regular state UI exhibit a highly seasonal pattern, with first-quarter outlays consistently higher than payments in later quarters. Although the Commerce Department (the source of the benefits data in Table 1.1 and for this analysis) seasonally adjusts the data on regular state UI benefit payments, it does not similarly adjust EB or TC payments. To be consistent, all series were used in seasonally unadjusted form. Because most young workers do not collect UI benefits, the cyclical indicator used was the unemployment rate for persons twenty-five and older. To control for inflation and changes in the scale of the economy, aggregate benefit payments were deflated by the personal consumption deflator from the National Income Accounts and expressed as a percentage of potential real GNP. Between 1969 and 1983 real benefits under regular state UI averaged 0.44 percent of potential real GNP.

Table 1.2 displays regressions that explain the pattern of benefit payments between 1957 and 1979. For regular state UI the explanatory variables are the unemployment rate, the base period unemployment rate, a linear time trend, and seasonal dummy variables. The time trend is included to control for long-term influences such as the gradual tightening of eligibility in the state programs and the increasing female share of adult unemployment. (A lower proportion of adult women collect benefits than of adult men.) The base period unemployment rate is included to control for the effects of lagged unemployment, which reduces eligibility through effects on worker base period earnings.[21] Both unemployment rates and the time trend are highly significant in equation 1.[22] Benefits respond positively to the unemployment rate, negatively to base period unemployment, and negatively to the time trend. All of these results are consistent with a priori expectations. The size and statistical significance of the coefficients hold up well in equation 2, which adjusts for serial correlation in the error terms. For the 1957–79 period over 97 percent of the variation in regular state UI benefit payments is explained by this straightforward specification.

Table 1.2. Regression Analysis of State UI Benefit Payments, 1957–79[a]

Independent Variables	Regular State UI Benefits		Federal-State Extended Benefits		Temporary Compensation Benefits[b]	
	(1)	(2)	(3)	(4)	(5)	(6)
Constant	.0047	.0109	.0366	.0491		
	(.3)	(.6)	(1.3)	(.7)		
Unemployment rate—persons 25 and older	.1542	.1521	.0250	.0179		
	(42.8)	(33.3)	(4.1)	(2.4)		
Unemployment rate national EB trigger "ON"			.0124	.0105		
			(5.4)	(4.8)		
Long term unemployment rate— temporary benefits "ON"					.1154	.1680
					(10.9)	(7.4)
Base period unemployment rate	−.0522	−.0534				
	(13.8)	(10.4)				
Time trend	−.0005	−.0005	−.0012	−.0010		
	(4.5)	(3.4)	(4.1)	(2.5)		
First quarter dummy	.0519	.0549	−.0269	−.0201	.0258	−.0092
	(5.9)	(6.9)	(2.9)	(2.5)	(1.5)	(1.0)
Second quarter dummy	.0619	.0623	.0074	.0072	−.0340	−.0231
	(7.6)	(8.5)	(.9)	(1.1)	(2.1)	(2.4)
Third quarter dummy	−.0093	−.0092	−.0033	.0032	−.0310	−.0284
	(1.1)	(1.4)	(.4)	(.6)	(1.8)	(3.4)
Serial correlation coefficient summary statistics		.334		.670		1.021
		(3.4)		(5.3)		(6.0)
Number of observations	92	91	36	35	24	20
R^2	.971	.974	.890	.912	.699	.855
Standard error of estimate	.027	.026	.018	.016	.029	.020
Durbin-Watson statistic	1.33	1.96	1.19	1.60	.69	1.62

[a]All regressions were fitted to quarterly data unadjusted for seasonal variation. Beneath each coefficient in parentheses is the absolute value of its t ratio. Equations 2, 4, and 6 were fitted using the Cochrane-Orcutt correction for first order serial correlation. The dependent variable is real UI benefits (in 1972 dollars) expressed as a percentage of potential real GNP.

[b]Equations 5 and 6 were fitted with no constant terms. Also, each observation was weighted by the fraction of the quarter that the temporary compensation program was in effect.

Payments under the EB program are examined in equations 3 and 4. Since these benefits were first available in 1971 the equations cover just the 1971–79 period. The unemployment rate, a time trend, and seasonal dummies are the explanatory variables. In this case the unemployment rate is interacted with a dummy variable for periods when the national EB trigger was in effect. Unemployment has a larger effect on EB payments when the national trigger is on. Both unemployment variables and the time trend have significant coefficients in equations 3 and 4. The effect of unemployment on benefit payments is raised by half when the national EB trigger is on. About 90 percent of the variation in EB over this nine-year period is explained by the equations.

Federal legislation has created a TC program five times since 1957.[23] The programs paid benefits to the long-term unemployed who had previously collected regular state UI benefits but had exhausted their benefit eligibility. Between 1957 and 1979 there were twenty-four calendar quarters when TC programs were in effect. Equations 5 and 6 explore the determinants of TC benefits for these periods. The cyclical indicator in these equations is the long-term unemployment rate: the number of persons unemployed twenty-seven or more weeks as a percentage of the civilian labor force. The equation omits a constant term under the assumption that benefit payments increase proportionately with the long-term unemployment rate. A time trend was also tested, but it proved to be insignificant. The long-term unemployment rate, however, is highly significant in both equations.[24] This should not be surprising since the TC programs were intended to aid precisely this group of workers.

The equations in Table 1.2 indicate that benefits in all three tiers of state UI programs are very responsive to unemployment. Unemployment coefficients in the six equations are highly significant, and the regressions explain most of the variation in real benefits payments as a percentage of potential real GNP. Since unemployment rose in 1980 and again sharply in 1982, the equations can be used to track the time paths of actual payments since 1979. Table 1.3 shows results of using the equations for this purpose. The top part traces actual and predicted payments from 1969 to 1979, the last eleven years of the estimation period. The four quarterly observations for each year have been averaged to produce the annual estimates appearing in the table. All three equations trace the actual time paths of benefits very closely for these years, including the sharp benefit increases in 1970 and 1975.

Next, projections for the 1980–84 period are displayed, and for regular state UI large errors are immediately apparent. The mean error for 1980 (−0.052) represents about 10 percent of actual payments,[25] almost twice the size of the largest average error for the 1969–79 period.[26] The percentage overprediction, that is, the error divided by actual payments, then grows to 24, 31, and 45 percent in the next three years, dropping to 40 percent in 1984. Clearly the close association between unemployment and regular state UI benefit payments observed in the preceding twenty-three years was seriously disturbed.[27] For a given unemployment rate much fewer regular state UI benefits were paid in 1980–84 than in earlier periods.

Since large prediction errors first appear in 1980, it is also clear that the changed relationship predates the advent of the Reagan administration. Because equation 1 included a control for base period unemployment, the pattern of sharply increasing errors in 1980–84 cannot be attributed to higher base period unemployment. Among unemployed adults, the tradi-

Table 1.3. Actual and Projected State UI Benefit Payments, 1969–83[a]

Year	Regular State UI Benefits— Equation (1)			Federal State Extended Benefits— Equation (3)			Temporary Compensation Benefits— Equation (5)		
	Actual	Forecast	Error	Actual	Forecast	Error	Actual	Forecast	Error
	Forecasts within the Period of Estimation								
1969	.222	.226	-.004	NA	NA	NA	NA	NA	NA
1970	.371	.382	-.011	NA	NA	NA	NA	NA	NA
1971	.445	.432	.013	.060	.051	.009	NA	NA	NA
1972	.376	.353	.023	.040	.052	-.012	.042	.019	.023
1973	.311	.292	.019	.011	.018	-.007	NA	NA	NA
1974	.406	.385	.021	.036	.027	.009	NA	NA	NA
1975	.722	.711	.011	.152	.146	.006	.128	.128	.000
1976	.515	.522	-.007	.129	.130	-.001	.155	.148	.007
1977	.438	.466	-.028	.088	.098	-.012	.063	.083	-.020
1978	.366	.363	.003	.032	.024	.008	NA	NA	NA
1979	.365	.382	-.017	.009	.012	-.003	NA	NA	NA
				1980–1984 Projections					
1980	.497	.549	-.052	.056	.063	-.007	NA	NA	NA
1981	.445	.550	-.105	.040	.045	-.005	NA	NA	NA
1982	.620	.813	-.193	.071	.149	-.078	.032	.064[b]	-.032[b]
1983	.510	.742	-.232	.048	.144	-.096	.152	.255	-.104
1984	.351	.493	-.141	.001	.034	-.033	.053	.156	-.103

[a]Forecasts for 1969–79 and projections for 1980–84 are based on equations (1), (3), and (5) from Table 1.2. Benefits are measured in 1972 dollars and expressed as a percentage of potential real GNP. Annual observations are averages of four quarterly observations per year.

[b]This projection was made assuming that FSC began as scheduled in mid-September 1982. Alternatively, if the program had been started at the start of April 1982, the forecast and error entries for 1982 would be .127 and -.095, respectively.

NA = Not applicable as there was no program in existence during the year.

33

tional group of UI recipients, lower application rates and reduced eligibility must be major factors behind the reduced benefit payments.

Determinations regarding benefit eligibility are made at the state level, and since 1980 the states have been under increasing pressure to reduce benefit payments. The number of states subject to penalty taxes because of outstanding debts increased from two in 1979 to nine in 1980. Due to the renewed borrowing by several states in 1980 it was clear that additional future penalty taxes were also in store. When federal loans started to carry interest charges in April 1982, there were increased financial incentives to reduce payments in order to minimize borrowing. Provisions of the March 1983 Social Security Amendments then offered debtor states an opportunity to reduce the costs of indebtedness in return for improving program solvency (raising taxes and lowering benefit payouts). Subsequent to that legislation most debtor states have enacted statutory changes to improve program solvency.

The reasons for the recent reductions in regular state UI benefit outlays are not well understood. Changes in laws and administrative procedures at the state level, especially in states with large debts, are undoubtedly a factor contributing to the reduced benefit payments.[28] Also, however, there could be measurable effects caused by several factors: high benefit exhaustion rates associated with the very prolonged recessionary period since 1979; different application behavior among eligible nonbeneficiaries in the 1980–83 period; a secular increase in the share of total unemployment arising in the South and West, regions that traditionally compensate a lower proportion of the unemployed than do states in the Northeast and North Central regions; and reduced utilization of state UI benefits by older workers who have been subject to more stringent old age unemployment benefit offsets since 1979.[29] Thus, changes in state UI laws and administrative practices provide only one (but not the only) important explanation for recent decreases in the utilization of regular state UI benefits by unemployed adults.

The Reagan administration's stance regarding the payment of regular state UI benefits could be characterized as follows. UI is a state program, and the states should have primary responsibility for ensuring that revenues match benefit payments. Furthermore, it is not appropriate for the federal government to make interest-free loans to states or to permit deferral of debt repayments, much less to forgive indebtedness incurred in current or prior recessions. In other words, keep the pressure on the states and they will eventually restore the fiscal balance in their programs. Given this perspective it is hardly surprising that the administration did not advance legislative proposals to lighten the financial burdens on the debtor state UI programs even after the severity of the 1981–82 recession became apparent and greatly increased the volume of benefit outlays.

To some extent, then, the reduced levels of regular state UI benefits in 1981 and later years can be attributed to inaction by the Reagan administration. Had it made proposals to lessen debt burdens, state UI benefits would undoubtedly be higher now and in future years. The size of this effect, however, is difficult to estimate with precision for at least two reasons. First, it is not clear how much of the reduction in benefit payments is due to state legislation and administrative inaction (as opposed to higher rates of exhaustion, reduced numbers of applications, and the other factors noted earlier). Second, it is also not clear how much the states would have done on their own to restore fiscal balance if they anticipated more financial help from the federal government. The absence of an administration policy initiative to reduce the cost of indebtedness is undoubtedly responsible for some of the benefit reduction, but it is not obvious what share of the total reduction is due to this policy stance.

The projections in Table 1.3 show that EB payments have also been reduced, particularly in 1982 and 1983. First, note the 1980 and 1981 projections that were made using the actual values of the explanatory variables in equation 3. For these two years the overpredictions represent 11.3 and 10.4 percent, respectively, of actual EB payments. Since fewer than average numbers of workers were receiving regular state UI benefits in these years, overpredictions of EB payouts would be expected. Using the actual values of the explanatory variables from equation 3 and considering the declining size of the regular state UI program, the projection errors in 1980–81 are not unusually large.

Reagan administration initiatives, however, have strongly affected actual EB payouts starting in the second quarter of 1982. If the national EB trigger had not been previously eliminated, it would have been activated in April 1982 and remained on into the third quarter of 1983. Using the adult unemployment rate–national EB trigger interaction variable in equation 3 causes the 1982 and 1983 predictions to increase sharply. The 1982 and 1983 projections are higher than the 1981 figures by 0.104 and 0.099 percent (calculated as a proportion of potential real GNP), and 0.060 and 0.056 percent of these increases were caused by the national EB trigger interaction term.[30]

State EB trigger thresholds were raised starting in late September 1982. Because unemployment was rising sharply in the last half of 1982, many state EB programs were activated despite the higher trigger thresholds. Thus not much effect was apparent in the fourth quarter of 1982. As 1983 unfolded, however, state EB programs were turned off despite the persistence of very high unemployment. At the end of March, June, September, and December 1983 the number of states in which EB had been triggered was twenty-six, ten, two, and zero, respectively. The combined effects of the higher trigger thresholds and the economic recovery were to sharply reduce actual EB payments in 1983, and by 1984 only $42 million was paid for the entire year.

The FSC program also paid out much less than the TC programs of earlier recessions. The average projection for 1983 yields an error of 0.104 percent of potential real GNP, exceeding actual payouts by 68 percent. This projection error is unusually large, particularly when it is recognized that FSC in 1983 was often being paid earlier in the unemployment spell, that is, immediately after regular state UI was exhausted, than under the TC programs of 1972–73 and 1975–77, in which EB payments had to be exhausted as well. A major reason for the overpredictions was undoubtedly the variable duration of worker FSC entitlement. Because potential weeks of benefits were directly tied to the state IUR they were typically shorter than the twenty-six-week maximum of the 1975–77 FSB program.

Long-term unemployment was particularly high in both 1982 and 1983. The unemployment rate of persons unemployed twenty-seven weeks or longer (as a percentage of the civilian labor force) averaged 1.61 percent in 1982 and 2.29 percent in 1983. The corresponding rates in the second and third quarters of 1982, just prior to the enactment of FSC, were 1.6 and 1.7 percent, respectively. These matched the highest rates for the entire 1975–77 period (1.6 percent in the third quarter of 1975 and 1.7 percent in the first quarter of 1976) and were higher than the highest rates in the prior recessions of 1957–58, 1960–61, and 1970–71. Thus, under a different administration in Washington, D.C., it is likely that FSC would have been enacted in the second quarter of 1982 rather than at the very end of the third quarter. The FSC projection for 1982 that appears in the body of Table 1.3 was made using the actual mid-September starting date for FSC eligibility. The forecast error was 100 percent of the observed rate of payout for 1982. Alternatively (as shown in footnote b of Table 1.3) the forecast could be made assuming FSC would have begun at the start of the second quarter of 1982. Under this assumption the 1982 forecast of FSC payments increased to 0.127 percent and the error increased to 297 percent of actual payments.

From these projections of state UI benefits in 1980–84, three findings stand out. First, using regression equations based on 1957–79 data the equations systematically overpredicted actual payments for the 1980–84 period. Second, in regular state UI the size of the overprediction errors grew sharply between 1980 and 1983. Expressed as a percentage of actual payments the average errors for the four years were 10, 24, 31, and 45 percent, respectively. Third, the largest errors were made in forecasting benefits for the long-term unemployed. In 1983, for example, the forecast error for EB and FSC benefits combined represented about 100 percent of actual payments. Actual real benefits, however, were 0.200 percent of potential real GNP, while projected payments were twice as high at 0.399 percent of potential real GNP.

From the preceding discussion it is obvious that UI benefit availability has been reduced during the 1980s. Reagan administration policy actions are clearly responsible for some of the cutbacks. In 1982 and 1983 cutbacks totaling $800 million to $1 billion a year in TAA, UCX, and public service jobless benefits can be attributed to administration initiatives. In the state UI programs, cutbacks of increasing size were apparent for the 1980–83 period. The cutbacks in state UI benefits began to occur in 1980, before the Reagan administration took office. Undoubtedly, these cutbacks are partly the result of actions taken by the states in response to the widespread funding problems they have encountered in the 1980s. State as well as federal actions have both contributed to the state UI cutbacks of the present decade, but it is not obvious how to estimate their separate contributions to the cutbacks.[31] What is obvious is that the state UI cutbacks have been of a large scale (30 to 40 percent in the 1982–84 period), and that workers receiving long-term state UI benefits have suffered the largest reductions.

4. The Economic Status of the Long-Term Unemployed

Two salient features of the U.S. labor market in the 1980–84 period were the high levels of long-term unemployment and the cutbacks in state UI benefits, particularly benefits paid to the long-term unemployed. This section examines the tabulations of the U.S. Census Bureau's Current Population Survey (CPS) for selected years between 1976 and 1983. The purpose of the analysis is to describe the economic status of the long-term unemployed and to explore the effects of state UI benefits and other transfers on their economic status. Attention is focused on those with the longest unemployment durations.

Long-term unemployment is measured in two different ways in the CPS. The monthly labor force survey asks questions about the duration of the current unemployment spell for each unemployed household member. Averages based on the twelve monthly survey responses to this question show there were between 1.0 million and 1.3 million persons who were unemployed twenty-seven weeks or longer in the years 1975–77. The corresponding annual averages were between 1.6 million and 2.6 million during 1982–84. In both absolute numbers and as a percentage of the labor force, this measure showed more long-term unemployment in 1982–84 than in 1975–77.[32]

A second CPS measure of long-term unemployment is based on responses to the "work experience survey" conducted in March of each year, which asks questions about total weeks of unemployment during the previous calendar year and combines unemployment from all spells experienced during the year. Because durations from all spells are combined, the work experience data show more long-term unemployment than do the annual averages based on the twelve monthly surveys. The work experience data indicate that more than four million persons were unemployed twenty-seven weeks or longer in each year of the 1975–77 period, whereas more than six million had such long durations in 1982 and 1983 and about five million in 1984. Like the annual averages, the work experience data show there was relatively more long-term unemployment during 1982–84 than during 1975–77.

Table 1.4 presents work experience data on unemployment duration for the years 1976, 1980, 1982, and 1983. It shows that 4.1 million persons were unemployed twenty-seven or more weeks in 1976. The corresponding counts were 6.8 million in 1982 and 6.2 million in 1983. The second panel of the table then shows that the long-term unemployed accounted for 21.1 percent of all unemployed persons in 1976, 26.7 percent in 1982, and 27.0 percent in 1983.

The March CPS questionnaire also includes a set of questions about the detailed income sources of each family member. One of the transfer payments that is identified is UI benefits. The bottom two panels in Table 1.4 show the numbers and proportions of unemployed persons who reported receipt of UI benefits by year and unemployment duration. Overall about one-third of the unemployed received UI benefits in each of the four years. The recipiency proportions rise with unemployment duration across the first three duration categories, but then decline among those unemployed forty to fifty-two weeks.

The recipiency proportions in the forty- to fifty-two-week duration category reflect changes in long-term benefit availability as discussed earlier. Recall from Table 1.1 that benefits were more available in 1975–76 than in 1982–83. Also recall that combined EB and FSC payments were much higher in 1983 than in 1982. In this longest duration category the recipiency proportions were 0.376 percent in 1976, 0.258 percent in 1982, and 0.329 percent in 1983.

The income status of the unemployed in 1976 and 1983 is examined in Table 1.5, which shows poverty rates for unemployed persons. Poverty status is measured in two ways: prior to the receipt of any transfer payments and after counting all transfer payments received. The table displays weighted counts of unemployed workers and poverty rates disaggregated by UI benefit status and unemployment duration.[33] There is a strong positive association between unemployment duration and the poverty rate in both years. In 1976, for example, the pre-transfer poverty rate increased from 17.1 percent for those unemployed one to thirteen weeks to 59.9

Table 1.4. Counts of Unemployed Workers and Unemployment Insurance Beneficiaries by Duration of Unemployment, 1976, 1980, 1982, and 1983

	1–13	14–26	27–39	40–52	Total
	Unemployment Duration (weeks)				
	Number of Unemployed (thousands)				
1976	10,943	4585	2135	2045	19,708
1980	11,293	5011	2174	2006	20,484
1982	11,872	6705	3110	3649	25,337
1983	10,852	5854	2804	3368	22,879
	Proportional Distribution of Unemployment				
1976	.555	.233	.108	.103	1.000
1980	.551	.245	.106	.098	1.000
1982	.469	.265	.123	.144	1.000
1983	.474	.256	.123	.147	1.000
	Number of UI Beneficiaries (thousands)				
1976	2441	1825	925	769	5960
1980	3015	2068	969	466	6518
1982	3502	2799	1389	941	8632
1983	2914	2378	1185	1107	7584
	Proportion with UI Benefits				
1976	.223	.398	.433	.376	.302
1980	.267	.413	.446	.232	.318
1982	.295	.417	.447	.258	.341
1983	.269	.406	.423	.329	.331

Source: Based on tabulations of the Current Population Survey conducted at the Urban Institute.

percent for those unemployed fifty-one to fifty-two weeks. This association reflects the importance of earnings in determining family income and poverty status. Family income is reduced as unemployment duration increases.

Unemployment insurance transfers and all other transfers each have measurable effects in reducing the poverty rate. Reductions in the poverty rate due to all transfers increase as unemployment duration increases, but the gradient of the reduced poverty rate is much steeper for those receiving UI benefits. In 1976, for example, transfers reduced the poverty rate by 4 to 5 percentage points among workers unemployed one to thirteen weeks. Among those unemployed fifty-one to fifty-two weeks, however, poverty rates were reduced by 38.8 percentage points when UI was received but by only 13.2 percentage points when UI benefits were not received.[34]

Note also in Table 1.5 that UI recipients generally had lower pretransfer poverty rates than nonrecipients with the same unemployment duration. Thus, UI beneficiaries have lower post-transfer poverty rates both because

Table 1.5. Poverty Status and Unemployment Duration, 1976 and 1983

Unemployment Duration	1976				1983			
	Worker Counts (thousands)	Poverty Rates			Worker Counts (thousands)	Poverty Rates		
		Pre-transfer	Post-transfer	Change		Pre-transfer	Post-transfer	Change
All Unemployed								
1–13	10,943	.171	.121	.050	10,852	.232	.187	.045
14–26	4585	.234	.152	.082	5854	.292	.224	.068
27–39	2135	.341	.182	.159	2804	.419	.297	.122
40–50	1247	.474	.262	.212	1922	.532	.388	.144
51–52	798	.599	.372	.227	1446	.665	.503	.162
Total	19,708	.240	.154	.086	22,879	.323	.247	.076
Recipients of UI								
1–13	2441	.089	.045	.044	2914	.111	.065	.046
14–26	1825	.174	.068	.106	2378	.205	.107	.098
27–39	925	.326	.104	.222	1185	.359	.174	.185
40–50	473	.463	.110	.353	662	.517	.272	.245
51–52	296	.591	.203	.388	445	.620	.387	.233
Total	5960	.207	.075	.132	7584	.244	.132	.112
Nonrecipients of UI								
1–13	8502	.194	.143	.051	7938	.277	.232	.045
14–26	2760	.274	.207	.067	3476	.352	.305	.047
27–39	1210	.351	.241	.110	1619	.436	.387	.076
40–50	774	.481	.355	.126	1260	.540	.448	.092
51–52	502	.604	.472	.132	1001	.684	.555	.129
Total	13,748	.255	.188	.067	15,295	.362	.304	.058

Source: Based on tabulations of the Current Population Survey conducted at the Urban Institute.

their pretransfer poverty rates were lower and because UI benefits caused larger reductions in poverty rates than among nonrecipients of UI. Overall, transfer payments reduced the poverty rate from 20.7 percent to 7.5 percent among UI recipients in 1976 while they reduced the poverty rate from 25.5 percent to 18.8 percent among nonrecipients of UI.

Comparing the poverty-reducing effectiveness of transfer payments between 1976 and 1983, three points are apparent from Table 1.5. First, the unemployed were generally somewhat poorer in 1983 than in 1976. For each of the five unemployment duration categories among both recipients and nonrecipients of UI, the 1976 pretransfer poverty rate was lower than the corresponding rate in 1983. For example, recipients of UI with one- to thirteen-week durations had pretransfer poverty rates of 8.9 percent in 1976 and 11.1 percent in 1983. Second, the poverty-reducing effectiveness of UI and other transfers was lower in 1983 than in 1976. For nine of the ten comparisons that can be made in the bottom two panels of the table, the 1976 poverty rate reduction was larger than the 1983 reduction.[35] Third, and most important, the diminished effectiveness of UI benefits in reducing poverty rates in 1983 is most apparent among workers with long unemployment durations. For those unemployed forty to fifty weeks and fifty-one to fifty-two weeks, poverty rates among UI recipients were reduced by 35-38 percentage points in 1976 but by only 23-25 percentage points in 1983. This finding is hardly surprising given the reduced availability of long-term UI benefits in 1983 compared to 1976.

5. Conclusions

Two traditional objectives of unemployment insurance are to reduce the size of income losses experienced by unemployed workers and their families and to provide automatic stability to the overall economy. Achievement of both objectives requires that benefit payments increase sharply during recessions. Although aggregate payouts from all UI programs did increase in the recessions of 1980 and 1981-82, the size of the increase (relative to real potential GNP) was considerably smaller than that in each of the previous four recessions. As documented in section 3, benefit availability was deliberately reduced in the 1980s while the economy was in recession. Two major causes for the benefit cutbacks were federal policy actions taken by the Reagan administration and state legislation enacted to improve state UI program solvency. Because of the cutbacks, UI has been less successful in the 1980s than previously in achieving its traditional micro (family-level) and macro (automatic stabilizing) income maintenance objectives.

Among all the transfer payment programs, unemployment insurance has a unique role to play in maintaining income and reducing poverty among the unemployed. In years of high unemployment, the average duration of unemployment spells lengthens and increased economic hardships are experienced by the long-term unemployed. Not only do UI benefits reduce poverty rates, but also its poverty-reducing impact is largest among the long-term unemployed. Much of this impact can be attributed to long-term jobless benefits paid to workers who have exhausted their regular state UI entitlement.

The recent cutbacks in UI benefits have contributed to the higher post-transfer poverty rates of the unemployed in 1983 compared with those in 1976. Increases in post-transfer poverty rates between 1976 and 1983 were particularly large among those unemployed twenty-seven weeks or longer. Cutbacks in long-term jobless benefits which were even larger than the cutbacks in regular state UI benefits in the 1980s have undoubtedly contributed to this outcome.

It can be argued that UI programs are best suited for addressing problems of short-term unemployment, and that they never were meant to compensate long-term unemployment. That may be true, and it may be appropriate to create a separate program (with more definite job search and job training components) to compensate these individuals. Nevertheless, it is clear that the long-term unemployed experience very high poverty rates and that UI benefits have a substantial poverty-reducing impact. In the absence of some alternative new program, and given the particularly large amount of long-term unemployment observed in the first half of the 1980s, the timing of the recent cutbacks in long-term unemployment benefits was particularly unfortunate.

To this author there is a continuing need for UI programs to make benefit payments and a need to provide jobless benefits to the long-term unemployed. The micro and macro income maintenance objectives of UI are no less valid in the 1980s than they were in the 1930s. New approaches for dealing with long-term unemployment are worthy of consideration, but in the meantime the provision of long-term jobless benefits will also be needed. At present state UI programs have no automatic mechanism for providing such benefits on a scale similar to their availability in the mid-1970s.

NOTES

1. For historic data on maximum duration by state, see U.S. Department of Labor (1960) and earlier issues of this publication.

2. One survey of the literature on labor supply responses is found in Vroman (1983), pp. 125–137.

3. A summary of recent UI legislative developments at both the federal and state levels is given in Chapters 1 and 2 of Vroman (1986).

4. Funding problems for the states through the end of 1984 are summarized in Chapter 1 of Vroman (1986).

5. Some states (Connecticut, Delaware, the District of Columbia, Pennsylvania, Vermont, and Washington) had been subject to penalty taxes for certain years prior to 1980.

6. In fact, Illinois and Pennsylvania did not enact major legislation to reduce their debts until 1983, and New Jersey enacted legislation only in 1984.

7. Not all of the administration proposals were enacted. The most important of those not enacted was a proposal to change the definition of "suitable work" which would have required that after they had received benefits for thirteen weeks UI claimants must accept any job paying an amount equal to (the higher of) the weekly UI benefit or the minimum wage. Suitable work has more frequently been interpreted as paying at least as much as the previous job.

8. The 1981 changes in UCX were partly reversed by the Miscellaneous Revenue Act of 1982 (P.L. 97-362). After October 25, 1982, veterans who had served two or more years and were not dishonorably discharged would collect up to thirteen weeks of UCX after completing a four-week waiting period.

9. U.S. House of Representatives, Committee on Ways and Means (1982), p. 309.

10. As mentioned in note 8, the UCX changes were partly reversed in late October 1982.

11. States with an IUR above 7.5 percent (Michigan, for example) were permitted to defer three-fourths of the annual interest payments on outstanding loans. Sharp increases in FUT penalty tax rates scheduled for 1984 and 1985 were eliminated in some states. See Hobbie (1982), pp. 11–15.

12. For a state forced to borrow in 1983 the increase in net solvency must be at least 25 percent in 1983 and then 35 percent in 1984, and 50 percent in 1985. Some states that made adjustments, such as Michigan, increased net solvency 50 percent immediately in 1983.

13. Chapter 2 in Vroman (1986) summarizes these state legislative changes.

14. The state could use either its current insured unemployment rate or an average rate starting on January 1, 1982, for determining the potential duration of FSC benefits.

15. Because coverage of regular state UI expanded sharply in 1978 there is less need for a SUA program in the 1980s. Nevertheless, about half of total benefits in the earlier SUA program went to workers covered by regular state UI. Benefits were available to these persons because SUA had more liberal eligibility requirements than did many regular state UI programs.

16. The higher amount in 1983 reflects increased UCX eligibility after October 1982.

17. From 1973 to 1975–76 benefits more than doubled. If the 1979 benefit level were doubled, $572 million would have been paid in 1982 and 1983, or $493 and $388 million more than was actually paid.

18. Deflating these current dollar magnitudes with the personal consumption deflator from the National Income Accounts causes the proportional reductions in real benefits to be even larger. Real benefits in 1975 and 1976 were $1.300 and $1.724 billion, whereas in 1982 and 1983 they were $.410 and $.412 billion, about $1 billion less in real terms each year.

19. The magnitude of dollars of 1972 purchasing power was $7.572 billion for 1975–76 and $5.083 billion for 1982–83.

20. When the number of persons unemployed twenty-seven weeks or longer is expressed as a percentage of the civilian labor force, this figure is 1.28 percent for 1975, 1.40 percent for 1976, 1.60 percent for 1982, and 2.29 percent for 1983.

21. The base period unemployment rate is approximated by an average of rates lagged two to five quarters with weights of 0.2, 0.3, 0.3, and 0.2 for each quarter.

22. Statistical significance of the coefficients is indicated by the t ratios that appear in parentheses beneath each coefficient. Ratios larger than 2.0 are significantly different from zero when tested at the 0.05 level of significance. A large t ratio means the associated coefficient is estimated with a high degree of precision.

23. The program names and time periods covered were as follows: Temporary Unemployment Compensation, July 1958 to June 1959; Temporary Extended Unemployment Compensation, April 1961 to June 1962; Temporary Compensation, February 1972 to September 1972; Federal Supplemental Benefits, January 1975 to November 1977; and Federal Supplemental Compensation, September 1982 to March 1985.

24. The large unemployment coefficients in equations 5 and 6 of Table 1.2 do not imply that TC benefits are as responsive to unemployment as regular state UI benefits. Recall that the TC equations utilize the long-term unemployment rate, which in 1981 was only 20 percent of the rate for adults twenty-five and older, or 1.07 versus 5.45 percent.

25. Recall that payments are measured in real terms and expressed as a percentage of potential real GNP.

26. Another way to gauge the 1980 projection error is to compare it with the standard error of estimate of the underlying regression equation. If projection errors were random the average error for the four quarters of a year would have a mean of zero and a standard deviation roughly half the size of the regression's standard error (which is 0.027 for equation 1). For 1980, however, the average error is about two times this standard error, or four times what would be expected.

27. In a similar type of investigation, Burtless found that the relationship between insured unemployment and job loser unemployment fitted to 1968–79 data shifted downward by 10 percent in 1980 and by an additional 13 percent in 1981–82; see Burtless (1983). This analysis was later updated with data through the third quarter of 1984 in Burtless and Vroman (1984), who found the cumulative downward shifts to be 10 percent in 1980, 21 percent in 1981, 28 percent in 1982,

and 34 percent in 1983–84. The direction and size of these changes over the 1980–84 period are quite similar to the results in Table 1.3.

28. Evidence from the four states with the largest amount of debt (Pennsylvania, Illinois, Michigan, and Ohio) is supportive of this interpretation. Between 1979 and 1983 the national ratio of insured unemployment to total unemployment fell by 0.080, from 0.397 to 0.317. In these four states, however, the average 1979–83 reduction in the ratio was twice as large, falling by 0.161 from 0.462 to 0.301.

29. Those who try to collect retirement and unemployment benefits simultaneously are now subject to an offset that reduces UI benefits on a dollar-for-dollar basis for most retirement benefits that are received.

30. The national trigger would have been activated on April 12, 1982. It is not clear exactly when the trigger would have gone off since EB recipients were previously included in the trigger calculations. After examining seasonally adjusted monthly IURs for 1983 it was estimated that the national trigger would have gone off in mid-August 1983, halfway through the third quarter.

31. One effort to distinguish the two causes for benefit reductions is made in Part 4 of Vroman (1984).

32. Long-term unemployment as a percentage of the labor force was 1.28 percent in 1975, 1.40 percent in 1976, and 1.04 percent in 1977. The corresponding percentages for the 1982–84 period were 1.61 percent, 2.29 percent, and 1.44 percent.

33. Most unemployed persons are members of households, and it is the poverty status of the household that is measured. Thus, the table shows proportions of unemployed persons who were members of poor households.

34. Part of this contrast is due to the fact that some in the fifty-one- to fifty-two-week duration category received no transfers of any kind. These persons are included with all other nonrecipients of UI in the bottom panel of Table 1.5. Among nonrecipients of UI who were unemployed for fifty-one to fifty-two weeks and did receive some kind of transfer payment, pre-transfer and post-transfer poverty rates were respectively 85.9 percent and 65.9 percent in 1976. In this duration category the poverty-reducing effect of other transfers was about half that of UI benefits.

35. The single exception is found among UI recipients with one- to thirteen-week durations. The 1976 reduction in poverty was 4.4 percentage points, compared with 4.6 percentage points in 1983.

REFERENCES

Burtless, Gary. 1983. "Why Is Insured Unemployment So Low?" *Brookings Papers on Economic Activity* 1: 225–253.

Burtless, Gary, and Wayne Vroman. 1984. "The Performance of Unemployment Insurance Since 1979." Paper presented at the annual meeting of the Industrial Relations Research Association, Dallas (December).

Hobbie, Richard. 1982. "Unemployment Insurance: Financial Trouble in the Trust Fund." Congressional Research Service, Library of Congress. Issue brief no. IB79098.

U.S. Congress. House of Representatives. Committee on Ways and Means. 1982. *Background Material and Data on Major Programs Within the Jurisdiction of the Committee on Ways and Means.* Committee Print WMCP 97-29.

U.S. Department of Labor. 1960. *Significant Provisions of State Unemployment Insurance Laws,* October 15. Washington, D.C.: U.S. Department of Labor.

Vroman, Wayne. 1983. *Employment Termination Benefits in the U.S. Economy.* Washington, D.C.: Employee Benefit Research Institute.

Vroman, Wayne. 1984. "The Reagan Administration and Unemployment Insurance." Washington, D.C.: The Urban Institute. Mimeograph.

Vroman, Wayne. 1986. *The Funding Crisis in State Unemployment Insurance.* Kalamazoo, Mich.: Upjohn Institute for Employment Research.

2

Unemployment Insurance and the Safety Net for the Unemployed

SHELDON DANZIGER AND PETER GOTTSCHALK

Introduction

This paper analyzes the unemployment insurance program as a component of the overall income maintenance system for the unemployed. We focus on two different income maintenance functions—protection against earnings losses and protection against poverty. The first line of defense against earnings losses arising from unemployment is UI, a social insurance program. As in other social insurance programs, benefits are available to covered workers regardless of income. The second line of defense includes income-tested programs, such as Aid to Families with Dependent Children or General Assistance, which explicitly take need into account and make payments to the unemployed who are not eligible for or have exhausted UI benefits, or still have low incomes after receiving UI. There are also other social insurance programs for the unemployed who leave the labor force through retirement or disability.

The paper is divided into five sections. We start by defining terms and describing our sample. The second section describes how the proportion of household heads with low earnings changed between 1976 and 1984. The third section documents changes in the probability of being unemployed and of receiving UI. We then turn to the receipt of other cash transfers by the unemployed. We conclude with some recommendations for modifying the "safety net" to better assist the unemployed, low earners in particular.

1. Definitions of Unemployment and Low Weekly Earnings

We analyze the unemployment experiences in 1976 and 1984 of households headed by persons whom we classify as "expected to work." Included in this group are heads who are between the ages of twenty-one and sixty-four, are not disabled or in school, and are not women with children under six.[1] Because of our focus on the UI program, we exclude the self-employed, who are not covered, from the analysis.[2]

The two years chosen had similar unemployment rates, 7.7 and 7.5 percent respectively, and both followed deep recessions. However, the UI program was quite different in the two years.[3] UI eligibility and benefit levels had been liberalized in response to the 1974–75 recession—supplemental payments were available for up to sixty-five weeks and benefits were extended to those who had not previously been covered. In contrast, benefits were restricted to twenty-six weeks for most of the unemployed as part of the budgetary retrenchment of domestic programs during the early years of the Reagan administration (see Burtless, 1983; Vroman, 1984). Thus, the two years chosen represent similar macroeconomic conditions and highlight the dramatic changes in UI that have taken place.

Since our primary interest is in the effectiveness of the safety net for the unemployed who are at high risk of being poor, we focus on household heads who have low weekly earnings. We define "low earners" as household heads with weekly earnings less than $204 in 1984 dollars. Such persons could not earn the poverty-line income for a family of four even if they worked fifty-two weeks a year at that weekly wage.[4] Households headed by low earners are not necessarily poor. Whether or not the household is poor depends on the household's own poverty line and its total cash income from all earners and all other income sources. Similarly, poor households do not necessarily have heads with low weekly earnings.[5]

We begin by classifying all household heads into one of three mutually exclusive groups based on their work experience and level of weekly earnings: those who worked at some time during the year and had low weekly earnings; those who worked at some time during the year and did not have low weekly earnings; and those who did not work at all during the year. We further distinguish, for low earners and those who are not low earners, between those who were unemployed for some part of the year (looking for work or on layoff) and those who were not unemployed during the entire year. We do not analyze the unemployment or UI experience of household heads who report no earnings or weeks worked, since we cannot calculate their weekly wage.

Figure 2.1 illustrates these distinctions. In 1984 there were 58.57 million households with a head whom we classify as expected to work.[6] Among these heads, 9.74 million (16.6 percent) had low weekly earnings, 43.34 million (74.0 percent) had weekly earnings above $204, and 5.49 million (9.4 percent) reported no earnings or weeks worked. Low earners were almost three times as likely to be unemployed and, if unemployed, only about half as likely to receive unemployment insurance as those who were

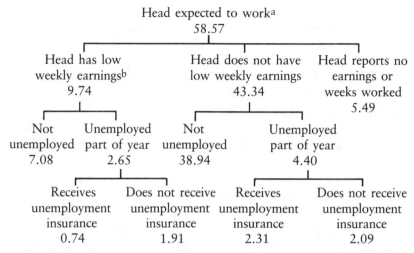

Figure 2.1. Households Classified by Whether Head Is Expected to Work, Has Low Weekly Earnings, or Is Unemployed, 1984 (all numbers in millions)

Source: Computations by authors from March 1985 Current Population Survey computer tape.

[a]Head is under sixty-five and not a student, disabled, self-employed, or a woman with a child under six.

[b]Weekly earnings below $204.

not low earners. About 27 percent of low earners (2.65/9.74) and about 10 percent of those who were not low earners (4.40/43.34) were unemployed at some point during 1984. About 28 percent (0.74/2.65) of unemployed low earners and about 53 percent (2.31/4.40) of unemployed non–low earners received UI. Thus by 1984, UI reached only a minority of all the unemployed, and coverage was minimal for unemployed low earners.

In the next two sections we examine how the composition of household heads and their unemployment probabilities and UI receipts changed over the 1976–84 period. We find that the incidence of low earnings increased and that the situation of low earners deteriorated, even though macro-economic conditions were similar in the two years.

2. Changes in the Incidence of Low Earnings

Table 2.1 presents changes in the composition of our sample between 1976 and 1984. Heads of households are classified on the basis of their work experience and level of earnings. Because there are large differences in the

Table 2.1. Percentage Composition of Households Whose Heads Are Expected to Work, 1976 and 1984

	Male		Female	
	1976	1984	1976	1984
Head has low weekly earnings	9.1	13.0	31.0	29.3
Head does not have low weekly earnings	85.1	79.5	50.2	55.1
Head reports no earnings or weeks worked	5.8	7.5	18.8	15.6

Source: For all tables in this chapter, computations by authors from March 1977 and March 1985 Current Population Survey computer tapes.

labor market experiences of male and female household heads, we distinguish between sex of household head in the analysis that follows.

Male household heads in each year were much less likely than female heads to be low earners and much less likely to report zero weeks of work or zero earnings. In 1984, about 80 percent of male heads earned more than $204 per week—that is, they did not have low weekly earnings—whereas 55 percent of female heads had earnings that exceeded this threshold.

The increase between 1976 and 1984 in the proportion of men with low or zero earnings is striking: the percentage of men who had low earnings increased from 9.1 to 13.0 percent, and the percentage who reported no earnings or weeks worked increased from 5.8 to 7.5 percent. The result was that while roughly one out of every seven male heads had low or zero earnings in 1976, this ratio jumped to one in five by 1984.

The trends differed for female heads. The proportion not working dropped from 18.8 to 15.6 percent and the proportion with low weekly earnings decreased from 31.0 to 29.3 percent.

3. Changes in Unemployment and UI Receipt

In this section we first describe changes in unemployment and unemployment insurance receipt. We then present a statistical model to account for these changes.

Tabular Evidence

Table 2.2 shows the change between 1976 and 1984 in the probability of unemployment at some point during the year for male and female household heads, classified by whether the head was a low earner. The unemployment probabilities shown are higher than published unemployment rates, which measure the probability of unemployment during a single

Table 2.2. Unemployment, 1976 and 1984

	Probability of Being Unemployed During the Year[a]			Mean Weeks Unemployed[b]		
	1976	1984	Percentage Change[c]	1976	1984	Percentage Change[c]
Head has low weekly earnings						
Male	0.299	0.302	+ 1.0	19.9	21.1	+ 6.0
Female	0.237	0.228	− 3.8	16.6	17.0	+ 2.4
Head does not have low weekly earnings						
Male	0.126	0.106	− 15.9	16.6	16.4	− 1.2
Female	0.114	0.079	− 30.7	15.4	14.3	− 7.1
All expected-to-work heads of household	0.145	0.133	− 8.3	17.0	17.5	+ 2.9

[a]Defined only for household heads who are expected to work and who report earnings and weeks worked. A head is classified as unemployed if she or he was laid off or without a job and was looking for work in at least one week during the year.
[b]Defined only for those reporting some unemployment.
[c]Defined as [(1984 value − 1976 value)/1976 value] × 100.

month.[7] Nevertheless, the trends are the same for both measures; the aggregate unemployment rate declined slightly, from 7.7 to 7.5 percent, and the proportion of our sample who reported some unemployment during the year declined from 14.5 to 13.3 percent over the period.

The decrease in the probability of unemployment was, however, not uniformly spread across all groups. Not only were household heads of either sex with low weekly earnings more than twice as likely to be unemployed in 1976 as those who did not have low earnings, but their unemployment probabilities were relatively constant between 1976 and 1984, while the probabilities for others declined. Thus the labor market disadvantage of low weekly earners increased over the period.

Table 2.2 also shows the change in the mean weeks of unemployment for those who reported some unemployment. Low weekly earners again had a greater and growing disadvantage. They had longer unemployment durations, and the difference between their mean weeks of unemployment and those of heads who were not low earners increased over the period. In 1984, an unemployed male low earner's mean unemployment duration, 21.1 weeks, was about a third longer than that of an unemployed male who was not a low earner.[8]

Table 2.3 presents changes in the probability that a household head who was unemployed for at least one week during the year received UI benefits and the mean value of those benefits.[9] As do previous studies, we find that a smaller percentage of all of the unemployed received benefits in 1984 than in 1976 and that those receiving benefits received smaller amounts.

Table 2.3. Unemployment Insurance Receipt among the Unemployed, 1976 and 1984

	Probability of Receiving UI[a]			Mean Annual UI Benefit[b]			Mean Weekly UI Benefit[c]		
	1976	1984	Percentage Change[d]	1976	1984	Percentage Change[d]	1976	1984	Percentage Change[d]
Head has low weekly earnings									
Male	0.346	0.282	– 18.5	$2,773	$1,987	– 28.3	$139.35	$94.17	– 32.4
Female	0.299	0.272	– 9.0	1,584	1,453	– 8.8	95.42	85.47	– 10.4
Head does not have low weekly earnings									
Male	0.569	0.541	– 4.9	2,644	2,060	– 22.1	159.28	125.61	– 21.1
Female	0.482	0.411	– 14.7	2,117	1,649	– 22.1	137.47	115.31	– 16.1
All expected-to-work heads of household	0.497	0.432	– 13.1	2,550	1,969	– 22.8	150.00	112.39	– 25.1

[a]Defined only for household heads who are expected to work, who report earnings and weeks worked, and who were unemployed in at least one week during the year.
[b]Constant 1984 dollars. Defined only for heads receiving benefits.
[c]Defined as the mean annual benefit (from this table) divided by the mean weeks of unemployment (from Table 2.2).
[d]Defined as [(1984 value/1976 value)/1976 value] × 100.

Male low earners fared less well in each year and had more negative trends for each variable than males who were not low earners. In each year female low earners were the least likely of the four groups shown to receive UI and received the smallest benefits. However, the declines in their probability of receipt and in their mean benefits were smaller than average. For example, unemployed male low earners were 18.5 percent less likely to receive UI in 1984 than in 1976 (a decline in the probability of receipt from 0.346 to 0.282). In 1984, unemployed males who did not have low earnings were about twice as likely to receive UI; their probability of receipt had declined by only 4.9 percent. Likewise, male low earners who received UI received annual benefits that were 28.3 percent lower after adjustment for inflation (a decline from $2,773 to $1,987), while benefits declined by 22.1 percent for other unemployed males. As a result, in 1984 an unemployed male low earner with a mean unemployment duration of 21.1 weeks (as shown in Table 2.2) was receiving an average UI benefit of about $94 a week, compared to $140 for his counterpart in 1976, who had a mean unemployment duration of 19.9 weeks.

A Statistical Model

The tabular evidence presented thus far is consistent with two different interpretations about the treatment of the unemployed by the UI system. The first is that if a randomly chosen individual became unemployed in 1984, his or her chances of receiving UI were lower than those of a similar individual in 1976. An alternative interpretation is that individuals who became unemployed were different in 1984 than in 1976. In any year some individuals have a lower probability of receiving UI because of the nature of their jobs or personal histories—for example, many younger or less skilled workers have insufficient weeks of employment to be covered by UI. If these people composed a greater proportion of the unemployed in 1984, then the proportion of the unemployed receiving UI would decline even if there were no changes in the probability that any person with given characteristics received UI. The descriptive data would make it appear that the UI system had changed, when in fact it was only the unemployed who had changed.

To distinguish between these two interpretations, we estimate a descriptive statistical model which controls for a variety of observed characteristics of the unemployed and takes account of the unobserved characteristics that may have affected those who became unemployed. We estimate bivariate probit models in which the probability of being unemployed and the probability of receiving UI are estimated jointly. Models are estimated for male and female household heads classified by whether the head had or did not have low weekly earnings. (See the appendix, pages 63–66, for detailed specification.)

The models answer the following questions: If a low earner were chosen at random, what is the probability that he or she would become unemployed? If he or she became unemployed, what is the probability that he or she would receive UI? Because we start with a sample of all low earners, not just unemployed low earners, we have taken into account how changes concerning who becomes unemployed affect the probability of receiving UI.

Note, however, that these models do not explain changes concerning who becomes a low earner. To do so requires the estimation of a trivariate probit model in which the first equation explains the probability that a person is a low earner and the remaining two equations are the ones we estimate—the probability that a low earner is unemployed and the probability that an unemployed low earner receives UI. We do not estimate such a model because we are primarily interested in how well the UI program serves low earners, whatever the cause of their low earnings.[10] Thus, we begin with separate samples of those who had and those who did not have low earnings.[11]

Table 2A.1 in the appendix (see pages 64–65) shows the regression coefficients from our biprobit estimation of the determinants of unemployment and of the probability that an unemployed household head received UI. Separate biprobit models were estimated for three of the four types of household heads discussed. For female heads with low weekly earnings, we estimated univariate probit models because the bivariate models did not converge. The independent variables in the unemployment equation included whether the head was white, black, or Hispanic as well as his or her region and area of residence, age, educational attainment, and industry. The unemployment insurance receipt equation included all of these variables except those of geographic location and education. Two unemployment duration variables not included in the unemployment equation were also included—whether the unemployment spell was longer than twenty-six weeks and whether there were multiple spells of unemployment during the year.[12]

Since we allowed all coefficients to change between 1976 and 1984, the change in the probability of being unemployed (or receiving UI) differs across individuals with different characteristics. In order to summarize the change in probabilities, we evaluated each equation at the sample mean of all people in the specified sex/earnings status category in 1976. By holding characteristics constant across the years in these calculations, we derived results that do not reflect changes in the composition of the population.

Table 2.4 shows the predicted probability (evaluated at the 1976 sample means for persons in each of the four groups) of being unemployed and

Table 2.4. Predicted Probability of Unemployment and Unemployment Insurance Receipt, 1976 and 1984[a]

	Probability of Being Unemployed			Probability of Receiving UI if Unemployed Less than 26 Weeks			Probability of Receiving UI if Unemployed More than 26 Weeks		
	1976	1984	Percentage Change	1976	1984	Percentage Change	1976	1984	Percentage Change
Head has low weekly earnings									
Male	0.276	0.281	+ 1.8	0.320	0.309	– 3.4	0.465	0.237	– 49.0
Female[b]	0.213	0.206	– 3.3	0.287	0.281	– 2.1	0.372	0.363	– 2.4
Head does not have low weekly earnings									
Male	0.094	0.095	+ 1.1	0.622	0.520	– 16.4	0.823	0.516	– 37.3
Female	0.099	0.072	– 27.3	0.417	0.409	– 1.9	0.589	0.520	– 10.6

[a]Probabilities are representative of a person with the average characteristics of persons in 1976 in each of the four sex-of-head and earnings status categories.

[b]Probabilities are based on univariate probit equations, as the bivariate probits did not converge.

of receiving UI. For example, the probability of unemployment for a male with given characteristics increased slightly between 1976 and 1984. Thus, the declines in the probability of unemployment for males shown in Table 2.2 were due to changes in the composition of the population. The predicted and observed probability of unemployment declines for each female group.

The estimated model allowed the probability of UI receipt to differ for those unemployed less than or more than twenty-six weeks in the preceding year. This specification was chosen since Vroman (1984) pointed out that the legislative changes made in the UI program since 1980 have disproportionately affected the long-term unemployed.

We find that the probability of receiving UI declined for each of the four household groups, both for those unemployed less than twenty-six weeks and for those with extended unemployment spells. While those unemployed more than twenty-six weeks had a higher probability of UI receipt than those unemployed for less than twenty-six weeks in 1976, they experienced larger declines over this period. Our results thus confirm Vroman's conclusion.

For example, the probability that a male with low weekly earnings received UI dropped by 3.4 percent (from 0.320 to 0.309) for those with spells shorter than twenty-six weeks but by 49.0 percent (from 0.465 to 0.237) for those with spells longer than twenty-six weeks. Thus, the decline in the proportion of the unemployed receiving UI found in Table 2.4 reflects changes in how the UI program served the unemployed and not just compositional changes in the population.

4. Other Income Transfers and Poverty among the Unemployed

The results from the previous section raise several questions concerning the relationship of the UI program to the rest of the income maintenance system. Given that so many of the unemployed received no UI benefits, were they recipients of other cash benefits?[13] How did the receipt of other transfers change as the receipt of UI declined? How effective were UI and other cash transfers in alleviating poverty among the unemployed?[14]

Receipt of Other Cash Transfers

Table 2.5 classifies households by the earnings status of the unemployed head and by whether she or he received UI, and presents the percentage receiving other cash transfers. These percentages were low and declined between 1976 and 1984 for almost all of the groups shown. In 1976, 17.1 percent of all UI recipients with low earnings received other transfers, as did 8.7 percent of all UI recipients who did not have low earnings. UI

Table 2.5. Receipt of Cash Transfers Other than Unemployment Insurance among the Unemployed, 1976 and 1984

	Probability of Receiving Other Cash Transfers: All Heads[a]			Probability of Receiving Other Cash Transfers: Male Heads[a]			Probability of Receiving Other Cash Transfers: Female Heads[a]		
	1976	1984	Percentage Change[b]	1976	1984	Percentage Change[b]	1976	1984	Percentage Change[b]
Head has low weekly earnings									
Receives UI	0.171	0.129	− 24.6	0.176	0.118	− 33.0	0.161	0.153	− 5.0
Does not receive UI	0.238	0.207	− 13.0	0.190	0.173	− 8.9	0.308	0.276	− 10.4
Head does not have low weekly earnings									
Receives UI	0.087	0.059	− 32.2	0.087	0.057	− 34.5	0.088	0.076	− 13.6
Does not receive UI	0.094	0.115	+ 22.3	0.083	0.115	+ 38.6	0.161	0.112	− 30.4

[a]Other cash transfers include Social Security, railroad retirement, government employee pensions, veterans' compensation and pensions, workers' compensation, Supplemental Security Income, Aid to Families with Dependent Children, and General Assistance. See note 15.
[b]Defined as [(1984 value/1976 value)/1976 value] × 100.

nonrecipients were only slightly more likely to have received other transfers. By 1984, among low earners the probability of receiving other transfers had dropped to 12.9 percent for those who received UI and to 20.7
percent for those who did not. Retrenchment had occurred both in UI
and in other transfer programs.

The receipt of other transfers by the unemployed was much less common
than the receipt of UI. In 1984, more than two-thirds of low earners did
not receive UI (Table 2.3, rows 1 and 2, column 2) and four-fifths of this
group received no transfers at all (Table 2.5, row 2, column 2). Other
transfers hardly provided any safety net for unemployed expected-to-work
household heads.

Once earnings status and receipt of UI have been taken into account,
differences in the receipt of other transfers between male and female heads
were small. Households headed by women had a somewhat higher probability of receipt, but all four of those probabilities also declined between
1976 and 1984.

Antipoverty Effectiveness of Transfers

How effective were UI and other transfers in reducing poverty among
the unemployed? Table 2.6 addresses this question. The first three columns
present three measures of the incidence of poverty for households classified
by the sex and earnings status of the unemployed head. Pretransfer poverty
(column 1) is calculated by subtracting all government cash transfers
received by household members from reported cash income. Column 2
presents a measure of poverty calculated by subtracting the head's UI
benefits from reported cash income.[15] Column 3 presents the official
measure of poverty, which is based on cash income from all sources (before
taxes). Columns 4 and 5 show, respectively, the percentage reduction in
poverty due to all cash transfers except the head's UI and the percentage
reduction due to the head's UI. The sum of these two columns, shown
in column 6, gives the percentage reduction in poverty due to all cash
transfers.[16]

Several points emerge. First, while transfers were received by a minority
of the unemployed, they significantly reduced poverty. Among unemployed
male low earners in 1976, poverty rates were 25 percent lower after the
receipt of transfers than they were prior to receipt (column 6). For household heads with higher weekly earnings, poverty rates were cut in half
by transfers. This reflects the smaller income deficit of these households.

Second, as might be expected, UI was more important than other
transfers in reducing poverty for three of the four groups. For example,
in 1984, 20.0 percent of pretransfer poor households headed by a male
who did not have low earnings were taken out of poverty by UI and

Table 2.6. Poverty Rates and the Antipoverty Effectiveness of Income Transfers among the Unemployed, 1976 and 1984

	Percentage of Households in Poverty			Percentage Reduction in Poverty Due to		
	Money Income Less All Cash Transfers (Pretransfer) (1)	Money Income Less Head's UI Benefit (2)	Money Income (Official Measure) (3)	Cash Transfers Other than the Head's UI Benefits[a] (4)	Head's UI Benefits[b] (5)	All Transfers[c] (6)
Head has low earnings						
Male, 1976	59.1	53.5	44.2	− 9.5	−15.7	−25.2
Male, 1984	61.0	57.3	53.4	− 6.1	− 6.4	−12.5
Female, 1976	60.5	51.3	45.4	−15.2	− 9.8	−25.0
Female, 1984	64.7	58.8	54.9	− 9.1	− 6.0	−15.1
Head does not have low earnings						
Male, 1976	10.2	8.9	5.0	−12.7	−38.2	−50.9
Male, 1984	11.0	9.3	7.1	−15.5	−20.0	−35.5
Female, 1976	11.7	8.9	4.5	−23.9	−37.6	−61.5
Female, 1984	11.5	10.2	8.4	−11.3	−15.7	−27.0

[a]Defined as 100 times the difference between the poverty rates in columns 2 and 1 divided by the rate in column 1.
[b]Defined as 100 times the difference between the poverty rates in columns 3 and 2 divided by the rate in column 1.
[c]The sum of columns 4 and 5 is the percentage reduction in poverty due to all cash transfers.

Table 2.7. Poverty Rates among the Unemployed, Classified by Receipt of UI, 1976 and 1984

	Percentage of Households in Poverty: All Heads			Percentage of Households in Poverty: Male Heads			Percentage of Households in Poverty: Female Heads		
	1976	1984	Percentage Change[a]	1976	1984	Percentage Change[a]	1976	1984	Percentage Change[a]
Head has low weekly earnings									
Receives UI	30.9	37.1	+ 20.1	29.6	36.5	+ 23.3	27.8	38.5	+ 38.4
Does not receive UI	52.3	60.3	+ 15.3	51.9	60.0	+ 15.6	52.9	61.1	+ 15.5
Head does not have low weekly earnings									
Receives UI	2.8	3.0	+ 7.1	2.8	3.2	+ 14.3	2.7	4.1	+ 51.9
Does not receive UI	7.7	12.0	+ 55.8	8.0	11.6	+ 45.0	6.2	14.0	+125.8

[a]Defined as [(1984 rate − 1976 rate) ÷ 1976 rate] × 100.

another 15.5 percent were taken out by other transfers. The corresponding 1984 figures for female heads who were not low earners were 15.7 and 11.3 percent. The exception to this pattern were female heads who were low earners in each year. This is the group most likely to receive AFDC, and for whom the antipoverty effect of other transfers exceeded that of UI.

Third, in almost all cases both UI and other transfers had a smaller antipoverty effect in 1984 than in 1976. For example, for males with low earnings, the percentage reduction in poverty due to all transfers in 1984 was only half the size it was in 1976.

While the failure to receive transfers compounds the problems of unemployed low earners, their high poverty rates are primarily a result of their low earnings capacity. Table 2.7 illustrates this dramatically. Poverty rates are shown for the unemployed, cross-classified by earnings status and receipt of UI. Holding earnings status constant, those not receiving UI had higher poverty rates than UI recipients. However, the largest differences in poverty rates were between households headed by unemployed low earners and those who were not low earners, regardless of whether or not UI was received. Again, male-female differences were small. For example, in 1984, 37.1 percent of all low earners who received UI were poor, while only 12.0 percent of all households where the head did not receive UI but had weekly earnings above $204 were poor. Poverty was not a particular problem for the unemployed who did not have low weekly earnings, since the 1984 poverty rate for all 58.6 million households in which the head was expected to work was 10.2 percent.

5. Summary and Policy Implications

Our empirical work has confirmed earlier findings that the UI system does not cover a majority of unemployed workers and that coverage was less in 1984 than in 1976. We have offered new evidence that the lack of coverage is most severe for households headed by persons with low weekly earnings. Furthermore, these households are not well covered by other transfer programs — about half received neither UI nor other transfers in 1984 — and have very high poverty rates. Although their poverty rates are primarily a reflection of their low earnings, the fact that less than half receive any transfers indicates that their safety net is imperfect. The evidence presented suggests extensions of coverage in both tiers of the income maintenance system for the unemployed — UI and the income-tested programs.

What about the efficiency losses associated with increased benefits? Since UI does have some impact on the duration of unemployment, there is a potential tradeoff between encouraging work and reducing poverty (see

Burtless, 1989). The question is whether the current UI program strikes the right balance between these two goals. We see little reason to be very concerned about the magnitude of work reductions that would result from extending coverage for persons with low weekly earnings. If wages are a rough indicator of productivity, then little production will be lost even if these low earners increase their duration of unemployment in response to an expanded UI system.

We have three proposals to shore up the safety net. First, we propose two changes in the extended benefit program (EB), which pays benefits for an additional number of weeks after the term of regular UI benefits has ended, if unemployment reaches a specified level in a state. We find that Burtless's (1983) arguments for using a trigger (the unemployment level at which EB benefits are authorized) based on measured unemployment rather than insured unemployment are compelling. Many of the administrative decisions about the availability of regular unemployment compensation reflect decisions about how many of the needs of the unemployed should be met, not about the existence of such needs. The EB triggers were originally set to allow the program to start only in states with demonstrated need. Since changes in regular UI receipt now no longer fully reflect changes in need, insured unemployment rates no longer serve their function.

We would also restore the number of weeks of coverage of the EB program at its (high) 1976 level but allow the benefit amount to decline with the number of weeks of UI receipt. This would gradually increase the incentive to leave the program without the sudden cessation of benefits that characterizes the existing program.

Our second proposal recognizes the fact that less than a fifth of the unemployed with low earnings received other cash transfers in 1984. This indicates that the second line of defense against income losses from unemployment is ineffective and that the safety net needs to be expanded. We endorse the provision in the Family Support Act of 1988 which changes the state-run AFDC-U program from an optional to a mandatory program for poor two-parent families in which the household head is unemployed. Coverage is still limited, however, as persons who have now worked enough to qualify as unemployed are excluded. Also, because AFDC-U provides income-tested benefits only for unemployed families with children, coverage problems remain for single individuals and childless couples, who are generally eligible only for Food Stamps.

Our third proposal reflects our finding that poverty among the unemployed is closely associated with low weekly earnings. This suggests that, where possible, the UI system should include a component to increase the earnings potential of the unemployed. This could take the form of expanded relocation or training allowances. Since training programs have been found cost-effective only for some participants (see Bassi and Ashenfelter, 1986), we propose that the unemployed worker who chooses to enroll in a program be asked to share part of the costs of training or relocation through lower UI benefits. In this way recipients would be encouraged to self-select the training or relocation program which best suits their needs. (See U.S. Congressional Budget Office, 1985, for a discussion of similar alternatives.)

We believe that these proposals represent an appropriate response to the current lack of coverage by UI and other transfers and the high poverty rates of the unemployed. However, they would probably have only a small impact on the very high poverty rates among households whose heads are unemployed low earners. They would, nevertheless, counter the trend of the past decade, characterized by rising hardship and reduced coverage.

APPENDIX

The model we estimate can be specified using a standard latent variable framework to specify the selection equation (whether or not the person was unemployed) and the primary equation (whether or not the unemployed person received UI). The selection equation determines whether the person was in the sample of those who were unemployed. The primary equation determines whether the person received UI.

A latent variable Y_1, which is a linear function of a vector of characteristics X_1 and a random component ϵ_1, determines whether the person is in the sample. If this latent variable exceeds the threshold C_1, a dichotomous variable, Y_1^*, is set equal to one, and the person is included in the sample. Similarly, a vector of characteristics, X_2, and a random component, ϵ_2, determine whether the dichotomous variable in the primary equation, Y_2^*, takes on the value of zero or one.

$$Y_1^* = 1 \quad \text{if} \quad X_1\beta_1 + \epsilon_1 > C_1; \text{ otherwise}$$
$$Y_1^* = 0;$$

$$Y_2^* = 1 \quad \text{if} \quad X_2\beta_2 + \epsilon_2 > C_2; \text{ otherwise}$$
$$Y_2^* = 0,$$

which yields

$$\text{pr}(Y_1^* = 1) = \text{pr}(\epsilon_1 > C_1 - X_1\beta_1); \text{ and} \qquad \text{Selection equation;}$$
$$\text{pr}(Y_2^* = 1) = \text{pr}(\epsilon_2 > C_2 - X_2\beta_2). \qquad \text{Primary equation.}$$

If ϵ_1 and ϵ_2 are independent, the selection and primary equations can be estimated separately. If they are not independent, the two equations must be estimated jointly.

We have no a priori expectation as to the sign of the correlation. For example, an unobserved factor, such as an individual's motivation, may result in her or his becoming unemployed in order to receive UI. In this case, ϵ_1 and ϵ_2 will be positively correlated. Or an unobserved factor, such as illiteracy, may increase the probability of a person's being unemployed and decrease the probability that the individual will receive UI, causing the correlation to be negative.

Our approach is to estimate the two equations simultaneously, using maximum likelihood, and to test for independence. This correction for selection is analogous to Heckman's well-known correction in the case in which the primary equation is continuous. By explicitly taking account of the cross-equation correlation between error terms, the procedure controls for the fact that large (small) values of ϵ_1 may be associated with large (small) values of ϵ_2, thus affecting the probability that the latent variable in the primary equation will exceed its threshold.

We estimated bivariate probit models for four demographic groups (sex of head × earnings status) for 1976 and 1984. Table 2A.1 shows the coefficients for male heads with low earnings for 1984. The other seven sets of estimated equations are available upon request. Included in both the unemployment and UI equations are the following variables: race, Hispanic origin, age, and a set of dummy variables for the worker's industry. In the unemployment equation we also included a set of urbanization and regional dummy variables to reveal geographic differences in employment opportunities, and an education dummy, since unemployment rates are highly correlated with educational attainment. The UI equation excluded the geographic dummy variables and educational attainment. The availability of UI should not vary systematically with these characteristics, even though the amount of UI might. The UI equation included measures of the number and length of unemployment spells to reflect differences in the treatment of the long-term unemployed by the UI program. The exclusions in the two equations help identify the parameters of the models.

The results shown in Table 2A.1 follow the expected patterns. For example, being older decreased the probability of being unemployed but raised the probability of receiving UI if the person became unemployed. Persons with multiple spells of unemployment or with spells greater than twenty-six weeks were less likely to receive UI. The significant negative correlation between ϵ_1 and ϵ_2 shows that unobserved factors which raised the probability of being unemployed lowered the probability of receiving UI. To ignore this correlation would have led to biased estimates of the probit equations.

Table 2A.1. Bivariate Probit Estimates, Males Who Have Low Earnings, 1984

Variable[a]	Coefficient	Asymptotic T Stat	D(PROB)/D(X)[b]
Results for the Primary Equation Probability of Receiving UI if Unemployed			
CONS	0.0122	0.0418	0.0042
BLAC	−0.1507	−1.5109	−0.0520
HISP	−0.0974	−0.8947	−0.0336
AGE	0.0146	4.4731	0.0050
2752	−0.1495	−1.8643	−0.0516
MSPL	−0.1211	−1.5640	−0.0418
FIR	0.2186	0.9857	0.0755
CNS	−0.1420	−0.8587	−0.0490
DM	0.2734	1.4888	0.0944
NDM	0.0271	0.1552	0.0094

Table 2A.1 (*continued*)

TCU	0.5185	2.3987	0.1790
WR	0.1733	1.2973	0.0599
PRS	0.0804	0.2760	0.0209
PAD	0.0224	0.0639	0.0077
SSV	0.0033	0.0207	0.0011

Results for the Selection Equation Probability of Unemployment			
CONS	0.3474	1.9963	0.1203
BLAC	0.1653	2.3094	0.0572
HISP	−0.0191	−0.2266	−0.0066
NCEN	−0.0281	−0.3768	−0.0097
SOUT	−0.2412	−3.3593	0.0835
WEST	−0.1055	−1.3409	−0.0365
CCIT	−0.0496	−0.7873	−0.0172
NSNS	−0.0046	−0.0747	−0.0016
NOID	0.0639	0.7256	0.0221
AGE	−0.0147	−7.0390	−0.0051
EDUC	0.0276	−3.0004	−0.0096
FIR	0.0699	0.4417	0.0242
CNS	0.4990	5.2421	0.1728
DM	0.1880	1.8743	0.0651
NDM	0.2037	1.7513	0.0705
TCU	−0.0079	−0.0608	−0.0027
WR	0.0434	0.5155	0.0150
PRS	−0.3250	−2.9254	−0.1125
PAD	−0.2671	−1.3290	−0.0925
SSV	0.0779	0.7236	0.0270

Correlation Estimate
RHO   −0.7979   2(Log Likelihood) = 4466.39
Standard Error   0.1653   "Degrees of Freedom" = 2956
Asymptotic T   −4.8257

[a]Definitions of variables:

CONS	Constant
BLAC	1 if individual is black
HISP	1 if individual is of Hispanic origin
AGE	Age
2752	1 if unemployed 27–52 weeks
MSPL	1 if individual has multiple spells of unemployment during the year

Industry dummies

FIR	Finance, insurance, or real estate
CNS	Construction
DM	Durable manufacturing
NDM	Nondurable manufacturing
TCU	Transportation, communication, or utilities
WR	Wholesale and retail trade
PRS	Professional and related services
PAD	Public administration

Table 2A.1 *(continued)*

SSV	Selected services
AGR	Agriculture, forestry, or fisheries (omitted)
	Regions
NCEN	North Central
SOUT	South
WEST	West
NE	Northeast (omitted)
	Geographic location
CCIT	Central city
NSNS	Not in metropolitan area
NOID	Area not identified
SMSA	In metropolitan area, but not in central city (omitted)
EDUC	Years of education

bDerivatives evaluated at the mean.

NOTES

Daniel Feaster, George Slotsve, and Douglas Wissoker provided valuable assistance; Nancy Rortvedt, clerical assistance. Gary Burtless and others provided useful comments on a prior draft.

1. Although childcare responsibilities may complicate market work for single-parent households with children over six, we nevertheless classify such persons as expected to work because this is consistent with existing welfare policies.

2. We also exclude household heads who reported receiving farm income, even if they received additional wages from another job.

3. Gary Burtless has pointed out that the reporting of unemployment insurance in the Current Population Survey (CPS) increased over this period. Thus, if the underreporting were corrected and the data adjusted to reflect actual UI receipt, the decline in benefits shown here would have been even larger.

4. In 1984, the poverty line for a family of four was $10,609. We define any household head with weekly earnings (defined as yearly earnings/weeks worked) below $204 as a low earner, regardless of his or her household size. The official poverty line is fixed in real terms and varies over time because of changes in the Consumer Price Index (CPI). We used the CPI-X, which employs a rental-equivalence approach to the cost of home ownership, to derive a low-earnings threshold of $118 per week for 1976. Between 1976 and 1984, the CPI increased by 82.4 percent while the CPI-X increased by 73.1 percent. If we had used the CPI, the low-earnings threshold for 1976 would have been $112 instead of $118.

5. The relationship between low earnings of the head and poverty of the household can be illustrated by considering a head of a household of four persons who earns $250 per week. She or he would not be counted as a low earner even if the person worked only ten weeks last year. If this were the household's only income last year, the household would be poor. However, the individual would not be classified as a low earner because her or his household could escape poverty through

full-year work. Also, consider a head of a two-person household who earns $150 per week for fifty weeks, or $7,500 per year. We classify this head as a low earner, but the household is not poor because the poverty line for a two-person household is $6,762.

In 1984 about 60 percent of households headed by low earners escaped poverty. The main reasons for escape were that family size was less than four and that the earnings of other household members and/or income transfers when combined with the earnings of the head exceeded the poverty line. See Danziger and Gottschalk (1986) for further details.

6. There were 93.50 million total households in 1984. Those not shown in Figure 2.1 include 28.17 million headed by someone who was elderly, a student, disabled, or a woman with a child under six, and 6.76 million headed by someone who was self-employed or received farm income. Households include both families and unrelated individuals.

7. The reported unemployment rate and our probability would be equal only if the same people were unemployed in every month. With duration of unemployment below fifty-two weeks, the probability of being unemployed during the year must exceed the monthly unemployment rate.

8. It is somewhat anomalous that female household heads who are expected to work have lower unemployment probabilities and shorter unemployment durations than their male counterparts. This is due in part to our exclusion from the computations in Table 2.1 of heads who report no weeks worked or earnings during the year. In 1984 female nonearners composed about 15 percent of all female expected-to-work heads, whereas males were about 7 percent of their respective group.

9. We measure mean benefits by dividing annual UI benefits by the number of weeks unemployed. This mean can decline either because the person received UI during a smaller proportion of the weeks unemployed or because the real value of weekly benefits declined.

10. Our model implicitly assumes that the receipt of UI benefits does not affect work effort and, hence, the probability that a household head is a low earner. See Burtless (1989) for a review of recent studies. He concludes that "the evidence does not support any firm conclusion about the effect of the program on aggregate work effort actually supplied in market jobs" (p. 102).

11. Because our model takes low-earning status as given, care should be taken in interpreting our results. For example, assume that a black person has a higher probability of being a low earner, but that black low earners and white low earners have the same probability of becoming unemployed. In this case, a trivariate model that begins with the entire population would show that a black person chosen at random would have a higher probability of being unemployed because she or he would have a higher probability of being a low earner. Our model, which begins with the selected sample of low earners, would find no effect of race on the probability that a low earner is unemployed.

12. Unemployment spells that span calendar years are mismeasured in the CPS because each person is asked to report only weeks unemployed during the calendar year. For example, if a worker was laid off July 1, 1983, and was reemployed

on July 1, 1984, she or he would report a spell of twenty-six weeks in 1984, even though the spell lasted fifty-two weeks. We have no way of correcting for this misreporting.

13. The CPS reports the amount of income received from the following major cash transfer programs: Social Security and railroad retirement; federal, state, and local government employee pensions; unemployment insurance; workers' compensation; veterans' compensation and pensions; Supplemental Security Income; Aid to Families with Dependent Children; and General Assistance.

Since 1980, the CPS has also gathered information on the receipt of major in-kind transfer benefits, such as Medicare and Food Stamps. Because we have focused on trends over the 1976–84 period, we restrict our analysis to the receipt of transfer benefits that are reported for both years.

14. Because poverty as officially measured is based on income from all persons and all sources, we focus on all cash transfers other than UI and not just those that are income-tested. Also, we do not distinguish between other transfers received by the household head and those received by other household members.

15. Because of the way the CPS data are reported, we overstate the amount of UI received for persons who receive UI and workers' compensation, UI and veterans' compensation, or UI and both of these other transfers. Since we have no way of allocating the reported benefits to the other programs, we count all income from these sources as UI for multiple-benefit recipients.

16. These comparisons are based on the assumption that transfers elicit no behavioral responses. Since transfers do induce labor supply reductions, the pre and post comparisons made here provide upper-bound estimates of the antipoverty effects of transfers.

REFERENCES

Bassi, Laurie J., and Orley Ashenfelter. 1986. "The Effect of Direct Job Creation and Training Programs on Low-Skilled Workers." In Sheldon Danziger and Daniel Weinberg, eds., *Fighting Poverty: What Works and What Doesn't.* Cambridge: Harvard University Press.

Burtless, Gary. 1983. "Unemployment Insurance and Poverty." Testimony presented to the Committee on Ways and Means, U.S. House of Representatives, October 18.

Burtless, Gary. 1989. "Unemployment Insurance and Labor Supply: A Survey." Chapter 3 in this volume.

Danziger, Sheldon, and Peter Gottschalk. 1986. "Work, Poverty and the Working Poor." *Monthly Labor Review* 109 (September):17–21.

U.S. Congress, Congressional Budget Office. 1985. *Promoting Employment and Maintaining Incomes with Unemployment Insurance.* Washington, D.C.: Government Printing Office.

Vroman, Wayne. 1984. "The Reagan Administration and Unemployment Insurance." Washington, D.C.: The Urban Institute. Mimeograph.

3

Unemployment Insurance and Labor Supply: A Survey

GARY BURTLESS

Unemployment and public-assistance programs have gone far beyond the stated goals of alleviating poverty and hunger, to the extent that in many cases a laid-off worker is better off . . . . Obviously, this creates a significant incentive for voluntary unemployment, and recent studies by the U.S. Department of Labor indicate that this problem may be reaching epidemic proportions.

—*The Wall Street Journal,* August 23, 1983

I find it much more believable that the adverse consequences of government policies have been largely the unintended and unexpected by-products of well-meaning policies that were adopted without looking beyond their immediate purpose or understanding the magnitudes of their adverse long-run consequences. . . . I believe the government never considered that raising the amount and duration of unemployment benefits to the current high levels to avoid hardship among the unemployed would encourage layoffs and discourage reemployment.

—Martin Feldstein (1980)

Introduction

These two statements reflect an attitude toward unemployment insurance that is increasingly common in the lay public and within the economics profession. Unemployment insurance is seen as a powerful disincentive to gainful employment and hence as an important explanation for rising unemployment and declining economic performance. This view is not entirely new, but it has gained greater currency as unemployment rates in the United States and other industrialized countries rose to postwar records.

In this essay I examine the proposition that UI has adversely affected

69

labor supply. Although I consider a variety of theories relevant to UI programs around the world, much of the discussion will center on the effects of the U.S. system. The American system is similar in basic outline to UI programs in other countries, but some of its specific features are quite distinctive. Hence, many of my conclusions are fully applicable only to the United States.

The organization of the paper is as follows. Section 1 briefly describes some historical statistics about the U.S. program. These statistics are given to provide a rough idea of the scope and significance of the program, both in relation to the aggregate economy and as a share of earnings lost through unemployment. Section 2 contains a simple theoretical model of the effect of UI on an individual worker's behavior, stressing the value of UI as a pure insurance program for workers subject to unemployment risk, and shows the distortionary labor supply incentives that can be created for unemployed workers. A third section considers the incentive effects that arise from specific features of the U.S. system, for example, the limited duration of benefits and the payroll tax mechanism for financing benefits. Section 4 considers findings from recent empirical studies of the program. These studies support some of the leading theoretical predictions about UI's effects, but the studies are very incomplete. Many avenues through which UI can affect labor supply have not been explored.

The paper ends with some conclusions. One point that I stress—and, indeed, that I emphasize throughout the paper—is the fragility of our current knowledge. Neither theory nor available empirical evidence permits us to predict unequivocally the net effect of unemployment insurance on labor supply. This uncertainty may come as a surprise to many critics, including some economist critics, but it follows from the fundamental nature of the program. By providing insurance to workers, UI offers something of value to people who become employed, and it thus may increase the attractiveness of market work. But by supplementing the incomes of workers who become unemployed, it can slow down the process of reemployment. Without better empirical evidence than we now have, it is impossible to predict which of these two basic effects of UI will predominate.

1. Background Statistics

Although the UI program is of vital importance to some categories of workers, especially currently unemployed workers, it does not loom very large in the context of the U.S. economy. It is not even especially large when compared to other social insurance programs created under the Social Security Act. Table 3.1 shows outlays on UI and three other social insurance programs during seven recent fiscal years. Outlays are measured in constant 1984 dollars. By far the largest is Social Security's Old Age and Survivors' Insurance program. This program pays out about 6.5 times more benefits than the UI program, for the very simple reason that the number of insured retired workers far exceeds that of insured unemployed workers. The Medicare program is likewise far larger than UI, and it has been growing much more rapidly. During nonrecessionary times, the UI program is approximately equal in size to the disability insurance program, the smallest listed in the table. When recessions occur, however, UI outlays rise rapidly in response to rising insured unemployment, and they then far surpass typical outlays on DI. Between fiscal years 1979 and 1983, for example, UI outlays more than doubled, and then fell 45 percent in 1984 when unemployment declined. No other social insurance program shows this strongly cyclical pattern.

Table 3.1. Outlays on Selected Social Insurance Programs (billions of 1984 dollars)

	Fiscal Year						
	1979	1980	1981	1982	1983	1984	1985
Unemployment insurance	14.6	19.8	20.8	25.7	33.3	18.4	16.9
Old age and survivors' insurance	125.3	130.4	141.6	150.1	159.0	159.8	163.8
Disability insurance	19.4	19.4	20.0	19.6	19.1	18.4	18.7
Medicare	40.5	44.3	49.2	54.9	59.3	62.4	63.7

Source: Budget of the United States Government, selected years.

UI is approximately the same size today as it was shortly after World War II. Unlike other social insurance programs, unemployment insurance "matured" very quickly after it was first introduced in the mid-1930s. Workers become fully insured and eligible to receive benefits within a year or so of entering covered employment. It takes several years of employment to become fully insured under Social Security and Medicare, and the benefits might not begin for many years after a worker becomes insured. Moreover, UI benefits attained their present level relative to earnings shortly after the war. There was some liberalization in the duration of benefits, particularly during the 1970s, but some of the liberalization that occurred in the 1970s was rescinded in the early 1980s. Most of the program liberalization effected since the war has involved extensions of coverage to new categories of workers—employees of small businesses, agricultural enterprises, and nonprofit and government organizations. Since several of these categories of workers experience relatively little insured unemployment, the extensions of coverage have not had a large effect on the percentage of unemployed workers collecting UI benefits. In recent years the effects of even these liberalizations have been offset by other factors. The share of newly laid-off workers qualifying for benefits has fallen sharply since 1980, possibly due to tighter administration and more restrictive eligibility requirements in some state programs (see Burtless, 1983; Burtless and Vroman, 1985).

Table 3.2 shows the historical relationship between UI taxes and benefits, on the one hand, and wage compensation, on the other. UI is ordinarily financed through federal and state taxes imposed on the covered payrolls of participating employers. In a few states, workers have been required to make tax contributions as well.[1] The first column in Table 3.2 shows the total of employer and employee payroll tax contributions in selected postwar years. The second column shows the gross compensation paid out to wage and salary employees, and the third column gives the ratio of the first two columns. As these ratio statistics make clear, UI tax contributions are a very small percentage of gross compensation in the United States — typically less than 1 percent — and the contribution rate has remained substantially unchanged since the Second World War.

The fourth column in the table shows the gross UI replacement rate, which is simply the average weekly benefit amount received by the insured unemployed divided by the average gross weekly wage of all employed workers. Once again, this ratio has shown surprisingly little movement over the postwar period. Much of the movement is in fact cyclical rather than secular. To show the cyclical component in year-to-year movements I display the civilian unemployment rate in the right-hand column. Note that the gross replacement rate declines as unemployment falls and can rise sharply in recessions. This pattern is explained by the changing composition of the insured unemployed over business cycles. In tight labor markets, unemployed workers tend to be somewhat more disadvantaged, so their weekly benefits are lower than average. (Weekly benefits are based on a worker's average earnings in a recent base period.) During severe recessions more highly paid employees are laid off, so weekly benefits tend to rise. Comparing years in which the civilian unemployment rate was roughly similar, there does not appear to be much difference between replacement ratios in the immediate postwar period and those in the past few years.

The relative constancy of the gross replacement rate for lost money wages may disguise movements in the net or after-tax replacement rate. Before 1987, UI benefits were either untaxed or lightly taxed for many unemployed workers. Since wage earnings were subject to ever higher marginal tax rates, the same gross replacement rate has actually replaced a higher fraction of after-tax money wages lost to unemployment. Partly offsetting this trend was the fall in money wages as a share of gross compensation. Workers now receive a greater share of compensation as untaxed health, disability, and pension benefits, and these items are excluded in computing the gross replacement rate reported in the table. Taking all of these factors into account, the net replacement of worker compensation

Table 3.2. Ratio of Unemployment Insurance to Gross Compensation and Earnings, 1947–52, 1979–84

Year	UI Payroll Tax[a] (in billions of 1984 dollars)	Gross Compensation (in billions of 1984 dollars)	Ratio of UI Tax to Gross Compensation (%)	Gross Replacement Rate[b] (%)	Civilian Unemployment Rate (%)
1947	5.9	538.2	1.10	39.1	3.9
1948	4.9	556.7	0.87	38.8	3.8
1949	5.0	558.2	0.90	40.8	5.9
1950	5.8	599.8	0.96	39.1	5.3
1951	6.4	658.3	0.98	36.4	3.3
1952	5.9	695.7	0.84	37.6	3.0
1979	21.7	1,981.5	1.10	40.8	5.8
1980	19.2	1,969.6	0.98	42.1	7.1
1981	18.3	2,000.5	0.92	41.8	7.6
1982	18.1	1,994.5	0.91	44.7	9.7
1983	21.3	2,048.1	1.04	44.0	9.6
1984	23.8	2,221.3	1.07	41.8	7.5

Source: U.S. Department of Commerce, Bureau of Economic Analysis, *The National Income and Product Accounts of the United States, 1929–76 Statistical Tables* (September 1981), and *The Survey of Current Business* (July 1983, 1984, and 1985); U.S. Council of Economic Advisors, *The Economic Report of the President* (1981 and 1985).

[a]Includes both employer and employee tax contributions to unemployment insurance.

[b]The ratio of average weekly unemployment insurance benefits received by the insured unemployed to average gross weekly earnings of production or nonsupervisory workers in private nonagricultural employment.

lost due to unemployment has probably risen somewhat over the postwar period.

This brief survey suggests three main conclusions. UI is relatively small as social insurance programs go. The tax used to finance it is no heavier today than it was immediately after the Second World War, when, incidentally, unemployment rates were far lower. And the growth in benefits has roughly kept pace with the growth in compensation over the postwar period. If the program causes larger adverse consequences on employer and worker behavior today than it did after the war, this fact must be due to changes in the structure of the program. The scope of the program has remained essentially unchanged.

2. Theory

Gains from Pure Insurance

Unemployment insurance is first and foremost a system of insurance for workers. The main goal of the program is to insure workers against the risks of earnings loss from unemployment. This goal has been emphasized in theoretical papers by Baily (1977b, 1978), Stafford (1977), Topel and Welch (1981), and Rosen (1983).

To see the possible welfare and labor supply effects of a pure insurance program it is helpful to consider a simple model. First, we assume that workers rely entirely on their wages and insurance benefits, if any, to finance consumption. During each period in a worker's career — say, each week or month — he is either employed or unemployed.[2] Unemployment is involuntary and occurs randomly. The probability that the worker will be unemployed is μ, while the probability of employment is $(1 - \mu)$. If he is employed, the worker earns a wage equal to W. We also assume that the marginal utility of consumption declines with consumption. This assumption requires us to believe that the first dollar of consumption in a given period yields greater marginal satisfaction than the one thousand and first. Economists and noneconomists alike generally find this to be plausible.

Figure 3.1 shows the relationship between consumption in a period and the satisfaction (or utility) that is derived from that consumption. The horizontal axis represents consumption levels; the vertical axis, utility levels. Assume for a moment that workers cannot save. They consume all of their net wages in periods when they are employed, and consume nothing when unemployed. Since on average a worker will be employed $(1 - \mu) \times 100$ percent of the time and unemployed the remainder, his average consumption will be $(1 - \mu)W$. His expected utility is the weighted average of utility while employed and utility while unemployed, or $\bar{U}(C) = \mu \times U(O) +$

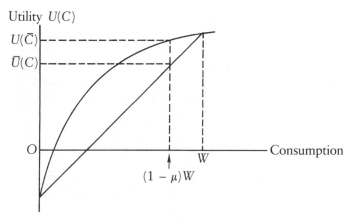

Figure 3.1. Utility of Consumption per Period

$(1 - \mu) \times U(W)$. From the diagram it is clear that the worker could do much better than this if he were willing to save and had access to unlimited credit. Without loss of generality, assume that the worker can borrow and lend at a zero interest rate. During periods of employment he should set aside μW as savings and consume only $(1 - \mu)W$. Then during each spell of unemployment he could spend $(1 - \mu)W$ per period out of savings. If his savings were exhausted, he could costlessly borrow $(1 - \mu)W$ per period until he becomes reemployed, thus maintaining his consumption at a constant level. The worker's expected utility from this strategy is $U(\bar{C}) = U([1 - \mu]W)$, which is clearly superior to utility in the no savings case.

For this level of utility to be fully attainable, it is necessary to assume that credit is available, on favorable terms and in potentially large amounts, to insolvent, jobless workers. To state the assumption is to reveal its absurdity. Bankrupt workers do not have easy access to credit when they are unemployed. If the worker expects to be borrowing constrained, he would be forced to rely on his own savings from periods of employment. During at least part of his life a prudent worker would therefore set aside more than μW per period to self-insure against unemployment, and even then an unfortunate string of unemployment spells might force him to reduce consumption to very low levels in some periods. As in the no-savings case, the variability of the worker's consumption—induced by the riskiness of his wage income—would keep him below the full maximum level of satisfaction $U(\bar{C})$. In fact, during many—perhaps most—periods in his life, prudence will prevent him from consuming $(1 - \mu)W$ per period. Not only will his consumption be variable, but his average consumption over much of his career will be below the level that is attainable with unlimited, costless credit.

The obvious solution to this problem is insurance. Assume to begin that the insurance can be provided without "moral hazard." The problem of moral hazard arises when the state of nature insured (unemployment) is to an important degree affected by the actions of the agent covered by insurance. In this case, moral hazard could arise if the worker exercised some control over the probability of unemployment, μ. Assume for a moment that this is not a problem. If the worker pays a fair premium of μW in each period during which he is employed, the insurance fund can pay him $(1 - \mu)W$ during each period in which he is unemployed. The fund will remain solvent (or close to solvent) by assumption because μ is the known probability of unemployment for all workers. With a large number of insured workers and independence across workers in the incidence of unemployment, the insurance fund can pay approximately the current period's claims out of the current period's premiums. Each worker could perfectly smooth out consumption so that it is identical to his expected wage income per period.

Before considering the problem of moral hazard and real-world features of UI programs, it is useful to consider how UI affects labor supply within the model just described. We begin by relaxing our previous assumption that a worker's wages while he is employed are fixed. Instead assume that $W = wH$, where w is an hourly wage and H is the number of hours worked during each period of employment. Although the worker might not have full control over the hours he works while employed, it is reasonable to assume that he has at least limited control at the time he is selecting a job.

How will the availability of insurance affect his choice of H? In the usual analysis of labor supply decisions, individuals are assumed to have well-ordered preferences across different combinations of weekly hours and consumption, $U = U(C,H)$, with $dU/dC > O$ and $dU/dH < O$. The attainable combinations of consumption and hours are shown in Figure 3.2. Average consumption per period is represented on the vertical axis, hours per period employed on the horizontal axis. When insurance is offered and workers are required to pay a premium of μw for each hour worked, the net wage during periods of employment is $(1 - \mu)w$. This also yields the optimum level of consumption per period during spells of both employment and unemployment. Hence the tradeoff between hours worked while employed and average consumption for the insured worker is represented as the solid straight line OB, with slope $(1 - \mu)w$.

Now compare this constraint with the tradeoff faced by an uninsured worker who is prevented from borrowing. What level of average consumption could this worker support at each level of hours? In expected value

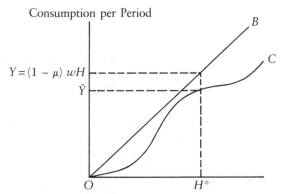

Figure 3.2. Tradeoff between Consumption and Hours, with and without Unemployment Insurance

terms the uninsured worker could consume just as much as the insured worker, namely $(1 - \mu)wH$. But for reasons described above, he could not consume his lifetime income in a steady pattern. One way to think about the difference between insured and uninsured workers is to consider the amount of certain (or constant) income that is required to make a worker as well off as he is when given a risky stream of wage income. As we have already seen, a worker who has declining marginal utility of consumption (or, alternatively, who is risk averse) would accept a lower stream of income if it was offered with certainty. Denoting this "certainty-equivalent" level of income as $\tilde{Y}$, we have $\tilde{Y} < Y = (1 - \mu)wH$ for risk-averse workers. The constraint relating $\tilde{Y}$ to H is drawn as the line OC in Figure 3.2. This constraint must lie below OB, since the worker is worse off at every $H > O$ if the income from working H hours per week is uncertain.[3]

The labor supply decision of a worker covered by UI can now be compared with that of a worker who is uncovered. OB is the work-consumption budget constraint faced by an insured worker, and OC is the constraint faced by an uninsured worker. As just noted, OC must lie below OB, implying that the certainty-equivalent average wage offered to the uncovered worker is below that offered to the covered worker. This implies as well that there must exist at least one range of H in which the slope of the certainty-equivalent constraint of the uncovered worker is below the slope of the covered worker's constraint. It cannot be shown, however, that the slope is everywhere below that for a covered worker without making some added assumptions about the worker's preferences. (For this reason, I have drawn OC as a curved line in which the slope is sometimes less than and sometimes greater than that of OB.) Even without this ambiguity, it would be impossible to predict conclusively the sign of the effect of insurance on the choice of H. This would clearly depend on the relative magnitudes of the income and substitution effects on labor supply, a subject on which economic theory is silent and empirical evidence contradictory. For low- and middle-income workers, the slope of the labor supply function may be positive, suggesting that UI might actually increase desired labor supply, although the effect must be slight. On balance, insurance has an ambiguous effect on a worker's labor supply while he is employed, and hence on the aggregate labor supply of insured workers. The most significant effects of UI in this simple model are then to raise the well-being and average productivity of workers, not to affect their average labor supply in any easily predicted direction.

Unemployment Varies by Industry

I have so far assumed that the probability of unemployment, μ, is the same for workers in all lines of work. This is not very plausible, however. Workers in some industries and occupations face persistently higher unemployment probabilities than average. Here we should carefully distinguish between predictable and unpredictable spells of unemployment. Farm laborers and construction workers may be unemployed every winter because there is nothing for them to do when the weather is bad. This type of unemployment is perfectly predictable and hence easy to provide for in a sensible savings and consumption plan. No insurance plan could raise the workers' well-being. The variability of earnings over the year does not imply any variability or unpredictability in consumption because the worker can save enough while employed to exactly cover a constant rate of consumption while unemployed. The hourly wage in predictably seasonal industries should exactly compensate for the expected incidence of unemployment over the year.

No savings plan can duplicate the benefits of insurance for a worker who faces the possibility of unpredictable unemployment. That is because if unemployment is unpredictable and the worker is borrowing constrained there is always the possibility that, with a constant consumption path, his experience of unemployment could cause him to exhaust all savings. For industries with systematically different patterns of unpredictable unemployment, provision of UI can affect the relative attractiveness of the industries to job seekers. For example, if there are two sectors, one with a low rate of unemployment, μ_1, and the other with a high rate, μ_2, provision of UI can raise the relative attractiveness of the second sector in comparison to the first.[4] Because income in the second sector is riskier to begin with, the potential welfare gains from insurance are greater there. In a general equilibrium model of response to UI, some workers in the first sector will be attracted to the second, and hourly wages will therefore fall in the latter sector and rise in the first. Whether aggregate labor supply rises or falls as a result of this sectoral shift is ambiguous. (It might seem obvious that work effort will fall when a high-unemployment sector grows at the expense of a low-unemployment sector, but the aggregate effect also depends on the average level of hours in the two sectors.) From the example just described, it is obvious that actuarially fair UI could encourage the movement of risk-averse workers from low productivity/low riskiness sectors to high productivity/high riskiness sectors.[5]

Effect of UI on μ

Within this simple model we have seen that theory provides a prediction about the welfare and productivity-enhancing effects of UI but not about its work effort effects. We have ignored, however, the effect of UI on unemployment itself, for by assumption the probability of unemployment, μ, has been assumed to be determined outside the model. UI can clearly affect this probability. If a worker is offered a guaranteed payment during spells when he is unemployed, the inducement to seek and hold a job would obviously be reduced. This incentive effect has been the focus of most theoretical and empirical studies of UI.[6]

When μ is unaffected by the provision of insurance and when the worker's earnings while employed, W, are known with certainty, we have just seen that the optimal insurance benefit for risk-averse workers is $B = (1 - \mu)W$, the benefit that totally eliminates consumption fluctuations arising from unemployment. But if μ is affected by, for example, the availability of benefits, because unemployed workers search less arduously for jobs, then provision of UI will give rise to moral hazard. Baily (1977b, 1978) has shown that in the presence of moral hazard the optimal insurance benefit must lie below $B = (1 - \mu)W$. Specifically, Baily shows that the optimal benefit will fall as the adverse unemployment effects of UI rise. In other words, at the optimum the benefit will only partially insure a worker against income losses from unemployment, and might not insure the worker at all against small losses (for example, the loss of a single week's wages).

The welfare and employment effects of an insurance system that offers only partial insurance are illustrated in Figure 3.3. This figure is similar to Figure 3.1. It shows the relationship between a worker's utility level and his consumption and wages in a given period. Assume for simplicity that workers are prevented from saving. This exaggerates the welfare gains from insurance, but it makes the graphical exposition much more straight-

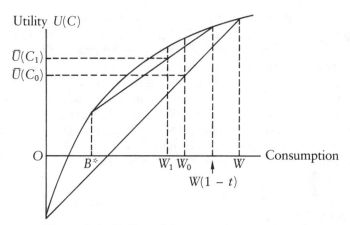

Figure 3.3. Utility of Consumption per Period

forward. As before, W is the worker's income and consumption while he is employed, and $\mu = \mu(B)$ is the probability in each period that a worker will be unemployed. Note that μ is now assumed to depend on B, the level of UI benefits, with $d\mu/dB > O$. If the benefit is set to zero, that is, if no insurance is offered, the worker's consumption will fluctuate between W when he is employed and O when he is unemployed. The worker's average consumption per period is $W_0 = [1 - \mu(O)]W$, and his average utility is denoted $\bar{U}(C_0)$, representing the weighted average of utility in employment and unemployment spells.

When unemployment insurance is offered (that is, when $B > O$), the worker's consumption will fluctuate between the benefit when he is unemployed, say B^*, and $W(1 - t)$ when he is employed, where t is the UI tax rate on earnings. We assume that the program is self-financing, so that $t = B^* \times \mu(B^*)/W[1 - \mu(B^*)]$, or, in words, t is the proportion of the worker's lifetime earnings that must be used to finance his expected lifetime benefits. In Figure 3.3 I have drawn $W(1 - t)$ so that it is greater than W_0, the worker's average consumption in the absence of UI. It could easily be less than that amount if B^* is sufficiently high and μ is extremely sensitive to the benefit level. That is, it is possible that the insured worker's after-tax income when employed is lower than the uninsured worker's average income across employed and unemployed periods. The important point, however is that the average income of the insured worker is $W_1 = [1 - \mu(B^*)]W$, which must be below that of the uninsured worker, $W_0 = [1 - \mu(O)]W$, because by assumption $d\mu/dB > O$. Even though his average consumption is below that of the uninsured worker, the insured worker can have higher average utility because the disutility arising from unpredictable income fluctuations has been reduced by insurance. This is shown in the figure where the weighted average utility of an insured worker, represented as $\bar{U}(C_1)$, is above that of the uninsured worker, $\bar{U}(C_0)$. Now the effect of UI is potentially to raise the worker's well-being but to reduce unambiguously his average earnings and labor supply.

Some analyses of UI stop at this point. Yet the conclusion is based on an assumption that is just as special as our previous assumption that UI does not affect the probability of unemployment. In particular, it rests on the assumption that UI has no effect on wages and labor supply while the worker is employed. For several reasons, however, this appears unlikely. First, provision of UI affects the certainty-equivalent value of wage income, as we have already seen. This can affect labor supply while a worker is employed. Second, UI might affect the outcome as well as the duration of job search. One conceivable outcome of a longer search is a better job. A job might be "better" in several dimensions. It might offer higher wages, more suitable hours, or lower likelihood of permanent separation. If UI leads to a greater amount of economically productive search, wage income while employed could easily rise, offsetting at least part of the adverse effects on unemployment duration (see Ehrenberg and Oaxaca, 1976).

The effect of UI on the outcome of job search has received a great deal of attention. The partial equilibrium effects seem rather clear-cut, at least in theory. An unemployed worker determines a set of reservation conditions with which he compares any job offer that is received. (For simplicity, most job search models focus on a single condition—the reservation wage.) If an offer is received that meets these conditions, it is accepted. Otherwise it is rejected, and the individual searches for another offer. By supplementing a worker's income during spells of unemployment, UI permits the worker to establish a more selective set of reservation conditions (see Mortensen, 1971; Feldstein and Poterba, 1984). Although receiving unemployment benefits prolongs the worker's search, it also results in accepted job offers that, on average, have more desirable characteristics, for example, a higher wage. Baily (1977b) has pointed out that UI may not only affect a worker's reservation conditions, but also the amount of effort devoted to search. If the amount of effort is reduced, the duration of job search will also increase.

UI may affect the reservation conditions and search effort of unemployed workers, but it does not follow that it will affect the distribution of wage offers. If wage offers are not raised, the duration of unemployment is increased without affecting the ultimate distribution of accepted wage offers. (In terms of Figure 3.3, W remains unchanged.) More plausibly, we might think that UI causes employers to raise their wage offers, but only because less labor is offered in the aggregate. To the extent that workers spend a smaller proportion of their time employed and the average number of workers in employment is reduced, then with a given capital stock the marginal product (and wage) of employed workers will rise. W rises, but not because UI has made originally employed workers any more productive. It has simply reduced the number of employed workers and hence caused employers to bid up wage rates.

In addition to the effect just mentioned, UI may increase the amount of economically productive job search. That is, it might raise the average productivity of workers by improving the match between jobs and workers. If there are two job vacancies and two unemployed workers, it can be economically productive to subsidize the workers to sort themselves into the two jobs so that their joint output and earnings are maximized. This example might seem farfetched, but I think it is a central reason why UI is offered in all high-wage capitalist economies and in virtually no low-wage economies. In high-wage societies, workers accumulate specialized skills through their own or their employers' considerable investments in education and training. Although these skills make a worker highly productive, their specialized nature can also expose him to considerable risk.[7] The number of jobs requiring his specialized skills will be limited, and this fact will affect his job search strategy should he become unemployed; with no secure source of income he will be tempted to accept a low-wage job offer that is unsuitable given his background and abilities. By partially replacing lost wages, UI increases the likelihood of a suitable match, both for the individual unemployed worker and for unemployed workers collectively. According to this view, prolonged job search is not an undesirable side effect of UI, as argued, for example, by Feldstein (1976); it is in fact the intended effect. In addition, as we saw above, provision of insurance increases the attractiveness of high productivity/high unemployment risk occupations and hence can raise the average productivity of workers.

In low-wage societies the economic advantages of UI are smaller. Many unemployed and underemployed workers in these societies have general rather than specialized skills, and a great majority of vacancies require only general skills. The social payoff from prolonging job search in this kind of labor market will be small, although the humanitarian payoff might nonetheless be large.

3. Other Features of Unemployment Insurance

I have argued that a stylized UI program can improve the welfare of workers. It can also increase the duration of a spell of unemployment, but that effect might in turn raise the earnings and productivity of employed workers. The overall effect on labor supply is ambiguous. The description of UI that I have given is general enough to cover basic features of UI systems around the world. But the U.S. system has important features that distinguish it from those in other countries. Five of these features have interested economists: (1) benefits are determined on the basis of a worker's recent earnings history; (2) benefits are limited rather than indefinite in duration; (3) entitlement to benefits is restricted to unemployed workers engaged in good-faith job search who are available for work; (4) entitlement to UI is generally restricted to workers on temporary and permanent layoff—unemployed new entrants and reentrants, persons who quit their last jobs, and persons discharged for cause are usually ineligible for UI; and (5) the source of financing for UI is a payroll tax imposed on employers with a tax rate that differs from one employer to another to reflect (imperfectly) the layoff record of each employer. These features of the U.S. system can affect the labor supply response to the program. Each will be considered in turn.

Relation of Benefits to Past Earnings

The fact that benefits are determined on the basis of a worker's past wage history might provide the worker with an incentive to earn more while he is working. For an employee who can reasonably expect to experience unemployment, at least occasionally, an earnings-based benefit schedule should encourage the worker to supply additional hours during spells of employment to insure himself more comfortably against large earnings losses from unemployment.[8] (See Yaniv, 1982; Hamermesh, 1979, has also shown that desired hours while working might rise.) This contrasts with the effect of the UI system in Britain, where the basic benefit is essentially independent of a worker's past average earnings.

Duration of Benefits

The limited duration of UI benefits in the United States also contrasts sharply with the situation in other Western economies. U.S. benefits are typically limited to twenty-six weeks, though they are regularly extended to thirty-nine weeks during periods of exceptionally high unemployment.[9] Benefits can last far longer abroad, particularly in northern Europe. The duration limit on U.S. benefits implies that the system does not provide coverage for catastrophic earnings loss due to unemployment. This may seem odd, inasmuch as workers are less able to self-insure against catastrophic loss than against more modest losses. However, only about a quarter of claims for UI ends in benefit exhaustion. The catastrophic protection is needed relatively infrequently for most insured workers. In addition, workers who exhaust benefits always have recourse to public assistance if their incomes and savings are low enough.

The limit on UI benefit duration also has an important advantage: it places a practical limit on the consequences of moral hazard. Workers who prolong their search for a job beyond twenty-six weeks will not receive any marginal subsidy for doing so. Burdett (1979) has argued that finite-duration UI benefits actually increases the likelihood of job acceptance as an unemployed worker approaches the end of his UI eligibility.[10]

Monitoring Search

Another feature of UI is also intended to reduce the problem of moral hazard. Those collecting UI benefits are monitored to ensure they are available for work and making good-faith efforts to find work. Benefits can be denied to workers who fail to provide evidence that they are searching for new jobs. In most states, workers are required to register with and report regularly to the U.S. Employment Service. In some, beneficiaries are asked to submit written evidence of job applications. In all states a worker can be denied benefits if a "suitable" job offer is refused.

Admittedly, most tests to ensure good-faith search and availability for work are weak. There is no method of guaranteeing that a worker will exert his best efforts to find a job. In this respect, the U.S. system provides weaker safeguards than those available to UI systems elsewhere. In particular, the U.S. Employment Service is relatively ineffective as a job-finding aid in comparison to comparable government services in Europe. Swedish employers, for example, are required by law to register vacancies with the Employment Service, so detecting a worker's refusal to accept a suitable job to which he has been referred is quite simple. The U.S. Employment Service is informed of only a small share of job vacancies, thus making enforcement of job search tests very difficult. Nonetheless, even the somewhat ineffective U.S. system of monitoring search is helpful in limiting the adverse effects of moral hazard.

Uninsured Unemployed Workers

Less than half of the stock of unemployed workers in the United States is typically insured by UI. Over two-thirds of the unemployed received benefits in 1976, but this coverage rate was extraordinary and not attained in any other postwar year. A more typical coverage ratio is 40 percent, and the rate has fallen below 30 percent in recent years. The low likelihood of coverage for unemployed workers is a direct consequence of the philosophy of the U.S. system. Because the program was designed to protect workers against earnings loss due to involuntary layoff and short hours, it does not provide insurance protection to new labor market entrants or to reentrants who have not established a recent earnings record. Benefits are also denied or substantially reduced in the case of workers discharged for cause and workers who voluntarily leave their jobs. For both these categories of unemployed, entry into unemployment is at the discretion of the worker, so full insurance protection does not seem warranted. It should be noted that the American philosophy of insurance is by no means universal. In Britain and Sweden, for example, new entrants and certain reentrants to the labor market can receive insurance payments.

The effects of the U.S. restrictions can be inferred by reference to Table 3.3, which shows the statistical breakdown of unemployment in two months in 1982 and 1985. October 1982 was a month of extremely high unemployment, and workers in some states were therefore eligible to draw benefits under the Extended Benefit and Supplemental Income programs for longer than twenty-six weeks. Unemployment had fallen substantially by October 1985, and its composition was more typical of what is observed during mature economic recoveries. As the table clearly indicates, job losers are a much higher fraction of the unemployed during severe recessions than during economic expansions. A higher percentage of unemployed workers consequently receives UI benefits during recessions. However, even during exceptionally severe contractions, such as the one in 1981–82, a very high percentage of the unemployed are in categories that are clearly ineligible for benefits—new entrants and reentrants—or that are relatively unlikely to receive benefits—job leavers and job losers unemployed longer than six months. In addition to these ineligible unemployed groups, there

Table 3.3. Composition of U.S. Unemployment

| | October 1982 | | October 1985 | |
	Number (in thousands)	Percentage of Total	Number (in thousands)	Percentage of Total
Total	10,942	100.0	7,917	100.0
Job losers	6,520	59.6	3,651	46.1
On layoff	1,942	17.7	923	11.7
Other	4,578	41.8	2,728	34.5
Unemployed under 6 months	5,001	45.7	2,950	37.3
Job leavers	847	7.7	999	12.6
Reentrants	2,357	21.5	2,301	29.1
New entrants	1,218	11.1	967	12.2
Insured unemployed	5,198	47.5	2,227	28.1
Regular programs	4,391	40.1	2,227	28.1
Supplemental program	807	7.4	0	0.0

Source: U.S. Department of Labor, *Employment and Earnings* (November 1982 and November 1985); and U.S. Council of Economic Advisors, *Economic Indicators* (March 1985 and April 1986).

are also potential labor market entrants who are not currently searching for work, perhaps because they are discouraged by the current state of the labor market. Since they are not actively seeking work they are defined as not in the labor force (NLF) and excluded from the count of unemployed. Any analysis of month-to-month flows between different labor market states would nonetheless show that many labor force participants in one month were reported as NLF in the preceding month.

The existence of uninsured unemployed and NLF workers has important implications for the theory of labor market response to insurance. These implications were scarcely considered in the early 1970s, when economists concentrated on the adverse effects of UI on the job search of insured unemployed workers. Yet the predicted effects on insured workers can be entirely offset by effects on uninsured and nonemployed workers. For example, if jobs are being rationed because of an inadequacy in the demand for labor, the longer job search of insured workers could be exactly counterbalanced by shorter unemployment duration on the part of uninsured job seekers (see Atkinson, 1981). Because insured workers are in competition for jobs with uninsured workers, an unattractive job offer that is rejected by an insured unemployed worker might be quickly snapped up by his uninsured rival. If UI has an effect on the number of unemployed workers at all, it is only because uninsured workers are drawn into the labor market by the prospect of easier job finding!

This view of labor market competition between insured and uninsured workers points up a defect in most methods of statistically estimating the effects of UI. If the average durations of unemployment of the insured and uninsured groups are compared for purposes of inferring the UI effect, the comparison will clearly exaggerate the size of the net effect. The insured workers' duration is increased by UI, but the uninsured workers' duration is reduced. Although on balance the average duration may be unaffected by UI, the statistical comparison will reveal a spurious effect.[11] This implies that a valid estimate of the overall UI effect can be obtained only by comparing the effects of different UI systems on comparable populations.

Several economists have noted that UI has a direct effect on the uninsured population in addition to the indirect "spillover" effect just described. Insurance should raise the attractiveness of finding a job. For a person who is currently uninsured and not employed, landing a job will not only provide a stream of wage income but also eventually give rise to entitlement to UI. If this entitlement has any value to the individual it should encourage him to enter the labor market and accept job offers with greater alacrity. Mortensen (1977) and Hamermesh (1979) have emphasized the importance of this entitlement effect on labor force decisions.

We should distinguish between two possible reasons why uninsured people find insurance coverage attractive. The first is that UI implicitly subsidizes workers who have intermittent employment experiences. Workers who occasionally work may expect to receive more in benefits while unemployed than they pay in insurance contributions while employed. If this is true, the offer of insurance raises the expected income associated with every level of hours of work while employed. This violates our previous assumption that in expected value terms, contributions equal benefits. If the UI program is to remain solvent, some workers must make net contributions to pay for the expected losses incurred in the claims of occasional workers. By implication, the net wages of these unsubsidized workers will be lower than they would be in the absence of UI. This might either raise or lower their labor supply while employed, depending on the relative size of the income and substitution effects on hours of work. If we assume that poorly and moderately paid workers have an upward-sloping supply function, the tax burden would be expected to reduce their labor supply.

It is not obvious that UI provides a subsidy to intermittent work patterns, however. For the intermittent employment strategy to be feasible in the United States, allegedly subsidized workers require the cooperation of their employers. As we have seen, voluntary job leavers are not generously insured in the United States, so workers would typically need to be discharged in order to file a valid claim. Since many employers expect eventually to fully reimburse the benefits paid out to their discharged workers (see below), there is no reason to assume employer cooperation. In addition, employers should discriminate against job applicants showing erratic employment histories or, alternatively, should pay these workers lower wages than they would to other workers without the same history of erratic labor force attachment. In either case, the implicit UI subsidy for occasional workers must decline or disappear.

A second reason that UI has value to uninsured workers is that it offers pure insurance protection against earnings loss due to unemployment. This would be the case even if the workers expect to pay fair premiums for their insurance. We have considered already the effects of pure insurance protection on the labor supply of the worker. For a person who would otherwise be employed the sign of the effect was ambiguous. For the currently uninsured and nonemployed person, the analysis is just the same, except that the offer of insurance can only *raise* desired labor supply. UI increases the certainty-equivalent value of wage income subject to unemployment risk. Therefore, if it has any effect at all on the work effort of a person not currently employed it must raise the probability of labor force attachment and employment. (Note that the probability of unemployment as well as employment is raised; the probability of nonattachment is reduced.) For an uninsured person who would otherwise be out of the labor force, it raises the likelihood of searching for work. For an uninsured worker searching for work, it raises the attractiveness of job offers which have associated unemployment risk, and hence it increases the probability that an offer will be accepted.[12]

Before closing this discussion of UI effects on worker behavior, it is worth mentioning the possible effects of insurance on workers who are on temporary layoff. Table 3.3 shows that a high proportion of people on layoff are not permanently discharged workers but workers who expect to be called back to their former jobs. For some workers on temporary layoff, the usual model of job search is not very relevant. These workers are not comparing sequential job offers to a precisely calibrated reservation wage and then selecting the first offer that satisfies optimizing first-order conditions. They are waiting by their phone for notice that they have been recalled to work. On the whole, it would be difficult to devise a more optimal "search" strategy than the one adopted. If they engaged in costly search, they are likely to find that the starting wage at other firms is below the one offered on their current job; that is, their productivity with their current employer, which reflects past investments in job-specific skills, is higher than their productivity elsewhere. Thus it hardly seems rational to seek a permanent job which will pay less than the wage that will be offered, with high probability, when the worker is recalled. This analysis is valid whether or not UI is available. Workers on very short-term layoff are probably unaffected by adverse UI incentives. Workers on longer-term layoff may refrain from seeking a temporary low-wage job. In both cases, the adverse effects of UI on the duration of unemployment may be quite small.

Referring again to Table 3.3, we can briefly summarize the predicted effects of UI on the labor supply of different classes of unemployed workers. New entrants, reentrants, and laid-off workers who have exhausted their claim to benefits should be induced to become employed faster than they would in the absence of UI. At least a few of these potential workers are probably attracted to the labor market by the availability of insurance. Uninsured job leavers should also be induced to take jobs more quickly, whereas insured job leavers should prolong their job search. In the few states where job leavers are generously insured, some workers will be induced to quit their jobs by the availability of benefits. As we have just seen, some workers on temporary layoff will be at most modestly affected in their job search by UI. Only workers who are on permanent layoff and who are not yet near expiration of benefits will have strong incentives to prolong their job search. Note that these workers constitute far less than half of all unemployed workers, even during a severe recession. The longer unemployment duration of these workers should be at least partly offset by shorter unemployment durations on the part of uninsured workers. Taking all of these effects into account, it appears likely that insurance will raise the number of unemployed workers. But, ironically, a major reason for this conclusion is not that UI discourages labor supply, but that it induces some people who would otherwise be nonparticipants to search for work. The overall effects of the program on employment and hours of work are ambiguous without a much more detailed model of market dynamics.[13]

Employer Effects of Experience Rating

Our assumption thus far has been that workers pay for unemployment benefits through a tax levied on earnings. The tax rate is determined by the expected unemployment experience of each worker. This assumption permitted us to focus squarely on the insurance aspects of the program and to see the adverse consequences of moral hazard on worker behavior. No assumption has been made about how expected unemployment experience could be computed or which economic agent would collect the premiums and distribute the benefits.

In principle, it might seem that private insurance companies could provide the insurance, or that employers themselves might offer UI benefits. Since there is an obvious welfare gain from insurance, it should be profitable to offer it in the market. However, no well-organized and universally available UI program is offered in the private market, nor was one available before the government intervened to create one. Government intervention thus seems required if insurance is to be offered universally.

Several theories have been advanced to explain the government's role. It has been argued that moral hazard creates a barrier to private insurance in this area, but I do not find this argument convincing. Moral hazard is a barrier to insurance in other areas (for example, casualty insurance for homes and motor vehicles), but the private market seems to overcome the problem well enough to offer insurance to those who want it. Adverse selection is also mentioned as a reason that private markets might fail to develop. Workers with the highest probability of layoff are the ones who would have the greatest motivation to seek insurance. Workers with less likelihood of layoff might therefore be forced to pay a premium that reflected the poor experience of workers who typically demanded insurance. It is easy to see how this premium could exceed the value of insurance to workers who are not prone to layoff. Although this is indeed a problem, government intervention could be limited to a law requiring each worker to be covered and specifying minimal criteria for the policies offered. As a parallel example, such is essentially the extent of intervention in the auto insurance market. Governments have chosen to go much beyond this level of intervention, however, and adverse selection thus does not seem a convincing explanation for the extent of intervention.

I find persuasive the suggestion of Rosen (1977) and Topel and Welch (1980) that private insurance would not be credible. One of the striking features of U.S. unemployment is its strongly cyclical nature. The peak rate of unemployment has varied widely in different cycles, ranging up to 25 percent during the 1930s. The duration of labor market contractions has also varied tremendously. The offer of unemployment insurance under such conditions would be akin to offering fire insurance in a crowded wooden city that lacked a fire department. Such insurance could undoubtedly be offered, but the firms offering it might be expected to go bankrupt the first time the city, or a sizable part of it, went up in smoke. For insurance to be effective, it must protect workers against losses in severe recessions—when many of the losses occur—as well as in normal labor markets.[14] Given its authority to tax and ability to borrow, government can feasibly provide an insurance policy that is credible to workers.

To finance this insurance, the U.S. government and the individual state governments levy a tax on the payrolls of covered employers. Each state government has established a unique set of tax schedules for employers within its boundaries. Generally, the tax rate charged to a given firm varies depending on the frequency of insurance claims filed by laid-off workers of that firm; as the frequency and cost of claims rise, the tax rate rises.[15] So far as I know, the United States is unique in financing its insurance in this way. In other countries UI is financed by taxes that fail to reflect, even imperfectly, an employer's (or a worker's) past experience of insured unemployment. In view of this difference between the United States and other countries, it is interesting that American economists have devoted so much attention to departures from perfect experience rating in their own system. Little if any attention has been given to this issue abroad, where of course it is far more relevant.

Most state UI tax schemes depart from perfect experience rating by establishing minimum and maximum tax rates chargeable to individual firms. Firms with exceptionally good layoff records are charged the minimum rate; firms with exceptionally poor records, the maximum rate. Firms with an intermediate experience face a tax rate that varies as their layoff experience varies. At the margin, these firms might expect to fully pay for the claims of a newly laid-off worker.[16] By contrast, firms facing the minimum and maximum tax rate do not bear the full cost of an insurance claim filed by an additional laid-off worker. In fact, they might not bear any of the cost of the claim.[17] Baily (1977a) and Feldstein (1976) argued that incomplete experience rating, together with the tax-exempt status of

UI benefits, provided an incentive for firms to engage in excessive layoff behavior.[18] The UI program essentially provides workers with benefits for which their employers do not pay the full price, but these benefits can be realized only if the workers are laid off.[19] Hence, employers will respond to variations in demand by laying off workers rather than adopting some strategy that on the margin is more costly to themselves and their employees — for example, accumulating inventories, reducing wage rates, or limiting weekly hours. These alternative strategies are more likely to be followed in the absence of subsidized insurance.

It does not follow, however, that the employer response will affect the amount of labor at work, measured in terms of average hours over the business cycle. During cyclical downturns fewer workers will be employed, but average hours worked by individuals will be higher than in the absence of excess layoff behavior. During cyclical upswings, when few workers are on layoff, employers will be forced to meet a greater share of current demand out of current output because less inventory has been accumulated. Either hours per employee or the number of employees will therefore rise. It might be argued that since incomplete experience rating provides an implicit subsidy to firms that engage in excessive layoffs, firms that prefer layoffs will prosper at the expense of those that do not. Although this situation will indeed raise the average number of workers on layoff, the general equilibrium effect on average labor supply remains uncertain. Those firms preferring layoffs might well use more labor at cyclical peaks.

The Baily-Feldstein model has attracted the attention of macroeconomists as well as economists interested more narrowly in labor market behavior. The model shows clearly how UI can raise the number of workers on layoff not only in normal times, but also during recessions. By contrast, during the 1950s and 1960s the program was regarded by macroeconomists as an automatic stabilizer that helped prop up consumer demand when other sources of demand were weak. According to this earlier view, the number of workers on layoff was reduced by the program because the consumption of unemployed workers was not reduced by as much as it would have been in the program's absence. Consequently, overall consumer demand was higher and layoffs less frequent. Baily and Feldstein would presumably agree with this view, but they would note that the same consumption stimulus could be achieved without UI's adverse effects on employer behavior. In thinking about the program's overall effect on layoffs, however, we must keep our comparisons firmly in mind. In comparison with a UI program financed by perfectly experience-rated taxes, the number of workers on temporary layoff is higher under the current program, as Baily and Feldstein show. But in comparison with no UI program at all—and with no alternative consumption stimulus—the number of workers on layoff might be lower under our current system of UI.

4. Empirical Estimates of UI Effects

In this section I will briefly describe our current empirical knowledge of the effects of UI on labor supply. The discussion is restricted to the four principal areas where statistical analysis has been concentrated: (1) effects of UI on the duration of unemployment of insured unemployed workers; (2) effects on the reemployment wage income of insured workers; (3) effects on the layoff behavior of employers; and (4) selected effects on uninsured workers or aggregate supply. Some or all of these effects have been reviewed in previous papers, notably Hamermesh (1977), Topel and Welch (1980), and Gustman (1982), all of which provide excellent summaries. Gustman in particular emphasizes that our current empirical knowledge is too fragmentary to permit any conclusion about the overall effect of UI on labor market transitions. This can be seen by comparing the list of empirical topics just given with the list of theoretical topics described in the previous two sections. In theory, there are a great number of ways in which labor market behavior can be affected by UI. Only a few of these have been explored. One of the most conspicuous omissions is the virtual absence of studies of UI effects on labor supply while workers are employed. (Hamermesh, 1979 and 1980, provide partial exceptions.) As we have seen, the theoretical effect of UI on labor supply while employed is ambiguous, but this does not imply that the size of the effect is small.

Effects on Unemployment Duration of Insured Unemployed Workers

Length of unemployment has been more intensively studied than any other effect, both by American and British econometricians. Researchers have sought to estimate the size of the effect because both common sense and economic theory provide an unambiguous prediction about its sign. In a simple labor supply model, UI gives rise to both income and substitution effects which should tend to prolong the spell of unemployment (see Moffitt and Nicholson, 1982). In the job search model, the insured unemployed worker is encouraged to set a higher reservation wage by the availability of benefits. The higher reservation wage should prolong search (see Mortensen, 1971). Empirical studies almost without exception have confirmed this theoretical prediction.

Feldstein and Poterba (1984) have shown that an unemployed worker's reservation wage is strongly affected by the availability and level of UI benefits. Feldstein and Poterba measure UI benefits by computing a net replacement rate—the ratio of UI benefits to the net after-tax earnings lost through unemployment. They measure the reservation wage ratio as the ratio of the reported reservation wage to the wage on the worker's last job. A 1 percent rise in the net replacement rate is found to raise the reservation wage ratio by 0.13 points in the case of workers on layoff, by 0.42 points for other job losers, and by 0.29 points for voluntary job leavers. Using a few simple assumptions about the distribution of wage offers, Feldstein and Poterba suggest that reducing the net replacement rate from 0.7 to 0.5 could reduce the expected duration of an unemployment spell by 29 to 37 percent for a worker with the average reservation wage ratio. This suggestion is purely conjectural, however, since we know little about the wage offer distribution facing individual workers, nor do we know how the reservation wage reported by an unemployed worker corresponds to the wage he eventually accepts. (He might accept a lower wage, for example.)

A number of writers have attempted to give a "best estimate" of the effect of UI on the duration of an unemployment spell given the large number of varying estimates. Hamermesh (1977) concluded that a 10 percent rise in the gross replacement rate leads to an increase in the average insured spell of unemployment of about half a week. Welch (1979) discussed in great detail the statistical problems of estimating UI effects. He estimated that the effect of UI on total unemployment duration—including the uninsured portion after benefit exhaustion—is approximately 1.5 weeks for every $10 rise in the weekly benefit amount. (Welch used 1970 as his reference year; because of inflation, the $10 in benefits in that year would translate to approximately $25 in 1986.) However, Welch noted that this estimate is typically based on the responses of recipients of UI. If we also included the response of insured workers who are unemployed too briefly to qualify for benefits, the average response to a $10 benefit rise on covered workers would be less than one week. Solon (1985) has investigated the effect of taxing UI benefits, which began in 1979. Although his published estimates are difficult to compare with earlier results, it appears that the taxation of benefits resulted in a significantly shorter average duration of insured unemployment spells. The average spell was reduced by approximately as much as would be predicted in view of the reduction in net replacement ratios that occurred.

Classen (1977, 1979) has performed some of the more careful studies based upon UI administrative records. Her estimates suggest that the elasticity of insured unemployment duration with respect to changes in the UI replacement rate is about 0.6 to 1.0 for average workers. That is, a 1 percent rise in the replacement rate (for example, from 0.500 to 0.505) will lead to a 0.6 to 1 percent rise in the average duration of insured unemployment. Lancaster (1979), Nickell (1979, 1980), and Atkinson and co-workers (1984) have obtained virtually identical elasticity estimates for the UI program in Britain. But Atkinson and co-workers warn that the elasticity estimate is not well determined. It is extremely sensitive to seemingly trivial changes in the statistical specification and to alternative methods of representing the UI benefit. Atkinson and colleagues note, in fact, that under plausible specifications the best estimate of the UI effect is zero.

Another problem with Classen's and the British estimates of response is that they are based on unemployment durations of workers who are insured under a single system. (Classen's estimates are based solely on the insured unemployed in Arizona and Pennsylvania; observations from the two states are not combined. The British estimates are of course based only on unemployed workers in the United Kingdom.) As mentioned earlier, this kind of sample restriction can bias the estimate of overall response to the program. The unemployment durations of well-insured workers are implicitly compared with those of poorly insured workers under the same system. Because the unemployment durations of the latter may fall as a consequence of the choosier job search strategy adopted by the former, the difference in unemployment durations between the two groups can overstate the net effect of UI benefit generosity. In spite of this, Classen in particular has interpreted her results as showing that the average duration of unemployment and the total number of unemployed are raised by more generous UI benefits (see Classen, 1977, pp. 442, 444).

A number of analysts have noted that UI should have a smaller impact on workers on temporary layoff than on workers permanently discharged from their previous jobs. Classen (1977, 1979) has confirmed this prediction and found that the effect on temporarily laid-off workers is only one-third to one-half the effect on other insured unemployed workers. Topel and Welch (1979) summarize past studies and estimate that a 10 percent rise in the benefit replacement rate extends the average unemployment spell of insured workers who change jobs by 1.2 weeks. The effect on temporarily laid-off workers is far smaller.

The duration of a current spell of unemployment should also affect the size of the UI impact. Workers might be strongly affected at the start of an unemployment spell, but much less affected as their eligibility for benefits draws to a close. So far as I can discover, this suggestion by Burdett (1979) has not been investigated empirically. However, the findings reported by Nickell (1979) are suggestive. Nickell examined the effect of the UI replacement rate on the probability of unemployed British men's finding jobs. The National Insurance (NI) unemployment benefit in Britain is a non-means-tested benefit similar to the regular UI benefit in the United States. The NI benefit can be received for a maximum duration of fifty-two weeks. During the period studied by Nickell it was supplemented by the Earnings Related Supplement between the third and the twenty-eighth weeks of unemployment. (A means-tested Supplementary Benefit is also given to some workers who exhaust their NI benefits.) Nickell found that the UI replacement rate had a much smaller effect on job finding once an individual had been unemployed for six months or more. His estimated coefficients indicate that the impact after the sixth month is one-third or less the impact during the first six months of unemployment. One explanation for this finding might be that the UI benefit has less effect on behavior when benefit exhaustion is near.

Moffitt and Nicholson (1982) have provided the best estimates of the effect of potential benefit duration on the actual duration of unemployment spells. Using a labor supply perspective rather than the job search model ordinarily applied, they found statistically significant responses to variations in both net replacement rate and potential benefit duration. They estimate that a rise of 0.10 in the net replacement rate will increase the average duration of unemployment by 0.84 to 0.98 weeks for typical insured unemployed workers. A one-week increase in the potential duration of benefits will raise the length of an average spell by 0.1 week.

We may summarize by saying that the best cross-sectional studies have found statistically significant, but sometimes rather small effects of UI on the unemployment spells of insured workers.[20] These studies fall well short of being ideal, but there is wide consensus that UI gives rise to a significant increase in time spent between jobs for unemployed workers covered by UI.

Effect of UI on Wages

A number of studies have examined the effect of UI on the wages of reemployed workers. Most studies agree that there is a beneficial effect, although possibly a modest one. The best-known study is that of Ehrenberg and Oaxaca (1976), who examined the effects of UI on both unemployment duration and reemployment wage gain. Their analysis sample consisted of men and women from different states (and hence subject to wide variations in UI incentives) and was drawn from a national probability sample rather than from UI administrative records. Ehrenberg and Oaxaca found with other analysts that UI has significant positive effects on the duration of unemployment for every insured group examined. But their results also show that the program has significant beneficial effects for the reemployment wage of adult men and women. (Small and insignificant gains were found for young men and women.) The authors estimate that a 10 percent rise in the UI replacement rate from 0.4 to 0.5 would increase a male's reemployment wage by 7.0 percent and a female's wage by 1.5 percent. Burgess and Kingston (1976) and Holen (1977) similarly find significant earnings gains on the part of insured unemployed workers.

Classen (1977, 1979) is much more doubtful that UI produces an earnings effect. Her results show a contradictory pattern of response in different samples and using different specifications, and she rejects the hypothesis that an earnings gain is present.

Welch (1977) has summarized some of the statistical problems with the reemployment wage studies, problems that he apparently finds insuperable. He also argues against the theoretical prediction that UI will increase reemployment wage rates. One point he stresses is that by lengthening the average duration of unemployment, UI makes insured unemployed workers less attractive in the eyes of potential employers. A long spell of unemployment carries with it a negative signal to potential employers, one that should lessen the chance of a job offer. The problem with this theory is that all insured unemployed workers are provided with the same "negative" signal. If each insured worker was out of work for, say, four extra weeks as a result of UI then it would be difficult for employers to discriminate against job seekers with somewhat longer unemployment. Every insured unemployed worker on offer has a longer duration. Rational, well-informed firms would be aware of this and set their hiring criteria accordingly. It might be argued that firms would thus be induced to discriminate in favor of uninsured unemployed workers, but a moment's reflection will show that this is unlikely. Uninsured unemployed workers consist of new labor market entrants, reentrants, workers who quit their last jobs, laid-off workers who have exhausted their benefits, and discharged workers who were fired for cause. None of these groups appears particularly attractive in comparison to experienced unemployed workers who are still eligible for UI. I would therefore expect UI benefits to convey a favorable rather than an unfavorable job market signal.

On the whole, the empirical evidence supports the prediction that reemployment wage rates are increased by UI, at least for some major groups. The evidence is not nearly so strong or plentiful as that available on the effects of unemployment duration, but this is largely because fewer economists have examined the wage-gain issue.

Effects on Layoff Behavior of Firms

According to the theory of Baily (1977) and Feldstein (1976), unemployment insurance should increase the frequency of temporary layoff unemployment. This hypothesis has been examined in at least three studies (see also the survey by Topol in this volume). Feldstein (1978) used data from the March 1971 Current Population Survey (CPS) to estimate the effect of the net UI replacement ratio on the incidence of temporary layoffs among survey respondents. In the month studied, 1.6 percent of respondents were on temporary layoff. Feldstein used a simulation program to predict the net UI replacement ratio of all sample members, whether on layoff or not, and then estimated the effect of this replacement ratio on the temporary layoff status of respondents.[21] His coefficients imply that UI benefits cause 46 to 53 percent of all temporary layoff unemployment in the United States, or 12 to 13 percent of 1971 unemployment. Because he finds the effect of the replacement rate to be nonlinear, his results imply that temporary layoff unemployment could be reduced even more sharply if benefits were limited to less than 50 percent of lost net earnings rather than reduced to zero. (His nonlinear results imply that 70 percent of temporary layoff unemployment could be eliminated by restricting the net replacement ratio to no more than 0.50.)

Recall that even if Feldstein's interpretation of these results is correct we could not conclude that labor supply over the business cycle is reduced by a corresponding amount. Workers who remain employed may work additional hours, and the number of employees at cyclical peaks may be higher. For at least two reasons, however, we should be cautious in interpreting Feldstein's estimates. The estimates reflect workers' reemployment probabilities as well as employers' layoff behavior. If laid-off workers are slow in accepting alternative employment because of generous UI benefits, they are more likely to be found on temporary layoff at any point in time. Even though the effect of UI on the unemployment duration of temporarily laid-off workers is small, it nonetheless affects the point-in-time incidence of temporary layoffs. Feldstein's estimates thus measure the effect of UI on the behavior of both firms and job-seeking workers.

Second, implicit in Feldstein's discussion is the assumption that workers on layoff would be employed in the absence of UI.[22] This is debatable. Some workers might be on permanent layoff or out of the labor market rather than on temporary layoff. If they are on permanent layoff, the count of unemployed workers is unaffected. If they are NLF the number of unemployed is reduced, but so is the size of the work force. In either case, labor supply would not be affected.

Close in spirit to Feldstein's work is a study by Clark and Summers (1982). These authors also use CPS data to measure the impact of UI on labor market status, but unlike Feldstein they estimate its effects on transitions between labor force states. Using combined data from the March and April 1978 surveys, Clark and Summers consider how the net UI replacement rate affects movements into and out of temporary layoff unemployment. They find that the probability of moving from employment to temporary layoff unemployment is very significantly related to a worker's net replacement ratio. A 10 percent fall in the replacement rate (from, say, 50 to 40 percent) would reduce the probability of temporary layoff unemployment by 0.05 percentage points. Complete elimination of UI benefits would reduce the probability of temporary layoff unemployment by 0.25 percentage points. For purposes of comparison, 2 percent of the sample employed in March 1978 was unemployed in April. This implies that about 12 to 13 percent of the movement from employment to unemployment in a given month is due to the UI effect on layoff unemployment. I should note that these estimates, as well as Feldstein's earlier ones, do not provide a direct confirmation of the Baily-Feldstein hypothesis. The estimates fail to isolate the effect of the implicit UI subsidy on excessive layoff behavior. When Clark and Summers tried to estimate the effects of imperfect experience rating on layoffs they could detect no effects on the flow out of employment.

Two other findings of the Clark and Summers study are relevant to our discussion thus far. In addition to the significant but comparatively small UI effect on movements from employment to layoff unemployment, Clark and Summers also found significant and quite large effects tending to reduce the movement of employed persons out of the labor force. Between March and April 1978, 3.3 percent of the employed population dropped out of the labor force. An employed person eligible for the average UI replacement rate (about 50 percent) was 2.2 percentage points less likely to drop out of the labor force than an otherwise identical worker who was ineligible for benefits. Clearly, many of the workers induced by UI to be unemployed would have been NLF in the absence of the program rather than employed, as is usually assumed. Clark and Summers also confirmed that UI benefits slow down the reemployment of insured laid-off workers. This effect appears to be quite sizable, but it is very imprecisely estimated.

A third study of employer behavior is more directly relevant to the Baily-Feldstein hypothesis than the two studies just mentioned. Brechling (1981) has tried to estimate the effects of imperfect experience rating on the layoff behavior of firms in different states. His primary objective was to estimate the impact of state differences in tax structure on layoff and rehire rates. Brechling finds that changes in the tax formulas which tend to reduce the relation between a firm's tax liabilities and its claims experience have the predictable effect: as effective experience rating declines, the frequency of layoffs increases.

The available evidence on the Baily-Feldstein hypothesis is preliminary and unsatisfying but appears to be consistent with the theory's basic prediction. Layoff unemployment is more frequent for workers with high net replacement rates, and temporary layoff unemployment occurs more frequently in states where employer tax contributions are not closely tied to UI claims experience. But although the evidence is consistent with the theory, it is very incomplete. It is not clear, for example, whether the higher number of workers on temporary layoff would be employed, permanent job losers, or NLF in the absence of UI. Nor is it known whether the countercyclical consumption stimulus provided by UI offsets part of the program's adverse effects, at least during cyclical downturns.

The Effect on Uninsured Groups and Aggregate Supply

Empirical studies of UI have focused largely on the behavior of unemployed workers who are insured by UI and the employers who finance it. Yet if insurance has any value to potential workers, the program should also affect behavior in groups which are not presently insured. As indicated above, the effects of UI on insured workers may, in addition, have spillover effects on uninsured job seekers. Few of these potential effects have received much empirical study. The significance of spillover effects has been completely unexamined so far as I know.

Hamermesh (1978, 1979) has completed two studies of the labor supply effects of UI on uninsured workers. His 1979 article on the entitlement effects of UI is the better-known study and the one on which I will concentrate here. Hamermesh notes that UI can provide work incentives to potential labor force entrants that partly or wholly offset its adverse incentives on insured unemployed workers. Some potential entrants may be attracted to employment by the prospect of the UI benefits, entitlement to which is restricted to workers who meet certain minimum earnings requirements. Using data on adult women from a nationally representative data set—the Panel Survey of Income Dynamics—Hamermesh finds that this prediction is at least weakly supported in the observed earnings distribution of women. There is a clustering of female earnings in the range just above the minimum earnings required for UI entitlement.

Hamermesh tries to estimate the effect of UI incentives on three groups of women: those with earnings below the minimum qualifying earnings for UI; those above the minimum but below the maximum qualifying earnings; and those above the maximum qualifying earnings. In theory UI should have differing impacts on these three groups. Hamermesh uses annual hours of work as his measure of labor supply. He finds the expected pattern of work response in the three groups, though the effects are very imprecisely estimated. On balance, the positive entitlement effect on women below or just above the minimum qualifying earnings level is approximately equal to the negative incentive effects on women who are comfortably eligible for benefits. According to Hamermesh's findings, a 20 percent boost in the weekly benefit amount would raise the number of working women by 1.1 percent as a result of the entitlement effect, while the same benefit increase would reduce female employment by 1.4 percent because of prolonged unemployment among comfortably eligible women. The net impact on women's employment is thus −0.3 percent.

The impact on annual hours is even smaller. The reader should note that these estimates are very imprecise. In his 1978 study, Hamermesh finds that easier UI eligibility requirements induce higher average weeks worked among adult women. This effect occurs primarily as a result of added weeks worked among women who work less than thirty-nine weeks per year. Presumably these women find insurance valuable and are encouraged by easier availability of benefits to seek and hold a job.

The most thorough analysis of the effect of UI on all types of labor market transitions is the study by Clark and Summers (1982) mentioned earlier. The authors examine the effects of the net UI replacement rate and certain qualifying provisions on each type of monthly transition (the transitions from employment to unemployment and NLF, from unemployment to employment and NLF, and from NLF to employment and unemployment). Although their results cast no direct light on the entitlement question studied by Hamermesh, several of the findings are suggestive. The transition probabilities out of unemployment are especially striking. As expected, increases in the UI replacement rate are found to raise the probability of transition from employment to unemployment significantly. Taking account of the increased frequency of temporary layoffs, permanent layoffs, and quitting, the average UI replacement rate raised the probability of transition to unemployment by 0.4 percentage points. As noted earlier, 2.0 percent of employees in one month are unemployed in the following month. According to the Clark-Summers estimates, this rate would be reduced to 1.6 percent if UI was eliminated. However, this effect on unemployment is dwarfed by the UI effect on transitions out of the labor force. At the average replacement rate, the probability of moving from employment to NLF is reduced by 2.1 percentage points as a result of UI benefits.[23]

If UI benefits are a pure work disincentive for employed workers, transitions to unemployment would be raised and transitions out of the labor force would be unaffected by UI. If UI simply affected workers' reported nonemployment status without affecting employment, then any induced rise in transitions to unemployment would be exactly counterbalanced by a fall in transitions out of the labor force. Here the idea is that workers report job search or temporary layoff in order to collect benefits. Their true labor market status is indistinguishable from their being out of the labor force altogether. But the Clark-Summers results show neither of these patterns. They show instead that transitions out of employment are significantly reduced by UI. The added flow into unemployment is much more than counterbalanced by a decline in the number of transitions out of the labor force. Taking account of the UI effect on all types of transition probabilities, Clark and Summers predict that total elimination of UI in 1978 would have reduced the unemployment rate in that year by 0.65 percentage points (or about 10 percent), but would also have reduced the employment/population ratio by 0.59 points (or about 1 percent). By implication the nonparticipation rate would have risen by nearly 1.1 percentage points. On balance, the program raises aggregate employment and labor force participation.

Although Clark and Summers express surprise at their findings (and some skepticism toward their believability), the overall pattern of results is in fact consistent with two leading theories of UI effects. First, the program provides a subsidy to unemployment and hence should encourage workers and their employers to increase it. But, second, the program insures workers against some of the riskiness of labor market income, so increases in UI generosity should encourage some potential workers to join the labor market and remain employed. It is difficult at this stage to judge the credibility of the Clark and Summers results. Their study is thus far the only one that investigates such a broad range of possible UI effects. Until further studies are completed, there is no other empirical standard of comparison.

5. Conclusions

As we have seen, economists have proposed a wide variety of reasons that UI might in theory affect the labor supply of workers. Insured workers who become unemployed have less reason to seek and to accept a new job. But by delaying their job acceptance, the workers may be encouraged to find more stable employment or jobs that are more suited to their skills. Moreover, the provision of insurance and the relation between insurance benefits and past earnings might stimulate some workers to work longer hours while employed. Uninsured persons who are either unemployed or potential labor market entrants are offered an incentive to become employed in jobs covered by insurance. Firms which face uncertain and variable demand are implicitly encouraged to engage in excessive temporary layoff behavior. But firms which would otherwise be tempted to permanently lay off temporarily surplus workers might be less inclined to do so when they are forced to bear some of the cost of the resulting insurance claims. The countercyclical consumption stimulus provided by UI might reduce the cyclical swings in unemployment, at least modestly.

Nearly all theoretical studies of UI represent partial equilibrium analyses, and even these analyses frequently lead to ambiguous predictions about the impact of UI on labor supply. Since some of the partial equilibrium effects — on insured and uninsured workers and on employers — go in opposite directions, it is difficult to make confident predictions about the size or magnitude of the overall effect. The general equilibrium effects of UI are even more elusive. The program has simultaneous effects on the composition and supply of and the demand for labor, and, in addition, it can affect the cyclical demand for final consumption. Consequently, theory alone cannot resolve the controversy over the alleged adverse consequences of UI. Theory tells us that provision of insurance can raise the welfare of workers subject to unemployment risk and that such insurance can distort allocative decisions on both the supply and demand sides of the market. But more precise conclusions about the net impact of insurance must be based on empirical studies.

The available empirical studies are on the whole rather one-sided. Most concentrate on the adverse incentives of UI on the reemployment of insured unemployed workers and on the layoff behavior of firms. These studies have generally confirmed the theoretical predictions that they set out to test: in comparison with less well-insured workers, better-insured workers spend more time in unemployment. In comparison with less generous programs, more generous programs encourage employers to increase the number of workers on temporary layoff. Unfortunately, these studies do not resolve the basic questions that they raise. By how much is unemployment raised, taking account of spillover effects on uninsured unemployed workers? Do firms reduce the number of workers in employment by their excessive temporary layoff behavior? Or do they simply substitute temporary for permanent layoffs, which they might otherwise effect?

In the smaller number of studies that examine the predicted beneficial effects of UI, economists have also found support for their partial equilibrium predictions. Better-insured workers appear to find higher-wage jobs than those found by less-insured workers. Uninsured persons are drawn into the labor market and into employment by the offer of more generous insurance benefits. In the only study examining UI's effects on all labor market states, Clark and Summers (1982) tentatively conclude that more generous insurance raises the probability of both unemployment and employment; only the probability of nonparticipation is reduced.

My conclusion from this survey is that unemployment insurance has both beneficial and adverse consequences for labor supply, and that both beneficial and adverse effects have been reasonably well demonstrated in available empirical studies. But the evidence does not support any firm conclusion about the effect of the program on aggregate work effort actually supplied in market jobs. Given the relative stability in the size of the U.S. program since World War II, the evidence does not even come close to supporting the idea held by some that unemployment benefits are a partial explanation for America's declining economic performance since the 1960s.

NOTES

Katherine Abraham, Martin N. Baily, Peter Gottschalk, and two anonymous reviewers provided helpful comments on an earlier draft. The research assistance of Sheila Murray is gratefully acknowledged. Any remaining errors are the sole responsibility of the author.

1. General revenues may be used to pay for certain extended and supplemental UI benefits.

2. A worker is referred to as "he" for simplicity. No stereotyping is intended or implied; the theory applies equally well to women and men.

3. Baily (1977b, 1978) emphasizes the welfare-enhancing effects of UI. See also Rosen (1983).

4. This is true even assuming that workers in the sectors are required to pay a fair premium for insurance, namely, μ_1 per dollar of wages in the first sector and μ_2 per dollar in the second. If instead the premiums in the two industries are identical, the comparative attractiveness of employment in the second sector would be raised even more.

5. The productivity-enhancing effects of UI have been shown more formally by Rosen (1983).

6. UI can also affect the probability that an employer will discharge or temporarily lay off a worker (see below). Hence employer as well as worker response can affect μ.

7. Stafford (1977) has made a related argument.

8. If the worker bears the entire burden of the taxes that pay for his UI benefits, the incentive to work longer hours while he is employed is less clear-cut.

9. Benefits were extended to sixty-five weeks in 1975–77, but this liberality was unique in the postwar period.

10. His theoretical predictions conform with those of earlier analysts, however, in showing that a newly laid-off worker will be less likely to accept a job when insured by UI. Hence, short-duration spells will increase in length even as long-duration spells decline.

11. Many statistical studies of UI are restricted to an analysis of only insured unemployed workers, but these studies are subject to exactly the same criticism. Unemployed workers with low benefits are less well insured and hence may indirectly benefit from the choosy job search strategies adopted by their better-insured competitors.

12. This analysis ignores the fact that many wage earners are members of income-sharing families. One way for families to insure themselves against earnings loss due to unemployment is to have multiple wage earners. The loss of one member's earnings represents a much smaller relative loss when there are two or more earners than when there is only one. The provision of unemployment insurance reduces the riskiness of having only a single wage earner and may thus reduce the incentive to self-insure with multiple earners. Of course the effect of this incentive could be to reduce the average size of income-sharing family units as well as to reduce the proportion of family members who work.

13. See Clark and Summers (1982) and Gustman (1982) for a more extended discussion of the offsetting UI effects on various groups.

14. To compound the problem of a private insurance company, its assets might fall in value when they are most needed. Equities purchased in the 1920s could not have paid off the claims of many unemployed workers during the 1930s; bonds bought in the 1960s would not have satisfied many claims in the inflationary 1970s.

15. For a description of some of the state systems, see Becker (1972) and Brechling (1977).

16. This would of course depend on the exact nature of the state's tax schedule; see Becker (1972).

17. Although it might appear that a firm facing the minimum or maximum rate bears none of the cost of a marginal layoff, this conclusion must be modified for firms which eventually expect to face an intermediate tax rate; see Wolcowitz (1984). Rosen (1983) argues that the maximum rate is based upon sound insurance principles. If the tax rate always went up to reflect a firm's past experience of unemployment—no matter how severe the experience—there would be no insurance. The maximum rate, therefore, provides true insurance against large losses. Note, however, that Rosen is referring to insurance that is provided to employers, not to workers. Most other economists writing about UI have implicitly or explicitly assumed that it provides insurance to workers, not to firms.

18. Feldstein (1974) in particular has emphasized the adverse consequences of exempting UI benefits from taxes. Because workers pay taxes on wage income but not on insurance benefits, the replacement rate on net wages lost through unemployment must be higher than the replacement rate on gross wages. Whether this implies that the net replacement rate is too high is debatable; exactly the same net replacement rate would result from eliminating the tax exemption on benefits but simultaneously raising the gross replacement rate. If the primary purpose of eliminating the UI tax exemption is to reduce certain distributional anomalies, then naturally the gross replacement rate should be raised to preserve the previous average ratio of insurance compensation to net earnings loss. If the main objection to the exemption is that it makes net replacement rates too high, then the gross replacement rate can be reduced as easily as the exemption can be eliminated.

19. Taxation of UI was introduced in 1979 for families with high gross incomes. In 1982, the income threshold for taxing UI was reduced, greatly increasing the fraction of UI that is subject to federal income taxation; see Solon (1985). Since 1987, UI has been taxed like ordinary income.

20. The aggregate time series studies sometimes find much larger effects, but I do not find these studies believable. See Atkinson (1981) for a discussion of the British time series studies and their problems.

21. Note that this does not really provide a direct test of the Baily-Feldstein hypothesis, because the replacement rate does not measure the net subsidy to employer layoffs. According to the theory, it is the subsidy, not the replacement rate, that encourages layoffs.

22. For the unemployment rate to fall by the percentage given by Feldstein, 46 to 53 percent of workers on temporary layoff would have to become employed.

23. This compares to an average probability of 3.3 percentage points of leaving employment to become NLF.

REFERENCES

Atkinson, A. B. 1981. "Unemployment Benefits and Incentives." In Jon Creedy, ed., *The Economics of Unemployment in Britain*. London: Butterworths.

Atkinson, A. B., J. Gomulka, and J. Micklewright. 1984. "Unemployment Benefit, Duration and Incentives in Britain: How Robust Is the Evidence?" *Journal of Public Economics* 23 (February/March): 3–26.

Baily, Martin N. 1977a. "On the Theory of Layoffs and Unemployment." *Econometrica* 45 (July): 1043–1063.

Baily, Martin N. 1977b. "Unemployment Insurance as Insurance for Workers." *Industrial and Labor Relations Review* 30 (July): 495–504.

Baily, Martin N. 1978. "Some Aspects of Optimal Unemployment Insurance." *Journal of Public Economics* 10 (December): 379–402.

Becker, Joseph M. 1972. *Experience Rating in Unemployment Insurance*. Baltimore: Johns Hopkins University Press.

Brechling, Frank. 1977. "The Incentive Effects of the U.S. Unemployment Insurance Tax." In Ronald G. Ehrenberg, ed., *Research in Labor Economics*. Vol. 1. Greenwich, Conn.: JAI Press.

Brechling, Frank. 1981. "Layoffs and Unemployment Insurance." In Sherwin Rosen, ed., *Studies in Labor Markets*. Chicago: University of Chicago Press.

Burdett, Kenneth. 1979a. "Unemployment Insurance Payments as a Search Subsidy: A Theoretical Analysis." *Economic Inquiry* 17 (July): 333–343.

Burdett, Kenneth. 1979b. "Search, Leisure and Individual Labor Supply." In S. A. Lippman and John J. McCall, eds., *Studies in the Economics of Search*. Amsterdam: North-Holland.

Burgess, Paul L., and Jerry L. Kingston. 1976. "The Impact of Unemployment Insurance Benefits on Reemployment Success." *Industrial and Labor Relations Review* 30 (October): 25–31.

Burtless, Gary. 1983. "Why Is Insured Unemployment So Low?" *Brookings Papers on Economic Activity* (Spring): 225–249.

Burtless, Gary, and Wayne Vroman. 1985. "The Performance of Unemployment Insurance Since 1979." *Industrial Relations Research Association Proceedings* 37: 138–146.

Clark, Kim B., and Larry H. Summers. 1982. "Unemployment Insurance and Labor Market Transitions." In Martin N. Baily, ed., *Workers, Jobs, and Inflation*. Washington, D.C.: Brookings Institution.

Classen, Kathleen P. 1977. "The Effect of Unemployment Insurance on the Duration of Unemployment and Subsequent Earnings." *Industrial and Labor Relations Review* 30 (July): 438–444.

Classen, Kathleen P. 1979. "Unemployment Insurance and Job Search." In S. A. Lippman and John J. McCall, eds., *Studies in the Economics of Search*. Amsterdam: North-Holland.

Ehrenberg, Ronald G., and Ronald L. Oaxaca. 1976. "Unemployment Insurance, Duration of Unemployment, and Subsequent Wage Gain." *American Economic Review* 66 (December): 754–766.

Feldstein, Martin. 1973. "Unemployment Insurance: Adverse Incentives and Distributional Anomalies." *National Tax Journal* 27 (June): 231–244.

Feldstein, Martin. 1976. "Temporary Layoffs in the Theory of Unemployment." *Journal of Political Economy* 84 (October): 937–957.

Feldstein, Martin. 1978. "The Effect of Unemployment Insurance on Temporary Layoff Unemployment." *American Economic Review* 68 (December): 834–846.

Feldstein, Martin. 1980. "Introduction." In Martin Feldstein, ed., *The American Economy in Transition*. Chicago: University of Chicago Press.

Feldstein, Martin, and James Poterba. 1984. "Unemployment Insurance and Reservation Wages." *Journal of Public Economics* 23 (March): 141–167.

Gustman, Alan L. 1982. "Analyzing the Relation of Unemployment Insurance to Unemployment." In Ronald G. Ehrenberg, ed., *Research in Labor Economics*. Vol. 5. Greenwich, Conn.: JAI Press.

Hamermesh, Daniel S. 1977. *Jobless Pay and the Economy*. Baltimore: Johns Hopkins University Press.

Hamermesh, Daniel S. 1979. "Entitlement Effects, Unemployment Insurance, and Employment Decisions." *Economic Inquiry* 17 (July): 317–322.

Hamermesh, Daniel S. 1980. "Unemployment Insurance and Labor Supply." *International Economic Review* 21 (October): 517–527.

Holen, Arlene. 1977. "Effects of Unemployment Insurance Entitlement on Duration and Job Search Outcome." *Industrial and Labor Relations Review* 30 (July): 445–450.

Lancaster, Tony. 1979. "Econometric Methods for the Duration of Unemployment." *Econometrica* 47 (July): 939–956.

McCall, J. J. 1970. "Economics of Information and Job Search." *Quarterly Journal of Economics* 84 (February): 113–126.

Moffitt, Robert, and Walter Nicholson. 1982. "The Effect of Unemployment Insurance on Unemployment: The Case of Federal Supplemental Benefits." *Review of Economics and Statistics* 64 (February): 1–11.

Mortensen, Dale T. 1970. "Job Search, the Duration of Unemployment, and the Phillips Curve." *American Economic Review* 60 (December): 847–862.

Mortensen, Dale T. 1977. "Unemployment Insurance and Job Search Decisions." *Industrial and Labor Relations Review* 30 (July): 505–517.

Nickell, Steven. 1979. "Estimating the Probability of Leaving Unemployment." *Econometrica* 47 (September): 1249–1266.

Nickell, Steven. 1980. "The Effect of Unemployment and Related Benefits on the Duration of Unemployment." *Economic Journal* 89 (March): 34–49.

"Poverty Rates and the Incentive to Be Unemployed." 1983. *Wall Street Journal*. August 23.

Rosen, Sherwin. 1977. "Comment." *Industrial and Labor Relations Review* 30 (July): 518–520.

Rosen, Sherwin. 1983. "Unemployment and Insurance." In Karl Brunner and Allan H. Meltzer, eds., *Variability of Employment, Prices, and Money*. Amsterdam: North-Holland.

Solon, Gary. 1985. "Work Incentive Effects of Taxing Unemployment Benefits." *Econometrica* 53 (March): 295–306.

Stafford, Frank P. 1977. "More on Unemployment Insurance as Insurance." *Industrial and Labor Relations Review* 30 (July): 521–526.

Topel, Robert, and Finis Welch. 1979. "Unemployment Insurance: What the Theory Predicts and What the Numbers (May) Show, Survey and Extensions." Los Angeles: UCLA (September). Mimeograph.

Topel, Robert, and Finis Welch. 1980. "Unemployment Insurance: Survey and Extensions." *Economica* 47 (August): 351–379.

Welch, Finis. 1977. "What Have We Learned from Empirical Studies of Unemployment Insurance?" *Industrial and Labor Relations Review* 30 (July): 451–461.

Wolcowitz, Jeffrey. 1984. "Dynamic Effects of the Unemployment Insurance Tax on Temporary Layoffs." *Journal of Public Economics* 25 (November): 35–51.

Yaniv, Gideon. 1982. "Unemployment Insurance Benefits and the Supply of Labor of an Employed Worker." *Journal of Public Economics* 17 (February): 71–87.

4

Financing Unemployment Insurance: History, Incentives, and Reform

ROBERT TOPEL

Introduction

The unemployment insurance system in the United States was federally mandated under the Social Security Act of 1935. By 1937 all states had enacted legislation providing for the payment of UI benefits to unemployed workers and their financing through various programs of payroll taxation. The United States was something of a latecomer in this area of social legislation—Britain instituted the first UI program in 1911, followed by Germany (1917), Italy (1917), and Austria (1920), among others.[1] One major characteristic of UI programs in the United States is unique, however. All state programs are financed by variable payroll taxes that are to some degree experience rated.[2] Here this term is used to mean that tax rates levied on individual employers depend in whole or in part on each employer's history of generating insured unemployment. In all other countries that provide UI, benefits are financed by flat-rate payroll taxes or out of general tax revenues, so there is no connection between an individual firm's behavior and its tax liability.[3] This characteristic, coupled with heterogeneity in methods of experience rating among state programs, makes the United States a unique laboratory for studying issues related to UI financing.

For economists, UI financing methods are interesting because they affect incentives, especially incentives that produce unemployment. Current financing methods encourage unemployment for two main reasons. First, the structure of UI payroll taxation in the United States allows firms with relatively high layoff rates (construction firms, for example) to pay consistently less in taxes than their workers collect in benefits. This subsidy leads sectors with unstable employment or high turnover to expand, increasing total unemployment. Second, employers in general are not liable for the full value of UI benefits generated by an extra layoff. This wedge raises the relative value of unemployment to workers and their employers, so layoffs are encouraged. As it turns out, both of these effects can be greatly reduced through fairly minor reforms of existing UI laws.

This paper addresses two sets of questions related to UI financing and its effects. The first is retrospective and empirical: How do methods of UI financing actually operate? What incentives for employers and workers are built into current financing systems? Empirically, are these incentives large enough to affect the allocation of resources? How much unemployment is attributable to UI in general and to methods of financing in particular? Briefly stated, the results of current research on these topics imply that the impact of UI on unemployment is substantial, and much of this effect is attributable to methods used to finance UI over the past fifty years. For example, a reasonable estimate is that incentives associated with imperfect experience rating of UI taxes account for approximately 30 percent of temporary layoff unemployment in the United States.

The second set of issues is mainly prospective. The goal of UI is to mitigate the loss of spendable income for persons suffering unemployment. Given that unemployment insurance in some form is here to stay as an element of social legislation, a key issue is how it should be financed in order to promote efficient resource allocation while at the same time achieving this goal. Options range from simple reforms within the context of the current financing structure to more fundamental changes in the way that benefits are provided to workers. I consider several such reforms in section 4 of the paper.

It is useful to note at the outset that the concept of experience rating of unemployment insurance taxes has very little relation to the idea of experience-rated premiums in the insurance literature. There "experience rating" means that premiums are adjusted so as to reflect expected future probabilities of a loss. In contrast, the existing UI system does not seek to estimate a firm's expected benefit outlay in the future, or to establish an actuarially fair tax rate (premium). Rather, I will show that even for experience-rated employers the current system of UI financing merely advances interest-free loans to cover current benefit costs, enforcing repayment through higher future tax rates. There is thus no "insurance" aspect of UI financing at all, since there is no risk spreading through cross-sectional diversification of risk.

The paper is organized as follows. Section 1 provides an analysis of UI financing methods and summarizes the incentives that they create for distorting the sectoral distribution of employment and production, and for increasing unemployment. Types of UI financing are also surveyed in this section. Section 2 presents empirical evidence on the actual extent of experience rating that exists in these programs, and on trends toward so-called insolvency of state UI funds. Section 3 summarizes the current state of evidence on magnitudes of UI effects on unemployment. Section 4 suggests possible reform in methods of providing and financing benefits, and section 5 concludes.

1. Financing Unemployment Insurance: Methods and Incentives

Under federal legislation in the United States, states have the option of designing their own schemes of benefit financing provided that taxes charged to individual firms are justified in some way on the basis of the firm's past experience. All states have opted for a dual system in which a firm's taxes are split into a uniform surcharge and a second component that depends on the firm's history of generating insured unemployment. The first component funds administration, benefits not charged to specific firm accounts (for example, because a firm has gone out of business), and deficits in the aggregate account. Taxes from the second component are credited to firm-specific accounts against which some benefits are charged. By design the state systems are self-financing, although the reality has sometimes deviated from this goal.

As with Social Security, payroll taxes collected to fund UI are paid as a proportion of a taxable wage base. This base can be no lower than a federally mandated minimum, although states are free to choose a higher base and most have done so. Federal guidelines and requirements for the form of state systems are quite loose, and as a result there is substantial heterogeneity both in methods of financing chosen by state systems and, for a given method, in the parameters that affect experience rating and incentives. Currently, there are four basic methods of experience-rated financing in use in the United States. The main features of each method are summarized in Table 4.1; these are analyzed in more detail below. Note that benefit ratio and reserve ratio methods account for over 80 percent of covered employment, a figure that has grown over time as states abandon benefit/wage ratio and payroll declines accounting.

The three main issues that I will discuss in regard to these accounting methods are cross-subsidization of labor costs via UI benefits and taxes; "moral hazard" and adverse incentives created by imperfect experience rating of tax liabilities; and aggregate UI fund dynamics and the so-called "solvency" of state UI systems. I begin with employment subsidies.

Cross-Subsidization of Labor Costs

A basic feature of all UI financing systems in the United States is that tax rates applied to the wage base are bounded by minimum and maxi-

Table 4.1. Methods of Experience Rating

Method	Major Features	Number of Systems	Share of National Covered Employment (%)
Benefit ratio	Rated firms pay taxes in proportion to the ratio of benefits paid to taxable wages, usually over the past three years. Taxes may be adjusted up or down depending on the solvency of the aggregate state system. Interest is neither charged nor credited to employer accounts.	8[a]	26.02
Reserve ratio	Rated firms depend negatively on the ratio of reserves (past taxes less benefit payments) in their accounts to taxable wages. Rate schedules commonly depend on current funds in aggregate state UI system. Interest is neither charged nor credited to employer accounts.	34[a]	57.81
Benefit/wage ratio	Taxes depend on the total number of compensable separations generated by an employer, but not on actual benefits paid. Some states do not charge for spells that end before a certain number of weeks.	5	10.09
Payroll decline	Taxes are based on variations in employer payrolls, so connection to unemployment is at best indirect, and may be remote.	4	5.76

[a]Michigan and Pennsylvania combine reserve ratio and benefit ratio methods.

mum rates. These extreme rates vary widely among systems. One obvious consequence of this fact is that firms with relatively high average unemployment, which pay the maximum rate, will consistently accumulate deficits of tax contributions relative to benefit withdrawals from the system. Since aggregate systems are self-financing, this deficit represents a net subsidy to the firm's labor costs that is financed by taxes collected from firms with low average unemployment.

The potential for cross-subsidization is illustrated in Table 4.2. The table shows some characteristics of the distribution of insured unemployment and tax liabilities for six major UI systems in 1967 and 1978. Row A shows the estimated proportion of total employment that occurred in firms whose accumulated past tax contributions were smaller than benefit withdrawals. This percentage averages about 10 percent of covered employment, yet

Table 4.2. Summary Statistics for Selected State Programs: Distribution of Insured Unemployment for Positive- and Negative-Balance Firms, 1967 and 1978

	California		Massachusetts		Michigan		New York		Ohio		Wisconsin	
	1967	1978	1967	1978	1967	1978	1967	1978	1967	1978	1967	1978
A. Proportion of total taxable wages paid by negative-balance firms	14.2	14.3	11.8	13.1	3.6	28.0	13.8	28.4	4.4	29.9	8.5	14.4
B. Proportion of total charged benefits charged to negative-balance firms	51.8	52.5	55.3	46.0	34.8	68.1	61.6	72.7	34.2	58.1	60.8	26.9
C. State insured unemployment rate[a]	3.9	3.3	2.9	3.1	2.6	3.6	2.9	3.8	1.6	2.1	2.1	2.5
D. Estimated insured unemployment rate for negative-balance firms[b]	14.2	12.1	13.6	10.9	25.1	8.7	12.9	9.6	12.4	4.0	15.0	4.7

Source: Becker (1972, p. 112; 1981, p. 83); U.S. Department of Labor, *Handbook of Unemployment Insurance Financial Data* (1978). Data for the insured unemployment rate in 1978 are unpublished, and were obtained directly from the Labor Department.
1 [a]Average weekly insured unemployment.
[b]Defined as (row B ÷ row A) × row C.

row B shows that roughly half of all UI benefits were received by employees of these firms. The implication is that firms that entered these years with negative balances due to high past unemployment had higher than normal unemployment during 1967 and 1978 as well. Thus the identities of deficit employers tend to persist through time. Row D reports estimates of average insured unemployment rates for negative-balance employers. These were roughly five times the implied averages for positive-balance employers in 1967, but this difference narrowed as greater numbers of firms achieved deficits during the high unemployment years after 1975 (see row A). One important message from these data is that firm-specific unemployment rates of 15 percent or higher are not unusual, even in a relatively stable aggregate economy such as that of the 1960s.

The estimates in Table 4.2 imply cross-subsidization, but are the magnitudes of these subsidies large enough to be empirically important? To answer this, let μ denote the average proportion of the year that workers in a particular firm spend unemployed and collecting benefits under the UI system. Thus μ is the firm's long-run average insured unemployment rate. Let ω be the taxable wage base per worker under a state's UI law, and let τ_{min} and τ_{max} be the minimum and maximum legislated tax rates in the state. Letting b denote UI benefits paid to an unemployed worker expressed at an annual rate, if tax contributions are to balance benefit withdrawals, there must be a tax rate τ^* that satisfies

$$\tau^*\omega = b\mu. \tag{1}$$

Obviously if the budget balancing tax rate satisfies $\tau^* > \tau_{max}$, a balanced account is not possible and the firm's workers will consistently receive more in benefits than is collected in taxes (and conversely if $\tau^* < \tau_{min}$). Thus equation 1 also defines the maximum and minimum unemployment rates that are consistent with a balanced account:

$$\mu_{min} = \tau_{min} \times \omega/b, \text{ and} \tag{2a}$$
$$\mu_{max} = \tau_{max} \times \omega/b. \tag{2b}$$

Labor costs of employers with unemployment rates $\mu > \mu_{max}$ are subsidized. The first column of Table 4.3 reports calculated values of μ_{max} for a set of illustrative state UI systems in 1977–81. By most standards the estimated upper-bound unemployment rates in the table are modest — the national average insured unemployment rate for this period was about 4 percent — so that heterogeneity of unemployment rates illustrated in Table 4.2 implies subsidies for many employers.

Bounded tax rates are not the only source of subsidy. Until recently, benefits received under state UI programs were not subject to income taxation, so a dollar received as UI was worth $1 ÷ (1 − t) in units of earned income, where t is the unemployed individual's marginal tax rate on earned income. A reasonable value for t is 0.30; thus it typically required $1.42 in wage income to equal the spending power of $1 in UI. Even today, benefits are taxed only for individuals with incomes over a stipulated limit. Accounting for this additional source of subsidy, some algebra implies that the total labor cost subsidy, S, expressed as a proportion of the annual wage bill per worker is

$$S = [1 - \text{Min}(\mu_{max}, \mu) \times \frac{1 - t}{\mu}] \times \frac{b\mu}{w(1 - t)(1 - \mu)} \qquad (3)$$

where w is the annual wage and μ_{max} is defined by equation 2. For example, if there was no tax advantage of UI (t = 0) and $\mu < \mu_{max}$, then S would equal zero. But if t is greater than zero, even firms that pay in taxes what their workers receive in benefits are subsidized in their hiring decisions. Since all firms benefit from this tax advantage, aggregate demand for labor is increased.

The labor cost subsidy in equation 3 is increasing in μ, so high unemployment firms benefit more. The magnitude of this cross-subsidization from within a financing system is shown for various levels of unemployment in Table 4.3. The important point illustrated is that the labor cost subsidy is relatively small for firms with modest unemployment — it averages about 1 percent of labor cost for firms with unemployment rates of 5 percent — but it looms large for employers with average unemployment

Table 4.3. Estimated Labor Cost Subsidy Due to UI, as a Percentage of Annual Wages: Selected States, 1977–81

State	μ_{max}	Unemployment Rate (%)				
		5.0	7.5	10.0	12.5	15.0
California	6.74	0.88	1.68	3.28	4.98	6.77
Colorado	5.30	1.09	2.83	4.82	6.93	9.16
Florida	4.45	1.03	2.46	3.97	5.58	7.27
Indiana	4.52	0.69	1.68	2.73	3.84	5.01
Iowa	6.64	1.20	2.28	4.46	6.76	9.19
Massachusetts	7.76	1.06	1.63	3.40	5.41	7.54
New York	5.42	0.90	2.28	3.93	5.67	7.51
Pennsylvania	3.62	1.71	3.54	5.47	7.51	9.70
Texas	5.41	0.88	2.25	3.86	5.57	7.39

Note: Calculations are based on equation 3 in the text, assuming that t = 0.3 and a benefit replacement rate (b/W) equal to the average for the state. Replacement rates are imputed for a random sample of individuals in each state, using qualifying provisions of each state's UI laws. Taxable wage bases for computing μ_{max} are those in effect during a given year, and w/b is the ratio of the taxable wage base to fifty-two times the average weekly UI benefit for the state.

rates of 10 percent or more. Referring to Table 4.2, the simple average
unemployment rate for negative-balance employers in the illustrated states
exceeded 15 percent in 1967. For unemployment rates of this magnitude,
the average employment cost subsidy in Table 4.3 approaches 8 percent.

These estimates have two important implications. The first relates to
resource allocation and the composition of aggregate output. With
subsidies that exceed 10 percent of labor costs for many employers, high
unemployment sectors are encouraged to expand, perhaps significantly.
This effect alone will raise aggregate unemployment. I know of no detailed
estimates of the impact of these subsidies on the industrial composition
of employment, but a rough calculation will serve to make the point. Average unemployment rates of construction workers in a typical year are about
10 percent nationwide, and in many states they are substantially higher.
As a rough (and probably conservative) approximation, a long-run labor
demand elasticity of unity implies an expansion of employment in construction on the order of 5 percent, using the estimates in Table 4.3. This
amounts to about three hundred thousand workers, given the current size
of the construction industry. Under these assumptions, the deadweight
efficiency loss in the construction industry from this misallocation is equal
to about 0.25 percent of the sector-wide bill.[4] In construction alone, this
inefficiency amounts to approximately $300 million a year.

These are underestimates of the true effect because they are based on
the average unemployment rate of construction workers. The subsidy is
a marginal concept, however, and so its actual effect will depend on the
amount of time spent unemployed by a marginal addition to the labor
force.[5] For example, suppose that seasonality of demand causes full
employment to occur for exactly half of the year. During the other half,
80 percent of construction workers are employed, so the annual unemployment rate in the industry is 10 percent. Nevertheless, the last unit of
labor hired works only half the time (though each worker may be employed
for 90 percent of the year), so the *marginal* unemployment rate is 50 percent. In this case, the subsidy is increased by a factor of five. The point
is that the allocative effects, and social costs, of cross-subsidization may
be much larger than even the estimates in Table 4.3 would imply.

The second point is simply that these subsidies create vested interests
that stand to gain substantially from maintenance of the status quo. It
should come as no surprise that in policy debates over reforming UI
financing, opponents of extending the range of experience-rated taxes are
from labor unions and representatives of such industries as construction
and apparel—traditionally high-unemployment sectors of the economy.[6]
Their argument is that unemployment is an event beyond the control of
workers or employers, so that limits on taxes are a form of insurance.
The point would have some validity were it not for the widespread per-

sistence in the identities of deficit employers, particularly those from certain sectors of the economy. These employers receive a pure employment subsidy.

Experience Rating and UI Financing

To this point I have focused on characteristics of UI financing that may affect the allocation of employment and other resources among industries or firms. Experience rating itself has its main impact on decisions that generate unemployment within a firm. I define *incomplete experience rating* to mean that an additional layoff spell generates UI benefit payments to an unemployed worker that have greater present value than the associated increase in tax liabilities to his employer. With incomplete rating, layoffs are subsidized because workers receive income while unemployed for which their employer is not liable. Thus the relative cost of unemployment declines and layoffs are encouraged.

One reason for incomplete rating is obvious from my previous discussion: since tax rates are bounded, taxes are completely insensitive to layoff behavior for firms that pay the maximum or minimum rates. The marginal cost of benefits to these employers is zero. A second reason is that even for firms whose tax rates fall between the minimum and maximum rates in a state, defined by equation 2, in cases in which taxes are sensitive to layoff behavior, incremental tax liabilities are spread through time. Current accounting systems do not charge interest on these deferred liabilities, so the degree of experience rating will depend on the time profile of tax changes. Even in cases in which the full nominal value of benefits is eventually repaid, which is the most common case, the timing of tax changes implies that current benefits are paid with what amounts to an interest-free loan to employers.

To illustrate these incentives, consider the benefit ratio method. Under this system of financing, the component of taxes that is sensitive to the firm's behavior is proportional to the ratio of total benefits charged against the firm's account over a past number of years, T, to total taxable wages for that period. This quantity is called the benefit ratio. States vary widely in criteria for determining whether benefits are charged against an employer's account. Noncharged benefits must be financed in the aggregate, however, and so in order to balance aggregate benefit payments to tax receipts states adjust the taxable wage base, the minimum and maximum tax rates, or the factor of proportionality that multiplies the benefit ratio. All of these changes affect experience rating.

Let $\alpha < 1$ be the proportion of benefits drawn by laid-off workers that is charged to an employer's account and $\rho = b/\omega$ the ratio of average UI benefits (expressed per unit time) to the taxable wage base per employee.

With ρ constant through time, the benefit ratio, BR, is a weighted average of firm-specific insured unemployment rates over the past T years:

$$BR_t = \alpha\rho \sum_{j=1}^{T} k_{t-i} \mu_{t-i}, \tag{4}$$

where k_{t-i} is employment in year $t - i$ as a proportion of covered employment over the past T years, and μ_{t-i} is the average proportion of year $t - i$ spent in insured unemployment by the firm's employees. Tax rates are determined from BR based on a common formula for all firms. In practice, this formula turns out to be linear:

$$\tau_t = \lambda_0 + \lambda_1 BR_t. \tag{5}$$

In equation 5 λ_0 is a constant determined by the size of the statewide reserve fund or by other solvency criteria, and $\lambda_1 \geq 1$ is the state's "experience factor." Thus λ_0 and λ_1 are parameters that are controllable by the state in order to achieve particular goals, and states differ widely in technical criteria for setting and adjusting these parameters. For example, under the UI law in Texas λ_1 is adjusted yearly to equal the ratio of total state benefit payments to those benefits that were charged against employer accounts. This ratio averaged about 1.3 during the 1970s. No state sets λ_1 below 1.0.

Equation 5 holds only when the indicated tax rate lies between the minimum and maximum rates in effect in the state. Equation 4 and the fact that employment shares, k_{t-i}, must sum to unity then imply the maximum and minimum insured unemployment rates that subject firms to experience rating:

$$\mu_{min} = \frac{\tau_{min} - \lambda_0}{\lambda_1 \alpha\rho}, \text{ and} \tag{6a}$$

$$\mu_{max} = \frac{\tau_{max} - \lambda_0}{\lambda_1 \alpha\rho} \tag{6b}$$

Firms with long-run average rates of insured unemployment that lie outside this range are nonrated in the sense that small changes in charged unemployment have no tax consequences. Note that the upper limit for experience rating depends positively on τ_{max} but negatively on all other adjustable parameters of the state's tax law. In particular, increases in λ_0, λ_1, or α that may increase revenues for a fixed range of tax rates also have the effect of reducing experience rating for high-unemployment firms.

Employers who lie within the range defined by equation 6 are experience-rated in the sense that current layoffs will increase future tax liabilities. This effect is apparent from equations 4 and 5. I define e as the present value of these taxes caused by a small, transitory increase in charged unemployment ($\alpha = 1$) relative to the present value of UI benefits received by workers. Thus e is the degree of experience rating. Note that interest is not charged on past benefit payments in calculating the benefit ratio. Because of this, some tedious calculations imply that

$$e = \frac{\lambda_1[1 - (1 + i)^{-T}]}{iT}, \tag{7}$$

where i is the nominal rate of interest. Equation 7 also holds for permanent increases in the layoff rate. When $\lambda_1 = 1$ the reader may verify that the full nominal value of benefits is eventually repaid in future taxes, but $e < 1$ because taxes are deferred relative to the current receipt of benefits. This relative present value is declining in T because payments are deferred further into the future when T is large. Experience rating also declines with the rate of interest because future dollars have smaller current value. A typical benefit ratio state sets $T = 3$ years, so with $i = 0.10$ and $\lambda_1 = 1$ the marginal cost of a dollar of UI benefits paid currently to workers is only $.83. This subsidy is partially or completely offset in states that set $\lambda_1 > 1$, and in fact it is possible to have e exceed unity by a substantial amount. In these cases, the UI system actually taxes unemployment for some employers and their workers.

These calculations imply that the benefit ratio method of accounting is nothing more than a system of providing interest-free loans to firms with a predetermined repayment stream. Hence my comments at the outset that experience rating of UI taxes has little connection with the idea of experience-rated premiums as it is applied in the insurance literature. From the firm's perspective, there is no insurance component at all: it receives a loan to make mandated benefit payments to workers on layoff. For nonrated employers who pay the maximum rate, there is no repayment of benefits at all, so the marginal subsidy to unemployment is the full value of UI benefits.[7]

Equation 7 is the firm's marginal cost of benefits when those benefits are charged against the firm's account. Obviously, noncharged benefits have zero cost. More generally, incomplete charging ($\alpha < 1$) of benefits widens the band of experience-rated unemployment rates (see equation 6) but reduces the marginal cost of benefits within that range. Given provisions for contesting the charging of benefits in current laws, we may expect that changes in τ_{max} and τ_{min} that shift the range of experience rating may increase challenges by employers to the charging of particular unemployment spells, and also increase political pressure for more generous non-charging provisions. These incentives mean that changes in some parameters of the UI law that would appear to enhance experience rating may be partially offset on the margin of benefit charging.

Reserve ratio accounting differs from the preceding analysis only in mechanical details. Taxes depend on the ratio of cumulative reserves (past nominal tax contributions less charged benefit withdrawals) credited to a firm's account to the firm's total taxable wage base (usually expressed as an average over several years). Interest is not charged on deficit accounts or credited to accounts with positive balances. Higher values of this reserve ratio generate lower tax rates. The key implications are virtually the same as in the above discussion, except that an increase in unemployment generates increased taxes that are spread over a longer period of time than under benefit ratio accounting. Again, the nominal value of current benefits is eventually repaid, but the longer average deferral of liabilities implies that the true marginal cost of benefits is usually lower under a reserve ratio system than under a benefit ratio system.[8] Detailed analyses of reserve ratio dynamics appear in Topel and Welch (1980).

Table 4.4 illustrates the range and degree of measured experience rating in thirty-eight benefit ratio and reserve ratio states that operated in 1977–81. I report estimates of the lower- and upper-bound unemployment rates for which experience rating is relevant (see equation 6), along with the estimated marginal cost of benefits to employers who operate within that range (see equation 7). Layoff costs are zero outside the indicated range. Differences in both the range and the degree of experience rating among states are important. For example, the maximum marginal cost of a dollar of UI benefits occurs in Pennsylvania, where some low-unemployment firms are charged $1.59 for each dollar of UI paid out to workers on layoff. To illustrate the range of costs, consider a typical worker in Pennsylvania who would earn about $300 a week in 1981 and qualify for weekly UI benefit of about $150 if laid off. If these benefits are not taxed, their earning-equivalent value would be $214 at a marginal tax rate of 0.30. The employer's cost for these benefits in terms of the present value of incremental taxes would be $238, for a net layoff tax of about $24 a week. At the other extreme, for the same benefits in Nevada an otherwise identical employer subject to positive experience rating would pay only $54, for a net layoff subsidy of $160 a week. The difference in the firm's cost of a layoff is $184 per week. Looking at the range of experience rating, any employer in Mississippi with an average insured unemployment rate above 3.3 percent would have zero cost of benefits for an additional layoff, whereas in Georgia this cutoff does not occur until the firm's unemployment rate exceeds nearly 11 percent. Below I summarize evidence indicating that differences in incentives for otherwise identical employers are large enough to significantly affect behavior.

Table 4.4. Experience Rating Parameters, Reserve Ratio, and Benefit Ratio States, 1977–81

State	$e(u)$	Minimum Rated Unemployment Rate	Maximum Rated Unemployment Rate	Method[a]
Arkansas	0.81238	1.14810	10.0357	RR
Arizona	0.72753	0.22030	6.2535	RR
California	0.63131	1.20617	6.7435	RR
Colorado	0.48755	0.54865	5.3039	RR
Connecticut	0.82895	0.74978	7.4978	BR
Florida	1.53999	0.02445	4.4515	BR
Georgia	0.81651	0.12986	10.5927	RR
Hawaii	0.73684	1.61238	8.4647	RR
Iowa	0.89317	0.25010	6.6495	RR
Idaho	0.68943	2.15722	9.5640	RR
Indiana	0.94127	0.90425	4.5272	RR
Kentucky	0.86518	1.58876	7.5169	RR
Louisiana	0.83871	0.49185	3.9721	RR
Massachusetts	0.67532	2.89437	7.7559	RR
Maryland	0.90256	0.00000	4.0334	RR
Maine	0.56140	4.55470	9.3844	RR
Michigan[b]	1.49001	0.93564	6.5719	BR/RR
Minnesota	1.03619	0.00000	7.5329	BR
Missouri	0.68354	0.88193	6.3499	RR
Mississippi	0.82895	0.00000	3.2854	RR
North Carolina	0.90074	0.16428	9.3638	RR
North Dakota	0.68750	0.57845	4.8590	RR
Nebraska	0.88138	0.15779	5.8383	RR
Nevada	0.36305	1.02210	5.1105	RR
New Hampshire	0.64871	0.10610	8.7401	RR
New Jersey	0.78402	1.71336	8.8524	RR
New Mexico	0.76905	1.18142	9.0000	RR
New York	0.73262	0.64588	5.4254	RR
Ohio	0.76744	0.53114	4.3553	RR
Pennsylvania[b]	1.58971	0.00000	3.6234	BR/RR
Rhode Island	0.55567	4.32371	8.7005	RR
South Carolina	0.82363	2.51252	7.6109	RR
South Dakota	0.92635	0.00000	7.3118	RR
Tennessee	0.64134	0.79718	6.6089	RR
Texas	1.35961	0.07781	5.4154	BR
Wisconsin	0.84834	0.00000	5.5223	RR
West Virginia	0.71810	0.46142	7.2701	RR
Wyoming	0.82895	0.00000	4.2350	RR

Note: Calculations are based on experience rating formulas in text. Figures refer to average values over the period 1977–81. In Michigan and Pennsylvania, a combination reserve ratio/benefit ratio system is used, and the reported value for $e(u)$ to the maximum payback ratio in the rated range.

[a]RR = Reserve ratio accounting; BR = Benefit ratio accounting.

[b]Payback ratio refers to segment of cost function where both reserve ratio and benefit ratio methods operate.

Costs and incentives are not so easily quantified for the two remaining accounting methods shown in Table 4.1. Incentives are likely to be worse, however. Consider the benefit/wage ratio method. This system makes no attempt to measure the actual amount of benefits paid out by an individual employer. The key concept is "benefit wages," which are simply the total number of compensated separations generated by an employer times taxable wages paid to those workers. Taxes are proportional to the benefit/wage ratio, which is benefit wages of the past T years divided by total taxable payroll over the same period. If all workers earn the taxable wage base, note that the benefit/wage ratio is simply the number of insured separations divided by total employment, or the employer's layoff rate.

If all layoffs are permanent in the sense that unemployed workers are never recalled to their former employer, then most of the analysis above goes through. The firm-specific unemployment rate that was relevant in benefit ratio and reserve ratio accounting systems is simply replaced by a firm-specific layoff rate. Maximum and minimum tax rates define bounds for experience-rated layoff rates, and so on. The duration of unemployment spells is not controlled by the former employer in this case, so this method would have the advantage of focusing tax changes on the variable that is controlled by employers. But empirical evidence indicates that not even the majority of layoffs are permanent. For example, Lilien (1980) finds that about two-thirds of layoff unemployment spells end with a rehire by the previous employer. When layoffs are temporary, the duration of unemployment spells is affected by the employer who initiates the spell, and the adverse incentive offered by this system is clear. An employer can reduce his taxes while keeping his temporary layoff unemployment rate constant by simply economizing on layoffs, while extending the duration of spells by postponing rehires. Thus employers for whom temporary layoffs are important may appear to be experience-rated, but in fact their workers can draw far more in UI benefits than their employers ever pay in taxes. Some states have evidently recognized this feature of the law: in Virginia and Illinois spells that last for less than a stipulated period (usually three weeks) are not charged to employers at all, so the firm has an incentive to rehire within this grace period. The implication is then that short layoff spells are free to all employers.

The final system is "payroll declines," which accounts for only about 6 percent of covered employment in the United States. Under this system, variations in an employer's payroll are used to determine tax liability, and the connection with insured unemployment is indirect at best. Employers with the largest declines pay the highest taxes. Here tax liability may actually be completely independent of benefit payments: employers with high average unemployment (due to high turnover) but stable payrolls may face no tax penalty. Thus, cyclic increases in layoffs are more likely to have tax consequences than normal turnover in an industry. Since the latter is more directly controllable by employers (as, for example, in seasonal layoffs), the incentive is the opposite of what is desired.

2. How Big Are the Effects?

That imperfect experience rating of UI taxes encourages unemployment is not debatable. Layoffs generate income for a firm's workers that has no corresponding cost for the employer, creating an incentive to compensate workers with UI rather than earnings. Unemployment thus becomes relatively more attractive. For temporary layoff spells, this implies that both the incidence and the duration of spells is increased. Are these effects large enough to be of concern to policymakers? Empirical research indicates that they are.

I have studied this issue in a series of papers (Topel, 1983, 1984a, 1984b, 1985). The key idea in this research is to use between-state heterogeneity in the cost of UI to employers (see Table 4.4) to mimic the conceptual experiment of changing experience rating for otherwise identical employers.[9] Because theory predicts that UI and experience rating will affect different types of unemployment in different ways, an important data requirement is that distinct categories of unemployment spells be identifiable in the data. For example, because of the continuing relation between employer and employee, temporary layoff spells should be more sensitive than permanent layoffs to the incentives offered by UI financing methods. This data requirement is met by the microdata available from the Current Population Survey (CPS), which form the basis for published government unemployment statistics. For large samples of individual workers drawn from these files, one may use personal, geographic, and industry information to estimate the amount of UI benefits available to each person under state laws, and the estimates in Table 4.4 yield the cost of these benefits to employers in terms of current and future tax liabilities.

The subsidy to unemployment that affects layoff decisions for an individual is $s = b[1 \div (1 - t) - e]$, where e is the degree of experience rating relevant to an individual's employer (the marginal cost of benefits) and b is UI benefits available if laid off. Holding benefits and tax rates fixed, smaller values of e increase unemployment (Feldstein, 1976). In addition, changes in the benefit level affect unemployment by influencing search decisions of workers. By how much would unemployment rise if benefits were increased? Microdata on individual workers yield an answer to this question by allowing comparisons of unemployment frequencies among individuals with different levels of the subsidy and with different levels of benefits. Illustrative effects drawn from Topel (1986) are shown in Table 4.5.

The table reports a decomposition of the impact of a 10 percent change in the level of UI benefits on the unemployment rate over the five years 1977–81. Separate effects are shown for temporary layoffs, permanent layoffs, and quits (which do not normally qualify workers for UI). Within each catgory, separate effects are reported for the UI subsidy, *s*, and for the level of benefits. For example, the estimate of 0.16 for the total effect of a change in UI implies that a 10 percent across-the-board increase in the level of benefits would increase the unemployment rate by about one-sixth of a percentage point. Of this effect, 0.149 ÷ 0.161 = 93 percent of the increase is due to the fact that benefit payments are imperfectly experience-rated. Put differently, if the subsidy were completely eliminated through full experience rating the estimates predict that the unemployment rate during this period would have been 1.49 points lower.[10] This reduction would have been accomplished without reducing the level of benefits available to unemployed workers. Since the total unemployment rate in the same was about 5.2 percent, this estimate means that methods of UI financing account for about 30 percent of all unemployment spells in the data. Finally, note the concentration of the impact of UI and the subsidy on increasing temporary layoffs: these spells are far more sensitive than either permanent layoffs or (of course) quits to the availability of UI. Since temporary layoff spells imply by definition a continuing relationship between worker and firm, theory indicates that they should be most sensitive to changes in the relative value of unemployment.[11]

Table 4.5. The Effect of a 10 Percent Increase in Unemployment Insurance Benefits on Unemployment, by Type of Unemployment and Source (%)

| Change in | Type of Unemployment Spell | | | |
	Temporary Layoffs	Permanent Layoffs	Quits	Total Effect
Benefit level	0.081	−0.060	−0.009	0.012
Subsidy	0.113	0.045	−0.001	0.149
Total	0.194	−0.014	−0.018	0.161

Source: Based on estimates in Topel (1986) from linear probability models for the incidence of unemployment. Other explanatory variables include experience and its square, education, marital status, race, sample year, twenty-seven industry categories, and nine occupation categories. The sample consisted of 76,106 prime-aged males.

3. Solvency of State UI Funds

As noted above, state UI programs are designed to be self-financing. In theory this means that current benefit obligations should be covered by an aggregate state fund accumulated from a past surplus of taxes over benefit withdrawals. In practice it was recognized early on that in some circumstances these funds would be inadequate. In these situations, states have the right to borrow federal funds to meet their current UI obligations. Until March of 1982 these federal advances were made at zero interest. The option to borrow was not exercised by any state until the 1960s, and then only on two occasions. The dam broke in the recession of 1975–76, however, when twenty-five states borrowed federal money to meet short-term obligations. Eight of those states continue to have outstanding loan balances, with Illinois, Michigan, and Pennsylvania each owing more than $1.0 billion (interest free). These debts were incurred before 1982, when financing laws were amended to charge interest on federal advances. They continue to be interest free. A brief examination of how UI funds have evolved over time will illustrate how this situation came to be.

Aggregate state reserves are determined by interest that accrues on past reserves, tax revenues, and benefit payments. If reserves per worker in a state are denoted by R_t in year t and $\bar{\tau}$ is the average tax rate on taxable payrolls, then per capita reserves evolve according to the formula

$$R_t = R_{t-1}(1 + i_t) + b_t \frac{\bar{\tau}_t \omega_t}{b_t - u_t} \tag{8}$$

where i_t is the nominal rate of interest, u_t is the insured unemployment rate for the state, b_t is the average weekly UI benefit, and ω_t is the average weekly taxable wage. The time path of aggregate reserves is determined by the bracketed term (neglecting interest). The evidence is that states have allowed average benefit levels to grow much more rapidly than either taxable wages or tax rates, so that per capita benefit years collected $(\bar{\tau} \frac{\omega}{b})$ have fallen far short of insured unemployment. The result is that reserves have declined through time.

These trends are illustrated in Figure 4.1, which shows that the decline in per capita reserves was fairly continuous from 1950 to 1977. The benefit/taxable wage ratio rose until 1972, when the federal minimum taxable wage base was increased from $3,000 to $4,000, and then again until 1978 when the base was increased to $6,000. These are the only two years that show important declines in the ratio. A plausible interpretation is that states have refused to increase taxable wages or tax rates unless they are required to do so, even when faced with declining reserves. And who can blame them when money to cover any shortfall was offered at zero interest? The figure also shows that the typical state system held sufficient reserves in 1950 to finance five average years of insured unemployment without collecting any taxes. By 1976 the corresponding figure was one month. Hence the rush to borrow federal money.

The increase in average UI benefits relative to both tax rates and taxable wages has implications for experience rating. Since upper-bound tax

Figure 4.1. Benefit/Taxable Wage Ratio and Years of Insured Unemployment Held in State Reserves.

Note: The benefit/taxable wage ratio is the national average weekly benefit amount divided by weekly taxable wages in covered employment. Covered spells of unemployment per worker are reserves per worker divided by the product of the annual benefit rate and the average insured unemployment rate, 1950–79.

rates were relatively constant over this period, equation 6 implies that if experience rating terminates, upper-bound unemployment rates must fall. Table 4.6 shows that this is what happened in most states. Between 1966 and 1975 the average ratio of benefits to taxable wages in reserve ratio states rose from 0.6 to 0.8, which forced a decline of 1.6 percentage points in the average upper bound for experience rating. Thus, experience rating became progressively less relevant to employment and unemployment decisions over this period. After 1976, states' efforts to replenish reserves by increasing taxable wages and tax rates caused the range of experience-rated unemployment to increase somewhat. It is difficult to argue that a desire to affect incentives via extended experience rating was the motive for these changes.

The tendency of state systems to hold constant the nominal wage base has one further important incentive effect. With a declining real base, the relative cost of employing low-wage workers—who earn less than the base—increases. This causes substitution in favor of high-wage workers. This effect is enhanced if financing authorities compensate by raising the average tax rate. Thus, the trend shown in Table 4.6 has probably reduced the demand for low-wage workers, which probably serves to lengthen unemployment spells for these individuals.

Table 4.6. Approximate Upper Bounds for Experience-Rated Unemployment, Selected
Reserve Ratio States, 1966–79

State	1966		1970		1975		1979	
	ρ_a	μ_{max}	ρ_a	μ_{max}	ρ_a	μ_{max}	ρ_a	μ_{max}
California	0.61	6.6	0.68	5.9	0.79	4.3	0.65	6.2
Colorado	0.78	3.8	0.91	4.3	0.97	4.0	0.86	7.3
Georgia	0.54	9.6	0.68	8.1	0.64	4.4	0.66	11.4
Indiana	0.57	5.2	0.64	4.9	0.75	4.2	0.68	7.2
Massachusetts	0.65	9.7	0.74	8.5	0.09	6.1	0.76	9.6
Michigan	0.66	7.6	0.78	8.7	0.83	7.9	0.82	9.7
New Jersey	0.66	7.2	0.80	6.0	0.81	5.9	0.74	10.0
New York	0.68	4.8	0.82	4.0	0.85	5.9	0.76	7.3
North Carolina	0.47	11.8	0.51	10.8	0.76	7.4	0.67	10.0
Ohio	0.66	8.4	0.78	6.4	0.94	4.3	0.98	5.1
Wisconsin	0.69	6.2	0.77	5.7	1.0	5.0	0.93	7.0
Average twenty-five systems)[b]	0.61	7.5	0.70	6.7	0.80	5.9	0.76	7.7

[a]ρ is the ratio of the average weekly UI benefit to the taxable wage base per employee.
[b]In addition to those listed, the systems were Arizona, Arkansas, the District of Columbia, Hawaii, Iowa, Maine, Nevada, New Hampshire, North Dakota, Rhode Island, South Carolina, South Dakota, Tennessee, and West Virginia. Complete data were not available for other systems. See notes to Table 4.1.

4. Reforming the System

Most workers who are laid off from their previous jobs receive benefits from the UI system. In 1976, for example, 75 percent of workers on temporary layoff received UI benefits, and the corresponding figure for permanent layoffs (who do not anticipate recall by their previous employers) was about 70 percent.[12] Thus the primary goal of the UI system — maintaining the spendable income of the unemployed — appears to be achieved. The goal of policy reform is to maintain this aspect of UI while minimizing the adverse incentives that misallocate resources and increase unemployment.

The previous discussion has identified four main sources of adverse incentives. First, employers have only limited liability for the UI benefits that are received by the workers they lay off. Layoff and rehire decisions are therefore distorted, and firms organize production in ways that destabilize employment. For example, layoffs are substituted for reductions in hours per worker during periods of low demand, and firms are less willing to accumulate inventories during these periods. Second, workers have zero liability for the benefits they draw from the system. Job search decisions are consequently distorted and the average length of unemployment spells is increased.[13] Third, benefits are subject to income taxation only for high-income workers, so the relative value of income while unemployed rises. This distorts both of the previously mentioned decisions. Finally, the cross-subsidization of labor costs implicit in all UI systems reallocates employment in favor of high-unemployment sectors of the economy. All of these incentives can be affected by changes in aspects of UI laws without significantly changing the availability of benefits to the unemployed.

Increased Experience Rating

The easiest type of reform to effect is that that may be accomplished without radically changing the machinery of the current system of financing and providing benefits. Little needs to be said about taxation of benefits; taxation of all benefits as earned income would eliminate a prime source of subsidy to unemployment. More important changes would come from the extension of effective experience rating to all firms. The easiest way to accomplish this is to extend the range of tax rates. Reduction in the minimum tax rate to zero and dramatic increases in maximum rates would have two effects. First, the employment subsidies illustrated in Table 4.3 would be sharply reduced, and the industrial mix of employment and production would therefore not be so severely distorted. Second, a primary source of the wedge in layoff and rehire decisions would be eliminated, which will have a strong impact on unemployment in general and especially on temporary layoffs. These effects would be largest among high-unemployment firms. For example, in my 1982 study I estimated that elimination of the subsidy to unemployment would reduce the temporary layoff unemployment rate by 2.2 points from a level of 7.1 percent in 1975. In construction the decline would have been 5.6 points (from 14.2 percent), in apparel 6.8 percent (from 12.5). Complete elimination of the unemployment subsidy would then be achieved by computing interest on employers' accounts. Since interest-free accounting reduces layoff costs by as much as 60 percent, there seems to be little reason for continuing the current practice.

The thrust of these recommendations rests on the assumption that the benefit payments in question are charged against employer accounts. As I noted above, increases in experience rating can be effectively "undone" by greater laxity in charging of benefits, and these recommendations provide additional incentives for employers to seek noncharging provisions via political action. Thus a corollary of these recommendations is that regulations on charging of benefit payments should also be strengthened so that a greater proportion of UI benefits are charged to employer accounts.

An additional reform achievable within current systems is to index taxable wages to benefits. As the discussion of solvency pointed out, political choices have apparently usually allowed benefit levels to grow much more rapidly than the base from which they are financed. The result has been sharp declines in the upper-bound unemployment rates that are relevant for experience rating and employment subsidies, with adverse effects on incentives. Indexing would eliminate this decline and, since taxes rise with the wage base, create additional employer opposition to increases in benefit levels. Perhaps because of the latter effect, only a few states have chosen to index the wage base.

Indexing or raising the wage base would have additional effects. Since taxes are paid only on the wage base, the incidence of the tax falls more heavily on employees who earn less than the base. These are low-wage workers and those with higher rates of turnover. Raising the wage base would reduce the average tax rates needed to finance UI, and also reduce the relative cost of employing low-wage workers. Since the incidence of unemployment is heavily weighted toward these workers, the implied substitution of low- for high-wage skilled labor will probably reduce unemployment even further.

These reforms would effectively enforce full liability of employers for benefit charges generated by layoff behavior. These changes would leave part of the system unfunded, however. For example, noncharged benefits caused by business failures and the like are now funded by interest on the general account, which is not credited to employer accounts, and by taxes paid by low-unemployment firms. These sources would be eliminated, so the system would not be self-financing. If self-financing is the goal, then these costs can be funded through nonvariable payroll taxes that may create minor distortions. But there is no fundamental reason why UI must be a closed system. Some costs may be funded out of general revenue, possibly with smaller distortions than would occur with a payroll tax.

Coinsurance

As I have noted previously, the insurance aspect of current financing methods is very small. Even full experience rating, in the sense used above, is nothing more than a system of loans to employers to cover UI costs. Risks are not diversified, except over time for an individual employer. I will have more to say on this point shortly. At the aggregate level, even state systems do not achieve the full degree of risk diversification that is possible. States, like firms, may borrow (under certain circumstances) to cover UI obligations, thus making any diversification that is achieved purely intertemporal.[14] Geographic regions are known to be specialized with regard to industry mix, however, and business cycles have long been understood to have non-neutral effects among industries. The implication is that the geographic incidence of unemployment, and hence UI obligations, is not uniform. For example, the 1970s were a period of relatively rapid contraction in sectors such as durable manufacturing, and the list of states that still have outstanding Title XII loan balances reflects this fact: the four largest balances are for the "rust belt" states of Illinois, Michigan, Ohio, and Pennsylvania. Future cyclical contractions may be concentrated on other industries, and thus on other regions.

Greate diversification of these risks may be achieved by coinsurance among state systems. By this I mean that under certain circumstances the UI obligations of one state, or group of states, may be paid by drawing on a common fund. These advances would not be loans. Of course, the opportunity for states to obtain true insurance raises moral hazard problems in state systems: the financing structure chosen affects the probability of the insured event, so states have an incentive to set average tax rates too low. This is the problem illustrated in Figure 4.1. For this reason, stronger federal regulations on the actuarial structure of state tax rates would be required. Coinsurance clearly implies a greater federal role in UI financing, which I think would be a good thing. It would bring greater uniformity to tax structures and extend the importance of true insurance in financing UI.

Starting Over

All of the forgoing reforms could be achieved within the current structure of implicit loans to employers. They eliminate some of the adverse incentives noted above, in particular those associated with the hiring and layoff decisions of employers. One important source of moral hazard remains, however: workers themselves are not experience-rated in any sense, and so their job search decisions would continue to be distorted by the provisions of UI.

The incentive of unemployed individuals to inefficiently extend their spells would be eliminated if experience rating was extended to workers. There are two ways of accomplishing this. Consider first a system that rates workers in the same way that employers are now rated in benefit ratio or reserve ratio systems, except that interest should be charged and credited to accounts. Each worker would have his own account with the UI system, and his tax rate would depend on the size of that account. A current insured spell of unemployment would raise subsequent taxes. Each account would be vested, so retiring workers would receive the current value of past net contributions. Since these systems represent implicit loans with a fixed pattern of repayment in terms of future tax liabilities, unemployed workers would properly internalize the cost of current benefits in their job search decisions. A worker who accepted a job offer would forgo future UI benefits, but he would also avoid future tax liabilities with the same present value.[15] Furthermore, since UI benefits are simply loans to workers which are properly valued, the relative value of becoming unemployed is not distorted. Thus employers will have no incentive toward excessive layoffs.

This system is simply self-insurance by workers through forced saving and guaranteed access to the capital market if borrowing becomes necessary (the worker's balance becomes negative).[16] Therefore, as above, any diversification of unemployment risk is intertemporal, in this case within an individual's labor market life. Theoretically, if individuals were very long-lived and interest rates negligible, full diversification of risk could be achieved in this way. But these conditions are not satisfied—business cycle risks are an example—so there is an obvious case for cross-sectional diversification of risk, that is, for true insurance among individuals. Can it be achieved while maintaining efficient decisions by employers and workers?

In practice it cannot. Even if workers were experience-rated in the actuarial (insurance) sense of categorizing individuals into risk classes, the probability of the insured event (an unemployment spell, or a longer spell) is affected by individual and employer decisions that are not monitorable by the insurer. This is moral hazard. The "second-best" solution to this problem is incomplete coverage, or partial self-insurance (see, for example, Ehrlich and Becker, 1972), which trades off the risk-spreading achievable through insurance against the improved incentives implied by individual liability for losses. This trade-off can take the form of a mixture of the two senses of experience rating. For example, tax rates paid by workers can depend partially on the worker's balance in an interest-bearing account, so the borrowing and lending aspect of a forced self-insurance scheme is partially maintained. A second component of taxes would depend on the worker's risk category. To illustrate, for a given account balance workers in high-unemployment construction firms would pay higher premiums. In this sense, the system of actuarial experience rating is no different from the current system of setting premiums for car or fire insurance. The latter component of the system allows some slippage in terms of moral hazard, so unemployment is encouraged, but it also achieves greater efficiency in allocating consumption due to partial insurance.

The details of this hypothetical system remain to be worked out. What, for instance, is the best mixture of "market" and self-insurance? The argument here establishes only that neither extreme is the best policy. How should tax rates be set for young workers on whom there is little personal information? Nevertheless, this system is clearly technically feasible since it implies little more computational burden than already exists in experience rating employers. It would certainly be no more computationally burdensome than experience rating of other premiums for market-provided insurance, such as automobile insurance. The proposed change would move the UI system closer to a system of true insurance, and the main technology for experience rating of individuals would not be new. It will meet with political opposition, however. Groups that now benefit from the structure of UI financing will surely claim that it is unfair to unemployed workers, or an excessive tax burden on workers in certain sectors. That is their right. Yet in fact it would merely shift the cost of financing unemployment to individuals and sectors that are more likely to generate unemployment. The result would be a substantial reduction in measured unemployment, and a more efficient allocation of resources.

5. Conclusion

For fifty years the unemployment insurance system in the United States stabilized the disposable income of unemployed individuals who are attached to the labor force. Methods of financing this program through payroll taxation have not changed appreciably since the 1930s, and they continue to provide a number of adverse incentives to employers and workers, most of which operate to increase unemployment. A growing body of empirical evidence from a variety of sources indicates that the effects of UI on unemployment are important. In a typical year as much as 20 percent of unemployment among covered workers may be attributable to UI. Most of these adverse incentives can be dramatically reduced or eliminated without affecting the availability of benefits to workers. Thus, after half a century of experience, the evidence indicates that important reforms are called for.

Most of the reforms that I have discussed can be achieved within the current structure of UI financing. These are

1. Eliminating the lower and upper bounds on payroll tax rates. This change would have two main effects. First, it would eliminate the cross-subsidization of employment costs that currently distorts employment and production decisions, favoring high-unemployment sectors of the economy. Second, it would reduce the incentive now offered to employers who pay the minimum and maximum tax rates to engage in excessive layoffs.
2. Crediting interest to employer "accounts" in current UI financing systems. The failure to apply interest to these accounts implies that even firms whose tax liabilities are sensitive to layoffs are subsidized, at the margin, by as much as 60 percent of the value of benefits. Accounting for interest would eliminate this source of subsidy. In conjunction with the extension of experience rating suggested above, this reform would imply full experience rating for most employers.
3. Abandoning payroll declines and benefit/wage ratio accounting methods. These systems provide additional incentives that encourage unemployment, and the economies that they offer in terms of calculating liabilities are largely irrelevant in an age of low-cost computing.

4. Taxing all UI benefits at standard rates. This reform will affect both layoff decisions of employers and search behavior of unemployed workers.
5. Increasing the taxable wage base and indexing the base to the level of benefits. Even if point 1 above is not adopted, increases in the base will extend the range of effective experience rating to high-unemployment firms, and discourage layoffs. In addition, the incidence of the tax will be shifted away from low-wage workers, which will encourage hiring and discourage layoffs among these individuals (who are usually most sensitive to the forces that generate unemployment spells). Indexation to benefit levels will eliminate the variability over time in the real base from which benefits are financed, and improve the solvency of state funds.
6. Instituting coinsurance among state UI programs. Since business cycles and federal government policies have localized effects, coinsurance provides diversification of risks that extends beyond state boundaries.

These reforms are achievable within the current structure of UI financing. To achieve them, it will probably require greater regulation of state UI systems at the federal level. For example, the availability of coinsurance (or federal loans in the current system) has encouraged states to maintain low average tax rates and to limit taxable wage bases. These are predictable responses to political pressures from particular interest groups, and to the desire of state governments to compete for new businesses through an attractive tax structure. Reform at the federal level also stands a better chance of overcoming political pressures from groups that now benefit from the subsidies built into current financing schemes.

I have also proposed a more ambitious set of reforms that entail a fundamental rethinking of the role of UI. This would shift nominal incidence of UI taxation to workers, which would have additional desirable effects on incentives. The key elements of the financing structure would be much closer to a system of true insurance, with limited coverage due to moral hazard. This system is clearly feasible, and it achieves the main goals for which the current UI system is designed.

NOTES

Arnold Harberger, Neil Bruce, Michael Waldman, and Finis Welch provided helpful discussions for which the author is grateful. Paul Burgess and two anonymous referees provided many insightful comments on an earlier draft. The remaining errors and omissions are the sole responsibility of the author.

1. The first state program was Wisconsin's in 1932. For a history of the development of private and public UI programs in the United States prior to the Social Security Act, see Nelson (1969).

2. For a relatively complete history of experience rating and the policy debates that led to the current system, see Becker (1972). Puerto Rico and the Virgin Islands also have UI systems governed by the Social Security Act, but they do not experience-rate UI taxes.

3. See Blaustein and Craig (1977) for an international comparison of UI laws and financing methods.

4. For a small change in the subsidy, the implied welfare triangle is approximately $L = 0.5s^2wN$, where w is the elasticity of demand for labor and N is total employment.

5. For development of this point in the context of a general equilibrium model, see Topel and Welch (1980).

6. See the report of the National Commission on Unemployment Compensation (1980) for illuminating views of industry and labor representatives.

7. Note that the subsidy to unemployment is for a marginal increment to unemployment. Firms that are subsidized in their layoff decisions may nevertheless pay aggregate UI taxes equal to the average value of benefits collected by their workers.

8. Another difference is that under reserve ratio accounting the marginal cost of benefits may not be constant throughout the experience-rated range. See Appendix A of Topel (1982) or Topel and Welch (1980) for a detailed analysis.

9. It would be desirable to estimate the effects of UI financing structure from firm-specific, as opposed to individual-specific, data. Note, however, that a simple comparison of firm-specific layoff rates and their costs would not be appropriate. High-unemployment firms have low marginal costs of benefits due to the upper bound on tax rates in current systems.

10. One should exercise care in interpreting this estimate, since it refers to a 100 percent change in the subsidy. If gains achieved through reducing the subsidy are smaller at low levels of S, then the estimate may be too large. I have not found such nonlinearities to be important, however.

11. Permanent layoffs are often generated by large-scale changes such as plant closings, which should be only weakly affected by the availability of UI to workers. Other evidence in Topel (1982, 1985) shows the effect of the subsidy on the duration and the incidence of unemployment spells. Both of these are increased by a reduction in experience rating.

12. The estimates are based on tabulations of a special questionnaire administered with the May 1976 Current Population Survey. To my knowledge more recent data are not available.

13. Hamermesh (1977) and Welch (1978) survey estimates on the effect of UI on the duration of unemployment spells. For more recent estimates, see Kiefer and Neumann (1981) or Nickell (1979).

14. There is no reason why funds that are borrowed to meet current obligations should be viewed as insolvent. In an actuarial sense, average tax rates should be sufficient to finance average levels of unemployment. Thus, the probability of running a current account deficit should be zero.

15. One problem is that workers who approach the end of their careers with small or negative balances will not internalize the cost of current benefits. Thus, tax rates should be sufficiently high so that the probability of borrowing is small.

The paper by Burgess and Kingston in this volume documents substantial misreporting of employment status among persons receiving UI benefits. Many recipients are not searching for new jobs at all, which is another source of moral hazard in the system. This incentive to misreport would also be eliminated if workers were experience-rated.

16. This forced saving is unlikely to have important distortionary effects for two reasons. First, since unemployment will be a rare event, the taxes will be small on average and hence so will the impact on consumption decisions. Second, since accounts will be vested, this forced saving to cover UI will, for most workers, be a substitute for other forms of saving, which will accordingly be reduced.

REFERENCES

Becker, Joseph M. 1972. *Experience Rating in Unemployment Insurance: An Experiment in Competitive Socialism.* Baltimore: Johns Hopkins University Press.

Brechling, Frank. 1977. "The Incentive Effects of the U.S. Unemployment Insurance Tax." In Ronald G. Ehrenberg, ed., *Research in Labor Economics.* Vol. 1. Greenwich, Conn.: JAI Press.

Brechling, Frank. 1981. "Layoffs and Unemployment Insurance." In Sherwin Rosen, ed., *Studies in Labor Markets.* Chicago: University of Chicago Press for NBER.

Ehrenberg, Ronald G., and Ronald L. Oaxaca. 1976. "Unemployment Insurance, Duration of Unemployment, and Subsequent Wage Gain." *American Economic Review* 66 (December): 754–766.

Ehrlich, Isiah, and Gary Becker. 1972. "Market Insurance, Self-Insurance, and Self-Protection." *Journal of Political Economy* 80 (July/August): 623–640.

Feldstein, Martin S. 1974. "Unemployment Compensation: Adverse Incentives and Distributional Anomalies." *National Tax Journal* 27 (June): 231–244.

Feldstein, Martin S. 1975a. "The Importance of Temporary Layoffs: An Empirical Analysis." *Brookings Papers on Economic Activity* 5 (1975): 725–745.

Feldstein, Martin S. 1975b. "The Unemployment Caused by Unemployment Insurance." *Proceedings of the Industrial Relations Research Association's 28th Annual Winter Meetings:* 225–233.

Feldstein, Martin S. 1976. "Temporary Layoffs in the Theory of Unemployment." *Journal of Political Economy* 84 (October): 937–957.

Feldstein, Martin S. 1978. "The Effect of Unemployment Insurance on Temporary Layoff Unemployment." *American Economic Review* 68 (December): 834–846.

Hamermesh, Daniel. 1977. *Jobless Pay and the Economy.* Baltimore: Johns Hopkins University Press.

Hamermesh, Daniel. 1981. "Transfers, Taxes and the NAIRU." In *Supply Side Effects of Economic Policy.* St. Louis: Center for the Study of American Business, Washington University in St. Louis, and the Federal Reserve Bank of St. Louis.

Keifer, Nicholas, and George Neumann. 1979. "An Empirical Job-Search Model, with a Test of the Constant Reservation-Wage Hypothesis." *Journal of Political Economy* 87 (February): 89–108.

Lilien, David. 1980. "The Cyclical Importance of Temporary Layoffs." *Review of Economics and Statistics* 62 (February): 24–31.

Nelson, Daniel. 1969. *Unemployment Insurance: The American Experience, 1915–1935*. Madison: University of Wisconsin Press.

Nickell, Steven. 1979. "Estimating the Probability of Leaving Unemployment." *Econometrica* 47 (September): 1249–1266.

Topel, Robert. 1983. "On Layoffs and Unemployment Insurance." *American Economic Review* 73 (September): 541–559.

Topel, Robert. 1984a. "Experience Rating of Unemployment Insurance and the Incidence of Unemployment." *Journal of Law and Economics* 27 (April): 61–90.

Topel, Robert. 1984b. "Equilibrium Earnings, Turnover, and Unemployment." *Journal of Labor Economics* 2 (October): 000–000.

Topel, Robert. 1986. "Unemployment and Unemployment Insurance." In Ronald G. Ehrenberg, ed., *Research in Labor Economics 7*.

Topel, Robert, and Finis Welch. 1980. "Unemployment Insurance: Survey and Extensions." *Economica* 47 (August): 351–379.

U.S. Department of Labor. Bureau of Labor Statistics. 1978. *Handbook of Unemployment Insurance Financial Data (1938–1976)*. Washington, D.C.: Government Printing Office.

U.S. Department of Labor. Bureau of Labor Statistics. *Unemployment Insurance Statistics*. Various issues.

Welch, Finis. 1977. "What Have We Learned from Empirical Studies of Unemployment Insurance?" *Industrial and Labor Relations Review* 30 (July): 431–437.

5

Monitoring Claimant Compliance with Unemployment Compensation Eligibility Criteria

PAUL L. BURGESS AND JERRY L. KINGSTON

Introduction

Unemployment compensation (UC) is generally viewed as a program of temporary income support for involuntarily unemployed workers who have (sufficiently) strong prior work attachments and who desire to return to work. Accordingly, eligibility criteria related to several dimensions of workers' past and present labor market circumstances are utilized to determine the eligibility of claimants for UC benefits. Within the federal-state partnership, most UC program eligibility criteria are formulated by the states themselves. However, a small but growing number of uniform criteria have been imposed on all states by the federal partner.[1]

All state programs contain monetary eligibility provisions designed to screen out those who do not have sufficiently "strong" prior work attachments. These monetary criteria must usually be evaluated only once for each UC benefit year.[2] Further screening of claimants occurs at the beginning of each unemployment spell to evaluate the "separation issues" causing claimants to leave their previous employment; the typical reason for separation that qualifies a claimant for benefits is a layoff due to lack of work. In contrast, benefits would generally be either delayed or denied to those who left their last jobs because of voluntary quits or discharges for cause. Further weekly (or biweekly) screening occurs in all states to determine whether otherwise eligible claimants are able to work, are available for work, have not refused suitable employment, and have not received disqualifying earnings for employment during periods for which UC benefits are claimed. In addition, and of particular interest in this chapter, thirty-nine of the fifty-three UC jurisdictions also include an active search requirement as a separate test of work availability.[3] Because a detailed discussion of these and other eligibility requirements in a typical state UC program is provided elsewhere, these general eligibility criteria are not discussed further in this chapter.[4]

The focus of this chapter is on incentives for and the extent of claimant noncompliance with the above UC eligibility criteria, and on possible responses to such noncompliance. Because the focus of the chapter is on claimant noncompliance, it should be strongly emphasized at the outset that some claimants also receive smaller payments than those to which they are entitled. Although existing empirical evidence suggests that such underpayments are likely to be a much smaller problem than the overpayments emphasized in this chapter, it should be noted that there is still no reliable evidence available to determine the extent to which incorrect benefit denials may also result in "underpayments" to claimants.[5] In any case, it should be noted that underpayments that result from either incorrect payment amounts or incorrect benefit denials are not analyzed in this chapter.

The chapter is organized in the following manner. In section 1 some conceptual difficulties associated with formulating UC eligibility criteria and some reasons why noncompliance with UC eligibility criteria is very likely a substantial problem are discussed. Section 2 contains a brief summary of available evidence that documents the existence of a significant noncompliance problem. Claimant incentives that contribute to noncompliance with UC eligibility criteria are explained in section 3. Section 4 contains an overview of some issues involved in responding to the problem of noncompliance by UC claimants. Some specific responses to claimant noncompliance then are discussed, with the elimination of the work search requirement analyzed in section 5 and the utilization of statistical screening profiles discussed in section 6. Concluding comments are provided in the last section.

1. The Problem of Claimant Noncompliance

Formulating and effectively ensuring claimant compliance with UC program eligibility criteria is a challenging task. In this section, some conceptual issues that indicate how difficult this task is are first considered; then some institutional features and other factors that contribute to noncompliance in the UC system are briefly discussed.

Conceptual Issues

The objectives of the UC program were summarized by the U.S. Department of Labor in a statement issued nearly thirty years ago:

Unemployment insurance is a program—established under Federal and State
law—for income maintenance during periods of involuntary unemployment
due to lack of work, which provides partial compensation for wage loss as
a matter of right, with dignity and dispatch, to eligible individuals. It helps
to maintain purchasing power and to stabilize the economy. It helps to prevent
the dispersal of the employers' trained work force, the sacrifice of skills, and
the breakdown of labor standards during temporary unemployment.[6]

Although disagreement might exist over the extent to which the UC program could or should be expected to accomplish each of the above
objectives, this statement indicates that UC benefits are intended for
involuntarily unemployed workers. The above statement also reflects the
view that only partial income replacement is to be provided to unemployed
workers, presumably a reflection of the trade-off between moral hazard
and benefit adequacy issues. Although these particular objectives have been
a part of the UC program since its inception fifty years ago, recent theoretical and empirical analyses of the labor market have cast doubt on the
possibility of easily separating eligible from ineligible workers on the basis
of these criteria. Some examples are provided below to illustrate the conceptual difficulties involved in three of these conceptual issues: voluntary
versus involuntary unemployment; expected versus unexpected unemployment; and benefit adequacy versus moral hazard.

Voluntary versus Involuntary Unemployment. Several years ago, Lucas
observed that

> Accepting the necessity of a distinction between explanations for normal and
> cyclical unemployment does not, however, compel one to identify the first
> as voluntary and the second as involuntary, as Keynes goes on to do. This
> terminology suggests that the key to the distinction lies in some difference
> in the way two different types of unemployment are perceived by workers.
> Now, in the first place, the distinction we are after concerns sources of unem-
> ployment, not differentiated types.
>   . . . the unemployed worker at any time can always find some job at once,
> and a firm can always fill a vacancy instantaneously. That neither typically
> does so by choice is not difficult to understand given the quality of the jobs
> and the employees which are easiest to find. Thus, there is an involuntary
> element in all unemployment, in the sense that no one chooses bad luck over
> good; there is also a voluntary element in all unemployment, in the sense
> that however miserable one's current work options, one can always choose
> to accept them.[7]

Lucas goes on to point out that it does not appear possible, even in principle,
to classify individuals as either voluntarily or involuntarily unemployed.[8]

Though not universally accepted, contemporary macroeconomic theory
places much greater emphasis on the concept of voluntary unemployment
than was the case during the formative years of the UC program. The

conceptual difficulties of this development for UC program eligibility criteria include the following questions. Is the historical emphasis on the payment of benefits to only (or primarily) involuntarily unemployed individuals still a reasonable program goal as the UC system begins its second half-century of operation? If so, how can such individuals be practically identified if they cannot even be conceptually classified? If not, what criteria, if any, should be imposed in lieu of current requirements designed to screen out those who are not involuntarily unemployed?

Expected versus Unexpected Unemployment. Another distinction that has received substantial attention by economists since at least the time of Adam Smith is that between expected and unexpected unemployment, a distinction that is obviously related to voluntary versus involuntary unemployment and one that has recently been reemphasized by Abowd and Ashenfelter.[9] This dichotomy is important because some workers may prefer employment that provides periodic layoffs, either on a seasonal or a more intermittent basis, while others may demand wage premiums for accepting jobs that offer less stable employment. Teachers, for example, are typically not employed full-time throughout the year, but their absence from work during the summer months or between semesters is clearly anticipated in the usual case. Whether teachers and other academic professionals are actually available for work during summer periods becomes an obvious issue for such employment situations.[10]

The same availability issue noted above for teachers is relevant for workers in many other occupations and industries in which definite periods of nonemployment regularly occur, either at scheduled times or somewhat unpredictably (in terms of specific days or months). Examples of the former include seasonal industries such as food canning, tourism, and many types of construction work, as well as industries with regularly scheduled shutdowns due to model changes (for example, the auto industry). Examples of definite periods of nonemployment that may occur somewhat unpredictably throughout the year include many types of construction activity in much of the country and many service activities that depend on the weather. Another UC program issue besides that of availability that arises for workers in such employment situations is the extent of "hardship" imposed on these workers by anticipated periods of nonemployment. In fact, such jobless periods may actually increase the utility of some (well-informed) workers who select employment in such industries or occupations. In any event, it is clearly the case that compensating wage differentials would be expected to compensate well-informed and mobile workers for employment conditions that are uniformly considered adverse, other things equal.[11] Thus, the existence of UC benefits that compensate workers for such anticipated jobless periods would be expected to reduce any wage differentials that would otherwise exist.

The above discussion indicates that at least the following five conceptual issues arise for formulating UC eligibility criteria because of the expected versus unexpected unemployment distinction. First, to what extent are periods of joblessness anticipated by different types of workers? Second, should anticipated periods of unemployment be compensated by UC benefits, since some workers may view such periods positively or receive compensating differentials for doing such work? Third, does the "hardship" of unemployment depend on whether it is expected or unexpected, and is income maintenance appropriate for expected periods of nonemployment? Fourth, do UC benefits actually stabilize employment or assist employers in retaining trained workers in instances of expected unemployment, or do such benefits simply reduce compensating differentials that would otherwise exist? Finally, are workers who expect regular periods without work actually involuntarily unemployed due to lack of work during such periods, and are they genuinely available for other work during such periods?

Benefit Adequacy versus Moral Hazard. UC benefits provide for only partial income loss for several reasons, including concerns that the receipt of such benefits may reduce individual incentives to return to work. Consequently, UC program provisions attempt to balance income support goals with the objective of enhancing the claimant's return to employment. The conceptual basis for attempting to balance these goals has become more difficult in recent years as two quite different concepts of the adequacy of UC program benefits have emerged. For the first forty years of the program, the adequacy of the UC weekly benefit amount (WBA) was assessed through comparisons of the WBA with expenditures undertaken by the beneficiary and/or household during a typical pre-unemployment period; these expenditure categories were alternatively denoted as nondeferrable, recurring, or necessary/obligated in nature.[12] Using this approach, benefits were deemed to be more nearly adequate if they constituted a large proportion (oftentimes denoted as half or more) of such pre-unemployment expenditure sets. Within the last decade, however, Hamermesh has developed an alternative approach to the concept of benefit adequacy that is based on the distinction between transitory and permanent income.[13] Also utilized by DePippo,[14] this alternative approach determines the adequacy of UC benefits by whether or to what extent household consumption expenditures are maintained during jobless periods.

The conceptual dilemma involved in these diverse strands of benefit adequacy research involves identifying those groups for whom UC benefits are or are not adequate (and, consequently, groups for whom moral hazard may be more or less an issue). The earlier studies tended to conclude that, because of the limitation imposed by weekly benefit amount ceilings, UC benefits tended to be less adequate for those with higher earnings.[15] In contrast with this view, the "new" benefit adequacy literature concludes that benefits tend to be most adequate for higher earners because of the greater availability to them of financial and real assets that, in turn, can be used to cushion the consumption decline that results from an unemployment spell.[16]

To the extent that the adequacy of UC benefits is an operational concept of use in achieving UC program goals, it would be helpful if a consensus on the concept of benefit adequacy could be reached. This would facilitate the formulation and administration of eligibility criteria that might more nearly reflect the balancing of income support and moral hazard issues. The benefit adequacy versus moral hazard issue relates to the emphasis in this paper because of the effects varying wage-loss replacement rates may have on worker incentives to comply with stated UC eligibility criteria, particularly the availability-for-work and active work search requirements. In addition, the moral hazard versus benefit adequacy issue is obviously related to the voluntary versus involuntary and expected versus unexpected unemployment issues discussed above.

Conceptual Issue Summary. Although there are many responses to the problem of claimant noncompliance emphasized in this paper, one approach might involve altering eligibility criteria so as to increase the likelihood of effective enforcement. Within this context, the importance of the above discussion revolves around understanding that the formulation of eligibility criteria that can be effectively administered will be constrained by conceptual as well as by operational and administrative considerations. However, no attempt is made to answer these broad conceptual issues in this paper. Instead, narrower administrative and operational considerations are primarily emphasized, even though the above (and other) conceptual considerations would be extremely important in any major effort to revise UC eligibility criteria.

Contributing Factors to Claimant Noncompliance

In addition to the difficulties involved in conceptually formulating UC eligibility criteria that can be effectively administered, a number of factors suggest that noncompliance with existing criteria—whether detected or not—is likely to be a substantial problem. Some of these factors relate to institutional features and constraints within the UC system itself, whereas others relate to issues that directly affect that system and the likelihood of claimant noncompliance.

A number of institutional features and constraints of the UC system itself limit the possibility of effectively administering the work search requirement (and other weekly eligibility criteria) in the existing UC program.[17] First, the eligibility criteria imposed on claimants in most if not all state UC programs are probably much more complex than could be justified on the basis of reasonable benefit/cost calculations that account for effective administration and claimant compliance with stated criteria. Second, given existing UC eligibility criteria, state UC programs are underfunded to a much greater extent than indicated by the shortfall between actual administrative funding allocations to states and those implied by UC cost-model studies and projected UC claims loads. Third, the increase in the volume of claims filed that began with the 1974–75 recession, combined with relatively limited administrative funding levels and increased federal emphasis on rapid claim processing, may also have contributed significantly to frequent noncompliance with UC eligibility criteria.[18] However, despite the difficulties indicated by the second and third points just noted, substantial increases in administrative funds for state UC programs are neither likely nor even desirable without other changes in the existing system. Furthermore, because of legal and other considerations, state UC programs are likely to continue to experience strong pressures for the timely payment of benefits. Another institutional constraint that may have contributed to claimant noncompliance in recent years is that Job Service funding reductions have reduced resources for administering the work test provisions of state UC programs through job referrals provided to UC recipients. A final institutional feature that has contributed to claimant noncompliance is that state UC agency personnel typically confront an incentive system that does not encourage and may even discourage their efforts to monitor claimant compliance with weekly eligibility criteria carefully.

Certain other factors have also contributed to claimant noncompliance. Employers typically have little incentive to incur substantial costs in assisting UC agency personnel in their routine monitoring of claimant compliance with the weekly eligibility criteria, such as claimant availability for work. Also, the cash economy provides opportunities for UC recipients to obtain earnings from "concealed" employment that need not be reported to UC agencies and that cannot be detected by conventional UC program operating procedures.

The above considerations strongly suggest that it is virtually impossible for state UC program personnel to fully monitor the compliance of most UC claimants with the weekly eligibility criteria in the UC system as it presently operates. Thus, these considerations, and others to be discussed in more detail below, are consistent with the view that noncompliance with UC eligibility criteria is a major problem. Responses to these problems, however, have been constrained until recent years by the lack of accurate evidence on the extent and nature of noncompliance with UC program requirements. Such evidence is discussed in the following section.

2. Evidence on Noncompliance with UC Eligibility Criteria

Prior to 1980, accurate evidence on claimant noncompliance was not available.[19] For example, in concluding the first comprehensive study of this topic in 1953, Becker stated that

> On the subject of willful violators—that is, the proportion of working violators who are cheaters—the most intelligent statement that can be made is that no one knows. . . . The figures are even less certain for nonworking violators. . . .[20]

Nearly two decades later, Adams concluded another comprehensive study as follows:

> . . . the problem of claimant abuse of the UI program was less significant at the end of the decade of the 1960s than it was during the immediate post–World War II period when Becker made his study. Furthermore, it is likely that the extent of abuse was less than the general public thought it was when the Gallup Poll was taken in 1965. It is probably less than most people, who are not familiar with the facts, are inclined to believe.[21]

Support for Adams's conclusion was evident in the official statistics published by the Department of Labor (DOL) during the latter half of the 1970s on overpayments detected by state UC agencies. These reports indicated that both fraud and nonfraud overpayments combined amounted to about 1.5 percent or less of total benefit payments nationwide.[22] Hence, notwithstanding the periodic concerns that appeared in the popular press about the issues of fraud, overpayments, and abuse of the UC program, the evidence available to document such concerns was primarily anecdotal.

Valid evidence on the true extent of claimant noncompliance first became available from the authors' study conducted for the National Commission on Unemployment Compensation.[23] Undertaken in Buffalo, Oklahoma City, Phoenix, Pittsburgh, Salt Lake City, and the Queens Borough of New York City during 1979 and 1980, the study relied on comprehensive audits of probability samples of UC payments to estimate the percentages of UC benefits that were overpaid in these cities. The comprehensive auditing procedures for each claim provided for verification of compliance with the UC eligibility criteria, including those regarding the claimant's prior earnings and/or employment (to determine if monetary eligibility criteria had been met); the claimant's reason for separating from his/her previous employer (to detect any disqualifying separation reasons); whether the claimant was able to work; whether the claimant was available for work and, if required to demonstrate availability, also actively seeking work; whether the claimant had refused any offers of suitable work; and whether the claimant had any disqualifying earnings during the week for which benefits were paid.[24] On average, these benefit eligibility verifications required between eight and thirteen hours of direct investigative time to ascertain the claimant's eligibility for a single week of compensated unemployment. Hence, both because of its experimental design (that permitted estimates of population error rates on the basis of sample evidence) and because of the comprehensive benefit eligibility verification procedures utilized, the study provided the first valid estimates of overpayment rates in the UC system since the inception of the program.

The estimated overpayment percentages for dollars of benefits in the six study cities ranged from 3.8 percent to 24.3 percent, with a simple average of 13.9 percent recorded for the six cities.[25] These estimates were much higher than the overpayment rates detected through conventional state procedures in these cities for the same periods. For example, estimated overpayment rates were at least four times as large as the routinely detected overpayment rates in five of the six study states, and the study rate was actually forty-two times the routine state agency rate in one of the cities. An important implication of these findings is that the noncompliance problem in the UC program has not been usefully approximated by the "official" DOL statistics that are based on overpayments detected by routine state UC agency benefit payment control procedures. Another major finding of the study was that violations of active work search requirements represented the major source of overpayments in the six cities combined (and only five of the six cities had such requirements).

Partly in response to these findings, the DOL launched the random audit program in 1981.[26] This program was designed to estimate overpayment rates in statewide UC programs (not just metropolitan areas) for entire years (to avoid potential seasonality problems that may have existed in the study, which encompassed only six months). The program was pilot tested in five states—Illinois, Kansas, Louisiana, New Jersey, and Washington—and evaluated by Burgess, Kingston, and St. Louis in 1982. Principal findings of the analysis include the following: overpayment rates ranged from 7.3 percent to 24.3 percent of total benefits paid, with a simple average for the five states of 13.1 percent; the estimated UC benefits overpaid in just these five states alone exceeded by 60 percent the total overpayments officially reported by the DOL for the entire nationwide UC system for approximately the same time period; and the primary cause of overpayments was violations of the continuing eligibility criteria, especially the requirement that claimants actively seek work.[27]

Following the pilot test period, the random audit program was ultimately expanded to include forty-six UC jurisdictions. Although the overpayment rate estimates produced by these programs had not been made publicly available as of this writing, the DOL has reported that, on the basis of findings for calendar year 1982 for fifteen states, the mean overpayment rate was approximately 12.5 percent.[28] If this average rate were applied to total UC benefits paid during FY 1985, the implied dollar amount of over-payments would amount to nearly $2 billion for that year. On this basis, and given the fact that the random audit program tended to produce low estimates of overpayment rates,[29] available evidence strongly indicates the existence of a major problem of noncompliance with UC program eligibility criteria.

3. Claimant Incentives for Noncompliance

Much previous UC research has focused on the impact of UC support pro-visions (for example, the size and duration of weekly benefits) on the labor market experiences of presumably eligible UC recipients. To the extent that ineligible claimants might respond differently to varying levels or dimensions of UC program support, however, the findings and implica-tions of these previous studies merit reconsideration, as discussed in two other chapters.[30] In contrast with the focus of most previous research on the incentive effects of the UC program, the focus in this chapter is on how UC eligibility criteria and the administration of these criteria create incentives for claimants to file for benefits to which they are not entitled. Overpayments may occur accidentally or by deliberate design. Given the complexity of existing eligibility criteria, it would not be implausible to argue that many mistakes do occur, and complexity as a contributor to claimant noncompliance and other administrative problems has been exten-sively analyzed elsewhere.[31] In fact, however, both theoretical considera-tions and available empirical evidence are consistent with the view that many overpayments—especially violations of the weekly eligibility criteria —may reflect deliberate noncompliance. In the analysis that follows, this approach is applied to violations of the availability-for-work and active search provisions of the weekly UC eligibility criteria. This approach is taken because (1) these violations accounted for the majority of overpay-ments detected in both the Kingston-Burgess study and the follow-up evaluation by Burgess, Kingston, and St. Louis, as noted above; (2) these violations are more likely to reflect claimant incentives and behavior than other types of noncompliance which may involve both claimant and employer motivations (for example, separation issues); and (3) compliance with these criteria would seemingly be less difficult to monitor than many other aspects of the weekly eligibility criteria (for example, nonrefusal of suitable work), so that the problems involved in enforcing most other weekly eligibility criteria would be expected to be at least as severe as those emphasized here.

A Simple Noncompliance Model

Consider a potential UC claimant beginning another week of continued unemployment.[32] Within the context of conventional job search models, the intensity of job search depends on the benefits and costs of searching more intensely.[33] Assume, for purposes of illustration, that these benefit/ cost calculations lead a claimant to engage in less search than is required to qualify for UC program support for the week in question. At this point, the potential UC claimant confronts a second set of benefit/cost calculations. Given that actual job search for the week in question does not satisfy state requirements, a decision to file or not to file for such support as an ineligible claimant must be made (assuming the claimant is aware of actual search requirements). The expected net monetary return E(NMR) to filing an ineligible claim is given by

$$E(NMR) \quad = E(BEN) - E(COSTS), \qquad (1)$$

where

E(BEN)	$= (1 - a)WBA;$
E(COSTS)	$= (d \times e \times f)(NOMPEN);$
a	= probability that an ineligible claim would be detected before the claim is paid;
d	= probability that a payment made to an ineligible claimant would be detected after receipt of the payment by the claimant;
e	= probability that an overpayment would be "established" (formally processed) by the state UC agency if an invalid payment was detected;
f	= probability that any nominal penalty (NOMPEN, defined below) would be effectively applied if an overpayment was established for an invalid claim;
WBA	= the UC weekly benefit amount; and
NOMPEN	= the dollar amount of the nominal penalty imposed for an established overpayment.

In this formulation, the expected monetary benefits of filing an ineligible claim, E(BEN), are given by the product of the likelihood that the claim would *not* be detected before payment $(1 - a)$ and the size of the weekly benefit payment (WBA). As is explained in more detail below, it appears that a is very low in many state UC programs, so that E(BEN) probably is nearly equal to WBA for many claimants. It should be noted, however, that E(BEN) includes only monetary returns and ignores any possible psychic returns that some individuals might experience as a result of filing an ineligible claim for UC support. Thus, to the extent that "beating the system" strongly enters the utility functions of some workers, E(BEN) understates the expected benefits of noncompliance for such workers. The expected monetary costs, E(COSTS), of filing an ineligible claim depend on *d, e, f,* and NOMPEN. Since each of these cost components is expected to be quite low (as explained in the following section), the net monetary return of knowingly filing an invalid claim may nearly equal the weekly UC benefit payment for many claimants. Accordingly, many UC claimants may be induced to file for UC program support to which they are not entitled. In contrast, the psychic costs of noncompliance may strongly enter the utility functions of some potential claimants, and noncompliance would thus tend to be discouraged for such claimants.

Evidence on Noncompliance Costs and Benefits

Some empirical evidence is available from both the authors' study and the Burgess-Kingston-St. Louis analysis of the random audit program pilot tests to suggest that the likelihood of detecting eligibility noncompliance is extremely low in the existing UC system. In the former study, it was found that routine state UC agency benefit payment control procedures detected fewer than one-fourth of the overpayments detected by the specialized auditing procedures in five of the six cities studied, as noted above. Similarly, in the Burgess-Kingston-St. Louis study it was estimated that the dollar volume of overpayments in just the five pilot test states exceeded by 60 percent the total of overpayments actually detected and established by all fifty-three UC jurisdictions combined for a comparable one-year period.[34] Similar conclusions follow from the evidence presented by Black and Carr; based on their analysis of UC recipients who participated in the Seattle and Denver income maintenance experiments, they found that nearly one-third of the "person-weeks" of compensated unemployment analyzed from the Seattle experiment involved the payment of UC benefits to individuals who were not searching for work, and that nearly one-fifth of such payments were received by individuals who were neither searching nor available for work.[35] Similar results were reported for their analysis of data from the Denver experiment.[36] Further analysis of the Burgess-Kingston-St. Louis study data revealed that nearly one-fifth of all claimants who were required to search for work and who had certified that they had done so in obtaining UC benefits had actually made no job search contacts for the weeks for which UC benefits were claimed.[37] Moreover, such tendencies for nonsearch were not random, but rather varied systematically by sex, age, duration of unemployment, and reason for job separation. The above findings, taken together, strongly suggest that the probability of detecting a violation of the work search/availability criterion after a payment has been made (*d* in equation 1) is very low.

Although there is no comparable direct evidence available for assessing the likelihood of detecting noncompliance prior to a payment (a in equation 1), the above considerations and other factors discussed in this chapter suggest it too is quite small.

The second determinant of the expected cost of knowingly filing an invalid UC claim—the likelihood that an overpayment will be established for a detected violation (e)—also tends to be quite low, at least in some state UC programs. Evidence to support this view is available from both the Kingston-Burgess and Burgess-Kingston-St. Louis studies.[38] In the Kingston-Burgess study it was determined that, in one of the participating states, state administrative policy prohibited the retroactive establishment of overpayments for detected noncompliance with stated work search criteria. Similarly, in three of the five Burgess-Kingston-St. Louis study states, overpayments could not be established for work search violations unless written documentation was available to prove that the claimant had previously received a formal warning that his or her work search activities were deficient. Further evidence from the study indicates that, even with an average of eight to thirteen hours of investigative time allocated to investigate a single claimant's eligibility for a single week of compensated unemployment, nearly half or more of all work search contacts *reported* by UC claimants could not be verified as either acceptable or unacceptable contacts; nevertheless, no overpayments were established for this lack of verifiable job search contacts in any of the five states. In addition, many states have "finality" rules in their employment security laws or policies that prohibit the establishment of overpayments after a certain number of days has elapsed, even if it is subsequently determined that an erroneous payment has been made. Finally, it should be noted that DOL pressures on state agencies to recoup overpayments that are established may have caused some states to establish overpayments for detected violations of eligibility criteria only (or at least primarily) in those instances in which the likelihood of obtaining repayment of overpaid amounts is high.[39] Taken together, these considerations suggest that some, and perhaps many, detected or partially detected violations of UC eligibility criteria may not be formally established as overpayments, thereby reducing d and E(COSTS) in equation 1.

The nominal penalty (NOMPEN) for most work search/availability overpayments that are established also tends to be quite modest. Nationwide, only about one-fourth of all overpayments are determined to be fraudulent in nature, and the majority of these fraud overpayments occur because of concealed employment during periods for which UC support is claimed.[40] Consequently, nearly all work search/availability overpayments in most states are classified as nonfraudulent in nature. The most common penalty assessed in such instances is that the benefits received (WBA) for the ineligible week must be repaid, so that NOMPEN = WBA.

Deliberate noncompliance with UC eligibility criteria is also not discouraged by the fact that the probability of effective application of any nominal penalties assessed (f) is quite low in most state UC programs, as indicated by the following five considerations.[41] First, in some states, overpaid amounts are simply "offset" against future benefit claims, and cash repayment is not required; in such circumstances, repayment is either delayed (if a subsequent claim is filed in the claimant's benefit year) or eliminated (if no subsequent claim is filed). Second, in most states, any overpaid amounts are immediately restored to the claimant's maximum benefit award so that the same number of dollars may yet be paid to the claimant before the end of his or her benefit year; for those who exhaust their benefit entitlements, the effective penalty for an overpayment amounts to nothing more than the delay involved in receiving the same amount of total support during their UC benefit years. Third, some states do not charge interest on outstanding overpaid balances so that, even if repayment does ultimately occur, the affected claimants receive interest-free loans during the interval before repayment occurs in such states (assuming overpayments are ultimately repaid). Fourth, federal law prohibited the utilization of offsets of benefits paid under federal programs to repay amounts overpaid under state UC programs until very recently. Finally, it should be emphasized that repayment rates for established overpayments tend to be quite low. As an assistant inspector general for audit in the Department of Labor reported several years ago:

> . . . SESAs [State Employment Security Agencies] are neither effectively nor efficiently detecting and collecting benefit overpayments. Because of the size of the UI benefit payment program—more than $15 billion in calendar year 1981—and the program's susceptibility to both fraudulent and non-fraudulent overpayments, changes in laws, policies and practices must be made immediately.[42]

Evidence from the FY 1982 results of the Department of Labor's quality appraisal program also supports the conclusion that repayment rates for established overpayments tend to be quite low; for that year, the DOL had a "desired level of achievement" for states to recoup at least 55 percent of all overpayments established that were subject to recovery. However, during FY 1982, only twenty-two states met or exceeded this criterion, and overpayment recoveries amounted to only about 53 percent of all overpayments subject to recovery for all UC jurisdictions combined.[43] Similar information was not released by the department for FY 1983, but the evidence for FY 1984 reveals that the comparable overpayment recovery percentage for all UC jurisdictions combined was about 56 percent.[44]

The empirical evidence discussed above strongly suggests that the expected costs of filing an ineligible claim for UC benefits are very low in the current UC system and are certainly low relative to the expected benefits of filing such an ineligible claim. In fact, the above discussion indicates that a claimant evaluating the benefits and costs of knowingly filing an ineligible (but nonfraudulent) claim would typically compare the benefits of such a claim ($[1 - a] \times$ WBA), which is approximately equal to WBA, with the costs ($[d \times e \times f] \times$ WBA), which is approximately equal to zero. Consequently, considerable deliberate noncompliance with eligibility criteria would be expected, at least by claimants for whom the (presumably self-imposed) psychic costs of noncompliance are relatively small. The moral hazard versus benefit adequacy issue discussed earlier in this chapter is, of course, directly related to the present discussion, since any increase in weekly benefits that is designed to improve benefit adequacy also entails an increase in the incentives for claimant noncompliance.

4. Responses to Claimant Noncompliance: Overview of Issues

The problem of claimant noncompliance with weekly UC eligibility criteria involves a number of issues, many of which have not received any emphasis in this chapter. Moreover, responses to the problem of claimant compliance could be devised in a number of different ways, depending on how many aspects of the overall noncompliance problem were addressed, value judgments, and state specific circumstances. Answers to the conceptual issues posed earlier in the paper would also affect the evaluation of various approaches to the problem of claimant noncompliance. In short, a large number of responses to the overall noncompliance problem might be considered, including approaches within the existing institutional framework of the UC system that would provide for (1) simplified UC eligibility criteria; (2) an improved administrative funding mechanism; (3) increased administrative funding for monitoring claimant compliance; (4) improved federal performance criteria for state programs; (5) improved incentives for employers to engage in monitoring claimant compliance with UC eligibility criteria; (6) improved incentives for state UC agency personnel to engage in monitoring claimant compliance with UC eligibility criteria; (7) the substitution of UC eligibility criteria that can be more effectively and less expensively administered than existing criteria; (8) the elimination of difficult-to-monitor eligibility criteria; (9) improved incentives for claimant self-compliance with stated UC eligibility criteria; and (10) improved administration of existing (or altered) eligibility criteria without any substantial increase in real administrative funding levels.[45] The above approaches, and still others, are not mutually exclusive. Moreover, value judgments on the appropriate roles of other UC system participants would be important in formulating any overall response to the problem of claimant noncompliance. However, the approach taken in this chapter is to focus narrowly on only selected aspects of the last three of the ten alternative approaches noted above. The elimination of the work search requirement (one aspect of approach 8 above) is analyzed in the next section of the chapter. In section 7 the use of statistical screening profiles to improve UC administrative operations and to increase claimant self-compliance (one aspect of approaches 9 and 10 above) is then discussed.

5. Elimination of Work Search Requirement without Compensating Changes

Thirteen UC jurisdictions do not currently impose a separate work search requirement, although claimants are required to be available for work in all jurisdictions.[46] In order to evaluate the merits of eliminating the active search requirement, it would be useful to identify both the costs and the benefits of imposing and administering this requirement.

Within the current institutional environment, the costs of imposing and administering this requirement may include the following: high actual overpayment rates (whether detected or not) because of the high expected net monetary returns of noncompliance to claimants, as discussed in section 4 of this chapter; violations of horizontal equity because the work search requirement cannot be uniformly enforced for persons in similar circumstances; a socially unproductive allocation of administrative resources for enforcement of this eligibility criterion, to the extent to which existing enforcement procedures fail to induce socially productive job search activities that result, for example, in reduced unemployment or enhanced reemployment experiences; a socially unproductive allocation of claimant and employer resources, to the extent to which the work search requirement promotes nonproductive job search and/or verification activities that consume resources with positive social opportunity costs;[47] and increased misreporting of labor force status and job search activities by UC claimants that could confound attempts to obtain meaningful policy interpretations of measured unemployment rates.[48]

The potential benefits of imposing an active work search requirement on UC recipients could include the following: more effective administration of other UC eligibility criteria, especially the availability-for-work requirement, given that the work search requirement presumably constitutes a more specific test of a claimant's availability for work than would exist in the absence of the work search requirement;[49] reduced claim filing by claimants who are actually unavailable for work and who, in the absence of the more specific work search requirement, would file for UC benefits (subsequently denoted as the "screening" effect);[50] increased job search activity by UC claimants that could reduce the duration of unemployment spells and enhance claimant reemployment experiences;[51] and increased public support for the UC program, to the extent to which such support depends on broadly held views that UC benefits are paid only (or primarily) to "deserving" claimants.[52]

Another effect of the work search requirement not included in the assessment provided above is the likely impact on the volume of legitimate UC claims both filed and paid, for any given level of overall labor market demand. This effect is discussed separately because it does not unambiguously constitute either a benefit or a cost of this eligibility criterion. An active work search requirement probably tends to reduce claim filing by eligible as well as ineligible claimants. Even otherwise eligible claimants may view the time, psychic, and monetary costs of complying with the work search requirement as unjustifiable, given the expected returns of such activities, so that claim filing by these individuals would tend to be reduced. Furthermore, given that a work search requirement could result in the erroneous denial of benefits to some otherwise eligible claimants, its existence would reduce the proportion of any given number of claims filed that are paid. Consequently, existing work search requirements likely reduce the total volume of UC benefit outlays (and hence employer tax rates) for any given overall level of labor market demand.

Even though a rational assessment of retaining or eliminating the work search requirement would be facilitated by evidence related to the above costs and benefits, little information is available on the benefits and costs of imposing and administering this requirement. Even though work search requirements are an integral aspect of the UC program in most states, there have apparently been no studies designed specifically to determine the impact of this criterion on the effective allocation of either public or private resources. Perhaps partly in response to this problem, the DOL issued a request for proposal in 1985 that sought to fund a research project to evaluate the effects of variations in active search requirements. According to the DOL:

> Finally, neither the study of denial rates nor the random audit data reveal any information about the effects that variations in active search-for-work provisions have on actual claimant behavior and/or on the job finding success of claimants. Very specific and consistently enforced active search-for-work requirements may increase denial rates and may either increase or decrease payment error rates but not lead to any significant change in the rate of reemployment among claimants or even to a significant decrease in benefit payments. Claimants may simply alter their benefit duration. Even more importantly, some types of specific requirements may lead to increased job-finding while others do not.[53]

Unfortunately, the proposed experimental design for this study emphasized comparisons of claimant unemployment and reemployment experiences in states with and without active search requirements. In our view, interstate differences in UC program requirements, administration, and other factors are so pronounced that it will be very difficult and perhaps impossible to isolate the impact of the work search requirement on these dimensions of UC claimant experiences in such an interstate study. A more appropriate design would involve making such comparisons within rather than among state UC programs.

What, then, would be the impact of eliminating the work search requirement within a state UC program? In simple point of fact, we do not know. In the absence of "within-state" experiments in which UC claimants would be randomly assigned to groups with varying work search requirements, it may not be possible to ascertain the effects of eliminating or altering UC program work search provisions on the unemployment or reemployment experiences of UC claimants, or the extent to which the existence of such a requirement effectively screens benefit claims by ineligible claimants or enhances the feasibility of administering other aspects of the continuing eligibility criteria.

Notwithstanding these considerations, however, it would seem likely that some or all of the following would result from elimination of the work search requirement: (1) a reduction in actual (and hence detected) overpayment rates; (2) increased claim filing for any given level of overall labor market demand; (3) an increased proportion of paid claims out of total claims filed; (4) increased difficulties in administering the availability-for-work and perhaps the nonrefusal-of-suitable-work provisions of the weekly eligibility criteria; (5) reduced actual job search by UC claimants (and perhaps an altered composition of search strategies), together with a change in whatever social and private returns had been associated with the amount and composition of previous search activities; (6) less misreporting of search intensity and labor force status that, of itself, would tend to reduce measured unemployment rates; and (7) reduced public support for the UC program, to the extent that the program would then be perceived as serving the needs of less deserving claimants who are not required to seek work actively.

6. Improved Administration of Existing (or Altered) Requirements and Increased Claimant Self-Compliance

Another approach for dealing with the work search "problem" in the existing UC system would be to improve the administration of existing (or even altered) work search/availability requirements. Although a number of such approaches might be considered,[54] only the use of statistical screening profiles to increase the likelihood of detecting ineligible claimants who file invalid claims for benefits (probabilities a and d in equation 1) is discussed in this section. Under such an approach, most UC claims would be paid routinely, with only a cursory review to determine if the certifications were properly completed and signed by the claimant; specifically, no resources would be allocated to verify the information reported by most claimants on their weekly or biweekly certification forms. The resources freed up by these altered procedures could then be reallocated for more intensive reviews of a selected group of high-risk claims targeted for such audits by statistical profiling techniques. A number of issues would be important in considering the revised approach discussed in this section.[55] Because very little work has been undertaken within the UC system to experiment with statistical profiles, however, the remaining discussion focuses on the technical aspects of constructing such profiles.

Although statistical screening profiles for eligibility issues apparently have no operational history in the UC system, there have been some very limited experimental efforts to develop screening profiles with special data sets.[56] Porterfield, Burgess, Kingston, and St. Louis utilized special data to explore the possibility of developing screening profiles to detect unreported earnings by UC recipients.[57] Black and Carr utilized self-reported data obtained from personal interviews with SIME/DIME (Seattle Income Maintenance Experiment/Denver Income Maintenance Experiment) participants who also were UC claimants to analyze admitted nonsearch and unavailability for work by UC recipients.[58] Burgess, Kingston, St. Louis, and DePippo utilized state UC random audit data to explore the possibility of developing screening profiles for detecting work search/availability overpayments in an unpublished report.[59] Because random audit data represent an ideal data source for administrative profiling purposes, one that is now available in forty-six states, the possibility of developing screening profiles with this data source is discussed in some detail below. First, the advantages of random audit data (and similar data from the Department of Labor's recently implemented Quality Control program) in constructing such profiles are briefly discussed. A conceptual framework for constructing screening profiles is then discussed, followed by an analysis of the empirical results of estimating such profiles for the five states included in the Burgess-Kingston-St. Louis study. Finally, some cautions in interpreting the results presented, as well as some considerations for future research, are briefly discussed.

Utilizing Random Audit Data for Screening Profiles

The data sets that have resulted from the random audit system have several advantages for administrative profiling purposes.[60] First, the payment samples selected in each of the states constitute probability samples of the UC payments made each year in these states. Second, these data sets have payments classified as proper payments versus overpayments on the basis of intensive eligibility verifications, so the possibilities of misclassification are much smaller than would be the case for operational data. Third, the random audit program data include information on a number of claimant and labor market characteristics that are not routinely available from state UC agency data files. Fourth, the random audit data bases were available for a total of forty-six states by FY 1985, allowing the profiling efforts discussed below to be replicated in most states. Finally, further analysis of the random audit program data could provide useful insights into the possible uses of similar data that will become available from the operational Quality Control program that was implemented in all states as of April 1986.[61]

Conceptual Framework for Work Search/Availability Profiles

The conceptual framework for developing statistical noncompliance profiles is provided by standard neoclassical search theory and the simple noncompliance model provided in equation 1 above. UC claimants conduct a given amount of search for any particular week, based on the benefits and costs of that search. For some workers, the search actually conducted would satisfy UC eligibility criteria. For others, actual search efforts would fall below UC requirements, and such workers must decide whether to engage in deliberate noncompliance with UC eligibility criteria and file for benefits, even though they do not satisfy those criteria. Thus, any factors that increase the net returns of *actual* job search would be expected to reduce deliberate noncompliance with UC eligibility criteria, whereas any factors that increase the net returns of noncompliance for a given level of search effort would be expected to increase noncompliance.

The data for the five random audit pilot states are utilized to illustrate the possibility of developing statistical profiles within the context of the above conceptual framework. The general model estimated for these states is the following one:

NONCOMPLIANCE =

$$c_0 + c_1(\text{WBA}) + c_2(\text{AWW}) + c_3(\text{SEXMALE})$$
$$+ c_4(\text{AGE1}) + c_5(\text{AGE3}) + c_6(\text{WHITE})$$
$$+ c_7(\text{EDUCATION}) + c_8(\text{UNION})$$
$$+ c_9(\text{CONSTRUCTION}) + c_{10}(\text{SPELLS})$$
$$+ c_{11}(\text{BENEFITSUSED}) + e, \qquad (2)$$

where

NONCOMPLIANCE = a work search/availability overpayment established or a formal warning issued for a work search violation. This variable takes

on a value of 1 if an overpayment was established or a formal warning issued, and
a value of 0 otherwise;

WBA   = the weekly UC benefit amount to which the
claimant was entitled on the basis of his or
her base period wages, measured in dollars;

AWW   = average weekly wages of the claimant in the
UC base period used to establish the claim-
ant's eligibility for benefits, measured in
dollars;

SEXMALE   = 1 if male, and 0 otherwise;

AGE1   = 1 if less than twenty-two years of age, and
0 otherwise;

AGE3   = 1 if more than fifty-four years of age, and
0 otherwise;

WHITE   = 1 if white (and non-Hispanic), and 0
otherwise;

EDUCATION   = number of years of formal education completed;

UNION   = 1 if the claimant was a union member and
allowed to register with a union hiring hall
in lieu of Job Service registration as a condition for receiving UC support, and 0 otherwise;

CONSTRUCTION   = 1 if the claimant worked in the construction
industry, and 0 otherwise;

SPELLS   = the number of spells of UC-compensated
unemployment the claimant had experi-
enced in the previous twelve-month period;

BENEFITSUSED   = the dollar amount of UC benefits received
by the claimant during his or her current
benefit year, as computed at the end of the
week of unemployment investigated; and

e   = a randomly distributed error term.

Before discussing the empirical results of estimating the above equation
for each of the five states, the variables included are briefly discussed.
The dependent variable, NONCOMPLIANCE, includes both formally
established availability and work search overpayments as well as detected
instances of work search noncompliance that resulted in formal warnings
(rather than formal overpayments). This choice of the dependent variable
reflects both the institutional features of the UC system and also the interest
in this chapter of exploring the possibility of developing profiles that could

be utilized to prevent as well as detect instances of noncompliance. In most states, including the five states analyzed here, work search activities are interpreted as evidence that a claimant is available for work. Under these circumstances, overpayments established because of inadequate work search efforts may be "written up" as violations of the availability eligibility criteria, and how the violation is established depends to a great extent on the unique facts of each case. In particular, at least some work search violations may be recorded in agency records as violations of availability criteria. A similar definitional nuance relates to instances in which formal warnings are issued to claimants for not complying with work search requirements. Some state laws or policies require that such warnings be issued before an overpayment can actually be established for a given week of compensated unemployment. Because the actions of claimants who commit work search/availability violations and are held ineligible may be identical to those of claimants who receive only formal warnings, the latter were included with persons for whom work search/availability overpayments were formally established.

Because the purpose here is not to test specific hypotheses, but rather to illustrate the possibility of operationally utilizing screening profiles in the UC system, the specific signs expected for the independent variables included in equation 2 are not emphasized here.[62] However, it may be noted that WBA, AWW, SEXMALE, AGE1, AGE3, WHITE, and EDUCATION are variables that would be included in conventional search intensity equations.[63] Nonetheless, some brief discussion is appropriate for the UNION, CONSTRUCTION, SPELLS, and BENEFITSUSED variables because they are included primarily in an attempt to reflect some particular institutional features of the UC system.

The UNION variable is included because of differences in the activities necessary for union versus nonunion claimants to satisfy state work search/availability requirements. In most instances, state requirements for union workers are satisfied when the claimant registers for work with a union hiring hall.[64] Hence, the activities required of union claimants to satisfy state work search/availability requirements were quite limited, and therefore few violations would be expected for such claimants. In contrast with union claimants, nonunion claimants are expected to demonstrate their availability for work, at least in part, through contacts with employers. Simply because of this difference in treatment by the UC system, work search violations are clearly much more likely for nonunion than union workers.[65]

The CONSTRUCTION variable is included because of certain characteristics of the construction industry. The regularly intermittent employment that often characterizes this industry could increase the likelihood that claimants in this industry may use jobless periods as planned periods of leisure or nonmarket activity, even though they continue to report themselves as unemployed for UC purposes. In contrast, it may be more difficult for UC personnel to verify job search contacts for construction workers because of typically informal job application procedures and because of the temporary nature of construction sites. The first effect would tend to increase detected noncompliance, whereas the second would decrease it.

The SPELLS and BENEFITSUSED variables are included partly as measures of claimant knowledge of the UC system. Greater knowledge of the system would suggest that claimants would be both more aware of UC eligibility criteria (reducing the possibility of accidental noncompliance because of limited information) and also more aware of the limited capabilities of the UC system to monitor compliance with stated criteria (increasing the possibility of deliberate noncompliance). These variables could also affect optimal search intensity by UC recipients through present-value comparisons of an active search strategy and continuing unemployment (in light of limited UC benefit duration).[66]

Some Empirical Estimates for Work Search/Availability Profiles

The data base for which equation 2 is estimated had work search noncompliance rates that varied for the total samples analyzed from 6.6 percent in Louisiana to 30.7 percent in Kansas, as reported in Table 5.1. Differences in work search noncompliance rates partly reflect differences in laws, policies, and administrative practices among the five states studied. However, the particular interest in this paper is whether claimants who do and do not engage in such noncompliance can be predicted on the basis of the types of personal, labor market, and UC variables for individual claimants included above in equation 2.[67]

Table 5.1. Total Samples and Work Search Noncompliance Rates for Five States

| State | Total Sample[a] | Cases with Work Search/Availability Overpayments or Formal Warnings | |
		Number	Percentage of Total
Illinois	306	25	8.2
Kansas	225	69	30.7
Louisiana	395	26	6.6
New Jersey	367	92	25.1
Washington	320	46	14.4

Source: Burgess, Kingston, St. Louis, and DePippo (1983).

[a]These sample sizes are smaller than the total samples selected during the random audit program pilot test period. In Illinois, Louisiana, and New Jersey, all of the cases removed from the original data base were excluded because the claimants were not required to satisfy the state's work search requirement. In Kansas, additional cases had to be removed for this analysis because of operational problems which involved the incomplete validation of work search efforts by claimants.

The dependent variable in equation 2 is a dichotomous one, and maximum-likelihood logistic regression analysis is thus an appropriate estimating technique. The specific coefficient estimates for each state are reported in Tables 5A.1–5A.5 in the appendix (pages 164–166). However, because the specific coefficients estimated are of less interest than the overall classificatory power of the equations estimated, some different ways of viewing the power of the results for equation 2 for each of the five states are summarized in Table 5.2. For comparison purposes, the mean noncompliance rate for the entire sample for each state is reported on row 1 of the table. Row 2 contains the predicted noncompliance probability estimates from equation 2 for the sample cases, classified by cases of actual noncompliance versus compliance in each state. Ideally, cases of actual noncompliance would have extremely high predicted probabilities that would approach 100 percent, whereas cases of actual compliance would have extremely low predicted probabilities that would approach zero percent. Obviously, these profiles fall far short of such ideal ones. More realistically, one would hope that statistical profiles such as these would result in much higher predicted probabilities than the mean rates for cases of actual noncompliance and much lower predicted probabilities than the mean rates for cases of actual compliance. Comparing the row 2 estimates with the row 1 sample means provides a basis for these latter comparisons. These comparisons clearly indicate that the overall predictive power of these equations is quite limited, particularly for New Jersey and to a lesser extent for Illinois and Louisiana.[68] Nonetheless, it may be noted that the predicted noncompliance probabilities are considerably higher for cases of actual noncompliance than for cases of actual compliance in each of the states except New Jersey.

Although the overall predictive power of the estimated equations is quite limited, it appears that the estimated profiles may hold more promise as a basis for allocating resources for eligibility reviews in the operational UC system than might be suggested by the above discussion. This is the case because it would not be particularly useful to utilize such profiles for predicting overall noncompliance probabilities for all claimants. Rather, given extremely limited administrative resources, the potential importance of statistical profiles as an administrative strategy hinges more on whether such profiles can be used to effectively identify especially high-risk claimants for intensive reviews. This would be the main issue in evaluating such profiles, particularly if their only use was to rank claimants for intensive audits from highest to lowest predicted noncompliance probabilities and then auditing just those claimants with the highest predicted probabilities. Alternatively, the above strategy might be supplemented by an approach that would attempt to group claimants into various categories, such as "very high-risk," "intermediate risk," and "very low-risk" groups. A large

Table 5.2. Maximum-Likelihood Logistic Regression Estimates of Work Search Noncompliance Probabilities for Equation 2[a]

	Illinois		Kansas		Louisiana		New Jersey		Washington	
1. Mean noncompliance rate for all cases	8.2%		30.7%		6.6%		25.1%		14.4%	
2. Based on equation 2, predicted noncompliance probability for										
(a) Cases of actual noncompliance	13.4%		40.7%		11.5%		27.6%		21.6%	
(b) Cases of actual compliance	7.7%		26.2%		6.2%		24.3%		13.2%	

3. Based on equation 2, predicted noncompliance probability intervals for individual cases

	Cases of Actual		Cases of Actual		Cases of Actual		Cases of Actual		Cases of Actual	
	N[b]	C[b]	N	C	N	C	N	C	N	C
0% up to 5%	3	102	1	21	3	184	0	1	2	34
5% up to 10%	7	109	0	14	10	113	1	8	9	96
10% up to 15%	7	49	1	16	7	49	4	24	10	58
15% up to 20%	2	12	8	13	2	15	8	33	3	40
20% up to 25%	3	4	9	13	3	6	21	75	4	18
25% up to 30%	1	2	5	12	0	2	31	93	6	12
30% up to 35%	2	0	5	18	1	0	12	18	2	6
35% up to 40%	0	2	7	14	0	0	6	11	1	5
40% up to 45%	0	0	11	7	0	0	5	8	2	3
45% up to 50%	0	1	21	9	0	0	3	3	2	1
50% or more	0	0	1	19	0	0	1	0	5	1
Total	25	281	69	156	26	369	92	274	46	274

Source: Burgess, Kingston, St. Louis, and DePippo (1983).
[a]Coefficient estimates for the five states are reported in Tables 5A.1–5A.5 in the appendix.
[b]N = noncompliance; C = compliance.

proportion of the very high-risk group could then be selected for audits, and a much smaller proportion of the intermediate risk group, and few or no claimants from the very low-risk group would be selected. Because this latter approach may be a viable alternative and because it also proves useful for comparison purposes, Table 5.3 summarizes the results from Table 5.2 for both high- and low-risk claimants, according to the predicted noncompliance probabilities from equation 2.

The results reported in Table 5.3 indicate that the estimated prediction profiles were relatively successful in identifying low-risk claimants. This is indicated by the fact that the actual noncompliance rates for claimants with low predicted probabilities of noncompliance (see row 2) were considerably lower than the (actual) mean noncompliance rates for all claimants in each state (reported for comparison purposes in row 1 of Table 5.3). Even for Illinois and Louisiana, the states with the lowest mean noncompliance rates, the actual noncompliance rates for claimants with predicted noncompliance rates of 5 percent or less were considerably lower than the mean rates for all claimants (2.9 versus 8.2 percent and 1.6 versus 6.6 percent, respectively). In each of the other three states, the claimants estimated to have low noncompliance probabilities also had actual noncompliance rates that were substantially lower than the mean noncompliance rates for all claimants.

The above results relate to identifying low-risk claimants, but Table 5.3 also provides information for evaluating the accuracy of the estimated equations in identifying high-risk claimants (see row 3). These results show that the actual noncompliance rates for claimants with high predicted noncompliance rates from equation 2 were much higher than the mean noncompliance rates for all claimants in each of these states, except for an unusual exception for one category in Illinois.[69] Even in Kansas and New Jersey, the states with the highest actual noncompliance rates, claimants with high predicted noncompliance rates still had actual noncompliance rates that were much higher than the average noncompliance rates for all claimants (47.3 versus 30.7 percent and 40.5 versus 25.1 percent, respectively). In the other three states, claimants estimated to be in the high-risk group often had even larger differences between their actual noncompliance rates and the mean rates for their states.

Cautions and Considerations for Future Research

The empirical results reported in Tables 5.2 and 5.3 clearly indicate that statistical profiles might be an effective technique for identifying low-risk versus high-risk claimants for differential treatment in selecting claimants for intensive eligibility reviews, either before or after payments have been made. However, the above results are only intended to illus-

Table 5.3. Actual Noncompliance Rates for Cases in Selected Probability Intervals, Based on Equation 2 Predictions

	Illinois	Kansas	Louisiana	New Jersey	Washington
1. Mean noncompliance rate for all cases	8.2%	30.7%	6.6%	25.1%	14.4%
2. Actual noncompliance rates for cases with relatively low predicted noncompliance probability intervals of[a]					
≤ 5%	3 of 105 cases = 2.9%	1 of 22 cases = 4.5%	3 of 187 cases = 1.6%	0 of 1 cases = 0.0%	2 of 36 cases = 5.6%
≤10%	—	1 of 36 cases = 2.8%	—	1 of 10 cases = 10.0%	11 of 141 cases = 7.8%
3. Actual noncompliance rates for cases with relatively high predicted noncompliance intervals of[b]					
≥15%	8 of 29 cases = 27.6%	—	6 of 29 cases = 20.7%	—	28 of 114 cases = 24.6%
≥25%	3 of 8 cases = 37.5%	—	1 of 3 cases = 33.3%	—	17 of 45 cases = 37.8%
≥35%	0 of 3 cases = 0.0%	44 of 93 cases = 47.3%	—	15 of 37 cases = 40.5%	7 of 17 cases = 41.2%

[a]Based on row 3, Table 5.2. Noncompliance rates for a state calculated only for intervals that have upper limits that are less than the mean noncompliance rate for the state.
[b]Based on row 3, Table 5.2. Noncompliance rates for a state calculated only for intervals that have lower limits that exceed the mean noncompliance rate for the state.

trate the potential benefits that statistical profiling may provide in more efficiently allocating administrative resources to improve payment accuracy and to induce an increase in claimant self-compliance. It is important to emphasize that utilizing the same group to estimate a prediction profile and then to test the predictive power of that profile obviously makes the results seem more positive than would be the case in an operational setting in which a profile estimated on the basis of one group's characteristics would be used to predict noncompliance probabilities for a subsequent group of claimants. This would be a particularly serious problem if the systematic determinants of work search noncompliance vary through time or change markedly over the business cycle. Nonetheless, the results discussed above, combined with the findings of St. Louis, Burgess, and Kingston on reported versus actual job contacts for the five states combined,[70] strongly suggest that work search/availability noncompliance is systematically related to the expected benefits and costs of noncompliance rather than randomly distributed among the claimant population. Accordingly, it appears that statistical profiles could be used to effectively identify high-risk versus low-risk claimants for differential administrative scrutiny.

It should also be noted that the above profiles were estimated for the total samples in each state simply to illustrate the possibilities this approach may hold. However, noncompliance determinants may vary importantly among various groups, consistent with the findings for much of the empirical literature on labor supply responses. In fact, an analysis of the claimants in the five states combined by St. Louis, Burgess, and Kingston clearly indicates that job contact misreporting behavior varies markedly between certain subgroups, particularly between union hiring hall and nonunion claimants and between men and women.[71] Thus, separately developing profiles for various subgroups within a state (especially given larger sample sizes than those utilized for the profiles discussed above) would be expected to produce more accurate prediction profiles.

7. Conclusions

Social payment systems must have eligibility criteria to separate those who are and are not eligible to receive support from such programs. Noncompliance with such eligibility criteria has been documented as a major problem within the existing UC system. Conceptual difficulties related to the fundamental goals of the program, together with possible conflicts among those goals, may hinder efforts to respond to the noncompliance problem through revision of existing eligibility criteria. Hence, other approaches merit consideration. Two possible responses were considered in this chapter: elimination of the work search requirement and improved

UC program administration through the use of statistical profiles. It is not possible to fully assess the costs and benefits of eliminating the work search requirement because the studies necessary for such an evaluation have not yet been conducted. A number of factors suggest, however, that elimination of the work search requirement is not likely to be a widely adopted strategy, at least until the effects of this approach are more clearly understood. The development and use of statistical profiles, on the other hand, appears to be a technically feasible approach that could significantly improve the allocation of UC program administrative resources. This approach would require no increase in the (real) level of resources devoted to UC program administration and could be implemented with existing or revised eligibility criteria. Furthermore, increased claimant self-compliance with UC eligibility criteria would be induced. Also, the technical feasibility of utilizing such profiles on an operational basis has been greatly enhanced by the availability of random audit program data in most states, and by the availability of Quality Control program data in all states, starting in April 1986.

Notwithstanding these considerations, statistical profiling has received very little consideration to date. The rather limited profiling efforts analyzed in this paper, however, illustrate the potential contributions of such an approach. It seems quite certain that further estimation efforts, based on either random audit or Quality Control program data, would result in more powerful statistical profiles than those discussed in this chapter. Hence, further investigation of this approach appears warranted.

APPENDIX

Table 5A.1. Results of Estimating Text Equation 2 for Illinois

Variable	Coefficient	Standard Error	t-statistic
Constant	−2.004	1.461	−1.37
WBA	−0.002	0.011	−0.20
AWW	−0.003	0.003	−1.13
SEXMALE	−0.528	0.488	−1.08
AGE1	−0.395	0.811	−0.49
AGE3	0.444	0.644	0.69
WHITE	0.471	0.522	0.90
EDUCATION	0.004	0.093	0.04
UNION	−1.464	1.160	−1.26
CONSTRUCTION	1.123	0.590	1.90
SPELLS	−0.142	0.236	−0.60
BENEFITSUSED[a]	0.032	0.025	1.24

Log of the likelihood function = −79.6131
Degrees of freedom = 293

[a]BENEFITSUSED coefficient and standard error are multiplied by 100 for reporting convenience.

Table 5A.2. Results of Estimating Text Equation 2 for Kansas

Variable	Coefficient	Standard Error	t-statistic
Constant	0.955	1.338	0.71
WBA	0.006	0.008	0.68
AWW	−0.004	0.003	−1.40
SEXMALE	−0.913	0.344	−2.66
AGE1	−0.293	0.496	−0.59
AGE3	−1.033	0.730	−1.41
WHITE	−0.340	0.426	−0.80
EDUCATION	−0.013	0.088	−0.15
UNION	−1.738	1.090	−1.60
CONSTRUCTION	−1.245	0.797	−1.56
SPELLS	−0.126	0.261	−0.48
BENEFITSUSED[a]	−0.019	0.021	−0.93

Log of the likelihood function = −119.721
Degrees of freedom = 212

[a]BENEFITSUSED coefficient and standard error are multiplied by 100 for reporting convenience.

Table 5A.3. Results of Estimating Text Equation 2 for Louisiana

Variable	Coefficient	Standard Error	t-statistic
Constant	−0.915	1.116	−0.82
WBA	−0.004	0.009	−0.47
AWW	−0.001	0.003	−0.38
SEXMALE	−0.524	0.589	−0.89
AGE1	0.295	0.642	0.46
AGE3	−0.730	0.870	−0.84
WHITE	−0.672	0.439	−1.53
EDUCATION	−0.114	0.081	−1.41
UNION	−1.772	0.836	−2.12
CONSTRUCTION	1.145	0.561	2.04
SPELLS	0.161	0.233	0.69
BENEFITSUSED[a]	0.037	0.023	1.62

Log of the likelihood function = −87.558
Degrees of freedom = 382

[a]BENEFITSUSED coefficient and standard error are multiplied by 100 for reporting convenience.

Table 5A.4. Results of Estimating Text Equation 2 for New Jersey

Variable	Coefficient	Standard Error	t-statistic
Constant	−1.460	0.900	−1.62
WBA	0.008	0.006	1.24
AWW	−0.002	0.001	−1.49
SEXMALE	−0.067	0.267	−0.25
AGE1	0.775	0.369	2.10
AGE3	0.250	0.395	0.63

Table 5A.4. *(continued)*

WHITE	0.138	0.281	0.49
EDUCATION	0.010	0.052	0.19
CONSTRUCTION	-0.187	0.480	-0.39
SPELLS	-0.379	0.209	-1.81
BENEFITSUSED[a]	0.007	0.015	0.47

Log of the likelihood function = -200.096
Degrees of freedom = 353

[a]BENEFITSUSED coefficient and standard error are multiplied by 100 for reporting convenience.

Table 5A.5. Results of Estimating Text Equation 2 for Washington

Variable	Coefficient	Standard Error	t-statistic
Constant	-1.618	1.208	-1.34
WBA	0.006	0.008	0.78
AWW	-0.001	0.002	-0.38
SEXMALE	-0.690	0.381	-1.81
AGE1	1.512	0.496	3.05
AGE3	0.275	0.607	0.45
WHITE	-0.249	0.517	-0.48
EDUCATION	-0.029	0.079	-0.37
UNION	-0.593	0.581	-1.02
CONSTRUCTION	-0.403	0.574	-0.70
SPELLS	-0.170	0.152	-1.12
BENEFITSUSED[a]	0.035	0.018	1.95

Log of the likelihood function = -119.621
Degrees of freedom = 307

[a]BENEFITSUSED coefficient and standard error are multiplied by 100 for reporting convenience.

NOTES

The authors gratefully acknowledge the substantial assistance of Robert St. Louis in developing some of the ideas discussed in this paper. The authors also benefited from the comments of Wayne Vroman on an earlier draft.

1. See Rubin (1983, Ch. 3) for a discussion of the growth of federal standards that relate to eligibility criteria.

2. A benefit year is typically the fifty-two-week period during which a claimant is monetarily eligible to receive a maximum amount of UC benefits on the basis of prior earnings and employment.

3. U.S. Department of Labor (1985a, Table 400).

4. For a detailed discussion of UC eligibility criteria and related issues, including the complexity it indicates for the UC system, see Burgess and Kingston (1987, Ch. 3).

5. For evidence of the relatively small magnitude of underpayments due to incorrect payment amounts, see Kingston, Burgess, and St. Louis (1986, Table 1).

6. Haber and Murray (1966, p. 26).

7. Lucas (1978, p. 354).

8. Lucas (1978, p. 355).

9. Abowd and Ashenfelter (1981); Smith (1937, Bk. 1, Ch. 10).

10. The National Commission on Unemployment Compensation (1980, p. 32) noted that portions of the Employment Security Amendments of 1970 and 1976 were specifically directed at schoolteachers because of congressional concern about their availability for work during summer months.

11. For some recent empirical estimates of compensating differentials, see Duncan and Holmlund (1983).

12. See Burgess, Kingston, and Walters (1978); Becker (1961).

13. Hamermesh (1982).

14. DePippo (1983).

15. Burgess, Kingston, and Walters (1978); Becker (1961).

16. Hamermesh (1982); DePippo (1983).

17. For a detailed discussion of these points, see Burgess and Kingston (1987, Ch. 3–6).

18. For a detailed discussion of administrative financing and time pressure issues as they relate to enforcing UC eligibility criteria, see Burgess and Kingston (1987, Ch. 4, 5).

19. For a comprehensive review of evidence on overpayments in the UC program, see Burgess and Kingston (1987, Ch. 2); Kingston, Burgess, and St. Louis (1986).

20. Becker (1953, pp. 310–311).

21. Adams (1971, p. 92).

22. U.S. Department of Labor (1979).

23. For details on the National Commission on Unemployment Compensation's overpayment study, see Kingston and Burgess (1981) and Burgess and Kingston (1980). A summary of this evidence is contained in Kingston, Burgess, and St. Louis (1981).

24. Details on the investigative procedures used in the National Commission on Unemployment Compensation's overpayment study are found in Kingston and Burgess (1981, pp. 1–12) and summarized in Kingston, Burgess, and St. Louis (1981).

25. For the findings discussed, see Kingston and Burgess (1981, pp. 32, 43, 46).

26. For the details of this program, see Burgess, Kingston, and St. Louis (1982). A briefer discussion of the program is contained in Kingston, Burgess, and St. Louis (1986).

27. Kingston, Burgess, and St. Louis (1986).

28. U.S. Department of Labor (1984c).

29. For a discussion of the likely underestimation of overpayment rates in the random audit program, see Kingston, Burgess, and St. Louis (1986).

30. Kingston, Burgess, and St. Louis (1986); St. Louis, Burgess, and Kingston (1986).

31. Burgess and Kingston (1987, Ch. 3).

32. The elements included in the noncompliance model developed in this section and discussed in the next are outlined and briefly discussed in Kingston, Burgess, and St. Louis (1986).

33. See, for example, Barron and Mellow (1979).

34. Kingston, Burgess, and St. Louis (1986).

35. Black and Carr (1980, p. 529).

36. Black and Carr (1980, p. 530).

37. For the results discussed, see St. Louis, Burgess, and Kingston (1986, Tables 1–4).

38. For the results discussed, see Kingston and Burgess (1981, pp. 37–39); and Kingston, Burgess, and St. Louis (1986), which contains a detailed analysis of work search noncompliance in the UC system.

39. As is discussed subsequently in the text, these considerations may have led the Department of Labor to temporarily drop this "desired level of achievement" for overpayment recoveries from the quality appraisal program. A similar criterion, however, was reintroduced in the 1985 quality appraisal program. For further discussion of these issues, see Burgess and Kingston (1987, Ch. 5).

40. In both the Kingston-Burgess and Burgess-Kingston-St. Louis studies, for example, concealed employment accounted for a large proportion of fraud overpayments in several states. See Kingston and Burgess (1981, p. 43) and Burgess, Kingston, and St. Louis (1982, pp. 132–156).

41. See Kingston, Burgess, and St. Louis (1986); Burgess and Kingston (1987, Ch. 6).

42. Peterson (1983, p. 1).

43. U.S. Department of Labor (1982, pp. 3, 26).

44. U.S. Department of Labor (1985c, p. 3).

45. For a detailed discussion of several of these alternatives, see Burgess and Kingston (1987); Kingston, Burgess, and St. Louis (1986).

46. U.S. Department of Labor (1985a, Table 400).

47. Corson, Long, and Nicholson (1984) found that attempts to provide for more effective (that is, stringent) enforcement of work test provisions did not result in a reduction in the period of job search or the acquisition of better jobs by UC claimants. Similarly, Keeley and Robins (1985, p. 355) conclude that job search requirements in government programs do not significantly reduce the duration of unemployment.

48. St. Louis, Burgess, and Kingston (1986).

49. Without a specific work search requirement, the primary tests of availability for work would be nonrefusal of suitable work and registration with the Job Service. For problems associated with detecting instances of refusal of suitable work, see Burgess and Kingston (1987, pp. 164–166). Some insights into the problems associated with even determining if claimants are effectively registered with the Job Service are found in Kingston and Burgess (1981, p. 70).

50. Nonmonetary determinations are written both to prevent payments and to establish overpayments once payments have been made. Unfortunately, available information does not permit identification of nonmonetary determinations written for work search/availability issues to screen payments before they are made. Separate classification of nonmonetary determinations written before versus after payment would be very useful in assessing the extent of any screening effects that occur. It may be the case, for example, that even though work search/availability violations are extremely difficult to detect once payments have been made, these

eligibility criteria constitute partially effective screens against the erroneous payment of benefits. Information on the total number of nonmonetary determinations written for work search and availability violations, however, is available; see U.S. Department of Labor (1984a).

51. As previously noted, however, available evidence does not support the contention that government-imposed job search requirements either reduce the duration of unemployment or result in enhanced reemployment experiences. See Keeley and Robins (1985, p. 355); Corson, Long, and Nicholson (1984).

52. See, for example, Adams (1971, pp. 21, 56); Curtin and Ponza (1980, p. 770).

53. U.S. Department of Labor (1985b).

54. Such approaches are discussed briefly in Kingston, Burgess, and St. Louis (1986) and in much more detail in Burgess and Kingston (1987, Ch. 7).

55. Three of these other issues — profiling objectives, burden of proof considerations, and the legal and political feasibility of developing profiles — are discussed by Burgess and Kingston (1987, Ch. 7).

56. These attempts have all relied on special data sets because routine operational UC system data include so many undetected overpayments as proper payments that such data could not be utilized for accurately classifying proper payments versus overpayments.

57. Porterfield, Burgess, Kingston, and St. Louis (1980).

58. Black and Carr (1980).

59. Burgess, Kingston, St. Louis, and DePippo (1983).

60. These data also have some clear limitations in the context of testing general search intensity models, including certain selectivity biases. For a discussion of these issues, see St. Louis, Burgess, and Kingston (1986).

61. For the announcement of the revised quality control program, see U.S. Department of Labor, "Unemployment Insurance Program Letter No. 4-86," December 20, 1985.

62. In any case, appropriate hypothesis testing would require that individual state data be pooled because of the definitional link between AWW and WBA in each state. However, this approach is not taken in this paper because the operational use of screening profiles in the UC system would have to involve screening profiles developed for each state, not profiles for groups of states.

63. For example, see St. Louis, Burgess, and Kingston (1986) for an analysis of the relationship of some of these (and other) variables to self-reported versus actual search among UC recipients.

64. New Jersey represents an exception among the five states analyzed. There registration with a union hiring hall is not sufficient to satisfy the work search requirement; thus the UNION variable is not included in the equation estimated for New Jersey.

65. For example, St. Louis, Burgess, and Kingston (1986) show that nonunion workers have much higher UC work search misreporting rates than union workers.

66. Burgess and Kingston (1981, pp. 263–265) show that potential benefit duration is an important determinant of the (reported) duration of compensated spells of unemployment.

67. Of particular importance for the profiles estimated in this paper, it was

possible to identify claimants excused from their states' work search requirements for the individual weeks analyzed, and the total samples reported in Table 5.1 have such persons excluded. For such claimants, compliance with work search requirements would be irrelevant in the profiling context analyzed in this paper.

68. In fact, the overall equations for these three states are not statistically significant at the 0.10 level, as indicated by the results reported in Tables 5A.1, 5A.3, and 5A.4 in the appendix.

69. The only exception is for a group of just three Illinois claimants who had predicted noncompliance probabilities of at least 35 percent. None of these claimants fell in the actual noncompliance group.

70. St. Louis, Burgess, and Kingston (1986).

71. St. Louis, Burgess, and Kingston (1986, Tables 1, 3, and 4).

REFERENCES

Abowd, John M., and Orley Ashenfelter. 1981. "Anticipated Unemployment, Temporary Layoffs, and Compensating Wage Differentials." In Sherwin Rosen, ed., *Studies in Labor Markets*. Chicago: University of Chicago Press.
Adams, Leonard P. 1971. *Public Attitudes Toward Unemployment Insurance*. Kalamazoo, Mich.: Upjohn Institute for Employment Research.
Barron, John M., and Otis Gilley. 1979. "The Effect of Unemployment Insurance on the Search Process." *Industrial and Labor Relations Review* 32 (April): 363–366.
Barron, John M., and Wesley Mellow. 1982. "Labor Contract Information, Search Requirements, and Use of a Public Employment Service." *Economic Inquiry* 20 (July): 381–387.
Barron, John M., and Wesley Mellow. 1979. "Search Effort in the Labor Market." *Journal of Human Resources* 14 (Summer): 389–404.
Becker, Joseph M. 1961. *The Adequacy of the Benefit Amount in Unemployment Insurance*. Kalamazoo, Mich.: Upjohn Institute for Employment Research.
Becker, Joseph M. 1953. *The Problem of Abuse in Unemployment Benefits*. New York: Columbia University Press.
Black, Matthew, and Timothy J. Carr. 1980. "An Analysis of Nonsearch." *Unemployment Compensation: Studies and Research*. Vol. 2. Washington, D.C.: National Commission on Unemployment Compensation.
Burgess, Paul L., and Jerry L. Kingston. 1980. "Estimating Overpayments and Improper Payments." *Unemployment Compensation: Studies and Research*. Vol. 2. Washington, D.C.: National Commission on Unemployment Compensation.
Burgess, Paul L., and Jerry L. Kingston. 1981. "UI Benefit Effects on Compensated Unemployment." *Industrial Relations* 20 (Fall): 258–270.
Burgess, Paul L., and Jerry L. Kingston. 1987. *An Incentives Approach to Improving the Unemployment Compensation System*. Kalamazoo, Mich.: Upjohn Institute for Employment Research.
Burgess, Paul L., Jerry L. Kingston, and Robert D. St. Louis. 1982. *The Development of an Operational System for Detecting Unemployment Insurance Pay-*

ment Errors Through Random Audits: The Results of Five Statewide Pilot Tests. Washington, D.C.: U.S. Department of Labor, Unemployment Insurance Service.

Burgess, Paul L., Jerry L. Kingston, Robert D. St. Louis, and Paul DePippo. 1983. "Predicting Worksearch Overpayments in Unemployment Insurance Programs." U.S. Department of Labor, Unemployment Insurance Service. Mimeograph.

Burgess, Paul L., Jerry L. Kingston, and Chris Walters. 1978. *The Adequacy of Unemployment Insurance Benefits: An Analysis of Weekly Benefits Relative to Preunemployment Expenditure Levels.* Washington, D.C.: U.S. Department of Labor, Unemployment Insurance Service.

Corson, Walter, Alan Hershey, and Stuart Kerachsky. 1984. "Application of Unemployment Insurance Work System Test and Nonmonetary Eligibility Standards." Princeton, N.J.: Mathematica Policy Research.

Corson, Walter, David Long, and Walter Nicholson. 1984. *Evaluation of the Charleston Claimant Placement and Work Demonstration Project.* Princeton, N.J.: Mathematica Policy Research.

Curtin, Richard T., and Michael Ponza. 1980. "Attitudes Toward and Experiences With Unemployment Compensation Among American Households." *Unemployment Compensation: Studies and Research.* Vol. 3. Washington, D.C.: National Commission on Unemployment Compensation.

DePippo, Paul David. 1983. *The Liquidity Approach to the Adequacy of Unemployment Insurance Benefits.* Ph.D. diss., Arizona State University.

Duncan, Greg, and Bertil Holmlund. 1983. "Was Adam Smith Right After All? Another Test of the Theory of Compensating Wage Differentials." *Journal of Labor Economics* 1 (October): 366–379.

Haber, William, and Merrill G. Murray. 1966. *Unemployment Insurance in the American Economy.* Homewood, Ill.: Richard D. Irwin.

Hamermesh, Daniel S. 1982. "Social Insurance and Consumption." *American Economic Review* 72 (March): 101–113.

Keeley, Michael C., and Philip K. Robins. 1985. "Government Programs, Job Search Requirements, and the Duration of Unemployment." *Journal of Labor Economics* 3 (July): 337–362.

Kingston, Jerry L., and Paul L. Burgess. 1981. *Unemployment Insurance Overpayments and Improper Payments in Six Major Metropolitan Areas.* Washington, D.C.: National Commission on Unemployment Compensation.

Kingston, Jerry L., Paul L. Burgess, and Robert D. St. Louis. 1981. "Overpayments in the Unemployment Insurance Program in the United States." *International Social Security Review* 34 (4): 462–476.

Kingston, Jerry L., Paul L. Burgess, and Robert D. St. Louis. 1986. "Unemployment Insurance Overpayments: Evidence and Implications." *Industrial and Labor Relations Review* 39 (April): 323–336.

Lucas, Robert E., Jr. 1978. "Unemployment Policy." *American Economic Review* 68 (May): 353–357.

National Commission on Unemployment Compensation. 1980. *Unemployment Compensation: Final Report.* Washington, D.C.: Government Printing Office.

Peterson, Gerald W. 1983. Memorandum for Albert Angrisani, Assistant Secretary of Labor. Letter of transmittal accompanying final report on audit of Unemployment Benefit Payment Controls: Improvements Needed. U.S. Department of Labor. May 16. Typescript.

Porterfield, Richard, Robert D. St. Louis, Paul L. Burgess, and Jerry L. Kingston. 1980. "Selecting Claimants for Audits of Unreported Earnings." *Unemployment Compensation: Studies and Research*. Vol. 2. Washington, D.C.: National Commission on Unemployment Compensation.

Rubin, Murray. 1983. *Federal-State Relations in Unemployment Insurance*. Kalamazoo, Mich.: Upjohn Institute for Employment Research.

Smith, Adam. 1937. *The Wealth of Nations*. New York: Modern Library.

St. Louis, Robert D., Paul L. Burgess, and Jerry L. Kingston. 1986. "Reported vs. Actual Job Search by Unemployment Insurance Claimants." *Journal of Human Resources* 21 (Winter): 92–117.

Stevens, David W. 1977. *Unemployment Insurance Beneficiary Job Search Behavior: What Is Known and What Should Be Known for Administrative Planning Purposes*. Washington, D.C.: U.S. Department of Labor, Unemployment Insurance Service.

U.S. Department of Labor. 1979. *A Briefing for the National Commission on Unemployment Compensation on Benefit Payment Control*. Washington, D.C.: U.S. Department of Labor, Unemployment Insurance Service.

U.S. Department of Labor. 1982. *Unemployment Insurance Quality Appraisal Results for FY 1982*. Washington, D.C.: U.S. Department of Labor, Unemployment Insurance Service.

U.S. Department of Labor. 1984a. "ETA-207 Tables 57A and 58A." Washington, D.C.: U.S. Department of Labor, Unemployment Insurance Service.

U.S. Department of Labor. 1984b. "ETA 5159 Table 1A." Washington, D.C.: U.S. Department of Labor, Unemployment Insurance Service.

U.S. Department of Labor. 1984c. "Unemployment Insurance Program Letter No. 19-84." Washington, D.C.: U.S. Department of Labor, Unemployment Insurance Service.

U.S. Department of Labor. 1985a. "Comparison of State Unemployment Insurance Laws." Washington, D.C.: U.S. Department of Labor, Unemployment Insurance Service.

U.S. Department of Labor. 1985b. *Request for Proposal: RFP L/A 85-12*. Washington, D.C.: U.S. Department of Labor, Office of the Assistant Secretary for Administration and Management.

U.S. Department of Labor. 1985c. *Selected Administrative Data on Benefit Payment Control (State UI)*. Washington, D.C.: U.S. Department of Labor, Unemployment Insurance Service.

Washington State Employment Security. Unemployment Insurance Division. 1985. "Statewide Work Search Activity Program." Olympia: Washington State Employment Security, Unemployment Insurance Division.

6

Unemployment Insurance in Western Europe: Responses to High Unemployment, 1973–1983

BEATRICE REUBENS

Introduction

The unemployment insurance systems of Western European countries have been subjected to strong pressures since 1975 because of substantially higher unemployment rates, prolonged spells of unemployment, and increasing concern that traditional UI programs are not up to the task of dealing with the current composition of unemployment. This has led to the search for new approaches in some countries and efforts to curtail expenditures on UI programs in others.

Unemployment rates in most Western European countries were considerably lower than those in the United States through the 1950s and 1960s, rising with the onset of the oil crisis in 1973, dropping back slightly for a few years, and then rising sharply in the early 1980s and remaining at what seem by all standards to be excessively high levels through 1985 (Table 6.1).

Several countries, like Austria, Norway, and Sweden, have maintained low unemployment through special circumstances or policies: Austria with effective fiscal and monetary policy, Norway with the exploitation of its oil resources, and Sweden with extensive training and employment programs (which may serve persons who would be recorded elsewhere as unemployed). While the U.S. unemployment rate dropped in 1984–85, few European countries showed improvement. By 1984 nine of the thirteen European countries had higher unemployment rates than the United States. (In 1970 only Italy and Ireland had rates exceeding that of the United States.)

Along with the rise in unemployment rates, the average duration of unemployment also increased, though less so in the United States than

Table 6.1. Annual Average Rate of Unemployment, Fourteen Countries, 1970–85 (percentage of labor force)

	1970	1975	1979	1982	1983	1984	1985[a,b]
Austria	1.4	1.7	2.1	3.5	4.1	3.8	4.0
Belgium	2.1	5.0	8.2	12.6	13.9	14.0	13.75
Denmark[a]	0.7	4.9	6.0	11.0	11.4	11.0[b]	9.25
Finland	1.9	2.2	5.9	5.8	6.1	6.1	5.75
France	2.4	4.1	6.0	8.2	8.4	9.7	10.5
Germany	0.8	3.6	3.2	6.1	8.0	8.6	8.25
Ireland[a]	5.8	6.4	6.1	11.4	14.1	16.0[b]	16.5
Italy	5.3	5.8	7.5	9.0	9.8	10.2	10.75
Netherlands	1.0	5.2	5.4	11.4	13.7	14.0	15.25
Norway	1.6	2.3	2.0	2.6	3.3	3.0	2.75
Spain	2.4	3.7	8.5	15.9	17.4	20.1	21.5
Sweden	1.5	1.6	2.1	3.1	3.5	3.1	2.75
United Kingdom	3.1	4.6	5.6	12.3	13.1	13.0[b]	12.0
United States	4.8	8.3	5.8	9.5	9.5	7.4	7.0

Sources: Standardized unemployment rates, according to methods described in OECD, *Quarterly Labour Force Statistics*. 1970–84 rates from OECD, 1985a, Table II-9. Estimated rates for 1985 from OECD, 1985b, Tables 13, 14.
[a]Based on national definitions and data.
[b]Estimated by OECD Secretariat.

Table 6.2. Long-Term Unemployment in Twelve Countries, 1973 and 1983 (percentage of total unemployment)

	1973	1983		
	12 months and over	6 months and over	12 months and over	24 months and over
Austria	7.4	25.8	9.0	na
Belgium	51.0	77.9	62.8	42.8
Finland	na	38.3	14.6	4.7
France	21.6	67.0	42.2	19.4
Germany	8.5	54.1	28.5	9.3
Ireland	na	50.9	31.0	na
Italy	na	na	41.9	18.4
Netherlands	12.8	69.6	43.7	na
Norway	na	20.0	6.7	na
Spain	na	71.0	53.6	29.8
Sweden	4.7[a]	24.9	10.3	na
United Kingdom	26.9[b]	58.1	36.5	17.1
United States	3.3	23.9	13.3	na

Sources: OECD, 1983a, Table 24; 1985a, Tables H and I-8.
[a]1977.
[b]July data for Great Britain only.

in most Western European countries. Between 1973 and 1983, European countries endured substantial increases in long-term unemployment of one year or more, with eight of the twelve countries under discussion having more than a quarter of the unemployed out of work for a year or more (Table 6.2). This can be attributed partly to the fact that European employment has grown slowly since 1975, in contrast with substantial U.S. employment growth in the same period.

The composition of unemployment has also changed, especially compared with the pre–World War II period when male heads of household constituted the bulk of the labor force and were the focus of social concern. Structural unemployment, with its impact on older workers and the length of unemployment, has reached new proportions, often overshadowing cyclical and frictional unemployment (OECD, 1984b, pp. 83–86). Furthermore, unemployment has risen for the young, females, and minorities—groups not considered when UI programs were first designed. Such changes are forcing a rethinking of UI programs, especially in international agencies.[1]

Because of the substantial differences between the U.S. and Western European UI programs, as well as variation among the European nations, it is important to provide a better understanding of a few representative systems. Section 1 begins by summarizing the main features of UI and other income replacement programs for the unemployed in West Germany, Great Britain, Sweden, and France. Section 2 traces the course and causes of the rise in expenditures on UI and policy responses. Section 3 examines the adequacy of UI benefits. Section 4 assesses the effects of unemployment benefits on work incentives. Section 5 reports on alternative uses of UI and complementary programs that may be of interest in the United States. Section 6 presents a summary and conclusions.

1. UI Systems in Selected Countries

West Germany

The Federal Republic of Germany maintains a three-tier system of income replacement: UI, which covers 90 percent of wage and salary workers and is based on mandatory contributions from workers and employers; means-tested, federally financed unemployment assistance (UA) primarily used by those who exhaust unemployment insurance benefits but also by those who fail to qualify for UI; and, as a last resort, local public welfare. Unemployed persons older than forty-five receive prolonged benefits; those over fifty-eight can remain on benefits until they reach retirement age. Since 1975, publicly funded family allowances paid to employed persons are also paid to UI beneficiaries, replacing dependents' allowances for those on UI.

In 1969 West Germany passed the Employment Promotion Act, a broad set of labor market programs under a self-governing public corporation with multipartite administration called the Federal Employment Institute (FEI). The act provides that mandatory contributions by employers and employees to FEI shall be used for multiple purposes: UI; UA; a variety of other income replacement programs for partial or total loss of employment; operation of the employment service; training measures to improve the employability of the whole labor force (not just the unemployed); and job creation through active labor market measures on the supply and demand sides. Austria operates a similar system (Bruche, 1984b). In both countries, the federal treasury covers deficits.

A feature of German financing has been the shifting of financial responsibility among various public budgets and trust funds (Bruche and Reissert, 1985a, p. 2). For example, the cost of maintaining the other social insurance rights of recipients of unemployment insurance was shifted from the federal treasury to the FEI in mid-1978. Also, the cost of unemployment assistance for those exhausting UI benefits was shifted from the treasury to the FEI when the latter had a surplus in 1966, but was returned to the treasury some fifteen years later (Bruche and Reissert, 1985a, pp. 9, 12). A consequence of such redistribution of financial burdens has been "a lack of continuity in entitlement programs for the unemployed and preventive measures to combat unemployment" (Bruche and Reissert, 1985a, p. 2).

Great Britain

Great Britain's provision rests on two programs. The first is flat-rate UI benefits (the earnings related supplement, introduced in the 1960s, was eliminated in 1982). Benefits are financed out of the mandatory social insurance contributions from employers and employees to the omnibus National Insurance Fund in the Department of Health and Social Security. Special UI schemes cover agricultural workers, seasonal workers, and domestics. More than 90 percent of all wage and salary employees are covered by the social security system, but some 10 percent of these are not fully covered by UI due to exclusions in the legislation or voluntary "contracting out," primarily by married women (OECD, 1976b; Reissert, 1985a, pp. 31–32). Unemployment benefits, including dependents' benefits, are paid through the Department of Employment, but the remainder, some 90 percent of all National Insurance Fund payments, goes to old age pensions, sickness and disability benefits, and payments by the

Department of Health and Social Security under other social insurance programs.

The second British program serving the unemployed, called Supplementary Benefit (SB), is a means-tested allowance of unlimited duration payable to persons sixteen years and older who are not working full-time and whose income from all sources falls below officially established standards. Besides the unemployed, elderly pensioners and single mothers at home are eligible. The division in SB between unemployed claimants and others fluctuates cyclically, with the unemployed accounting for 21 to 58 percent of total expenditures on SB from 1973–74 to 1983–84 (Reissert, 1985a, Table 8). SB can be paid in addition to unemployment benefits, or by itself to unemployed persons who have exhausted benefits or do not qualify; thus, school-leavers who have never worked are eligible. Of the registered unemployed who receive SB, the majority draw it alone, without unemployment benefits (OECD, 1976b, p. 28; Reissert, 1985a, Table 1).

A special program, redundancy payments, also compensates the unemployed. Paid out of a special fund started in 1965 and built on mandatory employer contributions, redundancy payments compensate qualified workers who are disemployed, individually or in groups, for economic reasons. The lump-sum payments are for loss of job and are paid even if the worker promptly obtains a new job or draws unemployment benefits. Beneficiaries of all three programs continue to receive family allowances, which are administered under an independent program.

Sweden

In Sweden, two parallel programs cover different sections of the labor force, including the self-employed. Eighty percent of the labor force is covered by forty-five unemployment insurance societies, operated mainly by trade unions. These are voluntary organizations, approved and regulated by the government, to which members pay variable but low contributions based on industrial or occupational vulnerability to unemployment. The funds pay the qualified unemployed a variable scale of daily unemployment benefits, based on prior earnings, with a maximum duration. Older workers have an extended duration. Workers' contributions cover only a small share of total costs, with the remainder made up by government, which, in turn, draws part of its contribution from a payroll tax on employers (Johannesson, 1984, p. 16; Schmid, 1984).

In 1974, Sweden introduced a cash assistance program (KAS) to pay daily unemployment allowances for a limited time period to people who were not members of insurance societies and who had a stipulated amount of qualifying employment. The principal targets are unemployed new entrants and reentrants, though some people who exhaust insurance benefits may also qualify. KAS is financed by the government, in part from the proceeds from the employer payroll tax. KAS payments are much smaller than UI benefits and, for families with children, they may be less than the social welfare payments of municipalities. These may supplement benefits or assist those whose UI or KAS has run out. The generous family allowances program continues to operate during unemployment, and no dependents' benefits are paid by UI or KAS.

France

France has frequently changed the programs, administration, and financing of its income replacement system for the unemployed (OECD, 1976d; Bruche, 1982, 1984a; Eurostat, 1984, pp. 84–86). Since 1984, one part of the program has insurance elements and is operated by forty-six associations (ASSEDIC) formed, regulated, and financed under collective bargaining agreements and reinforced by legislation. ASSEDIC unemployment benefits cover a high proportion of employees in the private sector, including agriculture, and are financed from contributions by covered workers and their employers. They offer two main benefit programs, basic benefits and end-of-entitlement allowances. Unemployed persons sixty years old or older who do not qualify for full old-age pensions can receive basic unemployment benefits until they have the required number of contributions or reach age sixty-five. The end-of-entitlement allowance resembles the unemployment allowance of West Germany or Austria, but the French system has no means test.

The second branch of current French unemployment benefit programs is financed entirely by the national government. Called "solidarity payments," it consists of three elements: an integration allowance for unemployed youth (sixteen to twenty-five years old) who have completed a recognized academic or vocational course, have been employed previously for three months or more, or have completed military service; a variable solidarity allowance for the long-term unemployed with previous insurable employment; and lastly, allowances to persons attending training courses, unemployed persons setting up their own businesses, and persons fifty-five and older taking early retirement under solidarity contracts in which jobs are created for younger workers (Eurostat, 1984, pp. 184–186). Family allowances are continued for all unemployed persons.

The European systems exhibit wide variation among themselves as well as significant departures from the American model. The variability is further increased by the specifics of provisions regarding coverage, eligibility for benefits, computation and levels of benefits, and duration of benefits (Eurostat, 1984; Garcia de Blas, 1985; EIRR, 1982; Blaustein and Craig, 1977; Sorrentino, 1976). Such differences, however, are not the focus of this paper, except as they bear on basic trends in European UI systems.

2. The Course and Causes of the Rise of UI Expenditures and Policy Responses

Growth of UI Costs

UI costs rose more sharply in the 1970s than in the 1960s. An OECD study (1984b, pp. 193–194) of seven countries for 1960–80 found that average UI benefits expenditures (in 1975 prices) almost doubled during the 1960s and more than trebled in the 1970s. Another OECD analysis of UI expenditures for 1960–75 (in constant prices) showed an average increase of 180 percent in the same seven countries: the United States, Japan, Germany, Canada, France, Italy, and the United Kingdom (OECD *Observer,* 1984). In the period 1973–82, the author's study of a group of six countries, which includes four of the countries studied by OECD, showed an even greater rate of increase (Table 6.3, column 2).

Between 1973 and 1982, four European countries experienced greater cost increases (in constant prices) than did the United States (Table 6.3); only Great Britain's costs rose more slowly. The OECD (1984b, pp. 193–194) analyzed the average annual real growth rate in UI expenditures for seven countries over the period 1960–80, dividing the time span into four periods. France, Germany, the United Kingdom, and the United States all showed more increases than decreases. Three of these four countries experienced the highest rate of increase in 1970–75; only the United Kingdom had its greatest rise in 1965–70.

UI expenditures as percentage shares of the GNP, while remaining modest, rose two- to threefold in the United States and five European countries from 1973 to 1982 (Table 6.3, column 4). The average rise in share of GDP (in 1975 prices) was greater in the 1970s than in the 1960s in the OECD seven-country study (OECD, 1984b, p. 194).[2] UI expenditures (in 1975 prices) generally increased as a percentage of total expenditures on income maintenance measures, according to the OECD study (1984b, p. 194). These varied among the nations, largely because of Western Europe's commitment to a more complex and generous set of additional income maintenance programs than are found in North America; disability pensions are a case in point. Canada spent between 8.43 and 17.35 percent of its income maintenance budget on UI benefits during 1960–80, with the United States next, ranging from 4.81 percent to 9.92 percent. Japan (except in one period), France, Germany, and the United Kingdom were under 5 percent, Italy under 2 percent.

Table 6.3. Expenditures on Unemployment Insurance, Six Countries, 1973–82

| Country | Change in Expenditures, 1973–82 (index numbers) | | | Expenditure on UI Benefits as Percentage of | | | | | |
	1 Total (current prices)	2 Total (constant prices; 1973 = 100)	3 Per Recipient	4/GNP 1973	1982	5 Total Expenditures on Employment Programs[a] (current prices) 1973	1975	1980	1982
Austria	681	401	343	0.15	0.43	37.0	38.8	39.1	43.4
France	2567	968	na	0.2	1.4	18.6	34.2	40.8	41.4
Germany	1292	861	143	0.15	1.13	20.4	43.0	36.8	47.0
Great Britain	852	245	51	0.25	0.56	34.1[b]	36.7[b]	30.9[b]	21.7[b]
Sweden[c]	786	333	121[d]	0.3	0.9	15.1	13.8	13.8	24.0
United States[e]	543	278	104	0.35	0.81	42.1	70.2	55.2	69.6

Sources: Bruche, 1984a, Tables 1, 2; Bruche, 1984b, Tables 1–3; Bruche and Reissert, 1985a, Tables 1, 2, 5; Reissert, 1985a, Tables 2–5, 16; Reissert, 1985b, Tables 1, 5, 7; Schmid, 1984, Tables 1, 3, 4; Wadensjö, 1985, Table A6; author's calculations.

[a]Called Labor Market programs in some countries. Totals include expenditures on all passive (UI, etc.) as well as active measures (training, etc.). In Germany totals exclude special federal government labor market programs and state and local measures. In Sweden totals exclude regional development and industrial policy programs.

[b]Budget years 1974–75, 1975–76, 1980–81, 1982–83.

[c]Data are for 1974–83 in columns 1–4; in column 5, 1974 data under 1973 entry.

[d]Calculated from average daily benefit during the year.

[e]Includes programs for special groups, such as railroad workers (Reissert, 1985b).

In four of the six countries, expenditures on UI benefits as a percentage of total expenditures on all public employment and training programs (including UI and UA) rose considerably from 1973 to 1982 (Table 6.3, column 5). In the United States, "passive" benefits dominate "active" training and employment programs, whereas the reverse is true of Sweden and recently of Great Britain.[3] Sweden's deliberate policy since the late 1950s has been to emphasize active labor market programs that foster the adaptability and mobility of the labor force and improve the position of disadvantaged groups, areas, and industries, rather than UI and other passive income replacement programs.[4]

Why UI Costs Rose; Policy Responses

Real expenditures on UI benefits can rise for several reasons: changes in the levels, composition, and duration of unemployment; changes in the size of the labor force and the share covered by UI; changes in coverage and eligibility rules and benefits; and changes in family circumstances and previous earnings of unemployed persons.

The OECD analysis for 1960–75 of seven large countries allocated the average annual percentage increase in real expenditure on benefits among three factors: changes in demographic patterns, changes in coverage, and changes in real benefit levels. Establishing changes in real benefit levels as the most important factor, this study also cited changes in the numbers covered by UI (growth of population, labor force, and unemployment), but found no influence from changes in eligibility for benefits (OECD *Observer*, 1984).

Another study by the OECD (1984b, pp. 193–204) of the same countries (France, Germany, the United Kingdom, the United States, Canada, Italy, and Japan) found that in the two decades from 1960 to 1980, changes in the unemployment rate and in discretionary policy were of the greatest importance in explaining expenditure trends. Less important and variable in their effect among countries and over time were the size of the labor force, the average level of UI benefits,[5] the average length of time during which benefits are paid, and the number of UI recipients (see Table 6.4).[6] The following general points emerged:

— The behavior of the individual factors has not been constant over the period and the contribution of each to UI expenditures has also been changing.
— Certain factors, such as number of beneficiaries, are more affected than others by changes in level of economic activity. Important lags in effect also occur.
— Cyclical influences and long-term trends tend to interact so that the influence of the underlying factors changes over time.
— The slowdown in annual growth rates of UI expenditure in 1979–80 has

Table 6.4. Number Receiving UI Benefits and Percentage of Unemployed Receiving UI Benefits, Six Countries, 1973–83 (monthly average)

	1973	1974	1975	1976	1977	1978	1979	1980	1981	1982	1983
Number of Persons Receiving UI Benefits (thousands)											
Austria	33.6		35.0		33.0			34.9		66.9	75.3
France	127.7	151.8	225.2								
Germany	154	352	707	615	557	516	448	454	698	926	1,014
Great Britain[a]	210	292	553	na	589	517	494	984	na	1,013	938
Sweden[b]		8,625	8,718	8,128	8,161	10,597	11,036	10,666	14,485	20,018	23,594
United States[c]	1,793	2,558	6,116	4,974	3,683	2,686	2,592	3,837	3,410	4,795	4,660
Percentage of Unemployed Receiving UI Benefits											
Austria	81.3		68.5		61.5			65.7		63.5	59.2
France	32.4	30.5	35.4								
Germany	56	60	66	58	54	55	51	51	55	51	45
Great Britain[a]	39.2	44.6	49.0	na	41.8	40.6	40.6	49.5	na	33.9	31.2
Sweden[b]		41	50	47	42	45	48	47	52	56	60
United States[c]	41.1	49.6	77.1	67.2	52.7	43.3	42.2	50.2	41.2	44.9	43.5

Sources: Bruche, 1984b, Table 3; OECD, 1976d, Table 6; Bruche and Reissert, 1985a, Table 2; Reissert, 1985a, Table 1; Reissert, 1985b, Table 5; Wadensjö, 1985, Table 3; author's calculations.
[a]November data.
[b]Number of persons not available. Data show annual total days of unemployment and percentage of days compensated by UI benefits.
[c]Includes all UI programs.

been reversed by the rise in unemployment since 1981. But the tightening of eligibility and payment criteria and slow or negative growth in the real value of benefits are containing expenditures (OECD, 1984b, pp. 203–204).

The main factors in increased UI expenditures in Germany during 1970–75 were the close correlation between UI expenditures and changes in total unemployment; extensions of UI coverage; a drop in the percentage of beneficiaries to total unemployed in 1970–73 (with a return to the 1970 level by 1975 due to changes in the composition of the unemployed by insurance status); changes in the composition and type of unemployment by age, sex, occupational status, and family situation; rises in the average amount of benefits received due to increased average earnings in current terms; a change in family supplement payments; a revised benefit formula adopted in 1975; and a lengthening of the average duration of unemployment, especially in 1974–75 (OECD, 1976a, pp. 11–27).

Reviewing the longer period, 1973–83, Bruche and Reissert (1985a, pp. 12–14) found that expenditures on UI in Germany rose sharply between 1973 and 1975 and between 1979 and 1982; from 1976 to 1978, there was a drop in outlays, although the level was above that for 1973 and 1974. The transfer in mid-1978 from the Treasury to the FEI of contributions to the pension systems on behalf of UI recipients increased per capita expenditures on UI by 31 percent between 1978 and 1979, despite a decline in the number of recipients. Significant savings in FEI outlays have resulted from the reduced contributions to pensions permitted in 1983 and reduced benefits for unmarried unemployed in 1984.

The rise in the number of UI recipients between 1973 and 1975 and 1980 and 1983 was the most important cause of increased spending in Germany from the beginning to the end of the period, although the proportion of the unemployed eligible for UI declined in almost every year from 1976 to 1983. This downtrend is attributed to the increased percentage among total unemployed of entrants and reentrants to the labor market with low or no insurance eligibility and the exhaustion of UI benefits by long-term unemployed. Between 1982 and 1983 the unemployed shifted from UI to UA due to changes in the composition of unemployment as well as tighter requirements for UI eligibility (Bruche and Reissert, 1985a, pp. 14–15, Table 2; Karr, 1978).

UI costs soared in many European countries due to enhancement of UI conditions and benefits during the first years of rising unemployment after 1973. In the first half of the 1980s these countries achieved cost containment through tightened eligibility criteria, slow or negative growth in the real value of benefits, and/or restructured programs to limit the UI portion of total income replacement programs for the unemployed (Reissert, 1985a; Bruche, 1984a; OECD, 1984b). Such cutbacks have been tied to the efforts of European nations to cover their rising UI costs without excessive demands on their financing sources. In face of sluggish employment growth, these nations are likely to maintain favorable UI benefit and other provisions for older workers as an incentive to reduce the labor force and recorded unemployment.

The main methods of augmenting funds available to UI systems are increased contributions from employers and workers, special assessments, income from reserve funds, drawing down reserve funds, borrowing, and an increased share of costs shifted to the government. The five European countries studied resorted to increased contribution rates, although they varied in extent (Table 6.5). Nevertheless, the total intake from employer and employee contributions formed a declining share of UI expenditures after 1973 in four European countries; no calculation was made for the United States (Bruche, 1984b; Bruche and Reissert, 1985a; Bruche, 1984a; Wadensjö, 1985; Reissert, 1985b). Further increases in payroll taxes to support UI would be unpopular and are feared in most European countries as an impediment to employment growth.

Some countries require drawing down reserve funds and others permit borrowing. When deficits continue in spite of these measures, governments provide subsidies, in most cases by law. Governments also assume certain costs, such as all or part of administrative costs or continuation of contributions to old-age, health, and other insurance, on behalf of UI recipients. The government's share of expenditures from 1973 to 1982 was highest in Sweden and lowest in Austria (Table 6.5, column 3).[7] The share decreased in Austria and increased in the United States but fluctuated elsewhere. In most countries, government funding offers only limited relief. Restraints on expenditures appear to be the main recourse.

3. Adequacy of UI Benefits

UI or Other Income Replacement for the Unemployed

The proportion of the labor force legally covered by UI systems has increased steadily in the postwar period.[8] However, the percentage of the unemployed receiving UI benefits is smaller than the share of the labor force covered by UI programs. This occurs in part because those most likely to become unemployed have lower rates of UI coverage than others, and in part because covered workers either fail to meet eligibility requirements or exhaust their benefits. The proportion of the unemployed on UI benefits in Austria, Germany, and Great Britain was lower in 1983 than in 1973, reflecting not only the further rise in unemployment in the 1980s, but also the tightening of eligibility (Table 6.4; Bruche and Reissert, 1985a; Reissert, 1985a; OECD, 1984b, pp. 200–202). This continuing

Table 6.5. Rates of Contribution by Employers and Employees to Unemployment Insurance, and Government Share of Total UI Expenditures, Five Countries, 1973–84

	1 Employer (% of eligible payroll)				2 Employee (% of eligible earnings)				3 Government Share of Total UI Expenditures (%)				
	1973	1975	1979	1984	1973	1975	1979	1984	1973	1975	1979	1980	1982
Austria[a]	1.0	1.0	1.05	2.2	1.0	1.0	1.05	2.2	8.4	6.1	6.6	6.5	4.9
France[b]	0.56	1.92	2.76	4.08	0.14	0.48	0.84	1.72	29.1	24.8	9.6	25.8	34.9
Germany[a]	0.85	1.00	1.50	2.3	0.85	1.00	1.50	2.3	0	40.8	0	8.5	21.0
Great Britain[c]		8.50	10.00	10.45		5.50	6.50	9.00	14.0	15.0	18.0	18.0	13.0
Sweden	0.4[d]	0.4[d]	0.4[d]	1.3[d]	e		e	e	73.5[f]	39.8[f]	50.9[f]	49.4[f]	40.4[f]
United States[g]									7.0	15.0	11.0	17.0	18.0

Sources: Hart, 1982, Table 1; Mittelstädt, 1975, Table 1; Blaustein and Craig, 1977, Table 2; Bruche, 1984b, Tables 4, 7; Bruche, 1984a, Tables 4, 5; Bruche, 1982, Table 1; Bruche and Reissert, 1985a, Tables 5, 6, 12; Reissert, 1985a, Table 6; Reissert, 1985b, Table 3; Schmid, 1984, pp. 20–23, Table 7; Wadensjö, 1985, Table A2; author's calculations.

[a] In Austria and Germany, contributions and expenditures are for active labor market programs as well as unemployment benefits, allowances, etc. Column 3 for Austria shows 1977 data under 1979.

[b] Employer and employee rates as of end of year. Data in column 3 not entirely comparable before and after 1979.

[c] Includes contributions and expenditures on all social insurance programs (old age, health, disability, maternity). UI accounted for 4 to 10 percent of all expenditures in 1973–84.

[d] For UI and KAS, 1974–82. From 1983, tax also for labor market training, previously under a separate payroll tax.

[e] Varies from fund to fund.

[f] From 1975, excludes part of government subsidy drawn from tax on employers imposed in 1974.

[g] Tax on employers varies from state to state. Most states do not tax employees; column 3 includes advances from General Fund for UI Trust Funds expenditures on special groups; and supplemental programs.

trend, not fully revealed by data ending in 1983, contrasts with the early 1970s in France, Germany, Great Britain, and the United States, when the proportion of the unemployed receiving UI benefits rose. These increases were a response to the influx into unemployment of workers with long employment records as well as to greater coverage, new programs, and easing of eligibility rules.

Whether the reduced share of the unemployed receiving UI benefits represents a deterioration in position depends on the alternative sources of income to unemployed persons. In Great Britain between 1973 and 1983, the emphasis shifted from UI to supplementary benefits.[9] During the same decade, the proportion of the unemployed who received neither UI nor SB shrank from close to one-fourth to 12.7 percent (Reissert, 1985a, Table 1).

The decline in the proportion of British unemployed not on any national income replacement program is a sign of progress. The shift from UI to SB is not necessarily adverse since the 1978 Cohort Study of Unemployed Men by the British Department of Health and Social Security found that the payments of UI and SB were quite similar and that family income replacement rates of men on SB alone were very close to those of men on UI alone (White, 1983; OECD, 1984b, pp. 121–133). However, earned UI benefits may yield higher psychic income than means-tested SB.

Germany showed a less favorable trend, although the proportion of the unemployed on UI was higher than in Great Britain. From 1973 to 1983, the proportion of the unemployed receiving unemployment allowances (UA) climbed from 8 to 21 percent. Unlike the British case, the maximum German UA payment is set at 10 percent below UI benefits, and in actuality, many UA recipients reveive less than the statutory maximum, since other resources, such as a spouse's earnings, reduce UA. In April 1983, it was estimated that about one-third of UA recipients were on reduced payments (Bruche and Reissert, 1985a, p. 82). The residual group receiving neither UI nor UA remained large and stable at around one-third of all registered unemployed (Bruche and Reissert, 1985a, Table 2).

Even if some unemployed subsequently entered training or employment programs that paid stipends equivalent to UI or obtained local welfare, the figures show a disturbing consistency year after year in the proportion reported as unemployed and without UI or UA. The number of unemployed recipients of public assistance grew dramatically in industrial cities. In response to the restrictions placed on both UI and UA, some unemployed Germans sought supplementation or full support from local welfare.[10] The burden on localities in aiding the unemployed has grown since 1978, when an insignificant share of the total cost was borne by local governments.[11] A stationary percentage of the unemployed without provision implies an even worse absolute position in the face of rising unemployment totals. Even in Great Britain the absolute number of unemployed without provision tripled between 1973 and 1983 (128,000 to 383,000), despite a reduced relative share (Reissert, 1985a, Table 1). The Austrian data, although not reliable, show a stabilization since 1975 in the high proportion of unemployed in neither program. From less than 10 percent in 1973, the proportion of unemployed in neither program settled at about 25 percent thereafter (Table 6.4; Bruche, 1984b, Table 3).

The proportion of the unemployed who are members of Swedish UI funds has risen dramatically over the years, especially among women. In 1963, one-third of males between the ages of sixteen and seventy-four were covered; by 1982 it was 60 percent. For females, the proportion increased from 7 percent in 1963 to 50 percent by 1982 (Björklund and Holmlund, 1983, Table 3). Not all of the unemployed members actually collect UI benefits, however. From 1974 through 1984, it is estimated that the percentage of the Swedish unemployed who received UI benefits rose from 41 to 69 percent, while the percentage receiving KAS increased from 10 to 18 percent. This leaves as many as one-half in 1974, descending to 13 percent by 1984, dependent on the social welfare payments of local governments (Schmid, 1984, p. 10; Wadensjö, 1985, Table 3). Because Sweden has no national unemployment assistance program, unemployed persons whose UI or KAS benefits expire have the legal right to publicly created jobs through which they acquire eligibility once more to UI or KAS. These "transitional measures," introduced in the 1970s and made a legal right in the 1980s, are credited with the much smaller proportion of long-term unemployed in Sweden than in other Western European countries (Schmid, 1984, p. 19).

The evidence for a few countries suggests that for much of the period fewer than half of the unemployed received UI benefits. At the same time, it is not well established how levels of payment on UA and local welfare programs compared with UI benefits.

Replacement Ratios

How well off are those on UI benefits compared with their prior earnings from full-time work? Although this appears to be a straightforward question, the definition and computation of appropriate replacement ratios (RR) are complex, especially for comparative purposes (OECD, 1984b, pp. 98–106). The first comparative efforts simply measured the percentage of average weekly earnings that were replaced by average weekly UI benefits (Mittelstädt, 1975; Sorrentino, 1976; Blaustein and Craig, 1977). The OECD has rejected this approach in favor of a more comprehensive RR that takes account of net loss of income while unemployed and net additions from all sources while unemployed. For example, net earnings may vary because of payroll deductions for income tax, social security, and other items that may also be deducted from UI benefits. On the other hand, the unemployed may collect benefits in addition to basic UI—benefits that may also be available to them when they work, often based on income or means testing. Net benefits may also vary by family size. Some countries have different systems in different regions or for different occupational groups. These and other factors can significantly affect the calculation of replacement ratios (OECD, 1984a, p. 92).

Efforts to measure replacement ratios in a comparative context with a more complex methodology resulted in a six-nation study by OECD in the mid-1970s (OECD, 1979; 1984b, pp. 107–108), a study in 1982 by the European Community of ten member countries, and a further OECD study for six countries (OECD, 1982; 1984b, pp. 108–117). All of these examined short periods of unemployment within a year, and most confined themselves to data for a single year, thereby making it impossible to draw conclusions about trends. The one exception was the UN Economic Commission for Europe (ECE), which examined replacement ratios from 1972 to 1982 in fourteen Western European countries, three south European countries, Canada, and the United States (UN, 1983, pp. 289–306).

Because the ECE results are for a large number of countries and cover a time period of interest to us, we present the conclusions (despite some limitations in the methodology).

- UI benefits were lower than previous take-home pay in all countries and at all times.
- The replacement ratios varied significantly among countries, with losses ranging from 8 percent to more than 50 percent.
- The income loss was greater for a single than a married man in most countries, though not in Austria, Denmark, Norway, Switzerland, Spain, or the United States.
- Replacement ratios for the majority of countries remained unchanged or fell between 1972 and 1982, but they rose markedly in France, Sweden (after 1975), Portugal (during the early 1980s), and less sharply in Italy.
- A study of Finland and the United Kingdom calculated earnings using an alternative method based on the base average earnings of typical unemployed workers while employed; it found a sharp decline over time in replacement ratios.

Another research issue is net replacement ratios for longer time periods, weighing all forms of replacement income, because unemployment may continue after UI benefits are exhausted. A study of hypothetical families entering long-term unemployment in five countries was conducted in 1982 by a French research agency (CERC). This was followed by an OECD study which assessed how the incomes of model families in five countries change as the principal earner moves from full-time employment into a prolonged spell of unemployment (OECD, 1984a, pp. 93–96). The conclusion was that there is a wide disparity in income replacement during unemployment. This is so both between countries for families of the same type at broadly comparable earnings levels, and between families of different composition at a range of earnings levels within countries. Unemployment generally implies a substantial drop in net income, although there are exceptions (OECD, 1984a, p. 96).

For a married couple on average earnings with no children, the RR during the first year of unemployment ranged between 35.9 percent in the United States and 68.5 percent in Canada; for single people the variation is even greater. Replacement ratios by family size as well as earnings level were as high as over 90 percent for two-child families previously receiving half or less than average earnings in Australia and the United Kingdom; when the more typical average earnings are assumed, the RR ranged from 41 percent in the United States to 72 percent in Canada. In most of the countries the continuation of the spouse's earnings means that family income during the first earner's unemployment falls relatively less, or in other words the replacement ratio is higher.

In addition, the study found that in some countries RRs tend to decline over time as UI benefits terminate and unemployed people move from a non-means-tested scheme on to a means-tested scheme; the value of the contribution of the second earner will tend to decline sharply, since it limits the means-tested benefit of the principal earner. This study demonstrated that the replacement ratios established for long-term unemployment are much lower than those for short-term and display much more variation.

Some national studies of replacement ratios, however, have discovered much higher replacement ratios than the series of comparative studies described here, leading to charges that UI benefits serve as a work disincentive, the next subject for discussion.

4. Effects of UI Benefits on Work Incentives

If workers lose only a small part of their disposable income when they become unemployed, they may be dilatory in beginning their job search, perhaps waiting until their UI benefits are about to expire. They may also search for a job less actively than they would with a lower RR. Finally, the level of replacement income will influence the wage they are willing to accept on a new job, the reservation wage.

In a cross-national framework, no correlation appears between the level of RRs in a country and the extent or depth of its belief that RRs are too high and act as a work disincentive. In fact, countries with relatively low RRs may be most vocal on the issue. Moreover, in countries where this issue has been raised, the volume of comment has not responded much to the downward trends in RRs noted by the UN Economic Commission for Europe:

> the fact that for the majority of countries considered the replacement ratio has either remained unchanged or has fallen since 1972 suggests that unemployment benefits have had little to do with the increase in unemployment since 1974, and especially with the large increase since 1979. (UN, 1983, p. 295)

The adverse effects of UI benefits on work incentives appear to concern the English-speaking countries around the world far more than continental Europe. Great Britain, the United States, and Canada provide the bulk of academic contributions on this issue. A partial list of output between 1975 and 1984, leaving aside the United States, shows a preponderance of British studies (for example, Atkinson, 1981, 1982; Benjamin and Kochin, 1979; Layard and Nickell, 1985; Maki and Spindler, 1975; Minford, 1984; Narendrananthan et al., 1983; Nickell, 1979; Spindler and Maki, 1978; Stern, 1984). Canada has also produced a number of studies (for example, Kaliski, 1975, 1976; Green and Cousineau, 1976).

For the most part, the academic multicountry studies find that UI benefits in some degree deter the search for a job and prolong the duration of spells of unemployment (Walsh, 1981). Grubel and Walker (1978) assembled ten country studies of which seven showed that by lowering the cost to the unemployed of not looking for work, UI benefits increase voluntary unemployment. Significant effects were found in the United States, Canada, Ireland, and the United Kingdom, but only limited evidence of induced unemployment was cited for France, New Zealand, and Belgium, and Germany and Italy showed no effects. In Italy, flat-rate unemployment benefits, financed by a payroll tax on employers, are very low and are used much less than an alternative system of benefits for temporary layoff and short-time working (EIRR, 1982, p. 12).

Great Britain has translated these academic findings into official doctrine; the Thatcher government abolished earnings-related UI benefits in 1982, leaving only the basic flat-rate benefit, on the grounds of adverse effects on job search (Reissert, 1985a; Disney and Metcalf, 1983, p. 14ff.).

In contrast, discussions and public concern are rarer in the continental European countries and in Scandinavia, where replacement rates are relatively high (Björklund and Holmlund, 1983, p. 108ff.; Bruche and Reissert, 1984, pp. 43–46). A recent German analysis contends that the UI system protects the existing wage structure, the skills hierarchy, and working conditions on the job against the adverse effects of unemployment. Reductions of UI payments or restrictive definitions strengthen the employers' bargaining position while undermining that of the unions (Bruche and Reissert, 1985a, p. 180). This social function might be regarded less benignly in other countries.

Continental Europeans tend to agree with an OECD multicountry report that declared:

> [A] small but not negligible amount of additional unemployment may be induced by the level of benefits, but that these benefits are intended to raise social welfare, and the fact that people prolong their job search by an extra week or two may well improve the match between their skills and job opportunities and reduce labour turnover in the longer run. (OECD, 1979, p. 14)

The OECD Secretariat addressed related policy issues at its 1982 international conference on income support policies during a period of high unemployment (OECD, 1984b, pp. 14, 81, 87–88). However, only a few in attendance mentioned work disincentives or other distorting effects on the labor market from UI benefits. Rather, participants pointed to factors other than replacement rates that affect unemployment durations. They suggested that governments could more accurately test UI recipients' willingness to work by taking responsibility for effective placement services and job offers (OECD, 1984b, pp. 95, 125, 134–136). An earlier review of the academic literature for OECD declared that although the phenomenon of insurance-induced unemployment exists, its importance should not be exaggerated, especially not in the post-1979 period (Walsh, 1981, p. 61).

Despite increased sophistication in recent economic studies of the work disincentives of UI benefits, many questions persist about the concepts, methodology, and data, including the way the RR is derived and interpreted. For example, RRs based on prior earnings—the usual measure for such studies—may be less relevant to reservation wages than the comparison of disposable resources during unemployment with those on the proposed new job (OECD, 1984b, p. 135).

The following selection of unresolved issues is drawn from a British presentation to the 1982 OECD conference on income support policies (1984b, pp. 121–133). Hypothetical rather than actual income data are faulted, as are the limited number of worker or family types studied compared to the great diversity in reality. The studies need a complete distribution of RRs, rather than averages. Although the most appropriate unit for measuring RRs may be the household, we still do not know enough about income sharing within households or whether decisions about working are made on an individual, family, or household basis. For most countries, it is misleading to compute the RR only for recipients of UI, omitting the unemployed receiving other income replacement. More insights are needed into the thinking of unemployed persons about RRs, their alternatives, and what time frame (weekly, monthly, annual) they use. Such information might indicate that some theoretical models are inappropriate for predicting behavior. For policy purposes it is important to know how the RR changes over time for particular unemployed individuals. Should RRs be computed for the working population also, so that studies can be made of the motivations of remaining in work when high RRs are available for not working? Might a high RR indicate too low a wage while unemployed?

Other questions have arisen in studies on the effects of UI on labor force participation and migration rates, the aggregate unemployment rate, the distribution of unemployment among various age-sex groups and those insured and not insured under UI, and registered versus unregistered unemployment (Walsh, 1981). Some economists have developed optimal UI programs to minimize work disincentives and have suggested reforms, some of which were implemented in the 1970s.[12]

Another approach to the subject stresses that existing analyses are lopsided, concentrating on the effects of UI on the supply of labor (Harrison and Hart, 1982). The reduced form equation in most analyses, with deviations from the trend in output used to capture influences on the demand side, is considered inappropriate for two reasons. First, the underlying structure of the labor market has not been explicitly outlined, and as a result the structural parameters cannot be retrieved. Second, the possible effects of UI programs on employment or unemployment via the demand for labor has been ignored by most analysts outside the United States, as has the potential of demand influences for confounding the estimation of a labor-supply response from a reduced form equation.

Specifying a complete model of the labor market and using British data from between World Wars I and II, Harrison and Hart (1982) found that UI influenced unemployment via the demand for labor, and at the same time discovered little evidence of the effect of UI benefits on the supply of labor or labor force participation. Hart (1982) found effects of UI on firms' employment and layoff strategies in European countries and the United States. This challenge to the most common analytic approach to work incentives and UI benefits suggests that the last word on work disincentives has not been said.

5. Expanded Use of Unemployment Insurance

European countries have utilized UI benefit funds in a number of ways that the United States has not tried at all or tried only in a limited way (OECD, 1984b, pp. 139–140). The main purpose of European innovation has been "to provide income support for employment-related activities other than job search" (p. 140). Such programs have been most common in periods when jobs were scarce. It should be emphasized that arrangements by which the unemployed who are entitled to benefits are instead moved into active labor market programs, as occurs routinely in Sweden, are not an illustration of an alternative use of UI benefit moneys. In fact such arrangements preserve the funds of UI systems instead of using them. A less clear-cut situation arises in Germany or Austria because a distinct fund for financing UI benefits does not exist, and the alternative use of UI moneys is not as relevant as is the division of total funds among passive and active labor market programs. Alternative uses of UI moneys are most significant when UI funds are legally and administratively separated from the funding of employment and training programs.

We can discern at least three major types of innovation in using UI funds. The first, common in Europe, compensates workers whose unemployment is less than full-time. The second permits fully unemployed persons on UI to draw benefits while undertaking an activity to improve their labor market position, such as training or education or, in the newest idea, establishing a business as an entrepreneur. In the last type, UI reserve funds are used to support particular programs, such as early retirement, public training courses or allowances, private firm on-the-job training, or temporary employment, as well as employment subsidies to employers making net new hirings of UI recipients.

The ability of a country to engage in these three types of alternative use of UI funds is heavily dependent on legal, financial, and administrative constraints. The legal issue is often overlooked when Americans refer admiringly to a specific feature of a foreign system. For example, German support for various types of training through the moneys collected to pay UI benefits is mandated by the 1969 Employment Promotion Act. In a nation such as the United States, where the UI system is firmly rooted in the job search concept and where availability for work and active job search are regarded as conditions for receiving benefits, it may not be legal to use benefit money for the second and third types of activity described above.

How UI is financed has a marked effect on whether there is the capability and incentive to use UI funds for alternative purposes. The main financing methods are

- Wholly or largely out of government general revenues (as, for example, in Australia)
- Mixed contributory and government financing in a changing program framework (France)
- Mostly contributory, but contributions finance labor market programs as well as UI (Austria, Germany)
- Contributory for basic UI (United States)

Each of these financing methods produces its own constraints and incentives. In Germany, for example, the prior claims of UI benefits limit expenditures on training and other active labor market programs, so that the desired countercyclical policy cannot be implemented. Moreover, the distribution of budgetary and fiscal net costs among agencies does not give the FEI, the main agency, financial incentives to direct recipients of UI benefits to alternative programs run by FEI (Schmid, 1983; Bruche and Reissert, 1985a).

Administrative considerations also constrain the use of UI funds for alternative purposes. If a training or education course lasts longer than an individual's entitlement to UI benefits, should such benefits be cut off? Is there a minimum benefit duration below which an alternative use of benefits should not be permitted? Is it possible to estimate the claims of future beneficiaries accurately enough to make allocations to other uses? These are questions that face all funds, but they may be more sensitive issues in some than in others. Differences between countries in the ease with which they can adopt an alternative use of UI benefits are significant. They should not be overlooked by Americans who are intrigued by a particular program and discuss its replication in the United States purely in terms of the details of the program itself. Notwithstanding these caveats, the rest of this section describes European programs that may be of interest to Americans.

Organized Partial Unemployment (Short-time Working)

A 1982 survey found that eleven OECD countries offer short-time benefits (OECD, 1984b, pp. 141–142). Short-time benefits are paid to a worker whose hours have been reduced by the firm. By allowing across-the-board reductions of hours, they make it possible for enterprises to avoid a choice between full-time work for some and layoff or dismissal for others when the economy is slack or when the firm has a loss of orders.

For example, the payment of benefits for short-time working is an established part of the German UI system, financed by the contributions of employers and workers.[13] These benefits are viewed not only as means for maintaining income and promoting social equity, but also as an active labor market program that tends to maintain employment while operating countercyclically (Schmid, 1983; Bruche and Reissert, 1985a; OECD, 1984b, pp. 160–166). The FEI has actively encouraged firms to use short-time work since 1975.

Short-time benefits are payable for reduced hours of work only in German firms that cut back production due to economic circumstances beyond the firm's control. Firms are not entitled to short-time benefits if they cut back due to seasonal patterns, customary procedures, or internal reorganization. (Homeworkers are also covered if they lose more than 20 percent of their customary earnings due to a lack of work.) Cutbacks lasting at least four weeks in which one-third of the work force loses 10 percent of its work time are reported to the local employment exchange office which must certify the firm. Firms make the payments to workers and are subsequently reimbursed by the FEI. Firms also pay both the employer and employee contributions to the health insurance and old-age pension systems for the lost working hours, receiving 50 percent reimbursement for the health contributions and 75 percent for the pension from the FEI (OECD, 1976a; Flechsenhar, 1978).

Payments are usually for a maximum of six months, with some exceptions. The Federal Ministry of Labor and Social Affairs may permit particular industries to draw short-time benefits for one or two years. Such extensions have been favored during the post-1973 period as a means of limiting full-time unemployment. Workers are eligible for short-time benefits if they continue to be in insurable work, have not been given notice of termination, and have the appropriate reduction in earnings. Their short-time benefits are paid at the same rate as for normal work benefits and are based on the percentage of net earnings lost through short-time.

The charge that German employers take subsidies for short-time and then make up the hours through overtime or apply for lost time that is not strictly necessary is rebutted on the ground that employers bear a part of the nonwage costs of the lost hours (OECD, 1984b, pp. 161–162). However, this same factor is cited as a reason that employers may not press for as much short-time work as might be socially desirable (Bruche and Reissert, 1985a, p. 120).

The average number of short-time workers fluctuates considerably in a countercyclical manner.[13] Stated as a percentage loss of usual working time, German workers lost 25–30 percent in the 1978–82 period, with each individual averaging 3.5 months on short-time benefits. Over a year, the total number of individuals on short-time was at least three times higher than the monthly average stock (OECD, 1984b, p. 161).

The reduction in full-time unemployment attributable to short-time benefits during 1974–82 ranged from a high of 147,000 saved jobs in 1975 to a low of 19,000 in 1979, with less than 50,000 total in most years (Schmid, 1983, Table 3; OECD, 1984b, p. 157). The official research agency of the FEI estimates that without short-time benefits Germany would have had 202,000 additional unemployed in 1982, of which 70 percent would have been registered unemployed; this is regarded as an upper limit, however (Bruche and Reissert, 1985a, p. 115).

Reviewing the experience of the 1974–80 period, Schmid (1983, Table 3, p. 22) concluded that, in current conditions, "short-time work—reasonably applied—is the most cost-effective instrument of active labor market policy." Costs of short-time benefits per capita were also considerably below those for advanced vocational training and retraining and general job-creation schemes. These same relationships also obtained when total fiscal costs were computed. However, a further analysis of 1982 gross costs and the budgetary offsets for short-time benefits revealed that the FEI bore a heavy net burden, while the federal budget and pensions system ended up with net financial relief (Bruche and Reissert, 1985a, pp. 119–120). In the world of policymaking, the distribution of net financial costs among various public agencies can have a greater impact on decisions than the general and social benefits discerned by economists.

Since the specifics of the German system are not an inherent part of short-time benefit payments, it is possible to devise a system that avoids the fiscal disincentives found in Germany. Other, more general issues in short-time benefits are the potential for subsidizing regular fluctuations in business activity, retarding the adjustment to structural change, helping inefficient firms to survive, or keeping workers in jobs for a while only to dismiss them later when the short-time benefits run out (Schmid, 1983, p. 22; OECD, 1984b, pp. 141–142). Despite such possible drawbacks, this type of benefit particularly recommends itself to American UI because it has a good track record and it raises fewer legal problems than most of the other alternative uses of UI benefits.

Promotion of Self-Employment

European countries have sought various ways of reducing the number of unemployed. One that has particular appeal is the transformation of jobless into self-employed persons who may create jobs for others (Friedman, 1985; OECD, 1985c; *Employment News*). The pressures in Europe to find alternatives to unemployment are more acute than in the United States because of persistently high unemployment rates with increasingly long durations (see Tables 6.1 and 6.2), the negative or very modest growth of total employment, the sluggishness of spontaneous entrepreneurship, and the slow or stagnant development in private sector service activities that could offset the drop in industrial employment and frozen or contracting public sector employment.

Friedman (1985) suggests that the European use of UI funds to encourage entrepreneurship merits replication in the United States. France and Great Britain do indeed offer heartening evidence of a strong response to general programs encouraging entrepreneurship, although the evaluations do not assess the displacement effects or how much new firm creation would have occurred without such programs (Bloch-Michel, 1983; Lachand and Denis, 1983; *Employment News* nos. 122, 133, 1983). More significantly, these countries do not provide usable evidence on the advantages of this type of program as an alternative use of UI benefits.

The Enterprise Allowance Scheme (EAS), initiated experimentally in Great Britain in 1982, serves the unemployed but operates outside of the UI system. EAS is not an alternative use of UI moneys; in fact, by aiding persons who might otherwise be drawing UI benefits, EAS actually relieves the UI fund of obligations. The administration of the program under the

Manpower Services Commission (MSC) and its financing out of the MSC appropriation from general revenues makes it roughly the equivalent of a program financed and operated by the Employment and Training Administration of the Department of Labor in the United States.

France began its program in 1979 with lump-sum grants to unemployed would-be entrepreneurs based on their entitlements under the complicated system of unemployment payments, only a portion of which resemble an American UI program (Bruche, 1982, 1984a). In 1984, the French government assumed complete financial responsibility for the self-employment program and opened it to a wider group of unemployed (OECD, 1985c).

Thus, if the United States were to undertake full-fledged programs to permit UI benefits to be paid to persons seeking to become self-employed, such measures could not currently draw on a body of valid European experience on the effects of the UI system since the European countries with variants of this program have begun operations too recently to provide useful information. One that will bear watching was introduced in 1984 in Sweden. Prior to receiving a monthly grant for a maximum of six months of the same amount as the UI benefit they would have received, newly self-employed persons in Sweden participate in a training course in entrepreneurship (Schmid, 1984).

Programs to Complement Unemployment Insurance

Many European countries compensate the employees of insolvent, reorganized, or otherwise financially incompetent firms for lost wages, fringe benefits, and other payments due them under advance warning of dismissal legislation and / or collective bargaining agreements. Such compensation programs, developed mainly during the period of economic dislocation and high unemployment, are financed by a tax on employers paid into a fund that may be a part of the UI fund or distinct from it. This type of compensation can be seen as complementary to UI benefits, in comparison to unemployment allowances, which are supplementary.

In December 1973 France gave priority to the payment by the official receivers for insolvent businesses of the wages, advance notice pay, and allowances owing to employees. A special employers' association (AGS) was created to establish a fund, financed by an employer payroll tax, out of which workers of insolvent firms are paid. The administration of the scheme was placed in the hands of UNEDIC, the overhead administrative unit for French unemployment insurance (OECD, 1976d, pp. 15–16, 34).

Germany, where an estimated 3 to 4 percent of new job losses in 1980–82 were due to insolvencies (Kohlhuber, 1983, p. 129), legislated a program in July 1974, after pressure from trade unions. The law guarantees employees of bankrupt firms all wages, salaries, and other compensation owed for the three months prior to the beginning of bankruptcy proceedings. Payments are made by the FEI, which recovers actual outlays plus administrative costs through assessments on employers for bankruptcy allowances. Actual collections are made by the FEI through prorated assessments on each trade association. In turn, the trade associations assess their individual members.

When the legislation was under discussion, employers' representatives proposed that bankruptcy allowances be paid out of the mandatory contribution by employers and employees that covers unemployment insurance. The law, however, assesses employers only, because employees were deemed to have already done their share by fulfilling their employment contracts (Bruche and Reissert, 1985a, pp. 36–38). Expenditures (in constant prices) on bankruptcy allowances in Germany rose threefold from 1973 to 1983, but much less than the increase in UI or UA expenditures. Moreover, the total amounts paid out for bankruptcy wage payments are only a small fraction of those for UI and UA and constitute only 1 to 2 percent of all FEI payments (Bruche and Reissert, 1985a, Tables 1, 8).

In 1978, Austria established an Insolvency Fund, financed by a special surtax on employers, in addition to the regular unemployment insurance tax. From 1978 to 1983, the surtax rose from 0.1 to 0.8 percent of payroll. The fund was to be self-financing, with deficits in one year financed by an increased rate in the following year. The payments to workers of bankrupt firms cover deficiencies in wages, salaries, pensions, and allowances with a variable time period, depending on the item in question. In 1982, bankruptcy payments constituted 12.7 percent of all expenditures on passive and active manpower policy; this exceeded the expenditure share of UA (Bruche, 1984b, pp. 21–22, Chart 1, Table 2).

Sweden established a wage guarantee for workers of failed or bankrupt firms in 1971, financed by a payroll tax on employers. It covers up to 12 months of pay loss up to a maximum monthly payment. Expenditures rose rapidly under this program, especially in the recession periods 1976–77 and 1981–82. At the high point in 1981–82, 15–17 percent of the total expenditures on the income maintenance programs—UI, KAS, and the bankruptcy wage guarantee—went to the bankruptcy guarantee. Critics of the program cited too large a deficit and the need to borrow to meet deficits, thus burdening taxpayers and consumers. They also said the program induced bankruptcies and evasion of wage payments by small firms that reorganized and reopened quickly under a new name. In 1984 the maximum annual payment was reduced and the period of compensable wage loss was shortened to six months prior to the bankruptcy (Schmid, 1984, pp. 13, 24, Tables 4, 6).

Finally, the British Redundancy Payments Act of 1965 created a fund and a system of lump-sum payments to workers dismissed for economic reasons, both from bankrupt firms and firms continuing to operate. Workers are eligible to receive redundancy payments regardless of whether they rapidly obtain another job and without prejudice to their UI benefits.

The reported crisis in the U.S. Pension Benefit Guaranty Corporation, established in 1974, gives added point to possible American considera-tion of the European approach (*New York Times*, November 8, 1985). In weighing the establishment of a bankruptcy fund based on employers' contributions, the United States might expand the coverage beyond pension rights to other payments owed to workers.

6. Conclusions

It is not clear which elements of the European UI systems might be feasible or desirable for the United States. European UI systems as a group and individually are not in themselves so superior to the American varieties that the analyst would draw general lessons for the United States from foreign UI statutes, structures, operations, or experience. Each UI system has its own strengths, weaknesses, and idiosyncrasies. None should be replicated elsewhere intact. The purpose of making comparisons among systems, as this paper has done, is to broaden the views of those who deal exclusively with U.S. UI programs, enabling them to draw their own con-clusions, both positive and negative. Although general lessons are not prac-ticable, specific ones may be drawn.

Since 1973, most Western European countries have felt severe pressures on their unemployment insurance systems due to elevated unemployment rates, longer spells of unemployment, and a changed composition of the unemployed since UI was first introduced to protect the prototypical male family breadwinner. A five- to tenfold increase in the number of UI recip-ients from 1973 to 1982 or 1983 was not unusual in European countries. As a result, the current issues for UI systems and employment policy are

—How to finance the added costs of UI benefits
—How to provide adequate UI benefits for recipients and establish programs for those who exhaust UI benefits or do not qualify for benefits
—How to increase the equity of the UI system in its coverage and eligibility, type, amount, and duration of benefits
—How to increase the efficiency of UI systems in aiding labor market adjust-ments and mobility, for example, through the effects of replacement ratios on work incentives and alternative uses of UI funds for more active em-ployment programs
—How to determine the place of UI in a rational employment policy—the division of resources and functions between passive and active labor market programs

The answers given to each of these questions have been as diverse as the basic UI systems themselves. A few common trends may be discerned. One is a tendency for finances to play a powerful role in policy changes and for general government revenues to bear a rising share of total costs of UI. Another is a failure to adjust UI programs to changing labor market and unemployment composition. Finally, alternative uses of UI funds have increased, as has been described above.

Because of the legal, financial, and administrative differences between state UI systems in the United States and national programs in European nations, straightforward replication of innovations in the use of UI funds is not feasible. Indeed, many specific ideas may simply require too much statutory change to be worth the effort. Among the features of European UI systems that appear to be tested, practicable, and within the legal range, one might commend compensation of organized partial unemployment as described in section 5. Also, it seems to be reasonable that all states should permit UI recipients to draw benefits while engaging in approved training or education, but it is more questionable whether a UI fund itself should organize, sponsor, or finance training courses.

Whatever merits are found in the European programs to convert unemployed people into entrepreneurs, there is as yet no body of European experience to support the view that it is better to support such a program through the UI system than through general government revenues. A good case can, in fact, be made that active labor market programs, of which promotion of self-employment is one, are best kept separate from UI which, in turn, can devote itself to serving those for whom no active employment program is provided. However, as long as separate employment and training programs are not adequate in type and financing and UI is not strictly a residual program, it is understandable that alternative uses of UI funds should be sought.

More generally, two other aspects of European practice bear closer examination by American social policymakers. The first is the long-standing provision of backup unemployment assistance programs for those who exhaust benefits or are not eligible. Whether provided by the states or the federal government, such a system is long overdue. AFDC payments are not a suitable equivalent. The second is the newer bankruptcy payments programs that serve as a complement to UI protection and, in some countries, are related to UI on the financing or administrative side.

European UI systems are not at present exemplary. They are in a state of flux and face stringency. The centenary of U.S. unemployment insurance may be a more tranquil time for making an assessment of unemployment insurance programs in European countries, when lessons for the United States may be more striking.

NOTES

1. Many of the UI policy issues were laid out by the Organization for Economic Cooperation and Development (OECD) at a 1982 international conference on income support (OECD 1984b, pp. 13–14, 78–89).

2. French UI expenditures as a share of GDP showed the strongest growth with considerable increases in Germany and the United Kingdom. The United States, Canada, Italy, and Japan, however, showed decreases in the share of GDP going to UI benefits in 1965–70, with only small changes in the United States, Italy, and Japan in each period. Canada tripled its percentage from 1965–70 to 1975–80. Canada ranked first in the share of GDP going to UI benefits in each time period, but the other rankings shifted. In 1970–75, the percentages ranged from 1.4 to 0.18 among the seven countries, with the United States second, followed by the United Kingdom, Japan, Germany, Italy, and France. By 1975–80, when the range was 1.74 percent to 0.25 percent, France moved to third place after Canada and the United States, with Germany, the United Kingdom, Japan, and Italy following in that order.

3. The countries also varied in the share of GNP for total public expenditures on active and passive programs together. France's share rose from 0.9 in 1973 to 3.3 in 1982. Less dramatic growth was experienced by Sweden (3.2 percent in 1983–84, up 2.1 percent in ten years) and Germany (2.4 percent in 1983–84, up from 0.75 percent in 1973). The United Kingdom, Austria, and the United States each hovered around approximately 1 percent during that decade (Schmid, 1984; Bruche and Reissert, 1985a; Reissert, 1985a, 1985b).

4. Research suggests that active labor market programs are more fiscally sound policy than passive programs (Persson-Tanimura 1979; Schmid 1984; Johannesson 1984; OECD 1984b, pp. 93–97). The rise in the UI share of Sweden's total labor market expenditure in 1982 reflects an increase in UI costs as well as a new emphasis on the less expensive forms of active labor market policy, e.g., placement rather than public works or public service jobs (Johannesson 1984, pp. 46–49).

5. Actual benefits grew moderately in the 1960s, in line with real wages, except in Italy. After the oil crisis of 1973, the growth of actual benefits accelerated, exceeding that of real wages in the beginning of the 1970s. The growth slowed down in the end of the 1970s when benefits showed a drop in real value in all but Japan and France.

6. Trends in the ratio of UI recipients to total unemployed, after dropping slightly in the latter half of the 1960s, except in Japan, rose sharply in the first half of the 1970s, except in Germany, and then dropped again in the late 1970s to early-1960s levels or below.

7. The comparability of the data in Table 5, column 3, is limited. In most countries the administrative costs are included in the base for calculating the government's share. Data for Austria and Germany refer to the government's subsidy to all labor market programs of the Austrian UI Fund and the German FEI, whereas French data refer to income maintenance for the unemployed other than through conventional UI programs. British government subsidies support all social insurance programs, but rising unemployment largely accounts for the increased

government share in the budget years 1973–74 and 1980–81; the drop in the next three budget years reflects the increased share of employer and employee contributions in total intake (Reissert, 1985a). Noncomparability of the data does not fully explain the extent of government sharing in UI expenditures. Germany probably has had no federal subsidy to the FEI for UI, since UI benefits are a first charge on the FEI fund, taking precedence over discretionary expenditures or active labor market measures. In the few years when the FEI required a federal subsidy, it was not necessarily used to cover expenditures on UI (Bruche and Reissert 1985a). The same would be the case in Austria (Bruche 1984b). If the French data concerned only the government share for the regular UI benefits of ASSEDIC/UNEDIC, the proportion would probably drop to the British or Austrian level.

8. As a percentage of the total civilian labor force, employees covered by UI programs increased from 38.2 percent in 1960 to 59.4 percent in 1975 in France, from 38.0 percent in 1957 to 47.7 percent around 1980 in Italy, from 50.2 percent in 1950 to 87.7 percent in 1975 in Canada, and 55.2 percent in 1950 to 89.5 percent around 1980 in the United States. In the United Kingdom, the coverage rate decreased from 88.9 percent in 1950 to 73.8 percent in 1974 (OECD, 1984b, p. 28).

9. British UI recipients constituted 39 percent of the unemployed in 1973, but rose to nearly 50 percent in 1975 and again in 1980, and fell to 31 percent in 1983. Means-tested SB took up most of the slack. From 1973 to 1976 about one-third of the unemployed received SB but not UI, rising to over two-fifths at the end of the decade and over half in 1982 and 1983 (Reissert 1985a, Table 1).

10. Between 1982 and 1983, three cities in the Ruhr reported a 70 percent increase in unemployed recipients of local public assistance (Bruche and Reissert, 1985a, p. 102).

11. By 1983 it had risen to 7 percent of the total expenditure and was of concern to local authorities (Bruche and Reissert, 1985a, Table 14).

12. The United Kingdom and Ireland set limits on RR at 85 percent; Canada reduced the rate of benefits; and Australia tightened eligibility criteria, widened the definitions of suitable jobs, and required more frequent registration by the unemployed. Some countries introduced taxation of UI benefits, but government financial stringency played a role, along with the aim of reducing work disincentives.

13. Recently, a separate assessment on employers to finance short-time working has been proposed, but the change is not likely to be introduced (Bruche and Reissert, 1985a, p. 201).

14. In 1970, there was a low of ten thousand, rising in the next three years, then reaching a high of seven hundred seventy-three thousand in 1975. Subsequently, there was a decline to eighty-eight thousand in 1979, rising again to six hundred twenty-five thousand in 1983, with a drop to three hundred eighty-four thousand in 1984, the last year of available data (BA, 1984, p. 56).

REFERENCES

Atkinson, A. B. 1981. "Unemployment Benefits and Incentives." In J. Creedy, ed., *Economics of Unemployment in Great Britain*. London: Butterworths.

Atkinson, A. B., et al. 1982. *Unemployment Benefit Duration and Incentives: How Robust Is the Evidence?* London: London School of Economics.

BA (Bundesanstalt für Arbeit). 1970–84. *Geschäftsbericht* (Annual Report). Nürnberg: BA.

Benjamin, D. K., and L. A. Kochin. 1979. "Searching for an Explanation of Unemployment in Inter-war Britain." *Journal of Political Economy* 87 (June): 441–478.

Björklund, Anders, and Bertil Holmlund. 1983. *Arbetslöshetsersättningen i Sverige-motiv, regler och effekter*. No. 151. Stockholm: Industriens Utredningsinstitut.

Blaustein, Saul J., and Isabel Craig. 1977. *An International Review of Unemployment Insurance Schemes*. Kalamazoo, Mich.: Upjohn Institute for Employment Research.

Bloch-Michel, C., et al. 1983. "Création d'entreprises par les demandeurs d'emploi." *Bulletin mensuel des statistiques du travail* 104, Supplement, March, pp. 6–14.

Bruche, Gert. 1982. *Die Französische Arbeitslosenversicherung*. International Institute of Management Discussion Paper. IIM/LMP 82-2. Berlin: Wissenschaftszentrum Berlin.

Bruche, Gert. 1984a. *Die Finanzierung der Arbeitsmarktpolitik: Frankreich*. International Institute of Management Discussion Paper. IIM/LMP 84-21b. Berlin: Wissenschaftszentrum Berlin.

Bruche, Gert. 1984b. *Die Finanzierung der Arbeitsmarktpolitik: Oesterreich*. International Institute of Management Discussion Paper IIM/LMP 84-21d. Berlin: Wissenschaftszentrum Berlin.

Bruche, Gert, and Bernd Reissert. 1984. *Manpower and Regional Adjustment Policies: The Case of West Germany*. Washington, D.C.: Institute for International Economics.

Bruche, Gert, and Bernd Reissert. 1985a. *The Financing of Labor Market Policy in the Federal Republic of Germany*. International Institute of Management. Berlin: Wissenschaftszentrum Berlin.

Bruche, Gert, and Bernd Reissert. 1985b. *Die Finanzierung der Arbeitsmarktpolitik — System — Effektivität — Reformansatze*. New York: Campus.

CERC (Centre d'Etude des Revenus et des Couts). 1982. *L'Indemnisation de Chômage en France et à l'Etranger*. Document no. 62. Paris: CERC.

Colin, J. F., and J. Gaudin. 1983. "Le financement de la politique de l'emploi en France." Typescript. Author's files.

Dilnot, A. W., and C. W. Morris. 1983. "Private Costs and Benefits of Unemployment: Measuring Replacement Rates." *Oxford Economic Papers* 35, supplement (November): 321–340.

Disney, Richard, and David Metcalf. 1983. "Financing Labor Market Policy in Great Britain." Department of Economics, University of Kent, Canterbury. Typescript.

EIRR (European Industrial Relations Review). 1982. *International: Unemployment Benefits in 12 Countries*. 105 (October).

Employment News. Department of Employment, Great Britain; monthly.

Eurostat. 1984. *Definitions of Registered Unemployment.* Luxembourg: Eurostat.

Flechsenhar, H. R. 1978. "Kurzarbeit-Kosten und Finanzierung." *Mitteilungen aus der Arbeitsmarkt-und Berufsforschung,* no. 4. Stuttgart: W. Kolhammer.

Flechsenhar, H. R. 1979. "Kurzarbeit-Strukturen und Beschäftigungswirkung." *Mitteilungen aus der Arbeitsmarkt-und Berufsforschung,* no. 3. Stuttgart: W. Kolhammer.

Friedman, Robert. 1985. *The Recipient as Entrepreneur.* Washington, D.C.: Corporation for Enterprise Development.

Garcia de Blas, Antonio. 1985. "Unemployment Benefits in Spain and Other European OECD Countries." *International Labour Review* 124 (March–April): 147–162.

Great Britain. 1984. *Economic Progress Report,* no. 173. November/December. London: Treasury, Information Division.

Green, C., and J. M. Cousineau. 1976. *Unemployment in Canada: The Impact of Unemployment Insurance.* Ottawa: Economic Council of Canada. Minister of Supply and Services.

Grubel, H., and M. A. Walker, eds. 1978. *Unemployment Benefits: Global Evidence of Its Effects on Unemployment.* Vancouver: Fraser Institute.

Harrison, Alan, and Robert Hart. 1982. *A Labour-Market Model of Unemployment Insurance.* International Institute of Management Discussion Papers IIM/LMP 82-19. Berlin: Wissenschaftszentrum Berlin.

Hart, Robert A. 1982. *Unemployment Insurance and the Firm's Employment Strategy: A European and United States Comparison.* International Institute of Management Discussion Paper IIM/LMP 82-11. Berlin: Wissenschaftszentrum Berlin.

Hofbauer, Hans. 1981. "Untersuchungen des IAB über die Wirksamkeit der beruflichen Weiterbildung." *Mitteilungen aus der Arbeitsmarkt-und Berufsforschung,* no. 3. Stuttgart: W. Kolhammer.

Johannesson, Jan. 1984. "Financing Active and Passive Labor Market Policy: The Swedish Case." Mimeograph.

Kaliski, S. F. 1975. "Real and Insurance-Induced Unemployment in Canada." *Canadian Journal of Economics* 8, pp. 600–603.

Kaliski, S. F. 1976. "Unemployment and Unemployment Insurance: Testing Some Corollaries." *Canadian Journal of Economics* 9, pp. 705–712.

Karr, Werner. 1978. "Leistungsberechtigten in der Arbeitslosenstatistik." *Mitteilungen aus der Arbeitsmarkt-und Berufsforschung,* no. 1. Stuttgart: W. Kolhammer.

Kolhuber, Franz. 1983. "The Importance of Unemployment Resulting from Insolvencies." *Mitteilungen aus der Arbeitsmarkt-und Berufsforschung,* no. 2. Stuttgart: W. Kolhammer.

Lachand, D., and J. Y. Denis. 1983. *Création d'entreprises.* Paris: UNEDIC.

Layard, R., and S. Nickell. 1985. "The Causes of British Unemployment." *National Institute Economic Review* (February).

Lenhardt, Gero. 1978. "Problems in Reforming Recurrent Education for Workers." *Comparative Education Review* 27 (October): 440–454.

Maki, D. R., and Z. A. Spindler. 1975. "The Effect of Unemployment Compensation on the Rate of Unemployment in Great Britain." *Oxford Economic Papers* (December).

Minford, P. 1984. "Response to Nickell." *Economic Journal* 94 (December): 954–959.

Mittelstädt, Axel. 1975. "Unemployment Benefits and Related Payments in Seven Major Countries." *OECD Economic Outlook*, Occasional Studies (July).

Narendranathan, W., S. J. Nickell, and J. Stern. 1983. *Unemployment Benefits Revisited*. Centre for Labour Economics Discussion Paper no. 153. London: London School of Economics.

New Society. 1983. London: Science Press. Weekly.

Nickell, S. J. 1979. "The Effects of Unemployment and Related Benefits on the Duration of Unemployment." *Economic Journal* 89 (March): 34–49.

Nordic Council. 1984. *Arbejdsløshedens Omkostninger i Norden*. Stockholm: Nordic Council.

OECD (Organization for Economic Cooperation and Development). 1976a. *Unemployment Compensation and Related Employment Policy Measures in Germany*. MAS/WP4(76)1. 1st Revision. Paris: OECD.

OECD. 1976b. *Unemployment Compensation and Related Employment Policy Measures in the United Kingdom*. MAS/WP4(76)1. 1st Revision. Paris: OECD.

OECD. 1976c. *Unemployment Compensation and Related Employment Policy Measures in Sweden*. MAS/WP4(76)1. 1st Revision. Paris: OECD.

OECD. 1976d. *Unemployment Compensation and Related Employment Policy Measures in France*. MAS/WP4(76)1. 1st Revision. Paris: OECD.

OECD. 1976e. *Public Expenditure on Income Maintenance Programmes*. Paris: OECD.

OECD. 1979. *Unemployment Compensation and Related Employment Policy Measures*. Paris: OECD.

OECD. 1982. *The Challenge of Unemployment. A Report to Labour Ministers*. Paris: OECD.

OECD. 1983a. *Employment Outlook*. Paris: OECD. Annual (September).

OECD. 1984a. *Employment Outlook*. Paris: OECD. Annual (September).

OECD. 1984b. *High Unemployment: A Challenge for Income Support Policies*. Paris: OECD.

OECD. 1985a. *Employment Outlook*. Paris: OECD. Annual (September).

OECD. 1985b. *Economic Outlook*. Paris: OECD. Annual (May).

OECD. 1985c. "Focus: Expanding the Opportunity to Produce." *Feedback ILE*, no. 1. Paris: OECD.

OECD *Observer*. 1978. *Unemployment Compensation: A Comparison of Six Countries*. Paris: OECD. Bimonthly (November).

OECD *Observer*. 1984. *Social Expenditure: Erosion or Evolution?* Paris: OECD. Bimonthly (January).

Persson-Tanimura, Inga. 1979. *On the Costs of Unemployment in Sweden*. International Institute for Management Discussion Paper IIM/LMP 79-16. Berlin: Wissenschaftszentrum Berlin.

Reissert, Bernd. 1985a. *Die Finanzierung der Arbeitsmarktpolitik: Grossbritannien.* International Institute for Management Discussion Paper IIM/LMP 1984-21c. Berlin: Wissenschaftszentrum Berlin.

Reissert, Bernd. 1985b. *Die Finanzierung der Arbeitsmarktpolitik: USA.* International Institute for Management Discussion Paper IIM/LMP. Berlin: Wissenschaftszentrum Berlin.

Reissert, Bernd, and Gunther Schmid. 1985. *Steuerungswirkungen von Finanzierungs-Institutionen auf Arbeitsmarktpolitisches Verhalten. Ein Internationaler Vergleich.* International Institute of Management. Berlin: Wissenschaftszentrum Berlin.

Schmid, Gunther. 1983. "German Labour Market Policy Under the Social-Liberal Coalition: Lessons from 1969–1982." *German Political Studies* 6.

Schmid, Gunther. 1984. *Die Finanzierung der Arbeitsmarktpolitik: Schweden.* International Institute for Management Discussion Paper IIM/LMP 84-21a. Berlin: Wissenschaftszentrum Berlin.

Sengenberger, Werner, and Burkhart Lutz. 1974. *Developments Related to the German Labour Promotion Act of 1969.* Paris: OECD/CERI.

Sorrentino, Constance. 1976. "Unemployment Compensation in Eight Industrial Countries." *Monthly Labor Review* 99 (July): 18–24.

Spindler, Z. A., and D. R. Maki. 1978. "More on the Effects of Unemployment Compensation on the Rate of Unemployment in Great Britain." *Oxford Economic Papers* 31, pp. 147–164.

Stern, J. 1984. *Repeat Unemployment Spells: The Effect of Unemployment Benefits on Unemployed Entry.* Centre for Labour Economics Discussion Paper no. 192. London: London School of Economics.

UN (United Nations). 1983. *Economic Bulletin for Europe.* Journal of the Economic Commission for Europe. New York: Pergamon Press. Quarterly (September).

Walsh, B. M. 1981. *Unemployment Insurance and the Labor Market: A Review of Research Relating to Policy.* MAS/WPS(81)1. Paris: OECD.

Wadensjö, Eskil. 1985. *The Financial Effects of Unemployment and Labor Market Policy Programs for Public Authorities in Sweden.* International Institute for Management Discussion Paper IIM/LMP. Berlin: Wissenschaftszentrum Berlin.

White, M. 1983. *Long Term Unemployment and Labour Markets.* P.S.I. No. 622. London: Policy Studies Institute.

7

Federal-State Relations in Unemployment Insurance

MURRAY RUBIN

Introduction

For almost fifty years, unemployment insurance thrived as a hybrid federal-state system. In no other public program were responsibilities so thoroughly shared between two levels of government. Few public programs were as dependent on intergovernmental cooperation, and few generated as much intergovernmental discord. Rarely has a public program's organizational structure had such an important influence on its direction.

The federal-state system was dictated by circumstances in 1935. Not enough was known then of the impact of the many ingredients of unemployment insurance to warrant imposing untried provisions on an entire nation. Moreover, there was doubt that such a system could even be enacted by a state-oriented Congress. Finally, President Roosevelt favored a "cooperative federal-state undertaking" (Haber and Murray, 1966), and Wisconsin had already established a precedent.

Fifty-one years later, unemployment insurance is still a hybrid system. But the characteristics that contributed to its success—continuity of objectives, dedicated leadership, and public support—have been severely eroded by recent developments. Persistently high unemployment, the consequent depletion of many states' reserves, and federal interest and loan repayment provisions have caused states to concentrate on fund rehabilitation and severely cut back benefit availability and adequacy. Federal deficits and a national leadership dedicated to reducing both federal costs and federal responsibilities crippled the extended benefit program and changed the federal focus from providing leadership in protecting the unemployed to guarding against overpayments and "moral hazards." One result of these developments is an unemployment insurance system that no longer meets the needs of a large majority of the unemployed.

Despite these shocks to the system, the federal-state arrangement survives. The purpose of this paper is to examine what ingredients made it successful, the causes of erosion, and what's to be done now.

1. Statutory Ingredients of a Successful Federal-State System

Self-Sufficient State UI Programs

The compelling issue in 1935 was not federal versus federal-state support of UI programs, but rather the best possible division of responsibilities. The system could be so structured as to render states little more than the federal government's administrative agents at one extreme, with total state autonomy at the other. The decision, expressed by President Roosevelt's Committee on Economic Security, and later by Congress in enacting the Social Security Act, was to give states as much autonomy as possible, consistent with certain prescribed national objectives:

> The plan for unemployment compensation that we suggest contemplates that the States shall have broad freedom to set up the type of unemployment compensation they wish. We believe that all matters in which uniformity is not absolutely essential should be left to the States. (Committee on Economic Security, 1935)

Accordingly, states alone determine what minimum wage or employment requirements must be satisfied by any individual to qualify for benefits. The formulas used to determine individual weekly benefit amounts, minimum and maximum benefit levels, the payment of partial benefits, and the availability and amount of dependents' allowances are also solely matters of state law. The formulas used to establish individual benefit duration and maximum potential benefits are state matters. States have almost complete authority in establishing the availability-for-work, ability-to-work, and work search requirements individuals must meet to maintain their eligibility for benefits. With minor limitations, states are free to establish the causes for disqualification from benefits and the particular disqualification penalty. States have wide discretion over how liability for taxes will be allocated among employers, and total authority to determine the amount of taxes to be collected.

The Committee on Economic Security's report does not discuss the reasons for granting states this "broad freedom." It notes only the "desirability of permitting considerable variation, so that we may learn through demonstration what is best." But the decision for state jurisdiction over substantive provisions and "primary responsibility for administration"

(Committee on Economic Security, 1935, p. 16) has stronger justification than merely the benefit of having fifty-three experimental laboratories. If unemployment insurance was operated on the basis of separate, self-contained state laws, the states must reasonably have substantial authority over the content and administration of those laws. It is not realistic to expect a state to support financially and manage efficiently a system over which it has little or no control.

Nor would such an arrangement be desirable. There is still no widespread agreement over the relative advantages of alternative UI provisions. Different approaches are regularly debated within state legislatures. Decisions on unemployment insurance must be made in the context of changing economic conditions. They must reflect consideration of the state UI program's potential and its limitations, competing priorities, and conflicting interests. When Congress enacts uniform program standards that are not essential to the national interest, affected areas of their UI programs are removed from states' jurisdiction and, most importantly, from the debates at the state level that are critical to the program's vitality and the key to its responsiveness.

Federal Responsibilities

But for the program to succeed, state autonomy must not be absolute. Certain federal requirements and leadership have proved to be vital in preserving the purpose of unemployment insurance and ensuring effective administration. The Committee on Economic Security identified four key federal responsibilities: providing an incentive for states to act; safeguarding unemployment reserves; ensuring efficient administration; and providing program standards where uniformity was essential.

Providing an Incentive Tax Credit. The immediate federal responsibility in 1935 was to provide an incentive for states to enact and maintain unemployment insurance laws.

> So long as there is danger that business in some States will gain a competitive advantage through failure of the State to enact an unemployment insurance law, few such laws will be enacted. (Committee on Economic Security, 1935, p. 16)

Accordingly, the Social Security Act provided business a competitive disadvantage if their state did *not* enact such a law. It established a federal unemployment tax (originally 3 percent, currently 6.2 percent) and allowed credit against the tax to employers who pay taxes under a state law that meets federal requirements. But the tax credit approach accomplishes more than providing an incentive. The federal tax is levied on wages, currently defined as the first $7,000 in remuneration paid to an individual during a calendar year[1] by an employer, defined as a person who either paid wages of $1,500 or more during any calendar quarter of the current or preceding calendar year, or who employed one individual for at least twenty weeks during the current or preceding year.[2] The remuneration must be for employment, defined as services (other than those specifically excluded) by an employee (also defined) for the person employing him.[3]

The tax credit provision thus embodies not only a compelling incentive for a state to adopt an unemployment insurance program, but also minimum coverage and taxable wage base standards. For all potentially eligible employers actually to receive credit against the 6.2 percent federal tax, the same employers, employment, and wages that are subject to the federal tax must also be subject to state law. A state that excluded the construction trades or the banking industry, for example, would deprive those employers of the opportunity to receive credit against the federal tax.

The national interest in making coverage almost universal was accomplished by gradually eliminating exclusions from the federal tax. In 1935 the tax applied to employers with eight or more workers in at least twenty weeks. The tax was extended to employers with four or more in 1950 and to the present one or more in 1970. Large farm employers and some domestic service employers were covered by 1976 legislation limiting the previous exclusions.

In 1970 and 1976 coverage was extended to nonprofit organizations employing four or more and to most state and local government workers. This last extension was accomplished, however, not by removing exclusions from the federal tax (they are still excluded), but rather by making their coverage under state law a condition for tax credit for all the state's employers.

The tax credit approach also embodies the principal penalty for failure of a state to enact an unemployment insurance law, or to conform with a multitude of federal requirements. Denial of tax credit is so formidable a penalty that few states are willing even to risk the hazard. In over fifty years, only one has actually incurred a penalty for violation of a tax credit-conditioned standard, and even that state managed to avoid the full potential penalty.[4]

Safeguarding Unemployment Reserves. A second key federal responsibility involved the handling of unemployment funds:

> We believe also that it is essential that the Federal Government assume responsibility for safeguarding, investing, and liquidating all reserve funds, in order that these reserves may be utilized to promote stability and to avoid damages inherent in their uncontrolled investment and liquidation. (Committee on Economic Security, 1935, p. 4)

Accordingly, the Social Security Act provides for the establishment of an Unemployment Trust Fund in the U.S. Treasury. It authorizes the secretary of the treasury to invest amounts in the fund not needed to meet current withdrawals. A separate bookkeeping account is maintained for each state UI agency, and the secretary is required to pay out of the fund to any state agency whatever amount in its account it requisitions.[5]

Both the Social Security Act and the Federal Unemployment Tax Act (FUTA) require that each state immediately deposit all contributions collected under the state UI law into the Unemployment Trust Fund—and that moneys withdrawn from that fund be used only for unemployment compensation.[6] "Unemployment compensation" is defined as "cash benefits payable to individuals with respect to their unemployment."[7] The "immediate deposit" and, particularly, the "withdrawal" standard have influenced the content of state laws more than any other federal requirements. Their justification is that in return for credit against the federal tax and administrative grants, it is reasonable to require that state unemployment reserves be available when needed, and used only for the purposes for which they were collected—to pay compensation. They have prevented enactment of a host of state amendments that would otherwise have completely altered the character of unemployment insurance in several states.

The withdrawal standard has been the major bulwark against a variety of regularly recurring state proposals for imposing income or means tests as conditions for benefits. These include state bills to deny benefits to individuals with prior earnings over a specified amount; to establish stiffer qualifying requirements for claimants with working spouses; to reduce the severity of disqualification for claimants with dependents; to require claimants with post-unemployment incomes over a specified amount to repay all or part of the benefits they received.

The most significant of these proposals was a 1963 amendment to the South Dakota law requiring claimants with base period wages over $6,000 to serve waiting periods of from seven to thirteen weeks, depending on the amount of their earnings. Following a formal hearing on the conformity of the state law with federal requirements, the provision was found inconsistent with the withdrawal standard, in that benefits would be paid or denied, under the state provision, on the basis of factors (income levels and presumed need) other than claimants' unemployment.

The standard has also prevented states from paying benefits to individuals separated from their jobs because of illness or disability. In such cases, it is argued, benefits would be paid to individuals on the basis of their physical condition rather than their unemployment due to lack of work. Similar reasoning applied to state proposals to exempt categories of claimants with certain characteristics from the state requirement that benefits be paid only to individuals who are available for work and able to work. States have proposed exempting from this requirement individuals unavailable for work because of compelling personal reasons, workers who are unemployed because of a labor dispute, workers who are unemployed because of their refusal to bump others with less seniority, pregnant women, and others. These proposals were held inconsistent with the withdrawal standard on the grounds that benefits paid an individual who is not available for work, who does not look for work, or who does not accept suitable work when offered would not constitute compensation payable for unemployment due to lack of work, but rather unemployment due to the individual's unavailability.

Finally, the withdrawal standard has prevented states from using moneys withdrawn from the Unemployment Trust Fund for a variety of payments other than compensation for unemployment. The following state proposals for the use of fund moneys were considered inconsistent with the standard: to use benefits as wages or wage supplements to claimants on public service jobs, and to claimants willing to take low-paying jobs; to satisfy claimants' penalties for fraud; to pay claimants' attorney fees; to provide loans to claimants; to pay interest to claimants when benefits have been delayed.

Efficient Administration. A third key federal responsibility was to ensure efficient administration of state programs:

> To encourage efficient administration, without which unemployment insurance will fail to accomplish its purpose, we believe that the Federal Government should aid the States by granting them sufficient money for proper administration, under conditions designed to insure competence and probity. Among those conditions we deem selection of personnel on a merit basis vital to success. (Committee on Economic Security, 1935, p. 19, 4)

These objectives were implemented, in large part, by two Social Security Act provisions. The first requires that grants shall be expended

> solely for the purposes and in the amounts found necessary by the Secretary of Labor for the proper and efficient administration of such State law. . . .[8]

The second requires that each state law include provision for

> such methods of administration (including . . . methods relating to the establishment and maintenance of personnel standards on a merit basis . . .) as are found by the Secretary of Labor to be reasonably calculated to insure full payment of unemployment compensation when due. . . .[9]

A third administrative standard requires each state UI law to include provision for

> opportunity for a fair hearing, before an impartial tribunal, for all individuals whose claims for unemployment compensation are denied. . . .[10]

Other administrative standards require payment of benefits solely through public employment offices and disclosure of unemployment insurance information to the secretary of labor and to various agencies.

Assigning states "primary responsibility for administration" (Committee on Economic Security, 1935, p. 16) but granting the federal government authority over administrative funds has guaranteed continual conflict between the two partners. More than in any other area, state freedom is circumscribed by federal requirements, which apply to the smallest details of administrative techniques and practices. At times, federal control has been shortsighted and authoritarian, allowing the states little flexibility and no input. Grant limitations have often been so unrealistic as actually to thwart rather than promote efficiency. At other times, federal authority, exercised in close cooperation with states, resulted in genuine reform of administrative practices.

Providing Necessary Program Standards. According to the Committee on Economic Security,

> We believe that all matters in which uniformity is not absolutely essential should be left to the States. (Committee on Economic Security, 1935, p. 20)

The committee made recommendations for state programs, but did not identify any specific areas of state unemployment insurance programs where it considered uniformity to be essential. The 1935 Social Security Act contained two program standards evidently considered by Congress at that time to be essential: experience rating and labor standards. Later congresses adopted a multitude of program standards, but only three can reasonably be considered to provide an essential uniformity: standards protecting interstate claimants, coverage of nonprofit organizations and state and local government workers, and extended benefits.

Experience Rating. The Federal Unemployment Tax Act permits states to provide additional credit against the federal tax on the basis of individual reserve, guaranteed employment, or individual experience.[11] Although a few state laws originally provided for the first two approaches, all states eventually permitted additional credit only on the basis of employers' experience. Additional credit is credit for the difference between what the employer actually pays in state taxes and 5.4 percent. Accordingly, an employer assigned a 1 percent rate, for example, would be eligible for normal credit of 1 percent (the amount actually paid) and additional credit of 4.4 percent against the 6.2 percent federal tax. Reduced rates (rates below the usual standard rate of 5.4 percent) and additional credit are permitted an employer only on the basis of his

> experience with respect to unemployment or other factors bearing a direct relation to unemployment risk during not less than the 3 consecutive years immediately preceding the computation date. . . .[12]

This provision was later amended, first to permit reduced rates on the basis of as little as one year of experience and later to newly covered

employers "on a reasonable basis" (but not less than 1 percent) until they
have enough years to qualify for a rate based on their experience. Aside
from new employers, experience rating is the only approach available to
a state wishing to lower an employer's rate below 5.4 percent.

The short, ambiguous standard (which many contend is not essential
to the national interest) generated an enormous volume of interpretation.
The most consistent challenges to federal interpretations have come from
state legislators' efforts to introduce factors into the determination of rates
which cannot reasonably be considered measures of employers' experience with *unemployment:* credits for employers over forty years of age;
those employing heads of households, providing approved training; for
hiring handicapped workers, or providing termination pay; employers
operating in an urban enterprise zone; and small businesses that expand
their annual payroll.

The second most frequent source of conflicts has been the efforts to
relieve employers of the responsibility for benefit costs under certain circumstances. According to federal interpretation, not all benefits must be
charged, as long as those that are charged provide a reasonable measurement of an employer's experience with respect to the unemployment risk
of his workers. Employers may be relieved of charges that may be
considered unreasonable, provided the noncharging would not result in
substantial distortion of the relative experience of employers. These are
vague criteria, and they have led to inconsistent rulings. Among the most
common noncharges that have been approved are benefits paid following
disqualification, federal-state extended benefits, certain benefits based on
earnings in more than one state, and benefits paid pursuant to a decision
that is later reversed. Many proposals for additional noncharging have
been rejected, ranging from a bill to relieve all employers of the first $400
of benefits otherwise charged, to proposals for special charging rules for
specific categories of employers (food processing employers, enterprise zone
employers, and so on).

There have been greater differences of opinion as to the desirability of
experience rating than with respect to any other single element of the program (Becker, 1982; Wagman, 1982).[13] Aside from those who recommend
outright repeal because of the incentive it provides to keep benefit costs
down, criticism has come from two different sources. On the one hand,
the standard is considered too restrictive; on the other, recommendations
have been made to permit states to reduce employers' rates on additional
grounds. If rates could be determined on the basis of employment practices
as well as unemployment experience, for example, lower tax rates could
provide an incentive for hiring handicapped or disadvantaged categories
of claimants, or for providing employees scheduled to be laid off work
search assistance, dismissal pay, retraining opportunities, relocation allow-

ances, or supplemental unemployment benefits. The chairman of the National Commission on Unemployment Compensation proposed to allow the states to experience-rate on the basis of employment as well as unemployment, and to eliminate the requirement for a "direct" relationship to unemployment risk (National Commission on Unemployment Compensation, 1980, p. 94). As in the case of past attempts to modify the standard, the chairman's efforts were rejected because of the opposition of employer representatives.

The second source of criticism has been employer groups who argue that experience rating has become ineffective in many states due to the Department of Labor's failure to enforce it more rigorously. They urge that states be required to reduce noncharging and remove other obstacles to the charging of virtually all benefits to employers' experience-rating accounts. This, they argue, is what the standard requires. It is true that to a substantial degree, employers' rates do not reflect their actual experience (Wagman, 1982, pp. 631–662). A substantial amount of benefits is not charged in many states which allow noncharging in almost every situation the federal law allows. In many states, a large amount of benefits is ineffectively charged in that benefits are made to employers already assigned the maximum tax rate, or are written off for employers with negative reserve balances. A number of states have thus chosen not to allocate a significant portion of benefit costs to employers on the basis of experience, but rather to finance them by charging a uniform rate in addition to experience rates.

Despite the federal standard and interpretations, states have considerable freedom in developing experience-rating formulas, qualifying them with secondary adjustment factors, determining what benefits may be noncharged, assigning emergency and other special rates, establishing tax schedules, and setting minimum and maximum rates. In effect, they can apply experience rating as rigorously as they wish.

Labor Standards. The 1935 Social Security Act also included the following labor standards requirement:

> Compensation shall not be denied in such State to any otherwise eligible individual for refusing to accept new work under any of the following conditions: (A) if the position offered is vacant due directly to a strike, lockout, or other labor dispute; (B) if the wages, hours, or other conditions of work are substantially less favorable to the individual than those prevailing for similar work in the locality; (C) if as a condition of being employed the individual would be required to join a company union or refrain from joining any bona fide labor organization.[14]

The purposes of conditions (A) and (C) are to prevent UI claimants from being used as strikebreakers, and to protect the rights of claimants to join unions of their choice. Condition (B) is intended to protect employed workers by preventing states from requiring claimants to accept depressed wages and substandard working conditions.

The standard is difficult to administer. First, it applies only to refusals of new work. This is easy to identify in the case of job offers from new employers. But the standard applies also to a change in the conditions of a current job (in effect, a change in the conditions of the contract), such as a downgrade in duties, or transfer to part-time status or to a different shift, which are not always recognized as new work. After identifying the offer as new work, the agency must determine whether the wages, hours, or other conditions of the offered work are substantially less favorable to the individual than those prevailing for similar work in the locality.

Aside from widespread failure of state agency personnel to apply the standard properly in identifying new work and determining prevailing wages, the most frequent conformity issues involve increasingly common state law amendments that define (as in the extended benefit requirements) suitable work as any work paying a specified minimum wage—but fail to indicate that the job must meet the prevailing wage, hours, and conditions of work requirements.

Despite these limitations and some reservations as to whether the standard is absolutely essential, there is no question that the labor standards have helped prevent the unemployment insurance program from being used as a means of depressing working conditions and otherwise undermining gains made by American workers.

Interstate Claimants. In 1970, federal law was amended to require that all states participate in a plan which combines the wages and employment of an individual who worked in more than one state so that eligibility for and the amount of benefits could be based on the combined wages and work when applying the provisions of a single state.[15] A related standard enacted the same year prohibits states from denying or reducing benefits to an individual solely because the claim is filed from another state (or Canada) or because of a change in residence to another state (or Canada) where the claim is filed.[16]

These standards were provoked by failure of some states to participate voluntarily in combined wage plans and by the discriminatory provisions of three states. In 1963 Ohio and Wyoming provided that an interstate claimant filing against these states may not qualify for a maximum higher than that payable in the agent state in which he filed his claim. As early as 1955, Alaska provided one maximum and dependents' allowances for claimants filing within the state and a much lower maximum and no dependents' allowances to claimants who filed claims against Alaska from outside the state.

Such provisions, if unopposed, would have justified the fears of those who had advocated a federal system in 1935 on the grounds that a federal-state system was not capable of handling the problems created by individuals who work in different states or cross state lines to look for work.

Coverage Standards. Federal legislation enacted in 1970 and 1976 required states to extend coverage to employees of nonprofit organizations with four or more workers and to most state and local government workers. Unlike past coverage extensions effected by removing exclusions from the federal tax, this coverage by a state was made a condition for tax credit like other program standards. Nonprofit organizations and public entities remained exempt from the federal tax, but failure of a state to cover them jeopardized tax credit for all the state's employers.[17]

The coverage standard fulfilled the national interest in extending unemployment insurance protection to most American workers. But it was accomplished at a high cost in terms of restrictions on state autonomy. First, any unauthorized exception, however insignificant, from the required coverage presented a conformity issue. Second, the standard required states to offer the newly covered entities the election of financing benefit costs on either a tax or a reimbursement basis.[18] This involved a large number of interpretations and rulings. For example, since employers must be permitted to change from one method of financing to another, interpretations were needed to establish the tax status of switching employers, whether they could recapture past favorable experience, their order in the charging sequence, and so on.

Third, states were required to deny benefits to school employees during breaks between school terms if they had "reasonable assurance" of employment for the second term. This was later extended to vacation and holiday periods and to employees of educational service agencies. The requirement was amended frequently in the 1980s. A huge body of interpretations and rulings extended to the smallest details of state operations.

Extended Benefits. The most significant federal standard since 1935 was the establishment in 1970 of a permanent standby program of extended benefits (EB).[19] It requires states to provide additional levels of benefits during heavy periods of unemployment for individuals who have exhausted their regular entitlement. The program is financed on a fifty-fifty federal-state basis. Up to thirteen extra weeks of benefits (for a maximum of thirty-nine weeks regular and extended) are permitted at the claimant's usual weekly benefit amount. The benefits are triggered on if the state's insured unemployment rate for the past thirteen-week period is 20 percent higher than the rate for the corresponding period in the past two years and the rate is at least 5 percent. The 20 percent requirement can be waived if state law so permits, provided the rate is at least 6 percent. Extended benefits cease to become available when the insured unemployment rate does not meet either the 20 percent requirement or the 5 or 6 percent requirement, whichever is applicable.

States have no choice other than to enact the EB program totally. They have no discretion over the terms and conditions under which extended benefits are paid.

Adoption of Unnecessary Federal Standards

After a hiatus of thirty-five years, Congress enacted new program standards or revised existing ones in 1970, 1976, 1981, 1982, and 1983. As indicated above, only three could reasonably be considered to provide an "absolutely essential" uniformity: coverage of nonprofit organizations and state and local government workers, establishment of the extended benefit program, and protection of interstate workers.

Three of the remaining post-1935 standards were reactions to state provisions considered too harsh with respect to claimants. They prohibited states from disqualifying claimants taking approved training (1970); from canceling wage credits or totally reducing benefits except for certain causes (1970); and from denying benefits solely on the basis of pregnancy (1976).[20] None of these had any significant effect or could be considered to provide an essential uniformity. The standard relating to claimants in training was undermined by the authority of states to approve any training for a claimant. The prohibition against cancellation of wage credits or total reduction of benefit rights did not restrain states from enacting severe disqualifications or developing new causes for disqualification. The prohibition against denying benefits on the basis of pregnancy was not needed because of an earlier Supreme Court decision holding that the practice violated the Constitution.[21]

The other remaining post-1935 standards were aimed at state provisions considered too lenient with respect to claimants. They required states to deny benefits to aliens not lawfully permitted to work (1976); to deny benefits based on participation in sports to professional athletes during the off-season (1976); to deny benefits to school employees between terms (1970, 1976, 1983); to deduct from a claimant's benefits generally any amount he is receiving for the same week in retirement pay (1976, 1980); to deduct from benefits generally any amount a claimant owes in child support obligations (1981).[22]

None of these standards represented a situation requiring uniformity. They represented unwarranted intrusion into areas better determined at the state level. In addition, for each standard, there are many interpretations and rulings that must be developed, applied, and enforced. Each represents a potential source of conflict and an issue of conformity. Most important, these standards removed from state legislators the opportunity to consider these subjects and fashion responses appropriate and consistent with each individual state's interest.

2. Nonstatutory Ingredients of a Successful Federal-State System

The statutory ingredients described above were not alone sufficient to ensure a successful federal-state system. Equally essential were elements that permitted both stability and responsiveness: checks and balances against domination by either partner, a fair and efficient means of resolving issues, a climate and pattern of cooperation, and effective federal leadership.

Checks and Balances

Conflict is inevitable when responsibilities for a single program are shared by two levels of government with different perspectives. The federal partner naturally seeks uniformity in both program and administrative areas. In the past, the Department of Labor (DOL) favored certain types of provisions, tried to persuade states of their desirability, and often lobbied Congress to impose them as standards. In the administration area, it seeks greater control over state practices, constantly promoting economy through standardization. In contrast, virtually every one of the fifty-three separate UI jurisdictions resists federal intrusion into the program area. Every state seeks as much independence over the administration of its law as possible. Each partner constantly seeks to prevail. The fact that neither has dominated the other is due to practical rather than statutory conditions.

The federal-state division of responsibilities rests on federal law, not constitutional grounds. There are no "states' rights" limitations on the authority of Congress to impose whatever provisions it wishes, or to substitute a national program for the present hybrid. However, there are practical restraints. Many of the reasons for rejecting a centralized system in 1935 are still valid. Congress is still inherently state-oriented, and after fifty years of success under the current arrangement, even less likely now to change the system. Strong vested interests at the state level would be difficult to resist, and substituting a large federal bureaucracy for current state administration is not a realistic prospect.

There are other practical restraints to federal domination. Each new federal program standard imposes still another burden on a federal UI staff that in 1980 the National Commission on Unemployment Compensation considered "too small to meet the responsibilities that go with a program of this size."[23] Ironically, as the number of federal standards increased dramatically during the 1970s and 1980s, federal staff responsible for their enforcement has been systematically reduced. From a strength of 221 in 1973, the national office of the Unemployment Insurance Service (UIS) has dropped to about 130 (as of June 1, 1986). Over 35 of those positions are devoted to the new quality control program aimed at cutting state costs and reducing state overpayments. Remaining UIS staff is too small and inexperienced to identify all potential conformity problems created by constantly changing state legislation, to conduct research, to provide program objectives, or to offer technical assistance to state agencies.

Nor has the federal partner even the inclination to exercise its full authority. The Department of Labor is no more anxious than a state to destroy the state's UI program by actually imposing the sanctions—of denying tax credit, withholding administrative grants, or both. Past actions against nonconforming states resulted, on three separate occasions, in Congress's amending federal law either to legitimize the challenged state provision, or to limit DOL authority over the issue in question. In 1947 Congress amended federal law to permit employers to pay voluntary contributions—a 1947 Minnesota law authorizing that practice had been held by the DOL to violate the experience-rating standard. In 1950, Congress amended federal law to prevent the secretary of labor from raising certain compliance issues with a state until the highest court in the state had ruled on the matter. This was the result of a conformity confrontation with California over the meaning of the term "new work" in the federal labor standards requirement (Haber, 1966, pp. 447, 448). In 1970, Congress provided for judicial review of any secretary's ruling adversely affecting a state's tax offset credit or eligibility for administrative grants.[24]

Finally, considerable research and legal efforts are prerequisite to successful conformity confrontations. These resources are now in too short supply to be used in other than critical situations.

There are corresponding checks on state action. Irresponsible state provisions have provoked federal standards in the past. The standards protecting interstate claimants, claimants in training, and pregnant claimants represent federal reactions to inequities or discriminatory state provisions. The most reliable safeguard against state excesses, however, has not been fear of federal retaliation. Rather, it has been the political process at the state level, manifested in legislative debate between reasonably balanced adversaries.

Resolving Issues

Checks and balances have helped to prevent each partner from dominating the other. But for the partnership to succeed, it is also necessary to keep conflicts from stalemating action. The system is constantly changing through both federal and state legislation. Its dynamic character has been one element of its success. But because of the constant input of new state proposals, each year issues arise over the conformity of proposed state program changes with federal requirements. The methods that have evolved for resolving these issues have permitted both progress and stability (Rubin, 1983, pp. 127–129).[25]

When proposed state legislation presents an issue of nonconformity with federal law, every effort is made to resolve the issue without the necessity for a formal hearing. The state agency is immediately advised why the bill presents an issue. If this notice does not defeat the legislation, the agency is advised of how the bill can be amended to preserve its intent, if possible, and avoid the problem. If the amendment is adopted without change, the agency may be asked to seek remedial legislation at the next session. If the amendment presents a major issue, the DOL will recommend adoption by the state legislature of a "savings clause" declaring the challenged provision void following a determination of its nonconformity by the secretary of labor pursuant to a hearing. This protects the state from being denied tax credit if the state legislature either is not in session or fails to take action to remove the provision. As indicated above, since 1970, states have the right to seek judicial review of a secretary's adverse decision.

The process has worked well. Although about fifty new issues are presented each year, most are resolved through negotiation. There have been fewer than two dozen formal conformity hearings over the program's fifty-year history. Only one state has incurred a penalty for nonconforming legislation, one lost part of its grant for failure to pay interest on time, and only two have had administrative grants temporarily withheld.[26] The system provides states full opportunity to challenge DOL interpretations of federal law at any step of the conformity process and in the courts. In effect, the system provides states the same opportunity for a fair hearing that federal law requires claimants be afforded. It has thus permitted the resolution of divisive issues, while preserving an essential stability.

Cooperation

Until recently, the dominant characteristic of the federal-state partnership was cooperative effort. Given the statutory and practical restraints on the authority of each partner, it became clear at the outset that the system can operate effectively only through cooperation. This was not accidental. President Roosevelt had recommended "a cooperative federal-state undertaking" (Haber, 1966, p. 79). The report of the Committee on Economic Security is replete with references to cooperative effort:

> Beyond this [federal tax, safeguarding reserves] the respective spheres of the State and local governments on unemployment compensation are not clearly

defined. Some standardization is desirable, but we believe that this should not be a matter of Federal control, but of cooperative action. A cooperative Federal-State unemployment compensation system should include the essentials we have outlined. (Committee on Economic Security, 1935, p. 17)

Even in the administrative area, the federal role was to be primarily of assistance, not domination:

> To encourage efficient administration . . . the Federal Government should aid the States by granting them sufficient money for proper administration, under conditions designed to insure competence and probity.
>   . . . The Federal Government, however, should assist the States in setting up their administrations and the solution of the problems they will encounter. (Committee on Economic Security, 1935, pp. 19, 20)

Cooperative effort was demonstrated early by federal assistance to the states in setting up their laws and administrative machinery. Throughout the years, the Department of Labor provided guidance to states in implementing changes in federal laws and commenting on proposed legislation. The avoidance of conformity confrontations has been a regularly occurring cooperative effort between state and federal administrators. States have cooperated with federal authorities in developing interpretations of federal law and administrative standards. Without state cooperation, the standards would have been unrealistic.[27]

A vital factor in establishing the long pattern of federal-state cooperation has been the presence at both state and federal levels of highly competent men and women strongly committed to the success of the program.

Federal Leadership

Important to the success of the program has been the leadership provided by the Department of Labor and its predecessors, particularly in providing broad as well as detailed unemployment insurance objectives. The first suggestions for state legislation were made by the Committee on Economic Security (Committee on Economic Security, 1935, pp. 20–23). The committee also recommended that a special insurance board within the DOL (later the Unemployment Insurance Service) be given power to decide whether state laws comply with the federal requirements,

> and that it be made its duty to assist States in setting up unemployment compensation administrations and in the solution of the problems they will encounter; also that it conduct continuous studies to correlate and make useful the experience developed under State laws. (Committee on Economic Security, 1935, p. 19)

In 1937, the Social Security Board issued *Draft Bills for State Unemployment Compensation of Pooled Fund and Employer Reserve Account Types*

(Social Security Board, 1937) which "meet the minimum standards set forth in the Social Security Act for State unemployment compensation laws." Subsequent draft bills, later called *Manual of State Employment Security Legislation,* were issued thereafter by the Department of Labor, usually at two-year intervals, and later when comprehensive changes (1970 and 1976) were made in federal UI laws. These documents contained not only provisions necessary to meet federal requirements, but also draft language and discussion of recommended provisions and alternatives in the effort "to make useful the experience developed under State laws."

Department of Labor recommendations were also incorporated in special legislative policy documents (U.S. Department of Labor, Bureau of Employment Security, 1962).[28] They were the subjects of legislative planning conferences held periodically with state agency personnel. Recommendations were also incorporated in periodic evaluations made of individual state laws. Comments on proposed legislation regularly included not only cautions about potential conformity issues, when appropriate, but comments on the technical adequacy of the proposed amendments and critiques of the state proposals from the standpoint of DOL objectives.

The recommendations covered every aspect of state UI provisions, ranging from computation of the weekly benefit amount to determination of the tax rate of successor employers. They represented what the DOL considered the most equitable and effective provisions, and they were invariably accompanied by the reasoning underlying each recommendation.

The draft bills, policy statements, state law evaluations, and policy comments on proposed state legislation were important for several reasons. They represented the only nationwide benchmark available for evaluating the fairness and adequacy of individual state provisions. In the context of legislative planning, they provided the focal point for discussion among and within states. They helped in the defeat of extreme state legislation and in the enactment of sound provisions. Most important, they provided background and information about unemployment insurance details not available elsewhere.

In its leadership role, the Department of Labor also served as clearinghouse for information and research studies on UI matters. It regularly distributed digests of decisions issued by state appeals authorities and courts covering a wide variety of eligibility and disqualification issues. Its monthly publication, the *Employment Security Review,* and later the *Unemployment Insurance Review,* presented forums for discussion of important UI issues by both state and federal administrations.

3. Weakening the System

A dramatic erosion of unemployment insurance protection occurred during the six-year period 1980–86. Persistently high unemployment rates, depletion of many states' unemployment reserves, and the election of a president and a majority of Congress dedicated to reducing the costs of domestic programs contributed to an array of crippling amendments at both state and federal levels.

During the six-year period, thirty-one states increased the amount of work or earnings necessary to qualify for unemployment benefits. Twenty states amended the formulas under which each unemployed worker's weekly benefit amount is computed to yield a smaller amount. The number of weeks benefits may be payable to unemployed workers was reduced by ten states. Most states made penalties for disqualifying acts more severe (U.S. Department of Labor, Employment and Training Administration, 1980; National Foundation for Unemployment Compensation and Workers' Compensation, 1986). During the same period of unprecedented state cutbacks, the federal-state extended benefit program was systematically dismantled by a series of federal amendments.

These state and federal actions occurred during a period when unemployment rates reached record high post-Depression levels (1982) and continued relatively high thereafter.

Crippling the Extended Benefits Program

During the recession years 1974–77, the extended benefit program was activated in all states, permitting workers who had exhausted regular benefits up to thirteen weeks of EB, making a maximum of thirty-nine weeks. An additional thirteen weeks of federal supplemental benefits (FSB) was made available as of January 1, 1975.[30] On March 29, 1975, President Ford signed a bill which provided an additional thirteen weeks of FSB, making possible a maximum of sixty-five weeks available until January 1, 1976.[31] By early 1975, between two-thirds and three-fourths of the 8.5 million unemployed were receiving unemployment benefits (Kolberg, 1978, pp. 67–71).

A June 30, 1975, amendment extended the program to March 31, 1977. It limited the twenty-six weeks of FSB to states with unemployment rates of at least 6 percent and the thirteen weeks to states with rates of 5 percent or more.[32] A law approved April 12, 1977, limited FSB to thirteen weeks in any state but extended the program to October 31, 1977.[33]

There is some question as to the desirability of adding as much as twenty-six weeks of emergency unemployment benefits even during a recession as severe as the mid-1970s. Although the emergency benefits "had a substantial antipoverty effect," there is evidence that they also produced work disincentive effects, and that "substantial benefits went to the nonpoor as well" (Corson, 1982, pp. 3–8). In any event, it is clear that the prevailing attitude of the administration and Congress was concern for "meeting the needs of the victims of the recession" (Kolberg, 1978, p. 70).

During the 1980s the federal response to high levels of unemployment has not been to add additional layers of emergency benefits, but rather to dismantle the permanent extended benefits program and provide incentives for states to restrict regular benefits.

Three administration-supported amendments effectively destroyed the extended benefit program. The first eliminated the national trigger, which provided that when nationwide unemployment rates reached prescribed levels, EB would become available in all states.[34] Elimination of the national trigger was necessary, according to an administration spokesman, in order to remove

a disincentive for the unemployed to become quickly reemployed in those states with low unemployment when the national trigger is on.[35]

The second disabling amendment increased the level of insured unemployment necessary to activate the state trigger. Prior to passage of the amendment, EB became payable when a state's insured unemployment rate (IUR) averaged 4 percent or more for thirteen weeks and was at least 120 percent of the average IUR for the corresponding thirteen-week period in the preceding two years. A state could opt to disregard the 120 percent requirement and trigger on if its current thirteen-week rate was as much as 5 percent. The 1981 amendment increased from 4 to 5 percent the required state IUR trigger level and from 5 to 6 percent the optional trigger level for states choosing to waive the 120 percent requirement (see note 34).

In support of the amendment, the administration indicated that "structural changes in the labor force have contributed to a generally higher level of normal unemployment," and that

The new laws for extended benefits will better reflect these changes and provide these additional benefits where they are truly needed. (See note 35.)

The third amendment changed the method of calculating the insured unemployment rate (IUR). Prior to the change, the IUR calculation included individuals filing claims for extended benefits as well as regular benefit claimants (see note 34). The amendment eliminated extended benefit claimants from the count. The administration explanation for the change was, in part, that the prior method was "technically flawed and produces several anomalies" (see note 35).

As the result of these changes in triggers, extended benefits have become available in fewer and fewer states. Since 1983, for example, there has been no month in which more than four states have triggered on.

A number of other amendments adopted in 1980 and 1981 limited eligibility for extended benefits in the now unlikely event a state managed to trigger on. The most severe imposed new work search requirements and changed the concept of "suitable work" for which EB claimants must be eligible.[36] Except for individuals whose prospects for work in their usual occupation within a reasonably short period are determined to be good, suitable work for an EB claimant is defined as any work within the individual's capabilities that pays at least the higher of the minimum wage or the individual's average weekly benefit amount, and is otherwise suitable within the meaning of state law except that state suitable work criteria concerning consistency with the individual's prior training, education, work experience, and wage levels must be disregarded. This amendment was estimated to reduce federal program costs by $94 million in fiscal 1981.

All extended benefit claimants, including those whose prospects for work in their usual occupation within a reasonably short period are good, must engage in a systematic and sustained effort to find work and must provide tangible evidence of that effort. Claimants who fail to meet these requirements must be disqualified for the duration of their unemployment and until they have been subsequently employed for at least four weeks, earned wages equal to at least four times their weekly benefit amount, and are then laid off for nondisqualifying reasons. In contrast, under most state laws, any regular benefit claimant who for whatever reason — temporary illness, absence to attend a funeral, need to care for a sick relative, and so on — is not available for a week is denied benefits for that week and thereafter only for as long as the condition that caused the unavailability continues to exist.

The administration attempted unsuccessfully to apply the same suitable work requirement to regular benefit claimants. The proposed new federal standard would apply after the first ninety days of unemployment. According to the secretary of labor,

> By allowing unemployed workers to draw up to six months of compensation unless jobs in their occupation are available, the present unemployment compensation system discourages workers from seeking employment in new industries. . . .[37]

Still other EB amendments passed in 1980 and 1981 were clearly intended to encourage states to make corresponding restrictive changes in their regular benefit programs. The first provides for elimination of the federal 50 percent matching share for the first week of extended benefits in any state that does not have a waiting period for regular benefits (see note 36). This applies to states with no waiting week provisions, to states that have a waiting week for which the individual is later reimbursed if still unemployed after a specified period, to states whose laws authorize the suspension of the waiting period under emergency conditions, and even to states that waive a waiting week requirement if it would interrupt a continuous period of unemployment.

The expressed intent was to encourage unemployed workers to seek work rather than "beat a hasty track to the government office."[38] However, since any delay in filing a claim means a delay in benefits regardless of whether or not there is a waiting week, it is not clear how the waiting week would induce claimants to delay filing. It would appear that the more compelling reason for eliminating the federal 50 percent matching share for the first week of EB in a state that has no waiting week for regular benefits was that it would save an estimated $25 million in federal costs in fiscal year 1981.

A second EB amendment intended to exert leverage on regular benefit programs prohibits states from granting federally shared extended benefits to any claimant with fewer than twenty weeks of work or an equivalent earnings pattern in his base period (see note 34). Thus, anyone who qualified for any regular benefits on the basis of fewer than twenty weeks in his base period must be denied even one week of extended benefits. A third requires all states to provide that extended benefit claimants, who were disqualified from regular benefits for a voluntary quit, discharge for misconduct, or refusal of suitable work, must meet a subsequent work requirement before they can qualify for extended benefits (see note 36). Any individual who served a different disqualification required under state law is barred from any extended benefits. This amendment was estimated to reduce federal program costs by $32 million in fiscal 1981.

The extended benefit amendments were highly successful in reducing EB benefit costs. On the basis of DOL estimates, outlays for extended benefits that were expected to amount to $4.9 billion in fiscal 1983 under the old law were cut to $1.2 billion. In fiscal 1984, EB outlays had been estimated at $3.3 billion. The changes reduced the total to $302 million.

> Put another way, 3.3 million people who would have been eligible for the 13 week extended benefits in fiscal 1983 will not be eligible. Another 2.6 million will be excluded in fiscal 1984 and about 600,000 in fiscal 1985. (Rich, 1982, pp. 7, 10)

Given the fact that since 1983 no more than four states have triggered on during any single month, the overall savings in benefit costs achieved by the amendments undoubtedly far exceeded all estimates. However, not all observers have been impressed with these results:

> It is bitterly ironic that the very unemployed who suffer most from the efforts to fight inflation by slowing down the economy must also suffer from the trimming of their safety net, the unemployment insurance program. (Eizenstat and Spring, 1982, p. 674)

In 1982 Congress enacted a temporary program of wholly federally financed emergency benefits, payable for fewer weeks than EB, to many of the same workers who would have qualified for EB before the 1980 and 1981 amendments.[39] Originally scheduled to terminate March 31, 1983, the emergency program was later extended for two years because of persistently high unemployment—and the failure of extended benefits to trigger on because of the 1981 amendments.

Federal Abdication of Responsibilities

Since 1935, the federal agencies responsible for unemployment insurance promoted provisions considered sound in terms of adequacy and fairness. This implemented the Department of Labor's mandate to contribute to the welfare of American workers. One important function was the development of broad and detailed objectives for unemployment insurance and sample state provisions to implement them. These were changed to reflect changes in federal law and state experience. The recommendations served as benchmarks against which state laws could be evaluated, and they provided a continuing focus on the principles and purposes of unemployment insurance.

In 1982, the Unemployment Insurance Service abruptly stopped its long-term practice of commenting on the desirability and technical adequacy of proposed and enacted state legislation. Since then, comments by national and regional UIS staff have been confined to potential conformity issues. It is likely that the practice was discontinued partly to avoid offending employer groups opposed to many of the DOL's prior recommendations, but primarily to prohibit any recommendations that would tend to increase benefit costs and reduce the federal budget.

This would be consistent with the policy of the Office of Management and Budget (OMB), which during the early 1980s assumed most of the direction of federal responsibilities for unemployment insurance. The federal legislative initiatives covering the program were developed by OMB, with no participation or input from the Unemployment Insurance Service and little from any other element of the Department of Labor. This may have been due to a combination of an unusually powerful OMB director and a secretary of labor perpetually plagued by investigations into his prior activities.

In the administrative area, the role of the Department of Labor changed from providing assistance to conducting audits. Unemployment Insurance Service staff responsible for analyzing and identifying state administrative problems and providing advice for their resolution was severely cut. For example, staff assigned to assist states in improving the quality of their appeals operations and in meeting federal performance standards for timely appeals decisions was reduced from eight to one. In contrast, a new "quality control" unit was established in the UIS, and staff of the Department of Labor's Inspector General's Office, created during the Carter administration, was increased substantially. Thus those responsible for auditing state agencies for the purposes of uncovering waste, fraud, and abuse now actually outnumber the entire remainder of the UIS staff, which is responsible for advice, conformity, assistance, research, and policy.

State Cutbacks in Protection

As a result of the recession of the mid-1970s and the heavy unemployment of the 1980s, many states' funds became depleted, forcing them to borrow from the federal loan fund (National Foundation for Unemployment Compensation and Workers' Compensation, 1986a, p. 63).[40] Loans made after March 1982 bear interest which must be paid promptly, and from a source other than the Trust Fund, as a condition for administrative grants and tax credit.[41] Employers in a state that has not repaid its loan within about two years face (as a means of recouping outstanding loans) an annual reduction in their federal tax offset credit.

Under certain conditions, payment on interest can be deferred and automatic tax credit reductions can be eased.[42] Generally, to qualify for these advantages, the average state unemployment tax rate must equal or exceed a prescribed level, no action must be taken to reduce the state's unemployment tax effort, and no action must be taken that will result in a net decrease in the solvency of the state fund. These constitute strong incentives for states with financial pressures to cut back on benefit availability and amounts. They are similar to other federally induced pressures for benefit cutbacks incorporated in the 1980 and 1981 extended benefit amendments discussed above.

Nor do the states now lack rationale for not moving ahead in establishing benefit adequacy. For the past few years economists and behaviorists have been successful in publishing studies usually based solely on quantitative data purporting to show that unemployment insurance creates as well as perpetuates unemployment (Hamermesh, 1977; Marston, 1980, pp. 431, 438). Other behaviorists have attempted to document, through involved methodology, that a significant portion of benefits is overpaid—if not as a result of claimant fraud, then by administrative incompetence (Burgess and Kingston, 1980, pp. 487–526).

For whatever reason, the states have cut benefits back dramatically (see note 29). Between 1980 and 1986, thirty-one states increased their qualifying requirements for benefits. This does not mean merely the increases in qualifying wages that automatically occur because the requirement is tied to increasing wage levels. Rather, these states changed the actual qualifying formula—in Virginia, for example, from thirty-six to fifty times the weekly benefit amount; Idaho, from 1.25 to 1.5 times high-quarter wages; Wisconsin, from fifteen to nineteen weeks of employment; New Hampshire, from $1,200 in the base period and $600 in each of two quarters to $2,600 in the base period and $1,000 in each of two quarters, and so forth.

During the same six-year period twenty states changed the method of computing a claimant's weekly benefit amount. The changes in eighteen of these states provided that a claimant's base period wages and employment would now yield a smaller weekly benefit amount than prior to the change—for example, Arkansas, North Carolina, and North Dakota changed their computation from one twenty-sixth of a claimant's high-quarter wages to one fifty-second of his wages in his two highest quarters; Delaware, from one twenty-sixth of the high quarter to one seventy-eighth of the three highest quarters; New Jersey, from 66.67 to 60 percent of the claimant's average weekly wage.

During the six-year period, ten states reduced (one state increased) the number of weeks of potential benefit duration either by reducing the maximum number of weeks of benefits available, by changing the duration formula, or by switching from a uniform duration for all claimants to a variable duration based on earnings. For example, maximum weeks in Utah were reduced from thirty-six to twenty-six; Pennsylvania changed from a thirty-week uniform duration to a variable duration ranging from sixteen to twenty-six weeks; Louisiana changed its duration fraction from 40 to 27 percent of base period earnings.

Thirty-six states provide a flexible maximum weekly benefit amount that is stated as a percentage (ranging from 48 to 70 percent) of the statewide average weekly wage. During the six-year period 1980–86, sixteen of these states suspended the operation of the automatic maximum temporarily or indefinitely; five lowered (two increased) the percentage; two made the percentage contingent on specified fund conditions—for example, Louisiana, South Dakota, and Wisconsin suspended the flexible maximum indefinitely; Illinois, Montana, and Ohio suspended the flexible maximum until January 1987; Utah lowered the flexible maximum from 65 to 60 percent of the statewide average weekly wage; Oklahoma lowered the flexible maximum from 66.67 percent to the greater of $197 or 60 to 50 percent, depending on the condition of the fund.

It is difficult to evaluate changes in other states because the maximum can be realistically evaluated only as a percentage of the statewide average weekly wage. The Department of Labor no longer provides information about states' weekly wage.

During the six-year period, three states (Iowa, Maine, and Pennsylvania) that had not had a waiting period requirement adopted one. Four states (Hawaii, Illinois, Louisiana, and Ohio) that had provided for compensating the waiting period after a specified period of unemployment deleted this provision.

Data with respect to changes in disqualification provisions are not available for the same six-year period, but for the four-year period between January 1982 and January 1986, nine states increased the severity of their disqualification for voluntarily quitting work without good cause—for example, Idaho increased the disqualification from the duration of the claimant's unemployment and until the claimant earns an amount equal to eight times his weekly benefit amount, to duration plus sixteen times his weekly benefit amount. Eleven states increased the disqualification for discharge for misconduct connected with the work—Wisconsin, for instance, changed from the week of the occurrence plus three weeks to the duration of the unemployment and until the claimant has had seven weeks of work and earned an amount equal to fourteen times his weekly benefit amount. Twelve states increased the severity of the disqualification for refusal of suitable work without good cause—for example, Wyoming changed the disqualification from the week the claim was filed plus the seven following weeks, to the duration of the unemployment and until the claimant has had at least twelve weeks of work and earned an amount equal to at least twelve times his weekly benefit amount.

The period 1980–86 constitutes the most regressive six-year period in the history of the unemployment insurance system from the standpoint of cutbacks in benefit adequacy and benefit availability. The changes described above, combined with the crippling federal amendments to the extended benefit program, help explain why only one out of about three unemployed workers now receives an unemployment insurance check, and why the program seems to be fast becoming even more irrelevant.

4. Future Directions

Despite the damage caused by recent economic and political shocks, the unemployment insurance system remains viable—because of its federal-state structure. Yet pressure continues to change the basic distribution of authority.

Federal Domination Alternative

There have always been advocates of new federal program standards. Those who find different treatment of unemployed workers by different states intolerable or deplore the inadequate protection provided by some states seek benefit amount standards. Such requirements have been proposed unsuccessfully by four national administrations,[45] a majority of the National Commission on Unemployment Compensation, and even, at one time, by a majority of state agency administrators composing the Interstate Conference of Employment Security Agencies.[46]

The labor representatives of the National Commission recommended not only federal standards governing benefit maximums, but also benefit computation, qualifying requirements, waiting periods, disqualifications, eligibility conditions, appeals requirements, benefits for partial unemployment, dependents' allowances, and job search requirements (National Commission on Unemployment Compensation, 1980, p. 94).

Employer groups that consistently opposed federal standards (except experience rating) in the past, on the grounds that program matters should be left to the states, enthusiastically endorsed Reagan administration proposals for changes in the extended benefit program and for forcing all states to disqualify claimants who, after three months of unemployment, refuse a job that they are capable of performing that pays wages equal to the higher of the minimum wage or their weekly benefit amount—regardless of their past experience, training, or income levels.[47]

But even if new federal standards and greater federal authority over program matters are desirable, the prospects are not bright that any future federal action in this area will benefit the unemployed. The reduction of federal deficits through cuts in government spending is destined to dominate national administration and congressional priorities for the foreseeable future. Given current federal priorities, the program is more likely to be weakened than strengthened by new federal program standards.

Recent changes in the federally financed and controlled program of Unemployment Compensation for Ex-Servicemen (UCX), adopted in 1954, suggest the probable fate of a federally dominated system. The program is administered by the states acting as agents for the federal government pursuant to voluntary written agreements. For the first twenty-seven years, federal law required generally the same treatment of ex-servicepersons as applied to claimants for regular state unemployment insurance.

Individuals leaving the service were considered to face the same problems as other unemployed workers, as well as unique problems of readjusting to civilian life. In 1981 Congress adopted an amendment requiring states to treat as a voluntary quit and deny benefits to any individual who could have reenlisted.[48] Thus anyone who served one or more enlistment periods and desired to return to civilian life was to be treated the same as a worker who had quit his job without good cause. Upon reconsideration, Congress deleted this provision in 1982. But instead of continuing the prior practice of treating ex-servicepersons on an equal basis with other claimants, Congress, under pressure of previously accepted budget restraints, imposed a four-week waiting period and a maximum benefit duration for any claimant in the program of thirteen weeks.[49]

Congressional treatment of ex-servicepersons is in sharp contrast to state treatment of regular benefit claimants. No state has more than a one-week waiting period for regular benefit claimants. All but Puerto Rico (which provides a uniform potential duration of twenty weeks to all claimants) provide to all claimants a maximum duration of twenty-six weeks for regular benefits and thirty-nine weeks for combined regular and extended benefits.

Greater State Autonomy Alternative—Devolution

To imagine the probable fate of a wholly state-controlled system, one need only consider some past state proposals that were defeated only because they violated federal conditions for grants or tax credits. State efforts described above to condition regular benefits on income or needs tests or to use fund moneys for purposes other than compensation are only a few examples of many proposals that were popular at one time or another in a state that, if allowed to spread, would have radically altered the nature of the program and destroyed its effectiveness.

However, a recent proposal that promises greater state autonomy in the area of administration (if not other areas) has received support at both federal and state levels. On May 1, 1985, the Office of Management and Budget submitted to the Interstate Conference of Employment Security Agencies for comment a draft proposal titled "Administration of Unemployment Insurance and the Employment Service, A Proposal for Reform."

According to the proposal, the reform is aimed at problems created by the current federal-state administrative financing arrangement. The principal problem, according to the proposal, is that federal authority over the distribution of administrative funds and federal control over administrative priorities unreasonably limit states' freedom of control over program matters. The current structure "imposes rigidities on the substantive policy spheres reserved to the states," and "involves unnecessary control of funds and program authority by the federal government for responsibilities the states should control."

The reform purports to correct the problem by removing all but essential federal administrative requirements and shifting to the states complete responsibility for raising administrative funds. To help the states raise revenue for administrative costs, the current net federal tax would be reduced, and the difference between the current net tax (0.8 percent) and the reduced net (that is, 0.3 percent) would be made available to the states by increasing the maximum tax credit against the federal tax (that is, from the current 5.4 to 5.9 percent).

For the first time, the costs of administration as well as benefit costs would need to compete with other state priorities. Employer tax increases for administrative costs will invariably be resisted, even in those states where the increase in the state tax is less than the corresponding decrease in the federal unemployment tax. In many states administrative grants are greater than the yields produced in those states by the federal tax. In any event, the result of the proposed reform in several states is likely to be even more inadequate administrative funds than the federal government now provides, or forced cutbacks in overall program expenses, particularly benefits.

Nor is it clear that the reform would "give the States full control over administration of their UI and ES programs"; or free the states from "detailed reports on State program operation and extensive budget planning documents"; or eliminate the "mountains of paperwork" now required; or "remove obstacles that deny State administrators the ability to improve their State UI programs." First, it is clear that state executive and legislative branches are no less likely than their federal counterparts to require reports on agency operations and budget planning information. Second, not all federal authority over administration would be relinquished. Under the reform, each state would continue to be required to adhere to certain "basic principles," including the payment of benefits "timely and properly" to eligible individuals, a work test that would require all benefit recipients to be "able, willing, and actively seeking to work," assurance of a "fair and timely hearing for all parties at interest," and perhaps more. These basic principles appear to be as ambiguous and as subject to federal interpretation as the "methods of administration" and "proper and efficient" requirements of current federal law.

Finally, one questions the reform's premise, that federal control over administrative matters limits state freedom over program matters. For fifty years, the Department of Labor's position has been that the secretary may deny granted funds to finance a particular implementing procedure, service, payment, or purchase which he determines is not necessary for proper and efficient administration. However,

> The Secretary may not deny administrative funds to a State necessary to administer a substantive provision of State law merely because he believes the provision is unnecessary or would be costly to administer. The Social Security Act was intended to permit the States wide discretion with respect to the type of unemployment insurance law they wish to enact. If the Secretary had authority to fund or not to fund substantive provisions, the result would be to deny the States the discretion the legislative history shows that Congress intended them to have.[50]

If decisions concerning administrative grants are now imposing "rigidities on substantive policy spheres reserved to the States," then it would seem that the Department of Labor or OMB has departed from this long-standing interpretation of federal law, without the public notice and invitation to comment usually required for changes in significant interpretations.

It is ironic that concern for greater state freedom of control over their programs is now being expressed by an organization that for more than a decade has consistently supported (or initiated, in the case of the cost/ savings requirements of 1982 and 1983) almost every federal standard considered by Congress that required states to restrict benefit costs in some way. But it is not surprising. The principal beneficiary of the proposed devolution would be the federal budget, assuming the savings in costs are not offset by equivalent tax reductions.

According to the proposal, state costs associated with paying benefits and collecting revenues for the UI program were estimated in fiscal 1985 at about $1.6 billion. The projections increase for each succeeding year. The benefit to the states would be a somewhat greater degree of freedom over administrative priorities in return for bearing the entire burden of their administrative costs.

Any new freedom over administrative matters has great appeal to state administrators. There is no doubt that the states are left too little discretion over administrative matters, and too little incentive to improve operations. State agencies and the Interstate Conference of Employment Security Agencies must continue to explore, promote, and demand alternative approaches to more adequate revenues for administration and greater state control of their use.

In any event, however, the remedy to the problem is not likely to come from a reform which promises fewer administrative resources for many states, substitution of state budget and reporting requirements for federal ones, and continued federal control over "basic principles."

New Considerations for Extended Benefits

Benefit duration, always a source of controversy, is the program's most critical issue, particularly since the destruction of the extended benefits program. Undoubtedly, the growing irrelevance of the program—evidenced by the fact that less than one of three unemployed workers now receives an unemployment check—is due in large part to inadequate benefit duration during current periods of relatively high unemployment.

Research is needed to determine who the unprotected are, why they are not receiving unemployment insurance, and what is happening to them. The answers are prerequisite to any decision about benefit duration.

In the past, maximum potential regular benefits of twenty-six weeks appeared adequate during nonrecessionary periods, provided the state's benefit duration formula yielded twenty-six weeks to both high- and low-wage workers on the basis of a reasonable test of labor force attachment, for example, thirty-nine weeks of work. To illustrate, Florida provides twenty-six weeks of benefits only for individuals with a full fifty-two-week year of employment.

Unemployment during recessions has generally been considered a federal responsibility, as evidenced by four prior federal ad hoc temporary benefit extensions.[51] The permanent extended benefit program, providing for a fifty-fifty federal-state sharing of benefit costs, represents at least a partial federal responsibility.

In recent years, federal responsibility for recession unemployment has been overshadowed by federal concern for reducing program costs. Given the virtual elimination of the federal-state extended benefit program, current federal priorities, and increasing federal acceptance of unemployment rates in excess of 7 percent as normal, it may be that restoration of the program's effectiveness in meeting the needs of the unemployed must come from state initiative — with federal benefit extension only when unemployment reaches near-Depression levels. The area would appear ripe for the same kind of state initiative and experimentation that characterized the regular benefit program's initial period.

Only eight states now provide extensions for those who exhaust regular benefits. Most extensions are activated when state unemployment rates reach prescribed levels. Others are targeted to special industry-wide unemployment situations, or to individuals taking approved training or receiving reemployment assistance (National Foundation of Unemployment Compensation and Workers' Compensation, 1986a, p. 47).

That so few states provide extensions to those who exhaust regular benefit entitlement is due in part to cost considerations and in part to federal preemption of the issue of long-term unemployment. Repeal of the now obsolete extended benefits program would have the desirable effect of removing the illusion that any realistic federal-state backstop now exists.

Although states must finance the benefit costs for any benefit extensions they provide, there is no obstacle to federal financing of the administrative costs of state additional benefit programs, provided they constitute unemployment compensation. This means that benefits must be paid as a matter of right to eligible individuals solely on the basis of their unemployment. Under current law, no federal grants for administrative costs may be paid under state additional benefit programs that use benefits as loans to unemployed workers, as wages for public works jobs, as subsidies to self-employed individuals, or as supplemental pay to individuals receiving on-the-job training. Nor are federal grants payable if the additional benefits are limited to the principal supports of families, or conditioned on any means or income test (National Foundation for Unemployment Compensation and Workers' Compensation, 1986b, pp. 34–36).

These restrictions on federal administrative grants should be reexamined, not for the regular benefit programs, where they are still appropriate, but with respect to state extended benefits. At a time of almost universal domestic program cutbacks at both federal and state levels, it may be that support for benefit extensions will come only if they include an income test. Such an approach has received serious consideration by supporters of the program.

Saul J. Blaustein has recommended a basic restructuring of federal and state responsibilities: reemployment assistance would become an integral aspect of unemployment insurance; the extended benefit program would be eliminated altogether; a three-tier program would be established, with each thirteen-week tier providing increasingly stiffer qualifying and work search requirements. Aside from the first thirteen-week tier, the program would be partly (in the case of the second tier) or wholly federally financed and controlled.

Blaustein calls for a federal program of unemployment assistance (UA) "as a major backstop to UI" to cover unemployed workers from low-income households who do not receive UI, including those who have exhausted the thirty-nine weeks of UI provided by the three tiers, as well as unemployed workers who are not covered by UI or do not meet UI qualifying requirements. Benefits under the program would be conditioned on the lower living standard budget developed and estimated annually by the Bureau of Labor Statistics (BLS), which represents a "below-normal" standard to which a family may be reduced because of a temporary loss of income. It is not a "minimal" or poverty-level standard. As indicated, the UA program would apply to UI exhaustees only after thirty-nine weeks of regular benefits (Blaustein, 1981, pp. 106, 107).

In recommending extension of the FSB program, which then paid up to twenty-six weeks of emergency benefits, secretary of labor Dr. John Dunlop recognized that at some point benefit extensions cannot reasonably continue to be considered unemployment insurance — without weakening the integrity of the basic program. He expressed concern that the benefit extensions were turning unemployment insurance into "a public assistance program." However,

> I do favor this extension at this time because we have not in this country placed into effect a comprehensive type of welfare program; [another] solution to these two problems would say after a certain point a person who was unemployed — I do not care for the moment whether you say 52 weeks, 65 weeks, 78 weeks or some other number — ought to be treated financially not as part of the unemployment insurance system, financed in the way an unemployment insurance system is, but ought to be treated as part of some welfare program.[52]

Finally, the authors of an appraisal of the Federal Supplemental Benefits Program also offer considerations about the feasibility of applying an income test to benefit extensions:

> FSB reduced the incidence of poverty by nearly one-third. [However,] almost 40 percent would have had 1975 incomes above two times the poverty level

without FSB while 10 percent would have had incomes above four times that level.

. . . Thus, although the FSB program was superior to the available means-tested programs in reducing poverty for UI eligibles, it was target inefficient because a substantial amount of benefits went to the nonpoor. (Corson, 1982, pp. 91–93)

According to the authors, if FSB had been restricted to individuals who, at the time of application, had a household income below the Bureau of Labor Statistics lower living standard for 1975 (Blaustein's recommended benchmark, which comes to about 1.8 times the poverty line), almost 90 percent of program benefits would have been paid to recipients with annual incomes below two times the poverty line, compared with the 64 percent paid under the actual 1975 program (Corson, 1982, p. 107).

The foregoing observations pose the questions of when benefits should appropriately be tied to an income test, and whether removal of current federal conditions for administrative grants, in the case of state benefit extensions beyond twenty-six (or more) weeks, would provide effective incentives for needed state initiatives.

Promoting Sound Objectives

The program's growing irrelevance to the needs of a huge majority of unemployed workers is not only the result of the destruction of the extended benefits program, but due also to cutbacks in protection at the state level.

State qualifying requirements are now higher than at any other time in the history of the system. Wage levels and employment patterns that were sufficient in the past no longer meet minimum requirements. State formulas for computing weekly benefit amounts and benefit duration have been tightened, and benefits now bear a smaller proportion of past earnings than before. Benefit maximums have not kept pace with increases in wages. Disqualifications have become almost universally severe and eligibility requirements sometimes border on harassment. The extended benefit program is now more illusion than reality.

These developments are due as much to changes in both federal and state priorities as to the economic pressures of the past several years. At both levels, cost criteria overwhelmed considerations of adequacy and equity. Cost saving was the principal reason for benefit cutbacks and stringent eligibility conditions, but they have been defended frequently on the grounds that the availability of unemployment insurance tends to discourage individuals from seeking new kinds of work, from relocating, from taking training, or from other behavior considered appropriate for them.

The main purpose of unemployment insurance, to provide adequate protection to workers unemployed through no fault of their own, has been obscured.

The Department of Labor's termination of its responsibilities, to develop, promote, and provide analytical and research support for sound program objectives, has created a serious void. It may be that given informed advice, the Virginia legislature would not have decided to require almost six months of work before any worker could claim a dollar in benefits. More information may have dissuaded the Delaware legislature from adopting a formula that yields a weekly benefit amount less than 50 percent of the average weekly wage for anyone who experiences even a week of unemployment in a nine-month period. Better understanding of the implications for lower-paid workers may have deterred the Louisiana legislature from changing the formula used to compute total potential benefits from a maximum amount equal to 40 percent of a claimant's base period wages to a maximum amount equal to 27 percent.

It may be that with DOL urging, the Wisconsin legislature could have been persuaded not to adopt the most severe penalty of any state for voluntarily quitting a job without good cause connected with the work. The penalty requires denial of benefits for the duration of the claimant's unemployment until he becomes reemployed for at least seven weeks and earns an amount equal to at least fourteen times his weekly benefit amount. In addition, the disqualified claimant's benefit entitlement from the quit employer is reduced by 50 percent. The disqualification applies not only to the claimant's last separation but to any disqualifying separation from any base period employer.

It may be that changes made in the last six years in the interest of cutting costs would have been made regardless of any federal persuasion. In any event, responsible state action must be based on objective information and data. In the absence of other resources, state legislators must often rely solely on state UI agency personnel for expertise. This is not always desirable, since agency opinions are often influenced more by the administrative implications of a provision than by equity or adequacy criteria. In states where management and labor advocates are interested, knowledgeable, articulate, and reasonably balanced in influence, unemployment insurance debates are likely to provide a sound basis for legislation. This is true also in states with active and knowledgeable advisory councils. Unfortunately, not all these elements are usually present.

There now exists no authoritative source of recommendations for state unemployment insurance provisions based on research and experience, no evaluation of particular provisions from the standpoint of equity and adequacy, no vehicle "to correlate and make useful the experience developed under state laws." Nor are existing organizations of state agency personnel likely to fill the gap. The Interstate Conference of Employment Security Agencies and the International Association of Personnel in Employment Security provide important forums for the discussion of UI issues, but they tend more to react than to initiate policies, and their focus is primarily on administrative concerns.

Given the need of the program for direction, it is appropriate and encouraging that the state that led the nation in developing and implementing basic concepts of unemployment insurance again assume leadership fifty years later. If the La Follette Institute and the Industrial Research Institute of the University of Wisconsin can produce new objectives and sound evaluations of the program, this would provide a needed step in halting the trend toward irrelevance.

NOTES

1. See Section 3306(b), Federal Unemployment Tax Act (FUTA).
2. See Section 3306(a), FUTA.
3. See Section 3306(c), FUTA.
4. New Hampshire ($500,000 penalty assessed).
5. See Section 904, Social Security Act (SSA).
6. See Sections 3304(a)(3) and (4), FUTA; 303(a)(4) and (5), SSA.
7. See Section 3306(h), FUTA.
8. See Section 303(a)(8), SSA.
9. See Section 303(a)(1), SSA.
10. See Section 303(a)(3), SSA.
11. See Section 3302(b), FUTA.
12. See Section 3303(a)(1), FUTA.
13. See, for example, Becker (1982); Wagman (1982).
14. See Section 3304(a)(5), FUTA.
15. See Section 3304(a)(9)(A), FUTA.
16. See Section 3304(a)(9)(A), FUTA.
17. See Section 3304(a)(6), FUTA.
18. See Section 3309(a)(2), FUTA.
19. Federal-State Extended Unemployment Compensation Program, Title II of the "Employment Security Amendments of 1970," P.L. 91-373 (approved August 10, 1970).
20. For the prohibition of states from denying benefits on the basis of pregnancy, see Section 3304(a)(12), FUTA; from disqualifying claimants taking training, Section 3304(a)(8), FUTA; from canceling wage credits, Section 3304(a)(10), FUTA.
21. *Mary Ann Turner* v. *Department of Employment Security and Board of Review of the Industrial Commission of Utah,* No. 74-1312 (November 17, 1975).
22. See Sections 3304(a)(14), FUTA (on aliens); 3304(a)(13), FUTA (athletes);

3304(a)(6), FUTA (school employees); 3304(a)(15), FUTA (retirement deduction); 303(e), SSA (child support).

23. National Commission on Unemployment Compensation (1980), p. 129. The commission recommended that "the National Office of the UIS should be staffed with at least 200 jobs."

24. See Sections 3310, FUTA; 304, SSA.

25. For detailed discussion of the administration of the federal UI laws and the conformity process, see Rubin (1983).

26. New Hampshire (1981), the Virgin Islands (1985), South Dakota (1939), and Arizona (1941), respectively.

27. For example, two key performance standards—benefit payment promptness (1976) and appeals promptness (1972)—were the products of close cooperation between federal and state officials.

28. See, for example, U.S. Department of Labor, Bureau of Employment Security (1962).

29. Data come from comparing U.S. Department of Labor, Employment and Training Administration (1980) and National Foundation for Unemployment Compensation and Workers' Compensation (1986).

30. P.L. 93-572.

31. P.L. 94-12.

32. P.L. 94-45.

33. P.L. 95-19.

34. P.L. 97-352.

35. Statement of Lawrence E. Weatherford, Acting Deputy Assistant Secretary for Employment and Training, U.S. Department of Labor, before the Subcommittee on Public Assistance and Unemployment Compensation, Committee on Ways and Means, U.S. House of Representatives, March 12, 1981.

36. P.L. 96-499.

37. Statement of Raymond J. Donovan, Secretary of Labor, before the Subcommittee on Public Assistance and Unemployment Compensation, Committee on Ways and Means, U.S. House of Representatives, March 12, 1981.

38. *Congressional Record* (March 4, 1980), Senator Boren, p. S2094.

39. Federal Supplemental Compensation, P.L. 97-248 (approved September 2, 1982).

40. As of January 1, 1986, fifteen states had total loans and interest outstanding of about $6.69 billion. This was down from the previous year's total of thirty states and over $10 billion. See National Foundation for Unemployment Compensation and Workers' Compensation (January 1986), p. 63.

41. See Sections 3304(a)(17), FUTA; 303(c)(3), SSA.

42. See Sections 3302, FUTA; 1202, SSA.

43. See, for example, Hamermesh (1977), pp. 32ff.; Marston (1980), pp. 431–438.

44. See Burgess and Kingston (1980), pp. 487–526.

45. Truman (1950), Kennedy (1965), Johnson (1965), and Nixon (1973).

46. 1975, although the organization reversed its position four years later.

47. Statement on Proposed Budget Reduction in the Unemployment Compen-

sation Program before the Subcommittee on Public Assistance and Means, for the Chamber of Commerce of the United States, by Samuel E. Dyer, March 11, 1981. Similar testimony supporting the same bill was provided in testimony on behalf of the National Association of Manufacturers, March 11, 1981.

48. P.L. 97-35.

49. P.L. 97-362.

50. Letter, Lawrence E. Weatherford, Administrator, Unemployment Insurance Service, Department of Labor, to Al Eastman, office of Senator John Tunney, November 26, 1976.

51. Temporary Extended Unemployment Compensation Act of 1961 (P.L. 87-6); Emergency Unemployment Compensation Act of 1971 (P.L. 92-224); Emergency Unemployment Compensation Act of 1974 (P.L. 93-572); and Federal Supplemental Unemployment Compensation Act of 1982 (P.L. 97-248).

52. Statement of John Dunlop, Secretary of Labor, before the Senate Finance Committee, 94th Cong., 1st Sess., June 16, 1975.

REFERENCES

Becker, Joseph M., S.J. 1982. "The Location of Financial Responsibility in Unemployment Insurance." *University of Detroit Journal of Urban Law* 59 (Summer).

Blaustein, Saul J. 1981. *Job and Income Security for Unemployed Workers.* Kalamazoo, Mich.: Upjohn Institute for Employment Research.

Burgess, Paul L., and Jerry Kingston. 1980. "Estimating Overpayments and Improper Payments." In *Unemployment Compensation: Studies and Research.* Vol. 2. Washington, D.C.: National Commission on Unemployment Compensation.

Committee on Economic Security. 1935. *Report to the President of the Committee on Economic Security.* Washington, D.C.: Government Printing Office.

Corson, Walter, and Walter Nicholson. 1982. *The Federal Supplemental Benefits Program— An Appraisal of Emergency Extended Unemployment Insurance Benefits.* Kalamazoo, Mich.: Upjohn Institute for Employment Research.

Eizenstat, Stuart, and William Spring. 1982. "The Future of Unemployment Insurance." *University of Detroit Journal of Urban Law* 59 (Summer).

Haber, William, and Merrill G. Murray. 1966. *Unemployment Insurance in the American Economy.* Homewood, Ill.: Richard D. Irwin.

Hamermesh, Daniel. 1977. *Jobless Pay and the Economy.* Baltimore: Johns Hopkins University Press.

Kolberg, William H. 1978. *Developing Manpower Legislation—A Personal Chronicle.* Washington, D.C.: National Academy of Sciences.

Marston, Stephen T. 1980. "Voluntary Unemployment." In *Unemployment Compensation: Studies and Research.* Vol. 2. Washington, D.C.: National Commission on Unemployment Compensation.

National Commission on Unemployment Compensation. 1980. *Unemployment Compensation: Final Report.* Washington, D.C.: Government Printing Office.

National Foundation for Unemployment Compensation and Workers' Compensation. 1986a. *Highlights of State Unemployment Compensation Laws.* January.

National Foundation for Unemployment Compensation and Workers' Compensation. 1986b. *Highlights of Federal Unemployment Compensation Laws.* January.

Rich, Spencer. 1982. "Jobless Aid Fraying as a Safety Net." *Washington Post,* November 6, 1982.

Rubin, Murray. 1983. *Federal-State Relations in Unemployment Insurance: A Balance of Power.* Kalamazoo, Mich.: Upjohn Institute for Employment Research.

Social Security Board. 1937. "Draft Bills for State Unemployment Compensation of Pooled Fund and Employer Reserve Account Types." Washington, D.C.: Government Printing Office.

U.S. Department of Labor. Bureau of Employment Security. 1962. "Unemployment Insurance Legislative Policy, Recommendations for State Legislation." BES No. U-212A, October. Washington, D.C.: Government Printing Office.

U.S. Department of Labor. Employment and Training Administration. 1980. *Significant Provisions of State Unemployment Insurance Laws, July 6, 1980.* Washington, D.C.: Government Printing Office.

Wagman, Theodore D. 1982. "The Mythology of Experience Rating in Unemployment Compensation." *University of Detroit Journal of Urban Law* 59 (Summer).

8

Administrative Simplification of Unemployment Compensation Programs

EDWIN M. KEHL

Introduction

This paper addresses the bifurcated structure of the administrative financing and control of the unemployment insurance program in the United States from the perspective of an administrator of a state program.[1]

Wisconsin, the first state to pass a compulsory unemployment insurance law, initially emphasized employers' responsibility for controlling unemployment levels and stressed the concept of "experience rating" to determine the degree of employer responsibility and liability for funding the system.

The unemployment compensation system has been one of the United States' major income maintenance programs. The system has transferred huge sums of money to unemployed workers in their time of need and has managed to provide a stabilizing influence to the economy during economic recessions.

The basic administrative structure of the program, designed by Congress in the mid-1930s, has remained essentially unchanged during the last fifty years. But changes in the intervening years in the structure and functioning of the labor market point to a need for change in this structure.

1. Historical Perspectives

Unemployment compensation originated in Europe in the mid-nineteenth century. A number of voluntary UI plans were developed, primarily by trade unions. The first compulsory law was passed in Great Britain in 1911. The idea spread to other European countries after World War I, and U.S. state laws were largely copied from European efforts, with two major differences. The first was that the U.S. programs required contributions from employers only. In many European nations, workers also contributed to the funding of the programs; general revenues completed the tripartite funding. The second was a variable tax rate applied to employers' payrolls depending on unemployment experience — the experience-rated system.

The first voluntary plan in the United States was developed in 1821 by a trade union. Voluntary plans were popular and grew rather significantly in the garment industry. After World War I several voluntary plans were financed by employers and became the first guaranteed employment plans. The first compulsory program was introduced in Massachusetts in 1916, and New York followed in 1921. Neither of these plans was enacted into law. In Wisconsin a compulsory plan was first proposed in 1921 and was reintroduced in each session of the state legislature until it passed on January 29, 1932.

Wisconsin's legislative leadership attracted considerable attention at the national level. Efforts toward federal unemployment compensation laws had begun as early as 1916 and included a noteworthy attempt by Senator Robert Wagner to draft legislation in 1931. None were successful, however, until provisions for the national unemployment compensation program finally came to fruition as part of the Social Security Act signed into law by Franklin Roosevelt on August 14, 1935.

There was considerable concern that the Supreme Court would declare a national UI program unconstitutional. To prevent such court action, a novel administrative arrangement was created to ameliorate the provisions of the law. States were given strong incentives, through a federal tax measure, to set up their own programs, and only minimum federal standards were provided. The program has been characterized by this unique federal-state partnership ever since. Thus, despite some serious constitutional challenges to the bill, the constitutionality of the law was upheld in May 1937.

It is not clear whether individual states felt bludgeoned into participating in the program by the taxing provisions of the federal unemployment tax act or whether they were encouraged by the opportunity to participate in a new social program. Regardless of motivation, all states passed enabling and conforming legislation by 1938.

Originally federal law stated that employers were liable for the tax if they employed eight or more workers who were on the job for twenty or more weeks. This was reduced to four or more workers on January 1, 1956, and one or more workers in 1970. Several other changes should be noted here. In 1938, railroad employees were separated and covered under their own Railroad Unemployment Insurance Act. The Servicemen's Readjustment Act in 1944 created the famous "52-20 Club," entitling unemployed veterans to receive $20 per week in benefits for up to fifty-two weeks. The 1944 act also provided for federal advances to states having difficulty with UI fund solvency.

The system also underwent several interesting administrative changes; these alterations increasingly included provisions that were only tangentially related to UI. The original Social Security Act required that states deposit all collected funds into the federal unemployment trust fund; that they pay all unemployment compensation benefit payments through public employment offices; that they use all money withdrawn from the fund to pay benefits; and that they repay any funds determined by the secretary of labor to have been improperly spent. In an effort to improve service, the 1939 Social Security amendments required states to use merit-based personnel standards in hiring employees in the program and stipulated that administrative funds allocated by the federal government to the states could be used only for "proper and efficient" administration of the law.

Later states were also required to provide information to other state and federal agencies to provide a method of cross-matching payments among various income transfer systems to control fraud and abuse. They were also required to compel claimants to disclose any child support obligations and to inform state or local child support agencies of benefits paid to claimants with such obligations. Administrative amendments also included provisions relating to interest owed by the state on UI debts to the federal government.

2. Description of the System — 1985

State-Federal Relationships

Although the unique state-federal relationship created in part as a protection against constitutional challenge has endured over the last fifty years, it has not been without its critics. Many state administrators espousing state independence have felt that the federal partner has been domineering, inflexible, and insensitive to individual states' needs. Many states viewed the Feds as power-grabbing bureaucrats who, having unsuccessfully attempted to nationalize the system through the legislative process, tried to achieve the same result through administrative fiat.

On the other hand, many federal representatives are dismayed at the lack of uniformity and persistent performance problems among different states because of limited national standards. They feel that the states use the program as a political strategy to appease either the employers or the labor community, and that states attempt to influence economic development and major industrial location and relocation through questionable statutory provisions.

A seasoned observer might conclude that controversy and conflict is inherent in a system in which responsibilities are shared unequally and the communication glitches in a highly complex system create unproductive attitudes and misconceptions. However, the program's successful performance over the years may, in some small measure, be due to the different parties in this relationship keeping each other relatively honest.

Taxing Authority

The Federal Unemployment Tax Act (FUTA) and the Social Security Act established the framework for financing the UI system: FUTA imposes a 6.2 percent federal payroll tax on all employers covered under the program, but employers may receive a 5.4 percent credit against the federal tax if the state unemployment compensation law meets the minimum federal requirements. If those requirements are met the state is also entitled to federal grants to cover all the necessary costs of administering the program.

If a state fails to comply with federal standards, the secretary of labor is empowered to eliminate the tax credit or deny the grants to cover the cost of administration. Therefore, compliance with the federal law is highly desirable, and noncompliance is a painful, costly alternative. This is a very potent weapon for one partner to wield.

The 0.8 percent federal tax resulting from the 6.2 percent federal tax base offset by the 5.4 percent credit is used to pay all state and federal administrative costs associated with UI and employment service programs, to provide funds for the 50 percent federal share of benefits paid under the Federal / State Extended Unemployment compensation program, and to maintain a loan fund from which individual states may borrow whenever their own trust funds are inadequate to pay unemployment compensation benefits. A complex system of loan guarantees and repayments provides additional incentives for states to restore trust fund solvency within specified time periods.

States pay benefits to unemployed workers through taxing liable employers. Four states also collect contributions from employees. The federal requirements in the taxing area are limited and allow states wide variation in taxing practices. They do, however, order states to deposit the taxes in the federal treasury, so as to prevent accumulation of interest by the states on these funds. In fact, the Department of Labor (DOL) will chide states that delay more than two or three days in making the UI deposits.

FUTA requires a wage base of $7,000, but many states have adopted higher tax bases to provide sufficient revenues to maintain trust fund solvency. In addition, most states provide for an automatic adjustment of the wage base to respond to changes in FUTA.

Employment Service

Under the Wagner-Peyser Act of 1933, each state is required to operate and maintain a public employment office system funded by the administrative account described in the last section. Among its other responsibilities, the Employment Service registers unemployed workers who are filing for unemployment benefits and, in many states, applies a work test against those claimants to assure that they are actively seeking work.

Recent amendments to the Wagner-Peyser Act, enacted with the passage of the Job Training Partnership Act (JTPA), established new administrative goals for the Employment Service. State employment services are now required to engage in more localized planning with private industry councils under JTPA. This involvement in local-level planning has made the job services more responsive to local needs and has also resulted, in Wisconsin at least, in more attention to the needs of JTPA clientele and a closer working relationship with training and employment development activities.

Interstate Benefit Payments

The federal government also developed a program to provide UI services to claimants who cross state boundaries in pursuit of work or who have worked for employers in more than one state. This program allows states to process claims and adjudicate disputes from other states. Once slow and cumbersome because it relied on mail transmittals and had to accommodate a variety of state laws and qualifications, this system has been computerized and now is only slightly less timely than a regular intrastate benefit process.

3. Administrative Relationships — 1985

Congress

Despite a number of modifications and changes in the administrative structure of the UI program in the last ten or fifteen years, the program itself has attracted little congressional attention. Congress has occasionally considered exempting a class of workers from coverage or providing for a new federal standard that the states must comply with. Congressional activity regarding UI has principally been to extend benefits during economic recessions when claimants in many states experienced a high level of benefit exhaustion and additional coverage was required.

Federal Extended Benefits (FEB) and Federal Supplemental Benefits (FSB) have been available to the long-term unemployed during severe, extended economic recessions. Claimants who have exhausted their benefit entitlement in states which have experienced high insured unemployment rates for thirteen weeks or more may be eligible for additional weeks of benefits, depending on their employment history.

States routinely receive inquiries from congressional representatives who have been contacted by claimants or employers unhappy with the results of the system's determination process. It has been Wisconsin's experience that representatives are content to accept state agencies' explanations of the nature of the problems encountered and the rationale for the decisions made. On occasion, they may question the philosophy of the program and its intent, but few question how the program is operated. As a source of political pressure congressional delegations can be helpful in attempting to get a favorable decision out of the DOL, although the complex nature of the program prevents congressional input beyond a certain level of detail.

In recent years Congress has affected the administration of the program in several ways. In the Deficit Reduction Act of 1983 Congress specified that states must have an income verification system in place by 1988 in order to prevent fraud and abuse in a number of income maintenance programs. Most states operate a wage reporting system that provides a suitable process for income verification, but states that do not have wage reporting systems (including Wisconsin) will need to create them.

The role of Congress in establishing budgetary allocations and appropriations for the program is also important. Since 1980 Congress has been more supportive of the Employment Service and the UI program than the Reagan administration, frequently increasing targeted amounts for the administration of these programs beyond the allocations the president's budget provided.

Severe reductions in DOL funding have resulted in less federal participation in the UI program. This might be a favorable trend from the states' standpoint, but many state administrators believe the DOL has played an important role in communicating innovative ideas for change among states and in developing objective performance standards and performance measurement criteria.

With the reduction of resources to influence programmatic relationships, the DOL has concentrated its efforts and resources on administrative and financing issues. In the last several years much effort has been directed toward establishing mandatory, standardized benefit payment control activities to improve the integrity of state benefit payment systems. Unfortunately, the DOL has focused little attention on funding activities to recover improper benefit payments or to design and implement better payment control systems. The DOL staff has, however, increased the number and diversity of audits of the programs.

Interstate Conference of Employment Security Administrators

The Interstate Conference of Employment Security Administrators (ICESA) is an organization of state administrators that provides a forum for discussing problems related to program administration and to state-federal relations. In its fifty years of existence the ICESA has shifted its focus from the unemployment compensation program to the participation of the Employment Service and the Department of Labor in a variety of employment and training programs. However, the ICESA maintains a strong continuing interest in the UI program.

ICESA was considered an adjunct of the DOL at one time and received its administrative funding through federal sources. In the 1970s the activities and functions of the organization became focused on issues and concerns that dictated that it could no longer be considered an adjunct of federal government. ICESA began to assert itself in opposition to DOL policy issues and funding and organizational issues. It now exists as an independent organization funded by membership fees from the individual states. The ICESA headquarters in Washington maintains a constant liaison with the Employment and Training Administration and other agencies, such as the National Governors' Association, that have an interest in employment, training, and UI programs. ICESA has been successful in representing the needs and desires of state administrators in response to federal guidelines, instructions, restrictions, and new programs.

State Legislatures

Successful state administrators must maintain a constant liaison with the leadership of state legislatures in order to assure appropriate consideration of required legislation and to be in a position to promote and defend legislative proposals to modify the program. They must be able to respond to legislative initiatives and provide comments and input on the fiscal and programmatic impact of such legislation.

State legislators are frequently involved in the processing of inquiries and complaints from their constituents regarding program operations.[2] An administrator must be capable of explaining the intricacies of the program as well as the philosophical background for its structure and its inherent decision-making process.

Necessary adjustments in the program can cause political problems. In recent years, when members of the Wisconsin legislature recognized that the state's benefits and tax processes required substantial alteration, they took bold steps to provide sufficient benefit adjustments, at the risk of losing considerable support from both the employer community because of tax increases and the working community because of benefit reductions.

As a result of actions taken since 1983, Wisconsin's trust fund is expected to become solvent by the end of 1986.

Labor Organizations

Although organized labor strongly opposed UI during the 1900–30 period, it has supported UI since the Great Depression. The AFL-CIO consistently called for federalization of the program in the belief that workers would benefit by the imposition of more federal standards, including standard benefit levels in all states.

My impression is that organized labor has focused primarily on UI; its concern has not carried over to the Employment Service or employment and training programs. This disinterest in employment-related programs could be because labor has little to gain from them. Labor may even view the employment services as intruders into the domain of labor organizations, particularly with regard to referral of applicants to employers for job openings.

Public employee unions have been particularly resistant to employment and training programs for disadvantaged or marginally employable workers within public agencies. Public employee unions contend that all agency work should be performed by union members. In some cases unions have supported limited public service opportunities for nonunion workers, but generally they have opposed widespread use of public job sites to provide on-the-job training experience for disadvantaged people.

Business and Industry Organizations

Although organized labor views UI primarily as part of the nation's broad social programs, business interests take a narrower view. In brief, UI is, in business's view, a temporary and partial wage replacement program. Organizations representing business and industry lobby effectively for business-oriented change in the statutes and are constantly promoting changes in the administrative process that favor employers in decision making. Most such organizations accept the need for a program to protect a part of a worker's income during brief periods of unemployment caused through no fault of the individual worker. Many view modern statutory provisions, however, at a considerable distance from this original intent and purpose. They are critical of statutory language that they interpret as "rewarding workers for not working."

Representatives of stable businesses and industries are naturally supportive of taxing provisions that stress experience rating, whereas representatives of seasonal or less stable industries support tax policies that allow for shared risk in the UI tax program. Business and industry organizations rarely become involved in specific case decisions regarding benefit eligibility or tax liability. They are, however, well informed about employers' experiences and concerns with both benefit and tax issues. They frequently promote statutory changes or change in the administrative codes and regulations that would benefit their members.

With the advent of severe tax increases across the board for all employers in recent years, these organizations have become much more active in promoting business interests and lobbying for controls on the extent to which their constituents are held liable for the cost of the program.

Advisory Council

Historically the Wisconsin Unemployment Compensation Advisory Council (UCAC) has been very influential in guiding the administration of the program and the development of related statutes. Legislators were willing to allow the council process, which is comparable to a collective bargaining process, to hammer out a bill each session of the legislature. All other attempts to modify the state UI statutes were referred to the council or beaten down in committee.

This era ended in 1983 when the council, unable to agree on changes in benefits and taxes necessary to resolve trust fund insolvency, was set aside in favor of a special task force that drafted the necessary statutes. Under that legislation, the Department of Industry, Labor, and Human Relations (DILHR) now has the responsibility of introducing legislation if the council fails to provide adequate responses to federal mandates or to state fiscal trust fund problems. The legislature, of course, finally determines what legislation is enacted.

The UCAC accepted this new role and, as noted earlier, has participated in the process that will eventually restore to solvency Wisconsin's unemployment trust fund. Its primary concern has been to assure a balance between the revenue-producing and benefit-payment processes that will satisfy their various constituencies. The council does not inject itself into the day-to-day administration of the program, except occasionally to question processes that appear cumbersome or that delay the collection of taxes or the payment of benefits.

Participation in the work of the council involves a considerable investment of time and effort in a very complex and politically sensitive role. Council members individually bear the brunt of considerable criticism when they take unpopular stands—even those necessary to maintain the fiscal integrity of the program. They are also subjected to considerable abuse when their proposals are viewed by various publics as detrimental to economic growth or minimum income maintenance for unemployed persons.

Lobbyists

Proposed changes in the UI statutes usually attract a large and varied number of lobbyists who frequently provide interesting, although perhaps not completely objective, evaluations of proposals. They have become increasingly well informed in recent years, as DILHR has begun to publicize UI-related issues regularly through the news media and UCAC, bound by the state's open meeting law, conducts all deliberations in open meetings.

Advocacy Groups

For lack of a better term, I define advocacy groups as groups that support a particular segment of the population rather than employer groups or organized labor groups — agencies or organizations that represent older workers, the handicapped, or who have constituencies related to ethnic background. These groups have learned to challenge the UI program on grounds of comparability of service. They occasionally object to a policy or administrative decision that is perceived as treating their constituents unequally or unfairly.

Some contact the department directly, others work through an interested legislator, others communicate directly with the governor's office to express their concerns. In the 1970s some of our district offices were picketed by groups claiming to represent the unemployed, particularly during periods when large numbers of unemployed persons had exhausted benefits or were never declared eligible for benefits. Facing difficulties with economic survival, they conducted demonstrations to call attention to their plight. In recent years we have seen little organized activity among groups representing the unemployed.

Groups representing older workers have cited the unfairness of federal and state legislation relating to pension payments and their effect on eligibility for benefits. We have been criticized by several public service groups for our attempts to collect overpayments from elderly people who were improperly paid because they failed to report pension payments. These organizations wish the department to seek authority to permit the elderly to collect both UI funds and pensions.

Groups representing the handicapped complain that some requirements, such as attendance at hearings, create additional hardships for the handicapped. Hearings have also been a source of concern for Spanish-speaking claimants who require translation of proceedings.

No organized effort has protested inequitable treatment of minorities, but the department is nonetheless conducting studies to identify the extent to which minorities are treated differently from nonminorities in the system.

4. Administrative Issues — 1985

Conformity with Federal Law

In the "good old days" the Unemployment Compensation Advisory Council's bills were considered "agreed" bills and received little attention from the legislature. The department could leisurely assess the elements and features of a legislative proposal with regard to conformity with the federal law and with some reasonable assurance of accuracy. Now that the UCAC's activity may be challenged, or the legislature may initiate efforts to amend the statutes, the department is frequently required during legislative sessions to respond on short notice to questions of conformity.

Conformity questions can be very complex and may require the advice of the DOL's solicitor — a time-consuming procedure. Under pressure from legislative leadership, the department may find it necessary to interpret conformity questions locally or to guess about how the federal solicitors will decide an issue. This can cause frustration among legislators, who may suspect the department is raising conformity questions just to delay or prevent action on substantive legislative proposals it doesn't support.

Historically Wisconsin has avoided major issues of conformity, in part because as the originator of the law the state has maintained a strong basic concept of what the law requires and allows. In recent years, however, conformity has presented a challenge to Wisconsin and a number of other states with regard to new legislative initiatives as well as to long-standing legislative doctrines.

We can understand when the federal government questions new legislation. We do have special difficulty when it challenges statutes that have been on the books since the initial law was passed. It suggests that our federal partner is using the conformity process to veer the interpretation of basic program philosophy toward more acceptable ideology. A case in point. Since the program's inception Wisconsin has always expected the employer to be responsible for raising issues regarding claimant eligibility. In the absence of employer notice of issues, except for those relating to continuing eligibility, the agency is not authorized or required to take "administrative notice" of eligibility issues it may become aware of. Recently the DOL has questioned Wisconsin's failure to take administrative notice, claiming that it may in some cases violate the federal requirement for payment of benefits only when due.

This issue raises several interesting questions. Who is the predominant determinant of initial claimant eligibility—the employer or the agency? Regardless of who raises an issue of initial eligibility, should the employer's willingness to allow benefits prevail? When charged against his account only? When charged against the balancing account? When charged against other employer accounts?

Employer representatives on the Wisconsin UCAC do not now support changing Wisconsin's statutes or administrative practices on these matters. Indeed, there is general resentment among council members about the imposition of federally supported philosophical changes in the program through conformity interpretations.

Funding for Program Administration

While preparing budget proposals for Congress, the DOL prepares estimates of the national insured employment rate for the coming years. The administration is naturally optimistic in projecting this politically sensitive economic indicator. Therefore, the national estimate is not likely to be a realistic basis on which to develop estimates of the administrative moneys needed for the UI program. The states develop independent estimates based on their previous workloads. The difference between the national and the states' estimates is considerable.

This process results in allocation that does not appropriately reflect the relationship between work loads and administrative funding needs. It also fails to allocate sufficient funds for capital equipment, travel, premises rent, communication, and other nonpersonal costs.

The methodology for allocating funds in the UI system is based on a time distribution and cost model process that does not adequately reflect the shift of the program costs from labor-intensive operations to a more highly automated system. Although states fund start-up and installation costs of automation, they do not recognize the necessity of maintaining and continuing to improve automated systems.

The estimating technique must become more reliable and less politically sensitive, and it must relate the workload needs not only to personnel requirements but also to long-term nonpersonal services that will provide incentives to improve automation and efficiency in the system.

The system needs to recognize more clearly and fully the historical relationship between the Employment Service and UI programs. Many states require the Employment Service to register UI claimants and supervise work search, but have no contingency or emergency funding for periods when the workload increases quickly. In order to obtain funding for special purposes states must operate within a cumbersome and unresponsive supplementary budget request process.

Restrictions on moneys for major capital equipment sometimes make it impossible to arrive at cost-effective acquisition decisions. The Reed Act provides a federal revolving fund with which states can purchase capital equipment and buildings. Used in this manner, it provides for long-term amortization of major costs. It may also be used for ongoing administrative costs, but on a one-time basis only. States that borrow to maintain trust fund solvency, for example, are not permitted to use administrative moneys from the Reed Act, a restriction that effectively ignores the fact that even states that are in debt have maintenance needs.

In general the administrative budgeting process does not allow an efficient planning process. States are frequently forced to spend funds before they know whether the funds are available. Many government agencies complain that annual funding prohibits long-range planning and efficient use of automation and other cost-saving techniques. UI funding is even more restrictive. The DOL authorizes the expenditure of funds one quarter at a time. If those funds are not used or if the state does not generate enough through workloads to justify the total amount allocated, the excess is withdrawn at the end of the quarter. In usual circumstances it cannot be carried forward to assist in preparing for expected workload changes in future quarters.

Although the DOL recognizes the problem and allows for carryover of portions of unused moneys from the first to the second quarter in any fiscal year, it still continues to pick up quarterly surpluses at the end of the second and third quarters. This quarterly pickup process incorrectly assumes that qualified staff members can be added or deleted from the system on a moment's notice to respond to changes in the workload. This is not valid in any kind of civil service system. It also assumes that the cost model system provides adequate time distributions of each function and that control of funding by quarter assures that all work related to a specific function can be accomplished within that quarter. This is also untrue and can lead to large amounts of unused earnings during high workload quarters and scraping to get by in low workload quarters.

The system provides a disincentive to efficient and effective operation since it is so difficult to obtain funding for improvements and those improvements frequently affect the level of funding adversely without recognition of the continued costs of operating a more modernized system.

In addition, the DOL frequently upsets the delicate balance of administrative funding and workloads by dictating that states absorb the costs of administering additional programs that were not in the original budget. Most recently the DOL required state UI programs to fund the administration of the Trade Adjustment Act, a program that requires considerable effort.

In summary, the administrative financing of the unemployment compensation program has a number of adverse features.

1. The funding system is highly complex.
2. The program is basically underfunded, primarily because the program is so complex.
3. The program consists of base funding for minimum workloads and a contingency funding for increased workloads. It penalizes states that must operate on a small base with a high contingency because contingency funding does not provide adequate support for nonpersonal service costs.
4. The underfunding of nonpersonal services limits management modernization efforts, and discourages flexibility, innovation, and automation.
5. The quarterly accounting is a disincentive for efficiency and may encourage more complexity in a state program.
6. The benefit payment system encourages timely payments but does not necessarily encourage accuracy of benefit payments.
7. The system has no direct financial incentive to prevent overpayments or to provide for efficient collection of overpayments.

Economic Trends

Wisconsin's economy fluctuates seasonally, with employment levels usually peaking in September or October each year and bottoming out in February and March. The number of UI claims is usually fairly low in the early fall and begins to rise around the middle of November, remaining fairly high until late February or early March.

The seasonal fluctuations, coupled with increasingly severe national recessions, put a strain on administrative structures, particularly because funding is based on unrealistic estimates of national insured unemployment rates. They also make it difficult to develop appropriate legislative proposals for employer payroll taxes to adequately cover benefits payments.

Historically trust funds were supported on a countercyclical basis, building adequate reserves during periods of high economic activity to sustain program costs during recessions. The length and depth of recessions during the late 1970s and early 1980s exhausted state trust funds in Wisconsin and many other states and required borrowing from the federal government. Wisconsin is not likely to be able to tax employers' payrolls sufficiently to get out of debt and create large enough trust fund balances to allow the luxury of countercyclical funding. Wisconsin will probably continue to borrow occasionally from the federal government, preferably on a short-term basis to avoid significant interest costs. The severity of economic fluctuations and inability to forecast the taxing policies has made fund management a critical necessity.

Organizational Instability

A new administration in the White House has always been accompanied by new appointments in the DOL. If these were to occur only subsequent to elections there would be a limited amount of stability, at least in the interim. In recent years, however, DOL leadership has changed between elections, creating instability in the leadership and direction of the program.

Stability has also been affected by serious funding reductions and staff cutbacks at the national level. The resulting shifts in priorities and "stop and go" administrative processes tend to be wasteful and confusing to states that are seriously trying to maintain a spirit of cooperation with the DOL.

The stability of Wisconsin's program has been negatively affected by funding reductions, changes in DILHR leadership, the reorganization of departments and divisions, and the creeping politicization of program leadership. At this writing, however, the Wisconsin program is on a fairly stable course with experienced leaders who are attuned to the political philosophy of the chief executive.

Political Climate

Wisconsin's UI program has received considerable legislative attention since the early 1980s, as a result of the state's indebtedness to the federal government. A number of related questions will continue to attract political attention. One is how to maintain continued solvency of the trust fund while assuring business leaders that tax burdens will be minimized. Another is how to assuage organized labor's desire to regain some of the UI benefits that were lost in the move to solvency. Another politically charged issue is the federal requirement that Wisconsin develop a wage reporting system by 1988 to be used by all income maintenance programs to cross-check for potential fraud and abuse.

Much of the debate concerning the future of the UI program reflects deep concern about economic development. In the strong competition among states to bring in new industry by offering attractive tax and benefit packages, Wisconsin has not fared well, in part because of its high UI benefit levels and taxes. Efforts will undoubtedly be made to maintain if not enhance our competitiveness, particularly with other midwestern states.

Program Integrity

The federal standard for states sounds simple—to pay benefits promptly when due—and it is obviously a worthwhile goal to provide support for the unemployed as well as maintain a cash flow in the economy. But it can cause significant administrative headaches. The pressure to pay benefits in a timely fashion is particularly great when the number of claims is growing, creating increased staff workloads.

One problem is that the system requires a number of complex checks to determine whether an individual is eligible, but the rush to pay benefits frequently results in shortcuts that may lead to payment of benefits that are not legitimate. The federal government frequently applies standards relating to accurate benefit payment and cross-checks the legitimacy of payments during periods of low claim workloads. These are more difficult to achieve during periods of heavy workloads. Yet the integrity of the program is measured primarily by the extent to which payments are made to legitimate claimants.

A federal quality control study that reviewed and analyzed a sample of payments found relatively high levels of overpayments. Many state administrators, however, considered the study's eligibility criteria too strict, resulting in overstated overpayment percentages. They argued that this post-payment audit did not take into account the necessity of paying benefits quickly and asserted that if states were allowed more time during the initial process of determining eligibility, overpayment errors could be considerably reduced.

The overpayments discovered by the quality control study were largely unintentional, although the study did uncover a small amount of fraud. In Wisconsin we investigate potential fraud cases and refer serious cases to district attorneys for prosecution. Claimants found guilty of deliberate intent to defraud the system forfeit future benefits; employers who have deliberately defrauded the system or have colluded with claimants to achieve inappropriate benefit payments also can be penalized.

5. New Issues

The State-Federal Relationship

The unique fifty-year-old state-federal relationship may require alteration in response to new circumstances: reduced funding coupled with increased employer interest in the administration of the program. Employer representatives, by applying business principles, suggest more efficient and less costly methods of administering UI.

The Office of Management and Budget and the Executive Office are calling for development of the program from the federal to the state governments, returning considerable administrative control to the states and changing tax collection and distribution methods. The DOL is investigating whether such a change would be appropriate and would resolve some current operating problems.

Neither the federal statutes nor the federal code prevents major modifications in the administrative financing of the program. Much of what is in place is the result of administrative fiat rather than legislative or federal code requirement. Nonetheless, significant changes in the level or content of federal standards for the program are not likely.

Program Direction

Several states have developed admirable innovative programs. These include encouragement of worksharing, coverage of dependents in variable benefit eligibility programs, exclusions of worker eligibility and employer liability to promote training and retraining of unemployed workers, and relocation and retraining, particularly of dislocated workers. Although the DOL supervises conformity issues and publishes informational bulletins and guidelines, the programs are not federally mandated but rather the result of state initiatives.

Reform

If UI program administration is to be simplified, reform of the state-federal relationship is essential. A system is needed to fund the administration of the program within acceptable fiscal management principles that provide adequate resources for planning and incentives to improve the efficiency of the program. Block grants to the states through an annual administrative budget could serve these purposes, as might modification of the funding process to eliminate the quarterly review and pickup of unspent funds.

A third alternative would be a more drastic modification of the system by devolving the collection of administrative funds to the states and allowing the states authority to determine the level of taxation required to produce sufficient administrative dollars. States would be responsible for the allocation and application of those funds to the administrative process. This would turn the political process back to the state legislators, which some state administrators fear. However, the program's integrity could be protected by a federal mandate requiring a minimum of administrative and trust fund financing in order to continue to receive offsets from the Federal Unemployment Tax Act.

The future of the Employment Service bears a significant relationship to the potential for administrative simplicity in the program also. The Employment Service has essentially been devolved to the states with the funding of the program still controlled at the federal level. If this process of devolvement continues, the process of identifying the level of spending for the state employment services may eventually become a state-level function that will require a change in fund collection so that state legislatures control both the source of funding and the distribution of revenues. Without companion devolvement of the UI program, state legislators will be vying for administrative dollars for the Employment Service while the federal government controls the taxing mechanisms. This can only draw legislators and the state political structure into the administrative seesawing that is now confined to UI administrators.

With more control, states would probably adopt program and funding decisions based on more widely accepted estimates than are currently used. The states must consider economic conditions beyond their own borders and thus have some interest in national economic projections, but are better able than the federal government to identify program areas they wish to maintain if cutbacks become necessary. States can also better evaluate the impact of income maintenance programs. Increased state control would enhance organizational stability, although some degree of instability will continue regardless of the organizational structure or the state-federal relationship.

It would be utopian to expect a program free from political pressure or unresponsive to the current political climate. If control by the federal government is limited, then the power to make changes in that control is limited. The political climate at the state level can reflect more fully the needs, desires, and pressures of state politics.

The states and the federal government do not agree on how to achieve program integrity and how to assess it. The states' UI programs should have complete responsibility for the integrity of the program and be answerable to their state legislatures and their own employer and labor communities. The federal government could require some minimum monitoring activity as a condition of continued certification and provide technical assistance to states in conducting necessary audits and investigations.

6. Summary

This paper has described the evolution of the current UI program over the years, suggesting that the program's strength and continued success are partially the result of its framework. I have also identified a great need to change administrative structure and financing and to shift control of the program. A continued but modified state-federal relationship could be appropriate if responsibility for operating the program was assigned to the same agency that funded and controlled it—unlike the current arrangement, in which responsibility for the program is primarily at the state level, but the control and funding is at the federal level.

In addition to the foregoing comments on needed changes, the following points summarize my assessment of the major administrative problems in the current system that could be changed or eliminated in the interest of administrative simplification.

— *Trust fund borrowing.* States are victimized by national or international economic trends they cannot control, resulting in heavy drains on their trust funds. States required to borrow to maintain trust fund solvency surrender much of their independence in benefit and tax decision. The requirements of the loan repayment and interest charging are punitive. Additional incentives to maintain trust fund solvency are needed.

— *Unrelated and unfunded program mandates.* Mandating the collection and sharing of data, the administration of unrelated programs, and complex, time-consuming negotiation with other agencies without adequate funding places extreme pressure on state agencies with already apparent resource problems. All such mandates should be limited to UI-related activities and should be accompanied by adequate administrative financing.

— *Conformity to federal standards.* Conformity and compliance are powerful weapons that can affect the philosophical direction of a program and jeopardize individual employer tax liability and administrative funding. Conformity issues should be limited to legitimate questions of compliance within a limited range of necessary federal requirements.

— *Cash management.* State capability in independent cash management should be easily recognizable and assessable. States with adequate capability should be given more authority and responsibility. The present system of state responsibility without financial incentive for good performance is outmoded and inefficient.

— *ES-UI relationships.* Separating the planning and funding of ES programs from UI is bound to strain the relationship of the two agencies and reduce the level of effective cooperation. The close ties between these programs need to be strengthened and adequately funded.

— *UI program support.* Congressional delegations, state legislators, employer and labor organizations, and the public all need to increase their understanding of the UI program and participate in program reform.

— *Administrative financing.* The current process of administrative financing is complex, cumbersome, and unresponsive to program needs. Streamlining the process and providing an equitable allocation of available resources with maximum recognition of the contribution level by each state is a necessity. The use of UI administrative moneys for unrelated program costs should be eliminated.

— *Planning.* Improvement in economic and work load forecasting techniques for use in program cost and revenue estimates would reduce the uncertainty and crisis management now rampant in the system. Smoothing out the funding process would free up considerable manpower and system support for direct program application.

I do not support complete devolvement of the program. The program is national in scope and should have a minimum set of standards and objectives that each state must achieve. Beyond that, the program can be effectively administered and funded at the state level. The federal government's role can be limited to an oversight process and to determining whether states are meeting minimum standards. Achieving this kind of reform will require considerable time and effort. A new structure can evolve over time as parts of the current structure are reviewed and modified.

The current DOL leadership appears willing to consider proposals for administratively simplifying the system so that it can become more responsive to program needs at the state level. This interest is appreciated, and we can only hope it will be matched by an equal amount of interest at the state level. Considerable care must be exercised to ensure that the strengths of the program and its acceptance by participants are not damaged by this evolution to a different kind of state-federal relationship. The process will require careful evaluation of the current system and of the potential impact of changes in that system, as well as an assessment of the appropriate relationships between the two levels of government so as to preserve the strengths and the basic objectives of the UI program.

NOTES

1. It is with some humility and trepidation that this paper is undertaken. The author is not an expert on the UI program nor academically qualified to construct a paper that would meet any criteria of scholarly intent. It is also extremely difficult for him to maintain complete objectivity in defining the existing system and identifying the problems inherent in such a system. The views and opinions expressed are solely those of the author and do not represent official agency positions.

2. Legislators may be contacted by constituents regarding the location or hours of a local office, handling of a specific claim, delays in the processing of initial claims, delays in the receipt of benefit checks, tax liability on the part of an employer, penalties assessed against employers for late payments or late filing of reports, concerns about the rationale for decisions in the claims process, and specific complaints about sections of the statutes that some employers or claimants may find disagreeable or unacceptable.

PART TWO

NEW DIRECTIONS

9

Unemployment Compensation and Retraining: Can a Closer Link Be Forged?

W. LEE HANSEN AND JAMES F. BYERS

Introduction

Just when states are finally moving to put their unemployment compensation systems back on a firm financial footing after the substantial excesses of disbursements over revenues during the high unemployment years of the late 1970s and early 1980s, new pressures are building to use UI system reserve funds to underwrite the retraining of displaced workers. Proposals such as this have a certain appeal because they attempt to go beyond the immediate problem of income replacement: they combine the goal of income replacement with the provision of retraining that is designed to enhance the future employability of unemployed workers. But in doing so they threaten the integrity and viability of the long-established unemployment compensation system by joining together two quite different functions that will be difficult to link effectively and will add considerably to the cost of the UI system.

The purpose of this paper is to explore the forging of closer links between the objectives of the UI system and programs to retrain workers who lose their jobs, particularly those who are permanently displaced. We focus on a variety of active proposals that sketch out how these links might be developed. The growing interest in merging or at least bringing together the goals of income replacement and retraining arise out of two recent developments. One is the widespread and increasing concern about dramatic changes occurring in America's manufacturing sector that are creating an ever larger number of people who will be permanently unemployed or reemployed only at substantially lower wage rates and in considerably less skilled jobs. The other is disappointment about the drastic reduction since the late 1970s in public expenditures for employment and training programs. Linking retraining programs to the UI system is viewed as an attractive solution and one that represents a sensible and integrated attempt to deal with the complex problems of unemployment.

Our approach in this paper is as follows. First, we review the original purpose and principles of the UI program and then show how its structure has been altered in response to the changing dimensions of the nation's unemployment problems. We then examine the evolution of training and retraining programs in this country and what is known about the effectiveness of these programs. This is followed by a review of attempts that have been made to tie training and retraining more closely to the UI system. We next summarize the array of proposals that have been put forth and we subsequently analyze them, with special attention to the interactions that any blending of the systems would produce. We then consider other policy options for improving UI and training functions. We close with a list of research questions.

We conclude that although a closer link through the UI system between retraining programs and worker displacement due to plant closings may be advisable on certain grounds, the problems arising from trying to merge two programs that are conceptually, financially, and politically ill-matched outweigh whatever gains might result.

1. Unemployment, UI, and Retraining

Unemployment insurance has traditionally been viewed as society's way of insuring individual workers against the uncertain incidence of unemployment spells that are beyond their control and for the most part beyond the control of their employers. Involuntary unemployment deserving of protection has normally been viewed as resulting from cyclical fluctuations in demand. In fact, the more predictable seasonal unemployment is usually covered. Structural unemployment is also covered, largely because of the difficulty of differentiating between cyclical and structural unemployment.

Coping with unemployment is never easy. Considerable effort has been made over the years to minimize seasonal unemployment. Cyclical declines in demand necessitate reductions in employment until demand increases again. Structural unemployment, by contrast, implies the permanent disappearance of particular jobs. The reasons for structural unemployment are complex, but they can be grouped as follows: reductions in labor demand because of permanent shifts in consumer demand, technological changes that reduce the demand for particular labor skills, the sometimes inexplicable demise of once profitable enterprises, and more recently, aggressive foreign competition that undercuts domestic production and thereby reduces the demand for domestic labor. Whatever the cause of unemployment, UI quickly minimizes individual and family hardships. As long as seasonal and cyclical fluctuations are moderate and predictable, and as long as the rate of structural change proceeds relatively slowly and smoothly, the unemployment compensation system is not seriously taxed. In recent years this situation has changed. The rate of structural change appears to have accelerated, with the consequence that larger proportions of workers are being displaced from their jobs and face an uncertain future. Because of the demise of numerous high-paying jobs, the chance for displaced workers to find comparable positions has diminished, as compared to the situation, say, twenty years ago. In addition, the slower growth of new job opportunities and the "de-skilling" of these new jobs resulting from low-wage foreign competition have made many of these positions relatively less attractive to displaced workers. Developments such as these have combined to increase the overall rate of unemployment, extend the average duration of unemployment, leave a hard core of displaced workers who are unable to make the adjustment to new employment, and at the same time increase the dissatisfaction of those who are reemployed.

The adverse impact of such structural changes is minimized if displaced workers gain access to other jobs offering comparable pay. The likelihood of this happening is enhanced if the skills possessed by structurally unemployed workers are in demand by other employers or if other employers are willing to hire and then retrain these workers for similarly skilled jobs. If neither of these situations holds, unemployed workers may have to take jobs in other occupations that are less remunerative and most likely less satisfying as well.

While unemployed, those workers who are covered by the UI system receive unemployment benefits to cushion the financial hardship they would otherwise experience. For those who are structurally unemployed, the longer the duration of benefits, the more likely it is that they can search for and find what they believe are suitable jobs. However, workers who recognize the need to gain new skills that will make them more reemployable face real difficulties. If they undertake formal retraining they face the prospect of being disqualified from receiving UI benefits, because it is unlikely they can state that they are available for and looking for work.

This seeming contradiction has impelled people to propose with increasing frequency some kind of merging of UI and retraining in the belief that such a merging is essential in developing an effective approach for reducing high and persistent structural unemployment. These proposals typically call for relaxing important UI program requirements.

Such changes would produce several results. First, the demand on UI funds for retraining will increase. Second, retraining will reduce future unemployment spells and hence UI costs, but whether these effects will be substantial enough to offset the added costs is not clear. Third, if costs rise to any great extent, employer taxes will have to increase, trust funds will go more deeply into debt, or benefit levels will have to be reduced. The only other possibilities are to use general purpose revenues to support retraining programs, either separately or as part of the UI program.

Since the whole UI system is based on insurance principles, and because retraining costs are so unpredictable, there is a fundamental contradiction between UI and retraining programs.

2. Unemployment Compensation: Theory and Development

Unemployment insurance, like most other social legislation, came into existence in response to a particular situation: in this case, the set of social and economic circumstances known as the Great Depression. The UI legislation, passed as Title III and IX of the Social Security Act of 1935, developed out of a theory about unemployment and what could or should be done to alleviate it. That theory evolved over time, manifesting itself in the 1931 legislation setting up Wisconsin's first-in-the-nation UI system. Proving to be basic to the enabling federal legislation, it became embodied in other state laws which put UI into practice.

As time passed and circumstances changed, the UI program also changed. Initially, slight modifications and adjustments were made, as is usually the case with social legislation, in order to fine-tune the program. But as other pressures began to mount, more fundamental alterations in the program took place. Indeed, we can divide the history of UI into two eras, which we designate as the unemployment insurance era (1930–60) and the reemployment training era (1960–present). The major differences between these two eras lie in perceptions of problems and in proposed solutions to those problems.

The unemployment insurance era faced the problem of cyclical unemployment and attempted to provide a temporary "bridge" of benefits to alleviate for workers the economic costs of normal labor market fluctuations as well as abnormal fluctuations in aggregate demand.

The reemployment training era should not be viewed as an immediate and drastic break with the past. For the most part the system continued to operate on the same assumptions and with the same responses as before. But the forces of change were strong and reflected, as already mentioned, growing concern about structural or technological unemployment beginning about 1960.

The response to this perceived problem was a gradual acceleration in federal and, later, state funding of retraining programs. The critical element in this response was the decision to allow and ultimately require the use of UI funds to support workers undergoing retraining courses or programs.

To understand the differences in these two eras and to appreciate the problems rooted in these differences, it is necessary to look more closely at the theory basic to the insurance era and then the developments occurring through the training era.

UI in the Insurance Era

American "Exceptionalism." Considerable literature exists which seeks to explain why the American industrial relations system developed so differently from that of Europe. We need not discuss this in any detail except as it pertains to the industry-related social insurance that developed in the United States. The earliest form of social insurance in this country is Workers' (Workman's) Compensation. That program came into existence in the United States two decades before UI, but the battles fought over the form of Workers' Compensation helped determine the shape of UI.

The chief adversaries in the struggle were John R. Commons, founder of the Wisconsin school of industrial relations, and Isaac Rubinow, a Russian-born doctor, actuary, and social scientist. Rubinow firmly believed that the proper goal for America was a comprehensive social insurance system of the European type. He lobbied for a blanket approach for the whole of society, a system at once both all-inclusive and redistributive in nature. Rubinow failed. What succeeded was the "American Plan," which Commons suggested as being more attuned to the unique political, economic, and moral philosophy of the American people (Lubove, 1968, pp. 33–46).

An essential element of the difference between the two approaches was the question of the source of rights. The European philosophy argued in favor of rights based on needs. The American approach, perhaps rooted in the self-reliant individualism of the American character, was wary of a system that weakened the need for self-reliance:

> Men were at all times as lazy as they dared to be. If they became accustomed to public support when earning capacity diminished, what inducement would they have to "make provisions for the future"? How could society maintain the "necessary degree of production and economy"? The working classes would provide for themselves and their families if an "unwise charity" did not "offer a bonus to incompetence." (Lubove, 1968, pp. 27–28)

This attitude shaped the UI system: rather than the needs-based European system, the American approach was a narrow, more "purely" insurance-style system based on the worker's prior attachment to the labor market as initial qualification for UI coverage, and proof ("able and available for work" test) of continuing attachment to the labor market. Three elements set the U.S. system apart from systems adopted elsewhere. First, the American system is narrowly focused and represents a radical departure from relief or welfare programs. Potential beneficiaries included only those labor force participants in covered occupations who had earned rights to benefits by their prior and present attachment to the labor market. Second, the U.S. system was completely wage-related rather than needs-related as in Europe. Even though the law establishing the American UI system was passed in the depths of the Great Depression when legislators were aware of enormous economic dislocation and resulting hardship, the decision was clearly made to reject the European approach. Indeed, American UI was the first system in the world to base benefits on a percentage of prior earnings rather than on the needs of the worker and the worker's dependents.

Finally, the American system was designed to be insurance. The legislative history of H.R. 7260 (the Social Security bill) makes it clear that Congress intended to create a reserve fund based on the income of a carefully defined group of workers that could provide an insurance-like source of funds to replace partially the lost wages of those covered workers who became involuntarily unemployed:

> Unemployment insurance cannot give complete and unlimited compensation to all who are unemployed. Any attempt to do so confuses unemployment insurance with relief, which it is designed to replace in large part. It can give compensation only for a limited period and for a percentage of the wage loss. . . . It will enable most workers who lose their jobs to tide themselves over, until they get back their old work or find other employment. . . . Unemployed workmen who cannot find other employment will have to be cared for through work relief or other forms of assistance. (Dahm and Finescriber, 1980, p. 85)

It took a severe depression to convince Americans that they needed a UI system. Even then, they remained so wary of the "moral hazards" of the welfare mentality that the system adopted offered insurance against the vagaries of the labor market, a temporary bridge to another job, not a dole that would tempt workers to rely on others rather than themselves.

UI as True Insurance. Although UI is social insurance and therefore in some ways different from personal insurance, it is clear that the American approach makes it truly insurance. UI meets the tests of insurance:

1. it insures against personal loss (only the identified worker is covered);
2. it meets the test that the occurrence of risk is verifiable;
3. it is subject to the "law of large numbers";

4. the contingencies insured against happen to only a portion of the insured at any one time;
5. risks are predictable within reasonable limits, and techniques exist to estimate costs and adjust premiums accordingly;
6. risks are insurable, with the result that unemployment created by individuals cannot be compensated. (Haber and Murray, 1966)

The final element is critical in understanding the operation of American UI. To keep the system true to its insurance goal, it was necessary to pay benefits only for involuntary unemployment. Workers cannot collect benefits if they cause the unemployment (by quitting or engaging in misconduct that leads to being fired). But just as important, workers who are involuntarily unemployed must act to end their unemployment. This point is important, for it is the basis of the distinction between the two eras referred to above.

Disqualification. A number of disqualifications are permitted in the UI laws, and their common purpose is to obviate the possibility of work disincentives creeping into the system. Measures to preclude the intrusion of such disincentives include setting the benefit levels low so that work is more attractive than continuing to collect benefits. Duration of benefits is limited to encourage prompt job search and quick return to employment. But the most important measure for understanding the relation of UI to retraining is what is called the "work test." To receive benefits in any state, workers who have involuntarily lost their jobs must be

1. able to work: UI insures against unemployment, not injury or illness; even workers who are covered by UI and who meet the "involuntarily unemployed" test will be denied UI benefits if unable to work for other reasons.[1]
2. available for work: this is interpreted as meaning that workers desire work and are willing to accept jobs that they are "reasonably qualified" to do; (Courts have even interpreted this to mean that if an unemployed worker moves to a geographic area of high unemployment [12 percent or above], the worker has rendered himself "unavailable" and may be denied benefits).[2]
3. actively seeking work: the minimal requirement is that workers must register with the Employment Service; beyond this, workers must take reasonable and usual steps to find employment. (Zell, 1976, p. 17)

All three disqualification rules and tests make good sense because of the insurance nature of the UI program. Their purpose is to get people back to work as quickly as possible, a reasonable goal for a system designed to provide benefits between jobs.

The problem is that these work incentive measures so critical to our insurance-based UI system operate as disincentives to retraining. Thus, it is no surprise that these measures came under attack and were weakened in the retraining era, thereby setting UI on a new and uncharted course.

The Retraining Era

As noted in the introduction, the natural focus of the architects of American UI in the 1930s was the volume of unemployment then threatening our society and economic system. But massive unemployment did not dissuade them from adopting an insurance rather than a needs-based solution to the problem. The question is whether changes in eligibility standards are now at odds with the original UI philosophy. The programs at issue are those begun two decades ago to meet a perceived national need for retraining.[3]

Interest in publicly supported training and retraining programs began to take shape about 1960 and can be associated with three noteworthy developments. One stemmed from the slowly developing view that resolving structural imbalances in the economy required an active manpower policy of the kind practiced with considerable success in Europe, particularly in Sweden.[4] Aggregate economic policies were viewed as too blunt to deal with the complexities of structural unemployment.[5] Another reflected a heightened public concern that automation, the term used to describe new technological advances, was destroying jobs, increasing the unemployment rate, and posing a threat to future economic prosperity. For example, the 1964 *Manpower Report of the President* proclaimed the dawn of a new era, arguing that the history of industrialization had three phases: first, the age of mechanization (the eighteenth century); second, the age of mass production (the early twentieth century); and finally the age of automation (begun with the 1951 introduction of the first commercial computer). Convinced that automation was creating problems for workers displaced by the advances of technology, the federal government embarked on a series of national training and retraining programs. Finally, the emergence of human capital theory provided a way of viewing training and retraining programs as forms of investment that would enhance people's future productivity, employability, and earnings.[6] The attractiveness of this view did much to overcome opposition to this expansion of public sector activity.

All of these developments came together and gave rise to the Manpower Development and Training Act of 1962. A principal aim of this legislation was to provide retraining for workers displaced by technological change. With the declaration of the war against poverty early in 1964, and fueled by efforts to promote greater opportunities for minorities in the second half of the 1960s, the focus of manpower retraining programs shifted away from displaced workers. The results of the 1966 Automation Commission showed that the threat of job displacement had been greatly exaggerated.[7] It was obvious that much more in need were people who had never had much training or work experience and who were seeking ways to gain a foothold in the labor force. This led to creation of the Job Corps, youth employment programs, and the like.

By the early 1970s another shift took place, this time to create public sector jobs for the unemployed and to concentrate employment and training programs in aiding the poor, the disadvantaged, and other special groups. This orientation was reflected in the Comprehensive Employment and Training Act of 1973; in fact, the focus on serving particular population groups became even more pronounced after the Carter administration began. Toward the end of the Carter administration greater attention was given to involving the private sector in retraining efforts. It was not until passage of the Jobs Training Partnership Act of 1982 that the shift became dominant. Interestingly, JTPA put renewed emphasis on retraining displaced workers at a time when the problems are far more serious, the resources available for retraining are more limited, and questions about the value and effectiveness of training and retraining continue to be raised.

The Use of UI to Support Trainees

Each of the federal or federal-state programs mentioned above represents a changing or developing response to the perceived need for retraining. What differentiates these programs need not concern us here. What is more important is what links them, namely, the decision to fund only the training component instead of funding both the training and the support of the workers undergoing the training. The crucial decision was to use UI funds to support workers in training.

The reasons for using UI to support workers in training qualifies as a separate research piece but probably includes some or all of the following:

1. *Political expediency.* It was easier to legislate a program that would fund training rather than merge two quite different systems.

2. *Political sagacity.* UI was already twenty-five years old and an accepted element of U.S. social policy. By combining this new program of government involvement with training to offset structural or technological unemployment, the convergence of the programs may have been designed more to protect this fledgling manpower initiative than to siphon UI funds.

3. *Fund stability.* In combination with either or both of the first two reasons is the fact that during much of the first twenty-five years of UI the state trust funds had been stable, some would even say fat. Especially after World War II it was not uncommon for trust funds to maintain solvency even when benefits were raised and employer taxes were lowered.

4. *Limited scope of training.* Finally, the training programs started on a small basis and seemed to pose no threat to the UI system.

The use of UI funds had several effects:

—*For workers:* Benefit levels replace 50 percent of prior wages to provide minimal support; low UI benefit levels operate as incentives for work search; incomplete coverage reflected in the difference between the unemployment rate and the insured rate; and limited duration of benefits if training period exceeds benefit period, with effects on the decision to enter training, to drop out when benefits expire.

—*For employers:* Continued use of an experience-rated tax may necessitate raising tax rates and/or introduce inequities in the taxation system because some employers are taxed for purposes that fail to benefit their workers.

—*For states:* The results could include a drain on state reserves or require borrowing, either of which would likely lead to higher tax rates on employers in their state. The effect could eventually mean frozen or lowered benefits for the regular users of UI.

3. What Do We Know About Retraining?

The Economics of Retraining

The concept of retraining is relatively new. It builds on the closely related concept of training that emerged as an integral part of the human investment literature that came to prominence in the early 1960s (Mincer, 1962, pp. 50–80). Training, like education, can be viewed as a form of investment whose purpose is to enhance the knowledge and skills of individuals, particularly younger people, thereby making them more productive in their jobs and enabling them to command higher earnings. The presumption is that both training and education "pay off"; the test lies in comparing the present value of the costs and benefits of these activities. Research shows that on average the rates of return on education and training have been at least equal to, if not greater than, rates of return on alternate investment opportunities (Becker, 1964; Hansen, 1963, pp. 128–141).

This same approach can be applied to retraining, but the results are less certain than for education and training. Resources allocated to retraining programs are less likely to be cost-effective for any of several reasons. First, the costs of retraining are higher than for traditional schooling not only because retraining generally occurs later in life when foregone earnings are greater, but also because the retraining must be tailored to the needs of particular groups of displaced workers. Second, the benefits of retraining are likely to be smaller, in part because the remaining years of worklife are fewer than for traditional schooling. Third, uncertainty exists about whether the knowledge and skills provided by retraining will be marketable; there are also questions about whether retraining will "take" on workers who for many years practiced a limited set of skills. Thus, reduced expected benefits and higher costs make retraining investments look less attractive than education and training investments which typically take place earlier in life.[8]

How might this assessment change as we focus on displaced workers? We can think of displaced workers as suddenly experiencing significant reductions in the value of their human capital, reflected by declines—in the most drastic case, to zero—in the rental value (earnings) received on that capital from their most recent employers. The magnitude of the decline depends on a variety of considerations. If the worker's employer simply goes bankrupt, the value of his human capital need not decline, provided that other employers still require his knowledge and skills. If demand for the employer's output drops, there may still be comparable employment opportunities with other employers. If, however, the demand for output drops for an entire industry, the need for particular skills also diminishes and with it the value of the worker's human capital.

Suppose that workers are displaced. What are their options? First, they can try to find employment that does not require retraining, utilizing the skills they already possess. Finding such jobs may be difficult for the same reasons that led to their displacement. Second, they can take jobs that utilize a reduced or lower set of skills; this could mean a significant reduction in earnings. Third, they can continue seeking similar employment and remain unemployed or drop out of the labor force. Fourth, they can try to find employment that carries with it a training component, hope that their earnings will reflect the effects of that retraining, and under the best of circumstances earn what they did before. Fifth, they can try to retrain themselves (which may be difficult) or enroll in (and pay for) training or retraining programs to acquire new skills and knowledge. Sixth, they can enroll in public institutions that offer training and retraining programs. Seventh, if proprietary retraining programs exist, they can seek to enroll in such programs.

Displaced workers who seek retraining must decide what kind of retraining to seek, where to obtain it (at what kind of training institution), and how much to pay. The choice of type of training institution and cost are not independent. Employer-provided training is probably optimal because it is targeted to employer needs and requires no direct outlays from the trainees. Self-retraining is relatively expensive, particularly for workers who lack the aptitude for acquiring new skills. Training programs offered by public education and training institutions (colleges, vocational or technical schools, and so on) are typically subsidized, that is, tuition and fees are set well below the costs of instruction. In private colleges tuition and fees are much more likely to approximate full costs, and in proprietary training institutions tuition and fees are more likely to equal full costs. By contrast, publicly sponsored retraining programs are free to the individual. Indeed, some may provide stipends for living expenses. Obviously, the best alternative for displaced workers is to find new jobs that include company-sponsored retraining and provide access to their prior wage level or something close to it.

Still, the uncertainties faced by displaced workers are considerable. They must search for another job or they must try to augment their skills at the same time that they search for another, better job, that is, one that utilizes their training and offers greater economic rewards as a consequence. Thus, these individuals are confronted with choices that go beyond the usual search theory menu of choices. The latter includes choices about what kind of job to search for, where to search, how long to search, and how intensely to search. Displaced workers must also consider when to drop their search and seek retraining, which involves balancing the costs of retraining (out-of-pocket costs) against the benefits, reflected by the likelihood that employability will be increased. If a decision is made too late, or if the retraining period is an extended one, UI benefits will run out and the subsequent job search must continue without any support. Or workers may find new jobs while retraining and have to forego completing the training.

Just as these many uncertainties make it difficult for the average displaced worker to arrive at a considered judgment about what to do, firms looking for new employees face an equally complex array of choices. One is whether to seek out displaced workers rather than hiring from traditional labor pools, including new entrants into the labor force. Although displaced workers may have accumulated considerable experience, they bring with them work habits, mental outlooks, and other impairments to their effectiveness in a new organization. Moreover, the reservation wages of displaced workers may, because of prior experience and financial responsibilities, exceed those of new labor force entrants. Offsetting these liabilities are the records of displaced workers that may give stronger assurances about their capabilities than is the case for new entrants.

Extent of Need for Retraining

The most comprehensive information available comes from a recent study by the Bureau of Labor Statistics (Flaim and Sehgal, 1985, pp. 3–16).[9] Based on a special supplement to the Current Population Survey, 11.5 million workers aged twenty and above were found to have lost their jobs because of plant closings and employment cutbacks from 1979 to 1984. Of this total, 5.1 million had worked at least three years on their jobs and were the focus of the analysis. Half of these workers lost their jobs because their plants or businesses closed; 40 percent lost their jobs because of slack demand, and the remaining 10 percent had their shifts or individual jobs abolished. Thus, it would appear that about 2.5 million experienced workers fit our conception of hard-core displaced workers.

What kind of reemployment experience did the 5.1 million displaced workers have, in a period (1979–84) when overall unemployment rose but was considerably lower in January 1984 than the peak unemployment year of 1982? Here are a few highlights. By January 1984, 60 percent of the displaced workers were employed, a quarter were unemployed, and the remainder were outside the labor force. Of those reemployed and working full-time in January 1984, about a quarter were making less than 80 percent of their previous earnings, 20 percent were making 120 percent or more of their previous earnings, and the remainder were within this range. About twice as many of this last group were earning amounts equal to or greater than their previous earnings. This record is less impressive than it might seem because the considerable inflation over this period reduced real earnings and hence left a majority of people worse off than before.

What is the relationship between displacement and the receipt of UI? Of the 2.5 million displaced experienced workers, 1.6 million received unemployment benefits; about half of them had exhausted their benefits. However, when we look at the 5.1 million total, we find that 3.5 million received unemployment benefits and about 1.7 million exhausted their benefits. It is clear from these data that the number of workers potentially eligible for various types of retraining depends crucially on how eligibility is defined.

The length of time people were out of work is also of interest. For those employed in January 1984 their average duration of unemployment had been thirteen weeks; for those still unemployed, it was thirty-two weeks; and for those not in the labor force it was fifty-seven weeks. Overall, almost a quarter of all displaced workers had been unemployed for fifty-two weeks or more. In this sense, many displaced workers would have had ample time to undertake some kind of retraining.

Obviously, many additional details can be elicited from this rich body of data that would help indicate the potential of retraining programs. Unfortunately, no information is provided on whether any of these workers obtained retraining through federal programs, employer training programs, or other programs the unemployed undertook on their own initiative. Thus we must turn to other evidence in order to assess the likely effects of expanded retraining programs for displaced workers. It is to this topic we now turn.

Effects of Retraining

What do we know about the likely effects of retraining/training programs? We now have more than twenty years of experience with a wide range of these programs. A substantial body of literature evaluating these programs has evolved, and as might be expected, the quality of these evaluations varies greatly (Betsey et al., 1986). Interestingly, relatively little of it focuses on permanently displaced workers because they are such a new phenomenon.

What we have learned from evaluations of retraining can best be answered in the context of the following questions:

—Can displaced workers be retrained? Are they retrainable?
—Do permanently displaced workers receiving UI want to be retrained?
—What kinds of retraining would be most appropriate?
—What is the likely effect of different types of retraining on the employment and earnings prospects of those who are retrained?
—How can retraining be delivered to displaced workers who want or need it?
—Do the benefits from publicly financed and/or provided retraining programs merit the investment of the funds required to mount these programs?

Can Displaced Workers Be Retrained? The answer to this question is obvious—some can and some cannot. Little information exists on what personal characteristics indicate or reflect the capacity of different individuals to be retrained. We do know that many workers undergo periodic training and retraining within firms, activity that is not precipitated by actual or threatened job loss. However, workers resistant to training or retraining are possibly not selected for retraining. Clearly, there are limits to what can be done, but it seems reasonable to assume that on average people have the capacity to be retrained up to a comparable level of skill in other jobs.

Do Displaced Workers Want to Be Retrained? No clear-cut answers are available. We expect that the desire for retraining varies inversely with age, health, and the like. More important, retraining programs may not be as appealing as long as displaced workers believe they can find another similar job, even if it carries lower remuneration than the previous job. Thus it would appear that relatively few workers are ready to begin retraining immediately after they become displaced.

What Kinds of Retraining Would Be Most Appropriate to Provide? Again, there are no easy answers. The private sector has useful ways of determining what kinds of training it wants to provide its workers. There is no comparable basis to use in planning public retraining programs. Studies of current market demand can indicate the types of training that are now needed by employers. What kind of skilled workers employers will need some months or years hence when people who start retraining complete that training is much more difficult to predict. Projections of future job and training requirements by occupation must be based on a whole chain of assumptions, assumptions that are difficult to choose among in making projections. Moreover, the record of accuracy in labor market projections over periods of even a few years leaves much to be desired (Hansen, 1984).

How Can Retraining Be Delivered to Displaced Workers? In principle, training programs can be established for all different kinds of occupational skills. But the costs will be high unless there are substantial and continuing concentrations of workers in need of retraining. To illustrate the difficulties, recall the size of the displaced worker group, 5.1 million experienced workers. If this is the accumulated number of displaced workers and if the rate of displacement is uniform over the period, then roughly 1.0 million workers became displaced each year. Given their geographic spread across nine major regions of the United States, and in light of the distribution of displaced workers by occupation and industry, there will be no large concentrations of people in need of retraining in more than a few large metropolitan centers (nine regions multiplied by ten major occupational groups and ten major industrial groups yields nine hundred cells of about a thousand workers in each cell in each year). Even this is a gross estimate because the finer locational, occupational, and industry categories around which retraining programs would have to be organized are ignored. Even if sufficiently large numbers of trainees can be brought together, training institutions are unlikely to be highly responsive to opportunities for providing retraining unless they see a large and continuing demand for retraining activities.

Do the Benefits of Publicly Provided Retraining Programs Pay Off? Although we have numerous evaluations of employment and training programs, we have considerably less in the way of evaluations of retraining programs. Most retraining programs operated in the early and mid-1960s after MDTA took effect. Since then much of the training has been focused on assisting groups whose labor market attachment was not very well developed. Only recently has more attention been given to retraining programs, but no comprehensive evaluations have emerged as yet.

If we had to hazard a guess, it would be that retraining programs at best simply break even, with the present value of their benefits equalling their costs. That is certainly the case for most other training programs, and it is difficult to believe that we would find any substantial difference for retraining programs.

Summary. We conclude that retraining programs are not likely to be very effective from an economic standpoint. This suggests caution in trying to marry an already successful program of protecting workers from the hazards of unemployment to a network of still-to-be-established retraining programs that would have to be integrated into the UI structure.

4. Results of the Decision to Support Trainees with UI

Having now reviewed the development of the UI system and training/retraining programs, we examine the interplay between these two elements. We discover that as the reemployment training era began, pressures mounted for the UI system to recognize that UI and retraining were related. Here we survey the results of that development.

Federal Level

In analyzing the historical development and the legal provisions of federal retraining programs, two major influences on UI emerge. The first, and perhaps the most significant, of these has to do with the "work test" described earlier. Through the first twenty-five years of American UI, every state required recipients of UI benefits to be available for work. In 1960, prior to the inception of federal retraining programs, "a strict interpretation of its laws would have required practically every state to disqualify a worker as unavailable for work if he was taking a course of training" (Haber and Murray, 1966, pp. 269–270). Just six years later, a survey of states showed that a total of twenty-two states had amended their state UI laws to consider a recipient of UI benefits to be "available for work" if the person was attending a training or retraining course approved by the employment security agency (Haber and Murray, 1966).

This action introduced into the UI system a fiction, namely, that unemployed workers attending approved training for ten, twenty, thirty weeks or more were available and searching for work when in fact these workers were out of the labor market and would likely collect the maximum number of weekly benefits available under state law rather than the minimum necessary to find another job.

This fundamental change in UI can be directly attributed to the influence of ARA and MDTA in the early 1960s when efforts were being made to retrain structurally unemployed workers. The continued federal push for this approach is evident in a 1970 amendment to the Federal Unemployment Tax Act (FUTA) which said:

> benefits shall not be denied to an otherwise eligible individual for any week during attendance of training with the State agency's approval. That means that an individual taking such training may not be found ineligible for benefits on grounds that he/she is not available for suitable work, is not making an active search for work, or has refused suitable work. A State must consider

a trainee in an approved training course entitled to benefits if otherwise eligible, and it is prohibited from denying benefits thereafter for the causes specified above.[10]

This still left states some discretion in determining what constituted appropriate training. Even that discretion was removed for "dislocated workers" under JTPA in 1982. Section 302(d) of JTPA preempts state agency discretion to approve training.[11] If this provision of JTPA seems a rather heavy-handed override of state discretion, another section of JTPA softens the blow. Retraining for dislocated workers under Section III of JTPA requires matching funds from states, but UI benefits can count for 50 percent of those matching funds.[12] Both the carrot and the stick in this approach produce the same outcome: more UI funds are distributed to workers who are guaranteed a lengthy stay out of the job market.

The second major influence of the federal government on UI through its retraining programs emanates from JTPA. The federal requirement that states provide matching funds, only half of which can be regular UI payments, has produced incentives for states to undermine the UI system, as described below.

State Level

The patchwork of state laws makes it difficult to generalize about how retraining programs influence the UI system. To elicit such information, the Unemployment Insurance Service of the U.S. Department of Labor prepared a questionnaire for the states, but neither the Labor Department nor the OMB have approved its circulation (Vroman, 1985). Nonetheless, it is possible to offer some evidence on retraining funds and nontraditional training.

Retraining Funds. The matching funds requirement of JTPA has influenced the behavior of states and thus affected the availability of funds for retraining. At least four states have initiated new programs since JTPA went into effect in 1982, with all four increasing the funds that can be used to attract matching JTPA dollars.

California has set up an Employment Training Fund (1983) as a source for retraining funds. California is in the enviable position of having a $5 billion reserve in its UI trust fund. This made it possible to move $55 million to the retraining fund in 1983, and through a tax maneuver a $55 million contribution is assured each year thereafter. The tax maneuver raised the UI tax for all employers in the state by 0.1 percent and diverted the money to the retraining fund; then the UI tax payable into the UI trust fund was lowered by the same 0.1 percent. Trust fund money can only be spent for benefits, but by this creative tax manipulation, California kept its tax rate unchanged but diverted trust fund money from benefits to retraining. California's huge reserve makes this a relatively safe gambit, but the same would not apply to states with little or no reserve.

The employment training fund must be used for retraining, and recipients must be current UI recipients, former UI recipients who have exhausted their benefits in the past twelve months, or workers likely to be laid off in the near future and who would qualify for UI benefits.

Delaware created the "Blue Collar Jobs Act" (1984) to support both training and retraining efforts. Dislocated workers are the prime target for the $1.6 million that is to be funneled annually into the retraining fund. The source of funds is a variation on the California approach. Unlike California, Delaware was in debt to the federal government for loans needed to fund its UI program during the last recession. A 0.6 percent surcharge was added to the tax paid by employers to repay the federal loan. When the loan was repaid, Delaware reduced the surcharge by only 0.5 percent and is using the 0.1 percent as a source for the retraining fund. As in California, this approach diverts UI tax money from the trust fund to another purpose. Thus, the insurance reserve envisioned by the architects of the system is being sacrificed for retraining goals.

Massachusetts followed the same route as Delaware, except that it reduced the surcharge from 0.6 percent to 0.2 percent and kept the 0.2 percent for retraining. Massachusetts also passed plant closing legislation that contains an interesting UI component. When a plant closes without advance notice or without giving workers severance pay, dislocated workers are eligible for thirteen additional weeks of UI.

Illinois passed the "Prairie State 2000 Fund" in 1983 to reduce unemployment by responding to skill requirements of new technologies. The goal is to reduce barriers to retraining for UI recipients by providing tuition vouchers equal in value to the tuition of local community colleges. Two elements of the Illinois plan are significantly different: training is college-oriented, and the only source of funds is voluntary contributions.

The Illinois experience points out a serious flaw in the reliance on UI as a source of retraining: states with depleted UI funds, or worse, states deeply in debt to the federal loan fund, typically have the greatest numbers of workers who need retraining. Illinois was $2.4 billion in debt to the federal loan fund when it passed its retraining program—no wonder it called for voluntary donations. Unlike California, it had no $5 billion reserve to siphon off, and many years will have to pass before Illinois can emulate Delaware or Massachusetts by siphoning off its debt repayment surcharge tax.

Nontraditional Training. A subject for further research is the kinds of training that have been approved for UI recipients. Based on available descriptions, there may well be a bias toward blue-collar training. This seems shortsighted in an economy with a shrinking industrial base and a growing service and white-collar sector.

One state that has clearly broken out of this mold is New Jersey. Two significant steps have been taken: first, the provision in New Jersey law prohibiting enrollment in high school or college credit courses has been rescinded.[13] Second, any person in the labor force for two years and presently unemployed or the recipient of a layoff notice may enroll tuition-free in any state college (except Rutgers) or community college in New Jersey.

Conclusions

The conclusions that can be drawn from this analysis seem fairly obvious. The federal government has considerable power to shape UI policy for its purposes, and it has used its leverage to alter a major component of UI, the work test. The states, for their part, accepted this change and adapted their programs to federal standards, sometimes in quite innovative ways. The results of this federal action and state reaction will be analyzed later. But first, we examine proposed changes in UI law that go well beyond the changes just discussed.

5. Proposed Legislative Changes in UI

Having examined the developments in UI and retraining, and having seen how these departures from the original operating theory altered the insurance character of UI, we now review the wide range of proposed amendments to UI law.

For the most part, these proposals are designed to assist dislocated workers, encourage voluntary movement out of declining industry, and even help workers become self-employed. Whatever their ability to accomplish these laudable goals, they seem certain to further weaken the UI system and strain its finances.

The following House and Senate bills are categorized according to the time frame in which they would provide benefits to qualified workers.

Pre-Layoff Benefits

A cardinal principle of American UI has been a denial of benefits to those voluntarily leaving their present employment. Several of the new bills propose that this provision be changed for those who find themselves in declining industries.

1. H.R. 758 and S. 2795 would allow workers to voluntarily quit their present jobs and receive UI while seeking other employment;
2. H.R. 758 would also allow workers to quit and enter training instead of seeking another job;
3. S. 395 would go further and authorize extra benefits for those who quit their present jobs to enter training;
4. H.R. 758 would authorize states to pay partial benefits to workers who work a reduced workweek in order to enter training.

In all of these proposals, workers presently holding jobs would be free to voluntarily quit working and would be eligible to receive regular, or even extended, UI benefits while they seek or train for other employment.

Start of Unemployment

With the "rebirth" of the entrepreneurial spirit in the United States, some have suggested that the solution to some workers' unemployment problems is self-employment. Proponents have looked to UI funds as the possible source of start-up capital for such workers:

1. H.R. 1690 and S. 1008 would provide entrepreneurial capital for unemployed workers by making a lump-sum payment of all prospective regular UI benefits plus extended benefits for which a worker qualifies.
2. A similar bill would fund the move toward self-employment: regular weekly benefits would be paid with a waiver of the usual requirement that the worker be available and seeking work. Instead of seeking work, workers would be assumed to be setting up their own businesses.

During UI Eligibility

Numerous suggestions have been advanced for modifying the payment of UI benefits during the period of worker eligibility.

1. *"Super-benefits"/extended duration.* S. 395 would actually answer one of the more important criticisms of using UI benefits to support a worker during training—that is, the question of inadequacy of benefits. UI benefits are purposely set low (50 percent wage replacement rate) as an incentive for work search. Since a worker in training is relieved of the work search requirement, the low replacement rate is unnecessary. In fact, the low rate could conceivably act as a disincentive to stick with a training program. Under this proposed legislation, higher benefits would be paid to unemployed workers in training than to those seeking jobs. A worker entering training by the eighth week of regular UI would qualify for 125 percent of the regular benefit for the duration of the training pro-

gram or for twice the number of weeks the worker was eligible for regular benefits (whichever was less).

2. *JTPA extended benefits.* S. 395 would provide ten weeks of federal extended benefits to JTPA trainees.

3. *State incentives.* H.R. 1947 would encourage states to promote training programs by reducing interest due the federal government by the state; there would be a dollar-for-dollar reduction for each dollar of UI benefits paid to workers in approved training programs.

4. *Lump-sum extended benefits.* H.R. 759 would provide a worker on regular UI a lump-sum payment of federal extended benefits for retraining, higher education, or relocation.

5. *"Cash-out" remaining benefits.* S. 2795 would allow a worker accepting a lower-paying job prior to exhaustion of benefits to receive his remaining benefits in cash.

6. *Two-track benefit schedule.* S. 2795 would allow a worker in training to opt for a reduced level of benefits paid for a longer time. Such a policy might raise administrative costs slightly but would not otherwise cost more—except that it does still assume a right to all benefits during training.

7. *Wage voucher.* This proposal would provide an incentive for employers to hire unemployed workers with remaining eligibility and to train them, since the remaining benefits would go to the employer for payments to workers during retraining.

8. *Direct use of trust fund.* Some would change the law to allow trust fund moneys to be used for training.

9. *Benefit taxation.* Already begun at certain income levels, the administration's plan to fully tax UI benefits would mean a reduction of benefits.

Lifetime Wage Credits

Some experts suggest more than mere modification of the UI system: they would substantially reform the entire program, beginning with a new theoretical approach to funding. An essential element of this type of plan is the introduction of employee contributions, which would establish some vested interest or right to benefits. The notion of a "right" to accrued benefits which bedevils our present system would become an accurate appraisal under an employee contribution system. This adoption of a European-style UI program would establish a vested interest by the worker, allowing use of accumulated credits for periodic upgrading of skills or to undertake mid-career job changes. Lump-sum payments at retirement would be another feature of this approach.

Non-UI Funding

For the sake of completeness, we include two proposals which would have no impact on UI trust funds:

1. *ITAs.* H.R. 26 and S. 934 would authorize Individual Training Accounts on the order of IRAs to which both employers and workers could contribute (at a 100 percent and 125 percent tax deduction, respectively).

2. *IRAs.* Another proposal would allow the penalty-free use of IRA money to fund retraining.

6. Analysis

This section proposes to analyze UI and retraining from three perspectives. First, we examine how present and proposed legislation squares with the original theory upon which the unique American system of UI was built. Second, we review the economic effect of incorporating a retraining component into UI. Third, we explore how altering the UI system might endanger it. Fourth, we review the policy options. Finally, we conclude with a research agenda.

Present Legislation

The analysis of the roots of UI and its legal precepts has shown it to be an insurance system for involuntarily unemployed workers rather than a European-style needs-based welfare system. Two elements essential to the insurance character of the UI system remained relatively undisturbed and unchanged during the first quarter-century of UI: the work test, which verified the continuing involuntary character of recipients' unemployment, and the Trust Fund, which, as the insurance reserve, can be used only for benefit payments.

The limited merging of federal and state retraining programs violates both of these principles. Federal initiatives first suggested and finally required that workers in retraining programs be considered eligible for UI benefits. The legal fiction that a person sitting in a classroom today who plans to be there six months, nine months, or a year from now meets the test of being "available for work" and "actively seeking work" is a major change in the system. What this represents is a government policy designed to meet the needs of workers in retraining (and therefore out of the labor market) with funds reserved for benefits to workers without a job but in the labor market. This change has, in turn, caused the second one, namely the pressure on states to divert UI trust fund moneys to pay for retraining costs.

The results of these changes are already beginning to show up. First, the Delaware and Massachusetts programs illustrate how states, as soon as they cleared their debts from the past recession, diverted UI tax money to fund retraining. Such action weakens the UI system in several ways. The more retraining money that is made available, the more likely it is that unemployed workers avail themselves of that training. This, in turn, leads more UI recipients into lengthy programs and thus stretches out the duration of their UI benefits. Hence, every million dollars set aside by a state for retraining is an x million dollar reduction in its reserve fund balance. This could become a disincentive for states to retrain workers, reduce the competitiveness of its work force, and impair overall productivity growth. Or it could become an incentive for states to freeze or lower benefit payments (penalizing all UI recipients) or to restore the trust fund by increasing employer taxes (making state employers less competitive and discouraging in-state business location or expansion).

Second, the California-Illinois comparison shows how states with no debt can offer lower employer tax rates and higher benefits, win a larger share of federal money with large sources of matching funds, increase duration of benefits so that even more lengthy and comprehensive training can be provided, and end up with an increasingly better-trained and more productive work force. States with high unemployment, large debts or no reserves, and many dislocated workers will be forced to move in the opposite direction. Thus, tying retraining to UI funds could hurt states that need help the most and lead to greater disparity between "have" and "have-not" states.

Third, a study now under way on the UI system's health identifies overpayment of benefits as the single most important threat to the system. Overpayments are due primarily to violation of the work search requirement (Burgess and Kingston, 1984, pp. 4–5). Retraining programs have quite clearly institutionalized publicly sanctioned violation of the work search requirement as well as guaranteed benefit payments that are unrelated to experience-rated contributions.

Fourth, use of UI benefits to provide support during retraining ignores two important facts about UI benefit levels. One is that these benefit levels were intentionally set low to avoid the moral hazard of undermining self-reliance by giving people an incentive to remain unemployed. For example, Workers' Compensation benefit levels, paid in case of injury to replace income, typically provide 65 to 90 percent wage replacement, whereas UI replacement rates are set lower, at 50 to 55 percent, so as to encourage work search. The second is that they are not based on need, with the result that dislocated workers with numerous dependents may be forced to pass up retraining because the benefits are inadequate to support a household through a lengthy retraining period.

Proposed Legislation

The legislative proposals discussed above have two things in common: they all follow the direction pointed by changes of the last twenty-five years, and they all undermine the insurance character of UI. Nonetheless, it is useful to indicate how they violate the insurance rationale for UI.

1. Pre-layoff:
   - Violates the premise that unemployment is involuntary by allowing benefits to workers who quit their jobs.
   - Encourages the best, youngest, and most highly motivated workers to exit, thereby interfering with personnel strategy.
   - May alter worker productivity so that a marginal industry becomes a doomed industry.
   - Rewards those who would have quit voluntarily.
2. Lump-sum entrepreneur:
   - The United States is a land of venture capital: perhaps this is needed to spur entrepreneurial spirit in Europe, but not here.
   - Assumes a "right" to the whole stream of benefits.
   - Further assumes a right to extended benefits. What if extended benefits are paid now, but twenty-six weeks into the future the rate of unemployment drops and the EB trigger level is not met; has the lump-sum recipient received a windfall?
   - The major fraud in UI is the failure to seek work: what verification could be made on the claim of seeking self-employment?
   - Could workers establish a new benefit year and then requalify for another lump sum?
   - What incentives are there for the new entrepreneurs to take fewer than twenty-six weeks to become self-employed?
3. During UI:
   - Offering higher benefits to workers in training is a good practice, but unless qualifications for training are stringent, there are strong incentives for all unemployed to enter training to obtain 125 percent benefits for twice as long.
   - Reducing interest on debt is unfair to states which practiced good fiscal management or penalized their workers with lower benefits or the state's employers with higher UI taxes.
   - All lump-sum payments are a violation of principle: relocation money is a good idea, but such aid should be separated from the generation and distribution of UI funds.
   - UI wage vouchers are a windfall for employers who would have hired workers anyway, as well as a disincentive to choosing the best workers:

the system encourages employers to choose workers with the greatest number of weeks of UI eligibility remaining.

— Any use of UI trust fund dollars other than for benefits violates UI theory and, especially, makes the experience-rated tax inequitable.

— Taxation of UI benefits: lowers real benefits, increases burdens on states in debt, raises administrative costs (for withholding), and reduces the countercyclical effects of UI.

4. Wage credits:
— Total violation of the system *unless* workers contribute.
— Worker contributions change the whole system.

5. Non-UI funding:
— ITA presumes ability to set aside money while employed, so that it favors high-income workers who may need training the least, and who definitely need help the least.
— IRA use could compound difficulties for workers by allowing them to draw from their retirement funds to finance their support while unemployed.

Economic Effects

We now contrast the effects of the various proposals. We take as our reference point the original conception of the UI system, that is, one without any retraining component. Our reason for doing this will become clear in the final part of the paper, where we examine the options — one of which is returning to the original conception of UI. We focus on several kinds of effects: first-round cost changes of providing additional benefits for permanently displaced unemployed workers who are covered by UI and are already in retraining programs; behavioral responses that can be expected to increase participation in retraining programs; and the induced costs of these responses. These effects, although interesting, are not the end of the story. Our principal interest is in knowing how these proposals affect lifetime unemployment, lifetime wage-rate levels, and ultimately lifetime earnings.

We have reorganized and recast the various proposals so as to make them more amenable to analysis. We try to use terms that are appropriately descriptive of the proposals listed in section 5. It is important to note that we purposely ignore certain effects that could be of potential interest, such as the effect on the overall unemployment rate. Such effects seem even more difficult to estimate than those discussed here; hence, we ignore them.

It should be obvious that we are in no position to offer precise quantitative estimates of the various effects. We can, however, suggest their relative magnitudes by using plus and minus signs. We take as our point of departure a pure UI system that has no retraining component. Because some of the options build on others, readers should pay careful attention to the notes. We recognize the complexity of our task and offer our results to provoke discussion and criticism that will help us arrive at a more refined set of estimates.

Our results are summarized in Table 9.1, beginning with the pure UI system, which is shown as the "no retraining" case under line 1. Introduction of retraining, indicated by the "Retraining OK" designation under line 1, shows the effect of the present hybrid system. We then deal with the other proposals; they become progressively more complicated to evaluate because they overlap to some degree with the "Layoffs with retraining option" under line 2. The notes are designed to help sort through these effects.

It is quite clear that introduction of these various proposals increases the program costs for present program participants (column 1), attracts additional workers into retraining programs (column 2), and further increases costs because of higher participation rates (column 3). In some cases there are offsets, but their magnitudes are difficult to assess.

The effects in columns 4–6 rest on a set of assumptions which are implicit in the various proposals. Because these assumptions are so crucial to the expected results of the various proposals, it is important to make them clear at the outset. As nearly as we can determine, they are as follows:

1. Retraining facilitates reemployment and higher earnings.
2. Retraining programs are viewed as attractive opportunities for permanently displaced workers.
3. Retraining can be started whenever unemployed workers decide they want to begin retraining.
4. Retraining is of relatively short duration and can be completed during the period of eligibility for UI benefits (this could include the period of eligibility for extended benefits).
5. Decisions to enter retraining programs are most likely to be made after unemployment commences, and in some cases after UI benefit eligibility expires.

We turn now to the results in columns 4–6. The entries in these columns indicate that the effects of special interest will be favorable. These results, however, hinge crucially on the assumptions just mentioned. If these assumptions do not hold, and earlier evidence suggests that they may not, then we must adjust the results in columns 4–6 to allow for this. Unfortunately, we cannot make exact adjustments but we offer our best guesses.

We present these results in columns 4–6 of Table 9.2, adjusting the results of Table 9.1 as seems appropriate. The net result is a less optimistic assessment of the longer-run effects of expanding the retraining and other options available under the UI system.

Table 9.1. Direction and Relative Magnitude of Effects of Various Proposals for Expanding Retraining Dimensions of UI System to Deal with Permanently Displaced Workers

Proposal Description	Cost for Retrainees (1)	Effect on Participation (2)	Additional Cost of (2) (3)	Subsequent		
				Lifetime Unemployment (4)	Lifetime Wage Rate (5)	Lifetime Earnings (6)
1. Present system (fixed benefit duration)						
No retraining						
Retraining OK	+	+	+ +	−	+	+ +
2. Layoffs with retraining option						
Delayed recognition of retraining need						
Reduced but extended benefits	+	−	+ −	+	+	+ +
Extended benefits only	+ +	+ +	+ + + +			
Higher benefits only	+ +	+ +	+ + + +			
Extended and higher benefits	+ + +	+ + +	+ + + + +			
Immediate recognition of retraining need						
All cases "delayed"[a]				−	+ +	+ + +
3. Layoffs with other options[b]						
Self-employed/subsistence	+ +	+ +	+ + + +	?	?	?
Entrepreneurial capital	+ +	+ +	+ + + +			
4. Expected quits anticipate layoff[c]						
Retrain while working	0	+	+		+	+
Retrain upon layoff	0	+ +	+ +	−?		
5. Quits to retrain key workers in vulnerable sectors[d]						
Extended benefits only	0	+ +	+ + + +	−?	+	
Higher and extended benefits	0	+ + +	+ + + + + +			+ +

[a]Indicates effects relative to those in line 2a.
[b]These effects would be partly offset by decline in line 2a.
[c]These effects would be in addition to those in lines 2 and 3, and in the long run would reduce lines 2 or 3.
[d]These effects would be in addition to those in lines 2, 3, and 4, and in the long run would reduce lines 2, 3, or 4.

Table 9.2. Direction and Relative Magnitude of Effects of Various Proposals for Expanding Retraining Dimensions of UI System to Deal with Permanently Disabled Workers (absent assumptions on p. 292)

Proposal Description	Cost for Retrainees (1)	Effect on Participation (2)	Additional Cost of (2) (3)	Subsequent		
				Lifetime Unemployment (4)	Lifetime Wage Rate (5)	Lifetime Earnings (6)
1. Present system (fixed benefit duration)						
No retraining						
Retraining OK	+	+	+ +	0	+ ?	+ ?
2. Layoffs with retraining option						
Delayed recognition of retraining need						
Reduced but extended benefits	+	−	+ −	0	+ ?	+ ?
Extended benefits only	+ +	+ +	+ + + +			
Higher benefits only	+ +	+ +	+ + + +			
Extended and higher benefits	+ + +	+ + +	+ + + + +			
Immediate recognition of retraining need						
All cases "delayed"[a]				−	+ ?	+ ?
3. Layoffs with other options[b]						
Self-employed/subsistence	+ +	+ +	+ + + +	?	?	?
Entrepreneurial capital	+ +	+ +	+ + + +			
4. Expected quits anticipate layoff[c]				?	+ ?	+ ?
Retrain while working	0	+	+			
Retrain upon layoff	0	+ +	+ +			
5. Quits to retrain key workers in vulnerable sectors[d]				?	+ ?	+ + ?
Extended benefits only	0	+ +	+ + + +			
Higher and extended benefits	0	+ + +	+ + + + + +			

[a]Indicates effects relative to those in line 2a.

[b]These effects would be partly offset by decline in line 2a.

[c]These effects would be in addition to those in lines 2 and 3, and in the long run would reduce lines 2 or 3.

[d]These effects would be in addition to those in lines 2, 3, and 4, and in the long run would reduce lines 2, 3, or 4.

Our considered judgment, then, is that while the objectives of the various proposals are laudable, the likelihood of achieving these objectives is more limited than sponsors of the proposals have acknowledged.

Policy Implications

It was suggested earlier in this paper that social programs normally undergo modification and amendment. This is to be expected because programs must adapt to changing social and economic circumstances. It comes as no surprise that we should find a training connection gradually added to the UI program.

In fact, however, the form of the training component of UI represents less an evolutionary development than a fundamental change in the UI system. When the program was established a choice was made as to what problems UI was designed to meet, and what kind of instrument would be used to solve those problems. Within that framework, many tactical changes are possible without doing violence to the system. But the addition of retraining to the UI system violates the fundamental basis of the system to the point of threatening the integrity and perhaps even the existence of the program.

Some of these dangers have been elaborated in the previous pages. The major problems may be summarized as follows.

Reserve Fund Balances. Several aspects deserve mention. First, UI funds were designed to pay the minimum amount of benefits necessary to see a worker through a layoff or during the transition from one job to another. Authorization to use benefits as support during retraining taps the reserve funds for an added, unforeseen use. A second negative element concerns benefit duration. A threat to fund solvency arises from the practice of releasing unemployed workers from the work search requirement. This guarantees a lengthy stream of benefits and may even assure exhaustion of benefits, depending on the duration of approved training. Fund balances may be further depleted by the use of extended benefits — originally intended to continue assistance to job seekers during economic downturns — to cover lengthy training instead of lengthy job search.

One might even speculate about a form of interaction effect. The policy of establishing a "right" to the full stream of regular and even extended benefits for those in approved retraining may have the unintentional effect of reinforcing the attitude of unemployed workers who are not receiving training that unemployment status automatically qualifies a worker for the reception of the full stream of benefits. Some authors (for example, Burgess and Kingston, 1984) have suggested that failure to engage in active job search represents the most common and costly fraud against the system.

In conclusion, whatever the present level of cost to the system due to past policy decisions, the legislation now proposed would only multiply the effect. Lump-sum distributions would further strengthen the attitude that workers have a right to the whole stream of regular and extended benefits. Quit provisions would undermine the theoretical basis of the UI system by covering voluntary instead of only involuntary unemployment. Authorization to use trust fund moneys for purposes other than benefit payment would lower reserves (or increase the debt of already insolvent states). Higher payments and extended duration to those in training would cost more and attract participation by those not in need of training, further raising the costs and depleting state reserves.

Tax Policy. The fundamental problem with the change introduced in the UI program is its violation of the insurance basis of the system. An analogy may help: UI was intended to operate something like auto insurance, but people have come to think of it—and increasingly use it—like life insurance. Auto insurance collects premiums from all those covered in order to pay benefits out to the small percentage of those who actually experience an accident and need the prescribed benefit. If individuals pay for auto insurance for forty years and never have an accident, they have received the value paid for, namely protection in case of need. They do not have a right to some kind of eventual payment, as might be the case with the accumulation of value in some life insurance policies.

To expect that the present form of UI should disburse lump-sum payouts upon layoff or retirement would be analogous to expecting an auto insurance policy to provide the down payment for purchase of your next car if you never had a wreck with your previous car. Put another way, to assume that UI should support a worker in retraining is analogous to expecting your auto insurance company to pay for your children's driving lessons. The driving lessons may be as valuable to the insurance company in avoiding future claims as good retraining may be to the UI system, allowing it to avoid repeated and prolonged failure benefit claims from a dislocated worker. No one disputes the valuable natural linkage between UI and retraining. The problem is the potential for damage to the insurance system if training support drains the reserves.

This problem manifests itself in two ways in the funding of UI. First, the UI tax is experience-rated. This attempts (admittedly in an imperfect manner) to relate the employer tax rate to the use of layoffs. Whatever else may be wrong with this theory, it is completely disregarded when layoffs are no longer related to an employer decision or the availability of other jobs, but rather to a manpower policy decision to retrain workers. This short-circuits any recall by employers, while at the same time raising the UI tax to employers.

Another effect on the tax structure is evident in the taxing of employers requiring only the most basic of job skills who will now be taxed to support a system whose new purpose is not to counter layoffs but to support retraining. An amusement park that lays off an unskilled ticket-taker may be forced to support his retraining into a skilled worker unwilling to return to low pay and boring work. If the value of retraining is a value to society, should not the price be shared by the broader constituency?

Equity Considerations. Workers may also suffer. Trainees may find inadequate support from benefit levels replacing only 50 percent of former wages, and the duration of benefits under UI may be too brief to see them through a meaningful retraining program. To the extent that use of UI to support trainees depletes state reserve funds, UI administrators may freeze or even reduce benefit levels paid to the original targets of the program: unemployed job seekers.

Behavior Scenarios. By way of conclusion, let us examine some scenarios that attempt to describe the future results of present trends. If the economy continues as it has the past couple of years, the lower levels of unemployment will result in less pressure on the UI system. Debtor states may reduce record debts to Washington, and others may even use the good times to build modest reserves. The good news is that under such conditions payments to trainees will not strain the system unduly. Indeed, if the economic situation improves even more, the UI system will feel even less pressure, and in a tightening labor market, employers may undertake more retraining on their own.

The bad news is that we are approaching the average limit of modern recoveries, and an economic downturn, when it comes, will increase the regular usage of UI. States which have just cleared their debts will be forced to borrow anew; states still deep in debt may be pressed to freeze or lower benefits and raise taxes, and still see themselves slide into a deeper hole as the next recession wears on. A serious recession could cause the failure of marginal firms and lead to even more dislocated workers.

The demographics of the future suggest a brighter picture. A smaller youth cohort in the future could mean both less unemployment and a greater willingness on the part of firms to engage in training as a device to attract new young workers. This tighter labor market could also provide incentives for firms to retrain in order to retain valuable employees. This picture could be changed, however, by an increase in the trend of female entrants into the labor market.

Technology also provides a countervailing force to the demographic picture. If the pace of technological development and implementation quickens, it could offset the labor market constraints of the smaller numbers entering the work force. Robotization could even increase the levels of structural unemployment, and thus increase the pressure for retraining programs.

Such pressure would be only one of a number of possible scenarios. A generally older work force with less potential return on investment in retraining might be more interested in regular UI benefits than retraining support. A political trend toward less government, as well as constraints caused by deficit reduction measures, could translate into reduced training expenditures, thus lessening the need for support of trainees. Two additional political wild cards are minorities and illegal immigration. High levels of minority unemployment could develop into political pressure for targeted training of persons who have been unable to enter the labor market rather than retraining for dislocated workers. Effective measures to stem the flow of illegals may tighten the labor market.

Policy Options

Just as one can describe the points of the compass without immediately deciding in which direction to travel, we now describe the alternative directions the UI system might take in the future. For the immediate future, of course, the present system will continue in effect. This means perpetuating a hybrid system, one that continues the original purpose of UI (seeing a worker through the change from an old to a new job), but now adds a new function (facilitating the reemployment of displaced workers whose reemployment opportunities in comparable work are limited) that violates the operational theory of benefit eligibility and trust fund use.

The qualitative change is a fact: more research is now needed to determine if and when this qualitative change has the potential to become a quantitative threat to the integrity and endurability of the system. In other words, the UI system was not designed for every unemployed worker to receive the maximum duration of regular and even extended benefits, as happens for trainees with the waiver of the work test. If large numbers of trainees are supported by UI, the drain on the reserve fund (and on employers' tax rates) during business cycle upturns may be enormous, and could become overwhelming during business downturns.

This potential for drained reserves, higher employer taxes, and massive state debts to the federal government become even more likely if some of the proposed legislation we have reviewed becomes law.

What, then, are the alternatives to this less than hopeful scenario? One could think of many variations, but we feel they would fall under one of three basic directions.

Joint Funding. If the present direction is to be continued, the system will need more money. This could come from any one, or a combination of sources: higher employer taxes, initiation of worker contribution to the UI reserve, or general revenue contributions to the system. All of these sources are tapped in European UI schemes. As the American program strays from its unique character and drifts toward a European benefit approach, it may become necessary to emulate the European financing model also.

Restoration of Pure Insurance. A second direction would be to turn the clock back and restore UI to its function of half a century ago and pay benefits only to workers who are actively seeking reemployment. Procedurally, this could be simply and easily accomplished by reestablishing the work test ("able, available, and actively seeking"). Politically, this would be much more difficult to bring about because a commitment to training makes sense to a lot of people, and a clientele once established is difficult to disenfranchise.

Separate Programs. What could make the second option politically feasible would be to recognize the need for a response to structural unemployment but to devise a program of both training and support entirely separate from the UI system. The advantage for the trainee is that the setting of benefit levels and duration would be free from the intentional disincentives built into the UI benefit schedule. The advantage to the employer would be a return to a tax based on labor market conditions and not to funding human capital investments in retraining.

Conclusion. This analysis of the broad advantages of a comprehensive, well-funded system seems to argue for a broad funding base for the separate training program. It would seem society would benefit greatly; the question is whether society has the political will to fund such a system. For those who think the answer to that question is no and yet are convinced of the need for retraining, the only alternative may be to support a continuation of the present system.

Future Research

This topic of the intertwining of retraining with UI is an important area for research, given the criticism of training programs, financial problems of the UI system, and continuing suggestions of more new ways to use already depleted UI funds. Some of the questions in need of answers may be grouped around the following topics:

— *What is "approved training"?* This amorphous category lies at the heart of present retraining laws and needs to be studied. Three elements need clarification: what kinds of training are approved (or disapproved); what categories of workers (based on personal characteristics like age, skill levels, and so on) are approved for training; and how are the training and the workers paired?

— *How much is the program used?* How many workers receiving UI benefits are out of the labor market because they are in approved retraining?

— *How much does the program cost?* What does it cost the UI system to support trainees? Part of the answer depends on the duration of training: how long are these workers out of the labor market?

— *Does the program work?* Are retrained workers finding jobs, replacing former income levels, and staying employed in their new jobs?

— *What incentives and disincentives are at work?* Does the availability of the program encourage participation in retraining by those who would otherwise accept available jobs? On the other hand, are prime candidates for retraining discouraged from participation by the intentionally low benefit levels and limited duration of UI?

— *What is the impact on trust funds?* What is the optimal trust fund level? Does the program drain these funds, and should nonbenefit uses be permitted?

— *Does the program encourage fraud?* What is the effect of this program on the attitude and behavior of both employers and workers?

— *Does the program cause administrative problems?* Does the additional training component complicate the administration of UI?

NOTES

1. In a very few states, workers pay for and are then covered by supplemental insurance to meet these circumstances, but this constitutes an auxiliary program.

2. In *Calvan* v. *Industrial Commissioner of New York,* the U.S. Supreme Court affirmed the constitutionality of the "12 percent rule," but held that it must be applied in a nondiscriminatory fashion (it was being applied only to Puerto Ricans returning home).

3. For a good summary of these developments, readers are referred to Levitan, Mangum, and Marshall (1982).

4. A major proponent of this view was Charles Killingsworth (congressional testimony, 1963).

5. The opposing view was presented in Walter Heller (1965, pp. 97–146).

6. This is exemplified by the work of Gary Becker (1964), as well as by the special supplement "Investment in Human Capital" in the *Journal of Political Economy.*

7. For evidence particularly for youth programs, see Betsey, Hollister, and Papageorgiou (1986).

8. The evidence continues to mount that the benefit/cost results of training and retraining are less than favorable, with perhaps the exception of the Job Corps. See Hollister, Kemper, and Maynard (1984, pp. 239–285); Cain (1967); Thornton, Long, and Mollar (1980).

9. See also the Office of Technology Assessment study, "Technology and Structural Unemployment: Reemploying Displaced Adults," February 1986.

10. Section 3304(a)(8), FUTA (P.L. 991-373, approved August 10, 1970, effective January 1, 1972).

11. P.L. 97-300 (approved October 13, 1982; effective FY 1984).

12. Section 3304(b)(2), FUTA.

13. New Jersey Division of Employment Security, *Local Office Claims Manual,* Section 245.815.

REFERENCES

Becker, Gary. 1964. *Human Capital*. New York: National Bureau of Economic Research.

Betsey, Charles L., Robinson G. Hollister, Jr., and Mary Papageorgiou. 1986. *Youth Employment and Training Program*. Washington, D.C.: National Academy Press.

Burgess, Paul L., and Jerry L. Kingston. 1984. "The Unemployment Insurance System: The Case for Major Reform." National Chamber Foundation, Washington, D.C. Typescript.

Cain, Glen. 1967. "Benefit/Cost Estimates for Job Corps." Discussion Paper 9-67, Institute for Research on Poverty, University of Wisconsin–Madison. Typescript.

Dahm, Margaret, and Phyllis H. Finescriber. 1980. "Examining Dependents' Allowances." *Unemployment Compensation Studies and Research*. Report of the National Commission on Unemployment Compensation (July).

Flaim, Paul O., and Ellen Sehgal. 1985. "Displaced Workers of 1979–83: How Well Have They Fared?" *Monthly Labor Review* 108 (June): 3–16.

Haber, William, and Merrill G. Murray. 1966. *Unemployment Insurance in the American Economy*. Homewood, Ill.: Richard D. Irwin.

Hansen, W. Lee. 1963. "Total and Private Rates of Return to Investment in Schooling." *Journal of Political Economy* 71 (April): 128–140.

Heller, Walter. 1965. In Garth L. Mangum, ed., *The Manpower Revolution*. New York: Doubleday.

Hollister, Robinson H., Jr., Peter Kemper, and Rebecca A. Maynard. 1984. *The National Supported Work Demonstration*. Madison: University of Wisconsin Press.

"Investment in Human Capital." 1964. *Journal of Political Economy* 70 (October).

Levitan, Sar A., Garth L. Mangum, and Ray Marshall. 1982. *Human Resources and Labor Markets*. New York: Harper & Row.

Lubove, Roy. 1968. *The Struggle for Social Security 1900–1935*. Cambridge: Harvard University Press.

Mincer, Jacob O. 1962. "On the Job Training, Returns, and Some Implications." *Journal of Political Economy* 70 (October): 50–73.

Office of Technology Assessment. 1986. *Technology and Structural Unemployment: Reemploying Displaced Adults*. Washington, D.C.: Government Printing Office, February.

Thornton, C., D. A. Long, and C. Mollar. 1980. *A Comparative Evaluation of the Benefits and Costs of Job Corps After 18 Months in Post-Program Observation*. Princeton, N.J.: Mathematica Policy Research.

Vroman, Wayne. 1985. "Innovative Developments in Unemployment Insurance." *Report to the National Commission for Employment Policy* (February).

Zell, Stephen P. 1976. "Unemployment Insurance Programs and Procedures." *Monthly Review* (February).

10

Unemployment Insurance and Short-Time Compensation

MARTIN J. MORAND

Introduction

Short-Time Compensation (STC), an "innovation in UC," is no longer an "experiment" but a permanent and growing feature of UC (Unemployment Compensation), having added five states (for a total of twelve) since the conference, "Unemployment Compensation: The Second Half-Century," was announced in mid-1985.[1] Nine other states are studying the possibility of enacting STC legislation.[2] The task of evaluating it is made more complex by the long-delayed Mathematica research report (hereafter, M/D)[3] for the U.S. Department of Labor (DOL) and the storm of controversy which it has engendered, particularly among members of the advisory committee of "employee and employer representatives" mandated by the congressional legislation which encouraged STC's development.[4]

This paper provides an introduction to the rationale for and practice of STC; suggests a variety of ways in which the existence of and research on STC provide insights into regular UI; reviews the literature regarding STC, with particular attention to the Canadian STC research; offers a detailed critique of the M/D research; hypothesizes that STC may play an important role in providing information on and directing attention to the question of a shorter workweek; concludes that STC, as a form of worksharing, may lay a foundation for a more sharing society; and suggests some strategies for future research on STC and its significance for both UI as an institution and the labor market in general.

STC — A Definition/Description

STC, worksharing supplemented by shares of regular Unemployment Insurance (UI) benefits in proportion to the reduction in worktime, is an

302

amendment which corrects the "pay off layoff" bias of the regular UI system.[5] Unlike job sharing—the holding of a full-time job by two part-timers on a permanent basis—worksharing is a collective process through which a group of workers share temporary down-time in much the same way that workers generally share overtime.

The essence of STC is most easily illustrated by example:

> Suppose, because of reduced demand, the employer of 100 workers is planning to lay off twenty of them. Instead, however, he reduces the work-week of all one hundred workers by 20 percent, and the same UI benefits that would have been paid to the twenty laid-off workers are divided among the one hundred. Even though there would be a slight reduction in earnings of all one hundred workers, none would suffer the traumatic hardship of total unemployment; the employer would maintain a balanced, skilled, and productive work force; and there would be no significant additional drain on the UI fund.[6]

STC and Traditional UI Principles

STC follows the principle behind UI partial benefits—that UI should not be a disincentive to work—and applies it to periods of one to three days off in a week. Partials do not address many employer worktime reduction needs because, ". . . the methods commonly used to deduct earnings from maximum weekly benefits usually make it impossible for individuals who work more than a day or two per week to collect benefits . . . discourag[ing] workers from accepting reduced work schedules even for short spells."[7] Partials are far more liberal with UI fund moneys than is STC because they pay out more benefits for a given reduction in hours than the *pro rata* STC formula allows.

The foregoing assertion is contrary to the conventional wisdom regarding the partial benefit system and is in direct contradiction to the Laurdan Report which states ". . . unemployed workers under an STC program obtain higher wage replacement levels than they would have, had they been totally laid off, and somewhat *higher wage replacement levels than they would have, had they received benefits under the states' partial benefits provisions*" (emphasis added).[8] Consistent with this assumption, the Laurdan Report asserts, "From an employer's perspective partial benefits achieve some degree of job attachment *at a lower level of benefit exposure*" (emphasis added).[9] Ronald L. Adler, President of Laurdan Associates, asserted in response to my telephone inquiry/challenge to these statements that they were true at the level at which partial unemployment did *not* enable the worker to collect partial benefits.

But the term "partials" in its normal usage (as by Mathematica) refers to benefits and, in that context, partial benefits *do* cost more to the fund and therefore to the employer's experience rating; indeed they are designed and structured to do so. STC, on the other hand, is designed and structured to pay out benefits directly proportional to benefits paid for full weeks of unemployment—proportional to the reduction in hours.

An example may make the point more clearly:

In Pennsylvania, the earnings disregard—the amount of money an individual may earn while partially unemployed without affecting his/her benefits—is 40 percent of the benefit rate. Assume a firm with one hundred workers, a scheduled workweek of forty hours, and a $5 hourly pay rate. Such workers regularly earning $200 per week would typically have a UI benefit rate of about $100. Should the firm be faced with a need for a massive reduction in its labor time of, for example, 80 percent, the common procedure would be to lay off 80 workers. These eighty workers would collect $8,000 in UI benefits. The remaining twenty workers would continue to earn $200 per week, for a total of $4,000. UI benefits of $8,000, plus earnings of $4,000, would yield a total income of $12,000. Should the employer choose to reduce the entire workforce to one day per week, the workers would earn $40 per day times one hundred workers, or $4,000. These one hundred employees would, under the partial benefit program, be eligible for the full $100 UI benefit (because the $40 is within the 40 percent of benefit rate disregard), for a total UI benefit of $10,000 and a total income to the workforce of $14,000.

The partials formula in the states varies: some use percentage disregards; some ignore a certain dollar-level of earnings; the percentages and dollar amounts vary; and New York uses a formula based on days worked rather than amount earned. But the principle is the same and the direction of the effect is the same, which is one reason that most state STC programs set the maximum level of hours reduction that an employer may make under the program low enough so that it does not lead to so short a workweek that the worker would be better off under the partial benefits formula. Whether under a percentage, a dollar, or a day of earnings disregarded, a partial benefits program uses more UI dollars per hour of unemployment than does regular UI or its *pro rata* equivalent, STC.

Despite their relative generosity, partial benefits are not, as is STC, viewed with alarm as a drain on UI and as a threat to the integrity of the trust funds. Presumably, once STC becomes as familiar as the partial benefit concept, its contribution to encouraging employment rather than subsidizing unemployment will achieve general recognition and acceptance.

Some employers, workers, and unions maintain a tradition of work-sharing (despite the inhibitions of the administrative requirements for weekly payouts of UI benefits) by employing rotational furloughs. Through this system of sharing the slack time by alternating full weeks of work with full weeks of layoff, employers preserve their workforce and employees obtain their full UI benefits—they beat the system by abiding by the technicalities of the rules. This rotational layoff system of work-sharing with full UI benefits is known to be practiced by many employers; it is perfectly legal; it is not challenged as imposing a burden on the trust funds or on other employers; it is not subject to special administrative procedures or surtaxes; it is sometimes combined with a voluntarism which permits some workers to elect longer layoffs in order to provide more work time for others; and it is generally characterized by benign neglect.

Because partials do not permit small reductions in the workweek and because, for some enterprises, the multiweek worksharing of a rotating schedule poses production, administrative, and marketing difficulties, the sharing of time by reducing the workweek for one to three days through an STC plan simply fleshes out the options of the UI system.

If this new flexibility is merely old wine in a newly shaped bottle; if STC is consistent with the purpose of UI: "encouraging employers to stabilize employment"[10]; if it conforms with the UI practice of preserving a trained workforce during periods of temporary business downturns; if STC corresponds with the American ethic of encouraging effort rather than idleness; if STC serves a fundamental UI goal of sustaining purchasing power by preserving consumer confidence; why, then, has STC met with and suffered such resistance from bureaucrats within the system and from academic observers without the system? And why, if it is viewed with such favor among employer, worker, and union participants and by the states which have adopted it, has it not "taken off" more quickly and fully? The Laurdan Report indicates some of the reasons; my own experience suggests some others. The study surveyed all state Employment Security Agencies and received responses from all STC states and thirty-three other states in April and May of 1986. While the survey confirmed the usual reasons for adoption of the program—employment stabilization; layoff avoidance; workforce preservation; affirmative action; and positive social, psychological, and financial impacts on the employed—it uncovered a great deal of apathy, ignorance, and confusion about the program. ". . . STC legislation was not being considered because there was a general lack of interest by employers, labor, and the general public . . . reservations about the effectiveness of STC . . . [and] serious concern for the trust fund impact of STC benefits."[11]

The lack of interest is clearly related to lack of information and understanding about STC and its relation to regular UI. Even in states which have the STC program, most potential participants haven't heard about it; it is, therefore, not surprising that in other states without STC programs the concept is so little known. It is a common option in Europe and was already in effect in Germany when the U.S. program with its antisharing bias was adopted. The personnel manager in the Toronto plant of a U.S. brand-name corporation indicated that he had never discussed his use of

STC with corporate headquarters and was surprised to learn that there was an STC program in the U.S. state where the headquarters was located. Unionists in California who were very favorable to the program had never notified their international headquarters in Washington about it. Mid-level UI system administrators in California were unfamiliar with and hostile to the program even in its third year; centralized administration of STC insulates regional and local office personnel from familiarity with it. A senior UI administrator in one state which still does not have the program asserted that "it would be morally wrong to give checks to people who are working four days in a week."

Misinformation is still prevalent; the Laurdan survey found states concerned that ". . . unions would continue to be less receptive to what is considered to be a program that undermines the seniority system."[12] This assertion was made despite AFL-CIO statements and testimony in favor of STC at least since August 1981.[13] "The major reason given by states rejecting STC programs was the anticipated negative impact STC benefits would have on the state's Unemployment Insurance Trust Fund."[14] This, despite the fact that ". . . states with STC programs reported that they did not anticipate or have not experienced a negative impact on their trust funds."[15]

Confusion concerning the place of STC in the UI income support system was evident as states gave the following contradictory reasons for not adopting STC: ". . . economic climate bright . . . less pressure to develop programs for the unemployed" and ". . . depressed economic conditions . . . would be unresponsive to temporary and short-term fixes."

Administrative Procedures

The Administrative Analysis produced by Mathematica, despite some shortcomings discussed below, provides a good summary of the common administrative procedures in the STC states:

> . . . Although other details vary, the states have adopted very consistent frameworks for defining their programs. All state programs are defined in terms of employer plan requirements, eligibility conditions for individuals, procedures for modifying plans, methods for determining benefit amounts, and provisions for financing shared work benefits.
>
> All states require employers to submit a shared work plan, and use the employer's plan as the primary basis for ensuring adherence to the program's purposes. All states require that a plan application be submitted at the initiative of the employer. Although the states vary in how they define an acceptable plan, their requirements cover common topics. Plans are generally limited to a certain duration, either six or twelve months. All states require a certain minimum level of employee participation, stated as a number of employees

or a percentage of the defined "affected unit," and require information about the extent of participation in the employer's application. States commonly limit the length of time that individuals can draw benefits, most commonly to 26 weeks in a benefit year. Employers' plans must usually specify the percentage by which employees' work hours will be reduced, and that reduction must fall within a range specified in the state law.

All of the state shared work programs acknowledge the possibility that employers' plans, once approved, may need to be modified, and establish procedures for doing so. Employers are allowed to change the roster of employees included in their shared work unit and the percentage by which their work hours are reduced. The formality of the modification procedure, and the nature of the changes for which it must be used, vary across states.

State shared work laws specify how benefits are to be computed. All states calculate benefits as a percentage of each employee's regular computed weekly benefit amount (WBA). The percentage of the WBA paid is based on a measure of the "employment reduction" imposed by the shared work plan. This measure varies in subtle ways across programs, but always uses the reduction in either hours or wages from the "normal work week." The state programs also vary in other respects, such as the treatment of earnings from employers other than the shared work employer, and the manner in which non-work time (absences, vacation, sick time, holidays) are treated in benefit computation.

Finally, all state programs specify how shared work benefits are to be financed. Provisions in each state's law define how participation in the shared work program and the payment of benefits affect each employer's UI tax obligation, and specifically what special tax obligations are imposed on participating employers with negative reserve balances or high benefit ratios. Two types of special tax obligations have been used: "percentage surtaxes," computed by adding an increment to the regular tax rate applied to employers' payrolls, and "additional contributions," computed to equal the amount of shared work benefits issued under employers' shared work plans. Under the percentage surtax method, a schedule is used to determine by how much the employer's regular tax rate should be increased: the more negative the reserve ratio or the higher the benefit ratio, the greater the increment to the tax rate. The states using this method have adopted a variety of schedules, and thus have different maximum increments that can be added as surtax percentages.[16]

Advantages of STC

The major advantages of STC have been summarized by Work In America Institute, Inc., as:

For Employers

1. Maintenance of productivity because of higher morale and preservation of employee skills.

2. Retention of skilled workers.
3. Reduction or elimination of the large costs associated with layoffs, particularly where "bumping" occurs, for example, distorted production scheduling, delayed start-ups when recession ends, retraining of bumped employees.
4. Greater flexibility in deploying human resources to keep operations going.
5. Savings in employer costs associated with severance pay, early-retirement incentives, and other layoff schemes requiring substantial financing.
6. Avoidance of postrecession costs of hiring and training new workers to replace those who found other jobs during layoff.
7. Reinforcing group loyalties and strengthening employee loyalty to the firm.

For Workers

1. Continued job attachment for workers who would otherwise have been laid off.
2. Continued fringe-benefit protection for employees and their families.
3. Retention of more minority and women workers, thus preserving the aims and achievements of affirmative action.
4. Security for older workers, who cost more, are often among the first fired in selective layoffs, and are discriminated against when they seek new jobs.
5. Opportunity for workers with high seniority to trade work for increased leisure, with only a small decrease in take-home pay, thus providing a "taste" of retirement without fear of unemployment.
6. More effective preservation of the family income of two-paycheck families than if one member continues to work full time and the other is on unemployment insurance, particularly if the wife is a new entry into the labor force. (Women's traditional jobs are generally low paying, and eligibility rules for unemployment insurance require workers to meet a combination of dollar amount and time in covered occupations. For some new entrants, these benefits may be low or nonexistent.)

For Unions

1. Preservation of union membership and members' ability and willingness to pay dues.
2. Greater ability to take into account diverse interests of membership and to fairly represent all employees in the bargaining unit.
3. Improved long-run prospects for the union. Layoffs generally pose problems for unions because some laid-off workers do not return, new employees have to be organized, and returning workers may have less enthusiasm for the union after extended unemployment.
4. Less polarization between groups represented by the union.
5. Increased support from new workers who would otherwise be laid off.
6. Greater bargaining flexibility when an employer suffers a downturn.

For Society

1. Protection of affirmative action and equal employment opportunity advances.
2. Less need for public service jobs.
3. Less need for public assistance for the unemployed.
4. No increase in net unemployment insurance costs.
5. Less disruption of the society as a whole.[17]

STC and the UI System

The UI system will be strengthened and sustained during the next half century by the addition of the STC option. Apart from the benefits which will accrue to stakeholders in the system—employers, employees, unions, and governments—the system itself will benefit as STC addresses specific problems associated with UI and as discussion and debate regarding STC encourage that reexamination of the role of UI within the larger society suggested in Saul Blaustein's *Job and Income Security for Unemployed Workers.*[18] The following are a few problems facing the UI system which STC addresses:

1. The UI system is subjected to impossible demands that it become a zero-defects program. The complaints are legion: the Employment Service is ineffective; job search is unenforceable and may be unnecessary; it is hard to check up on ineligibles who get checks; some eligibles are improperly denied; the appeals process is time-consuming and costly, over-burdened and expensive. Efforts to reform the system are caught up in conflicts between labor and management, between Democrats and Republicans. In contrast, STC can be cheaper to administer—for workers, employers, and the system; it requires no job search to be policed or subverted; it keeps people out of the Employment Service's hair; it does not lead to denials and appeals. It is the only labor market legislation enjoying support from corporations and unions, conservatives and liberals.

2. UI is publicly perceived as legislation for losers; benefits for the unsuccessful; care for the least skilled, least senior, lease secure, least wanted. The Job Service is seen as securing undesirable low-end jobs for undesirable low-end people. To the extent that STC encourages and subsidizes job preservation for a work group as a whole rather than paying only to the laid off, it contributes to a more positive image and enlarges the constituency of supporters. The lack of such a constituency for UI stands in sharp contrast to the well-nigh universal support for its parent Social Security system. STC participants—workers and employers—are strong supporters of a UI system in need of such support.

While U.S. workers do not generally make direct payments to UI funds, they have been told in many ways that employer contributions are a form of deferred compensation, a fringe benefit, something coming to them. They may have heard this across a bargaining table as an employer response to a union negotiating demand, or through an employer informational program designed to gain recognition of, and credit for, the host of labor costs that do not show up in the pay envelope. Many of these employees are insulated from layoff and are consequently aloof from, or even hostile to, the fact that they have "given" at work and received nothing in return. (It is precisely this sentiment to which employers respond when they offer cafeteria benefit plans.) STC addresses this concern as it makes more workers shareholders in the system.

Reports from employers to state UI agencies include: "It is a wise expenditure of government funds that benefits all parties involved. An excellent creative idea!!" (Washington).[19] "The program has shown . . . that a state bureau can respond creatively to the short-term welfare of the *contributing* members of society" (Oregon, emphasis in original).[20] The California Industrial Relations Committee reports: "Employer representatives in the state capital strongly endorse the shared work UI program . . . including the California Chamber of Commerce which vigorously opposed the program originally. . . ."[21] "Morale is high, and we've maintained a highly trained workforce. It's that rare thing, a win-win situation" is the way one executive summed up the STC program.[22]

3. For most of its contributors and beneficiaries—and by many of its staff—the UI system is seen as nothing more than a check collecting and check issuing system. As evidence mounts that STC contributes to worker and family stability, morale and productivity, reduction of other government transfer costs, and encouragement of a sense of community in the workplace, it will foster and force a reexamination of the UI system and its place in the total economy and society.

4. UI benefits replace a smaller percentage of earnings in the United States than they provide in other industrialized nations. Levels of UI benefits in the states are in no way related to rational public policy but are rather the result of a tug of war periodically waged in state capitals by business and labor lobbyists. Relatively high wage states with very healthy UI reserves often have much lower benefits than states not so richly endowed. In several heavy industry states major corporations joined labor unions in lobbying for higher UI benefits following negotiation of supplementary unemployment benefit (SUB) plans (higher UI payments reduced their costs since SUB only requires the company to pay the difference between UI and a fixed percentage of regular wages). States with STC programs report employer comments such as: "I wish it were possible to allow the people with higher incomes to get more compensation."[23] AFL-

CIO has voiced the similar concern that more senior, higher wage workers have a smaller portion of their incomes protected in STC programs than do the junior, lower paid workers. When the normal demands of workers and unions for "more" are joined by at least some employers seeking similar goals, politicians are likely to respond positively. (Such was the case when increases in Social Security benefits followed on the heels of steel industry negotiated pension plans which required employers to make up the difference between Social Security and $100.)

5. Regular UI provides some cash for some weeks but does little to aid workers who must change jobs and learn new skills. While STC is not intended to deal primarily with other than temporary downturns, it may be used, at least in Maryland, Washington, California, and Canada as a transitional mechanism leading to a permanent downsizing or elimination of the labor force. (Maryland conditions using STC for permanent workforce reductions on inclusion by the employer of a reemployment assistance plan as part of its worksharing program.) In Canada there are specific provisions in the STC program for federally financed retraining programs run by tripartite committees during the days when work is not scheduled. As state and federal policy makers increasingly look toward the UI system as a cheap and easy vehicle for addressing employment and training problems they will want to examine the role of STC in providing time and money to support such training. In addition, STC is sometimes a means of paying for prevention instead of catastrophe: the quicker and more efficient response to upsurges in demand available through STC may enable temporary worksharing to prevent permanent plant closure.

6. Small businesses are often critics of regular UI because they see themselves as squeezed between the power of big business and big labor. This is true to the extent that, over the past half century, the cap on taxable wages has been kept down while maximum benefits have gone up; the smaller businesses which pay lower wages and salaries have been burdened with a greater percentage of the cost of the system. In 1986 in Pennsylvania, for example, a worker earning about $8,000 per year might receive a weekly benefit of $80; a worker earning about three times as much would be eligible for the maximum payment of $232. Yet the employer of the higher benefit worker contributes to the fund only on the first $8,000. STC does not, of course, automatically correct this problem. But STC may contribute to remedying this discriminatory feature of our so-called experience rating schemes. The states, DOL, and business and labor organizations are watching closely the relationship between trust fund income and expenditures in this new program and evidences of cost shifting will be highlighted and addressed. If, as is believed by some, senior higher wage workers (who would not have been laid off but who participate in STC) draw higher benefits, and if these are disproportionate to

their employers' contributions, STC may call attention to this larger problem. More important, studies of STC are identifying and calling attention
to the larger question of the true cost of layoff, particularly to governments, thus giving rise to a reassessment of the appropriate balance between
individual employer experience-based charges and the extent to which UI
costs ought to be shared, not only among all employers, but possibly by
the general funds.

7. One criticism of regular UI is that by maintaining income it discourages job search, that is, UI creates unemployment. UI has certainly
not been the cause of unemployment but, in addition to easing the conscience of a society whose social conscience is too easily eased, reporting
the cost of trust fund payouts has become a convenient substitute for
measuring the true cost of unemployment to society. The costs to society
are costs to government and to our sense of comfort in our communities—
costs in money for food stamps and for jails, costs in hunger and in the
harm done by and to the social deviants whose crimes are so highly correlated with levels of unemployment.[24] In just one preliminary effort to
inquire into the cost difference to state government between regular UI
and STC it was discovered, not surprisingly, that the Child Support
Enforcement program was finding, at considerable expense, and at a rate
in excess of one hundred to one, more regular UI delinquent parents than
STC recipients.[25] The congressionally mandated study of costs and benefits
to employers, and particularly to workers and communities, has not been
carried out by DOL. But it will be and, as employers, workers, unions,
and particularly government, become more aware of what we spend to
prop up unemployment, a broader constituency of reform—not just of
the regular UI system but of our entire jobs/income policies—will emerge.

8. The unemployed include particularly the "newly hired employees,
minorities, and women"[26] whose special problems were highlighted in the
congressional legislation. While regular UI, in the absence of STC, does
not by itself create disparate treatment of recently hired minorities and
females, in combination with seniority (almost as widely practiced in nonunion as in unionized enterprises), it certainly leads to disparate impact
and the perception of discrimination. With STC, particularly with a legislated stipulation that it cannot be used to lower the proportion of protected classes in the work group, such charges of discrimination could not
even be made.

9. There were basic philosophical ideals associated with the initiation
of UI which STC may more meaningfully address than does the regular
program. There is evidence and logic that, as a countercyclical tool, STC
does a better job in maintaining purchasing power than does regular UI,
since consumer confidence is greater among workers who are working and
layoffs lead to reduced spending readiness of those not yet laid off.

10. To the extent that job stabilization and not just income security was

one of the rationales for the UI system's experience rating scheme: ". . . to promote the financial security of workers by encouraging employers to stabilize employment . . . ,"[27] that dream has been too long deferred. Most workers don't get fired, they get laid off. STC encourages a rightful expectation that everyone willing to work will continue to do so.

11. Creators of the UI/Social Security system had an additional goal which was dropped from the 1935 legislative package—national health insurance. Unlike 1935, most large employers are now paying for health insurance and are finding this per-worker cost the major inhibitor to adopting sharing instead of layoff. As more employers examine the STC option and become aware of the full cost of layoff, they may become part of a coalition of support for national health insurance. There is, after all, a long tradition of big business socializing its layoff costs, as is evidenced by recent calls for national health insurance from Chrysler, Goodyear, etc.

12. The most serious challenge to the regular UI system is the fact that the vast majority of the unemployed went without UI benefits last year. Whether this was caused by exhaustions or denials, STC does and can address both of these phenomena whose existence challenges the very *raison d'être* of UI. STC recipients are earning credits even while collecting benefits. If the practices adopted in California and Arizona (of extending eligibility for STC based on a trigger point of high unemployment) are universalized, exhaustion would never occur where STC is in use. While most states have mechanically applied their regular UI standards to STC eligibility, some have made appropriate exceptions. As STC is increasingly understood as a *collective* approach to work preservation, eligibility standards which apply to individuals who are being pushed out on the job market will be modified to eliminate denials to any worker designated as a member of an employer STC work group.

13. A major contribution of STC to the regular UI system is to make it inescapably clear that there is no UI *system*. "One of the first real innovations in UI in many decades,"[28] whether it were STC or something else, would probably have forced some recognition of how disconnected and, indeed, competitively hostile, the fifty-two separate systems are. Whatever the creators' intent may have been fifty years ago, we do not today have a meaningful federal-state system. The budget and staff assigned to UI in DOL are minuscule in relation to the smallest of the state administrative operations. Congress may call for technical assistance, model language, and extensive research on STC, but DOL has neither the resources, the power, nor the will to exert federal leadership.

These potential contributions of STC to the UI system will be frustrated (or at least delayed) should the recent research report submitted to Congress by DOL be accepted at face value.

STC Research

What can be said regarding research on STC in the United States to date is that it remains to be done. What has been studied and published until now is more helpful in sharpening the questions than in providing the answers; more useful in highlighting the difficulties in various research methodologies than in providing a model for future work; more significant in what has been ignored than considered; more valuable in exposing the limits of available data than in expanding the data base; more intent on using the data that are relatively cheaply, quickly, and easily assembled than in defining the full scope of data collection needs; more focused on the statistical exactness of the results than on their relevance. Researchers dare not be so concerned with mathematical verifiability that they over-look the primitive state of our knowledge and the limits of the data. They must acknowledge the need to expand our understanding of STC by description, anecdote, critical speculation, and cooperative development of appropriate methodologies, while we await the time when stringent proofs of mathematical hypotheses can be advanced. In many respects, the research reflects the economists' curse that ". . . often we know little about what is really going on (for example, when we estimate a production function for the cement industry without even having been in a cement plant)."[29] It is to be hoped that future STC research will heed the advice contained in a report to DOL by Thomas Kochan that labor market research include ". . . a richer blending of institutional and quantitative methods [and that] more attention should be given to the functioning of micro institutions."[30]

Research on STC falls into several categories: case studies; reports by state UI systems; econometric models combining data and theory; and best known and most extensive, major studies of STC conducted for the Employment Development Department (EDD) in California, the Canadian Employment and Immigration Commission, and the U.S. Department of Labor.

Case studies have been undertaken of particular firms' experiences with STC, including analysis of the implications to the firm of utilizing the sharing versus layoff option. The most extensive example of this kind of firm-based study is one carried out for Motorola Corporation by Ben Burgoon and Robert St. Louis.[31] They assert that, despite deliberately erring on the side of conservatism in their estimates, they found corporate savings through STC of $1,868 per worker, who would otherwise have been laid off. Of particular significance is the study's finding that STC paid out fewer dollar benefits than would have been expended through regular UI, thereby reducing the experience-rating effect on the firm and the drain on the fund. Since we do not know the extent to which the absence of extra costs for maintaining insurance coverage for the additional employees kept on the payroll through STC was a factor in the Motorola results (Motorola maintains such coverage during short-term layoff), it is difficult to generalize to other employers from this single plant study. But the experience may explain why Motorola was the major moving force behind the legislation in four states (Arizona, Florida, Illinois, and Texas) and why Motorola's representative on the Department of Labor advisory committee was so strongly critical of the M/D report.

Indeed, what the Motorola effort underlines is the need for further case studies which will attempt to identify the types of firms and the economic circumstances under which STC works best. Unfortunately, the next recession may be upon us before such further studies are undertaken, even though the need for this kind of microanalysis was pointed out as long ago as May 1981 in comments regarding the EDD study made by Frank Schiff at the First National Conference on Work Sharing Unemployment Insurance:

> . . . the most valuable aspect of the evaluation study has been the very careful and sophisticated way in which the authors have sought to assess the full range of elements that go into determining the cost of worksharing with partial UI relative to complete layoffs. . . . they have included not only direct employment costs but the cost of various fringe benefits, of investment in training that would be lost by layoffs, of rehiring and retraining costs entailed if new employees had to be taken on, etc. The fact is that most firms (even large ones) typically do not take the full range of these cost and benefit factors into account when they are faced with decisions on how the employment consequences of reductions of demand should be met . . . a really meaningful accounting format for such firms [would] enable them to carry out a true cost-benefit analysis of the comparative merits of outright layoffs and short-time compensation. If such an analytical tool were more widely available, it might well turn out that a larger number of firms than at present will see that it is to their advantage to use worksharing as an alternative to layoffs.[32]

Other case studies are reported in *Work Sharing Case Studies;*[33] in the transcript of the first national conference on Work Sharing Unemployment Insurance at which employers and union representatives described their experiences; in reports issued by the Work in America Institute; and in various news articles.

A second source of published information is the reports, generally issued annually, by the participating states to their legislatures and to the general public. These reports contain statistics on utilization of STC, results of surveys of employer users, and, occasionally, recommendations for legislative revisions. The most comprehensive of these state reports (the EDD evaluation aside) come from Arizona which also conducted a survey of employers, workers, and unions *before* it adopted its program.

There are some European sources, but the only one of these which deals directly with the U.S. situation is "Short-Time Working as an Alternative to Layoffs: The Case of Canada and Càlifornia."[34]

The Canadian STC Story

The Canadian research is interesting and important to U.S. observers perhaps as much for the way it directs attention to comparisons with the entire Canadian UI system as for the specific information which it provides on Canada's STC program. The program was announced and almost immediately begun in January 1982, and in its first year it had ". . . over twelve times as many firms and employees as the California program did during its second year of operation,"[35] despite the fact that Canada's population is approximately the same as California's. This is partly explained by the program's aggressive implementation by the Employment and Immigration Commission and the Industrial Assistance Services, and also because Canada's STC program is more generous in worker benefits (as is Canada's regular UI) and less costly to employers (because Canada's national health insurance program sharply reduces the cost of maintaining extra workers on the payroll).

One phenomenon which was barely mentioned in the Canadian research is the requirement that even nonunionized workers must affirmatively approve an STC program before employers can be certified to participate. When a similar suggestion was made by Frank Schiff in 1981, it was viewed by some as radical and unrealistic. Worker participation in Canada's program is so much taken for granted that it was not seen as an issue that needed to be researched. This presumption of worker participation in the decision-making process in Canada (and in Europe) is a logical outgrowth of workers' contributing directly to the UI fund.

Early in 1982, the Canadian government initiated studies of STC far more extensive than any conducted in the United States. A Preliminary Evaluation of the Work Sharing Program was issued in March 1983, and Evaluation of the Work Sharing Program in March 1984.[36] During this time eleven other specialized studies were published by the Employment and Immigration Commission. The total cost of this research was approximately equal to what DOL allocated for its multistate study. One must, of course, be wary of international analogies, but the similarities and interdependencies of these North American economies (particularly corporations and unions which span the border) and the equally interesting differences in their STC and UI program commend themselves to our consideration. As the National Commission on Unemployment Compensation noted: "Canada's economy closely resembles our own. . . ."[37]

STC Research in the United States

The first large-scale U.S. study was done in California for the Employment Development Department under the direction of Fred Best.[38] Although the research involved extensive surveys of employers, workers, and unions, it also used elaborate scenarios constructed partly on empirical data and partly on economic assumptions. Both the interview basis for much of the data and some of the economic assumptions of the scenarios have been criticized. Nevertheless, the study became the primary resource for an understanding of STC. It served to identify the extensive support for STC among the stakeholders; it provided the first evidence of senior worker and union support for STC; and it was most useful in focusing on the cost-benefit issue not just for the UI system but for workers, employers, and society as a whole. The strong constituent support for STC which the study uncovered encouraged California's EDD to merchandise it much more extensively and the legislature to delay its sunset, to liberalize its benefits, and to reduce its financial and administrative inhibitions to employer participation.

Mathematica Evaluation

The largest U.S. study undertaken to date was mandated by the Congress as part of the Tax Equity and Fiscal Responsibility Act of 1982. The contract was awarded to Mathematica Policy Research, which reported:

> The results of the study are highlighted here according to the nine questions explicitly raised by Congress:
>
> 1. STC participation did seem to reduce the extent to which layoffs were made during the 1982–1983 primary study period. The extent of these reductions in layoffs varied among the three states (average reductions were largest in Oregon and the smallest in California). Most STC participating employers used a mixed strategy of employment reductions that featured both reduced hours and layoffs.
>
> 2. Although total hours of regular UI collection were lower for STC participating firms, the average total hours of compensated unemployment (including both regular UI and STC benefits) were somewhat higher for those firms. Again, the extent of this additional compensated unemployment varied significantly by state (it was greatest in California and smallest in Oregon).
>
> 3. Patterns of employment and layoffs for minority and female employees were quite similar between STC participating firms and nonparticipating firms. Hence, no significant impact of STC participation on affirmative-action outcomes was observed.
>
> 4. STC benefit payments were generally more effectively experience-rated than were regular UI benefit payments. STC participants tended to experience

somewhat greater increases in UI tax rates during the study period than did nonparticipating employers.

5. On a per-employee basis, average total (UI plus STC) benefit charges were higher among STC participating employers than among employers in the comparison group. Although such additional charges may have imposed a short-term drain on UI trust-fund reserves, the longer-term impact was significantly mitigated by the more complete experience-rating of STC benefits.

6. Practically all employers retained health and retirement benefits for workers who were placed on reduced hours. Although state laws generally did not require that benefits be maintained as a condition for STC participation, firms seem to have followed that practice anyway.

7. In general, STC programs seemed to be administered in a similar manner across the various states, although many differences in specific details were observed. Through their procedures, all states tried to limit STC use for the purpose of acting as an alternative to layoffs during temporary downturns. However, the small number of states in the study precluded any precise evaluation of their success in doing so.

8. STC participation did help firms save on the hiring and training costs that would have been associated with layoffs. However, for some firms, these savings were counter-balanced by the higher fringe benefit costs involved in STC participation. The effects of STC use on productivity were not measured, and it is possible that such effects dominated these other cost considerations.

9. The administration of STC benefit payment activities on a per-layoff-equivalent basis was somewhat more expensive than the administration of regular UI. The additional costs associated with extra weekly benefits activities outweighed the savings on initial claims and ongoing eligibility determinations that occurred under STC. However, the costs of STC administration may decline over time as experience with the program accumulates.

A major issue not addressed in the congressional mandate for the present study concerns the determinants of STC participation. The reasons for the currently low levels of participation (less than 1 percent of all employers) are not well understood. Whether they are due to deterrents that may diminish in importance over time (possibly including the lack of information on the program) or to more permanent problems (possibly including the unsuitability of the program for many employers) could not be determined within the scope of the present study. Hence, the study offers only a very limited basis for extrapolating STC participation rates into the future.[39]

The Advisory Committee Comments

Congress targeted no special funds for the study and there has been an ongoing critique of the Department of Labor's failure to carry out the congressional mandate to provide technical assistance and research. The legislation called for an advisory committee of employer and employee representatives, which, however, did not meet until after a request for proposal had been issued and a contract awarded despite the fact that the legislation "clearly required consultation prior to the implementation of the study."[40] Members of the committee have been critical of their restricted role in the process and of the research design and its conclusions. The flavor of the debate, which took place over many months among members of the advisory committee, DOL staff, Mathematica researchers, and congressional aides has begun to appear on the record as members of the advisory committee have gone public.

The fall 1982 federal legislation had concluded that: "Not later than October 1, 1985, the Secretary [of Labor] shall submit to the Congress and to the President a final report . . . including recommendations as to necessary changes in the statistical practices of the Department of Labor."[41] Congressional sponsors complained about DOL's slowness in initiating the study (it had not commenced one year after the law's passage) and agreed to extend the deadline rather than receive a report clouded in controversy.

Nevertheless, the controversy continued and advisory committee members insisted upon and were granted the right to submit comments to be forwarded to Congress in addition to the "official" report. Further on, I will repeatedly refer to the views of one member of the advisory committee, Frank W. Schiff, Vice President and Chief Economist of the Committee for Economic Development. The comments of C. F. Koziol, Vice President and Director of Personnel Administration, Motorola, relate to:

> . . . three major concerns that have not been satisfactorily addressed in Mathematica's Report. . . . The methodology used to identify comparison companies is inappropriate. . . . The study is misleading in that it succeeds in quantifying many of the disadvantages of using STC, but quantifies almost none of the advantages. . . . The layoff conversion rates are not reported appropriately. . . . the vast majority of those who have participated in STC programs: a) strongly feel that the advantages of the program outweigh its disadvantages; and b) would use the program again if business conditions warranted. . . .[42]

Dr. Robert G. Spiegelman, Executive Director of the W. E. Upjohn Institute for Employment Research, reaches a contrary conclusion that Mathematica "has done a fully satisfactory job in presenting its findings. . . . I feel that the general findings of the report; i.e., that the total unemployed hours will be greater under STC than would be the case under regular UI alone, has been substantiated for the sum of the three states represented in the sample." He then asks "do these results provide a sufficiently credible base for policy decisions," and answers that it is "difficult to make an affirmative answer."

> This difficulty stems from the wide range of results among the three states. . . . It is hard to believe that none of the STC hours represent substitute hours,

and the credibility of these results is not enhanced by the evidence . . . showing that STC failed to cause any significant movement of California employers into higher UI tax rate classes . . . Thus, the MPR report provides no basis to support an STC program, but also inconclusive evidence that the net benefits are negative.[43]

The comments from the AFL-CIO member of the advisory committee, John Zalusky, go beyond the critique of the study itself "to note inadequate funding, support and performance by the Department of Labor. . . . Congress clearly asked for a broad analysis. . . . What it received was a narrow look. . . . The result . . . deliberately conveys a politically unpopular impression of STC by stressing costs, while narrowly considering benefits. . . ." He goes on to charge:

> The bias is first evident in the way the Secretary of Labor assigned responsibility for the study. The Office of Assistant Secretary for Policy Evaluation and Research . . . had been considering STC since at least 1977 — more than four years prior to passage of the bill directing this analysis. Rather than using these in-house policy research assets with broad knowledge and experience to guide this work by Mathematica, the Secretary of Labor assigned the responsibility to the watchdogs of the unemployment trust funds in the Employment and Training Administration (ETA). . . . The assignment of the task to ETA insured a limited and parsimonious view of the concept through the window of UI compensated hours. This view excludes many of the benefits of the concept that would have been available by a broader analysis, and certainly avoids looking at the plight of workers who have their hours and earnings cut while the employer avoids UI costs with work sharing. If the assignment of the task was not motivated by a desire to bias the analysis against the positive elements of STC, it certainly had that result.
> The limited scope of the study was then confirmed by the extremely limited funds provided. . . . The result is that a comparison group study design was chosen.
> The basic advantage of this type of study is its low cost. . . . This type of analysis was unsuited for the task assigned by Congress.[44]

The Mathematica Study Criticized

An earlier portion of the study, *Shared Work Compensation: An Administrative Analysis of State Programs*,[45] was issued by Mathematica in March 1985. This report met with little controversy, contains valuable data about the administration of the program in several states (primarily California, Arizona, Oregon, and Washington), and makes some valuable suggestions for more efficient methods of administration and promotion of the program. However, even this study reflects some of the same biases (in its consideration of controls, surtaxes, cost shifting, and trust fund effects) that critics of its successor have noted. As indicated in note 8, while the administrative analysis suggests that all states have imposed surtaxes, the fact is that four did not. They rejected the assumption that there are necessarily additional costs to the trust funds from employer use of STC.

Neither this report nor its successor "evaluation" examines the potential administrative *savings* to the Employment Service but focuses solely on *costs* of UI administration—despite the fact that a consultant to the Mathematica study, Robert St. Louis, had pointed out with regard to Arizona that ". . . clearly such potential savings [a saving to the Job Service equal to more than one-half of STC benefits paid out during the first ten months of the program] cannot be ignored when attempting to evaluate the desirability of an STC program—especially when it is reasonable to assume that after this initial start-up period the program can be administered more efficiently."[46]

The Canadian and California EDD studies deal with issues similar to the M/D report and reach different conclusions; a thorough review of the quality of their data and analyses will be essential in future research. Where EDD found a saving in labor cost per worker who would otherwise have been laid off of $3,023, Canada concluded that the figure should be $944, and M/D reports $175 to $250. As Noah Meltz noted, the M/D "figure apparently does not include off-the-job training, on-the-job training, and the results of below normal productivity. . . ."

> Given the importance of the calculations it would have been useful to compare their results with those for California (1982), since the two studies reach opposite conclusions. It is also worth noting that the recent analysis of STC at Motorola in Arizona, as indicated by Schiff, is consistent with the findings of the California study that the benefits of STC to employers exceed the costs even excluding less easily quantifiable impacts on health and social aspects.[47]

Since M/D did not itself study certain of the most basic questions (productivity, worker reactions, government and community effects) which were dealt with in the EDD and Canadian reports, one would have expected the report to devote more attention to these studies and their conclusions, even if M/D disagrees with them. Regarding productivity issues, M/D reports correctly that it is an important and complex issue but asserts that "the existing state-of-the-art does not permit such a refined analysis";[48] it would have been helpful to at least acknowledge the Canadian estimate that STC saves $325 in productivity loss per laid-off employee. More important, since Congress requested but M/D was unable to report on attitudes of and effects on worker participants, the remarkably consistent positive findings from both Canada and California warrant greater attention. Finally, the M/D study states that "broader questions about the effect of STC on other components of government or on the welfare of the community at large were outside the scope of the study,"[49] but does not recognize the effort by EDD and the Canadian Employment and Immigration Commission to address precisely these societal issues.

While the primary thrust of the challenge to the M/D evaluation centers on methodology, concerns have also been raised about the failure to address the broadest congressional requirement: "a comparison of costs and benefits to employees, employers, and communities from use of short-time compensation and layoffs."[50] The M/D Report's comments concerning this omission are essentially that the exigencies of time and the limitations of funding prevented a fuller study. Both of these explanations are undoubtedly valid; but even the request for proposal issued by the DOL focused more on the UI system than on the economy and society as a whole, leading some researchers to conclude that a negative cost-benefit assessment of STC was inevitable.

Trust Fund Effects

The research issue of greatest concern and controversy, from a public policy point of view, is whether STC costs the trust funds more than regular UI, either immediately or ultimately. The position which DOL has taken for many years, a position endorsed in the study conducted for it by Mathematica, is that STC costs more. Even prior to the M/D report, this DOL assumption had already had important policy implications. The DOL's advice to states whose trust funds are in debt to the federal government, when they contemplate adopting STC, is, to oversimplify, "Don't." To be more specific, states whose trust fund deficits led them to borrow from the federal government were required to make commitments not to change their UI program in any way which would increase costs. These commitments are a condition for obtaining a cap on the repayment schedule and/or interest-free loans. A state which has undertaken such a commitment may adopt changes which lead to increased costs, even if only temporarily increased, only if these are balanced by other benefit savings or other revenues. There have been about eighteen states in this debtor status during the period since Congress instructed the DOL to "assist states . . . in developing, enacting, and implementing" STC.[51] Some of these states have been discouraged from adopting STC programs by DOL's position that doing so will violate their loan agreements, a position which is based on an assumption for which I contend there is no compelling empirical evidence. The future growth and development of STC will be inhibited unless and until a satisfactory study lays this question to rest.

The feared negative impact of STC on the trust funds, particularly with regard to employers whose experience-rated tax was already at maximum, led to the adoption by the first three STC states—California, Arizona, and Oregon—of surtaxes on such employers when they use STC. This a priori assumption leads to a research problem: if the fear is well-founded, there might have been a drain on the trust funds from STC employers, but the discouraging effect of the surtax on participation might prevent or diminish this result. Fortunately, at least from a researcher's viewpoint, the fourth state to adopt STC, Washington, had no experience rating system in effect at the time (1983) and therefore imposed no surtax. Shortly after adopting STC, Washington moved to experience rating, which necessitated a study of income versus expenditure for all its firms. That study found no disparate effect on the trust fund from STC users and, although the Washington UI system recommended other legislative amendments to its STC law (making it easier for employers to participate), it has not found any need to institute a surtax.

Maryland adopted STC in 1984 and, even though it had an experience-rated contribution system, it made an affirmative decision (as did Louisiana and Arkansas in 1985) not to impose a surtax unless and until evidence was developed that there was a need for one. The Maryland experience with STC has not demonstrated any need to impose a surtax. A review of Maryland and Washington experience deserves particular attention in future STC studies, with specific attention to the question: Did STC usage lead to higher UI benefit payments than would otherwise have been the case for these firms?

Does STC Cost the UI System More?

Because the UI system's concern is more with fund cash flow than with socioeconomic effects, the M/D assertion of extra cost, even though acknowledged by M/D as, at most, a short-term problem, is crucial. I therefore explore it in some detail.

A case study of one of the largest users of STC, Motorola Corporation, concluded that the firm's UI charges are lower with STC (and therefore that the trust fund does not expend additional dollars even in the short run); this is in sharp contrast to the findings of the more general studies.[52] (Motorola was excluded from M/D study in Arizona on the grounds that they could not find a comparable firm; since it represents 40 percent of the total STC usage, its inclusion would have dramatically reversed the results of that study.)

The arguments which hold that STC will lead to increased costs assume higher benefit payments per worker and more hours of compensated unemployment. We consider these assumptions in some detail because they are critical to the future development of STC.

Will UI Benefits Be Higher with STC?

The prediction is that average weekly benefits will be higher under STC because more senior workers with higher earnings, who would not have been laid off, will draw benefits. The premise underlying this assumption seems unarguable and the California EDD study made just such a finding. But EDD had built the assumption of a higher wage–more senior worker linkage into its model, and its conclusion was therefore inevitable. The other side of this higher-benefit-for-senior-workers belief is the concern expressed by the AFL-CIO that employers will, by reducing the work time of senior higher-paid workers, cut labor costs at the expense of their workers. There are, however, industrial relations realities which need to be weighed against these theories.

The thesis that everyone knows that employees with more years of service at a company normally receive higher pay than comparable employees who have spent less time with the same firm[53] is based on data dealing primarily with salaried, not hourly wage, personnel. The extent to which it is true in American private enterprise, "particularly in the range between minimum wage and something under $10 an hour (at which point maximum UI benefits are received anyway)," is not clear.[54]

To the extent that there is some truth to the assumption of a direct relationship between tenure and earnings, a variety of other workplace "facts of life" may offset its effect. For example: Many hourly wage jobs are also rewarded on a piecework or other incentive pay basis, and there is a dearth of data on the seniority–incentive bonus nexus; younger workers sometimes turn out more product and receive higher pay. Without knowing the pay system of a firm, it is impossible to predict the effect of STC on UI benefit rates.

As another example, higher earnings for longer service are often the result of promotions to better job classifications and/or to different departments. Layoffs are seldom made on a pure wall-to-wall seniority basis; rather, they are made by job categories or employment areas within the firm. The wage rate spreads within such layoff units are much smaller than over the total firm. My study of fifty-five unionized companies participating in STC in California identified only one collective bargaining agreement with a "pure" seniority unit — and in that one unit the wage spread among all job classes was only fifty cents an hour. One large California company did a computer model estimate of what the wage level would have been if it had laid off workers instead of instituting worksharing. In the bargaining unit representing its skilled workers, the average wage of the remaining work force would have been 1.5 percent higher if it had laid off. In its production unit the use of STC instead of seniority layoff reduced the average wage by less than 5 percent. In neither case would layoff versus STC have had any effect on the UI rate—all the workers were earning at a level which entitled them to full UI.

In addition, to the extent that collective bargaining agreements and non-union seniority systems balance seniority and ability, the effect of length of service will be moderated. In California, "several business agents were quick to point out, they have rarely seen a 'pure seniority' contract provision with respect to layoff. The classic clause provides for some interaction between seniority and ability, leading to constant tension within the union and potential fair representation problems in handling grievances"[55] and affects the seniority-earning correlation.

Finally, the apparent logic behind the union assumption of employer payroll savings through worksharing instead of layoff is moderated by the fact that senior workers who are not laid off because they bump down to lesser-paid positions do not generally retain their higher wage rates. A California union agent offered this fact as a reason why more senior workers prefer sharing to layoff; through bumping down their employment is protected, but at the expense of being assigned to a lower-wage, less satisfying (harder, dirtier, duller) position.

Will STC Lead to More Hours of Compensated UI?

Another assumption is that STC will lead to more total hours of compensated unemployment. There is an initial plausibility to this basis for predicting higher costs for STC than for regular UI. Some laid-off workers find other jobs; STC workers are neither required nor intended to seek other employment; the "survival rate" of STC recipients will be longer, the duration of their unemployment will be greater. Though plausible, this assumption needs to be balanced against one of the major reasons offered by employers for preferring STC: it permits a much more rapid return to full production. Not only may this mean a shortening of the duration of down time through adoption of the STC option, but, in some cases, the ability to respond rapidly and economically to a market upsurge may preserve a firm that would otherwise fail.

In addition, were the program not available, the type of firm which opts for STC might elect other alternatives which would affect the amount of UI benefits drawn by its workers. It could utilize rotational layoff which has exactly the same effect on the trust fund as does STC. It might request—and such requests will be honored for varying periods of time depending on state UI policy, the area demand for labor of the type laid off, and, not least important, the relationship between the firm and the personnel at the local UI office—that its work force not be dissipated, that is, that its workers not be required or encouraged to engage in job search.

A third basis for the assumption of an increase in UI hours with STC is that it is based upon the assertion that it is easier to institute an STC program than to lay off workers and that STC thus encourages hours reductions which would not otherwise have occurred—that is, that STC discourages labor hoarding. This assumption that STC reduces labor hoarding because employers are more willing to institute an STC program than to layoff, flies in the face of some of the realities of the program. First, STC requires an application and approval process (with a union sign-off in unionized firms). An employer cannot simply announce one afternoon to a group of workers that they are temporarily or permanently laid off, an event which certainly does occur in the real world of regular UI. STC requires preplanning and a part of the planning preparation, with or without a union, is "selling" the program to the work force. My interviews in California and Canada indicated that a great deal of time, energy, and thought goes into this process. A firm which stated to its work force, "we have to go on a four-day week for the next few months" in at least one instance perceived itself as making a commitment—and was then reluctant to make greater work-time reductions, even when business conditions deteriorated more than it had anticipated.

The EDD report, a simulation based on survey data, assumed no duration increase from use of STC versus layoff UI. The M/D study found a dramatic increase in benefit usage under STC and explains this increase by asserting that many employers used STC who would otherwise have hoarded labor. In fact, the M/D conclusion that the California results indicated that all STC benefits were extra expenditures was so startling that it drew the following comment from Frank Schiff:

> . . . the basic finding for California—that STC use essentially did not substitute for layoffs *at all*—strikes me as totally implausible. Since STC firms had to submit affidavits indicating that STC represented an alternative to layoffs, one would have to believe that all these firms were cheating 100 percent. Still less credible is the implication that unions would willingly have gone along with an arrangement that involved some wage cutbacks for all of their members even though it entailed no benefits in terms of reduced layoff potentials.[56]

Since the hours on UI issue is critical to accurately defining and determining the relative cost to the trust fund of STC and regular UI; since the M/D study submitted to Congress and the president is the most recent, most extensive, and most "official" study; since the DOL has consistently, before and after the study, operated from the assumption of increased cost; therefore certain workplace and UI administration realities and research/data phenomena which may help explain the "totally implausible" conclusion reached by DOL require serious consideration.

The Comparison Group Problem

The major criticism of the M/D study arises from the use of a comparison group methodology. Indeed, one question concerning this approach is acknowledged in an earlier, draft version of the report (extensive criticism of the report led to some revisions, but the fundamental methodology remains unchanged), which states that if the STC and comparison samples were not comparable, the results of the analysis would be unreliable due to selection bias. This concern was carefully considered and then rejected by Mathematica, but it does seem that participants were certainly a self-selected group in at least two senses: they were all employers who did know of the program while "among employers in the comparison group . . . approximately half had not heard about the program"[57] and they made an affirmative decision that the program would be useful to their firms. While Mathematica remains confident that its analysis utilizes statistical procedures to control self-selection, labor and management representatives on the advisory committee and other researchers disagree.

The challenge to the comparability of the user and the nonuser group does not only focus on the theoretical question of the effect that awareness of the option may have on the choice or rejection of STC. Rather, the major challenge to the M/D methodology is that, whereas all the STC users were presumably faced with a need to reduce labor time, the nonuser group includes a sizable number of firms that had no layoff during the period in question — in essence that apples are being compared with a mixture of apples and oranges.

Firms that use STC are inherently different from firms that do not — in ways not addressed by the comparison group factors utilized in the M/D study. To quote Schiff again:

> There is a major question, in particular, whether STC-users and comparison group employers faced similar economic circumstances. Only three primary characteristics were used in selecting comparison group firms: industry classification (according to three digit SIC codes); employment size; and UI tax rate. The UI tax rate has little relevance to current economic conditions. The relatively broad industry classifications used did not automatically assure that firms in the comparison groups were subject to the same degree of economic stress as those which used STC. One specific indication of such stress would have been evidence that these firms were laying off people. In fact, however, a significant number of comparison group firms registered no layoffs. If there were conclusive evidence from other sources that the two sets of firms faced similar economic conditions, the exclusion of no-layoff firms from the comparison group might be justified, but this was clearly not the case in this instance. When one does exclude firms that made no layoffs from the comparison group, the excess in total hours of compensated unemployment for firms using STC over those in the comparison group falls from eleven per-

cent to seven percent. Moreover, when the figures are adjusted to take account of delayed impacts of STC use in the first two quarters after the year covered by the study, the differential almost disappears.[58]

The M/D report shows a dramatic 29 to 1 difference in the effect of STC on insured unemployment between California and Oregon. "In Oregon . . . STC . . . hours spent in STC were almost precisely balanced by fewer hours spent on regular UI."[59] This is almost precisely the 100 percent substitution effect one would predict in the ideal STC program. California, on the other hand, ". . . appeared to be associated with a 29 percent average increase in total hours of compensated unemployment"[60] in STC firms; that is, all STC expenditures were additional costs with no offsetting reduction in regular UI. This dramatic 29 to 1 difference, M/D speculates, ". . . may have arisen from differences in how STC was administered, from differences in the general economic environment, or from the nature and quality of the records data."[61]

Unfortunately neither these explanations nor other statistical problems mentioned by the authors stop them from reaching the confident conclusion that ". . . one general result was apparently the customary example of STC's substituting for regular UI use on an hour-for-hour basis did not seem to be supported by the data."[62]

The wildly disparate results from Oregon and California are incorporated with an estimated 12 percent increase in UI hours for Arizona (where, if Motorola had not been excluded, the result might have been a reduction, not an increase), and they are "averaged." The study then concludes that STC uses more UI hours than does regular UI. Although the mathematics are doubtlessly accurate, the irrelevance of such averaging is apparent. Imagine a Department of Agriculture study of the effect of DDT on the lives of animals and humans which was undertaken to help decide whether this pesticide should be encouraged, allowed, or banned. Imagine a finding of 2900 percent difference in its effects in two neighboring states that *might* be explained by differences in climate, method of application, the quality of the data, or statistical error. Then imagine averaging such a range of results to reach *any* policy conclusion.

Another agriculture analogy has been used by Robert St. Louis in criticizing the Mathematica methodology. He says:

> The major concern I have about the report is a probable selection bias in the sample analyzed. Consider the following hypothetical situation. The U.S. Department of Agriculture (USDA) wants to determine the impact on yield (in bushels per acre) of a farm support program designed to help farmers whose yields were low this year. Toward this end they divide farms into those which applied for support (support users) and those which did not apply for support (support nonusers) this year. The USDA feels the yield for this year

is influenced primarily by soil nitrogen content, soil phosphorus content, the weather this year and the support program. They select samples of support users and support nonusers which are matched on soil nitrogen content, soil phosphorus content, and the weather last year (classified as good or bad). Because the samples are matched on these three variables, the USDA concludes that the difference in yields betwteen the two samples is due to the support program.

Clearly the USDA would not be justified in inferring that the difference in yields this year is due to the support program. Last year's weather is not a good indicator of this year's weather, and it is this year's weather which caused some farms both to have poor yields and to apply for the support program.[63]

This selection bias problem is the critical one, relating to the question of possible inherent differences between STC users and nonusers not identified in the comparison factors selected by Mathematica. One of the things that may be more important than SIC, size, and UI tax rate — because of the way in which it can influence the reality of the job search requirement — is the firm's business philosophy and employment policy, particularly its perception of the need to retain its labor force. A company opting for STC is saying that it values its labor, believes in stabilizing its work force, and anticipates returning to full employment in the foreseeable future. Absent such an attitude and assessment, it would be foolhardy to undertake the very significant burden involved in retaining unneeded workers on the payroll. The AFL-CIO representative on the Advisory Committee, John Zalusky, in his dissent to the M/D report, made a similar point:

> Each firm also has different personnel policies and these are almost as unique as signatures. These differences go to the heart of the problem of matching employers on this issue. Layoff and STC are only two methods employers may use to adjust to economic downturns. They, in turn, are responses to employer views of their labor markets. Some employers care little whether they retain employees — an attitude that is not limited to fast food shops — while others train and promote from within and see employer-employee loyalty as a two-way street. Some employers in the same SIC can shift work between locations of the same firm and are dealing with multiple labor markets while others are not. Some within the same SIC can unilaterally cut hours of work without STC but others cannot because of union contracts; some firms can simply cut wages or benefits — and a number did during the last five years — while others cannot. In short, a comparison of firms controlling all variables would be nearly impossible and doing so would make the number of observations quite small indeed.[64]

Since the expectation of laid-off workers being available when recalled is a key factor in reaching the decision to share or layoff, future research may need to take into account the *local* labor market and the availability of alternate employment for laid-off workers: ". . . some establishments in the same SIC operate in localities with high unemployment while other establishments may be in tight labor markets."[65] A comparison methodology which examines only the state-wide and firm-wide data maintained in state UI records and does not distinguish the geographic labor market location of the workers who are laid off or placed on STC has a severe limitation.

The research problem is not amenable to easy solution. To limit the comparison group to firms that had some threshold level of compensated unemployment unless ". . . there were conclusive evidence from other sources that the two sets of firms faced similar economic conditions,"[66] seems eminently reasonable, but there are four potential objections.

First, by including only firms that utilized layoff and whose laid-off workers drew benefits one prejudges one of the reasons given for higher UI costs, namely that STC makes work-time reduction so much easier that some firms use it even though they would otherwise have hoarded labor.

Second, some firms that might otherwise have been in the comparison group will be omitted because, although they had layoffs, many of their workers did not draw UI because of a firm policy—perfectly legal in every jurisdiction but Colorado—that it will fire workers who are temporarily laid off if they apply for benefits.

Third, some firms reduce their employees' work time by a day or two per week but do not apply for STC. This practice was advanced by one rural Arizona employer as an argument against the state STC law—he didn't need it and didn't want his workers to expect that they had a right to compensation for the shortened time. This practice of workspreading without UI benefits has led the AFL-CIO to propose that STC benefits be available to workers as a matter of right, not subject to employer veto. Herbert Gans, a Columbia University sociologist expert on worksharing in Europe, characterizes the announcement that some federal agencies might use "shortening workers' hours . . . as a way to help bring spending and the deficit within targets set in the new budget balancing law . . . instead of layoffs"[67] as worksharing Herbert Hoover style.

Fourth, many workers, particularly recent or illegal immigrants, out of fear or ignorance, will not go near government offices of any kind. Precisely such differences in behavior by his minority group members between participation in STC (with which they were comfortable) and behavior when laid off (where they avoided signing for UI) led one Mexican-American union officer in California to recommend STC and take "the time to learn the WSUI system and translate instructions into Spanish for his members."[68]

Mathematica recognizes that the matching is inherently imperfect, but believes its use of regression analysis, controlling statistically for observable sample differences, overcomes this problem. Other researchers question whether, from available data, one can identify characteristics that will permit creation of an adequate comparison group and whether statistical manipulation can eliminate the selection bias. It is partly for this reason that Schiff recommends "more intensive efforts . . . to assure that comparison groups face equivalent economic circumstances . . . utiliz[ing] survey data . . . as a cross-check to other types of information."[69]

Another phenomenon which might have occurred in California that would account for the very different figures (from Arizona and Oregon) on the extent to which STC usage substituted for regular UI may relate to the period of the study. The period covered, mid-1982 to mid-1983, would have limited the Arizona and Oregon STC employees to first-time users since these programs were new at the time. California had adopted its law in 1978 and by 1982–83 some of its STC employer-users were repeaters. A non-STC user with the same number of employees and a comparable UI tax rate would have had fewer workers eligible for UI benefits than the STC employer for two reasons: First, the STC employer who has used the program previously would have more high-tenure workers; the new hires in the firm that regularly practiced layoff may not have sufficient base-period earnings to qualify, whereas its previously laid-off workers would have had periods without earnings which might reduce or eliminate their eligibility for UI. Second, STC workers are less likely to lose their UI eligibility because they are continually earning wage credits even while drawing their *pro rata* benefits.

Data: Readily Available vs. Most Relevant

The fault in the findings that California STC was an additional burden to the fund rather than a substitute for layoff UI may lie less in these unexamined externalities than in the nature of the data which was used. UI data are aggregated for the entire firm; STC plans are for work groups *within* the company. Thus, the supposed "match" is between employers that may share certain macro characteristics, but not between comparable work groups. In a typical STC situation, the firm might be sharing work in the machine shop while laying off in the shipping room. Since STC firms used the program for only 10 percent of their work-time reduction, while continuing to use regular UI as their primary method of cutback on labor cost, unless one knows which work groups are involved in STC and which workers are subject to layoff the fundamental research question remains not only unanswered but unaddressed. The appropriate question is: What would have been the regular UI experience for the workers who were on STC if STC had not been used? The M/D study does not tell us whether any of the STC recipients were also regular UI recipients, prior or subsequent to the STC plan. The fact that other locations, departments, shifts, job classes, etc., within the STC firm had substantial regular UI usage may indicate nothing more than that businesses that use STC are facing more severe economic problems that those (presumed comparison firms) which do not.

STC and Affirmative Action

This same phenomenon, that STC plans are for groups of workers within the firm and that the employer may designate any collection of workers it chooses as an STC work group, may go a long way toward explaining the failure of STC research to identify the anticipated affirmative action effects of substituting sharing for last-hired, first-fired layoff.

> Neither in individual firms nor within the smaller work units within plants is the workforce stratified randomly with regard to sex or minority status. Instead there are employers who do or do not hire workers of protected classes. Particularly in the initial hiring assignments and consequently in the eventual location of workers within a plant, assignments are not made at random but to male and female jobs, black and white jobs, etc. This is a problem with respect to equal employment opportunity, but not one especially influenced by work sharing because the sharing is within relatively homogeneous work groups. As one business agent put it pithily, "Hey, man, we all minority here."[70]

In a segmented work force, the work groups in which minorities and women are concentrated may not be the work groups in which the employer instituted worksharing. The influence of STC on affirmative action can only be measured by targeted studies of what would have been the layoff experience for the work groups that use STC, not by comparing them to the minority or female composition of laid-off workers in the entire firm of a comparison group.

There are other possible explanations for the absence of a finding that STC protects employment for minorities and women, an issue focused on by the congressional legislation and by the original proponents of STC who hoped to overcome the disparate effect of "last-hired, first-fired." Schiff offers this possibility:

> It is quite possible, for example, that differences in the characteristics of STC-using firms and comparison-group firms had a significant impact on the results. Thus, the proportion of inexperienced workers in the comparison group (many of whom may have been ineligible to receive regular UI when they

were laid off) was apparently significantly higher than for STC-using firms. To the extent this held true, the relative extent of layoffs of women, minorities, and younger workers from the comparison group may have been understated. The report mentions this possibility in a footnote, but states that "given the data available, it was not possible to examine these issues. . . ."[71]

Zalusky, on the other hand, believes that the absence of a finding of an affirmative action effect of STC is because

the AFL-CIO believes the STC programs in the three states studied have weak affirmative-action designs, and therefore we are not surprised that the study produced the result that there was little positive effect on affirmative action goals with these STC plans. However, the study lacks direct evidence to support its conclusion and offers no foundation on which to develop sound public policy. Recognizing the limitations of the research design on this aspect of the Congressional charge, one must observe without admiration the courage of Mathematica in drawing the bold conclusion that STC had little effect on affirmative-action goals.[72]

The Motorola case study, while it does not deal with affirmative action effects, also notes the under-collection phenomenon that a "significant number of employees did not draw UI for the fifth [STC] day."[73] For a variety of reasons, a similar conclusion was reached in California: some workers don't want to bother applying (particularly where the state's system requires signing up at the local UI office—an unnecessary burden on the worker and the office) for one day's UI pay; some workers use up earned vacation credits on their off days (the AFL-CIO strongly objects when employers "require employees to use earned vacation time");[74] some workers fear that the temporary reduction may presage a later layoff and don't want to draw down their UI entitlement. This fear led to an AFL-CIO recommendation to eliminate the charging of STC benefits drawn by workers, most of whom would *not* have been laid off, against their total entitlement (in line with the Canadian approach). Union agents worry that if STC is followed by full layoff, workers will need and deserve their full UI benefits. This reason for not drawing STC benefits is based on a failure to understand the system; STC workers are earning UI credits even while drawing STC benefits; more extensive use of STC would counteract the growing tendency for most of the unemployed not to be UI eligible.

STC: Too Little to Warrant the Worry?

M/D emphasizes that, ". . . STC remains a very small operational program, consistently accounting for less than 1 percent of all regular state UI payments and involving fewer than 1 percent of all employers in each state."[75]

The difficulty (and potential danger) of this attempt to use quantitative analysis of a new public policy in order to assess its potential importance and effect is demonstrated by the following data *not* included in the report. (Some of these data became available after the study was completed, but before it was published, and some were apparently missed during the study.) In 1985 in California, there were "88,000 shared work UI claims in September of this year. This represents roughly *six percent* of all weeks claimed for UI in September" (emphasis in original).[76] For the same month in Arizona the figure was approximately 25 percent.

How are these much higher figures of 6 percent and 25 percent, compared with the M/D report's "less than one percent," to be understood? Are they merely irrelevant outliers? Or is any effort to assess the *potential* of a new program an unexplored area where means and medians are meaningless? Might not the *range* of utilization experiences provide the most meaningful insights into the possibilities of STC?

Before reaching a conclusion on how these data should be evaluated, other data, which were either not gathered or not reported (but which were available during the mid-1982 to mid-1983 period of the M/D study) should be considered. For example, the Arizona Department of Economic Security's Unemployment Insurance Administration Report for the last quarter of 1982 (the initial year of their program) shows the "percent of shared work total weeks filed to total weeks filed–UI program" ranging close to 10 percent.[77]

Do Administrative Procedures Affect Program Size?

Having noted, inaccurately, the low level of employer participation, Mathematica makes a number of assertions regarding administration (focusing primarily on costs based exclusively on Arizona data) without considering connections between administrative regulations and procedures and level of participation. It commends Oregon, which is "more restrictive than . . . most other states"[78] and which rejects a proactive role for the agency in "promoting" STC, but ignores the relationship (whether causal, coincidental, or indeterminate) between administration and participation. For example:

Oregon, with a UI-covered work force of slightly under one million, reports, "The number of workers claiming Workshare benefits has approached 4,000 in 1982–83 and again in the fall of 1985."[79] Arizona, with an only slightly larger covered work force (almost 1.2 million), "during its first year . . . included a total of 25,889 employees in STC."[80] This 500 percent contrast between STC participation of less than 0.5 percent in Oregon and over 2 percent in Arizona may have many explanations, but any effort to understand participation rates must take into account both the letter of the law (more liberal in Arizona) and the attitude of its administrators (more proactive in Arizona).

Arizona's law was set up following extensive research, including surveys of workers, employers, and unions. An attempt was made to make the legislation fit its purposes, rather than force-fit STC into the Procrustean bed of existing UI regulations. Oregon, on the other hand, "tended to adopt the most stringent regulations on program use."[81] A few of the differences between the two states are reported in the M/D's Administrative Analysis: In Arizona an employer may extend an STC plan for an additional 52 weeks; Oregon requires a delay of 52 weeks after final benefit payment under the previous plan (and is the only state with such a requirement). Arizona permits an employer to have more than one STC plan; Oregon permits only one (and is the only state with such a restriction). Arizona considers an employee who earned $1,000 from a shared-work employer to be eligible for benefits; Oregon requires six months of full-time or one year of part-time work before an individual can join the plan (the most restrictive rule of any state). Arizona decided, "Moonlighting income should not be deducted from STC benefits";[82] Oregon determined that it was appropriate that "work-sharing benefits be impacted by other income such as pensions and earnings in the same manner as regular benefits, since work-sharing benefits are charged against the employer in the same manner as regular benefits."[83] Finally, Arizona permits STC benefits to be paid under the federal-state extended benefits program, whereas Oregon does not.

The process of participation in STC varies in detail and difficulty from state to state. Each state has been very much on its own in developing its STC program and administration. There has been so little federal assistance that Washington state's shared work coordinator complained that there is no mechanism to provide for interstate cooperation even between states which have STC programs. Many state administrators express the wish that the federal governmen not "help" them. Arizona complained that the model legislative language which Congress instructed DOL to prepare, rather than encouraging the states to experiment in line with the congressional mandate to do so, "not only includes the minimum guideline provisions but has additional and sometimes restrictive provisions added by the Department of Labor. . . . the more restrictive provisions are included, the less likely the states will adopt a program, or that much experimentation will take place."[84]

A more elusive but potentially more important variable than the law itself is the attitude of those who administer and enforce it. It seems to be the philosophy and policy of the director of the Employment Division of Oregon's Department of Human Resources, Ray Thorne, that government should not be in the business of selling or promoting its programs.

Contrast this with the views of Thomas Vaughn, UI program administrator in Arizona:

> I think it's the greatest thing since sliced bread. I also believe one of the
> main reasons for Arizona's success was an attitude on the part of the adminis-
> tration to make it as easy and flexible as possible, to encourage participa-
> tion, and to try whatever was necessary to make it work so that the benefits
> of the program can be realized. In my mind, some of the programs in other
> states are overly restrictive, and I don't believe they will be as successful.[85]

As the Laurdan Report notes, "employer participation rates are low.
To an undetermined extent this may be due to the limited efforts of most
states to 'market' these state programs."[86] "This lack of a marketing orientation may be an inherent problem in all state-sponsored programs or may
be a reflection of the state's commitment to STC. The enactment of STC
legislation, in the first place, and program participation and 'success' later
on, seems to be more closely linked with the energies and creativity of
a 'champion' (e.g., a major employer in the state, a state administrator,
or legislator) than to the routine efforts of the state agency."[87]

Although Oregon reports, based on a 1983 survey, that participating
employers were overwhelmingly supportive of the program, it also points
to "areas of concern to employers" which emphasize a demand for a more
flexible and liberal program.

"The program would be better if it were set up with a flexible percentage, e.g., an employee would work 24 hours one week and 32 the following and 24 again without being penalized—percentage compensation
should 'slide' with work available."

"In a service business such as ours, we have no way of knowing when
the work loads will increase or decrease on a day-to-day basis. With our
people eligible for Work Share, more flexibility as regards hourly changes
within the reporting period would be beneficial."

"It would be beneficial if we could modify our program with a phone
call. We do not always know how much time we need to cut some people
back as far as two weeks in advance. It seems to be a little too easy to
get disqualified on technicalities."

"I think some of the regulations should be changed—the six-month limit
on employment, for example, and the stipulation that an employee has
to work part of the week to collect benefits."

"I wish we could extend the program beyond the 26-week period, as
the . . . economy has not rebounded as quickly as we had hoped."

"The 'waiting week' is not appropriate for this program."

"I wish it were possible to allow the people with higher incomes to get
more compensation."

"Program needs more publicity—no one I told about it had heard about it."[88]

There are other experiences with the administration/participation relationship worth considering not only because of what insight they may provide concerning participation rates but also because of what this uncollected or unreported data suggests about the limited nature of the research. First a look at Washington, the fourth, and Florida, the fifth, state to adopt. The Mathematica Administrative Analysis notes, "Washington's program could be regarded as the least restrictive of the four earliest programs,"[89] but the participation implications of this are ignored. Florida, with over four million UI-covered workers, reports that, "In 1984 there were only three employers with approved S.T.C. plans and a total of $2,173 in S.T.C. benefits were paid."[90] In 1985 there were forty-five plans and $300,000 in benefits. Contrast this with Washington with only one-third as many UI-covered workers where the participation figures for 1984 were 152 employers, $387,000 in benefits, and 1,603 workers; for 1985, they were almost 400 employers, nearly $1,000,000 in benefits, and over 6,000 workers.[91]

Washington not only had the least restrictive program, it "does not provide for any surtax addition to regular UI tax rates"[92] and was the first state (followed by Maryland, Arkansas, and Louisiana) to reject this participation-discouraging additional employer burden. Washington also mounted a massive public relations campaign, not only printing its own informational material and using the mass media extensively, but also creating a narrated slide show to present and "sell" the program. The use of radio announcements in July 1985 resulted in a 500 percent increase in inquiries and a 700 percent increase in applications for plan approval in succeeding months. During 1984 Florida printed but did not distribute an informational brochure about its program (there was no money specifically budgeted for this purpose).

Even though they sit in different political, economic, and social insurance contexts, there are administration/participation aspects of STC in Germany and Canada worthy of note.

In Germany, where STC has been in existence since 1927, one would not expect to find significant differences in utilization among the federal states, particularly since there is one national law for UI and STC. Nevertheless, sharp differences exist. In 1983, STC payments in the Federal Republic were 18 percent of regular UI payments, in 1984 they were 12.8 percent, and in the first half of 1985, 12.4 percent. However, in the state of Baden Württemberg the comparable figures were: 1983, 27 percent; 1984, 16 percent; and 1985, 21 percent. The head of the relevant state agency, Harry Meisel, attributes a large part of this difference to the active efforts of his staff to promote STC.[93]

The Canadian STC program was initiated in 1982 with a $10 million appropriation. It was aggressively promoted by the director of the Manpower Consultative Service (since renamed the Industrial Adjustment Service) to conduct seminars and meet at worksites with interested employers, unions, and workers. Before the year was out, in response to demand, the cabinet had increased the budget to $190 million.[94]

To criticize a new program for failing to attract large-scale support while at the same time praising the most restrictive administrative regulations without evidence that they are needed, is unfair. More to the point, it obscures the promise of the program that lies not in its past but in its potential. If STC is, after serious study, found to live up to its advocates' expectations as it is tested in the labor market, then not only administrative impediments but substantive programmatic components will need to be reviewed with an eye to making the program more attractive and thus more widely used.

Stakeholders' Opinions of STC

What the M/D study significantly ignores is that the reactions to actual experience with STC from those who have vested interests in the program (but varying and potentially conflicting interests) reveal a unanimity of support differing in degree but not in direction.

Public Officials

Since most of the research has been ordered and paid for by public policymakers, usually legislators, it seems prudent to inquire into their responses to experience with the STC legislation after they have adopted it. A brief summary would include these points:

1. No state which adopted STC reversed itself.
2. States which adopted STC as sunset legislation extended its life and/or made it permanent.
3. States which modified their initial legislation did so exclusively in the direction of liberalization with amendments such as:
   a. Duration of benefits for worker claimants has been extended either absolutely and/or during periods of high unemployment.
   b. Surtaxes, in some states which imposed them, have been reduced and/or replaced with other formulas.
   c. States without a surtax have, reviewing their experience, affirmed the decision not to impose one.

d. Prior earnings and employment standards for benefit eligibility have been eased.

e. Application and reporting procedures for participating firms have been simplified.

f. Procedures for amending STC plans have been made more flexible.

g. Administrative regulations which restricted eligibility were removed by administrative action where feasible and by legislative amendment where necessary.

4. Bills to amend existing STC laws were greeted by greater—to the point of unanimity—legislative support than the initial legislation.

5. Shifts in control of the governor's office from Democratic to Republican or vice versa did not diminish support and have been, causally or coincidentally, associated with liberalizing the programs.

6. Where initial STC legislation met with indifference, opposition, or skepticism from state capital labor and management lobbyists who watchdog UI legislation, such negativity has been replaced with support.

7. Whereas early STC initiatives found some UI administrators opposed to the concept of making state payments to persons nearly fully employed, or concerned that the program would suffer from "abuse" by "weak" employers who did not carry their "full tax load," administrators have become increasingly positive about the program, willing to "advertise and promote" it as they found constituencies praising government for "doing something right for a change."

8. The Canadian STC program, introduced by a Liberal government, was made permanent by its Conservative successor. Ideologically rooted opposition expressed by the Canadian Manufacturers Association and the Canadian Labour Congress has been replaced by qualified endorsement based on their constituencies' positive experiences. There are two elements in the Canadian situation which deserve mention and consideration in any effort to evaluate the extraordinarily high level of support for the program from worker participants (91 percent)[95] and from employer participants (82 percent).[96] First, all Canadian workers, union-represented or not, must affirmatively endorse their employer's application to participate before it can be approved. As in the United States, unionized workers do so through their collective bargaining representative; unorganized work groups designate two of their number to represent them in discussions with the employer and government, and then each worker is individually solicited to sign a petition authorizing the program. Second, employer participants are not faced with the major cost (and inhibition to use) of STC found in the States because national health insurance, which covers the laid off as well as the employed, reduces the cost of keeping additional workers on the payroll.

9. In Germany where STC originated in 1927, the 1969 Employment Promotion Act made STC payable for up to six months, with extensions to "12 months in cases of high or prolonged unemployment in certain indus-

tries or areas." If the entire economy is distressed, the benefit may be extended to 24 months. In 1982 legislation was adopted "providing for an extension to 36 months of benefit eligibility for the steel industry."[97]

Workers

Workers who have been covered by STC programs grow more supportive with that experience.[98]

1. Although they initially indicate a willingness to make the commitment and sacrifice for well-defined and severely limited time periods, experience leads them to be willing to extend that time.
2. Senior workers who are relatively immune from layoff increase their level of support and willingness to participate after experience with the program.
3. Participation makes workers more aware of the economic and nonmonetary benefits and value of leisure time.
4. Where worker participants have been interviewed (California, 1982, and Canada, 1984), they indicate strong support for the program.

Unions

Union representatives, despite initial suspicions that STC would undermine collectively bargained, seniority-based layoff clauses and the principle that all workers willing to work full time have a right to do so, have, following experience with STC, become increasingly supportive of its concept and application.[99]

1. The AFL-CIO, in its 1981 Executive Council Statement of support for STC, cited positive reports from its California locals as a basis for this policy initiative.[100]
2. Business agents who experienced it recommended it to others in their unions.
3. Union officials describe their locals' attitudes toward the experience as having been "well satisfied and, faced with a need for a layoff, would use STC again."[101]
4. Unions utilized the STC program with their own employees (and found it useful) before recommending it to their membership.

Employers

"The decision to adopt STC is primarily a management decision." While "employers cannot choose to grant or withhold from their employees the benefits of protective labor legislation . . . the fact that this is not true of Short-Time Compensation focuses attention on the centrality of management attitudes."[102] What have been these management attitudes?

1. All studies conclude that, with variations only in degree, management that has experienced STC wants it to continue to be available and will, when appropriate circumstances arise, use it again.
2. Over time, many employer users are repeaters — often for additional plants or work groups beyond those covered in the initial application.
3. Employers have indeed been critical of the program, as reported in a number of studies, but those criticisms have most often been of restrictions and limitations in the program, and corporations and their organizations have been one of the major forces behind expanding the benefits of and access to the program.
4. Employers who have invested in affirmative action programs find that they can preserve that investment by using STC in place of last-in, first-out layoff schemes, and they can be reasonably certain that an STC program will protect them against the reverse discrimination charges which inverse seniority or quota layoffs might trigger.

Others

There are public interests, financial as well as moral and political, at stake in the layoff versus sharing scenario. These public interests include the affirmative action/civil rights community, which first made STC a public policy issue in the United States and which continue to support the program. They also include government income and benefit support agencies as well as private, nonprofit agencies whose services are disproportionately called upon by the unemployed. These too have a public policy interest in the STC alternative to layoff and their support has been encouraged by the Canadian research on STC.

The Canadian studies look at the six-month period most typically involved in an STC option and find that

although a six-month period is a very brief interval during which to observe changes in patterns of behaviour, the study pointed to a number of key changes in the unemployed person's behaviour, lifestyle and general health. Unemployment not only generates financial problems but creates emotional stress which translates itself into altered patterns of behaviors and attitudes. Negative effects are evident in most of the changes associated with lifestyles — eating, drinking, sleeping, and sports habits were changed over the period, showing more instability in the case of the unemployed worker than in that of the work sharer. There was also a definite increase in the number of health related symptoms (headaches, loss of appetite, dizzy spells, etc.) which the unemployed worker experienced. Interviewees related these back to the stresses of their job situation. They also mentioned changes in their moods with increases in aggressiveness, irritability, depression and worry. There was also a generally lower level of socially appropriate responses to a number of psychological statements.[103]

It is for reasons such as these that social work and health care spokespersons have joined business and labor in support of the STC alternative to layoff. Although it is unquestionably true that this litany of advocates does not prove that STC is a worthwhile program, the M/D report, which gives no weight to the judgment of stakeholders in the program and which focuses on the UI system as if it existed for its own ends, reminds one of R. H. Tawney's famous comment, "They make a darkness and call it research."

Shorter Hours—The New Deal Reconsidered

To the extent that STC removes the layoff-to-collect bias of regular UI regulations which have contributed, in combination with other New Deal labor legislation, to the shelving for fifty years of labor's historic thrust toward shorter hours, it makes major corrective contribution. To the extent that STC provides employers, workers, unions, government, and society with a factual basis for the renewal of serious and practical consideration of the shorter work week, it makes a major prospective contribution.

It is ironic that labor laws that were intended to spread the work have conspired, unintentionally and unconsciously, to inhibit the tendency of workers and their unions to strive to reduce regular hours of employment. Social Security benefits were expected to encourage older workers to leave jobs to younger workers; child labor regulations were intended to discourage the displacement of adult workers by minors. The UI portion of the Social Security Act became a disincentive for labor to follow its past practice of preserving jobs during economic downturns by sharing the shorter hours. (On the other hand, the STC experience with working shorter hours has served to reinforce workers' demands for a permanent reduction in hours—one of the few negative concerns expressed by Canadian employers about the program.) The forty-hour week aspect of the Fair Labor Standards Act (FLSA), particularly when combined with the National Labor Relations Act's (NLRA) legitimizing and strengthening of unions' bargaining power, became a minimum rather than a maximum. Admittedly, this is a very serendipitous interpretation of these New Deal laws whose intent, as expressed by one of FDR's braintrusters, Harry Hopkins, was "to get these ten or twelve million back to work [through] a universal five-day week."[104] The conclusion that, at least in the area of societal sharing of the available work through shorter hours, UI, FLSA, and the NLRA were two-edged swords, requires several words of explanation and justification.

One example of UI's discouragement of worksharing follows:

> Because of the importance that American unionists attach to the principle of seniority—indeed, to some it is almost synonymous with unionism—it is

easy to forget that the practice of dealing with a reduced demand for labor in a given workplace by laying off workers in inverse order of seniority is a phenomenon of relatively recent vintage. The more common practice during most of our industrial history has been to share available work through a reduction in the normal hours of work. Given union controls that prevent arbitrary or discriminatory employment decisions, such as closed shops, hiring halls, and standardized wage rates, sharing was more common than seniority in early union contracts and practice. In 1935, at the time of the passage of the Wagner Act, few collective bargaining agreements outside the railroad industry contained the seniority clauses so familiar in contemporary agreements.

Indeed the practice of sharing was so common and accepted that, as recently as 1938, a UAW leader in Michigan, Emil Mazey, had to patiently explain the advantage of layoffs over work sharing to UAW members. Mazey used an example to make his point: "In a plant working 24 hours per week with an average wage of one dollar per hour, if we worked one shift, each worker would receive $24 per week. If this work was equally divided by working two shifts, the average income would be $12."

Mazey pointed out that if half the workers continued to work 24 hours per week and earn $24, the other half could be laid off and obtain WPA jobs at $15 per week — giving the entire group average weekly earnings of $19.50 instead of $12 per week. A few months later, when Michigan made its first unemployment compensation payment, Mazey would have substituted UI benefits for WPA jobs.[105]

Mazey's focus on the collective income of the work group was pragmatically correct but it hardly comported with labor's historic position articulated by Samuel Gompers that "as long as we have one person seeking work who cannot find it, the hours of work are too long."

The effects of FLSA and NLRA on the length of the workweek were equally unintended. The Wage and Hour Laws provided not a ban on but a bonus for overtime work. With collective bargaining, particularly under the impetus of the War Labor Board's wage increase restraints, unions focused on fringe benefits and premium pay. The fringes were so extensive that John L. Lewis claimed to have woven a full blanket of protections out of them and they effectively offset the cost of time and a half, leading employers to prefer and require overtime to new hiring. The premium pay principle was expanded from time and a half over forty hours to premium pay for working scheduled days off, for working beyond regular daily hours, and so forth, and workers, encouraged by easy credit and consumerism, sought and even fought for overtime work.

John L. Lewis's demand for a 30-hour week, made in his address on Labor Day 1936, was aimed to give workers the leisure to play an active role in a democratic society, not to serve as a ploy to get double time on holidays. When Philip Murray testified before the Temporary National Economic Committee on April 12, 1940, asking for a cut in the maximum hours in technologically highly developed industries, he did not envision some steelworkers working a second shift at time and a half while their brothers were on layoffs from which US Steel refused to recall them.

The UI contribution system itself, because of an unrealistically and unfairly low cap on taxable wages, encourages employers to work incumbents overtime rather than to hire extra help.

Shorter Hours—The STC Experience

STC, by providing a corrective to the layoff bias of regular UI, encourages a return to sharing shorter hours. The STC experience with shorter hours provides employers, workers, unions, and government with new insights into the reality and practicality of publicly legislated and/or privately arranged reduced work schedules.

Employers have traditionally assumed that a reduction of hours would lead to a reduction in profits. STC experience is revealing that shorter workweeks may lead to fewer unscheduled absences from work; a reduction in stress-related accidents and illnesses (with reduced expenses for sick leave, Workers' Compensation, sickness and accident insurance, and experience-rated health insurance); more effective utilization of preventive health and dental care (which employers buy because their use cuts insurance costs); and other cost savings. All this is in addition to the direct productivity improvements per hour of work usually associated with shorter hours. Actual experience, as it displaces historic prejudice, may lead to more informed employer reactions to proposals for work-time reductions. The largest corporations in Holland are doing just that—conducting experience-based studies of the potential effects of the reduced work weeks for which Dutch unions are calling.[106]

Workers who have tried shorter hours as part of an STC program find that they like it. STC has created a new awareness of the extent to which workers value leisure per se and an awareness of the changing needs and expectations of a changing workforce. When calculating the net cost of a day off with STC, workers have measured the psychic and social value of free time and the economic cost of going to work—transportation, meals, clothing, babysitting, and so on. As consumers they have discovered that, with a scheduled weekday off, they can shop more effectively, visit lawyers and doctors without taking unscheduled time off, fix up their homes, and so forth. The cost of absenteeism and accidents has usually been thought of as an employer cost, but they cost the worker at least as much. For workers, STC reduces their cost of absenteeism and accidents, gives them time during the normal workweek to schedule preventive dental and medical examinations, and contributes to their more efficient consumer and home owner behavior.

Shorter Hours—The Union Role

May 1, 1986, marked the centennial of the labor movement's call for a nationwide strike for the eight-hour day—a call which led three days later to the Haymarket tragedy. The motto "eight hours for work, eight hours for sleep, and eight hours for what we will" was the moral inspiration for the labor movement during the next half century, just as shorter hours had been the dominant theme in the previous half century. The reasoning in that earlier period of a general shortage of labor had not been to counter unemployment; the notion of a premium pay reward for excess hours would have violated the democratic and humanitarian rationale for the hours reduction: "Let the mechanic's labor be over when he has wrought ten or twelve hours in the long days of summer, and he will be able to return to his family in season, and with sufficient vigour to pass some hours in the instruction of his children or the improvement of his own mind."[107]

In the early days of the New Deal, labor supported the Black-Connery Bill, which would have restricted all goods in commerce to those produced under the limits of a thirty-hour week, whether in the United States or abroad. Neither that bill, which failed, nor the Wage and Hour Act, which passed, provided for compensating wage increases. But it is the perceived need for such guarantees against loss in take-home earnings which inhibits strong labor support for legislative reductions in the standard workweek and weakens labor's demands for contractual cuts in the workweek. Unions do not imagine that the 15 percent increase which a 35-hour week would suggest nor the 33 percent increase which a 30-hour week would imply are immediately achievable. So, while unemployment stagnates at what, until recently, was considered an intolerable level, the shorter hours solution is essentially ignored.

It must be acknowledged that, to the extent that shorter hours would reduce unemployment and its disciplining effects on workers' demands, STC might well lead to an increase in effective labor pressure on wages. To the extent that shorter hours are associated with productivity increases, there might also be a lessening of employer resistance to such demands. In any event, the shorter hours solution, partly because of productivity increases associated with it, is more likely to slow the rise in the growth of unemployment than to create additional jobs.

I have already suggested that what employers and workers learn from the temporary shorter hours experience of STC can provide food for fresh thought. How does STC affect unions' thinking on the subject? First, some facts, then some speculation.

The California Machinist representative who was one of the strongest advocates of STC—even going to other West Coast states to spread the gospel—included in every speech for temporary sharing a call for a permanent reduction in maximum hours. He recommended, as do other union spokespersons for such legislation, that overtime be penalized by a double-time premium since time and a half is no longer a sufficient disincentive. For any legislative initiative for shorter hours to gain labor support it would probably need to include a ban on compulsory overtime except under rare and compelling circumstances. Another business agent in California reported that when the (then) twenty-week limit on STC expired, workers were willing to continue on shortened hours for additional months without any UI payment rather than accept the layoff alternative.

Many union representatives have reported that workers were reluctant to return to full-time once they had experienced the personal and financial benefits—the improved quality of their total lives—of the shorter week. In a reversal of the classic story of the coal miner who, when asked why he was consistently putting in four-day weeks, responded, "Because I can't quite make it on three," many workers were discovering that they could make it on four and preferred to do so.

Union negotiators, like most of us, still think in terms of the classic nuclear family: the working father, the housewife mother, the thirteen-year-old boy, the eight-year-old girl, the bike, and the dog. STC highlights the changing composition of the workforce and the shift in worker preference for leisure versus work. STC provides more compelling evidence of this growing desire than do survey reports to the same effect because worker responses to shorter hours with STC are experience-based, not hypothetical.

Unions as institutions need the additional members which shortened hours promise, not only to pay the revenues to run the organization but, more important, because the reserve army of the unemployed is the major threat to union power and survival.

Short Hours, STC, and Social Change

Finally, STC may suggest—not just to unions, which have traditionally taken the lead in movements for shorter hours, but to government policy-makers as well—a rationale for and a means of moving toward this socially urgent goal. STC is a cut in hours partially subsidized by the government. It is the expenditure of moneys which would otherwise be paid for full unemployment to preserve some employment. It also exposes to greater scrutiny many other government costs of unemployment and focuses attention on the question of whether public policies to encourage more employment with fewer hours may be more feasible than we have hitherto imagined. German employers receive partial government reimbursement for the additional health insurance and pension costs of STC. Other governments, many U.S. industries loudly complain, subsidize the cost of production and one way they do this is by spending money to delay or prevent layoff. Proposed public policies to encourage wage/price restraint include corporate and individual tax relief for those employers and workers who adhere to such policies. If the openness of direct subsidy for encouraging employment through hours reductions seems too "foreign," certainly the use of tax credits to accomplish public policy has been a very traditional congressional ploy.

STC will not of itself lead to a shorter workweek. It will offset some of UI's negative impact on the traditional business and labor practice of sharing the shortage of demand for labor by spreading the work. Most important, it will create that critical mass of worker-employer-union-government experience which will encourage a sharper and more objective examination of paths to a shorter workday, -week, or -year.

Conclusion

For a final comment on STC, I offer not my own judgment but an excerpt from a paper by James Byers, in which he views STC in the way we have been challenged to examine "Unemployment Compensation: The Second Half Century":

> . . . a central element of the work-sharing unemployment compensation system . . . relates to the question of the unity of workers and the community of interest between the employer and employees of a firm. Whether they realize it or not the legislators who authorize this experiment in their state and the personnel directors and union officials who implement it are doing more than just adjusting a system of payments. A substantially different way of viewing work and the possession of—indeed the right to—a job is a factor in this experiment. If this experiment succeeds it will be interesting to see how far its success can go in spreading a more democratic attitude toward work. . . . The basic question: Will a spirit of democracy, a feeling that workers and employers are in this together, win out over the traditional attitude of "every worker for himself"? . . . If it results in a greater feeling of unity among workers, the combination of that increased solidarity with everyone getting a taste of the unemployment problem could just be the source of a lot of pressure for meaningful full employment programs in the United States. In any case, short time compensation seems to be an idea whose time has come.[108]

Appendix: Future Research

The body of this chapter has identified many areas of necessary research on STC, UI, and their relationship. This listing will merely reiterate and underline a few of those which seem most useful and urgent.

1. The Impact of STC on the Trust Funds: Benefits and Taxes. This issue was the major focus of the M/D research and several criticisms of its methodology have been dealt with above. There is now an additional vantage point from which to examine the STC fund effect issue. The first states—California, Arizona, and Oregon—made an a priori assumption that selecting the STC option would lead some employers whose contribution rate was already at the maximum to shift this experience to other non-STC-using employers. They therefore imposed a surtax which made it impossible to fully test that assumption because, if employers who might be subject to surtax were discouraged from participating, we cannot know whether or to what extent their participation might have adversely affected the trust fund. Because Washington, Maryland, Arkansas, and Louisiana have not imposed a surtax, their experience is "purer" and using their data would contribute to a fuller study.

Their inclusion, while necessary, is far from a sufficient component of such a fuller study. With maximum tax rate employers, as with other STC participating employers, one must ask: What would these employers have done were STC not an available option? Would they have laid off? Would that layoff have been for a comparable duration and depth? Would such employers have utilized a rotational layoff approach? If they had used a seniority layoff system, might more of those drawing benefits have been so recently hired that their benefits would be chargeable to prior employers or socialized to the fund?

By examining this new facet of the STC impact on fund benefit payments—the states without a surtax or other penalty for employer participation in STC—and by focusing on the issue of the options that employers might have chosen if STC were not available, we will gain additional insights into the problem.

2. *The Impact of STC on the Trust Funds: Administration.* Administrative costs have been considered, to a limited extent, in prior research. No consideration at all has been given to the Employment Service (ES) aspect of administrative cost. Nor have alternative methods of administration been examined in terms of their effect on cost or on participation rates (an increase in which might reduce administrative costs per claim). Such administrative alternatives include: batch filing of initial and continuing claims; centralized versus local administration of STC; delivering benefit checks through the place of work rather than mailing them to claimants' homes (as in Canada in 1982); permitting employers to process the applications for continuing benefits rather than requiring individual applications (which would require ignoring outside earnings as in Arizona); utilizing computer tapes instead of processing paper (as in Germany); permitting employers to make the payments and take credits against their tax obligation (as in Germany); and so on. Administrative costs for both UI and ES are paid for by the same employer payroll tax; they should be examined in tandem.

3. *Other Costs and Savings to Governments.* The data in Washington

and California have already hinted at UI system savings within the Child Support Enforcement program. Tracing those savings through the welfare and criminal justice systems might suggest methods of identifying other short- and long-term savings in those systems. The long-term (two years plus) effects of layoff on health and social systems were identified by M. Harvey Brenner and Gordus and McAlinden[109] in their reports to the Joint Economic Committee of Congress in July 1984; the Canadians have found parallel short-term (six-month) effect differentials between STC and layoff. The STC option provides an opportunity to begin to measure these costs.

4. *Reasons for the Low Level of Employer Participation.* This issue and the potential for increased participation were targeted by M/D as important research questions. Such an examination will be strengthened by considering the higher participation rates in Canada and Western Europe and the reasons therefore.

5. *Productivity.* This has been identified in the M/D report as a major but difficult issue to be investigated. Efforts to measure it have been made by California EDD and Canada. Difficult as it may be to accurately assess, the importance of productivity to the U.S. trade balance problem is so obvious that if STC makes a difference, we need to know the direction and extent of that difference.

6. *STC and Labor-Management Cooperation (LMC).* The potential influence of STC on LMC is clearly related to the productivity question. While there is a fair amount of anecdotal and theoretical material (I have discussed it in a book [see note 3] and in a paper at the 1985 Industrial Relations Research Association Annual Meeting), there has been no systematic effort to measure the influence of STC on LMC or vice versa.

7. *Effects on Workers.* The effects of the STC alternative on workers and the way their well-being and satisfaction affects the larger society and its concerns for equity and efficiency are obvious areas for further investigation.

8. *Union Attitudes.* While related to both the LMC and worker effects of STC, the issue of the changing attitude of unions toward STC fits with the broader, ongoing inquiries into the changing roles of unions in society, which in turn relate to the productivity question.

9. *Countercyclical Effects.* Does STC, as some have claimed, maintain consumer confidence and affect purchasing power in ways that layoff does not? This is not an easy question, but one that is related to the Keynesian presumptions behind UI.

10. *Measuring the Cost of Layoffs to Firms.* As employers make choices between layoff and STC they examine questions of turnover costs and alternative fringe benefit approaches that are important to individual firms but also have broader economic implications. Fitting into the UI system as structured has tended to obscure this question; STC surfaces it for firms and for society.

11. *Affirmative Action.* Neither M/D nor EDD found that STC pre-

served jobs for women and minorities. Further research is warranted, particularly because this finding flies in the face of the conventional wisdom about last-hired, first-fired seniority layoffs.

12. *Shorter Hours.* We have asserted that experience with STC will lead some employers, workers, and unions to develop a new appreciation of the value of shorter hours. This is an essentially untested assumption.

13. *A Sharing Society.* This is not a separate topic so much as a question that warrants consideration in much of the other research that is done. To the extent that UI was conceived as more than a simple insurance scheme, it was intended as a piece of a more equitable political economy. Does STC really contribute to that goal?

NOTES

1. "Unemployment Compensation: The Second Half-Century," a project of the Robert M. La Follette Institute of Public Affairs and the Industrial Relations Research Institute of the University of Wisconsin–Madison, February 20–22, 1986, Wingspread Conference Center, Racine, Wis. The states, in order of implementation, are: California (August 1978); Arizona (January 1982); Oregon (July 1982); Washington (August 1983); Florida (January 1984); Illinois and Maryland (both in July 1984) (since the Illinois program of work sharing benefits does not operate through the UI system, since the employer must therefore prepay the cost of the benefits, and since no employer had made use of the program during its first two years of existence, it is debatable whether to count it); Arkansas (July 1985); Texas (September 1985); Louisiana (January 1986); New York (January 1986); and Vermont (July 1986).

2. Ronald L. Adler and Robert A. Hitlin, "A Report on a Survey of State Work Sharing Programs," prepared by Laurdan Associates for the National Foundation for Unemployment Compensation and Workers' Compensation, June 1986 (hereafter, Laurdan Report), p. 3.

3. Stuart Kerachsky, Walter Nicholson, Edward Cavin, and Alan Hershey of Mathematica Policy Research, Inc., "Summary Report: An Evaluation of Short-Time Compensation Programs," prepared for the Office of Strategic Planning and Policy Development, Employment and Training Administration, U.S. Department of Labor, December 1985.

4. Public Law 97-248, Section 194, "Tax Equity and Fiscal Responsibility Act of 1982."

5. Ramelle MaCoy and Martin J. Morand, eds., *Short-Time Compensation: A Formula for Work Sharing* (Elmsford, NY: Pergamon Press/Work in America Institute Series, 1984). The phrase is from Ruth Blumrosen, an affirmative action advocate who conceptualized STC as a way of encouraging an alternative to last-hired, first-fired seniority layoffs. See her chapter, "Work Sharing, STC, and Affirmative Action," pp. 139–157.

6. Ibid., pp. 3–4.

7. Alan Hershey, "Shared Work Compensation: An Administrative Analysis of

State Programs," Mathematica Policy Research, Inc., prepared for the Office of Strategic Planning and Policy Development, Employment and Training Administration, U.S. Department of Labor, March 1985, p. 2.

8. Laurdan Report, p. 13.

9. Ibid., p. 12.

10. "Unemployment Compensation," *Labor Relations Expediter* (Washington: Bureau of National Affairs), 1981, p. 795, as cited in "A Prospectus for Short-Time Compensation Research," unpublished Master's thesis, Michael Haberberger, Indiana University of Pennsylvania, 1983.

11. Laurdan Report, p. 10.

12. Ibid., p. 11.

13. Statement by the AFL-CIO Executive Council, August 5, 1981.

14. Laurdan Report, p. 10.

15. Ibid., p. 9.

16. Hershey, pp. 5–7. Note the implication in the final paragraph that all states have imposed special tax obligations on participating employers when, in fact, neither Washington, Maryland, Arkansas, nor Louisiana have done so.

17. Jerome M. Rosow and Robert Zager, *New Work Schedules for a Changing Society* (Scarsdale, N.Y.: Work in America Institute, 1981), pp. 89–90.

18. Saul J. Blaustein, *Jobs and Income Security for Unemployed Workers: Some New Directions* (Kalamazoo, Mich.: W. E. Upjohn Institute for Employment Research), 1981.

19. Randall Yule, Shared Work Program Coordinator, State of Washington, letter to author, December 18, 1985.

20. "Workshare Survey: Final Report," Employment Division, Oregon, 1983.

21. Allen Davenport, Consultant to California Senate Committee on Industrial Relations, letter to author, December 12, 1985.

22. Ken Phillips, Motorola Executive, in *Industry Week*, August 8, 1983, p. 19.

23. "Workshare Survey."

24. M. Harvey Brenner, *Estimating the Effects of Economic Change on National Health and Social Well-Being*, a study prepared for the Subcommittee on Economic Goals and Intergovernmental Policy of the Joint Economic Committee, Congress of the United States (Washington, D.C.: Government Printing Office, 1984); and Jeanne Prial Gordus and Sean P. McAlinden, *Economic Change, Physical Illness, Mental Illness, and Social Deviance*, a study prepared for the Subcommittee on Economic Goals and Intergovernmental Policy of the Joint Economic Committee, Congress of the United States (Washington, D.C.: Government Printing Office, 1984).

25. Yule.

26. Public Law 97-248.

27. "Unemployment Compensation," p. 795.

28. "Unemployment Compensation: The Second Half-Century."

29. Zvi Griliches, "The Use and Abuse of Econometrics: Data and Econometricians—The Uneasy Alliance," *AEA Papers and Proceedings* 72 (May 1985): 196.

30. Thomas Kochan, *Labor Management Relations Research Priorities for the*

1980's: Final Report to the Secretary of Labor (Washington, D.C.: Government Printing Office, 1980), pp. 24–25.

31. Bennett Burgoon and Robert D. St. Louis, "The Impact of Work Sharing on Selected Motorola Units," prepared for Motorola, Inc., 1985.

32. Frank Schiff, "Comments, First National Conference on Work Sharing Unemployment Insurance," Employment Development Department Transcript, May 15, 1981.

33. Maureen E. McCarthy and Gail S. Rosenberg, with Gary Lefkowitz, *Work Sharing Case Studies* (Kalamazoo, Mich.: W. E. Upjohn Institute for Employment Research, 1981).

34. Juan M. Mesa, *Short-Time Working as an Alternative to Layoffs: The Case of Canada and California* (Geneva: International Labor Office, 1982).

35. MaCoy and Morand, p. 106, "Canada's STC: A Comparison with the California Version," chapter by Frank Reid and Noah Meltz.

36. Both reports published by Program Evaluation Branch, Employment and Immigration, Hull, Canada.

37. *Unemployment Compensation: Studies and Research III,* compiled by the National Commission on Unemployment Compensation (Washington, D.C.: Government Printing Office, 1980), p. 829.

38. "Shared Work Unemployment Insurance Evaluation Report," prepared by the Employment Development Department, Sacramento, California, May 1982.

39. Kerachsky et al., pp. iv–v.

40. Linda Ittner, Legislative Assistant to the Honorable Patricia Schroeder (D-Colorado), prime congressional sponsor of the Federal STC legislation, memo to the author, Casey Young, and Bea Walfish, June 6, 1983.

41. Public Law 97-248.

42. C. F. Koziol, "Comments on Mathematica's Short Time Compensation Report," February 8, 1986.

43. Robert G. Spiegelman, letter to Stephen Wandner, Employment and Training Administration of the U.S. Department of Labor, February 10, 1986.

44. John L. Zalusky, "Dissent of Advisory Committee Member Concerning the Report 'An Evaluation of Short-Time Compensation Programs,'" February 19, 1986.

45. Hershey.

46. MaCoy and Morand, p. 94, "Arizona, Motorola, and STC," chapter by Robert St. Louis.

47. Noah Meltz, "Comments—Work Sharing: New Experiences," Thirty-Eighth Annual Meeting of the Industrial Relations Research Association, New York, December 30, 1985.

48. Kerachsky et al., p. 31.

49. Ibid., p. 5.

50. Public Law 97-248.

51. Ibid.

52. Burgoon and St. Louis.

53. Katharine G. Abraham and James L. Medoff, "Length of Service and the Operation of Internal Labor Markets," *Working Paper Series,* No. 1085, National Bureau of Economic Research, Inc., March 1983.

54. MaCoy and Morand, p. 33.

55. Donald S. McPherson and Martin J. Morand, "Union Leader Responses to California's Work Sharing Unemployment Insurance Program," paper presented at the First National Conference on Work Sharing Unemployment Insurance, San Francisco, May 15, 1981; reprinted in *Daily Labor Report,* Bureau of National Affairs, May 28, 1981, pp. D1–D10.

56. Frank W. Schiff, "Comments on the Mathematica Research, Inc., Report, 'An Evaluation of Short-Time Compensation,'" February 21, 1986, p. 2.

57. Kerachsky et al., p. 37.

58. Frank W. Schiff, "Issues in Assessing Worksharing," *Industrial Relations Research Association Annual Meeting,* New York, December 30, 1985.

59. Kerachsky et al., p. 12.

60. Ibid., p. 14.

61. Ibid.

62. Ibid., p. 18.

63. Robert St. Louis, letter to Stuart Kerachsky, September 22, 1985.

64. Zalusky, 1986, p. 4.

65. Ibid.

66. Schiff, 1985.

67. "U.S. Denies It Has Plan To Shorten Workweek," *New York Times,* January 11, 1986, p. 8, col. 6.

68. McPherson and Morand.

69. Schiff, 1985.

70. McPherson and Morand.

71. Schiff, 1986.

72. Zalusky, 1986, pp. 5–6.

73. Burgoon and St. Louis.

74. Zalusky, 1985, p. 8.

75. Kerachsky et al., p. 5.

76. Davenport.

77. Arizona Department of Economic Security, November 1985.

78. Hershey, p. 13.

79. Libby Leonard, Deputy Administrator, Employment Division, Department of Human Resources, Oregon, letter to author, November 21, 1985.

80. Arizona Department of Economic Security.

81. Kerachsky et al., p. 30.

82. MaCoy and Morand, p. 87.

83. Ibid., p. 102, "Oregon Tries the 'Workshare' Idea," chapter by Donna Hunter.

84. Donald B. Mathis, Acting Director, Arizona Department of Economic Security, letter to Carolyn Golding, Director, Unemployment Insurance Service, U.S. Department of Labor, January 19, 1983.

85. Thomas Vaughn, UI Program Administrator, Arizona, letter to author, December 12, 1985.

86. Laurdan Report, p. 3.

87. Ibid., p. 7.

88. "Workshare Survey."

89. Hershey, p. 13.

90. Talmadge Harrison, Chief of Bureau of Claims and Benefits, State of Florida, letter to author, December 17, 1985.

91. "Shared Work Compensation Program: Annual Report," Washington State Employment Security, January 1986.

92. Hershey, p. 13.

93. Harry Meisel, President, Federal Employment Institution, State of Baden-Württemberg, Federal Republic of Germany, letter to author, July 7, 1985.

94. MaCoy and Morand, p. 106.

95. *Evaluation of the Work Sharing Program,* p. 72.

96. Ibid., p. 82.

97. MaCoy and Morand, p. 56, "The Pioneers: STC in the Federal Republic of Germany," chapter by Harry Meisel.

98. Ibid., pp. 36–50.

99. Ibid.

100. Statement by the AFL-CIO Executive Council, August 5, 1981.

101. McPherson and Morand.

102. MaCoy and Morand, p. 14.

103. *Evaluation of the Work Sharing Program,* pp. 99–100.

104. Henry H. Adams, *Harry Hopkins: A Biography* (New York: G. P. Putnam's Sons, 1977), p. 59.

105. MaCoy and Morand, pp. 37–38.

106. Herbert Gans, conversations with the author concerning his (unpublished) studies for the German Marshall Fund of the United States on Short-Time Compensation in Western Europe.

107. MaCoy and Morand, p. 49.

108. James Byers, unpublished paper on Short-Time Compensation.

109. Brenner; Gordus and McAlinden.

11

Controlled Experiments and the Unemployment Insurance System

ROBERT G. SPIEGELMAN AND STEPHEN A. WOODBURY

Introduction

Since the late 1960s, most economists have placed increasing emphasis on the importance of so-called frictional and structural factors in explaining the high unemployment rate in the United States. In a wave of contributions perhaps best represented by the well-known volume edited by Phelps (1970), frictional unemployment—the unemployment resulting from turnover in the labor force and job search—was espoused by an important part of the profession as a major source of unemployment. Concurrently, inadequate demand—the Keynesian explanation for unemployment—began to receive less prominence as an explanation of unemployment. The shift in emphasis away from demand deficiency and toward frictional factors in explaining unemployment appears to have permeated the profession and is now widely accepted and taught. Indeed, with the current estimate of the natural (or constant inflation) rate of unemployment at 6 percent, less than four-tenths of the unemployment at the peak of the last recession (9.7 percent) could be attributed to deficient demand. Furthermore, only one-seventh of the unemployment rate of 7.1 percent experienced in 1985 could be attributed to deficient demand (see, for example, Gordon, 1982).

This shift in the way most economists view unemployment has had important ramifications for economic policies that act on individual households and firms (as opposed to aggregate demand policies). Martin Feldstein was early to single out the unemployment insurance system for reform, and an outpouring of research (reviewed elsewhere in this volume by Gary Burtless and Robert Topel) followed his criticism. Essentially, Feldstein argued that the UI system both encourages covered employers

355

to lay off too many workers too often, and creates incentives for UI beneficiaries to engage in excessive job search (see, for example, Feldstein, 1975). Both arguments imply that the UI system contributes to turnover (or search) unemployment, making the natural rate of unemployment higher than it would otherwise be. The conclusion, that the UI system creates unemployment, differs greatly from the traditional conclusion that UI reduces unemployment by providing automatic countercyclical stimulus.

Employment Security administrators and legislators have responded to these criticisms of a system that was once viewed as uniquely beneficial, perhaps even inviolable.[1] Since 1979, UI benefits have been taxed as income when their beneficiaries are part of higher-income households (see Solon, 1985, for an analysis). Furthermore, state Employment Security administrators seem willing to experiment with the system and ultimately to make changes that might meet some of the criticism. Indeed, there has been a recent wave of controlled UI experiments that could — properly designed, executed, and evaluated — greatly enhance our understanding of the UI system and the problems it may pose.

In this paper we explore what these controlled social experiments can contribute to our understanding of the UI system and (by implication) of labor markets. We first set out, in section 1, the central issues in experimental design and operations. In section 2, we offer a treatment of the key issues in research on the UI system, and appraise the extent to which experiments can make a contribution to each of these main issues. Our own interest and involvement in UI experiments stems from two experiments that were conducted by the State of Illinois during 1984 and 1985. In section 3, we discuss these experiments, and three other UI experiments that have been conducted or are in progress. A final section summarizes the potentialities and the limitations of UI experiments.

1. Central Issues in Social Experimentation

Why Conduct Social Experiments?

Since the late 1960s, experimental methods have been applied to the study of several major social programs. Income maintenance programs, housing subsidies, educational vouchers, health insurance, and time-of-use pricing of electricity have all been the subject of large-scale controlled experiments.[2]

Social experiments have had a dual purpose. Their main purpose has been to measure and predict the effects of new and untried social programs — indeed, it is hard to imagine that policymakers would have advocated and approved the large expenditures that have gone into social experimentation if there were not a large payoff to those who must recommend and devise social and economic policies. But social experimentation, especially when conducted by economists, has been carried on in the framework of mainstream economic theory, and has frequently been used to conduct tests of various aspects of that theory. These two objectives of social experimentation—one a matter of measurement and prediction, the other more ambitious—have not always coexisted without some tension. Policymakers want to determine the efficacy of specific policies. Economists are often at least as interested in seeing whether the predictions of economic theory can be supported, and in estimating the parameters of economic models.[3] In any case, the emphasis that social experiments have placed on evaluating policies distinguishes social experimentation from experimentation in the biological sciences, for example, where matters of policy are further removed from the concerns of experimenters and their grantors alike.

To use the experimental method to test a social policy option, either existing or contemplated, it must be possible to translate the policy objectives into a concrete program whose effects can be measured. In a social experiment, the evaluation usually consists of comparisons between a group of individuals who receive a treatment and a control group. One great advantage of the experimental method is that the evaluation can be relatively "model-free" in the sense that with a large enough sample size it should be unnecessary to impose theoretical or other restrictions on the data in order to obtain results in which analysts can have some confidence.[4]

The central feature of social experimentation is random assignment of experimental subjects to either the treatment group or the control group. What random assignment accomplishes can be stated in two ways. First, properly done, it can provide experimenters with control over all variables, known or unknown, that might influence the outcomes that are of interest. Second, with a large enough number of subjects, it assures that the members of each subsample (control and experimental) will on the average differ only in the treatment received. That is, no other variable should be correlated with the treatment variable. This last implies that a simple comparison of experimental means with control means will be sufficient to isolate the effects of the treatment on behavior and outcomes.

The last point may be put another way: An ordinary least squares regression of the dependent variable that is of interest (denoted by y) on a constant term and the treatment variable (T, which equals one for individuals assigned to the experiment, zero otherwise) will yield an unbiased estimate of the effect of the treatment on y:

$$y = b_0 + b_1 T + e. \tag{1}$$

In equation 1, b_1 gives the effect of the treatment on y, and a confidence interval may be constructed around b_1 from the standard error associated with b_1.[5] (The constant term is b_0, and e represents a normally distributed error term.) There is no need to control for additional variables as long as individuals have been randomly assigned to the experimental and control groups.

The number of treatments administered in an experiment need not be restricted to one as long as individuals are randomly assigned to each experimental group. Indeed, the ability to create such variation in the incentives facing different groups is a unique advantage of experimentation.

In most social experiments, the control group represents a group of individuals or households who face whatever set of incentives and constraints currently exists—the status quo. This status quo environment may already include a program that contains elements of the newer program that is represented by the experimental treatment. In such a situation, the difference between the outcomes for the experimental group and for the control group must be interpreted as the change that would result from modifying the current program to reflect the experimental treatment. That is, the difference should not be interpreted as the effect of the experimental program, as if it were a totally new program acting on a mythical clean slate.

Two examples will illustrate the point. First, in an experiment to test the effects of intensive job search assistance as part of the unemployment insurance system, members of the control group would have access to whatever level of job search assistance already existed. A treatment that offered additional help in finding a job would show the effects of intensive job search assistance relative to the level of assistance currently offered by the Job Service, not relative to a total lack of job search assistance. Second, during all of the income maintenance experiments of the late 1960s and 1970s, members of the control group had available to them the existing set of state and federal income maintenance programs. The results of the income maintenance programs showed how household behavior would be affected by moving from the existing set of policies to the policies represented by the experiments—the results could not show the effects of an income maintenance program introduced into an environment without such programs. Indeed, the income maintenance experiments were limited to using experimental income support treatments that represented improvements over the existing system because participation in the experiments was voluntary, and it is clear that no one would volunteer to participate in an experiment that would make them worse off.

Comparison of Experimental and Other Evaluative Techniques

There are many nonexperimental approaches to estimating the impact of proposed or existing programs. Already-gathered survey data may be used to estimate behavioral parameters that can in turn be used to simulate the effects of a program. A so-called quasi-experiment—that is, a program

that is not universal, so that a group of individuals who did not participate in the program can be used as a comparison group—may present
itself.[6] Or a demonstration program may be developed.

The demonstration program provides a useful vehicle for illustrating
the difficulties encountered in evaluating a program by nonexperimental
methods. A demonstration involves implementing a program that is being
considered on a limited basis, and using observation (sometimes called
process evaluation) and statistical techniques to estimate the effects of the
limited program. A demonstration is simpler to administer than an experiment in that it avoids the need for an assignment process; anyone who
is eligible for the program may participate. In that sense, a demonstration
can be operated more like a real program. Indeed, one of the purposes
of a demonstration is to try out the actual operation of a program. Furthermore, the data needs of a demonstration will be fewer if reliance is placed
on process evaluation and other nonstatistical methods of appraising the
program's effects.

But statistical evaluation of a demonstration program requires the
researcher to control, using various econometric techniques, the effects
of extraneous variables on the outcomes that are of interest. Whereas with
an experiment one can rely on the random assignment of individuals to the
experimental and control groups to control all measured and unmeasured
determinants of y, we must now find other ways of controlling for the
determinants of y. Rather than use the model stated in equation 1 to estimate the effects of the program, one must construct a more elaborate model
that may embody a complete theory of how the outcome variable is determined. Such a model might be written as

$$y = b_0 + b_i T + c_i x_i + \cdots + c_M x_M + d_i w_i + \cdots + d_N w_N + e \qquad (2)$$

where x_i denotes measurable influences on y, w_i denotes unobserved determinants of y, and c_i and d_i are coefficients to be estimated. A model like
equation 2 might be estimated using a sample of individuals, some of whom
participated in the demonstration (for these individuals $T = 1$), and some
of whom did not (for these, $T = 0$).

The most serious problem that one encounters in trying to implement
this approach is that of controlling for unobserved variables that affect
the program's outcome (the w_i in equation 2). The problem arises because
access to the demonstration program is uncontrolled, so that anyone who
is eligible may enroll. Individuals who choose to participate in the program may well have unobserved characteristics that systematically alter
their performance in the program. When they do, it is virtually impossible
to distinguish the effect of the program from the effect of unmeasurable
traits that are specific to the individual. The problem is known as selec-

tion bias—individuals who select themselves into different treatment categories will perform differently—and has been widely discussed and researched.[7]

Three examples will illustrate the problem posed by selection bias. First, suppose that we want to determine the effect of the Job Service (JS) on reemployment, but without randomly assigning individuals either to an experimental group that would receive the assistance of the JS or to a control group that would receive none. A problem arises immediately if individuals who choose to get assistance from the JS are somehow different from those who do not. In fact, there is evidence that JS users do tend to differ from nonusers: the unemployed do not use the JS until they have exhausted all other means of obtaining a job, which suggests in turn that JS users tend to be less employable than nonusers (Johnson, Dickinson, and West, 1985). A second example would be a program that encourages unemployed individuals to search for jobs. If individuals who are most motivated to obtain a job are the most likely to take advantage of such a program, we would obtain a biased picture of the effectiveness of the program by comparing outcomes for those who took part in the program with outcomes for those who did not. Finally, consider the evaluation of a job counseling program. If unemployed individuals who decide to receive counseling are those who have the greatest need for counseling and have performed poorly in the labor market, then again we would obtain a biased view of the effectiveness of counseling by making a nonexperimental comparison of those who were counseled with those who were not. Selection bias is serious in all these cases because the same traits that lead someone to participate in a program lead also to different outcomes for that person—to different earnings or duration of unemployment.

There are statistical means of attempting to handle selection bias in evaluating a program; all attempt to control variables that are otherwise uncontrolled. One method is to statistically match program users with a group of "comparable" nonusers, and then to compare the two groups (see, for example, Westat, 1984; Dickinson, Johnson, and West, 1986). Another is to construct a variable that may capture the unobserved individual trait that leads to participation or nonparticipation, and to use this variable in a regression model (like equation 2), thus "controlling" the unobserved variable (see Barnow, Cain, and Goldberger, 1980, for a reivew of these methods). But these methods are widely viewed as less reliable than an experiment using random assignment, and indeed they can require even more data and data processing than experimental evaluation. For example, statistical matching demands a large population from which the comparable sample can be drawn. Such a large population is often unavailable for a small-scale demonstration. For its part, the approach of constructing a variable to capture the unobserved trait involves an identification problem that is often difficult to solve effectively (Johnson, 1986).[8]

To summarize, the main problem posed by nonexperimental evaluation is the need to measure and include in a model such as equation 2 all determinants of the outcome variable y. Failure to do so will result in estimates of the program's effect (b_1) that are biased. But failure to do so is almost inevitable. Indeed, the goal of all nonexperimental methods is to achieve the same kind of control over both measured and unobserved variables that is achieved by a controlled experimental design. Nevertheless, it is difficult to imagine a nonexperimental research technique that equals the ability of an experiment to control for both measurable and unmeasurable variables.

Pitfalls in Social Experimentation

Although experimentation can offer improved control over the variables that influence outcomes, such as unemployment duration or earnings, a variety of problems may arise in the design of a social experiment. These problems need to be recognized and handled appropriately if an experiment is to yield reliable results.

Learning Effects. Learning effects are changes that occur over time in the behavior of experimental participants. There are at least three varieties of learning effects. Some occur as participants become more convinced of the legitimacy and authenticity of the experiment. Others occur because participants may become increasingly aware of the consequences of their behavior as the experiment progresses. Still others occur because it takes time for individuals to make adjustments and rearrangements in response to new incentives.[9]

If learning effects are an inherent part of a program, then it is likely that a short-term experiment designed to test the effects of that program will obtain biased results. Specifically, if an experiment is too short to allow participants to understand and respond to the incentives created by an experiment, then of course the experimental results will underestimate the long-run response to a fully implemented program. The bias associated with learning effects can be avoided by designing the experiment so that it is long enough for participants to understand and respond to it.

The income maintenance experiments exhibited all three kinds of learning effects. First, participants were reluctant to give up jobs to obtain income transfers until they were convinced that those payments would continue. Second, they needed time to determine what kind of job alternatives might be available to them, and to understand how a job change would in turn affect their payments under the income maintenance program. Third, it took time to actually adjust their work schedules to the new incentives. An experiment of long duration was needed to overcome the problems associated with these lags.

In one of the two Illinois unemployment insurance experiments — the job search incentive experiment — new claimants for UI were offered a bonus of $500 to induce them to become reemployed quickly. (Because we will make frequent reference to the Illinois UI experiments in the remainder of this section, some readers may find it useful to refer to pp. 379–382, where we summarize the experimental treatments and results.) Such an experiment might be relatively free of problems associated with learning effects. It is simple to understand, its credibility is easily established, and participants need little time to adapt to the program.

On the other hand, the other UI experiment conducted in Illinois may have encountered problems resulting from learning effects. In this experiment (the hiring incentive experiment), a group of randomly chosen UI claimants was given a voucher worth $500 to potential employers — that is, if an employer hired a voucher-carrying claimant within eleven weeks of the individual's filing for benefits and retained the worker for four months, the employer would receive $500. This experiment is more complex in that it requires the understanding and activity of both claimants and employers. As a result, it may require more time to learn and could suffer from learning effects if it is of short duration.

Time Horizon. A related but distinct set of problems arises from the inevitably limited duration of experiments: participants' planning horizons may exceed the length of the experiment. If so, then the behavior of participants during an experiment may differ from what it would be if the experimental program were adopted and made permanent.[10]

The time horizon problem was a serious concern during the conduct of the income maintenance experiments. The concern was that participants would be reluctant to give up jobs and adjust their labor supply because the experiments were scheduled to end after a few years, whereas they would have been more willing to give up or change jobs if they expected the experiments to last indefinitely.[11] Charles Metcalf (1973) first discussed the problem, and concluded that a foreshortened experiment would result in the understatement of income effects (since the income guarantee would be provided for only a short time) and the overstatement of substitution effects (since the effective wage rate of participants was temporarily lowered during the experiment — leisure was, in effect, on sale during the experiment). In the Seattle and Denver income maintenance experiments, programs of varying duration were conducted in order to test the effects of an experiment's duration on labor supply. The results show that, for male household heads, a shorter experiment did significantly understate the program's effect on labor supply (which in turn suggests a serious understatement of the income effect). But for wives of male heads and single female household heads, the labor supply effects of the three- and five-year experiments were quite similar (Robins, Tuma, and Yeager, 1980, Table 3).

The time horizon problem should be less troublesome for certain experiments with the unemployment insurance system. Consider, for example, the Illinois job search incentive experiment. Because the length of such an experiment would have no effect either on the present value of the $500 bonus, or on the wages offered to participants, it is highly unlikely that a time horizon problem would be encountered in this experiment. The experiment, that is, should yield correct estimates of what would occur under a permanent program.

Displacement. Any experiment that is intended to improve employment possibilities or to upgrade the jobs of its participants may face the problem of displacement. Displacement occurs when improvements that are experienced by experimental participants come at the expense of others. For example, if a program to upgrade the skills of low-skilled workers was conducted in a local labor market where there were few job openings, the increased employment of the program's participants might well occur at the expense of others who in the absence of the program would have obtained jobs.

When it occurs, displacement can bias the results of an experiment, or it can hamper the use of experimental results in gauging what results would be achieved if an actual program based on the experiment were implemented. For example, if the individuals whose performance in the labor market has been harmed are members of the control group, then comparing the performance of experimental participants with that of controls will result in an overstatement of the true effect of the experiment on participants. Only if the experience of controls is what it would have been in the absence of the experiment does a comparison of experimentals with controls yield proper experimental effects. We refer to this problem as one of *internal validity*.

On the other hand, if the individuals who are harmed by the experiment are completely outside the experiment (that is, they are neither controls nor experimentals), then a comparison of experimentals with controls will yield correct estimates of the experiment's effects, but may nevertheless overstate the benefits of a full-scale program based on the experiment.[12] The overstatement results because a comparison of controls with experimentals correctly estimates the benefits that accrue to experimentals, but fails to count the harm done to nonparticipants. This is referred to as a problem of *external validity*.

The hiring incentive experiment in Illinois, which paid a bonus to employers who hired UI claimants, provides a useful example of how displacement can hamper the use of basically unbiased experimental results to gauge what would occur if a program based on the experiment were implemented (see Spiegelman and Woodbury, 1987). In the experiment, the number of job applicants carrying $500 vouchers was small enough that the experiment probably had little effect on control group members. Thus, comparing controls with experimentals should yield correct estimates of the effect of the experiment on participants.

But a problem arises in using the experimental estimates to gauge the effects of a real program based on the experiment. The potential for such a program to suffer from displacement effects is large. The $500 bonus would be like a dowry paid to employers who hire certain individuals. Employers could benefit from passing over job applicants without the dowry and hiring similarly qualified applicants who happen to have the dowry. Unless an increase in the rate at which vacancies are filled led to increased employment, or unless employers' demand for labor was increased by the program, any positive measured effect of the program could merely be the result of displacement.[13]

In the other Illinois UI experiment, claimants received a bonus if they became reemployed within eleven weeks (also in Spiegelman and Woodbury, 1987). It is unlikely that a comparison of the performance of those who participated in this job search incentive experiment with controls would be marred by displacement, because again the number of participants was small. Also, there was no incentive for employers to hire participants rather than other applicants. The effectiveness of the experiment derived from the increased intensity of job search, which is likely to increase the efficiency of job matching but is unlikely to displace other job seekers in a large and growing labor market. However, a permanent statewide program based on the experiment could pose a displacement problem if the number of participants became a significant proportion of all job openings.

Scale Effects. Increasing the size or universality of an experiment may affect the outcomes of an experiment in at least two ways. First, increasing the scale of an experiment may alter the tastes of participants. Second, increasing the scale of an experiment may alter the way information about a program is transmitted. These so-called scale effects are especially likely to arise when an experiment is expanded and implemented as a program.

The income maintenance experiments offer an example of how the universality of a program could alter individuals' tastes. An income maintenance experiment put into practice would be a negative income tax system, under which everyone would be entitled to income support if he or she did not work. It is possible that the stigma associated with receiving transfer payments in lieu of work would be lessened by the universality of the negative income tax system, and that, in effect, the taste for transfer payments would increase. The problem this change of taste poses for experimentation is clear: because of the change, reductions in work effort in response to an income maintenance experiment would be smaller than reductions under a universal negative income tax.

The scale of an experiment may also affect individuals' behavior — and hence the outcome of an experiment — by changing the way in which knowledge of the program is transmitted. For example, in the hiring incentive experiment knowledge of the bonus and the conditions under which it would be received was transmitted solely by claimants. In a full-scale program, knowledge of the bonus would be transmitted to all employers through the news media, possibly changing employers' perceptions and awareness of the program. If employers became more receptive to the program as it became generally understood, then the effects of an actual program would be understated by the experiment.

An unemployment insurance experiment being conducted in New Jersey offers another example of how enlarging the scale of an experiment would alter the flow of information and affect the results of a program. In the experiment, selected UI claimants are given special job search assistance during the fourth week of benefit receipt. Then in the seventh week, if they have still not found employment, they are told that they may receive a bonus if they find employment within the following ten weeks. (We discuss the New Jersey experiment in greater detail on pp. 385–386.) The problem with the experiment is that if it were turned into a program, there would be general knowledge that a UI claimant who meets certain criteria and has not found employment by the seventh week of benefit receipt will be offered a bonus for reemployment. This knowledge would undoubtedly affect the job search behavior of many claimants during their spell of unemployment. But in the experiment, participants are unaware that they will be offered a bonus until the seventh week. Information available during the experiment differs fundamentally from the information that would be available if a program based on the experiment were adopted. Thus, there is no way of telling from the experimental results what would happen to job search behavior if the experiment were turned into a full program, and the experimental results are bound to give biased estimates of the effect of a program based on the experiment.

The Hawthorne Effect. The Hawthorne effect takes its name from experiments at the Hawthorne plant of Western Electric Company in Chicago, in which changes in lighting and room color were undertaken to determine the effect of such changes on workers' productivity. The experimenters did find that productivity improved, but they discovered that the improvements resulted not from the tested changes in lighting and color but rather from the increased attention that was paid to workers whose work spaces were changed. A Hawthorne effect exists if, as in this experiment, subjects respond to an unintended treatment rather than to the designed treatment.

Participants in the income maintenance experiments were required to prepare monthly income reports in order to receive payments. A Hawthorne effect could have resulted if preparing such reports changed families' behavior by increasing their awareness of the relationship between work effort and income. To test for the existence of such an effect, a proportion of the control group was asked to prepare identical forms (in return for a small fee that was unrelated to income). No effect of preparing forms could be detected.

In the Illinois job search incentive experiment, a Hawthorne effect could have existed if participants increased the intensity of their job search not in response to the bonus offer, but simply to please those conducting the experiment. However, because UI claimants already face a work search requirement and are monitored by the Department of Employment Security, it seems unlikely that the participants' awareness of the experiment would alter the environment enough to result in changed behavior.

The main defense against a Hawthorne effect is to prevent participants from knowing what behavior the experimenters are seeking to measure. Participants in the income maintenance experiments, for example, were not told of experimenters' interest in work effort and labor supply, and participants in the Illinois UI experiments were not told of experimenters' interest in the programs' effect on benefit payments.[14]

Selective Attrition. The validity of an experiment is jeopardized if attrition from the experimental sample occurs nonrandomly. Starting with those who initially refuse to participate, and ending with those who for any number of reasons withdraw from the experiment, it is possible that attrition is nonrandom and that those who remain in the program (and in the sample) are somehow special and systematically different from members of the control group.

Nonrandom attrition destroys the essence of the experimental advantage. For example, refusal to participate in an income maintenance experiment is likely to be associated with a strong work ethic and a desire not to accept "handouts," or with a desire on the part of welfare recipients not to risk the loss of existing benefits. Those who refuse to participate would respond less dramatically than those who enroll in the experiment, and the experimental results would give an overstatement of an eligible population's response to income maintenance. In the Illinois job search incentive experiment, those who refused to participate may have been less serious about finding a job than those who participated. A comparison of controls with only those who participated would lead to an overestimate of the effects that would be observed if the program were implemented.

The most credible solution to selective attrition is to compare the behavior of all those who were offered the experimental treatment with the behavior of the control group. This comparison is clearly unbiased, since random assignment assures that the characteristics of the treatment group are the same as those of the control group. There are at least two problems with this solution. One is that the solution is not always available. If evaluation of an experiment relies on surveys during and after the experiment to collect data on outcomes, then attrition implies the loss of necessary data on those who drop out of the experiment. This, by the way, is an advantage of an experiment that can use administrative rather than survey data. Since administrative data are gathered to meet the needs of an ongoing program like Social Security or unemployment insurance, they are less subject to attrition than survey data because of legal reporting requirements.

The other problem with comparing the full treatment group with the control group is one of measurement. Including nonparticipants in the treatment group dilutes the treatment group, and may make it difficult to detect statistically a treatment effect that in fact exists. This is a statistical problem that can be mitigated by a large enough sample.[15]

Summary: Internal and External Validity. If any of the pitfalls described above is encountered, then either the internal or the external validity of the experimental results must be questioned. Internal validity refers to lack of bias in results obtained by comparing the control group with the experimental group—that is, to the validity of the results on their own grounds. External validity refers to the validity of the experimental results in another context or environment, or to the "transferability" of the results, as Aigner (1985) has called it. External validity is a concern mainly in determining whether experimental results give an accurate picture of what would occur if the experiment were turned into a program. Note that for experimental results to be externally valid, it is necessary (but not sufficient) for results to be internally valid.

Learning effects, Hawthorne effects, and selective attrition can destroy the internal validity of experimental results. The presence of any of these implies that a comparison of the experimental group with the control group may yield results that give a biased view of an experiment's effects on behavior. Time horizon and scale effects, in contrast, can destroy the external validity of experimental results—that is, their presence limits the extent to which inferences can be made about an actual program based on an experiment.

Displacement effects are more complicated. If participants in an experiment benefit at the expense of members of the control group, then the experimental results are biased and the internal validity of the experiment is compromised. If, on the other hand, the benefits obtained by partici-

pants do not come at the expense of members of the control group, then
the internal validity of the experiment is preserved, but the external validity
of the results may still need to be examined, especially if the anticipated
program is large in relation to the affected labor market. If expanding the
experiment into a program would cause displacement of individuals not
enrolled in the program, then the experimental results would be a poor
indicator of what would be achieved by the full-blown program. A more
general approach, such as that of Johnson (1979), would be required to
evaluate the effects of the full program.

Often, designers of experiments pay too little attention to the question
of whether the results of an experiment will be transferable or externally
valid. Clearly, the reason for devoting public funds to social experiments
is to learn about the likely effects of programs before they are implemented.
To ignore the external validity of an experiment is to invite experimental
results that will say little if anything about what we really want to
understand.

Elements of Experimental Design

The main elements of an experimental design are treatment selection,
eligibility criteria, sample selection, and site selection. A variety of operational issues also need to be addressed in designing an experiment—management of client flow, training of personnel to run the experiment, data
acquisition, and monitoring of performance, for example. Although these
operational issues are important, we focus here on the main elements.

Treatment Selection. A program that experimental subjects are offered
or required to accept is referred to as a treatment. An experiment may
comprise a single treatment or a set of related treatments, and the selection of treatments depends on the objectives of the experiment. In the
income maintenance experiments, the principal objective was to measure
the impact of various formulations of a negative income tax on work effort.
A payment formula was specified in which the payment to a family was
a function of a guaranteed support level (the payment to a family with
no other income) and a benefit reduction schedule (a tax applied to earned
or other income). Each treatment was a combination of a guaranteed
support level and a benefit reduction schedule, and each eligible household was randomly assigned to one of the treatments.

In each of the Illinois UI experiments, there was a single treatment—a
$500 bonus paid either to a claimant or to an employer who met certain
conditions. More than one treatment could have been tested in each experiment—various bonus levels could have been offered to different randomly
selected groups. But the main purpose of the experiments was to com-

pare the effectiveness of bonuses paid either to employers or to claimants. Hence, a single bonus level was adequate.[16]

Only policy options that are precisely represented by a treatment can be experimentally tested. Experiments designed with combinations of programs are suitable to evaluate only those combinations. For instance, if a treatment provided participants an option to receive either training or a subsidy to move to a new location, then the measured effect would be for a program providing that combination—it would not measure the effect of a program that provided training only or a moving subsidy only. Since a goal of the income maintenance experiments was to test separately the effects of changes in the guaranteed support level and of changes in tax rates, treatments had to be designed that provided changes along each dimension independently.

Eligibility and Sample Design. Two considerations arise in determining who should be eligible to participate in an experiment. The first is who would be eligible (and likely) to participate in an actual program based on the experiment. For example, although all families would be eligible to participate in a universal negative income tax program, families with high incomes would be unlikely to participate. Hence, very high income families were not enrolled in the income maintenance experiments. Similarly, experiments designed to test methods of reducing UI payments would be limited to UI claimants.

The second consideration that arises in determining eligibility is mainly statistical. It may be possible to improve the efficiency of experimental estimates by confining attention to a relatively homogeneous group of individuals. This would be the case if, for example, a group that is of special interest—prime-age workers, say—displayed less randomness in their behavior than younger and older workers. By confining the sample to prime-age workers, it would be easier to detect a statistically significant effect of the experimental program if one existed.

These two considerations—the first bearing on policy, the other statistical—must be weighed in determining who is eligible for an experiment. Although there are advantages of analyzing a homogeneous sample, there is a danger that overly restricting the groups included in the experiment may limit the usefulness of the results in guiding policy. For example, even though there were reasons to suppose that low-wage workers would respond most strongly to the job search incentive experiment, limiting the experiment to low-wage workers would have precluded testing of this hypothesis. Furthermore, limiting the experiment to low-wage workers would have been inappropriate if no such limitation would be imposed in the actual program.

Decisions about the number of individuals (or households) to enroll in an experiment also represent a balancing of two conflicting considerations: a larger sample is desirable in that it improves the reliability of results,[17] but a smaller sample is less costly to gather. In choosing the size of enrollment, it is important to have a prior subjective estimate of what the response to the experiment might be (or of how small a response would be useful to know about) in order to determine the sample size needed to detect that response. In the Illinois experiments, for example, it was estimated that, given the budget for the experiment, an increase as small as seven percent in the proportion of UI claimants obtaining reemployment within eleven weeks could be detected. Since an impact smaller than seven percent would be of no interest, it was decided that the sample size implied by the budget would be adequate.

Because some minimum number of subjects must receive a treatment in order to detect an effect of given size, the trade-off between cost and statistical reliability also determines the number of treatments that can be tested. In an unemployment insurance experiment in Tacoma, the State of Washington was originally interested in testing six different treatments, but it was forced to test only four because the budgeted sample divided among six treatments would not have allowed detection of likely effects.

Site Selection. Selection of the site or sites in which to conduct an experiment can determine whether the results represent what would occur under a fully implemented program. If the site chosen does not contain a sample representing the population that would be exposed to a full program, the results of the experiment may not be useful in predicting the effects of the program.

To illustrate, in 1969 researchers conducting the Seattle income maintenance experiment became concerned that the unusually high rates of unemployment in Seattle would significantly reduce the transferability of the experiment's results to regions where unemployment was closer to the national average. Hence, the experiment was replicated in Denver. In the end, the Seattle and Denver results were comparable, but this could not have been known in advance.

A second issue in site selection is the number of sites to operate. With more sites, there is greater certainty that the results of an experiment will represent the outcome of a full-blown program. Also, conducting an experiment at several sites may allow experimenters either to determine whether site-specific characteristics influence the experimental results, or alternatively to average out these effects by pooling the samples from various sites. By conducting the Illinois UI experiments in twenty-two separate Job Service offices, experimenters could be confident that the pooled results would represent the whole region, and further could determine whether experimental effects varied from site to site.

The main elements of experimental design—treatment selection, eligibility, sample design, and site selection—involve decisions that bear on the reliability, interpretation, and transferability of an experiment's results. Decisions about each will determine both the internal and external validity of an experiment and must be made with a clear view of its goals.

2. Central Issues in UI Research

What are the principal issues that have generated calls for reform of the UI system? How have they produced an interest in controlled UI experiments? To what extent are each of the perceived problems with the UI system susceptible to remedies that could be tested experimentally?

UI Benefits and the Duration of Unemployment

The most-researched aspect of the UI system is its tendency to prolong the duration of job search of UI claimants. The source of this prolonged job search is that, with UI benefits available, the pressure to accept a new job (or to return to an old one) is lessened; hence, UI claimants' duration of insured unemployment has been estimated to increase by roughly half a week in response to a 10 percent increase in the gross replacement rate (the ratio of the UI recipient's benefits to pretax earnings received before the spell of unemployment).[18]

Questions surrounding UI benefits and the duration of unemployment can be readily addressed through controlled experiments. Because the questions concern individual behavior, the unit of analysis for such experiments is the individual UI claimant, and random assignment of new UI claimants to control and experimental groups is easily achieved.

The basic approach of these experiments is to subject different randomly drawn groups to different benefit treatments. A variety of experimental treatments that would yield insight into the central issues can be imagined. The most direct approach would be either to alter the weekly benefit amount or to change the potential duration of benefits for members of the treatment group. Although straightforward, it is difficult to obtain legal approval for changing the weekly benefit amount or potential duration of benefits for some but not all. As a result, more circuitous ways of attaining the same goal must be found. For example, a bonus can be paid to a claimant who returns to employment within a short time, as in the Illinois job search incentive experiment. Alternatively, several weeks of benefits (perhaps five) could be paid in a lump sum at the time eligibility for benefits is determined.

Either of these treatments may be viewed as making leisure less desirable (by raising the net wage) or as decreasing the cost of obtaining work (by decreasing the costs, in terms of UI benefits forgone, of obtaining employment). Either treatment effectively shifts the budget constraint facing UI recipients so as to create an incentive to find reemployment sooner than would otherwise be the case.[19]

Interpreting the results of an experiment that provides job search incentives requires attention to both the internal and external validity of the experiment. The internal validity of the experiment will be violated if participants in the experiment increase their speed of reemployment at the expense of members of the control group. This is the problem of displacement that we discussed earlier. Estimates of the effect of the job search incentive would be biased upward because the speed with which controls became reemployed would be slower than in the absence of the experiment.

But even without displacement of controls during the experiment, the external validity of the experimental results could come into question: if expansion of the experimental treatment into a program increased the job search intensity of a large number of UI claimants, then job seekers without the same motivation as the UI claimants could be displaced. As a result, improvements in the speed of reemployment exhibited by UI claimants in response to the program would be at least partly offset by the increased trouble job seekers other than UI claimants would have finding a job. Experimental measures of the program's effects may be correct, but they would overstate the social benefits that could be expected from a full program.

What should be clear is that, although legal hurdles must first be cleared, and although experimenters must be wary of displacement, experiments offer a nearly ideal way of examining the relationship between UI benefit and unemployment duration. The range of treatments that can be designed, the ease of access to the population in question, and the availability of UI administrative data all contribute to the promise of such experiments.

UI Financing and Layoff Unemployment

The payroll taxes levied on an employer in order to finance UI benefits paid to his former employees are only partially experience-rated — that is, only within limits do they depend on the unemployment for which that employer is responsible. It follows that layoffs may be partially subsidized by the UI system, and that there is little disincentive for some employers to avoid laying off more workers more frequently than would occur under full experience rating. The effect of partial experience rating of UI benefits on employers' inclination to lay off workers has been analyzed by Robert Topel (see the review in this volume), who concludes that about 30 percent of all spells of layoff unemployment would be eliminated if employers were fully responsible for the UI benefits paid to their former employees.

Although available estimates of the contribution that less-than-full experience rating makes to layoff unemployment are carefully constructed, it is conceivable that controlled experimentation would improve the credence that could be placed in such estimates, and increase the confidence with which reforms might be undertaken. The strength of an experiment would be that it would put into practice "the conceptual experiment of changing experience rating for otherwise identical employers" that Topel has simulated using nonexperimental data (see page 123).

However attractive an experiment that varied the UI tax schedule facing different establishments might be, such an experiment would face at least four difficulties in practice. First, the unit of analysis would be the establishment, not the individual. Random assignment of establishments to control and experimental groups would require great care because establishments are far scarcer than individuals, and the accuracy of statistical inferences drawn from an experiment depends on whether two homogeneous random samples can be taken from a population. Constructing representative samples that could be assigned to two different treatments would probably require stratification by at least industry and firm size. Whether this could be accomplished successfully is a good question because there are so few large firms. To our knowledge, no social experiment to date has used the establishment as its subject.

Second, because the effects of experience rating could vary over the business cycle, and because it would take a full business cycle to observe the effects of different UI tax schedules on the trust fund, the experiment would need to be conducted over at least one full business cycle. In addition, the current capital stock and organization of production may be at least in part the result of decisions made in light of the UI tax system. If so, and if the effects of experience rating on the organization of production was a serious concern, a still-longer experiment would need to be planned.[20]

Third, there is wide variation from state to state, not only in the UI benefit and tax structures, but also in other factors affecting layoff behavior. If the results of an experiment on experience rating were to be widely applicable, it would have to be conducted in several states.

Finally, one would need to address the legal problem of treating similar firms differently — making some firms worse off (and others better off) by increasing the experience rating of the UI tax schedule they face.

We conclude that the design and implementation of an experiment to test the effects of increased experience rating would pose difficulties that make this issue less susceptible to experimentation than others (such as the relationship between UI benefits and unemployment duration). Nevertheless, imperfect experience rating may greatly increase the amount of layoff unemployment that occurs and seriously distort decisions about resource allocation. The importance of obtaining highly reliable estimates is surely great enough to justify further exploration of an experimental approach to the question.

Expanded Uses of UI Benefits

Two innovative and untraditional ways of using UI funds have been suggested in recent years and implemented in some states. The first, called short-time compensation or worksharing UI, entails the use of UI funds to compensate workers whose hours have been reduced but who have not been laid off. The second is the payment of UI benefits to workers who are undergoing retraining. What unites these untraditional uses of UI funds is that both result in payment of UI benefits to workers who have traditionally been ineligible for UI. Ordinarily, a worker must be separated from an employer to receive benefits, but under short-time compensation a reduction in hours is enough to qualify a worker for benefit payments. Similarly, workers who would be eligible for benefits but who have entered a training program are ordinarily declared ineligible for benefits, on the grounds that they are no longer available for work.[21] Whether short-time compensation and the extension of UI benefits to workers who undertake retraining become commonplace will probably depend on the pecuniary costs and benefits each entails. Can controlled experiments contribute to the debates over whether these new uses of UI funds are sensible?

Short-Time Compensation. The purpose of short-time compensation (STC) is to encourage employers to implement worksharing arrangements when demand is slack rather than to lay workers off. The paper by Martin J. Morand in this volume offers a positive view of STC, and presents the potential advantages (to both workers and employers) of worksharing compared with traditional layoff. Morand also points to the concerns held by many, including officials in the U.S. Department of Labor, about the strains STC may place on state UI trust funds. The question is whether STC programs will increase the burden on UI trust funds and ultimately require a realignment of UI tax schedules facing UI-covered establishments.

Controlled experimentation could make an important contribution to the debate over the costs and benefits of STC. Indeed, as Morand notes, the main criticism that has been leveled against existing studies of STC is that they have compared establishments that have used STC with those that have not, without controlling for unmeasurable differences between the two. In particular, there has been no way of controlling for self-selection in the use of STC. Clearly, an experiment could take care of this problem through random assignment of establishments to either a control or an experimental group, with STC as an option only to the experimental group.

This is not to say that experimentation provides a simple solution to questions about the costs and benefits of STC. Because the establishment would be the unit of analysis, an experiment on the effects of STC availability would encounter some of the same problems discussed earlier in regard to UI financing and layoff unemployment. In particular, the experiment would need to be conducted over a long period of time—at least long enough to encompass a full business cycle—in order to capture an establishment's behavior during a contraction. Furthermore, it might be necessary to stratify the sample of establishments by a number of categories such as size and industry, and to include in the experiment only establishments in size and industry categories for which there were enough establishments to make random assignment meaningful. Providing an estimate of the budget required to conduct such an experiment would pose a significant problem, because it would be so difficult to predict the actual incidence of layoff or the use of STC. The budgetary needs of the experiment could be estimated only with considerable error.

Despite the obstacles, an experimental examination of STC could in principle yield an understanding of the pecuniary costs and benefits of STC by sorting out the degree to which reduced hours (that is, worksharing) may serve as a substitute for layoff. The feasibility of such an experiment is well worth further exploration.

Payment of UI Benefits during Retraining. During the 1980s, displacement of workers from declining industries has been perceived as one of the major problems of labor market policy. It is in such a period that the extension of UI benefits to claimants who choose to undertake retraining has become an alluring idea. W. Lee Hansen and James F. Byers have concluded that because UI is essentially an insurance system for workers who find themselves unexpectedly and involuntarily unemployed, two elements are central to it (see chapter 9). The first is the work test, which verifies that an individual's unemployment is involuntary. The second is the trust fund, which serves as the insurance reserve. Hansen and Byers believe that both of these central elements are subverted by the use of UI to support retraining—unemployment is no longer involuntary as workers choose to undergo retraining and effectively withdraw from the labor force, and the trust fund is drawn upon for purposes for which it was never intended. They conclude that some program other than UI is needed to address the retraining needs of displaced workers.

Although the debate over use of UI funds to subsidize retraining will probably be settled on grounds such as those raised by Hansen and Byers, it is possible that controlled experimentation could contribute to the debate. Such an experiment would seek answers to at least three kinds of questions. First, what proportion of claimants would participate in UI-subsidized retraining, and what would be the characteristics of participants? Second, would UI-subsidized retraining improve the employment and earnings prospects of claimants? And third, would UI-subsidized retraining improve the earnings stability of those who receive training, so that some or all of the cost of retraining might be recouped in the long run through reduced dependence on the UI system? This last question highlights the implications of UI-subsidized retraining for the solvency of the UI system, and is closely related to the concerns raised by Hansen and Byers.

The design of an experiment to examine the above questions would be straightforward. The UI claimant would be the unit of analysis, and the treatment could be easily specified: for the experimental group, participation in an approved training program of specified maximum length would satisfy the work search test for benefit eligibility, whereas for the control group the standard work search tests would apply.

There are two main difficulties of such an experiment. The first is that it would need to be conducted over a long period of time. If the option of obtaining training while receiving UI benefits was available only briefly, some participants who would not seek training under an ongoing program might do so during the experiment in order not to lose the option. The result would be exaggerated estimates of the rate of participation in the program, and possibly biased estimates of its effects. Thus, a long enrollment period would be required to preserve the external validity of the experiment.

The second difficulty of the experiment concerns the data needed to evaluate it. Examination of the program's effects on the longer-term stability of employment, on subsequent use of the UI system by those who took advantage of UI-subsidized retraining, and hence on the finances of the UI system would require following each claimant's employment experience over a long period of time—two years might be desirable. Conducting such an extended experiment would be possible, although it would require considerable forethought. Our conclusion is that, if these two difficulties could be overcome, an experimental examination of UI-subsidized retraining could achieve a high degree of internal and external validity.

Effectiveness of the Job Service

The U.S. Employment Service (or Job Service) has played a central role in the UI system since its beginning. By providing a formal mechanism for matching unemployed workers with employers who have job vacancies, the JS attempts to improve the future earnings and employment stability of the insured unemployed. Whether the formal (and public) mechanism provided by the JS is more efficient than other, usually informal, methods used by most job seekers has rarely been examined; the only recent exception is the study by Johnson, Dickinson, and West (1985). Nevertheless, the JS has received increasing criticism and declining federal support.

The experimental approach offers a nearly ideal way of testing the effectiveness of the JS. By randomly assigning unemployed JS registrants either to a control group (whose members would receive the usual JS services) or to an experimental group (whose members would receive some reduced level of assistance), a simple and direct test of the importance of the services provided by the JS could be made. Random assignment would dispense with the main difficulty faced by nonexperimental evaluation of the JS, that of constructing a group with whom the performance of users of the JS could legitimately be compared. (The problem in constructing a comparison group is that users of the JS are self-selected.) A further advantage of an experimental approach would be the ability to determine which of the services provided by the JS is most effectve. Doing so would require specification of several treatments. One treatment might provide access only to a listing of available jobs; another might provide a listing of available jobs and placement services; a third might provide a listing of jobs, placement services, and counseling. Such a design would assume that these services are additive—that it would make no sense to provide counseling without placement services.

The main problem with testing the effectiveness of the JS rests in the political and legal difficulties that may be encountered in providing less assistance to individuals assigned to the experimental group (or groups). In an evaluation of the JS by SRI International, an experimental design was rejected because it was believed that denying services to a JS applicant would be illegal.[22] More recently, however, the State of Washington has implemented an experiment in which one of the treatments involves reducing the requirements placed on individuals to obtain services (see discussion, pp. 384–385).

Eligibility and Work Search Requirements

In recent years, Jerry L. Kingston and Paul L. Burgess have documented large overpayments of benefits to UI recipients (see their review in this volume). These overpayments come mainly in the form of benefits that are paid to claimants who search for work less than they are required to in order to receive UI benefits. (In the jargon of the UI program, these claimants have met the monetary and separation requirements of the program, but fail to meet the work search requirements while they are receiving benefits.) Clearly, overpayment of benefits places a strain on the UI system that could in principle be avoided. The question is whether any of the feasible ways of reducing overpayments would save more than they would cost—that is, would they be efficient?

Kingston and Burgess have considered at least three administrative approaches to alleviating the strain on state UI trust funds resulting from overpayments. One is to increase the stringency of the so-called monetary eligibility requirements that a claimant must meet in order to qualify initially for UI benefits. The idea behind this approach is to make eligibility for payment of UI benefits contingent on a more substantial work history than is required by the current system. This would eliminate many of those currently eligible who are unlikely to search seriously for work, and thereby eliminate the need for (and the benefit from) work search requirements. A second approach is simply to eliminate the work search requirement. Because enforcement of the work search requirement uses administrative resources, its elimination would be efficient if elimination did not lead to longer spells of unemployment and hence greater benefit payments. A third approach is to implement "statistical screening" of UI recipients, which would entail auditing mainly UI recipients who, based on their characteristics, are most likely to abuse the system. Since under statistical screening claimants who are less likely to search for work would be more likely to be followed up, administrative resources would be more efficiently directed.

The first of these three approaches, increasing the stringency of UI eligibility requirements, does not lend itself to experimental evaluation. Most of the potential administrative benefits of such an approach could be ascertained by a combined examination of existing administrative records and a random audit like that used by Kingston and Burgess to obtain many of their findings. That is, administrative records could reveal the number and characteristics of claimants who would fail various monetary eligibility criteria that were more stringent, and the random audit would suggest the degree to which claimants who remained eligible would actually search for work while receiving their benefits. To choose a new monetary eligibility criterion would be a matter of examining the actual work search behavior of groups who would remain eligible under various criteria.[23]

On the other hand, experiments could contribute to an understanding of the effects of eliminating the work search requirement. As Kingston and Burgess note, we simply do not know how actual work search behavior or the duration of unemployment would be altered by eliminating the requirement that UI recipients look for work during their spell of unemployment. But controlled experimentation is ideally suited to the task. One randomly selected group of new UI claimants would be assigned to a treatment that exempted them from any work search requirement, while a control group would experience the normal work search requirement. Comparing the insured unemployment spells of the two groups would reveal the degree to which current work search requirements lead to shorter spells of unemployment. Such an experiment would be both internally and externally valid; in particular, no problem of displacement could arise because no group would have an increased incentive to search for work. Indeed, an experiment similar to the one envisioned here is currently underway in the State of Washington.

Similarly, an experimental approach could be fruitful in determining the efficiency of statistical screening in the selection of which UI recipients to follow up. The question to be addressed here is whether enforcement of the work search requirement, particularly for UI recipients who tend to be lax about job search during their spell of unemployment, could reduce the duration of insured unemployment. A straightforward way of addressing the issue is to divide a cohort of new UI recipients into two groups: claimants in one group would receive no special treatment, whereas claimants in the other group would receive statistical screening and follow-up according to whether their profile suggested they had a low probability of complying with the work search requirement. If administrative costs could be kept equal between the two treatments (by assigning no special staff to follow the statistically screened group), the benefits of the program would be appraised by comparing any differences in the length of unemployment spells of the two groups. It is the possible behavioral response to the tougher enforcement of the work search requirement that gives the experimental approach an edge in handling this issue. The State of Washington experiment has some features of the experiment we are describing. Again, a high degree of both internal and external validity could be expected from such an experiment.

3. Experiments with the UI System: Some Examples

We noted in the introduction that there has been a recent wave of UI experiments that could greatly increase our understanding of the UI system. In fact, three UI experiments have already been conducted, and a fourth is in progress at the time of writing. We now turn to review these experiments, each of which has been intended to answer particular questions about how one or more reforms would affect the performance of the UI system.

The Illinois UI Experiments

Between late July of 1984 and June of 1985, the Illinois Department of Employment Security conducted two experiments designed to test the effectiveness of cash bonuses paid either to employers or to UI claimants in reducing the duration of insured unemployment (Spiegelman and Woodbury, 1987). In one experiment, called the hiring incentive experiment (HIE), a random sample of new claimants for unemployment insurance were instructed that their next employer would be eligible for a cash bonus of $500 if they, the claimants, found full-time employment before the end of the eleventh week following their initial claim, and if they held that employment for four months. Once the eligibility of these claimants was determined, each was mailed a packet of materials instructing him or her to advise prospective employers of the experiment and the possibility of receiving a bonus. The intent was to provide a marginal employment subsidy, or training subsidy, that might reduce the duration of insured unemployment.

In the other experiment, called the job search incentive experiment (JSIE), a random sample of new claimants were told that they would receive a cash bonus of $500 if they found full-time employment within eleven weeks of filing their initial claim, and if they retained that employment for four months. The intent here was to create an incentive for claimants to become reemployed more rapidly than they otherwise would.[24]

In the final experimental design, individuals between the ages of twenty and fifty-four, inclusive, who filed new claims for UI and registered at one of twenty-two selected Job Service offices in northern and central Illinois were randomly assigned to one of the experimental groups or to a control group.[25]

Analysis of the experiments relied on data obtained for the 12,101 claimants who were eligible both for UI benefits and to participate in the experiments — 3,952 of these were members of the control group, 3,963 were offered the opportunity to participate in the HIE, and 4,186 were offered the opportunity to participate in the JSIE. The random assignment of claimants to the control group, the HIE group, and the JSIE group allowed each to be treated as a random sample from the population of fully eligible initial claimants for UI benefits who were aged twenty through fifty-four. It follows that, for example, a simple comparison of the mean weeks of insured unemployment for members of the HIE group with the mean weeks for members of the control group will show the effect of the HIE on the duration of insured unemployment.

The results of the HIE were rather complex. First, the HIE suffered from low participation; employers of only 3 percent of the 3,963 eligible claimants assigned to the HIE group collected bonuses. Second, although there may have been an initial reduction in regular benefits received by the HIE group in the spell of unemployment immediately following the initial claim, there was no evidence (in the full sample) of a reduction over the full benefit year. Nor was there strong evidence of an impact of the bonus on the number of weeks of insured unemployment, either in the first spell of unemployment or over the benefit year, for the HIE group taken as a whole. Third, although there was no statistically significant effect of the experiment for the HIE group taken as a whole, disaggregating the results by sex and race turned up an important finding: offering a bonus to employers did reduce the duration of insured unemployment and benefits paid to white women, causing a $164 reduction in the benefits paid and a one-week reduction in their weeks of insured unemployment, both on average over the full benefit year. We have concluded elsewhere (Spiegelman and Woodbury, 1987) that, although the overall results of the experiment were weak, further study of the determinants of participation in the experiment, and of use by employers of the HIE voucher, would be worthwhile.

In contrast, the effects of the JSIE program on UI benefits received and the duration of insured unemployment were very strong. On average, UI benefit payments to eligible claimants assigned to the JSIE group were $158 less (over the full benefit year) than were benefit payments to controls. The number of weeks of insured unemployment experienced by the JSIE group was 1.15 weeks less than the number experienced by controls. The results are especially striking when it is recalled that these effects were achieved over the entire sample of 4,186 JSIE enrollees, only 570 of whom actually collected a $500 bonus. From the state's point of view, a program modeled on the JSIE would seem to be extremely attractive: for each $1.00 of bonus payments made, state regular benefit payments were reduced by about $2.32.

Because the results of the JSIE were so strong, it was important to address at least three additional questions about it. (We have discussed these issues in greater detail in Spiegelman and Woodbury, 1987, Chs. 5 and 8.) First, it is possible — indeed, the theory of job search suggests — that the shorter search time induced by the job search incentive may have led to a less-favorable match between worker and job, which would manifest itself in lower earnings in the subsequent job. We have found, however, that a comparison of the earnings of JSIE enrollees and controls in the quarter after they stopped receiving benefits reveals no significant difference between the two groups. Hence, we have concluded that the relatively rapid reemployment of JSIE participants was the result of more intense job search efforts by JSIE enrollees, and did not come at the expense of lower earnings.

Second, the improved performance of claimants who were enrolled in the JSIE group could have come at the expense of the control group — that is, JSIE participants may have "displaced" controls — in which case our estimates of the effect of offering a bonus to workers would be biased upward. This concern must be addressed somewhat more speculatively. In discussing the issue elsewhere (Spiegelman and Woodbury, 1987, Ch. 8), we have noted that the number of JSIE participants was quite small relative to the number of vacancies in the northern Illinois labor market in late 1984. As a result, we are fairly confident of the internal validity of the JSIE's results. Whether a program based on the JSIE would result in displacement of job seekers who were not UI claimants is a different question; the issue here is one of external validity. To ascertain whether UI claimants compete for jobs with other job seekers is a separate research issue, and an important one from the point of view of determining the merits of implementing a program based on the JSIE.

Third, it may have been that the JSIE did succeed in shortening the unemployment spells of participating claimants, but that not all claimants who qualified for a $500 bonus actually submitted a voucher. If these claimants were to cash a voucher, then the favorable cost/benefit ratio calculated above could be upset. The problem here might be thought of as a learning effect, since if the JSIE were turned into a program, we presume that over time nearly all eligible claimants would cash their vouchers. This concern is also one of external validity. We have estimated that 1,395 of the 4,186 JSIE enrollees (that is, about 33 percent) were reemployed within eleven weeks of filing their initial claim. Only 765 of these submitted notices of hire, and 570 of these cashed vouchers. If we suppose participation in the program increased so that all 1,395 claimants who could have submitted notices of hire did so, and that 75 percent of these stayed with their new jobs for the required four months and cashed a voucher, bonus payments would have increased to about $523,000.[26] Even if this increase in participation was unaccompanied by any reduction in unemployment duration or benefit payments, the JSIE program would still have a favorable and attractive, albeit a lower, cost/benefit ratio: the state would save $1.26 in benefits paid for every $1.00 spent on bonuses. It is likely, of course, that if actual participation in the program increased, there could be an accompanying reduction in unemployment duration and benefit payments. That is, increased participation of the kind envisioned would not only increase bonus payments, but could have a positive effect on behavior that would reduce UI benefit payments as well.

The Wisconsin ERP Pilot Project

From March through August of 1984, the Wisconsin Job Service conducted an experiment designed to test whether a special one-day, six-hour job search workshop could decrease the duration of insured unemployment and thereby reduce the total amount of benefits paid to UI recipients. The experiment became known as the eligibility review process (ERP) pilot project because its objectives came under the federally mandated eligibility review process—to promote "an active search for work by assisting claimants in their job search plan"—and hence drew federal ERP funds (Wisconsin Job Service, 1984).

The design of this experiment is clean and straightforward: new UI claimants in six Job Service offices in the state were randomly assigned to either a control or an experimental group. (Approximately two thousand claimants were assigned to each.) Those in the experimental group were told that, in order to remain eligible for benefits, they would be required to attend a one-day job search workshop conducted by Employment Service staff. The Wisconsin Job Service staff prepared a project program and trained local office staff so that the programs offered in the six offices would be as uniform as possible. There were, nevertheless, the expected differences in the program from office to office: the local labor market, characteristics of claimants, and administrative procedures of the office, for example. An additional interoffice difference that could in principle have been eliminated was the starting date of the project, which ranged from March 14 in Eau Claire to May 23 in Milwaukee. The project's evaluators concluded that the program's effects were unrelated to the week in which claimants entered the project, and this potential source of variation does not seem to have interfered with the experiment.

The ERP pilot project's evaluators found that claimants who were in the experimental group received 0.62 fewer weeks of UI benefits than those in the control group. (This point estimate is significant at the 85 percent confidence level, which means that there are three chances in twenty that the 0.62-week difference could have been observed even if there was no true difference between controls and experimentals.) The point estimate of 0.62 weeks implies a gross savings to the Wisconsin UI trust of nearly $165,000. Subtracting estimated program costs of $50,000, the net saving to the UI trust was nearly $115,000.

Based on the results of the experiment, the evaluators of the project recommended that job search workshops be provided routinely and made a requirement for UI benefit eligibility; that is, attendance at such a workshop would become part of the work search requirement. This recommendation is quite in accord with the findings of the experiment. But we would note two qualifications. First, the 85 percent level of confidence associated with the experiment's main finding might be considered low by some evaluators. We would suggest that a second experiment of greater duration or extended to additional offices would permit a larger sample that would in turn yield results in which we could place greater confidence.

Second, potential problems of predicting the results of an actual program from the experimental results were not addressed by the ERP pilot project's evaluators. The questions of external validity or transferability that have been raised before arise here: Did some of the benefits experienced by those who attended the workshop come at the expense of controls, who in effect became disadvantaged for lack of the same job-seeking skills? If the experiment were turned into a program (that is, if its scale were increased), would the improved job-seeking skills of UI claimants — who would be required to attend the workshop — put job seekers who were ineligible for UI at a disadvantage in searching for a job? If so, then some of the gains to UI claimants would be at the expense of those who were ineligible for UI. These questions are difficult, but well worth considering. A start could be made by conducting a second experiment on a larger scale, as we suggested above in regard to increasing the statistical power of experimental results. Because the benefits of the ERP pilot project appear to have greatly outweighed the costs, there is every reason to conduct an extended experiment and to improve understanding of whether and how such a program works.

The State of Washington Experiment

The State of Washington's Employment Security Department has implemented an experiment that is intended to answer two questions about the efficiency of its system. The first is whether increasing the stringency of its work search test for benefit eligibility, or increasing the services to be provided to UI recipients, would decrease the duration of insured unemployment (and hence benefit payments) by enough to offset any resulting increases in administrative costs. The second is whether relaxing the stringency of its work search test would reduce administrative costs by enough to offset any resulting increases in the duration of insured unemployment (and hence benefit payments).

Currently, the Washington system works as follows. (1) When a claimant is certified to receive benefits, he or she is instructed in the work search requirements for continuing eligibility, and signs a statement guaranteeing his or her availability for work and agreeing to search for work. (2) Every two weeks, a continued claim form must be submitted by the recipient to retain eligibility. On the form the individual lists the names of employers he or she has contacted (at least three are required) and the method of contact. (3) The continued claim forms are monitored to ensure that the minimum job search requirement is met. (4) In the twelfth to fourteenth weeks of benefit receipt, an employability review interview is conducted to initiate additional work search requirements and services, such as workshops.

The experiment comprises four treatments:

1. *Elimination of the continued claim form:* The recipient is required only to sign a statement on the weekly benefit check that he or she is still unemployed and available for work. There is no specific work search requirement or monitoring, but each recipient is expected to inform Employment Security of any changes that would result in ineligibility for benefits. A telephone hot line has been installed to simplify communication between recipients and the UI office.
2. *The current standard work search system:* This treatment serves as the control treatment, and is similar to the systems used in other states.
3. *The Washington work search activity program:* This is the current system with the addition of individualized work search requirements that become more stringent as the spell of unemployment lengthens. Under this treatment, the employability review interview is set earlier (between

the fourth and eighth weeks of benefit receipt), and more stringent work search requirements (at least four employer contacts per week) may be set at this time.[27] During the ninth to sixteenth weeks, Job Service specialists begin ongoing review of work search activities, increase work search requirements, and increase the number of contacts with the recipient.

4. *Intensive work search services:* This is the current system with the addition of a two-day job-finders' workshop for recipients who are still unemployed in the fourth or fifth weeks of benefit receipt. The workshop is shorter than that given after the twelfth week under the current system in order to encourage participation. For the three weeks following the workshop, recipients are required to use a telephone bank at least twice a week. If still unemployed after the eighth week, claimants are treated the same as under the work search activity program (treatment 3), with more stringent work search requirements and more intense monitoring imposed.

Note that the Washington experiment tests whether the duration of unemployment is affected by decreasing or increasing work search requirements (treatments 1 and 3) or by offering increased services in the form of workshops and a telephone bank (treatment 4). The experiment is being conducted in an office in Tacoma, one that is reasonably representative of the state's urban caseload, and will enroll about ten thousand participants over one year. Only claimants filing initial claims will be assigned to one of the four treatments.[28]

The New Jersey UI Reemployment Demonstration

An experiment with work search services and incentives recently implemented in New Jersey represents one of the major current research projects of the U.S. Department of Labor. Eligibility for this experiment is limited to new UI claimants who, based on their demographic characteristics, are likely to have a long spell of unemployment and to exhaust their benefits. Participants receive basic job search assistance, including orientation, a week-long job search workshop, individual assessment, and counseling, starting in the fourth week after filing for benefits (one week after receipt of the first UI benefit payment). Assignment to one of three treatments (two experimental and one control) is made in the fourth or fifth week, and participants are told during their counseling session about the experimental services that are available to them if they have been assigned to one of the experimental groups.

The two experimental treatments tested in the New Jersey experiment are (1) a choice of either training taken in a program approved by the counselor (the training may be either in the classroom or on the job) or assistance in relocating (if relocation is preferred by the claimant and judged suitable by the counselor); and (2) a bonus paid to an eligible claimant for rapid reemployment. A maximum bonus equal to ten times the weekly benefit amount is paid to an eligible claimant who becomes reemployed by the end of the seventh week after filing the initial claim. The bonus declines by 10 percent of the maximum amount in each following week if a job is not found, so that the bonus for early reemployment vanishes after the sixteenth week.

The New Jersey experiment could have provided potentially valuable tests of the effect of services and incentives on reemployment. But as we noted in section 1, the design of the experiment was flawed in that it could not provide externally valid results. The assignment of claimants to the control group or one of the treatment groups was hidden from claimants until the fourth or fifth week after filing. If the bonus program were adopted, all initial claimants for UI who met eligibility requirements would have the bonus available to them starting in the seventh week, but they would know about the availability of the bonus from the start—their eligibility could not be hidden from them as in the experiment. It follows that job search behavior during the early weeks of unemployment would be different for claimants in an actual program than for claimants in the experiment. It is likely that, under an actual program, claimants would tend to postpone accepting a job until after they became eligible for the bonus in the seventh week. Therefore, the results of the New Jersey experiment are likely to be biased toward showing a greater decrease in unemployment duration than would occur under a program modeled on the experiment. This is the essence of external invalidity: the New Jersey experiment cannot give a correct picture of what would occur if the experimental program were adopted.

4. The Potential and Limitations of UI Experiments

Controlled social experiments cannot be expected to meet all the needs of policymakers, or to solve all the problems of nonexperimental research. But when experiments can be conducted so as to avoid or overcome the pitfalls we described in section 1, social experimentation offers a promising way of obtaining reliable answers to some of the most pressing questions facing policymakers. Indeed, for many questions no nonexperimental method can provide the same assurance of unbiased results that a properly designed controlled social experiment can offer.

We discussed in section 2 some general questions about the UI system and its reform that might be usefully addressed by methods of social experimentation. Some of these questions, such as how the UI system affects unemployment duration and firms' layoff behavior, have been addressed in nonexperimental research but have not been wholly settled. Other issues, such as the effects of the work search requirement, the effects of short-time compensation, the effects of allowing UI recipients to enroll in retraining programs, and the effectiveness of the Job Service, virtually require an experimental approach if credible answers are to be obtained. Because experiments have only recently been conducted with the UI system, these latter issues have either gone unexamined, or have resulted in nonexperimental studies that remain open to criticism.

Our descriptions of the UI experiments that have been recently completed or are now under way should suggest the feasibility and credibility of an experimental approach to several issues that are of interest to policymakers interested in reform of the UI system: the effects of the system on unemployment duration, the effects of additional job search assistance, and the effects of work search requirements, for example. Equally important, the cost of these experiments has been modest compared with the cost of the income maintenance experiments of past decades. Although care must be taken in designing such experiments if their results are to be internally valid and transferable to the actual operation of a program (that is, externally valid), the success and relatively low cost of most of the UI experiments to date make us highly optimistic about the contribution such experiments can make to improving the effectiveness and efficiency of the UI system.

NOTES

For helpful comments on an earlier draft of this paper, the authors are grateful to Saul J. Blaustein, James F. Byers, W. Lee Hansen, Timothy L. Hunt, and Susan Pozo.

1. See the introductory remarks of Hamermesh (1977). Even recently, so strident a critic of social spending as Charles Murray (1984, p. 230) has suggested that UI is the only social program that does more good than harm.

2. On the income maintenance experiments, see, for example, Robins (1985) and the references cited there; on housing subsidy experiments, see Rosen (1985); on an experiment with educational vouchers, Rand Corporation (1972); on health policy experiments, Harris (1985); and on the time-of-use pricing experiments, Aigner (1985).

3. This tension can be seen as the tension that exists between those who believe that the goal of science is only to make good predictions (so-called instrumentalists), and those who believe that the goal of science is to explain phenomena (scientific realists). See Hausman (1984, pp. 5–6).

4. See Hausman and Wise (1985) on the relatively model-free aspect of experimental evaluation. That experimental evaluation can be relatively model-free does not preclude the use and testing of models with experimental data. Indeed, Stafford (1985, p. 97) disputes the "model-freeness" of experiments, arguing that an experi-

ment designed to test the effects of one policy does not permit one to "generalize to a 'nearby' alternative [policy] without an explicit or implicit model." Stafford considers this to be a "fundamental deficiency in a solely experimental approach." Although there may be some truth to Stafford's view, we find it to be overly critical: how can one fault experimentation because generalization of experimental results requires a model, when nonexperimental methods require even more restrictive models just to obtain estimates of effects? Furthermore, an important motivation for experiments has been the distrust of economic theory by policymakers and the reluctance of some economists to rely on theory (equally, perhaps, their willingness to subject theory to test). Stafford's view neglects this; it implies that policymakers must accept a theoretical structure if they want answers, and that economists should accept their theory as given, not test it.

5. The mean value of y for the control group equals b_0, and the mean value of y for the experimental group equals $b_0 + b_1$. Hence, b_1 represents the difference of means between the experimental and control groups.

6. The Job Corps and the Youth Entitlement Demonstration are examples (Stromsdorfer and Farkas, 1980). Note that the comparison group in a quasi experiment is not randomly assigned to control status, which is what distinguishes the quasi experiment from a controlled social experiment.

7. Barnow, Cain, and Goldberger (1980) offer one of the most readable synopses of the problem.

8. It is worth emphasizing that selection bias arises because of unobserved or unmeasurable variables. It may be that we can observe the traits that are correlated with both self-selection into a program and the outcomes that are of interest. If so—if the traits resulting in selection into the sample were age, race, and sex, for example—then these observed traits could be included in a regression model in either an experimental or a nonexperimental analysis, and unbiased estimates of the program's effects could be obtained.

9. Learning effects may also occur as a result of changes in the behavior of those who administer the program or the treatment, but we do not treat such effects here.

10. Note that the problems stemming from learning effects are distinct from those stemming from a time horizon that exceeds the duration of the experiment. An experiment could be long enough for participants to be fully convinced of its legitimacy, to understand fully the consequences of their behavior in relation to the program, and to have all the time needed to make adjustments, yet if their planning horizons exceed the experiment's duration, time horizon problems will arise.

11. The degree to which behavior during a short experiment would differ from behavior if an experimental program were made permanent depends on the value that an individual places on future as against present income. Those who place a relatively low value on future income will be more likely to adjust their supply of labor and work effort in response to a short-term experiment.

12. However, in cases where there are positive externalities associated with moving low-wage workers into higher-paying jobs, a comparison of experimentals with controls can actually understate the benefits of a full-scale program, as George Johnson (1979) has noted.

13. If the hiring incentive experiment induced its participants to search more intensely, then the program could have some of the attributes of the job search incentive experiment, and it would have a positive effect even without a net increase in labor demand.

14. It is nevertheless true that the relationship between experimental programs that offer cash bonuses for rapid reemployment and the duration of unemployment is so obvious that it could have resulted in a Hawthorne effect. Also, the extent to which office personnel made the experimental subjects aware that they were part of an experiment is unknown. To the extent that they did, Hawthorne effects could result.

15. To compare the behavior just of participants with the behavior of controls would require a model of the participation decision. The problem here is essentially one of selection bias, which was discussed earlier.

16. Although we refer to the Illinois UI experiments as two experiments (the hiring incentive and the job search incentive experiments), each with a single treatment, they may alternatively be referred to as one experiment with two separate treatments.

17. That is, the standard error of estimated parameters decreases as the sample size increases.

18. This is the oft-quoted summary estimate (Hamermesh, 1977). See also Burtless (in this volume). More recently, the influence of the potential duration of UI benefits (as opposed to their level) has been investigated by Moffitt and Nicholson (1982).

19. Because both of these treatments have income as well as substitution effects, it is possible for certain workers to increase the duration of their unemployment in response. Analysis suggests, however, that the income effects would either be small or affect very few claimants.

20. It is highly unlikely that an experiment that was conducted long enough to observe changes in the organization of production would be feasible. One would almost surely have to settle for a partial approach and observe the effects of different tax schedules over a single cycle. Indeed, the nonexperimental work on this subject has in effect had to settle for such a partial approach.

21. Since 1970, a federal standard has prohibited states from denying benefits to claimants who are in training programs that have been approved by the state Job Service agency. Hence, the door is open to partial subsidy of retraining by UI benefit payments. Also, a few states have set up separate UI-like trust funds to provide training.

22. The evaluation that was undertaken was nonexperimental and resulted in the Johnson, Dickinson, and West (1985) study. This nonexperimental evaluation used a statistical matching procedure to create a group of individuals with whom users of the JS could be compared. Although statistical matching was the best available method given the nonexperimental context, many characteristics of individuals that influence their behavior in the labor market cannot be observed, and therefore cannot be included in the matching procedure.

23. An experiment seems not only unnecessary but problematic. First, conducting an experiment would require denying benefits to certain claimants (those in

the experimental group) who would normally be eligible (indeed would be eligible if they were members of the control group). Second, since changes in UI eligibility rules could affect labor force participation, changes in the rules would have to be communicated to individuals even before they made their decision to participate in the labor force. An experiment in which claimants who were assigned to an experimental group learned of changes in UI eligibility requirements only when they filed for benefits would not only be unfair, but would lead to externally invalid results.

24. Technically, the HIE and JSIE may be considered two treatments within a single experiment since the participants for each were drawn from the same population, to be compared with the same control group.

25. In addition, claimants who were recently separated veterans or recently separated federal employees were excluded from the experiment. Note that claimants on layoff with a definite recall date and members of unions who would find employment through hiring halls were excluded automatically because assignment of claimants to the treatment groups took place at Job Service offices.

26. Of claimants who submitted a notice of hire, 75 percent cashed a voucher. Many of these were ineligible to cash a voucher because they failed to remain employed for the required four months. But experience with other programs, such as Food Stamps and AFDC, indicates that, for many reasons, individuals who are eligible to receive benefits do not always receive them.

27. Training may also be authorized at the time of the employability review interview in order to enhance work opportunities.

28. Because persons in similar circumstances receive different levels of service and must meet different requirements during this experiment, questions about the legality of the experiment arose. The solicitor of the Department of Human Services in the State of Washington ruled that the experiment could be conducted under present law.

REFERENCES

Aigner, Dennis J. 1985. "The Residential Electricity Time-of-Use Pricing Experiments: What Have We Learned?" In *Social Experimentation,* edited by Jerry A. Hausman and David A. Wise. Chicago: University of Chicago Press and NBER. Pp. 11–53.

Barnow, Burt S., Glen G. Cain, and Arthur S. Goldberger. 1980. "Issues in the Analysis of Selectivity Bias." In *Evaluation Studies Review Annual,* edited by Ernst W. Stromsdorfer and George Farkas, vol. 5. Beverly Hills, Calif.: Sage. Pp. 43–59.

Burtless, Gary. 1989. "Unemployment Insurance and Labor Supply: A Survey." Chapter 3 of this volume.

Dickinson, Katherine P., Terry R. Johnson, and Richard W. West. 1986. "An Analysis of the Impact of CETA Programs on Participants' Earnings." *Journal of Human Resources* 21 (Winter): 64–91.

Feldstein, Martin. 1976. "The Unemployment Caused by Unemployment Insurance." In *Proceedings of the Twenty-Eighth Annual Winter Meeting of the*

Industrial Relations Research Association, edited by James L. Stern and Barbara D. Dennis. Madison: IRRA. Pp. 225–233.

Gordon, Robert J. 1982. "Inflation, Flexible Exchange Rates, and the Natural Rate of Unemployment." In *Workers, Jobs, and Inflation,* edited by Martin Neil Baily. Washington, D.C.: Brookings Institution. Pp. 89–152.

Hamermesh, Daniel S. 1977. *Jobless Pay and the Economy.* Baltimore: Johns Hopkins University Press.

Hansen, W. Lee, and James F. Byers. 1989. "Unemployment Compensation and Retraining: Can a Closer Link Be Forged?" Chapter 9 of this volume.

Harris, Jeffrey E. 1985. "Macroexperiments versus Microexperiments for Health Policy." In *Social Experimentation,* edited by Jerry A. Hausman and David A. Wise. Chicago: University of Chicago Press and NBER. Pp. 145–186.

Hausman, Daniel M. 1984. "Introduction." In *The Philosophy of Economics: An Anthology,* edited by Daniel M. Hausman. Cambridge: Cambridge University Press. Pp. 1–50.

Hausman, Jerry A., and David A. Wise. 1985. "Technical Problems in Social Evaluation: Cost versus Ease of Analysis." In *Social Experimentation,* edited by Jerry A. Hausman and David A. Wise. Chicago: University of Chicago Press and NBER. Pp. 187–219.

Johnson, George E. 1979. "The Labor Market Displacement Effect in the Analysis of the Net Impact of Manpower Training Programs." In *Research in Labor Economics, Supplement 1: Evaluating Manpower Training Programs,* edited by Ronald G. Ehrenberg and Farrell E. Bloch. Greenwich, Conn.: JAI Press. Pp. 227–257.

Johnson, Terry R. 1986. *A Guide for Net Impact Evaluations* (JTPA Evaluation Design Project, Volume 5). Olympia: Washington State Employment Security. April.

Johnson, Terry R., Katherine P. Dickinson, and Richard W. West. 1985. "An Evaluation of the Impact of ES Referrals on Applicant Earnings." *Journal of Human Resources* 20 (Winter): 117–137.

Kingston, Jerry L., and Paul L. Burgess. 1989. "Monitoring Claimant Compliance with Unemployment Compensation Eligibility Criteria." Chapter 5 of this volume.

Metcalf, Charles E. 1973. "Making Inferences from Controlled Income Maintenance Experiments." *American Economic Review* 63 (June): 478–483.

Moffitt, Robert, and Walter Nicholson. 1982. "The Effect of Unemployment Insurance on Unemployment: The Case of Federal Supplemental Benefits." *Review of Economics and Statistics* 64 (February): 1–11.

Morand, Martin J. 1989. "Unemployment Compensation and Short-Time Compensation." Chapter 10 of this volume.

Murray, Charles. 1984. *Losing Ground: American Social Policy, 1950–1980.* New York: Basic Books.

New Jersey Unemployment Insurance Reemployment Demonstration Project. 1987. "Interim Report." U.S. Department of Labor, Employment and Training Administration, April.

Phelps, Edmund S., ed. 1970. *Microeconomic Foundations of Employment and Inflation Theory.* New York: W. W. Norton.

Robins, Philip K. 1985. "A Comparison of the Labor Supply Findings from the Four Negative Income Tax Experiments." *Journal of Human Resources* 20 (Fall): 567–582.

Robins, Philip K., Nancy Brandon Tuma, and K. E. Yeager. 1980. "Effects of SIME/DIME on Changes in Employment Status." *Journal of Human Resources* 15 (Fall): 545–573.

Rosen, Harvey S. 1985. "Housing Behavior and the Experimental Housing-Allowance Program: What Have We Learned?" In *Social Experimentation,* edited by Jerry A. Hausman and David A. Wise. Chicago: University of Chicago Press and NBER. Pp. 55–75.

Solon, Gary. 1985. "Work Incentive Effects of Taxing Unemployment Benefits." *Econometrica* 53 (March): 295–306.

Spiegelman, Robert G., and Stephen A. Woodbury. 1987. *The Illinois Unemployment Insurance Incentive Experiments: Final Report to the Illinois Department of Employment Security.* Kalamazoo, Mich.: Upjohn Institute for Employment Research.

Stafford, Frank P. 1985. "Income-Maintenance Policy and Work Effort: Learning from Experiments and Labor Market Studies." In *Social Experimentation,* edited by Jerry A. Hausman and David A. Wise. Chicago: University of Chicago Press and NBER. Pp. 95–143.

State of Washington, Employment Security Office, UI Program Analysis. 1989. "Washington Alternative Work-Search Experiment." Preliminary draft, February.

Stromsdorfer, Ernst W., and George Farkas. 1980. "Introduction." In *Evaluation Studies Review Annual,* edited by Ernst W. Stromsdorfer and George Farkas, vol. 5. Beverly Hills, Calif.: Sage. Pp. 13–31.

Topel, Robert. 1989. "Financing Unemployment Insurance: History, Incentives, and Reform." Chapter 4 of this volume.

Westat, Inc. 1984. *Continuous Longitudinal Manpower Survey: Summary of Net Impact Results.* Report prepared for the U.S. Department of Labor (ORE/ETA) under Contract No. 23-24-75-07. Rockville, Md.: Westat.

Wisconsin Job Service. 1984. *ERP Pilot Project Final Report.* Madison: Wisconsin Department of Industry, Labor, and Human Relations. December.

Woodbury, Stephen A., and Robert G. Spiegelman. 1987. "Bonuses to Workers and Employers to Reduce Unemployment: Randomized Trials in Illinois." *American Economic Review* 77 (September): 514–530.

PART THREE

THE WISCONSIN CASE

12

Unemployment Compensation in Wisconsin: Origins and Performance

RAYMOND MUNTS

> The development of unemployment compensation has involved "a combination of ideological commitments, political maneuvers, social myths, and that elusive substance, national character."
>
> —Nelson, 1969, p. 221

This paper selectively reviews highlights in the development of unemployment compensation in the United States and specifically in Wisconsin. The focus is on how this state influenced the program elsewhere.

Beginnings

Unemployment insurance programs in the United States, now marking their fiftieth anniversary, started with the merging of two historical trends. One derives from our history of private sector programs developed by labor and management, either jointly or separately, which sponsored "cash unemployment benefits" or "guaranteed employment plans." This is the voluntary thread of UI (Lubove, 1968). The other thread is the development of compulsory government plans, which first started in Europe. England's adoption of a compulsory program in 1911 stimulated the interest of Americans in the possibility of dealing more effectively with the problem of unemployment in an industrializing society.

The Voluntary Approach

The voluntary approach to social problems characterizes our own history. One form it took was the "New Emphasis" philosophy of voluntary planning by industrial leaders. In the 1920s this philosophy was used to argue against compulsory law on the grounds that American industrial leaders would or should assume responsibility for alleviating unemployment. According to the New Emphasis theory, the problem was one of business management and business statesmanship. Justice Louis Brandeis was a severe critic of inefficient management. He believed that employers rather than union leaders held the key to solving the unemployment problem:

> Society and industry need only the necessary incentive to secure a great reduction of irregularity of employment. In a scientifically managed business, irregularity tends to disappear. (Nelson, 1969)

In Wisconsin, a leading spokesperson for the New Emphasis approach to industrial capitalism was the noted economics professor, John R. Commons. Commons had helped to develop the Wisconsin Worker's Compensation program in 1911, which relied on a system of insurance to compensate workers who were injured on the job, and he saw the need for a similar approach to UI. He regarded social insurance as one more way to

> make capitalism at the same time more efficient and more humane. . . . [We] do not seek to eliminate profit motivated forces of the market but to guide them . . . to make a market yield both profits and a greater social good. (Nelson, 1969)

Commons' view of the role social insurance could play was optimistic because it assumed the ability of business to control unemployment. His position gained substantial support and was translated into public policy through his influential students.

The Compulsory Approach

The second thread in American UI came from abroad. The obligatory European programs, particularly those in England (1911) and Germany (1927), were not wholly satisfying to American scholars, who could not see much similarity between the cultural background of the old societies and the new American one. According to Beatrice Webb (1926), the British plan that made UI compulsory in 1911 represented a response to the guilt felt by successful industrialists who lived on the wealth their workers created while these same workers lived in poverty and destitution. English reformers argued that citizenship required greater equality of treatment, and that no one should suffer extreme deprivation because of unemployment.

In Germany, by contrast, where more social inequality still lingered, citizenship did not have the same connotation of equal rights as it had in England. Instead, Germans in socially subordinated positions had a claim to protection in return for obedience and deference to those above them (Rimlinger, 1968). This was the basis for its compulsory system.

Americans could not identify with either view. The English view seemed to be an unacceptable attempt to impose equality on the operation of the labor market, whereas the German approach reflected a hierarchical view of society distasteful to Americans. The American approach would have to come to terms with a mobile and classless society that valued both independence and competition. It was this groping for an indigenous framework that characterized the Wisconsin experience from 1921 to 1932.

Prevention First

If the underlying philosophy was philanthropy in England and paternalism in Germany, the New Emphasis philosophy of employer regularization of employment popular in America could be characterized as prevention. J. J. Hanley, secretary of the Wisconsin Federation of Labor, articulated the prevention argument:

> if the burden of the fund rests on industry, it will be more apt to cause the employer to take an active part in working rules and orders that will prevent and eventually eliminate unemployment rather than the payment of a small pittance of unemployment insurance. . . . (Nelson, 1969)

The prevention theory of UI was widely circulated by one of Commons's students, John D. Andrews, who helped organize the American Association of Labor Legislation (AALL) in 1906 and became its permanent secretary. He and his wife, Irene Osgood Andrews, devoted themselves to disseminating information and ideas and providing technical help. Having achieved its first goal of Worker's Compensation laws, AALL turned its attention to UI. In 1915 Andrews expressed the prevention philosophy underlying the approach to problems of both injury and unemployment:

> Professor Commons and I . . . have thought first of prevention and second of relief in dealing with each form of social insurance in this country. (Nelson, 1969)

The emphasis of the Wisconsin school was on the employer, who was believed to have the power to regulate employment levels, rather than on the worker, who merely passively suffered the unemployment when it occurred.

The practical application of the prevention theory came through the development of experience or merit rating. According to this approach, the payroll tax on the employer varies with the amount of benefits his own employees receive, which in theory provides the incentive that Brandeis said was needed: the less unemployment in the firm, the smaller next year's UI tax bill would be. This idea came to be so firmly established that every UI bill submitted to the Wisconsin legislature from 1921 to 1932 provided for employer contributions only, and for strict accounting of each firm's contributions and claims.

The first UI bill was submitted in 1921 by Assemblyman Henry A. Huber. In drafting this bill, Commons and Wisconsin Federation of Labor leaders faced a choice between incorporating the English approach as refined in the Massachusetts bill of 1916, or the Wisconsin prevention approach as developed in the Wisconsin Worker's Compensation Act of 1911. The English approach focused on workers, whose needs were to be met by a program funded by contributions of employers, workers, and general revenues. The Wisconsin approach focused on employers, who alone would be taxed, and these experience-rated taxes would then provide employers with the incentive necessary to regulate their employment levels.

The Huber Bill embodied the Wisconsin approach with a few English elements not incompatible with the prevention philosophy. Provisions of the Huber Bill include the following:

1. Benefit levels were set at $1.75 a day for unemployed men and women of age eighteen or over; 75 cents a day for males and females between the ages of sixteen and eighteen.
2. The entire cost of the compensation was to be borne by the employer, who would be required to insure his liability with a mutual insurance company controlled by the State Compensation Control Board.
3. Any insurance company authorized to sell Workman's Compensation insurance was authorized to offer UI.
4. Employees were to keep records of previous work on employment cards.
5. Rail tickets were provided to workers needing to travel to other areas where there were jobs available.
6. The state was to be subdivided into employment districts for administrative purposes.

Variations of these provisions were reintroduced in every session of the Wisconsin legislature for ten years; in fact, these proposals were intensely debated around the country during the 1920s. Still, no state was ready or able to take the lead in establishing a UI program.

Commons used his influence to recruit businessmen to the cause of preventing unemployment through the Huber Bill. One important convert was Herbert Johnson of the Wisconsin-based Johnson Wax Company, who in 1923 explained his methods and ideas for combating unemployment. He argued that the Huber Bill would encourage industry to cooperate on a gigantic scale to tackle this very business irregularity which brings on unemployment. . . . It assists industry in correcting a most damaging condition to business. (Nelson, 1969)

Enactment in Wisconsin

The conservative politics of the 1920s killed all efforts to pass an unemployment insurance bill, and it was not until the Depression and the election of Phil La Follette as governor of Wisconsin that passage became a possibility.

Two different bills were introduced in the state legislature in 1931, the Nixon Bill and the Groves Bill. The Nixon Bill was similar to the Huber Bill but provided for a state fund and a flat employer contribution of 1.5 percent of payroll. Although organized labor on the national level opposed UI, the Wisconsin AFL was convinced by Professor Commons to support the idea, and labor favored the bill. However, it had a serious defect that hurt its political feasibility. Employers had made it very clear during the ten years of debate about the Huber-type bills that they would not support a compulsory bill. They were also concerned about any bill that would leave uncapped the extent of the financial commitment of each participating employer. The Nixon Bill failed both these tests. What employers wanted was a voluntary system with reserves held on a plant-by-plant basis.

The second bill was introduced by Harold Groves, a young University of Wisconsin professor of economics, who had been elected to the assembly after running on a platform advocating a UI program. Groves had given much thought to the objections to the Huber Bill and designed an approach to calm the employer community. He proposed establishing a single fund but with an accounting of each employer's contribution and of the claims by his employees. Workers would receive a maximum of ten weeks of benefits a year at a rate of 50 percent of their average weekly wage, not to exceed $10 in any week. Employers would each contribute 2 percent of payroll until the fund balance reached $55 for each employee; they would then contribute 1 percent of payroll until the fund balance reached $75 per employee. If there were no claims, then no additional taxes would be collected until the fund dropped below the $75 level. The stickler in this bill was that if an employer's account dropped below $55 per employee, the maximum benefit for his unemployed workers would drop $1 for each $5 that the fund dropped below the $55 minimum.

State AFL leaders favored the Nixon Bill until it became clear that the Groves Bill had the best chance of winning. The Groves Bill effectively placated the opposition. The final accommodation came when Governor La Follette announced he would accept a bill that would become compulsory only if private employer plans failed to reach one hundred and seventy-five thousand workers by June 1, 1933. With the limited reserves approach and a voluntary alternative left open, the bill's opponents were disarmed. The legislature enacted it and the governor signed it on January 28, 1932.

After enactment, Wisconsin employers began to see the legislation in a different light. They became enthusiastic backers of the Groves Act, especially when they saw neighboring states seriously considering more costly plans:

> Wisconsin employers rejoiced that they had gotten off so easily. . . . The first consideration of the employers was the lower cost of the Groves bill, but there was more to their friendlier outlook, once the pressure of the legislative campaign had passed, than the lower tax rate. They had always taken a nominal interest in the idea of business reform through unemployment prevention; in 1931–32 these concepts became familiar to every businessman in Wisconsin and throughout the nation. (Nelson, 1969)

Opponents of the Wisconsin approach were associated with a group in Ohio that favored pooled reserves, opposed experience rating, and favored tripartite financing. Its proponents included Paul Douglas, Isaac W. Rubinow, William M. Leiserson, Eveline Burns, and others, who were, in the eyes of the Wisconsin school, impractical purists who were overly concerned with UI from the workers' point of view rather than that of employers, whose political support was needed to get any bill enacted. The purists, on the other hand, argued that the purpose of UI should not be primarily to influence the performance of employers but to recompense the unemployed.

The chief spokesperson for the Wisconsin approach was Commons's student Paul Raushenbush. A young instructor at the University of Wisconsin, Raushenbush was a lobbyist for UI in Wisconsin and later became director of the Wisconsin UI Agency. For years he emphasized the state's role, the importance of reserve accounting by separate establishments, and experience rating. He deserves credit for the offset device first suggested by his father-in-law, Louis Brandeis. He rarely changed his opinion and was outspoken if anyone dared question his views. However, although he argued vociferously against federal benefit standards, he also pleaded with other states to improve their benefits so that states would have a creditable record and deserve their freedom from federal standards. He also worked hard to assure that benefits provided by the Wisconsin law were not too far out of line with those of other states.

The enactment of a UI law brought considerable prestige to Wisconsin. The state won the battle for action at the state level, for segregated employer accounts, and for 100 percent experience rating. These principles now had considerable visibility. As a result, the new Roosevelt administration looked to Wisconsin for support as it began to develop its ideas for Social Security legislation.

The Social Security Act

The need for unemployment insurance became more and more evident as the Depression put an ever-increasing number of jobs at risk and the unemployment rate moved upward. Voluntary unemployment plans—even the most carefully conceived ones—proved too fragile for the circumstances. Other states seemed paralyzed and unable or unwilling to follow Wisconsin's lead. In Congress, Senator Robert Wagner introduced a UI bill in 1934 with tax offset provisions and benefit standards, but it was delayed at President Roosevelt's request until a special committee of his cabinet, the Committee on Economic Security, could complete a study of the proposals. At the suggestion of Arthur Altmeyer, who was the assistant to Labor Secretary Frances Perkins and a former secretary of the Wisconsin Industrial Commission, the committee selected University of Wisconsin professor Edwin Witte as its executive director. Altmeyer and Witte agreed with Roosevelt and Perkins that UI required a cooperative federal-state approach. However, not all those who had helped bring about passage of the Wisconsin act agreed. Merrill Murray, for example, and even Arthur Altmeyer at a later period favored a fully national approach.

Roosevelt's Committee on Economic Security had three options for structuring unemployment insurance: a purely federal system that might be rejected on constitutional grounds; a tax offset plan such as in the Wagner-Lewis Bill; or a state-controlled system augmented with federal subsidies. Roosevelt expressed preference for a cooperative federal-state system, thereby limiting the committee's choices to the latter two alternatives. Although numerous forces, including the AFL, favored the subsidy approach, the committee decided on a tax offset or credit as in the Wagner-Lewis Bill, but with the fewest possible standards.

Altmeyer explained that the committee's decision was based on two grounds. First, since the tax offset plan, unlike the subsidy plan, would require states to enact their own laws, the committee suggested that there was a greater likelihood of achieving some progress should the Supreme Court strike down federal participation. Second, because difficult policy questions would have to be addressed in formulating benefit standards, the committee preferred to put maximum responsibility for writing them on the states. Among the policy questions were how to determine the amount and duration of weekly benefits, whether protection should be provided for seasonal and partial unemployment, whether employees should contribute, and whether employers should be experience rated. Altmeyer (1966) leaves the impression that although the question of constitutionality constrained the choices, the decision was heavily influenced by a practical desire not to endanger the bill's passage by loading it with two decades of controversy. In short, the strategy was to avoid substantive policy questions. The constitutionality question was later settled by the Supreme Court (which had been chastised by the president's threat to pack the court) in a decision that would have permitted any of the alternatives considered by the Economic Security Committee, including the purely federal approach. William Green of the AFL spoke in dour tones about the UI provisions of the Social Security Act:

> It leaves the states almost complete freedom of action in the adoption of unemployment insurance laws. There are no standards set for the state laws to follow. Each is free to determine the waiting period to be imposed, the amount of benefit which shall be paid, the length of time benefits should continue, the wage earnings group which shall be included in the act, the type of funds which shall be set up, and the manner in which such funds shall be administered. (Taft, 1957)

Many of the benefit and financing issues remain unresolved to this day.

Experience Rating for All States

No account of the origins of UI can overlook the tremendous influence of the Wisconsin school in promoting the use of experience rating. The issue was complex because it involved the question of pooled versus segregated funds, along with individual employer accounts and limited liability. It also involved the question of employee contributions. Witte (1962) has said that this issue was not fully resolved until the last meeting of the Committee on Economic Security. Several members of the committee opposed separate employer accounts such as those in the Wisconsin law. The committee finally agreed to permit the states to authorize employer accounts, provided that employers were required to contribute at least 1 percent of their payroll to a central pooled fund. This solution was recommended by Arthur Altmeyer.

The House Ways and Means Committee deleted the provision for state experience rating on the grounds that it was inconsistent with the objective of putting the states at an equal competitive advantage in attracting industry. In the Senate, however, an amendment was offered by Wisconsin senator Bob La Follette, Jr., permitting states to receive the additional credit. In the same amendment, the Senate abolished the 1 percent minimum tax rate, thereby permitting the state portion of the tax to go to zero for the most favored employers if the state so desired.

The La Follette Amendment offered in conference was reportedly drafted in part by Paul Raushenbush. It permitted reduced rates only for the experience of the individual employer or firm and thereby blocked the states from taking any other approach. It prohibited reduced rates for other kinds of experience, such as uniform reduction for all employers equally or by industry classification. The much-lauded principle of the states' right to experiment, although touted for benefit levels, was prohibited by the La Follette Amendment for the financing of UI. It was in this way that the Wisconsin school imposed single-employer experience rating on all the other states.

The attractiveness of experience rating to many kinds of employers resulted in all states having one or another variation, but all in terms that applied to the single firm. The surveillance of this standard has occasioned much of the conflict between federal and state officials in the administration of the program.

In succeeding years, the justifications for experience rating have shifted. As the ideas of scientific management and the reform of capitalism by regularizing employment levels become quaint memories, the proponents of experience rating gradually altered their rationale to encompass the beneficial effects of an economically efficient allocation of costs, and employer interest and involvement in claims administration (Becker, 1972). Most of the opponents of the La Follette Amendment, if they are still alive, have become resigned to the fact that not much can be done about it now. The more important concern is solvency.

Two other issues were overlooked in consideration of the Social Security Act: employee benefit levels and employee contributions. In a retrospective mood, Altmeyer acknowledged his mistakes during the formative years of unemployment insurance:

> I think the present unemployment insurance system would have been much more adequate in compensating for wage loss if the administration had made different recommendations in 1935 and 1939, which it could have done without altering the fundamental federal-state character, without increasing the danger of unconstitutionality and with fair likelihood that its recommendations would have been accepted by Congress. . . . In 1935 the Benefit Advisory Council of the Department of Commerce recommended that there be employee contributions [in UI]. . . . So did a considerable minority of the advisory council of the Committee on Economic Security. . . . If employee contributions had been included in the 1935 bill, I believe that the adverse effects of experience rating in keeping benefits low would have been far less. . . . In retrospect, I believe that the establishment of the principle of minimum benefit standards, regardless of the level of the initial standards, would have led to incorporation of far more adequate standards in the federal law than now exist in most states. And of course, the absence of such standards has resulted in average contribution rates far below 2.7 percent in practically all the states. (Altmeyer, 1966)

AFL-CIO president George Meany, during a conversation the author had with him in 1960, recalled the time in 1936 when, as an officer of the AFL in New York, he was confronted with the unemployment insurance issue. He said that in hindsight, unions may have made a mistake in not supporting employee contributions. He now thought employee contributions might have given labor more influence on policy. At the time, however, nobody really knew much about the subject, and employee contributions seemed to constitute a pay reduction in exchange for an unknown, elusive, and difficult to understand kind of protection.

The States' Response to the Social Security Act

The states responded quickly to the passage of the Social Security Act. Within two years every state had enacted its own legislation. The Social Security Board sent out a couple of draft bills that many states used as a model. The act permitted pooled funding with separate bookkeeping for the transactions of individual employers. Most states took this approach. A second approach permitted the benefit fund to be organized into separate employer reserves. In its purest form, no pooling occurred; this amounted to self-insurance for each firm, with liability limited to that firm's reserve, as in Wisconsin's Groves Bill. Only a few states adopted the employer reserve system, and most of those, including Wisconsin, soon added a pooling element in the form of a re-insurance fund to assure that workers would not be denied benefits to which they were entitled simply because their employer's reserves were exhausted. A third approach allowed states to set up guaranteed employment accounts for individual employers, but this method was never used. Because of the influence of the Wisconsin school and the La Follette amendment, three-quarters of the states immediately adopted some form of experience rating, with the others following in due course.

The states did not all adhere to the views of the Social Security Board. For example, some decided to go beyond the minimum coverage requirement. In addition, nine states adopted employee contributions.

Having started much earlier, Wisconsin on August 17, 1936, became the first state to pay unemployment benefits. Other states came along in 1937 and 1938. Many claims were paid in the recession of 1938.

The Altered Mission

During the early years of the UI program state governments believed with increasing fervor that the 2.7 percent tax would raise more revenues than they needed to finance benefits. Labor began to pressure the states to increase benefits, particularly the duration of benefits, and employers asked for lower tax schedules. This pattern of liberalizing benefits and at the same time reducing tax rates become commonplace due to the huge reserves accumulated during the Second World War. The process of "something for everybody" continued until about 1958–60, when most of the reserves were gone. As a result, in the late 1970s and early 1980s states had to borrow massive amounts from the federal government. Many states, including Wisconsin, still do not have an explicit policy establishing or maintaining reserve levels.

UI programs in the 1930s usually provided up to sixteen weeks of benefits if a worker could not find a job in that time. The actuaries estimated that sixteen weeks was the limit that could be handled by a 3 percent payroll tax. Yet in 1942 the Social Security Board recommended an increase to twenty weeks. Two years later the director of the War Mobilization Board, anticipating high unemployment rates after World War II, recommended a uniform duration of twenty-six weeks, which became a national objective. Wisconsin eventually raised its duration of benefits to thirty-four weeks.

After a couple of interventions by the federal government because larger numbers of covered workers exhausted their benefits in 1958 and again in 1963, the states and federal authorities developed a permanent extended benefit plan for the long-term unemployed (beyond twenty-six weeks). This legislation was enacted by Congress in 1971. It provided for additional weeks of benefits half again as long as what each state provided but no more than thirty-nine weeks, and only when the rate of unemployment reached specified levels. The state and federal governments shared the cost of the extensions fifty-fifty. This was significant because it marked the first time the federal government contributed to financing benefits in a permanent program.

In 1972 and 1976, the federal government also extended benefits further by emergency or supplemental benefits paid for up to fifty-two weeks and in some cases even up to sixty-five weeks. These additional benefits were financed completely from federal general revenues.

The idea of extending UI benefits beyond the normal periods had not been considered in setting up the UI system. In the absence of other programs to take over the support of the unemployed, Congress solved its political problem during recessions by simply extending benefits.

Other Changes, 1936 to Present

A variety of important changes have occurred since 1936. One of the most important is in the coverage of UI. The objective has been to carry through on the original design, which was to offer universal coverage. The Committee on Economic Security wanted to cover nearly all wage and salary workers, but Congress opted instead for limited coverage. By 1976, however, approximately 95 percent of workers in wage and salary employment were protected. The remaining gaps are agricultural workers and household employees.

The second change came in response to public criticism of the disqualification provisions, which set the ground rules for eligibility and relationship to the labor market. In general the provisions covering those who quit or are discharged for cause have been stiffened considerably in conception, administration, and the length of time during which penalties apply.

A third change has been in the composition of the labor force, particularly the large increase in the number of working women and part-time workers. Multi-earner families with one earner unemployed do not suffer as much as families with a single wage earner who is unemployed. This has been used to justify counting benefits as income for income tax payable by higher-earning families.

Fourth, changes have occurred because of shifting features in the economic climate in which unemployment insurance functions, particularly the movement in average wages and salaries. Rising earnings levels have brought frequent adjustments in the maximum weekly benefit amounts, and also in the base-year earnings requirements. Rarely, however, has this updating kept pace with wage movements, particularly during inflationary periods. The introduction of the flexible or indexed maximum in 1959 was a partial solution to the problem, but the larger states have not yet enacted it. In 1983, Wisconsin repealed its sliding maximum and froze the maximum at $195, with the result that an increasing number of unemployed workers received the maximum while a decreasing number received benefits equal to half their weekly wage loss. In Wisconsin, $195 was 66.6 percent of average wages in 1983, but in 1987 represented only 57 percent.

Net Effects of Changes

The interplay of rising wage levels and amendments has resulted in some liberalization of benefits but at uneven rates. It also altered the mix of benefit features.

In the years 1938 to 1951 the weekly benefit amounts declined relative to wage levels and since then have improved only slightly. As a consequence, weekly benefits have not yet received the 50 percent wage replacement rate they were pegged at in the beginning. From 1941 until 1960 the average potential duration of benefits improved rapidly; since then the emphasis has been on temporary extensions, and the regular duration provisions have been liberalized only slightly.

The combined result of changes in the weekly benefit rate and the regular duration provisions (entitlement) can be seen in three stages, a general decline until about 1942, a gradual increase until 1960, and stability since then. In the late 1950s, however, states began to tighten up eligibility and disqualification provisions and their administration.

The net effect of these changes and trade-offs has been twofold:

1. To increase the protection of benefits by 20 to 40 percent, depending on whether the measure is the median state (unweighted by size) or the program mean of all states weighted by covered population. ("Protection" is used here in the sense of total entitlement for an average claimant for a given level of insured unemployment.)
2. To increase the range of differences in protection among the states compared with each other. Some states offer only half the protection offered by the most liberal states (Blaustein, 1980; Munts, 1976; Elterich and Graham, 1975).

These differences in protection are fairly persistent. A state that is high in protection is likely to stay that way, whereas a state that is low will likely remain so. Using average entitlement as a measure (average replacement rate times average potential duration) we know that between 1947 and 1983, Maryland and Utah were at the top, while others prominently near the top — at least since 1966 — were the District of Columbia, Wisconsin, Rhode Island, New Hampshire, and North Dakota.

On the other hand, near the bottom during the same period were Virginia, Texas, Alabama, Louisiana, Georgia, West Virginia, Florida, Indiana, Oklahoma, and Alaska. There is definite persistence in the ranking of states by their UI performance.

Benefit Performance in Wisconsin

A comparison of Wisconsin's benefit performance with that of other states shows that although Wisconsin does not rank first in every respect (see Table 12.1), the most inclusive measures place the state in the top rung (before the 1983 changes).

Table 12.1. Numerical Rank of Wisconsin among the States on Various Benefit Measures, 1966 and 1983

	1966	1983
1. Average weekly benefits/average weekly wage	6th	5th
2. Maximum weekly benefit/average weekly wage	9th	10th
3. Average potential duration	2nd	4th
4. Average potential benefit/average weekly wage (row 1 × row 3)	1st	3rd

How expensive is the Wisconsin UI program compared with those of other states? Table 12.2 shows the cost rate for various periods. The conclusion to be drawn is that the long-range cost of UI in Wisconsin is very close to the average for all states. During 1979–83 the Wisconsin rate was appreciably above the average, but it was a long way from being the most costly. Finally, the longest term (1943–83) shows Wisconsin just above the median.

Table 12.2. Cost Rate Averages, Selected States, 1940–1983 (ratio of benefits to total covered wages)

State	1940–78	1979–83	1940–83
Rhode Island (high state)	1.80	2.33	1.85
Wisconsin	1.20	1.71	1.26
Median, all states	1.20	1.32	1.21
Texas (low state)	0.50	0.52	0.50

Source: *Handbook of Unemployment Insurance Financial Data, 1938–1983.*
Note: These cost ratios do not include extended benefits.

Considering that benefits in Wisconsin have been relatively high, why then are the costs about average among the states? The answer is in part that Wisconsin is now more vulnerable to nationwide recessions than it used to be. Another part of the explanation is that the state may be employing some trade-offs that make its program less costly than the benefit dimensions would suggest. For example, Wisconsin may be a harder state in which to qualify for benefits and a liberal state once a claimant has passed through eligibility screens. Wisconsin shows, relative to other states, more emphasis on high benefit levels along with more exclusiveness on eligibility and qualifications (see Elterich and Graham, 1975).

Speculation on the Next Fifty Years

The political history of Wisconsin is studded with innovations in social and labor legislation. Behind these is the backdrop of independence and confidence that constituted the progressive movement headed by Robert La Follette.

In unemployment insurance, the Wisconsin school experimented for ten years before its proponents found the formula for a bill that could be enacted. It is probably true that proponents could have waited without making so many political concessions and become subject to the tax offset device which prodded other states into enactment in 1936–37. However, the fact that Wisconsin did enact a UI program earlier had an important demonstration effect, showing the nation that it could be done. The leadership from Wisconsin aided passage of the Social Security Act.

Wisconsin misused its power, however, in the La Follette Amendment, which imposed one narrow kind of experience rating on all the other states. This action clearly stamped unemployment insurance in this country as "made in the USA." As it worked out, experience rating has done serious harm to the financial solvency of the system.

In the fifty years since the inception of the unemployment insurance system, Wisconsin has done rather well compared with other states in offering a good benefit package at a reasonable cost. It risks problems in the future, however, because of the absence of a reserve policy.

Even if the Bush administration should follow through with devolution, Wisconsin will continue to offer a good program. But what will happen to the laggard states that have fallen far behind? Interstate differences are already severe and inequitable, and, without a federal partner, they may get worse. The quality of administration will decline as the more rural states, where subsidy is needed and now provided, will have to finance all their own administrative costs.

Wisconsin has earned respect among the states for its program, and it can provide leadership to keep the federal-state partnership alive and well. A national policy of devolution will influence Wisconsin directly and indirectly by what happens in other states. Wisconsin has always asserted its interest in the big picture and may again have an opportunity to help shape it. The times are a-changing, but this is no reason for the state to give up its heritage of concern for those dependent on wages and salaries, wherever they may be.

REFERENCES

Altmeyer, Arthur J. 1966. *The Formative Years of Social Security.* Madison: University of Wisconsin Press.

Becker, Joseph. 1972. *Experience Rating in Unemployment Insurance.* Baltimore: Johns Hopkins University Press.

Blaustein, Saul J. 1980. "Diverse Treatment of Claimants by States." In *Unemployment Compensation Studies and Research.* Vol. 1. Washington, D.C.: National Council on Unemployment Compensation. Pp. 187–263.

Bulletin of the Proceedings of the Wisconsin Legislature. 1921.

Elterich, Joachim, and Linda Graham. 1975. *Interstate Analysis of Unemployment Insurance Provisions and Proposed Changes.* Washington, D.C.: U.S. Department of Labor, Manpower Administration.

Epstein, Abraham. 1938. *Insecurity: A Challenge to America.* New York: Random House.

Haber, William, and Merrill Murray. 1966. *Unemployment Insurance in the American Economy.* Homestead, Ill.: Richard D. Irwin.

Handbook of Unemployment Insurance Financial Data, 1938–1983. N.d. Washington, D.C.: U.S. Department of Labor, Employment and Training Administration.

Lubove, Roy. 1968. *The Struggle for Social Security*. Cambridge: Harvard University Press.

Munts, Raymond. 1976. "Policy Development in Unemployment Insurance." In *Federal Policies and Workers' Status Since the Thirties*. Madison: Industrial Relations Research Association.

Nelson, Daniel. 1969. *Unemployment Insurance: The American Experience, 1915–1935*. Madison: University of Wisconsin Press.

Raushenbush, Paul, and Elizabeth Brandeis Raushenbush. 1979. *Our "UC" Story 1930–1967*. Privately published, Madison.

Rubinow, Isaac M. 1913. *Social Insurance*. New York: Henry Holt.

Rimlinger, Gaston V. 1968. *Princeton Symposium on the American Systems, Social Insurance*. New York: McGraw-Hill. P. 215.

Taft, Philip. 1957. *The AFL in the Time of Gompers*. New York: Harper and Row.

Webb, Beatrice. 1926. *My Apprenticeship*. London: Longman Green.

Witte, Edwin E. 1962. *The Development of the Social Security Act*. Madison: University of Wisconsin Press.

13

The Challenge in Unemployment Compensation: The Wisconsin Case

CLIFFORD J. MILLER

Introduction

The UC program is like many areas of public policy today—it is studded with issues which are both controversial and complex. Unavoidably, much of the material presented in this paper involves contentious recent developments and touchy issues which have not yet been resolved. Moreover, because of the technical nature of some of these issues, the paper makes for rather difficult reading in places. In this regard, I hope that the reader will agree with a couple of propositions: first, that it's not a good principle of public policy to avoid issues because they are difficult or controversial; second, that the surest way to convert a difficult problem into an unmanageable one is to ignore it.

The first section of the paper provides background on the recent problems in Wisconsin's unemployment compensation system and summarizes the major changes—legislative and other—which have taken place between 1983 and 1985. Sections 2 through 7 then deal with a broad set of issues involving the UC program. Some of these are new issues; others are old ones that must now be considered in a new (and radically different) setting. The final section presents a summary and some recommendations.

1. The Financial Woes of the Wisconsin UC System

Beginning with Connecticut in March 1972, twenty-five states found it necessary during the 1970s to borrow from the federal government in order to continue paying unemployment compensation benefits. During the 1980s, fifteen of those states borrowed again, and fifteen additional states (including Wisconsin) borrowed for the first time. Overall, forty states have borrowed at one time or another. The total borrowing amounted to $25.8 billion, with repayments of $19.6 billion and $6.2 billion in outstanding loans as of October 31, 1985. Wisconsin has borrowed $940 million and repaid $612 million, leaving some $328 million outstanding in December 1985.

Thus, the matters discussed in this paper are by no means peculiar to Wisconsin: the financial problems of the UC system; the strenuous efforts needed to resolve these problems; and the tangle of economic, political, bureaucratic, and legislative undergrowth which confronted those who became engaged in these efforts. This is an account of events in Wisconsin, but there are many parallels in other states.

In February 1982, Wisconsin's UC fund was exhausted and borrowing became necessary for the first time in the fifty-year history of the program. It had been known for some time that the system was in deep financial trouble, but Wisconsin's policymakers were unable to take action. Financial disaster arrived with a bang. In 1982, it was necessary to borrow over $400 million; about 70 cents of every benefit dollar was being covered by federal borrowing. It was clear, moreover, that the program's problems were not merely financial, and that an economic recovery—even one of miraculous proportions—would not cure the ills of the system.

Early in 1983, newly elected Governor Earl created a special panel to deal with this problem. The panel was chaired by the secretary of the Department of Industry, Labor and Human Relations and included the four leaders of the Wisconsin legislature. This panel did three things. First, it produced a bill which provided for sharp tax increases and benefit cutbacks to stem the flow of red ink. Second, with some augmented membership, the group made a thorough study over several months of the origins of the UC problem. And, third, the group provided for a complete restructuring of the UC policy machinery.

A reconstituted Unemployment Compensation Advisory Council was appointed and began extensive work in the summer of 1984, leading to the passage of major legislation in May 1985. This provided for major tax changes (state tax increases to avoid equivalent increases in the federal payroll tax, or FUTA) and laid the groundwork for future major revisions of the structure of UC benefits in Wisconsin. These restructuring activities are now well under way.

The author participated in these various efforts. This is an account of some of the major UC program and financing issues which have been explored and debated in Wisconsin over the past few years, and of some of the major changes which have taken place.

How the Problem Developed

The origins of the unemployment compensation financing problem in Wisconsin involves a blend of economic trends, overcommitment, and institutional failure.

Economic Trends. In dealing with the financing problems of Wisconsin's UC program, one frequently encounters the idea that the system worked well for nearly half a century, and that the problems were caused by the twin recessions of the early 1980s. In these terms, the problems of the UC system were viewed as transitory, related entirely to highly unusual economic conditions which, we could expect, would soon pass. These attitudes are changing, and there is an increasing awareness that our problems go a good deal deeper than that.

It is suggested in this paper that we view the matter in these terms: that the UC system indeed worked fairly well for a long time, but only when unemployment was at abnormally low levels, from the late 1940s through the 1950s and 1960s. Since the early 1970s the UC system has consistently been in trouble.

A bit of background is important here. From 1932 through 1945, the UC program simply wasn't much of a factor. The UC system (the nation's first) began in Wisconsin in January 1932, and the first benefit check wasn't written until August 1936, some four and a half years later. The highest yearly level of benefit spending in Wisconsin during the Great Depression of the 1930s was $3.6 million in 1939, scarcely a major amount in the context of the massive levels of unemployment of that time. In the early 1940s, of course, unemployment nearly disappeared because of the war.

For the next quarter century, roughly from 1946 through 1970, unemployment rates were very low and the UC system did work smoothly and well. During the 1970s and 1980s, unemployment has been much higher than during those halcyon years after the Second World War, and the UC system has been consistently in trouble.

As for unemployment levels, from 1954 through 1970 (seventeen years, inclusive) the total unemployment rate in Wisconsin averaged 3.7 percent. The rate reached 5 percent only twice: in 1958 (5.1 percent) and in 1961 (5.0 percent).

The figures changed radically during the 1970s and 1980s. From 1971 through 1979 unemployment averaged 4.9 percent, and for 1980–85 the average was 8.4 percent. Unemployment is estimated at 8.0 percent or higher for 1986 and the next several years.

Thus, each year we experience unemployment rates which are much higher than the highest rates reached during the 1950s and 1960s, and we may expect this condition to continue. Average rates are projected to be more than double those of the 1950s and 1960s.

As unemployment levels rose sharply in the 1970s, Wisconsin's UC program began encountering major financial troubles. The cash balance dropped to $162 million in 1975, equivalent to about six months of benefit spending—the lowest relative level by far since the program's beginnings. The UC Advisory Council deadlocked, and legislation was enacted in 1976 only when the governor acted to resolve the deadlock—and that legislation provided only temporary relief while ensuring even more serious problems for the future. This set the stage for the crisis of the early 1980s, which will be discussed presently.

It needs to be recognized, then, that we do not have a record of coping successfully with levels of unemployment such as we are now experiencing or can reasonably expect for the future. That's the economic ingredient of our UC financing problem.

Overcommitment. As economic problems were deepening, Wisconsin's policymakers were at work during the 1960s and 1970s increasing the commitments of the UC system. This overcommitment extended to both workers and employers. For workers, Wisconsin law provided one of the most generous UC packages in the country. For employers, Wisconsin's UC taxing provisions were among the nation's most lenient. As a rough measure, it could be said that Wisconsin in the early 1980s ranked about sixth nationally in benefit costs and about thirtieth in the degree of its tax effort.

The benefit pattern was expanded in stages. Around 1960, regular benefits were increased from twenty-six to thirty-four weeks, almost the highest in the country, and the maximum benefit payment was indexed to the trend in state average wages, increasing twice each year. From 1976 (the year of the last tax increase passed before 1983) to 1982, when UC borrowing began, the average UC benefit check increased by 60 percent.

In 1971, the multiplier for calculating the maximum benefit was increased from 52.5 percent of the state average wage to 66.67 percent, and the quit provision was considerably relaxed. Prior to 1971, a worker who quit a job without good cause could draw no benefits based on work for that employer. This was changed in 1971 to permit drawing such benefits after requalifying with at least four weeks of work with at least twenty hours each week. In 1976, this was further modified to require four weeks of work (not necessarily in employment subject to a UC law) with total earnings of $200—almost the most-lenient quit provision in the country.

In 1974, the number of weeks required to qualify was dropped from eighteen to fifteen; in 1976, the requirement for a waiting week was dropped.

While the benefit load was growing, the tax structure that had to bear the load—never very robust—was being progressively weakened. From 1967 to 1976, Wisconsin law included a provision which provided for the imposition of a special tax (calculated by the state agency) sufficient to prevent the fund balance from falling below a specified level. This provision was dropped in 1976—paradoxically enough, to "give something to business" in return for dropping the waiting week in accord with the position of certain labor groups. Beginning in 1980 and continuing through 1983, Wisconsin law required no tax (a "zero rate") of the most stable employers. Beginning in 1982, Wisconsin ceased charging the state share of extended benefits to employer accounts, thus causing a further drain on the fund.

Wisconsin's law provided that employers could write off any negative balances in excess of 10 percent of taxable payroll. From 1980 through 1983, about $500 million in negative balances was thus written off—in effect, forgiven. Wisconsin's top tax rate (7.4 percent of $6,000, or $444 per employee) would cover just over two benefit checks per employee per year. Even if all employers in the state had paid the top tax rate on their entire payroll, tax receipts would have been insufficient to cover benefits in 1982. Only 7 percent of the state's payrolls were taxed at the top rate, and 20 percent were not taxed at all. Employers could "buy" lower tax rates by making "voluntary contributions," increasing their balances by exactly enough to qualify for a lower tax rate (sometimes as much as ten brackets lower than the rate which would otherwise have applied). An employer's tax could not be more than 1 percent higher than the rate paid in the preceding year. These three provisions—write-offs, voluntary contributions, and the rate increase limiter—interacted in such a way as to produce some garish results. One firm, for example, ran up $56 million in benefit charges, paid $6 million in taxes without ever paying the top rate, and wrote off the remainder.

Institutional Failure. As these problems were developing, Wisconsin government simply failed, for a good many years, to deal with them effectively. Since the 1930s, UC matters in Wisconsin had been the exclusive province of the UC Advisory Council. By the 1970s, the pattern was simplicity itself: what the council approved was enacted into law, and what the council did not approve was not enacted. With one limited exception (in 1976), governors, legislatures, department heads, and state agencies gave the UC area a wide berth—the delegation to the council was absolute. The council consisted of ten members, five representing labor and five employers. In effect, each member had a veto.

It became apparent in the late 1970s, and especially in 1980 and thereafter, that Wisconsin's UC program was in very deep financial trouble. The employer representatives on the council indicated that they were willing to support major tax increases, but only if there were also extensive cutbacks in benefits in areas in which they believed Wisconsin's benefit package was far out of line. The labor representatives refused to accept any benefit reductions. The council deadlocked on this point, and continued in deadlock for over two years, until the governor assigned the problem to a special panel in March 1983.

Two points should be emphasized here. First, the UC problem had become (in the context of a middle-sized state such as Wisconsin) a massive one. By 1982 and early 1983, state UC taxes were covering just 30 percent of benefits; the other 70 percent had to be borrowed. The magnitude of the problem is suggested by the fix that ultimately was undertaken: state UC taxes have more than doubled, and benefits were cut by about 20 percent. Second, the council was, after all, a part-time, uncompensated advisory body, not a part of the formal structure of government. It is not surprising that it could not handle the problem. It is surprising, though, that through 1982 the governor, the legislature, and the state executive agencies were essentially silent and inactive.

2. The Federal Pattern and Wisconsin's Arithmetic

The Federal Pattern

As Wisconsin's political leaders began to pay serious attention to the UC problem around the beginning of 1983, two sets of questions assumed great importance. The first of these involved gaining an understanding of the exact terms of the federal loans, especially with respect to taxes and interest and the options available to borrower states; these questions are discussed in the paragraphs which follow. The second set of questions was internal to Wisconsin and involved, basically, the political arithmetic of the UC program in Wisconsin; this is covered in the next section.

The heart of the problem involves the benefit payments and tax collections marked with an asterisk in Table 13.1. All other benefit payments are covered, dollar for dollar, by reimbursements, mostly from the federal government, as shown. The bulk of the benefits, though, must be covered by state UC taxes or by borrowing. Since tax collections have not been sufficient, substantial borrowing has been necessary.

Federal Guidelines and State Discretion. The UC program is a combined federal-state program, involving, as shown in Table 13.1, a mixture of state and federal funds. The program operates in the context of federal guidelines of various degrees of rigor and specificity, with broad areas of

Table 13.1. UC Programs and Their Financing, 1981–85

	($ millions)				
	1981	1982	1983	1984	1985
Regular benefits, private sector	435	626	488	347	408
State share extended benefits, private sector	17	62	31	–	–
Subtotal, supported by state UC tax or borrowing*	452	688	519	347	408
Federal share extended benefits	17	47	23	1	–
Federal supplemental compensation	–	28	159	58	18
Other federal programs	70	18	18	12	10
Reimbursable (state and local governments, nonprofits)	19	25	23	20	17
Total benefit payments	558	806	742	438	453
State UC tax collections*	215	221	301	562	576
Federal reimbursements	87	93	200	70	28
Other reimbursements	19	25	23	20	17
Total collections	321	339	524	652	621
Surplus or deficit (–), annual*	–237	–467	–218	+214	+168
Fund balance, net, 12/31*	49	–416	–637	–419	–251

417

state discretion. Within the federal guidelines, the states are allowed a great deal of latitude in key areas such as qualification for UC benefits, the weekly benefit rate, duration of benefit payments, treatment of such items as voluntary quits, and so forth. By adopting a very austere approach in these discretionary areas, Wisconsin could develop a UC program which would cost, say, $100 million a year. By adopting a much more liberal approach, benefit outlays of perhaps $1 billion a year could result. Both programs would meet all federal guidelines. This is offered simply to illustrate, and to underline, the point that the discretionary areas left to the states are very broad indeed.

The Federal Pattern with Respect to Loan Repayment. By the spring of 1983, the federal pattern with respect to UC program loans was about as follows: first, that all loans after March 31, 1982, would bear interest; second, that unless a state reduced its debt in accordance with a certain schedule, an additional (and progressively rising) federal payroll (FUTA) tax would be levied in the state; third, that states could sharply reduce interest costs and avoid added FUTA taxes by acting to get their own house in order; and, fourth, that these provisions would be enforced—there would be no pattern of forgiveness or sunsetting.

For Wisconsin, the consequences of inaction were stark. Interest payments would have been over $40 million for 1983 and $100 million for 1984, and would have reached $200 million annually by about 1987. The added FUTA tax would have been $31 million for 1984 payrolls, $62 million for 1985, and so on, reaching $186 million for 1989—and rising thereafter if necessary. Putting it together, added FUTA taxes and interest charges would have reached about $300 million a year by 1987 and $500 million by 1989. The minimization of these added federal charges (interest and FUTA) became the pacing element in the development of Wisconsin's 1983 legislation. The objective was to lower these costs for the years 1983–88 cumulative by $1 billion. The mix of carrot and stick in the federal pattern provided a very strong inducement for states to act to get their UC finances in order.

The Road Not Taken. The bulk of this paper deals with the course which Wisconsin has followed since 1983: a difficult and painful course which has involved sharp reductions in UC benefits, substantial increases in UC taxes, a thorough (and often embarrassing) public airing of problems, the dismantling of the prior policy structure, and the development of a new one. In addition to considering what has actually occurred, though, it is instructive to pause for a time and to consider what hasn't happened: the road not taken.

Wisconsin did not have to enact UC legislation in 1983 or thereafter. Wisconsin's UC program could have gone on as it was for a few more

years. Had this course been chosen, several different things would have
occurred.

First, it would not have been necessary, for a few years at least, to enact
cutbacks in UC benefits. Under the old law, for example, benefit payments
in 1985 would have been about $100 million higher than they actually
were.

Second, it would not have been necessary to raise state UC taxes. Again,
under the old law, state UC tax payments would have been about $280
million lower in 1985 than they were.

Third, though, the debt would have been much greater: over $1 billion
at the end of 1985, instead of $328 million.

Fourth, as a consequence, the state's employers would have had to pay
$100 million in interest charges (instead of $20 million) in 1985, and $61
million (instead of zero) in added FUTA taxes.

Fifth, these added charges would have continued to soar, reaching $300
million a year by 1987, $500 million a year by 1989, and crossing the
$1 billion mark annually sometime in the 1990s. Meanwhile, the debt
would continue to grow, probably stabilizing at about the $3 billion mark
sometime in the 1990s.

Under this course, as noted, Wisconsin legislation could have been
deferred for a few more years.

Much higher benefit levels could have been paid, for a while at least.
Interest assessments and increased federal payroll taxes, both levied on
Wisconsin employers, would have covered these costs without state legislation. The rising payments to the federal government would have been
gradual. In political terms, it would have been difficult to relate these rising
payments to failures in Madison. After all, the amounts would be assessed
on federal tax forms.

Thoughts along these lines obviously occurred to policymakers in many
states. In January 1985, for example, added FUTA taxes were levied on
payrolls in every state bordering Wisconsin, and in every UC borrower
state nationally except for Wisconsin and Colorado. As noted, Wisconsin has taken the painful steps necessary to avoid the added FUTA tax
every year so far, and plans to continue doing so. Other states (except
for once each in Michigan and Colorado) have generally not managed this,
and over $4 billion in added FUTA taxes have been levied in these states.

Wisconsin resisted this temptation, for reasons which indicate that the
Wisconsin idea is still very much alive, together with the political courage
which gives it meaning. Had Wisconsin's political leaders done what those
elsewhere did—allowed deadlocks to develop, found excuses to delay—
then the added federal taxes and assessments would have been levied, and
the chance to reform the system would have been lost. If Wisconsin had

let 1983 go by without acting, the corrective measures required would have grown greater each year—and they would have been imposed at a time when sharp federal increases were already taking effect. We would probably have drifted into a situation in which a very substantial and growing benefit package would be financed primarily by a flat FUTA tax levied in Washington rather than by an experience-rated state tax levied in Madison.

Wisconsin's Arithmetic

Millions in Madison. In the transition from a federal to a Wisconsin perspective, it is necessary first to understand that hundreds of millions are, in Wisconsin, immense amounts of money. In 1979, for example, Madison's newspapers exposed abuses by state legislators. One who got a great deal of attention in the press had run up $7.60 for personal phone calls at state expense.

Which Employers Pay? A second aspect of Wisconsin arithmetic involves the basic financial relationships within the UC system. The highest UC tax that a firm could pay in 1983 was $518 per employee (7.4 percent of $7,000). The top UC benefit check was $196 a week. Under the old law, then, a firm's UC tax would cover (on the average) less than three weekly benefit checks per employee per year. If a firm's layoff experience was greater than that, the top UC tax wouldn't cover the resultant benefits. The problem was that the preponderance of UC benefit payments involved precisely such firms. In relatively prosperous 1978–79, 67 percent of Wisconsin's UC benefit payments involved firms whose employees were drawing an average of more than three benefit checks a year. In years of high unemployment (as in the period 1980–83), 82 percent of benefit payments were in this category.

Thus, the great preponderance of Wisconsin's UC benefit payments could not be recovered from the employers who had laid off claimants. The system's solvency tax, which was supposed to cover this gap, proved far from adequate. In 1982, when ineffectively charged benefits amounted to over $400 million, the solvency tax yield was $57 million. About one-fourth of state payrolls, it will be recalled, were not taxed at all.

Makeup of the Employer Community. The third aspect of Wisconsin's UC arithmetic involves the makeup of the state's employer community. Table 13.2 presents data for 97,617 firms, which is virtually the entire number of private firms subject to the state UC law. These data are broken down into the four categories, based on the unemployment experience of firms, presented in Table 13.3.

Note that 66,387 firms with 769,844 employees have few layoffs. This represents about 68 percent of the firms, and 51 percent of total employ-

Table 13.2. The Wisconsin UC Program: Key Data by Industry Group

	1984		Average per Employee per Year, 1984		Surplus or Deficit ($ millions)		Write-offs, 1980–83 ($ millions)
	Number of Firms	Employment	Benefits	Taxes	1980–83	1984	
Very low unemployment							
Construction	1,292	7,788	$ 5	$185	$ -1.1	$ 1.4	$ 0.1
Manufacturing	2,700	46,165	17	238	6.8	10.2	—
Subtotal	3,992	53,953	15	230	5.7	11.6	0.1
Other industries	50,042	399,633	10	119	62.6	43.4	—
Total	54,034	453,586	11	132	68.3	55.0	0.1
Low unemployment							
Construction	583	2,894	95	302	0.2	0.6	—
Manufacturing	998	51,953	62	268	5.5	10.7	—
Subtotal	1,581	54,847	64	270	5.7	11.3	—
Other industries	10,772	261,411	75	188	23.0	29.6	0.1
Total	12,353	316,258	73	202	28.6	40.9	0.2
Cycle-sensitive firms							
Construction	4,344	35,064	845	835	-41.3	-0.3	39.0
Manufacturing	4,000	393,899	324	666	-411.6	134.5	176.4
Subtotal	8,344	428,963	367	680	-452.9	134.1	215.4
Other industries	12,302	229,092	281	461	-80.4	41.2	33.6
Total	20,646	658,055	337	603	-533.3	175.4	249.0
Persistent high unemployment							
Construction	3,808	22,032	2,252	920	-278.5	-29.4	167.9
Manufacturing	694	10,002	1,463	677	-276.1	-7.9	56.6
Subtotal	4,502	32,034	2,006	844	-554.5	-37.2	224.6
Other industries	6,082	47,980	690	335	-178.4	-17.0	55.2
Total	10,584	80,014	1,217	539	-732.9	-54.2	279.7
Wisconsin total							
Construction	10,027	67,778	1,174	765	-320.6	-27.7	207.0
Manufacturing	8,392	502,019	292	585	-675.4	147.5	233.0
Subtotal	18,419	569,797	397	607	-996.0	119.8	440.0
Other industries	79,198	938,116	129	233	-173.3	97.2	89.0
Total	97,617	1,507,913	230	374	-1,169.3	217.0	529.0

Table 13.3. Benefit Payments by Wisconsin Firms for 1984

Firm Category	Number of Firms	Employment	Average UC Benefit Payments per Employee
Very low unemployment	54,034	453,586	$ 11
Low unemployment	12,353	316,258	73
Subtotal	66,387 (68%)	769,844 (51%)	36
Cycle-sensitive firms	20,646	658,055	337
Persistent high unemployment	10,584	80,014	1,217
Total	97,617	1,509,713	230

ment. UC benefit payments for these firms average $36 per employee per year, which computes to about one-fourth of a weekly UC check per employee per year. For a firm with one hundred employees, for example, two workers might each draw twelve checks a year, and the other ninety-eight not be laid off at all.

In 1984, most low-unemployment firms (and some of the cycle-sensitive firms as well) had no layoffs at all—about seventy thousand firms in all. Only a few thousand of Wisconsin's stable, low-unemployment firms have layoffs in a relatively prosperous year such as 1984; the composition of this group shifts.

About half of these stable firms, which account for about half of Wisconsin's insured private sector employment, paid average annual wages in 1984 of less than $9,000. In this large slice of the state economy, UC benefits are virtually unheard of. Many of these are family businesses involving a great deal of part-time work and work at or near the minimum wage. It is often the task of the wife to piece together a work force to accord with the peaks and valleys of the day, the week, and the season. The work patterns are often tailored to the needs and the availabilities of people in the neighborhood. Layoffs are virtually unknown. In such a setting, UC—paying someone $196 a week for not working—is seen (even in Wisconsin in the 1980s) as the spawn of the devil.

For the stable firms just discussed, UC benefit payments are low at any time and are not much influenced by the economic cycle. Note, in Table 13.2, that these firms produced large surpluses in the recession years 1980–83. For the firms accounting for the other half of state employment, though, UC benefit payments are much higher than for the stable firms, and show a pronounced cyclical pattern.

For the 20,646 cycle-sensitive firms, benefit payments averaged $337 per employee in 1984. These firms ran up large deficits ($533.3 million) in the fund in the years 1980–83, but produced a surplus of $175.4 million in 1984.

The final group of firms (those with persistent high unemployment) pay much more in benefits per employee than any other group; they incurred large deficits not only during the recession, but in 1984 as well. These firms account for only 5 percent of state unemployment, but for 45 percent of benefit payments and—as we shall see later—for a very large part of the continuing financing problem in the UC system.

As the lines formed in Wisconsin's UC financing battle, these various divisions within the Wisconsin employer community became quite pronounced. There are a small number of firms, accounting for about 5 percent of state employment, for which UC is a way of life. These include certain construction, manufacturing, and other firms. In these firms, layoffs due to weather conditions, model changeovers, and other reasons are normal, frequent, and accepted. There's a much larger slice of the state economy, as we have seen, where UC benefits are extremely rare. Many of these stable employers had not paid a state UC tax since 1979. For such employers, the financial crisis involved the threat of large added FUTA and interest charges, as well as a large state UC tax—and perhaps all of these. The crisis caused all Wisconsin employers to become involved in UC financing questions for the first time in many years. In this sense, the problem burst the bounds within which UC issues had normally been considered.

Wisconsin Legislation and Policy Changes, 1983–85

Wisconsin's political leadership (the governor and the majority and minority leaders in each chamber of the legislature) devoted a great deal of time throughout 1983 to the UC program—far more attention than had been devoted to UC matters for decades. Two major packages of legislation resulted. The first (Wisconsin Acts 8 and 99, 1983), which provided for sharp increases in taxes and cutbacks in benefits, aimed at stabilizing the fund for the next few years. The second (Wisconsin Act 388, 1984) involved legislation dealing with the UC policy structure and process. A third major legislative package (Wisconsin Act 17, 1985) was the first developed under the new policy structure. This provided for tax changes—specifically an increase in the state UC tax to avoid equivalent increases in the federal payroll tax—and laid the groundwork for major revisions in the structure of UC benefits in Wisconsin. These and other legislative changes are summarized in the sections which follow.

Tax and Financing Changes. As to taxes, the wage base has been increased from $7,000 under the old law to $8,000 in 1983, $9,500 in 1984 and 1985, and $10,500 in 1986 and thereafter. The zero rate was abolished; the lowest rate was set at 0.4 percent for 1984 and 1985. For 1986 and thereafter, the lowest rate continues at 0.4 percent for firms with a taxable payroll below $100,000. For larger firms, the lowest rate is 1.1 percent. The balance required to qualify for the lowest rate was increased from 8.5 to 10 percent of taxable payroll. The top rate was increased from 7.4 to 8.5 percent for 1984 and 1985; for 1986 and thereafter, the top rate is 10 percent.

The limiter on rate increases was moved from 1 to 2 percent for all firms for 1984 and 1985. For 1986 and thereafter, the 1 percent limiter is restored for firms with positive balances. Write-offs have been banned outright in connection with rate determinations for the years 1984 through 1987, and will be permitted thereafter only for firms which have paid the top tax rate for the two preceding years. Voluntary contributions can be used only to reduce the rate by a single bracket, and the size of the brackets has been greatly decreased. Provision was made to charge the state share of extended benefits to employer accounts. Changes in the Wisconsin UC law also increased state UC taxes from $222 million in 1982 to $563 million in 1984 and $576 million in 1985—roughly double what they would have been under the old law.

Benefit provisions were significantly tightened. The number of weeks of regular benefits were reduced from thirty-four to twenty-six. The number of weeks required to qualify for benefits was increased from fifteen to eighteen in 1984 and 1985, and to nineteen weeks in 1986 and thereafter. A wage qualification was introduced. During the base period, the claimant must have earned 30 percent of the state average weekly wage times the number of weeks required to qualify. Benefit rates were frozen indefinitely at a maximum of $196 and a minimum of $37 weekly.

For some time, Wisconsin law has provided that, if an employee is discharged for misconduct, all credits applicable to that employer are canceled. This provision is continued. Under the old law, though, the employee had to wait only three weeks to draw benefits based on other employment. Under the new law, a requalification is required: seven weeks of work in covered employment, with earnings equal to fourteen times the benefit rate.

As to quits, the old law required a requalification involving four weeks of work, not necessarily in covered employment, and earnings of $200. There was no reduction in benefits. The new law continued the various good-cause justifications for quitting. Other changes included the following:

— To meet the quit-to-take provision, an employee must have had another specific job offer when he or she quit the other job; the new job must be in covered employment; the claimant must work at least four weeks in that job and must satisfy one of four other conditions. If all these criteria are met, the employee can draw benefits based on the quit employment without reduction.

—Otherwise, the employee can requalify only after seven weeks of covered employment, with earnings of fourteen times the benefit rate. The benefits based on work for the quit employer are cut in half.

These various benefit cutbacks reduced benefit payments, relative to what they would have been under the old law, by 17 percent in 1984, 20 percent in 1985, and 23 percent in 1986.

Policy Structure and Process. In August 1983 a second group was appointed by the governor to develop a new policy structure and process for the UC program. This group included all five members of the first group (with the secretary as chair and the four legislative leaders) plus three others: the president of the state AFL-CIO, the president of the Wisconsin Association of Manufacturers and Commerce, and a prominent labor attorney. The presidents of the Wisconsin AFL-CIO and the Association of Manufacturers and Commerce had been active on the UC Advisory Council for many years.

It is necessary to mention the setting in which this new group began its meetings. The spring legislation, which involved substantial tax increases and the first significant benefit cutbacks in the half-century history of the program, had caused a great deal of controversy. The state's political leaders were shocked and dismayed at what they found as they began delving into the condition of the UC program—the depth and complexity of unresolved problems, the harsh choices available, and the demonstrated failure of state institutions (not just the advisory council, by any means) to do what was reasonably expected of them. There was a great deal of bitterness. The sessions in the fall of 1983 contributed greatly to a necessary process of healing and rebuilding.

These sessions came to involve a top-to-bottom reconsideration of the UC policy structure and process in Wisconsin. Many alternatives were considered, and at first the clear preponderance of opinion was to abandon the council approach—or, at most, to provide a very weak council.

After considering alternative approaches at considerable length, however, it was decided to continue with a strong council. Wisconsin's political leaders concluded that the council should have real power so that it could attract to membership persons who could commit a significant constituency. A policy structure including such a council was deemed to be more promising than the more traditional approach centered on an executive department and standing committees of the legislature. This decision was the product of about ten meetings of the UC advisory panel over a period of about four months, each meeting of several hours' duration. At each of these meetings, Wisconsin's political leaders considered the pros and cons of various alternatives.

What emerged had three main elements. First, a strong council was mandated, all members of which were to be newly appointed. Appointment was to be by the secretary of the Department of Industry, Labor and Human Relations, not by a quasi-judicial body. The council was expected to vote on recommended changes in UC law, with the votes of seven of the ten members necessary for it to support a position.

Second, a strong new policy role was prescribed for the Department of Industry, Labor and Human Relations. On January 15 of every odd-numbered year, the department was to provide to the governor and the legislative leaders projections of UC receipts, benefit payments, and fund status over the next several years, together with related legislative recommendations. The report was to show the position of the council on each recommendation.

Third, the governor and the legislative leaders would have the month from January 15 to February 15 (when the department was to report to the entire legislature) to decide whether to handle the UC package through a special panel. At the request of any two of the four state leaders, the governor was to convoke a special panel (the four leaders, chaired by the secretary, as in 1983) in lieu of following the normal legislative route.

The New Advisory Council and Act 17. The ten members of the new UC Advisory Council were appointed in the spring of 1984 and began meeting in June of that year. A great deal was accomplished in the first eighteen months of the council's existence. First, new working relationships with the Department of Industry, Labor and Human Relations evolved. Under these arrangements, for example, the department takes specific positions (for or against) on certain issues, and the council votes on specific issues. In other cases, the council is advised of a line of action which the department is considering and is publicly briefed at length. There is an opportunity for individual members of the council to offer advice or opinions, and to put matters to a vote in cases in which that seems warranted. One such case involves the financial policy followed by the department with respect to the repayment of UC program debt and related matters, discussed below.

The second major accomplishment since the new council was created involves the development of a comprehensive set of legislative proposals, the product of several months of cooperative effort by the department and the council late in 1984 and early in 1985. This package included these major elements: an increase in the state UC tax, in order to avoid an increased tax on Wisconsin employers under FUTA which would otherwise have occurred; long-needed technical reforms in certain aspects of UC benefits and the charging of benefits to employer accounts; and an outline of a new benefit structure to take effect in Wisconsin incidental to developing a wage-record system in accord with federal law.

These proposals were supported by the Department of Industry, Labor and Human Relations and, initially, had the virtually unanimous support of the council. (At first, the only exception was that one labor member dissented with respect to one item.) Two employer representatives later sought to withdraw their votes in support of the package.

With the governor's endorsement, the bill was introduced in the Senate as S.B. 76. There was lively and extensive debate, with strong efforts made to delay or significantly amend the bill. Passage was essentially along party lines, with virtually all Democrats supporting the measure and all Republicans opposed. It was quite clear that the time was past when the council's recommendations would be accepted by the legislature without murmur. Most of the controversy involved the state UC tax increase and the absence of further benefit reductions, which, it was maintained by some, produced an unbalanced (antibusiness) package. These matters are touched on in the sections which follow.

In the remainder of this paper, I address a number of broad problem areas in Wisconsin's UC program which have been dealt with, to varying degrees, in the 1983–85 legislation. They are the kind of problem for which there is no complete and final solution in the real world, although textbook solutions are simple enough to devise. These are the issues with which UC policymakers will have to deal in the years ahead.

3. State UC Taxes and Benefits: Mismatches at the High End

Firms with High and Persistent Deficits

In making a serious assessment of the financing of Wisconsin's UC program, this point is fundamental: for many firms, the amount of benefits which employees will draw will far exceed state UC taxes paid by the firm, year in and year out. Employees of a construction firm, for example, might be laid off and draw UC benefits, for an average of fifteen or twenty weeks a year. UC benefits in such a case, with the maximum benefit rate at $196 a week, can readily amount to an average of $3,000 to $4,000 per year per employee. At the top state UC tax rate (10 percent of $10,500), that firm would pay a state UC tax of $1,050 per employee per year. Thus, many construction firms (and some in other industries as well) incur substantial deficits each year. Even in "good" years, when unemployment is generally low, the taxes paid by these firms cover only a fraction of the benefits drawn by their employees.

Two misconceptions need to be cleared up at this point. First, we are not dealing here with recession conditions. These problems arise even when unemployment is at very low levels. Quite simply, the top state UC tax ($1,050 per employee) covers about 5.4 weekly benefit checks. Many firms experience much higher layoffs than that, even in a good year, due to seasonal factors, model changeovers, and other conditions. Second, we are not concerned with weaknesses in the system for charging UC benefit costs to employers. About 98 percent of UC benefit payments in Wisconsin *are* charged to employers. The problem is that, even at the top rate, taxes are insufficient to cover the benefits thus charged.

The condition is illustrated in Table 13.4 for the 10,584 firms with persistent high unemployment. Note that these firms incurred a deficit of $732.9 million during the recession years 1980–83; the deficit amount for 1984 was $54.2 million.

During 1984, UC benefit payments were at very low levels—much lower than they have been since, even in relatively good years. There are several reasons for the relatively low level of benefit payments in 1984: many workers had exhausted UC benefits and were unable to requalify for UC because of high unemployment from 1980 through 1983; and, in 1984, the economy was in a general recovery period. Benefit payments climbed from $347 million in 1984 to $408 million in 1985, indicating that 1984 was indeed a trough.

On the tax side, 1984 was also a good year. The new tax provisions were in full effect, and were applied to higher levels of employment in the state. The mechanics of UC financing are such that there is an especially sharp growth of revenue in the first year in which tax increases take effect.

Regarding both taxes and benefits, then, 1984 was a very good year. Yet this particular group of firms covered in Table 13.4 ran up a deficit of $54.2 million. Under more normal conditions, in nonrecession years, these firms would incur deficits (under the 1984 tax laws) of about $80 million a year. In years of high unemployment, the deficits would be much higher than that.

Role of the Cycle-Sensitive Firms

As shown in Table 13.2, there are about 20,646 firms in the state which experienced very heavy benefit payments and incurred heavy deficits in the recession years 1980–83; in 1984, benefit payments fell sharply, and these firms provided a surplus of $175.4 million.

These firms employ 658,055 people, some 44 percent of the jobs in Wisconsin's private sector. It is significant to note that the trends in this large part of the state economy are so thoroughly interwoven with the UC program. It is also worth noting that manufacturing is a very large factor in the cycle-sensitive area. Note, too, in Table 13.2 that manufacturing firms in total accounted for $675.4 million (about 58 percent) of our deficits during the recession. Manufacturing firms also contributed a surplus of $147.5 million in 1984—about 68 percent of the total surplus in that year.

Table 13.4. Wisconsin UC Program: Key Data by Industry Group for Firms with Persistent High Unemployment

	1984		Average per Employee per Year, 1984		Surplus or Deficit ($ millions)		Write-offs, 1980–83 ($ millions)
	Number of Firms	Employment	Benefits	Taxes	1980–83	1984	
Construction	3,808	22,032	$2,252	$ 920	$−278.5	$−29.4	$167.9
Manufacturing	694	10,002	1,463	677	−276.1	−7.9	56.6
Subtotal	4,502	32,034	2,006	844	−554.5	−37.2	224.6
Agriculture, forestry, and fisheries	368	2,916	1,003	470	−9.9	−1.6	6.0
Mining	75	779	2,217	1,017	−10.4	−0.9	6.5
Transportation, commerce, and utilities	630	5,454	1,037	467	−34.0	−3.1	12.0
Wholesale trade	441	5,689	1,327	326	−48.6	−5.7	14.5
Retail trade	2,284	16,344	428	254	−40.5	−2.8	5.8
Finance, insurance, and real estate	338	1,101	555	269	−5.4	−0.3	0.9
Services	1,946	15,697	486	323	−29.5	−2.6	9.6
Subtotal	6,082	47,980	690	335	−178.4	−17.0	55.2
Total	10,584	80,014	1,217	539	−732.9	−54.2	279.7

In the recession years 1980–83, cycle-sensitive firms incurred deficits of $533.3 million, as shown in Table 13.2. Some of that deficit will be recovered through unusually high surpluses in 1984 and (to a diminishing extent) in 1985 and 1986, but about $400 million will not be recovered (including $249 million that has been written off).

The heavy losses in this area during the 1980–83 recession years stemmed primarily from serious weaknesses in the tax structure: a low maximum tax and the interaction of provisions with respect to write-offs, voluntary contributions, and the rate increase limiter. As noted above, these problems have been largely corrected.

In a future recession, cycle-sensitive firms will again be in deficit in the UC fund—benefit payments will exceed taxes as unemployment rises. The deficits should be much smaller than those of 1980–83, and financial recovery following the recession should be much greater due to the corrective tax legislation.

It is reasonable to hope that these firms will come close to paying their way over the cycle, with deficits in bad years and surpluses in good years. For 1986 and the following years (until the next recession occurs) it is reasonable to expect these firms to generate a modest surplus.

Effects on Other Employers

So far we have outlined a set of conditions under which 87,033 Wisconsin employers (all except the 10,584 firms with persistent high unemployment, as shown in Table 13.2) are required to pay sufficient UC taxes to do three things:

— Cover their own benefit charges;
— Cover the deficits incurred by the high-layoff firms; and
— Provide a further margin for debt reduction.

These objectives will be covered in one of two ways: either by a state UC tax alone, or by a combination of a state UC tax and an added FUTA tax. As noted elsewhere, virtually all other borrower states have opted for the added FUTA tax. Wisconsin practically alone has chosen to take the steps necessary to avoid this tax.

Thus there is a built-in deficit, and the federal government is ready to levy a higher FUTA tax in the state to cover it if the state does not act to prevent such a measure. This is the central ongoing financial problem facing the Wisconsin UC system.

4. Old Issues and New Ground Rules: Experience Rating

The financing problem involving the mismatch at the high end was entangled with several others, many of which have been debated for decades in the UC world. In the context of the 1980s, though, these issues take a much different form. Experience rating is one of those issues which had to be addressed in formulating the legislative package for 1985.

Experience rating means, quite simply, that employers with high layoff records should pay a higher state UC tax than those with a record of lower layoffs. Experience rating has been required in federal law, and embodied in some form in the UC systems of the various states, since the 1930s.

Reasons for Experience Rating

The purposes in requiring an experience-rated system are to give employers a strong incentive to control their work force in such a way as to minimize layoffs; to provide employers with a strong incentive to challenge UC claims whenever that is warranted, thus helping to police and administer the system; and to further effective resource allocation, reflecting the costs of unemployment (along with other factor costs) in the price of the goods or services involved.

These objectives continue to make sense. For example, with respect to employer control of layoffs, a case was mentioned earlier in which for the years 1980–82, a firm ran up $56 million in benefit charges, paid $6 million in taxes, wrote off the difference, and never paid the maximum UC tax rate. If the state law had been such that the UC tax would have covered a much higher proportion of benefit payments—say, 80 percent instead of about 10 percent—it is almost certain that this firm would have followed a very different set of personnel policies. For example, there could well have been a different mix of permanent separations, temporary layoffs, part-time work, and so forth.

A construction contractor who is quite familiar with the UC system offers this example: on a Thursday morning in February, the weather has warmed up enough so that some construction work can be done. The contractor might call one worker who has not worked that week and has some UC eligibility remaining. If this worker does not work on Thursday and Friday, he will receive $196 in UC benefits for the week. If he works on Thursday and Friday, he might receive about $200 in wages and (in the pre-1985 system) nothing in UC benefits. Thus the person would, in effect, work the two days for nothing. Under these circumstances, a contractor might instead call another worker who has already worked that week or has exhausted UC benefits. In that case,

— The first worker could stay home the rest of the week and draw $196 in UC benefits.
— The second worker would receive $200 in wages for working Thursday and Friday, which he wouldn't have had if the first worker had been called instead.

— The contractor would pay $200 in wages.
— If the contractor's UC tax was already at the maximum rate, the contractor would not pay any higher amount, whether or not the first worker drew UC benefits for the week.

The outcome is quite different if the contractor is not paying the top UC tax rate. Then the contractor faces a choice:

— Paying $500 in total: $200 to the second worker for working Thursday and Friday, plus $300 in UC tax (basic and solvency) to cover the first worker's UC check for the week; *or*
— Paying $200 in total to the first worker for working Thursday and Friday.

Clearly, the contractor would have strong incentives to operate differently under an experience-rated system than would otherwise be the case.

Another set of considerations arises in connection with seasonal work. Consider, for example, a firm that offers twenty-five weeks of work a year at $200 a week, or $5,000 a year. In such a case, employees could routinely draw $2,000 a year in UC benefits (twenty weeks at $100 a week). The employer would pay a UC tax of $500 per employee at most (10 percent of $5,000). One need not have an especially fertile imagination to sense the possibilities in such a situation.

Obviously, experience rating doesn't make it possible to avoid layoffs altogether. There are cases in which experience rating makes little or no difference. If products simply are not selling, cutbacks are unavoidable. But in cases such as those illustrated above, there are many ways in which experience rating can give employers a strong incentive to act differently than they otherwise would.

The second reason for experience rating is that, because increased applications for benefits result in higher employer tax rates, it provides an incentive to employers to challenge any claims suspected of being fraudulent, and thus ensures that eligibility criteria are met. The conditions regarding eligibility for UC benefits (monetary and other) are generally items which the employer is in a good position to know. Did the claimant quit, for example, or was he or she laid off or discharged for misconduct?

As to cost allocation and resource flows, if construction of roads or houses in Wisconsin inherently involves high layoffs and high UC benefit payments, then this ought to be reflected in the cost of the houses or roads. It's hard to justify the practice of shifting large parts of these costs to other products and services through the vagaries of the UC tax and benefit system.

In short, it's difficult to mount a logical argument against experience rating. There are plenty of good reasons for it, including the sanction of federal law.

Experience Rating and Shared Risk

Experience rating is a concept which applies to the state UC tax, which is paid by private sector firms. It has always been recognized that the state UC tax would include two components: an experience-rated and a shared risk component. It has never been expected that all UC benefit payments would be recovered through the experience-rated component alone. The shared risk component of the tax was intended to cover certain benefit payments, as follows:

1. Benefits paid based on a job which was voluntarily quit.
2. Benefits in certain cases in which decisions were later reversed and over-payments not recovered from the claimant.
3. Benefits based on employment with firms which have failed, gone out of business, have no further payroll in the state, and so on.
4. Ineffectively charged benefits—that is, cases in which the maximum tax rate is insufficient to cover benefits charged to a firm, or where provisions of the law (for example, write-offs) made it possible for firms to avoid the tax consequencs.

There isn't much argument concerning the first three areas; that is, there seems to be general agreement that the shared risk component of the UC tax must be adequate to cover these costs. There is a great deal of dis-agreement concerning the fourth item, however. Spokesmen for stable employers (including paper manufacturers, banks, insurance companies, utilities, and retail concerns, among others) make the case along these lines: under extreme recession conditions, such that a firm that normally pays its way is hit very hard, there is some logic in permitting the firm to avoid some of its benefit payments. It's an entirely different matter, though, when a firm routinely incurs benefit payments of $2,000 or $3,000 per employee per year, and pays UC taxes sufficient to cover only, say, one-third of those payments. Why should other employers, year in and year out, be expected to pick up the remaining two-thirds of these benefit charges? What is the logic of requiring paper manufacturers, for instance, to pay part of the UC benefit charges stemming from layoffs by construction contractors or resorts?

There's no good answer to questions such as these. For example, some have observed that, if high-layoff firms were charged an extra $2,000 or $3,000 per employee per year, this might drive them out of business. Rep-resentatives of stable employers counter along these lines: not all such firms would go out of business; at least some of them are probably quite profit-able, and many of them could control UC benefit payments much more tightly if they knew they would have to pay for them. Beyond that, if a firm needs such high subsidies on a continuing basis, perhaps it shouldn't be in business at all. Thousands of firms do in fact go out of business because they can't pay their costs. If such subsidies are indeed necessary for a firm and justifiable in terms of public policy, such critics say, prove it and ask the legislature for the money through the front door—don't provide the subsidy through out-of-sight bookkeeping adjustments in the UC program. Moreover, if subsidies are necessary, why, specifically, in the UC area? Why not subsidize the cost of raw materials, or wages, or utilities, or the sales tax?

Two kinds of answers can be provided to such questions, neither completely satisfying. First, it can be pointed out that the top UC tax in Wisconsin has been increased very sharply in recent years: from $444 per employee (7.4 percent of $6,000) in 1982 and the years preceding to $1,050 per employee (10 percent of $10,500) in 1986 and the years following. Thus, high-layoff firms are required to pay a much larger share of the cost, and the subsidy is much smaller than it used to be. Second, it should be noted that Wisconsin's top UC tax payment ($1,050 per worker—that is, 10 percent of $10,500) ranks first or second nationally, as state laws now stand (the top rate under Michigan law is variable and cann be either higher or lower than Wisconsin's in any given year).

Major Elements of Experience Rating: Past and Future

In the late 1970s and early 1980s, there is no question that Wisconsin's experience rating system performed very poorly. Major examples of this condition have already been presented in this paper: the fact that over $500 million in benefit charges was written off the accounts of employers who laid off claimants; and the fact that one firm ran up $56 million in benefit charges, paid just $6 million in taxes, wrote off the remainder, and never paid the maximum tax. A report by the inspector general of the U.S. Department of Labor covering the years 1970–83 for Wisconsin and certain other states noted major weaknesses. For example, the report maintains that, in 1983, $281 million in Wisconsin benefit payments—about 40 percent of the total—were ineffectively charged, that is, charged to an employer who wouldn't wind up paying taxes to cover these costs. This was a major problem area, then, but there have been major reforms in the past few years. Among the states, Wisconsin should be at the top—if not at the very top—of the experience-rating list. There are four major aspects of experience rating. The paragraphs which follow address developments and comparisons in each of these areas.

Charging and Noncharging. Most benefit payments are charged directly to an employer's account; some are "noncharged"—that is, paid from a general account (called the balancing account in Wisconsin) and (in effect) allocated among all employers. In 1982, $74 million (10.8 percent) of benefit payments was not charged to the accounts of Wisconsin employers. In 1985, primarily because of two legislative changes, this noncharging had shrunk to $8 million (1.8 percent). Under present Wisconsin law, over 98 percent of benefit payments will be charged annually. In these terms, Wisconsin now ranks in the top six among the states.

Effective Charging: The Maximum UC Tax Payment. Charging benefits to an employer's account (just discussed) doesn't mean much unless these charges will actually have an effect on the state UC taxes which an employer pays. If $1,000 in benefits is charged to an employer and if, at the top rate, his or her UC tax bill is $200, then $800 of those benefits (80 percent of the total) is not effectively charged. Wisconsin's top tax, translated into dollars per employee, now ranks first or second nationally (depending on the variable rate assessed in Michigan). Once again, Wisconsin now ranks very high indeed.

Effective Charging: Removing Loopholes. In 1983 and 1985, Wisconsin law was tightened up to eliminate many large loopholes which had contributed to ineffective charging in earlier years. The major items included an outright ban on write-offs for four tax years (1984 through 1987) in succession; sharply curtailing the possibility of securing a rate reduction by making voluntary contributions; and providing for faster increases in tax rates. Prior to 1983, an employer's basic rate could not increase by more than 1 percent from the prior rate, no matter what the reserve position was. For the fall of 1983 and that of 1984, this limiter was stepped up to 2 percent for all employers. For the fall of 1985 and thereafter the limiter will remain at 2 percent for firms with negative balances, but will drop to 1 percent for firms with positive balances. Prior to 1983, provisions allowing write-offs, voluntary contributions, and rate increase limiters—especially when used skillfully and in combination—had had a massive adverse effect on the solvency of the Wisconsin UC system. These loopholes have now been closed, or in any case narrowed significantly.

Borrower States: Paying or Avoiding an Added FUTA Tax. For the forty states which have had to borrow from the federal government in order to continue paying UC benefits, a key question involves the extent to which the loans will be repaid through either the state UC tax system or the imposition of a progressively greater federal unemployment tax in the state. The debt must be repaid, one way or the other. To employers, though, there's a big difference between the two approaches:

—State UC taxes are experience-rated; FUTA taxes are not—they are levied on the first $7,000 of wages paid, regardless of a firm's layoff experience.
—The proceeds of an added FUTA tax are applied first to reduce interest-

free debt. If instead the state repays the loan from state UC tax receipts, the interest-bearing portion of the debt is the first repaid. The added FUTA tax is avoided and the interest burden on the state's employers is reduced.

Wisconsin's position is better than that of most states. In January 1985, an added FUTA assessment was levied in every state bordering Wisconsin, and, nationally, in every subject UC borrower state except for Wisconsin and Colorado. In January 1986, an added FUTA tax was levied in ten states, but not Wisconsin. Among Wisconsin's neighbors, employers in Minnesota paid an added 1.1 percent and in Illinois an added 0.9 percent.

In Minnesota, for example, a firm with no layoffs was assessed a state tax of 1 percent and added FUTA of 1.1 percent for a total tax of 2.1 percent. In Wisconsin, the total tax for that firm was only 0.4 percent (if the firm had a taxable payroll of $100,000 or less) or 1.1 percent if it was larger.

Considering the state UC tax alone, over twenty thousand stable (low-layoff) Wisconsin firms paid a lower tax in 1986 than the lowest rate which could possibly apply in Minnesota. If the comparison is broadened to include the state UC tax and the additional FUTA tax together, over forty thousand stable Wisconsin firms paid a lower rate. For large numbers of firms, the presence or absence of an additional FUTA tax is a very significant item.

It is significant, then, that Wisconsin and Colorado are the only states which have been able to avoid the added FUTA tax in every year in which it could have been levied. Of all the other states, only Michigan has been able to avoid the added FUTA tax for any year in which it might have been levied (and that involved a single year). Those commenting on the experience-rating systems of various state UC programs seem to overlook this point altogether.

5. Old Issues in a New Setting: Economic and Financial Policy

Three criteria have been stated for state UC financing systems: "(1) adequacy—ensuring that the system can match income and outlays; (2) timing—ensuring that the system is responsive to the economic cycle; and (3) equity—ensuring that there is a fair distribution of taxes among employers" (National Commission on Unemployment Compensation, *Final Report,* July 1980, p. 86). The third point, equity, has already been covered at some length in the discussion of experience rating. The other two points, adequacy and timing, will be discussed here.

Assumptions and Policy Prescriptions

The three criteria just noted are intertwined with several assumptions and policy prescriptions which have played a major role in the UC system for many years. It might be helpful to analyze some of these assumptions and prescriptions, and to consider how they relate to the world of today.

First, note that borrowing for state UC programs is simply ignored in guidelines such as those presented above—in effect, assumed away. The intelligent use of debt is a major element in UC policymaking in the 1980s since forty states have borrowed since 1972. There are no guidelines on dealing with this matter. Debt is either ignored outright, or treated as an aberration which will, it is hoped, soon go away.

Second, there is an assumption that UC funds should fill a countercyclical role in the economy, building up surpluses in good years and incurring deficits in bad years. UC financing was seen as the leading member in the family of economic stabilizers, drawing buying power out of the economy in boom periods and adding buying power to the economy in the downswing. Implicit here is the notion that unemployment is something that comes and goes. That isn't quite the way things are in the 1980s. In 1980, for example, a very bad year, benefit payments from the UC trust fund were $479 million—the second highest amount in the half century of the Wisconsin UC program's existence. In 1985, a very good year, benefit payments were about $408 million—the fifth highest in history, and higher than those for any year prior to 1980. That's not quite the kind of ebb and flow of benefit payments which the automatic stabilizer school had in mind. The economic impact of UC financing continues to be important, but in a considerably different context than suggested in the traditional approach.

Third, fund adequacy (or solvency) has generally been defined in terms of multiples of benefit payments. A minimum standard would be 1.5 times the highest yearly amount of benefit payments in the state's history; a more adequate fund would be double that, or three times the highest amount of payments ever made (National Commission on Unemployment Compensation, 1980, pp. 86, 90). Under these guidelines, Wisconsin would need a fund balance in 1986 ranging from $1.2 billion to $2.5 billion. This kind of benchmark really has no utility for a state such as Wisconsin. Of this, more later.

Fourth, it was assumed that UC policymaking would proceed in very long-term cycles. Tax rates and benefit provisions, once set, would continue in place for extended periods of time. It was not anticipated that the UC program would be subject to annual or biennial review and revision. In this sense, UC would be treated considerably differently from programs which were subject to the federal or state budgetary and appropriations process.

Fifth, it was thought that UC policymaking would be handled by specialized councils or other groups that were not part of the normal political and legislative structure. The general idea was that UC matters were too complex and too important to be handled through regular political channels. In this connection, it's important to bear in mind that, when the UC program began a half century ago, the role and the capabilities of government were very different from what they are today. Withal, the idea that "UC is a matter best left to experts such as myself" still has some strong adherents.

Sixth, most studies of UC policy have been presented in a programmatic vacuum, as if other government programs simply don't exist. For purposes of UC policy discussion, the world is a rather simple place—it includes a private economic sector, which sometimes lays off workers, the workers themselves, a UC program, and not much else. For example, how should UC taxation be related to the general tax picture in a state? The legislatures and governors who deal with UC taxes must also address much broader tax matters, often affecting the same sets of taxpayers. UC literature is silent on such relationships. Similarly, there are obvious relationships between UC and many other types of government programs: health and medical, income maintenance, education and training, housing, and others. A state's UC program might be shaped to some degree by the extent to which various kinds of needs were met through these other programs. Once again, these relationships have been largely overlooked in the literature and discussions of UC policy.

The foregoing assumptions about UC economic and financial policy, both as to content and means of formulation, have limited the program's relevance in the 1980s.

Policy Guidelines for the 1980s and Beyond

Some Wisconsin policy guidelines appear to be emerging from the events of recent years. These are summarized in the following sections.

No Large Fund Balances. There won't be any large UC fund balances. There is no serious possibility for Wisconsin to achieve in the near future a fund balance of $2.5 billion (to have a "fairly adequate fund") or even $1.2 billion to meet the "minimum" standard of the 1.5 multiple. For the foreseeable future, the outlook is for a UC fund that alternates between a relatively small debt and a relatively small cash balance. Wisconsin law provides for a tax/benefits package which (even with top tax rates in effect) doesn't allow the accumulation of much of a fund balance and, as an added precaution, provides for an automatic 50 percent tax cut to take effect if a significant balance should nonetheless materialize.

There are several reasons why the decision has been made to avoid large fund balances. From a political perspective, such balances are regarded as a temptation to extravagance, an excuse to increase benefits. With very sharp state UC tax increases necessary just to balance income and outgo, legislators don't have much inclination to levy the even greater taxes which would be necessary to provide ample cash margins for UC program managers, especially in light of the recent track record.

Economically, the levy of additional taxes to build an adequate fund would be extremely difficult. Since such funds are deposited in the U.S. Treasury, we would (in effect) be levying a heavy additional tax upon Wisconsin employers and using the proceeds for a low-interest loan to Washington.

A large fund balance is not necessary to pay benefits in a recession. Under present federal law, borrowing is possible, under quite favorable terms. For a variety of reasons, then, there should not be a large balance in the Wisconsin UC fund in the foreseeable future. This has a very profound effect on UC policy structure and process.

Intelligent Debt Management. Under present federal law, borrowing conditions for state UC programs are very favorable, *so long as the debt is under control.* For example, the federal government will advance any amount that is needed to pay benefits on very short notice. If the money is repaid by September 30 of the year in which the borrowing occurred, and if there is no borrowing after September 30 of that year, the loans are interest-free. In Wisconsin, there are large benefit payments in the first several months of each year. Meanwhile, there are no significant tax collections until about May 1. About $200 million can be borrowed in the early months and repaid in May with no interest charges.

Several factors, then, must be considered: unlimited availability of federal loan funds at low rates of interest, plus the severe economic and political constraints on the accumulation of a large UC fund balance. These factors together mean that intelligent debt management must be a feature of the Wisconsin UC system unless and until federal law is changed.

Shorter Policy Cycles. Major UC legislation was enacted in 1983 and again in 1985. It is quite likely that an even more complex and comprehensive package will be proposed in 1987. Wisconsin law now requires comprehensive analyses and legislative proposals in January of each odd-numbered year. In this regard, UC will become like other state programs, subject to biennial review. There isn't much support for a ten- or twenty-year fix.

Relationship to Regular Legislative and Budgetary Process; Comparison with Other Governmental Programs. The policy process for UC has varied greatly in recent years. Prior to 1983, as noted above, the UC Advisory Council had virtually absolute control in this area. In 1983, the council was simply set aside, and a special panel was formed to handle UC policy. In 1985, a legislative proposal was developed based on a long period of cooperative effort by the newly formed council and the Department of Industry, Labor and Human Relations. This legislation was enacted, with some amendments, only after a lengthy period of debate and discussion — during which a number of moves to delay or significantly revise the package were rejected. As major UC legislative packages are submitted each biennium, it is likely that legislators will develop the skills and the interest to deal with the program as they do with state programs generally.

To the extent that this process occurs, it is reasonable to expect that the UC program will increasingly be compared with, and placed in competition with, other programs. This can occur on both the tax and benefit sides. For example, a change in one form of business tax may be bargained as a UC tax change. A change in AFDC may be bargained in the context of a UC benefit change.

Recent Experience. Several aspects of Wisconsin's recent history are illustrative of the economic effects of the UC program in the context of today. From January 1, 1980, through April 30, 1984, benefit payments exceeded tax collections by $1.2 billion. This did two things. First, it injected a net of $1.2 billion of buying power into the economy of the state. Because of UC benefit payments, the drop in real (adjusted for inflation) per capita personal income in the state from 1979 to 1983 was about half of what it would otherwise have been. In 1982, one of every four workers in the state's private sector received UC benefit payments. Second, the excess of benefit payments over collections transformed a $462 million cash balance as of January 1, 1980, into a $738 million deficit in April 1984. With the fund balance gone, that effect can't be duplicated.

Although deficits were incurred in the worst years, thereby helping to sustain the economy, the sharp benefit cuts and tax increases needed to restore the fund to solvency did not begin to take effect until 1984, when the economy had considerably improved. The debt was reduced from its $738 million peak in May 1984 to $328 million in December 1985.

Wisconsin has been following, with a great deal of success so far, a strategy of financing the UC program to the maximum practicable extent with low- or no-interest federal loans, and has avoided the imposition of added federal payroll taxes in the state. These actions have minimized the cost of the program to the state's employers and, in that sense, have had a favorable economic effect.

Wisconsin's Ability to Pay. A final point concerning the economic impact of the UC program involves, quite simply, the state's ability to pay. This issue becomes involved with economic development policy, differential tax rates and "business climates" among states, and many other considerations.

In the early 1980s, Wisconsin's UC benefit package ranked about sixth nationally in relative generosity or liberality. This situation has changed dramatically. Benefits were sharply curtailed in the legislation enacted in 1983, which took effect beginning in 1984. The passage of time, and the continuing effect of this legislation, are producing a major change in the relationship of Wisconsin's UC benefit package to those of other states. The Wisconsin package, which, in total, ranked near the top nationally a few years ago, is moving to the midpoint among the states. This trend is not very well understood.

The perception persists that the Wisconsin benefit package is near the top nationally, and that this has been so for many years. Actually, although Wisconsin had the first UC program in the nation, for many years it was not the most generous one. The benefit/cost ratio (the ratio of UC benefit payments to total state payrolls) is, in the author's judgment, the best single indicator for interstate comparisons. From 1972 to 1978, for example, Wisconsin's rank among the states on its cost/benefit ratio ranged from twentieth to twenty-fifth. This rank began to climb in 1979 and, in the years 1980–83, ranged between fourth and seventh. Wisconsin occupied a high rank for only a short span of time, and it is now returning to the middle position it long occupied.

6. Old Issues in a New Setting: UC and the Unemployed

Coverage

The Employed. In July 1985, about 85 percent of the people employed in Wisconsin were covered by UC and 15 percent were not. Table 13.5 shows the approximate breakdown. Aside from agriculture, coverage of wage and salary employment in the state is virtually complete.

Table 13.5. Profile of Wisconsin Workers, 1985

	Number of Workers	Percentage of Work Force
Workers covered by state UC	1,864,600	
Federal and railroad workers covered separately	33,100	
Total covered	1,897,700	85
Workers not covered by UC		
Self-employed	188,000	
Agriculture	103,000	
All other	46,400	
Total not covered	337,400	15
Total Wisconsin employment, July 1985	2,235,100	100

The Unemployed. The situation for the unemployed is considerably different. In 1984, an average of 176,000 persons were unemployed in Wisconsin; insured unemployment averaged 60,000 workers, or 34 percent of total unemployment. As shown in Figure 13.1, this percentage has been

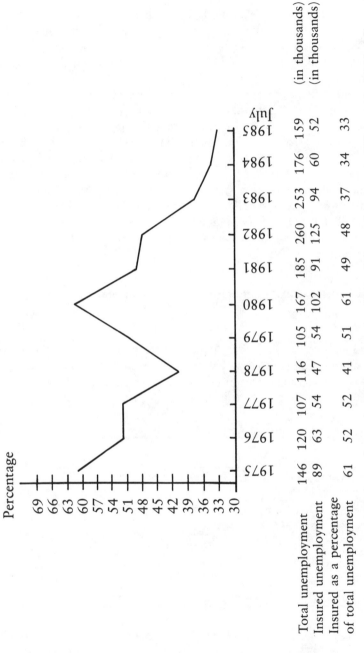

	1975	1976	1977	1978	1979	1980	1981	1982	1983	1984	1985 July	
Total unemployment	146	120	107	116	105	167	185	260	253	176	159	(in thousands)
Insured unemployment	89	63	54	47	54	102	91	125	94	60	52	(in thousands)
Insured as a percentage of total unemployment	61	52	52	41	51	61	49	48	37	34	33	

Figure 13.1. Insured Unemployment as a Percentage of Total Unemployment in Wisconsin, 1975–85

dropping sharply. In 1975 and again in 1980, insured unemployment was 61 percent of total unemployment. This proportion dropped to 37 percent in 1983, 34 percent in 1984, and—as noted in the figure—stood at 33 percent in July 1985.

The situation is actually somewhat worse than these figures suggest. Both of these statements are true for July 1985:

—Total unemployment was 159,400 and insured unemployment was 51,942, or 33 percent of total unemployment.
—Of the 159,400 unemployed, only 39,110 (25 percent) drew a UC check.

Table 13.6 presents details of Wisconsin unemployment in July 1985. Note that 120,290 people, 75 percent of the unemployed, did not receive a UC check. Most of these (71,295) were new workers and those reentering the labor force who did not qualify for UC because they had little or no recent employment. Layoffs from noncovered employment amounted to 6,815, indicating that further extensions of UC coverage would not do much to reduce the number of unemployed who don't receive UC. Although UC coverage is generally thought of as nearly complete, it is important to note that recently only about a quarter of the unemployed in Wisconsin have been receiving a UC check.

Table 13.6. UC Status of Unemployed Workers in Wisconsin, 1985

	Insured Unemployment	Total Unemployment
Drew full UC checks, state program	38,342	38,342
Federal employees	—	187
Railroad employees	—	581
Total drawing full UC checks	38,342	39,110
Partial checks	10,738	a
Disqualified	2,862[b]	3,266[b]
Delayed filers and never filers	—	10,403
Exhaustees	—	28,511
Total from covered employment	51,942	81,290
Laid off from uncovered employment	—	6,815
New and reentrants	—	71,295
Total unemployed	51,942	159,400

[a]Counted as employed.

[b]These figures are generally comparable, but they are affected in different ways by timing and other factors.

There are several possible reasons for the downturn just noted. Recent changes in legislation have made it harder to get UC benefits. Employers have had strong incentives to tighten up in this area because of rising UC taxes, the closing of loopholes in the UC tax system, and increasing pressure to cut costs in order to survive economically. The increasing use of temporary help arrangements is probably a factor here. (The number of employees in temporary help companies in Wisconsin rose from 7,721 in 1983 to 14,301 in 1985.) The increasing proportion of women in the labor force adds somewhat to the number of jobless who do not qualify for UC because women tend to enter and leave the labor force more frequently than men and are thus less likely to meet the UC qualifying requirements. The number of those who have exhausted UC benefits is up from the late 1970s.

Whatever the reasons for this condition, we have reached the point that, paradoxically, virtually all wage and salary workers are covered by UC but only one-fourth of the unemployed receive UC checks. It should be noted that this percentage will probably rise sharply at the onset of the next recession as workers now employed lose their jobs and (due to discouragement) the number of new entrants and reentrants declines. The long-term trend, though, is clearly down.

The Employer-Employee Relationship

The employer-employee relationship gives rise to many complex issues in the UC program, and is the source of a great deal of misunderstanding. There are strong reasons in many cases for a laid-off employee to be reluctant to sever the relationship if there is any chance of recall. These include seniority, wage prospects, fringe benefits (medical, retirement, vacation, and so on), location, commuting, and other factors. The employer also has strong reasons to wish to rehire the employee after a layoff. The employee may be trained, skilled, and a proven producer. Some employers make it quite clear that the last thing they want is to have their laid-off employees encouraged to seek other work.

This situation creates conditions in which laid-off workers drawing UC are not looking for other work, and are not expected to be. For example, a claimant who expects to be called back in a few weeks will normally not apply for a regular job with another employer—nor would that employer be inclined to hire the claimant under such circumstances. As a related matter, "reverse seniority" can arise in cases in which senior employees elect to be laid off, a practice which is closely analogous to using UC as partial compensation during a vacation. In cases such as these, the employer often expects—indeed, encourages—the claimant to draw UC. Employers sometimes protest, for example, if the claimant is required to undertake a work search. A claimant might thus wind up "basking in Florida" in February, rather than staying in Wisconsin looking for work.

Two points can be made in this connection: first, examples such as those cited make it especially important that benefits be effectively charged. If the employers in the foregoing examples are paying for the benefits, then no harm is being done to other employees. If the tax pattern allows shifting of such benefit payments to other employees, there are serious possibilities for abuse. Second, it is important that employers be candid with both employees and the UC agency regarding reemployment prospects. There are difficulties when claimants are encouraged to believe that recall is likely and imminent when this is not the case.

Repeaters

For many, unemployment is unexpected and, when it comes, a source of personal tragedy. The consequences are not only economic, but can involve problems with physical and mental health, family breakup, drug and alcohol abuse, and suicide. For others, unemployment is an accepted fact of life, something that is expected and accepted, built into personal plans and spending patterns. There are many types of occupations in which workers expect to be out of work, and to be drawing UC, for a part of each year. Those making UC policy must recognize that both kinds of situations exist. It is heartless to ignore the first; it is mindless to overlook the second.

Unemployment "repeaters" can be considered in terms of certain seasonal industries, geographic areas, family patterns, and recreational activities. Construction is the major example of a seasonal industry in Wisconsin in its effects on the UC program. There are high layoffs during the cold months in certain areas of transportation and tourism as well, and in smaller industries such as quarries.

There are strong geographic considerations in the Wisconsin UC program. Some cities and towns in the state, unfortunately, are in dire economic circumstances — conditions are very bad in the summer, and worse in the winter. In large areas of the state, there is a reasonable amount of economic activity in the summer, with farming, tourism, construction, and related kinds of work, but things close down for the cold months.

There is a family dimension as well. Women, for example, sometimes select certain types of work which permit them to be home during school vacation periods. In other cases, family members select types of jobs which permit them to be available for work in the family business during peak periods. A wife or a son may be essential during certain weeks on a farm during the summer, or in a resort in the late summer and on Labor Day. A farmer may cut and haul pulpwood during most of the year, laying off during peak periods on the farm. The farmer can't draw UC during such layoffs, but the neighbors and relatives he employs in the pulpwood operation can.

As to the recreational aspect, there is a pronounced upsurge in UC claims each year during deer hunting season. Certain layoffs (because of inventory periods, model changeovers, and so on) are timed to occur during desirable vacation periods.

In considering all these examples, a bit of arithmetic is important: for a person who works only part of the year, the potential benefit payments are at least four times the UC tax payment. For example, if a person works twenty-five weeks at $200 a week, the figures line up as follows:

— Total earnings are $5,000 (twenty-five weeks at $200).
— The maximum UC tax payable would be 10 percent of $5,000, or $500.
— Benefits payable would be twenty weeks at $100, or $2,000.
— The spread is thus at least four to one: $2,000 in benefits compared to $500 in taxes.

We have many cases, then, of people choosing to work in jobs in which they know that there will be layoffs, and of people continuing to live in areas which they know will have no work in the winter.

There are many ways to view the situation of a laid-off worker in a sparsely settled northern county. From one perspective, it is pointless to hassle such a claimant regarding work search. From another perspective, the fact that the person continues to live in the county means that he or she is not really looking for year-round work.

The effect of the UC program, under current conditions, is to provide repetitive annual income supplements to certain people, and to make it possible for people to continue to live in certain areas of the state. This is another problem area in which experience rating appears to be a large part of the answer. That is, the maximum tax should be increased to cover a much higher share of benefit payments. As noted a few paragraphs ago, the top tax for such workers now covers (at most) one-fourth of potential benefits. If the top tax could cover all, or virtually all, benefits payable, many of the problems (including the potential for abuse) would be greatly reduced.

Present law provides some examples which might be helpful in the area named above. School-year employees generally cannot draw benefits during school vacation periods. There are special provisions in the law with respect to wages earned during designated food canning and freezing seasons for certain types of crops. In general, there are limitations on benefits payable based on work during these seasons.

Another possibility would be to relate benefit payments to a longer period of time than one year. For example, benefit payments might be the lesser of

— 40 percent of the wages earned in the past year, or
— 30 percent of the wages earned in the past two years, less any benefits drawn one year ago.

In this way (possibly by extending the formula to a third and fourth year) a claimant could not indefinitely draw eight weeks of benefits for each ten weeks of work.

Causes and Attitudes

What causes unemployment? There are all kinds of answers, with varying degrees of plausibility. Here are some:

— There simply aren't enough jobs to go around, due to foreign competition, mismanagement of macroeconomics in Washington, unresolved structural problems in the economy, the baby boom, and so on.
— Some people are unemployable due to mental handicaps and other conditions, and some simply don't want to work—they won't commute or migrate, won't accept lower wages or different hours, and so forth.
— Labor costs (wages and fringes) are so high, and work rules so burdensome, that jobs are driven elsewhere.
— Shortcomings in management and finance—inability to adapt and compete effectively in national and international markets—have decreased the number of jobs.
— Joblessness is fostered by high taxes and a poor business climate.
— Bottlenecks in labor exchanges, problems in training and job skills, and racial or sexual discrimination result in higher unemployment.
— The state's climate and location affect job availability.

Obviously, the choice of a definitive cause of unemployment has a definite bearing on attitudes toward the UC program. If one believes that unemployment is primarily the fault of the unemployed worker (and some express this belief), the attitude toward UC is apt to be negative. Those who believe that there simply aren't enough jobs to go around will take a different view.

The position here is that—although there are exceptions, some of which have been noted—unemployment is not primarily the fault of the laid-off worker. Most unemployed workers in Wisconsin want jobs, especially during recessions. Desperation is not too strong a word for their desire and need to work. Thousands of Wisconsin people have stood in lines, in below-zero weather, to apply for a handful of jobs—not once, but many times. Note in Table 13.6 (page 443) that in July 1985, an estimated 10,403 people who were eligible for unemployment compensation were not drawing it. There are significant numbers of people who do not claim UC even though they are entitled to it, or who let several weeks go by and claim only when they become hard-pressed ("I didn't think I'd need it"). That says something about the work orientation of people in Wisconsin.

There's a corollary, though. The fact that Wisconsin employers lay off large numbers of workers also tells us something: those companies are not doing very well. And the fact that those workers can't find other jobs means that other companies haven't got work for them either. Wisconsin employers are hard-pressed at the same time that laid-off workers are.

In short, we have some very real needs: tens of thousands of workers (in recessions, hundreds of thousands) who are out of work through no fault of their own, who are desperate for work, and who, failing that, need help. At the same time we have some very serious shortages: employers who can't afford to pay wages to these workers also can't afford to pay high levels of UC benefits for extended periods of time. A virtually unlimited need, but severely limited resources: that's the matter we'll consider next.

7. New Issues in a New Setting: UC in a World of Limitations

The Basic UC Trade-off

Where the Money Comes From. UC taxes are paid initially by employers, but the process does not stop there. Looking at economic incidence, the tax is paid by some combination of the following sources:

- Reduced wages and other fringe benefits — if an employer's UC tax bill rises, the employer may cover some of the increase by paying lower wages than he or she otherwise would, or by curtailing other fringes.
- Higher prices — to some extent, UC taxes (like other costs) can be passed on to consumers.
- Lower profits — to some extent, the employer has to "eat" UC taxes. This, in turn, translates into some combination of lower investment and/or lower personal income for the owners of businesses.
- Different rates for other taxes, the net of (1) the need to raise other tax rates because lower taxes are paid on lower profits, (2) the need to cover the cost of federal lending at less than market costs, and (3) lower levels of spending on other public programs than would otherwise pertain.
- Reduced labor costs through job cutbacks, with increases in overtime, contracting out, and recourse to temporary agencies. As noted earlier, the number of employees in temporary help companies in Wisconsin rose from 7,721 in 1983 to 14,301 in 1985.

Where the Money Goes. UC benefits are paid initially to claimants. Again, the process does not stop there. As claimants receive and spend the money, several things happen, including the following:

- Some claimants have a better level of living than they otherwise would. This includes claimants who cannot find other work, or qualify for other forms of assistance, which would provide as much as UC.

—The pressure on claimants to take less desirable work is decreased.

—Migration from the most depressed areas of the state is slowed.

—Public spending in areas other than UC is lowered, the result of lower general tax revenues (as noted above) and a lesser need for public assistance on the part of certain UC claimants.

—Personnel management and layoff practices of certain companies are affected.

—A skilled work force for certain industries is maintained.

—Personal savings patterns are altered.

The Trade-off in the 1980s and Beyond. The basic justification for the UC program is to provide benefit payments—money—to laid-off workers, to help them through times of trouble, and thus to help sustain the economy. Benefit payments have traditionally been viewed as an unmitigated economic plus. When small businessmen complain about the UC program, the UC traditionalist will respond with questions such as, How many UC checks did you cash in your store? How much of your business would have disappeared if there had been no UC program?

Another set of questions could also be posed—and, in fact, can no longer be avoided—along these lines: How much in sales was lost because less family income was left for businesspersons after higher UC taxes were paid? To what extent did these taxes result in lower wages, lower investment, or a loss of jobs?

Putting it bluntly, Wisconsin's UC program today is like virtually any other public program: it involves taxing money from some people and giving it to others. For example, if there are UC benefit payments of $600 million in a given year, that amount enters the Wisconsin income stream through payments to claimants. At just about the same time, $600 million has to be withdrawn from the income stream through taxes on employers. To justify the program, it's necessary somehow to show that the gains of the program are worth the costs. The gains are the economic benefits stemming from $600 million in benefit payments; the costs involve the adverse effects of laying a $600 million tax on the state's employers.

This rather obvious point has not been given much attention. There are several reasons for this oversight. For one thing, in the early days of the program, coverage was much more limited, and it was possible to think of employers as industrial giants, far removed from workers. Such a perception was not unreasonable in 1940, when there were eleven thousand covered employers in Wisconsin. It's not a realistic view today, when one hundred thousand covered employers include every mom-and-pop establishment in Wisconsin. The average firm now subject to Wisconsin's UC law employs fifteen workers (the 1940 average was forty-three). About eighty-five thousand of the one hundred thousand employers who pay UC taxes have less than twelve workers. In many cases, employers are small family businesses which have less income than many of the workers covered by UC.

A good deal of misunderstanding stems from the fact that UC taxes are initially paid by employers. The matter of ultimate incidence, discussed above, is not grasped very clearly. The use of the word "fund" also causes confusion, as does use of the term "employer accounts" in connection with the fund. Some people believe that, since their employers have paid into their accounts taxes based on their wages over many years, there must exist in the fund a huge amount of cash available to pay any amount of benefits they might draw.

Actually, the fund is pooled. As of September 30, 1985, the net fund balance was a negative $267 million: the net of $524 million in positive employer balances, minus $772 million in negative employer balances, and minus $19 million, net, in balances for other items not reflected in employer accounts. Many employers have indeed paid taxes far in excess of the benefit payments attributable to them, but this is offset many times over by the reverse condition. In the net the fund is far in the red. As a financial benchmark, consider that if all workers in the state were to draw all the UC benefits to which they were entitled, the payments would amount to about $9 billion.

It's necessary to recall, too, that the UC program was developed at the same time as the Social Security program, and the people (many from Wisconsin, by the way) who developed and sold these programs were some of the most adroit semanticists that our country has produced. There has been a good deal of attention in recent years to Social Security financing, and much has been said concerning myths, massive misunderstandings, and the like. The public has become much more aware that there really hasn't been a Social Security fund as commonly assumed, and that the taxes paid in by a person years ago really weren't financing the benefits being drawn now. The term "compact between generations" has been coined to describe what's really taking place. Certainly there are similarities in the type of confusion which arises in UC and in Social Security financing.

In the same vein, the UC world is studded with semantic gems: the taxable payroll is called the "defined" payroll; the UC taxes that employers pay are called "contributions"; unemployment compensation is often (outside Wisconsin) referred to as unemployment insurance; and employers who escaped UC taxes altogether (as many did for a number of years) were said to be assessed at a "zero rate."

Finally, it should be noted that Wisconsin's UC fund did, for many years, have a large balance in the U.S. Treasury. In the early 1950s, for example, the fund balance was equivalent to twenty years or more of benefit spending. Under those circumstances, there could indeed be huge increases in state buying power through additional UC benefit payments without the need to draw additional UC taxes out of the economy at the same time. But today the fund is in the red, and there is little likelihood of raising a large fund balance in the foreseeable future.

This brings us back to the first proposition. Wisconsin's UC program today is like virtually any other public program: it involves taking money from some people and giving it to others. To justify the program, it's necessary to show that the gains (where the money goes) outweigh the costs (where the money comes from).

The Economic Crisis

For the next several years, the story of the UC program will be interwoven with America's efforts to deal with the emerging economic crisis. It's hard to overstate the gravity of the situation we face. The key elements of the problem appear to center in three deficits: in the balance of payments, in the federal budget, and in our investment sector.

It is far beyond the scope of this paper to offer predictions or prescriptions as to how these matters will be resolved. However, the process will almost certainly involve very sharp downward pressures on personal income: wages, salaries, and pensions. Real personal income will probably decline sharply. This will be accomplished either by a reduction in dollar incomes, or by significant price increases (inflation) that are not matched by wage increases.

All of this will affect the UC program in two primary ways. First, there will probably be a great deal of economic turbulence as we work our way through these problems. This means, at best, that we will probably experience high unemployment levels from time to time for a considerable time into the future.

Second, the UC program will be affected by severe resource constraints. There will be intense pressures on the federal and state budgets, and on wages and business costs, which will come to bear on the UC program. It will be very difficult for employers—who will be affected by the developments outlined above—to pay additional state UC taxes. There will also be strong pressures for federal cutbacks. Under the circumstances, there is a good possibility that the existing benefit pattern will have to be significantly curtailed.

8. The Mid-1980s and Beyond

What Has Been Accomplished

The crisis which erupted in Wisconsin's UC program in the early 1980s involved a blend of three elements: economic trends, overcommitment, and institutional failure. The economic trends—a long-run increase in unemployment levels and a number of other unresolved economic problems—are something which can't be solved in Wisconsin. A great deal has been done in the other two areas.

As to overcommitment, by the early 1980s Wisconsin had a UC benefit package which provided far more than the UC tax structure could support, even under favorable economic conditions. Both sides of the problem have been addressed. Legislation providing for sharp benefit cutbacks was enacted in 1983, and the provisions began taking effect in 1984. Under these provisions, it's more difficult to qualify initially for UC benefits in Wisconsin, or to requalify following a voluntary quit or discharge for misconduct; the top weekly benefit rate has been frozen indefinitely at $196, instead of being indexed to the wage trend in the state by automatic semi-annual adjustments; the maximum number of weeks of regular benefits payable has been trimmed from thirty-four to twenty-six; and the package has been tightened in a number of other ways.

With that legislation, and with the passage of time, Wisconsin's benefit package is moving from about sixth place nationally, where it was in the early 1980s, to a middle rank among the states (about twenty-fifth). In this connection, two points ought to be cleared up. The first involves, quite simply, emphasizing what's just been said: Wisconsin's UC benefit package no longer ranks near the top among the states. It did in the early 1980s; many have not yet caught up with the fact that this is no longer so. Second, many believe that Wisconsin has historically had one of the most generous UC benefit packages in the nation. That's not true. During most of the 1970s, for example, Wisconsin's rank ranged from twentieth to twenty-fifth. The state's rapid climb toward the top of the list began in the late 1970s; it is now returning to the position it occupied historically.

To support this reduced benefit package, to pay off the debt which was accumulated in the early 1980s, and to avoid the imposition of higher federal payroll taxes and interest charges in Wisconsin, the state UC tax has been sharply increased. This has involved major changes in three areas: first, the taxable wage base has been stepped up, as have the tax rates; second, all employers are now subject to a significant state UC tax—employers with the lowest layoff experience pay the lowest tax rates, but they don't escape payment altogether, as was the case for some twenty-thousand firms a few years ago; and third, we have closed or narrowed a number of loopholes through which more than $500 million was lost in the early 1980s. In line with experience-rating principles, about 98 percent of benefit payments are now charged to specific employers—essentially the highest percentage in the nation.

These measures have been painful. Benefit payments in 1986 will be about $150 million lower than they would have been under the old law, and total employer payments (the sum of state UC taxes, federal payroll taxes, and interest charges) will be about $150 million higher than the old law would have required. What has emerged is a benefits package which is much more in line with Wisconsin's economic capacity and a tax structure which will finance those benefits and provide for taking care of the debt. The current tax structure can support the current level of benefit payments and could support—for two successive years—payments at the 1982–83 level, the highest in Wisconsin's history. If unemployment became significantly worse than that, there would be trouble.

The problem of overcommitment, then, has been dealt with, barring an economic cataclysm. The benefits package provided for laid-off workers in the state can be financed with the state taxes being levied on Wisconsin employers.

Institutional Reform. It was clear for some time prior to 1983 that the UC program was in serious trouble, but until that time Wisconsin government simply failed to act. This failure involved the governor, the legislature, the state executive agencies, and the UC Advisory Council. Culprits were not hard to find; as one participant observed, "there's plenty of blame to go around." A great deal of time was spent during 1983 by key people in Wisconsin—legislative leaders, the governor and other executive officials, labor and business leaders—assessing the reasons for this failure and developing a new approach.

The new structure which emerged has three main elements: a strong UC Advisory Council, with membership newly appointed by the secretary of the Department of Industry, Labor and Human Relations; a strong policy role for the department, including the submission of comprehensive reports (analyses, projections, and legislative recommendations) to the legislature every second year; and prescribed roles for the governor and the legislative leadership. The department has been reorganized: a separate Unemployment Compensation Division has been created, and staffing and other changes made, leading to significant strengthening in the administration of the UC program. The structure is in place, in law and in practice, and so far has worked very well.

Other Features of the Wisconsin Approach. A major objective of the revised UC system has been to retain control of the program, and its financing, in Wisconsin, not Washington. If we had lost control of the debt, for example, Wisconsin's UC benefits would have been financed to an increasing extent by special add-ons to the federal payroll (FUTA) tax levied on Wisconsin employers. These additional taxes would have reached about $186 million a year by 1989, and would have grown thereafter as necessary (up to, potentially, about $560 million a year) to cover debt repayment. Wisconsin chose instead to do the job with the state UC tax.

Under the Wisconsin approach, about fifty-seven thousand small firms in the state with records of low layoffs (those with positive fund balances and taxable payrolls below $100,000) are exempt from the special increment of the UC tax which is directed at getting rid of the debt. The larger employers who do pay the special tax increment are assessed at different rates, depending on their layoff experience. None of these distinctions would apply if the added FUTA tax was being levied; that tax would be levied at the same percentage on all employers in the state, large or small, high layoff or low. Moreover, the proceeds of the tax would be applied to reduce the interest-free portion of our debt, whereas under the Wisconsin approach the interest-bearing portion of the debt is reduced. Since employers are assessed (separately) to cover interest costs, this aspect is also important.

The debt in Wisconsin has been managed in such a way as to take advantage of every break provided in federal law: reductions in interest rates, deferrals (without penalty) of interest payments, and avoidance of added federal taxes on state payrolls. No other state has accomplished these aims. For the years 1983 through 1988, inclusive, the 1983 and 1985 legislation saved Wisconsin employers about $1 billion in additional interest charges and FUTA taxes.

In economic effect, the timing of tax and benefit changes was also an important feature of Wisconsin's reforms. As noted elsewhere, it was necessary to enact very sharp tax increases, and benefit cutbacks, to heal the UC system. These actions took effect beginning in the spring of 1984, when the economy was in a strong recovery mode. It is hoped that the bulk of these adjustments will be behind us before the next recession begins in earnest.

Where We Are: UC in the Zero-Sum Society

About That Term. Lester Thurow uses the term "zero-sum society" to summarize our economic situation. He outlines the imposing set of economic and structural problems we face, "whose solutions require that significant economic losses be distributed to politically powerful interest groups. . . . America cannot go back to the 'effortless superiority' of the immediate post–World War II period. We aren't smarter than everyone else. America can, however, regain parity; America can remain one of the world's economic leaders. It won't happen automatically—social organization will be required—but America can have a world-class economy" (Thurow, *The Zero-Sum Solution,* pp. 11, 385).

Thurow's term, although inelegant and a bit abstruse, is nonetheless descriptive of the conditions under which the UC program must be conducted in the years ahead. To put it very bluntly, it is going to be virtually impossible to get additional money for UC. In fact, it is going to be extremely difficult to hold the UC benefit package at current levels. Given the kind of resource competition that's in store in Washington and in state capitals, many highly regarded programs are going to have to be trimmed, quite painfully. Under the circumstances, there will be strong pressures to make cutbacks in UC so as to reduce the amount of pain which must be inflicted elsewhere.

Much of the remainder of this paper will be, unfortunately, quite gloomy. There will be a strong tendency to believe that things can't really be this bad, that there must be happier possibilities which will surely materialize if we simply wait a while longer. Our recent history demonstrates, however, that "impossible" and highly undesirable things have a way of occurring. In its standard of living, for example, America has slid to eighth place in the world—indeed, lower than that if several small northern European countries are added to the count (Thurow, 1980, p. 51). For the first time in our history, and extremely rare in any society, the upcoming generation faces a lower standard of living than the older one. "Young adults now have a harder time making ends meet and face a far stiffer tax burden than their parents did when they were the same age. In the new America, the present is being financed with tax money expropriated from the future, and one of the legacies children appear to be inheriting from their parents is a diminished standard of living" (*Milwaukee Journal,* January 19, 1986). These are not things that were generally expected to happen. Indeed, many would have dismissed them as impossible a few years ago.

Other "impossible" things which have nonetheless occurred include the gas shortage and general energy crisis of the 1970s; the balance of payments crisis (some of us are old enough to remember when there was a dollar gap which, it was believed, would persevere for generations); federal budget deficits in the $200 billion range; the high inflationary levels of the late 1960s and 1970s; the record level of interest rates of recent years; and the rate of economic growth in Western Europe and east Asia. In 1962, for example, total (worldwide) Japanese auto exports amounted to just eight thousand cars. In 1985, we became a net debtor nation for the first time since World War I.

The developments recounted here were generally not expected, and they certainly led to many results that were neither planned for nor desired. For the future, we've simply got to do better. We must get rid of the notion that bad things cannot happen because there's a certain Providence which takes special care of drunkards, small children, and the United States. There isn't. Nor is there any law of history which forgives us or mistakes because our actions are explicable in the context of our political difficulties.

There's no painless way of dealing with a federal budget deficit in the $200 billion range, nor with a balance of payments deficit of a similar magnitude. That ought to be as clear now as it will surely be in retrospect. To provide a world-class economy in Wisconsin in the decades ahead, a very high level of research and investment spending by Wisconsin industry will be required. Wisconsin employers are going to find it difficult to accomplish that and simultaneously pay higher wages, higher UC taxes, higher federal taxes (a spinoff of solving the federal deficit), and higher prices (a spinoff of solving the balance of payments deficit).

UC, then, is not going to be treated in a vacuum, insulated from what's taking place in public spending and the economy generally. UC will be treated much more like the public spending programs, state and federal, than it has been in the past. The arrangements necessary to bring this about—political and economic, organizational, procedural, and legislative—are already in place. Various facets of this matter are covered in following sections.

UC on a Pay-as-You-Go Basis. For the foreseeable future, UC in Wisconsin will be conducted on a pay-as-you-go basis. This development, which is not very well understood, has some profound implications.

From January 1980 through April 1984, state UC benefit payments in Wisconsin amounted to $2.2 billion, and state UC taxes amounted to $1 billion (excluding federal UC programs). Thus, during this critical time, the state UC program pumped a net of $1.2 billion (benefits minus taxes) into the state economy. As bad as economic conditions were in Wisconsin during this period, few would disagree that they would have been considerably worse without this injection of a net of $1.2 billion in buying power into the state economy. That's the traditional automatic-stabilizer role of the UC program. For the foreseeable future, the UC program will not be able to play such a role.

If UC benefits amount to $2.2 billion during a future economic slump, UC taxes levied on state employers will amount to about $2.2 billion as well, in about the same period of time. There will be no net injection $1.2 billion of buying power into the state economy. UC is now like most other state programs: the amounts paid out have to be covered by taxes in essentially the same period of time.

There are two reasons for this change. First, there isn't any large fund balance. In the past, recessions usually began with a sizable fund balance ($462 million in January 1980, for example). A large part of the positive economic effect in the past resulted from drawing down this large pre-recession fund balance. The fund is in debt now, and for reasons detailed above, it's extremely unlikely that a significant fund balance will be maintained in the future.

Second, we're at a very different point on the federal financing curve. The federal financing package was developed to allow the states time to get their houses in order, and thus provides for increasingly stiffer requirements as time passes. States were, for example, given two years (two Januaries) before debt reduction was necessary to avoid imposition of an added FUTA tax. Thus, we were able to borrow extensively through 1982, 1983, and well into 1984 before reversing the flow, without suffering a FUTA penalty. But the grace period has ended. Moreover, the potential penalty grows stiffer each year. Had extra FUTA been assessed on 1984 payrolls, the bite would have been 0.3 percent ($31 million). For 1989 payrolls, this could be 1.8 percent ($186 million). Under federal law, the extra tax could ultimately amount to $560 million annually.

In a future economic slump, then, it's highly likely that one of these two things will happen: (1) state UC taxes will be high enough to cover benefit payments, or (2) state taxes won't do the job, so the added FUTA tax will take effect, and this will cover payments. Either way, the taxes paid by Wisconsin employers during the slump will essentially match benefit payments. There will be no net injection of buying power. The system is thus, essentially, operated on a pay-as-you-go basis.

It is possible that some limited favorable net economic effect can be achieved in a future slump, if we can reach debt-free status before the slump begins. That demands a very high level of skill and a good deal of luck. Even then, the net favorable effect will be considerably smaller than in the past.

A High Threshold of Benefit Payments. Wisconsin UC benefit payments amounted to $408 million in 1985. In one view, UC benefit payments should have been very low in that year: the general level of unemployment was (relatively) very low, and there is no serious expectation of a significantly lower level of unemployment in the foreseeable future; the UC benefit package had only recently been very sharply cut through legislative changes; and, in 1985, only one unemployed person in four was receiving a UC benefit check.

From another perspective, though, that $408 million is extremely high. It's more than was spent in any year prior to 1980. And in only two years in the history of the program (1984 and 1985) has the program collected that much in UC taxes.

In short, UC benefit payments are at near-record levels under the best economic conditions we're likely to see in a long time. That provides some indication of what we might expect in a future slump, when many more workers are unemployed and a higher proportion of them receive a UC check. We're in something like the condition of a family in northern Wisconsin which is pondering the fact that it's all the furnace can do to keep the place warm — in July.

The Trade-off: UC Benefit Payments and Taxes. In a future recession, benefit payments might amount to $800 million a year; that much in buying power will be placed in the hands of UC claimants. In the past, a large part of these benefits was a net addition to buying power in the state, thus helping to sustain the economy. In today's pay-as-you-go system, however, this is not so. That $800 million required for UC benefits in an economic recession must be taxed from Wisconsin employers at about the same time. We need to consider the incidence, and the economic effects, of levying $800 million in UC taxes. Although the taxes are initially paid by employers, the incidence of the tax involves some combination of reduced wages and other fringes; higher prices; lower profits, which translate into lower investment and/or lower personal income for the owners of businesses; different rates and yields for other taxes; and cutbacks in employment. UC policy must be formulated with a much better awareness of this trade-off.

The Wisconsin Economy in the Decades Ahead. In formulating public policy in any broad area affecting Wisconsin's economy, it's essential to have some clear idea of what we want that economy to look like in the future.

Our hope is that we will have a truly world-class economy, fully competitive in quality and price with the best in the world. We would wish that large parts of Wisconsin business would be led and staffed by people who understood the languages and culture, the legal, financial and business practices, and the tastes and preferences of people in many other countries in which Wisconsin products and services are sold. Producers thousands of miles away would still sell products in Wisconsin, but generally at the sufferance of Wisconsin producers—because, that is, Wisconsin producers had chosen to concentrate on more profitable items.

That sounds visionary, but it had better not be. If that isn't a reasonably realistic description of where the Wisconsin economy will be, a lot of things are going to have to change for the worse—including the UC program.

Obviously, all this cannot be brought about by people in Wisconsin alone. There have to be major changes at the national level. But a large part of the job *does* rest on people in Wisconsin. Wisconsin industry, in particular, will have to spend massive amounts for training, research, investment, product testing, setting up dealer networks, and taking the whole range of steps necessary for such an economy to come into being. This structural adaptation will have to take place in a national economy that is reacting to the profound depressant effects of reducing or eliminating two massive deficits: in the federal budget and in the international balance of payments. The former will involve, in some combination, reduced federal spending and higher federal taxes—both depressants. The latter will, as a minimum and at best, put strong upward pressure on prices, which won't help our competitive position.

In the process, there will be extreme downward pressures on personal income of all types. In fact, real personal income (that is, adjusted for inflation) will almost certainly drop sharply. That applies to wages, salaries, after-tax profits, interest income, pensions and other transfers—and to UC benefit payments. For wages and salaries, such a drop represents a continuation—and, probably, a considerable acceleration—of the current trend. Real wages and salaries declined 7 percent between 1970 and 1985.

The Outlook: Changes in UC Benefits

As regards both benefits and taxes, the suggestions which follow are not painless, and they will not be popular. They are the type of measures, though, which certainly must be considered in any realistic assessment of the future of the UC program. Anyone who has suggestions for reform which will be painless is certainly welcome to go to the head of the line.

Benefit Increases. Increases in payments are strongly indicated in certain areas. First, the maximum benefit rate had been frozen at $196 a week since January 1983. As this continues, half and then more of benefit payments will be at this single rate. This will increasingly undermine the policy objective of replacing 50 percent of lost wages. The freeze will have to be removed at some point, to provide some increase in the top rate.

Second, very close attention must be given to coverage. Something surely is out of line when only one unemployed worker in four receives a UC check.

A third area which should be considered is an allowance for dependents, which fourteen other states now provide. Such an allowance seems mandatory if the pressure to hold the line on benefits is to continue, as appears to be the case. A UC benefit of, say, $150 per week means one thing to a young single person living at home; it is quite a different matter to the head of a young family.

Fourth, the matter of medical insurance. Many Wisconsin workers have excellent medical insurance, which is lost to them (under conditions which vary from one firm to another) when they are unemployed. Consideration should be given to extending this medical coverage as part of the UC package. Claimant payments could be required; for example, if a claimant paid $10 a week for medical insurance while working, the charge could be $5 a week when he or she shifted to unemployed coverage status. If possible, this coverage should extend for longer than the normal UC term (twenty-six weeks).

Benefit Cutbacks. Decreases in payments will be necessary in some areas to cover the costs of any increases that are adopted and perhaps, beyond that, as part of a package which may be necessary to maintain the solvency of the program.

The first candidate for cutback should be Wisconsin supplemental benefits (WSB), added to the law in 1983. At that time, the maximum duration of regular benefits was reduced from thirty-four to twenty-six weeks, the duration in most states. An exception was provided, however, if the insured unemployment rate (IUR) reached specified levels for a thirteen-week period (either 5 or 4 percent *and* 1.2 times the rate for the corresponding period in the two preceding years). If the IUR reaches these levels, claimants who have sufficient weeks of work in their base period can draw up to thirty-four weeks of benefits. If federal extended benefits trigger on, they would override Wisconsin supplemental benefits. Most states provide a maximum of twenty-six weeks of benefits, unless extended benefits are in effect. If WSB payments were eliminated, Wisconsin would be in line with the national norm.

Second, a waiting week should be required, as was the case before 1976. Nationally, twenty-eight states (plus Puerto Rico, the District of Columbia, and the Virgin Islands) require an unconditional waiting week; twelve require a waiting week subject to certain conditions; and ten (including Wisconsin) do not require a waiting week at all. In some of the twelve conditional states, for example, the waiting week becomes payable if the claimant is unemployed for a certain period of time.

If an unconditional waiting week was required in Wisconsin, benefit payments would be reduced by about $35 million in the first year and about $25 million a year thereafter. Moreover, the federal government would reimburse Wisconsin about $5 million a year more when extended benefits were in effect.

In Wisconsin, if a person works fifty-one weeks a year and is unemployed for just one week, UC benefits are payable for that week. At a time of budgetary bloodletting, this is not an easy provision to defend.

Third, something like a two-week claim period should be considered. At present, a claimant might earn $600 in one week and zero in the next week. The claimant is paid no UC benefits for the first week, but full benefits (say, $196 per week) for the second week. Under the claim period approach, the two weeks would be considered together—in effect, as if the claimant had earnings of $300 a week. No state has such an approach. This was suggested by an employee of the State of Wisconsin (not the author) who wishes to remain anonymous.

Fourth, the matter of repeaters: unemployment is, for some, unexpected and, when it comes, a personal tragedy. For others, unemployment is an accepted fact of life, something that is expected and accepted and built into personal plans and spending patterns. There are many situations in which workers expect to be out of work, and to be drawing UC, for a part of each year.

Those making UC policy must recognize both situations. Few insurance programs would treat those who claim repeatedly the same as those filing their first claim after years of coverage.

It is suggested that claimants who have repeatedly drawn UC benefits should be treated differently from those who have not. One way would be to consider two or more years together. For example, the maximum number of weeks of benefits payable might be the lesser of (1) twenty-six weeks, or (2) forty minus the number of weeks drawn in the preceding year. Another approach would be to prescribe a season for certain types of work. For example, a construction worker laid off in July could draw benefits; one laid off in February could not.

The Outlook: Changes in State UC Taxes

Three related changes should be made in the state UC tax structure: a sharp increase in the taxable wage base; a reduction in the tax rates for employers with the lowest layoff experience; and an increase in the tax rates for employers with the highest layoff experience. These changes should be phased in over a few years, and should net to zero in revenue yield (that is, the increased tax payments by some employers should be offset by reduced tax payments for others). In broad outline, the changes would be about as set forth in Table 13.7.

Table 13.7. UC Taxation of Wisconsin Employers, Present and Proposed

	Firm with Low Layoffs (minimum rate)	Firm with High Layoffs (maximum rate)
Present:		
Wage base	$10,500	$10,500
Tax rate	1.1%	10.0%
Tax per employee	$ 115.50	$ 1,050
Proposed:		
Wage base	$20,000	$20,000
Tax rate	0.4%	20.0%
Tax per employee	$ 80	$ 4,000

Many Wisconsin firms pay relatively low wages to each worker in a given year. This includes firms with a seasonal business pattern; those which make extensive use of part-time help; and firms which pay hourly wages of $6 an hour or less. For such firms, the $10,500 taxable wage base means that virtually all wages (that is, virtually their entire payroll) are subject to the state UC tax. For higher-wage firms, only a fraction of the payroll (as little as one-fourth) may be taxable. An increase in the wage base to $20,000 would go a long way toward correcting this inequity.

It should be noted that, for many years after the two programs began, both UC and Social Security used a $3,000 taxable wage base. In those early days, that covered virtually all wages. In 1986, the taxable wage base for Social Security is $42,000, whereas the base for the Wisconsin UC tax is $10,500 (and that for FUTA is only $7,000).

The lowest rate would include a basic tax of 0.3 percent and a solvency tax of 0.1 percent, a total of 0.4 percent or $80 per employee. It is possible that this rate would work out to be a bit lower. With a wage base as high as $20,000, it should no longer be necessary to provide a special rate schedule for smaller firms.

At present, the top tax rate includes a basic tax of 6.7 percent and a solvency tax of 3.3 percent, a total of 10 percent. Only the basic tax (6.7 percent) is credited to the employer's account. At most, that amounts to $703.50 (6.7 percent of $10,500) per employee per year. The maximum UC check is $196 a week. The top basic tax, then, covers about four weekly UC benefit checks per employee per year at the top benefit rate, or about five checks at the average rate. This means that, if a firm's employees draw an average of five weekly UC checks a year, the firm pays the top UC rate. If they draw an average of ten checks a year, or fifteen, the firm still pays the same top rate. Under present arrangements, once that threshold of about five benefit checks per worker is crossed, the number of UC benefit checks drawn makes no financial difference to the employer.

Under the proposal the basic tax would be about 15 percent (and the solvency tax 5 percent), for a maximum basic tax of $3,000 per employee per year. This would raise the threshold just described from about five to about fifteen checks (allowing for increases in benefit rates). That is, it would matter greatly to the employer whether his or her employees drew an average of five UC checks a year, or ten checks, or fifteen checks. Given Wisconsin's seasonal employment pattern and the layoff practices in some companies, this five-to-fifteen-week range is significant, and should not be lumped.

Another consideration to bear in mind is the pattern in many seasonal firms (often those which are relatively small and pay relatively low wages) in Wisconsin. For such firms this change means that the top UC tax will cover one-half rather than one-fourth of the benefits payable.

In this example, a claimant could draw $2,000 a year in benefits while (under present law) the employer pays a maximum of $500 a year in state UC taxes; thus, $1,500 a year of benefit payments to this worker is not covered by taxes paid by the employer who laid the claimant off. In other cases involving higher wages and benefit rates, the unrecovered sums can amount to $3,000 or more per worker per year. These amounts must be financed by levying higher taxes on employers with few layoffs—that is, stable employers must pay UC taxes sufficient to cover (1) the amount of benefits paid to their own employees, plus (2) the deficits (benefit payments exceeding taxes) which are run up by high-layoff firms. Through this mechanism, stable employers are paying a part of the costs of—that is, subsidizing—unstable ones. In the aggregate, this subsidy now amounts to about $80 million a year in good years, and to over $100 million a year in years of higher unemployment. Under these tax proposals, such subsidies would be sharply reduced.

It has long been recognized that the UC tax embraced two elements: experience rating and shared risk. The shared risk principle allows for the fact that not all benefit payments can be recovered by taxes levied on the employer involved. The taxing proposal presented here is fully consistent with these precepts. What is proposed is to draw a much sharper distinction between firms which normally have relatively few layoffs, but which encounter a bad spell (either during a recession or otherwise) when layoffs (and UC benefit payments) are very heavy; and firms which have high layoff rates in their normal operations, in years of economic recession and in years when the general unemployment level is relatively low, and whose employees draw UC benefits each year which far exceed the amount of UC taxes paid by the firm.

Even with enactment of the tax changes recommended here (a wage base of $20,000 and a top rate of 20 percent), firms in the first category would be amply protected by three features of the UC financial system. The first is the lag period. If benefit payments accelerate rapidly, from twelve to twenty-four months will elapse before any related increases in taxes are actually payable. Second, because of the rate increase limiter, the basic UC tax cannot increase by more than 1 percent a year for firms with positive balances, or by more than 2 percent a year for firms with negative balances. Thus, it would take several years before a normally stable firm reaches the top UC tax rate. It's important to recall, too, that during the most difficult times for such a firm, the higher taxes are being levied on a relatively low payroll (those who are still working during the period of heavy layoffs). Third, the write-off provision allows a firm which has reached the top rate and paid it for two years in a row to write off any remaining negative balance in excess of 10 percent of taxable payroll. Thus if the firm has a stable record, it can work its way back down to a lower rate.

In short, normally stable firms which encounter a run of bad luck will not have a huge rate increase slapped on them overnight. The increases will begin well after the downturn begins, and will be phased over several years, with provision for some forgiveness (write-offs) after the firm has made substantial payments.

The firms which will be most affected by this proposal are those in the second category—those which have high layoff rates in their normal operations and whose employees, year in and year out, draw UC benefits far in excess of the taxes paid by the firm. Very few Wisconsin construction firms, for example, keep their employees at work for forty-eight weeks or more a year. That is, these workers are normally going to be laid off — and drawing UC benefits — for much more than five weeks a year. At a maximum benefit rate of $196 a week, it's not surprising that many construction workers draw UC benefits of $3,000 (fifteen weeks) or more a year. What's not clear is the reason for charging the construction employer for only a fraction of these benefit payments and shifting the bulk of the cost to other employers, such as paper manufacturers.

The changes recommended here should be phased in, and not imposed overnight. The message ought to be clear, though, that the present pattern of cross-industry subsidization is being ended.

As state laws now stand, this proposal would make Wisconsin's top UC tax rate the highest in the country by a wide margin. This point will certainly be raised as an argument against this proposal. The response would have to be along these lines: firms would pay such a tax only if their layoff record warrants it. Other firms could be offered a much lower tax, because they wouldn't be expected to pick up large parts of someone else's costs.

The point will be made that this will drive some firms out of business, or discourage others from doing business in the state — or, to put it another way, that the firms involved need this large subsidy to survive in Wisconsin. In connection with the threat to take payrolls elsewhere, we need to recall that large parts of what are involved here — building homes, roads, and bridges, for example — are not normally considered mobile.

The subsidies we are discussing, which amount to $80 to $100 million a year for the firms involved, appear to be unique to the UC program. That is, these firms do not receive special discounts in other state taxes. The legislature does not make appropriations to offset part of their costs. Their supplies don't provide goods to them at below-market prices, nor do their workers volunteer to accept wages that are far below scale. In other words, for these firms, it appears to be 100 cents on the dollar everywhere except at the UC window.

As noted, the matters discussed in this section involve a drain on the fund of about $80 million a year in good years, and well over $100 million in bad years.

Of Wisconsin's 100,000 employers, about 57,000 are small, stable employers who are now exempt from the special solvency tax; these employers would not be much affected by these proposals either way. Of the remaining 43,000, most (about 33,000) would realize a significant cut in their state UC taxes. The remaining 10,000 would be subject to sharp increases in their state UC taxes — as much as a fourfold rise if present layoff practices are continued. Overall, it is emphasized, this package should be so designed as to be revenue-neutral—that is, the total state UC tax payments under this proposal would be no higher than under current law.

The Write-off Provision. An account is maintained for each employer subject to the Wisconsin UC tax. That account is credited with the employer's basic tax payments and charged with the amount of benefits paid to people who worked for that employer. The ratio of the firm's account balance each June 30 to its taxable payroll for the preceding twelve months is the reserve ratio. The firm's UC tax is determined by this reserve ratio. To qualify for the lowest tax, a firm must have a reserve ratio of 10 percent or more. Firms with a negative reserve ratio of minus 6 percent or more pay the minimum tax. Intervening tax brackets are determined by reserve ratio intervals.

Normally, any negative balance in excess of 10 percent of the firm's taxable payroll at the time of the rate determination can be written off (forgiven) subject to certain conditions. Such write-offs have been forbidden, however, for a certain period of time. Specifically, they are not allowed from the fall of 1983 through the fall of 1986—that is, for the rate determinations for the years 1984 through 1987, inclusive. Write-offs were again permitted in the fall of 1987 for the 1988 rate determination.

It is suggested that write-offs not be permitted—that the ban be extended—until the third year after the $20,000 wage base and 20 percent tax rate have been in effect. After that, they should be permitted again, subject to the conditions provided in present law: that, in order to write off, a firm must have paid the top tax rate for at least the two preceding years; and that, if a firm writes off UC taxes, no voluntary contributions for the purpose of securing a reduced rate may be made for at least five years.

Federal Action

Any proposals for federal action in the UC area have to be in line with federal budgetary realities, which are about as follows: the federal government isn't going to be looking for new ways to spend money in the foreseeable future, and the UC program is a good candidate for cutbacks.

In this vein, we offer three proposals. First, the FUTA wage base, currently set at $7,000, should be increased sharply, to something like $20,000. At the same time, the effective net rate, 0.8 percent, could be adjusted if desired. Any additional federal revenues would lower the federal deficit. FUTA revenues would help build up a balance in the UC fund, which could reduce the pressure for cutbacks in the federal contribution to extended benefit payments and in administrative funding. And, most important, taxable wage bases in the states would also rise to the higher figure, ending a serious problem in states such as Wisconsin which are constrained, by reason of bogus interstate comparisons, from raising their wage base to a realistic level.

Second, it is recommended that the federal government take strong action to encourage effective charging in state UC programs—that is, arrangements under which a high proportion (80 percent or more) of benefit payments are covered by taxes levied on the employers involved. An increase in the FUTA wage base would be one such measure. The federal government could also offer preferential interest rates, different extended benefits sharing percentages, and other inducements to states to produce more effective charging. These steps would improve the overall financial soundness of state UC programs, and should considerably reduce the need for states to borrow from the federal government. The federal financial savings through a lower loan volume should outweigh the costs of the incentive provisions.

Third, in terms of priorities, if some area has to be cut, it is suggested that the last thing should be the federal UC loan provisions. These are the arrangements under which loans are available to states in unlimited amounts at the federal securities rate (but not to exceed 10 percent), and with no interest on amounts repaid by September 30 of each year. It is suggested that this area be given the highest priority.

In Conclusion

A great deal has happened in the Wisconsin UC program in the past few years. Many changes have been made. A great many problems have been encountered, and many issues raised. Many of these have been dealt with, in whole or in part; some are still unresolved. Any attempt to address these matters fully is, unfortunately, going to be time-consuming, technical, and difficult.

Given the realities—the economic outlook, the shape of the federal and state budgets, the competing demands for resources in both the public and private sectors, and the internal arithmetic of the UC program itself—we should not expect additional money, federal or state, for the UC program. Given the needs, it's hoped we can keep what we have. This paper, therefore, recommends a benefit package which would involve about the same level of benefit payments as the current package. Within that fixed total, though, there would be considerable redistribution—significant increases in some areas matched by cutbacks elsewhere. Total employer tax payments would be the same as under current law. There would, however, be a considerable redistribution within the employer community, with about ten thousand employers paying much more, about thirty-three thousand paying much less, and fifty-seven thousand small employers relatively unaffected.

In the same vein, we generally don't recommend that the UC program venture into new or untried areas—at least not the ones which have been suggested so far. Specifically, we don't recommend that UC payments be provided in lump amounts, and we don't recommend that UC funds be used for such purposes as training, relocation grants, reemployment vouchers, or short-term compensation (worksharing) agreements.

We've ruled out, then, additional funding and radically different approaches. But within what remains—the traditional areas of UC—major changes are recommended. Although these changes would be far-reaching, they are in accord with traditional UC principles.

As for benefits, a number of measures are proposed which would help those who are out of work through no fault of their own—those that the UC program was designed to help. These include increases in the maximum weekly benefit rate, in order to keep closer to our wage-replacement objectives; allowances for dependents, in recognition of the fact that $150 a week means one thing to a single worker (perhaps living at home) and something entirely different to the head of a family; some improvements in coverage, acknowledging that (recently) only one unemployed worker in four qualified for a UC check; and (our only nontraditional item) consideration of the possibility of using UC funds to help extend medical insurance coverage for the unemployed. Two further changes, not covered in this study, are now under active consideration by the Department of Industry, Labor and Human Relations and the UC Advisory Council. These would make it possible for a claimant to qualify for the maximum number of weeks of unemployment for two or more years in succession (not generally now possible) and would provide up to six months of earnings as a "banked" amount against which benefits could be drawn in a future recession. Together these measures would provide much better support than the provisions of present law to those laid off in a future recession.

The costs of these measures would be covered by cutbacks in other benefit areas. Wisconsin supplemental benefits, which in certain circumstances provide benefit payments for the twenty-seventh through the thirty-fourth week of unemployment, would be eliminated; we would have to rely, as other states do, on federal extended benefits. A waiting week would be required, as in most states and in Wisconsin before 1976, recognizing that (as an example) providing one weekly UC benefit check to a person who has had fifty-one weeks of work is a matter of much lower priority than other parts of the UC benefit package. Benefits for those who have high but sporadic earnings would be trimmed by a claim period approach, and there would be phased cutbacks in the benefits payable to those who draw UC year after year.

If the proposals presented in this paper were adopted, the Wisconsin UC system would draw a much clearer distinction in awarding benefits between claimants who are unemployed through no fault of their own, under circumstances which they could not reasonably have foreseen, and those for whom spells of unemployment (and UC benefits) are a recognized fact of life—expected, accepted, planned for, and built into personal finances and lifestyles.

On the tax side, the name of this game is experience rating—specifically, effective charging. For no particularly good reason, we've moved a long way from traditional UC principles by permitting certain employers to be heavily subsidized by others, year in and year out. Employers with even a moderate pattern of layoffs—say, six or eight weeks a year, which isn't much for seasonal industries, considering the Wisconsin climate—pay only a fraction of their benefit costs. The remainder must be borne by other employers. This internal deficit amounts to some $80 million a year in good years, and it greatly—and needlessly—complicates our financing problems in bad years. Our recommendations would greatly reduce this problem.

No additional federal spending is proposed in these recommendations, but it is suggested that the federal government cease compounding the problems of the states by adopting a realistic FUTA wage base and by taking concrete steps to encourage effective charging.

The UC program has played a vital role in the economy of Wisconsin and in the life of its people. We believe that the changes proposed here will make it possible for the program to continue to fulfill that role, when and where it's needed most.

CONTRIBUTORS

INDEX

Contributors

Paul L. Burgess, born in 1943 in Salt Lake City, Utah, is Professor of Economics at Arizona State University. He is the author of numerous articles and technical reports on the unemployment compensation system, and coauthor (with Jerry L. Kingston) of *An Incentives Approach to Improving the Unemployment Compensation System* (1987).

Gary Burtless, born in 1950 in Auburn, New York, is a senior fellow in the Economic Studies Program of the Brookings Institution. His primary research involves econometric studies of the behavioral effects of social welfare programs. He is the coeditor, with Henry Aaron, of *Retirement and Economic Behavior* (1984) and the editor of *Work, Health, and Income Among the Elderly* (1987).

James F. Byers, born in 1945 in Latrobe, Pennsylvania, is Chairperson of the Industrial and Labor Relations Department of Indiana University of Pennsylvania. Professor Byers served as coordinator of the conference Unemployment Insurance: The Second Half Century while pursuing doctoral studies at the Industrial Relations Research Institute of the University of Wisconsin–Madison.

Sheldon H. Danziger, born in 1948 in Houston, Texas, is Professor of Social Work and Public Policy at the University of Michigan. From 1983 to 1988 he was Director of the Institute for Research on Poverty, Professor of Social Work, and Romnes Faculty Fellow at the University of Wisconsin–Madison. His research analyzes the effects of social welfare programs on poverty, work effort, and the family. He is the coeditor of *Fighting Poverty: What Works and What Doesn't* (1986), *State Policy Choices: The Wisconsin Experience* (1988), and *The Distributional Impacts of Public Policies* (1988), and is the author of numerous scholarly articles.

Peter Gottschalk, born in 1942, is Professor of Economics at Boston College. His primary research areas are the economics of poverty and inequality. He has written extensively in scholarly journals and has disseminated the findings of his research in more popular journals, government reports, and congressional testimony.

W. Lee Hansen, born in 1928 in Racine, Wisconsin, is Professor of Economics and of Educational Policy Studies and former director of the Industrial Relations Research Institute at the University of Wisconsin–Madison. He is the author of numerous papers and books on labor economics, the economics of education, and public policy analysis, and past editor of the *Journal of Human Resources*. He recently coedited and contributed to *The End of Mandatory Retirement: Effects on Higher Education* (1989).

Edwin M. Kehl, born in Madison, Wisconsin, in 1926, is a graduate of the University of Wisconsin–Madison. He has a long public career in government employment and training and unemployment compensation programs, his most recent position being Administrator in the State of Wisconsin's Unemployment Compensation Division. He has authored legislation on manpower policy and government organizational reform as well as unemployment compensation.

Jerry L. Kingston, born in 1941 in Wayne, Nebraska, is Professor of Economics at Arizona State University. His primary research interest is the unemployment insurance program. He has published numerous articles and special studies on UI-related issues, including the book (with Paul L. Burgess) entitled *An Incentives Approach to Improving the Unemployment Compensation System* (1987).

Clifford J. Miller, born in 1924 in Duluth, Minnesota, is Director of Unemployment Compensation Policy Research in the Wisconsin state government. He is the author of a number of articles and papers dealing with the history of Wisconsin's unemployment compensation program, its financing problems, and recent legislative changes.

Martin J. Morand, born in 1927 in New York City, is Professor of Labor Relations at Indiana University of Pennsylvania and director of the Pennsylvania Center for the Study of Labor Relations. He and Ramelle MaCoy edited "Short-Time Compensation: A Formula for Worksharing" published by the Work in America Institute (1984).

Raymond Munts, born in 1923 in Morris, Illinois, is Professor Emeritus of Social Work at the University of Wisconsin–Madison. He was director of research and evaluation for the National Commission on Unemployment Compensation in Washington, D.C., 1977–1980. Formerly he was director of Social Security for the AFL-CIO. His publications are in the fields of social insurance and health delivery systems.

Beatrice Reubens, born in 1917 in New York City, is Senior Research Associate at the Conservation of Human Resources program, Columbia University. A specialist in comparative studies of employment and education, she is the author of *The Hard-to-Employ: Western European Programs* (1970), *Bridges to Work: International Comparisons of Transition Services* (1977), and *Policies for Apprenticeship* (1979); coauthor (with J. Harrison and K. Rupp) of *The Youth Labor Force 1945–1955: A Cross-National Analysis* (1981); and editor and coauthor of *Youth at Work: An International Survey* (1983).

Murray Rubin, born in 1930 in Providence, Rhode Island, was president of a consulting firm on unemployment insurance matters at the time of his death in 1989. A former director of the U.S. Department of Labor's Division of Program Policy and Legislation, he was the author of *Federal-State Relations in Unemployment Insurance—A Balance of Power* (1983), a periodical *Highlights of State and Federal Unemployment Insurance Legislation,* and monographs in *Unemployment Compensation: Studies and Research.*

Robert G. Spiegelman, born in 1928 in San Francisco, California, is Executive Director of the W. E. Upjohn Institute for Employment Research in Kalamazoo, Michigan. He was previously director of a research program at SRI International in which he was responsible for numerous social experiments and evaluations of social programs. He is the author of several articles and papers on the Seattle-Denver income maintenance experiment, which he directed.

Robert Topel, born in 1952 in Los Angeles, California, is Professor of Economics and Industrial Relations at the University of Chicago. Prior to moving to Chicago he was a professor of economics at UCLA. He is the author of numerous articles related to labor markets and is associate editor of the *Journal of Labor Economics*.

Wayne Vroman, born in 1940 in Schoharie, New York, is Senior Research Associate at the Urban Institute. In earlier research on unemployment insurance he developed a microsimulation model of benefit payments in individual state programs. He has also examined a number of other unemployment insurance subjects such as the program's macroeconomic effects and replacement rates, legislative developments, and program performance in the first half of the 1980s. He is the author of *The Funding Crisis in State Unemployment Insurance* (1986).

Stephen A. Woodbury, born in 1952 in Beverly, Massachusetts, is Associate Professor of Economics at Michigan State University in East Lansing and Senior Research Economist at the W. E. Upjohn Institute for Employment Research in Kalamazoo, Michigan. He is the author of several articles on the economics of nonwage benefits and of *The Tax Treatment of Fringe Benefits* (1989).

Index